To:
Peter -
All the books are good - Reading is
brd!
Dan d'Monte — 2014

A DIARY OF THE UNDERDOGS

JAZZ

1960's SAN FRANCISCO

By

DON ALBERTS

Featuring

Sonny Buxton, John Handy, Pearl Wong, Vince Lateano, Bishop Norman Williams, Dick Conte, Si Perkoff, Art Sharky Lewis, BJ Papa, Buddy Barnhill, Frank Passantino, Eddie Duran, Vince Wallace, Mal Sharpe, Terry Hilliard, Dick Saltzman, Larry Vuckovich, Dean Reilly, Larry Dunlap, Bobbe Norris, George DiQuattro, Richard Hadlock, Ron Marabuto, Chuck Peterson, Al Molina, Richard Brown, Mark Levine, Mike Lipskin, Mel Martin, Dick Fregulia, Donald Duck Bailey, Dick Whittington, and many others

Copyright December 9, 2009
Chill House Publishers-lulu.com
ISBN 978-0-557-23270-3
Third Edition

A Diary of the Underdogs

THE CITY

At the top of Nob Hill in the very heart of the city, stands the magnificent Grace Cathedral, so precious and stark, yet bleak, most assuredly a grounding spire, a monolith rising above the land pointing to God, declaring a city of faith and dedication, a place of supreme spiritual wealth, a healing chamber for the city's past and ongoing wounds.

It stands unclothed, openly displaying its steel genitals to the world, its metal, its droll and ostentation, its sanctity and elegance seen in the chiseled faces of many men.

The dawn turns the gray stone towers to gold in morning light and glistens damp behind the chill of a night's fog.

It stands as a candle in a dark hallway, stirring echoes in the mind and moving stiff hearts to release within its shadowy corridors where whispers ascend in silence to a cloudless heaven.

It is the touch, the robust hand of the mighty that flows within the visceral, the muted plasma pressing the genes with ineffable reverence.

Here, in the cleft of grief, in hidden goodbyes, in the halls of last sight and farewell, and in the fountains of new christening dwells the spirit of man, his internal joy and his struggle. The doors are open beyond wishes, past imaginings and desires, past memories.

A Diary of the Underdogs

PREFACE

Jazz in San Francisco in the 1960's is a lost history, a story that has never been told. There are torn pieces that fit jaggedly together and form a vague picture, but some pieces are still missing, yet these pieces remain vivid and alive in the memories of those who were there. This book gathers those stories, from the author's experience and as told first hand by his fellow survivors, told from within. They are about the feeling of living in that time, the details, the lives of forgotten musicians and the historical events, the musician's experience, and the life.

"A Diary of the Underdogs" is an effort to reveal some of the vital life impressions of the 60's, through the eyes of the musicians; the political fears, the passions, and the wonderment. It can only be told as it is told here, by those who lived it, those who recall the music and remember a time when the city was filled with celebration, with struggle, and with creativity, at a time when San Francisco was a focus for the world.

* * *

A Diary of the Underdogs

INTRODUCTION

This account begins with the political and emotional feeling of a nation in shock over the assassination of President John F. Kennedy in 1963, the bewilderment of the public and mounting mistrust of the presiding government and elected officials. It was a time of civil unrest. Immediately after Vice President Lyndon Johnson was sworn in as President his problems rose to a new high. The war in Viet Nam became an ugly reality, one that touched everyone at home as well as in Viet Nam. The continuing cold war with Russia was very real; there was an inherent fear among the population of the United States of the possible massive destruction of civilization by the terrible effects of the "H" bomb, a feeling producing a despondency that bore down on daily life in America. It could not be hidden or dispelled. People began to take chances with their lives, to live outside of rationality, to experiment with religion, music and drugs, and to rebel against unfairness and the pious middle-class materialist values that were out of reach for many. Resistance to the war was rampant and visible everywhere, not only because the war a living horror and terribly wrong, but also because it was rapidly becoming obvious that the war in Viet Nam could not be won, and because of the fear in the hearts of youth, the fear of being drafted into an army of fools where bad decisions were being made on the battlefield and death was know to be a high probability. Many revolted against the draft in the later sixties by burning their draft cards, some fleeing to Canada, willing to renounce their citizenship to avoid being sucked into service. Demonstrations became commonplace. Seemingly spontaneous assemblies of citizens with anti-war slogans, bloody flags and peace symbols, rallies with bull horns and rock bands on flatbed trucks singing songs of freedom and protest against this war became daily events in city squares and on college campuses. This was an easy cause to be joined by the young wide-eyed youth of America who came to San Francisco searching for meaning, adventure, love, and ultimately, the psychedelic experience.

Many factors stirred the City in the Summer of Love, 1964. The Haight Ashbury drug and music explosion, the dangerous and unpredictable Hell's Angels motorcycle club, Chet Helms' Family Dog concerts, Mario Savio and the Free Speech movement in Berkley, the Black Panthers in Oakland, the Bill Graham concerts, the progressive voices of underground papers like the "Berkley Barb" and the Haight Ashbury "Oracle," theologian Alan Watts' televised lectures which turned to accounts of his LSD experiences. Poet Allen Ginsberg, author of "Howl" and the messenger of the free society had become a sage among the Hippies. Timothy Leary had helped advance the use of LSD through the medium of television with his philosophy of "tune-in, turn-on, and drop out" which many followed exactly, quitting their jobs and abandoning small towns to flock to the Haight Ashbury district in San Francisco to experience the new high.

Prankster Ken Kesey, LSD veteran and student of psychedelic experiment, authored the novel "One Flew Over the Cuckoo's Nest," and, after leaving the Stanford Veteran's Hospital where he conceived the story, began his intrepid meanderings in the "Magic Bus," picking up psychedelic neophytes along the way. The presence of specific Yoga Masters brought the influence of Eastern religious practices to the City. These many factors were in evidence in the daily life in San Francisco and other large cities across the nation where news of the San Francisco phenomena had traveled, although San Francisco was considered the source of everything, the *place to be* among seekers of the new enlightenment and peers of similar discontent experiencing the overpowering need to break away from tradition.

Leading icons in music came from throughout the nation. Folk music was a strong factor in

A Diary of the Underdogs

uniting the people's fledgling coalition and singer Bob Dylan, heroic both in originality and lyric content, brought voice to the emotional feelings of the people. There were others, and the song was basically the same; "Get out of Viet Nam."

The English bands seized upon the great opportunity to expand into the U.S. "The Beatles" broke the ice in America with the song "I Want to Hold Your Hand" and instantly won hearts. Their example in music and behavior, even style, (long haircuts) seemed to show the way and during the mid 60s they reigned supreme. Meanwhile locally, blues and rock bands continued to bludgeon away in nightly concerts at the Fillmore Auditorium and the Avalon Ballroom where everybody was very "high" and the dance halls were blue with a mixture of marijuana smoke and patchouli oil accompanied by flashing colored light shows. The Grateful Dead concerts were a favorite for clandestine followers of the LSD genres although many bands had similar hypnotic attraction including early bands of the Haight, The Charlatans, Sons of Champlin, Big Brother and the Holding Company, Jefferson Airplane, Sopwith Camel, The Steve Miller Band, Quicksilver Messengers, Country Joe and the Fish, and others including Carlos Santana, and Frank Zappa. But the "Dead" remained the real "stoner" band with a certain mystique the others failed to cultivate.

The whole movement reached a high frenzy and remained. It became reliable. This was the new San Francisco and it seemed it would always be the celebrated fun town it had become since the Gold Rush days of 1849 but with a new twist, and quite a "twist!" Everything had changed; it was an organized turmoil that seemed to somehow accommodate the expansion it required to continue. It was "San Francisco in the Sixties."

However, despite the merriment it wasn't all good. There were shortages. The masses that flowed in from the mid west and the eastern states created a mild famine among the hoards of the Haight and there were problems feeding everyone. The "Diggers" was a nonprofit organization established to distribute food for those in need. The young unknown actor Peter Coyote was among the early founders.

Other problems included crime. Within the new influx of character types were drug dealers and addicts. There had always been drug use in the City but now it was blatant and "buys" were common on the corners of the Haight as well as in the Fillmore, which had heretofore been the main area of hard drug use and sales of narcotics like heroin and cocaine. The news of murders taking place in the Haight Ashbury district brought darkness to the joyful free-spirited "flower children" identity and the police quickly moved in. The Hippie movement was on the wane. There had been great pressure from the local government on the Haight establishment for some time but these events were the signal of the end. On October 6' 1966 the last "human be-in" was held at the Polo Fields in Golden Gate Park presided over by poets Allen Ginsberg and Michael McClure, and it was also the day LSD became illegal. It was the "Death of the Hippie," and an effigy was symbolically carried to the park and burned.

A Diary of the Underdogs

CONTENTS

A Diary of the Underdogs

Chapter 1-Kennedy, America, the Coming of Change

When they shot John Kennedy the whole country was in an uproar, divided and bewildered. After that it soon went crazy. With the news of the President's assassination the Nation was in shock. We held to each other and watched the replay on television. Lyndon Johnson, the Vice President, was being sworn in as President on "Air Force One" on the way back to Washington D.C. John F. Kennedy had been assassinated on the streets of Dallas in his motorcade. Texas Governor, John Connelly was traveling with the President as was First Lady Jacqueline Kennedy. Connelly was wounded but he survived. Lee Harvey Oswald, a known dissident who had spent some time in the Soviet Union was soon arrested as the suspected assassin. There was good evidence he had shot the President from the third floor of a building along the Presidential motorcade route called the Book Depository. A high powered rifle was found in the building and evidence that the rifle had been recently fired from a window overlooking the parade route. This was not "conclusive" evidence but enough reason to detain Oswald while an investigation continued, and the F.B.I. needed to provide the country with a perpetrator, an assassin, as quickly as possible. The following morning Oswald was escorted down the basement hallway of the Federal Building to court to be formally charged. Many reporters crowded in for pictures along the corridor as the Sheriff's deputies walked him along. Reporters thrust microphones before Oswald with questions which he refused

President John F. Kennedy in Dallas, November, 1963, seconds before assassination

to answer while the television cameras held a steady focus on Oswald and the accompanying police authorities. Suddenly an unknown man burst from the crowd and shot Oswald while the nation watched in horror on national television. Oswald died shortly after without a confession. He had always maintained he was innocent. Jack Ruby, a Dallas striptease club owner, was the gunman and was assumed to have "Mob" connections. The story goes on in vivid detail as history, well documented but never definitively clear. Ruby died mysteriously a few years later but always insisted he was acting alone in Oswald's murder.

In response to these events the -Warren Commission- was created, headed by Chief Justice Earl Warren, a commission whose sole purpose was to investigate the assassination of the President, collect all evidence and prepare a report that was to get to the bottom of the mystery of the President's death and provide conclusive facts as to the assassin and his motives. The report contained many possible scenarios and theories- which, with numerous variations, survive to this day. The real story can only be called a

A Diary of the Underdogs

"cover up" for the sake of national security, meaning the people of America couldn't handle the truth without being outraged, something that would promote a lack of trust and cohesion in the American body of States and the entire Federal system, but the end result was worse. The information was to be archived for 50 years which created even more suspicion.

That loss of the President and the ensuing mystery and unclear resolution of the event dominated the United States for some time. Few trusted LBJ and Washington seemed far away and remote. Though Lyndon Johnson was a powerful politician he could not win the people nor could he avoid the continuing conflicts and the coming war with Viet Nam, a war that was not to be won, an unpopular war causing a bitter loss of many young men, a war spawning angry protests, frequent demonstrations, and continuing upheaval at home.

Free Speech—

Mario Savio in 1964 at UC Berkeley Campus

On this unsettling format demonstrations erupted at UC campus in Berkeley California on October 1, 1964, following a student revolt over the failure of the University Faculty to be responsive to their individual needs and the lack of communication, believing that their course work was irrelevant and that their most difficult assignments were merely tedious busy work with little or no educational value. Meanwhile, a rebellious coalition was developing due to failed attempts to communicate with the University Regents on issues of student fund raising, recruitment, and off campus social and political advocacy groups. This prompted a group of students to set up unauthorized tables for distribution of materials outside the campus offices in rebellion. They were promptly confronted by University faculty led by Arleigh Williams, then Dean of Men. The participants, Mark Bravo, Brian Turner, Donald Hatch, Elizabeth Gardiner Stapleton, and David Goines, were summoned to the Dean's office for discipline. This was the first formal dissidence and these were the charter members of what later was to become "the free speech movement." An innocuous reserved and quiet young man of concern and dedication magically emerged from the crowd gathered in front of the University's Sproul Hall on a very historic

day and became a hero, overwhelmed by the injustice of what was taking place before him, he was moved. The University Regents accompanied by the Berkeley police were in a standoff with the angry student population. On October 1, 1964, the student spokesman, Jack Weinberg, ignoring the faculty warnings continued speaking at the rally and was arrested by the police and placed in the back seat of the waiting car whereupon the crowd closed in so tightly the car was surrounded and unable to proceed. As the angry roar of the students pitched to a new high, the hero spokesman materialized from within the crowd. Moved by unknown forces he leapt to the roof of the car using it as a podium and began. This was no infidel, no neophyte to protest or to public outcry. Mario Savio had come from the civil rights battlefields of Mississippi urging; "The rights to participate as citizens in a democratic society, the right to due process of law and to be judged by committees of their peers, and that regulations be considered as arrived at legitimately from the consensus of the governed." These complaints of the education system were eventually heard, though not before some long days of conflict and the arrest and beating of many of the dissenting students by the local police.

A Diary of the Underdogs

The San Francisco Hell's Angels, a powerful long standing motorcycle club led by a man named Sonny Barger, became involved in the student standoffs stemming from the problems at the University of California at Berkeley and at first taking the side of the police. The Hell's Angels, known for strong even violent vigilante type action, appealed to the regents of the University. They toyed with the idea of their usefulness and the "Angels" seemed willing at the outset and participated as "rough" police to demonstrators during an Oakland rally. But they soon found their cause with the students and the struggle for free speech and the rights to the very freedoms that allowed -their own- existence. They soon became a protection group for the ongoing Free Speech Movement, protecting the students in ongoing demonstrations staged on flatbed trucks in the streets of Berkeley.

Martin Luther King speaking before the Abraham Lincoln memorial statue after the historic "March on Washington" August 28, 1963

But that first significant rebellion had brought a brilliant and passionate man from the crowd to lead them and help bind their cause in organized protest. Mario Savio was considered shy and quiet, withdrawn, even to stutter at times, but as the cause took importance before him he became a hero involuntarily, something lifted him. He rose to leadership, to speak for them all with conviction and dedication and a personal urgency to be heard. As he mounted the surrounded police car, holding the first arrested student Jack Weinberg, within, he shouted from the roof. A microphone was handed him and he continued to address the intense crowd of students, police, and faculty gathered before the Hall. The student complaints were clearly heard voiced through this man, this common dedicated man of conviction, Mario Savio.

Others joined the causes of free speech and freedom; Allen Ginsberg, Jerry Snyder, Yippy leader Jerry Rubin, Joan Baez, and many other notables, and on December 8, 1965 the freedom was won. The University of California revised the student agenda to include distribution of political materials and the right for various organizations to recruit members on campus, "Free Speech." Mario Savio died November 7, 1996 in California.

Civil Rights

The Anti-segregationists, a black coalition which included many prominent whites, fought hard for racial equality in Mississippi and Alabama. Mario Savio had been active in their numbers before coming to Berkley. On August 28, 1963 the Southern Christian Unity led by Reverend Martin Luther King and his followers gathered together for the "March on Washington" to plead their case to the White house and speak before the statue of Abraham Lincoln. "The Civil Rights Movement" was now a protest carried to Washington sighting the racial violence in Selma, Alabama where blacks were being abused and killed by "segregationist" whites over "bussing," the forced integration of blacks in public schools and facilities, on public transportation, on busses and in restaurants. Martin Luther King had led a good fight, and while speaking in Memphis in 1968, he was assassinated by a man named James Earl Ray, an assumed radical acting alone.

A Diary of the Underdogs

Chapter 2 Protest Music: Folk, Rock and Roll, the Beatles

The Beatles in San Francisco, 1964

There was a lack of trust in the government. The various police authorities and the FBI had their hands full. Every visible organizer and protestor was being filmed by agencies of the federal government and kept in files by the authorities of national security. The whole country was experiencing a wave of drug infusion, dissidence and radicalism.

The population was politically divided yet there was cohesion and a unity in music, in Rock and Roll, in Folk music, and in jazz. In the midst of this civil turmoil, the music flourished. It seemed the only thing that wasn't whirling around, that was honest and that wasn't killing people was the music. It was a cry from within, something we could all identify with, where we found each other, something "*real*," and those who played for us became our heroes. The British invasion, as it was labeled by the media at the time, was the sudden appearance of rock and roll and pop bands from the UK who were becoming popular in the US and Canada. The period is roughly 1964 to1967 and began with the Beatles first appearance on the Ed Sullivan show and included the discovery of US born Jimi Hendricks who had gained recognition in the UK. In August, 1964 the "Beatles" invasion began with a sold out concert at the Cow Palace. Following that appearance in San Francisco and the subsequent exposure on the national television media, the music of the Beatles was heard everyday everywhere, and some songs touted drug experiences like, "Lucy in the Sky with Diamonds," "A Day in the Life," and "Sergeant Pepper's Lonely Hearts Club Band." The music was based on the idea of mystical excursions into Eastern philosophy, LSD, change and experimentation. Other British bands soon appeared during that time leading to a major cultural realignment of values; "The Byrds," "The Beau Brummels, "Paul Revere and the Raiders," "Todd Rundgren," "The Rolling Stones," "The Animals," Eric Burden and "War," "The Kinks," "The Who," all part of a long list of strong rock and roll patriots focused on San Francisco and the world. Joe MacDonald of "Country Joe and the Fish," and others of the San Francisco cadre, sang Viet Nam protest songs on flat bed trucks Sundays in the Golden Gate Park Panhandle. But nationally, Bob Dylan, the "prophet elite" became a giant among the "Folkies," (the folk-rock musicians). Dylan, with Joan Baez became the rock on which our hearts stood. Many others that followed culled a similar message, "Get out of Viet Nam."It was a war that had begun in 1959 and was still raging in the mid '60s, "band together because we can't trust the government." Those, and other similar sentiments, converged into "free love" and exotic drug experiences that took root in the "Haight Ashbury" neighborhood in 1965.

Songs that touted sexual freedom and referred to drugs quickly became favorites among the young population streaming into San Francisco from all over the country, forging a unity of common emotions through the explicit lyric music of rock and roll through which various seminal bands established their success, among them; "The Grateful Dead," "Jefferson Airplane," "Big Brother and the Holding Company," "The Moody Blues," and "The Doors."

Later in 1966 the innovative Frank Zappa would burst onto the music scene with "The Mothers of Invention" to the delight of many fans. Though hotly controversial, this iconoclast, easily the Thelonious

Ticket stub, Beatles at the Cow Palace, August, 1964

109E 4
SECTION   ROW   SEAT
RESERVED SEAT
COW PALACE — SAN FRANCISCO
WEDNESDAY NIGHT
AUG 19 1964   19
Hancock Bros. S.F.

A Diary of the Underdogs

Monk of the rock idiom, was more than mildly offensive to some. His promotion poster depicted him sitting pants down on the commode. He was once said to have defecated on stage to the revulsion and delight of his audience. He thrived on shock value and the unexpected. His music was powerfully intellectual and creative with a wry comical bent and lyrics of strong sexual content such as found in "The Zombie Woof" and "Dynamo Hum" which won him many fans instantly and caused his concerts to be sold out. Moving into the seventies when jazz was struggling with the preponderance of Rock and Folk music and the popularity of groups like the "Kingston Trio," his bands often included known jazz musicians such as pianist George Duke from San Francisco and bassist Pat O'Hearn from Oregon.

But there was one man who could not tolerate his very existence and he was quite explicit, Senator Slade Gordon of California. He railed against Zappa and his "Mothers of Invention" for his youth-corrupting and sexually exploitive songs. There were indictments and a Senate hearing in 1980, and finally he got his crack at Zappa. The outcome was pathetic. Gordon was obviously under equipped to deal effectively with Zappa's wit and the whole thing became a joke but with good solid Supreme Court concurrence. The idea of obscenity raised its ugly head again in favor of Zappa, that idea that obscenity was held within the mind of the beholder, something previously established in the Lenny Bruce case in 1963.

But, the incident served as an example and evidence that certain persons of the government were dissatisfied with the ruling icons of the new society, wealthy rock and roll musicians. The government had nearly lost the people and was considered aloof, profane, arrogant and deaf to their cries, not able to recognize or deal with the passions of the evolving young populations. The "Old Guard" was on the way out but they didn't know it. It was a time of obvious decay from within.

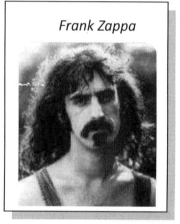

Frank Zappa

As the Viet Nam casualties began returning home, the dead in boxes, others missing limbs, or seriously addicted to drugs, they found a chaotic mess of a society with dwindling national welcome, receiving little thanks for their contribution in war. They had dutifully become the expendable forces of an impossible war. The nation had gone sour over Viet Nam. It was a war not to be won; it was rather, the nation's first embarrassing and tragic defeat. The Communist Chinese could not be bombed into submission, a sobering hopeless fact. Later in 1973, the U.S. withdrew from Viet Nam under President Richard Nixon as he resumed the control of America during his second term, a term from which he later resigned due to his implications with the "break-in" of the Democratic National Headquarters now known as "Watergate." Nixon's political life was over. Once again the nation was baffled, shaken over the lack of trust in government and the shoddy behavior of elected officials.

Gerald Ford, the Vice President, took office as President and ran the country lightly with golf and skiing at his retreat in Vale, Colorado though he was, by discovery to finalize the American activity in Viet Nam and pulled back the nation from all involvement. However, the original purpose of American forces there was to hold off the Communist forces from overtaking the new democratic government in South Viet Nam that had been installed by the United States. With American withdrawal from Cambodia the outnumbered army of South Viet Nam soon fell to the Communist North as they entered the city of Phnom Penh without resistance, allowing the return of the country back to Communist control, to what it was before the war began. The loss of millions of lives in that region was a tragic mistake.

Historically, Ford's was the most "wave-less" administration of record. Although he managed some international negotiations with Russia, the best thing to come out of that period was from First Lady,

A Diary of the Underdogs

Betty Ford who founded the "Betty Ford Clinic," subsequently helping many drug dependants back to useful lives including many wealthy elitists.

But it began with Kennedy and before. His assassination was the snap heard around the country, the twig in the still woods that set the forest to turmoil, disconsolately, an unrest spawning a creeping fear of dwindling national freedom and vulnerability, something not previously experienced in America since the great depression of the thirties.

Chapter 3-Jazz, Charlie Parker, Miles Davis, Dizzy Gillespie, San Francisco Clubs

Jazz music has always been the cry of freedom, born in the oppression of the American South, during the many years of slavery. It was "field calling," calling back and forth through the work day as in song and

Bird-Charlie Parker

answer, much the same as in the black churches. The music developed through the blues. Robert Johnson, Blind Lemon, Lead-Belly were just a few in the long line of music development and the jazz evolution which included Buddy Bolden, Jelly Roll Morton, influential trumpeter Louis Armstrong and later Bix Beiderbecke and others. The era of swing music also contributed greatly to the evolution of jazz music in America. Kansas City, Missouri was a musical hub in the 1930's and 40's, a place where musicians like, Coleman Hawkins, and Charlie Parker developed their style playing in the Jimmie Lunceford and Count Basie bands.

Jazz music exploded to new prominence in a modern form during the latter half of 1946 following World War II. The voice was "Bird," Charlie Parker, and he came from Kansas City. He held the *seed* of the "*bean stalk*" and "*Bird*" ultimately became "*Jack,*" but he wasn't acting alone. There were others around him that understood the music and carried him along, the cadre of musical torch bearers that allowed him to flourish in spite of his own

proclivity to drugs and dissipation, a product of his intense life style and the overwhelming fire of his own creativity. Sadly, at the age of thirty four, in 1955, he was consumed within his own flame. He left a scorching musical road for his diligent devotees to follow, a brilliant golden web of creativity and a legacy still being unraveled today.

Bird's early groups included Dizzy Gillespie, bright and talented trumpeter and energetic composer. Together they became the authoritative source of early "Bebop" music. Though surrounded by many competent musicians, only a small significant group could execute the complex musical forms with validity. There were already strong voices in Bird's fertile roost, players that had definitive styles and reputations; "Bean" (Coleman Hawkins) Lucky Thompson, Don Byas, and Thelonious Monk, all of whom improvised in much the same manner with the melody identified within the solo, while Bird played in a way revealing none of the original melody, creating something entirely new and fresh each time he played, like on the standard "*Quasimodo*" based on the chords to "Embraceable You."

Very quickly, during that period of the forties, ('46 to '48) others emerged with a firm grip on the

A Diary of the Underdogs

music that included precocious trumpeter Miles Davis from East Saint Louis who became a permanent part of Bird's band. Miles had followed Fats Navarro and as he later confessed in his book, "Miles, The Autobiography," by Quincy Troupe, published in 1986 by Simon and Schuster, that he was quite intimidated with what he had to live up to in Bird's band and talked about being insecure early on. Bird's ferocity, his energy and ability to scorch through burning fast tempos, exploding with rich spontaneous musical ideas seemed too immense a task for young Miles. Though he often went home after the gig perplexed and beat, he soon rose to the level of playing compatible with Bird but within his own style. Through that experience Miles began to develop his unique personal sound and style which propelled him on to his long creative career.

That historic Charles Parker band also revealed the brilliance of Max Roach, the quintessential drummer of the "Bop" movement. The pianist was Duke Jordan and the bassist was Tommy Potter, but there were stints with piano genius Bud Powell who was also making his own way with his powerful and innovative trio. Though Bud was considered erratic and to be plagued by mental problems he was undisputedly brilliant and had a strong hold on the new music. His compositions and playing showed that he was a tremendous force at the piano and at that time rivaled by none except the great Art Tatum. Bud pursued Tatum, and as one story indicates, they got together. That meeting was historic. Bud demonstrated

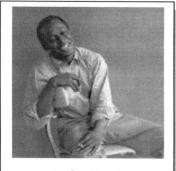

Miles Davis

his ferocious ability to Tatum who, after hearing Powell, imitated him, with embellishments, playing only with his left hand. The *"master"* was unassailable. None the less, Bud was prolific, a raging, hard swinging Bebop pianist, a power that eventually set him apart in the world of jazz and modern piano.

Bird was challenged by many New York musicians, all wanting to demonstrate their abilities with Bird, the "source." Many imitated his style, forgetting to search for their own voice. The new jazz music touched many players indelibly with an imprint that would follow them their whole musical lives. Throughout the early fifties vital recordings were made by Bird and as his story reveals, they were made under various moods and states of mind. Generally, they are considered pristine, full of color and emotion. Savoy Records believed in Bird and marketed the new Bebop music. In the fall of 1945 producer Teddy Reig of Savoy Records set up a recording date for Bird with Sadik Hakim on piano, (Dizzy Gillespie on some tracks) Curly Russell on bass, Max Roach on drums, and Miles Davis on trumpet, with Dizzy Gillespie on three of the tracks, "Warmin' up a Riff," "Meandering," and "Ko-Ko," Bird's take on "Cherokee," which Miles shied away from. Again, quoting from the "Miles Davis Biography," "I wasn't going to get out there and embarrass myself. I didn't really think I was ready to play tunes at the tempo of Cherokee, and I didn't make any bones about it." Later, Miles recalls being asleep on the floor in the studio while Dizzy played his part of the recording session. It wasn't until later, when the record came out, that Miles heard what Dizzy had done and marveled at the beauty of his solos. Miles had the heart to admit to Dizzy's greatness, his power and sensitivity. The record came out as "Charlie Parker's Reboppers," on Savoy Records, a classic.

Blue Note eventually became the strongest most successful record company to harbor jazz exclusively over the long haul during that early era of bebop, consistently signing good artists, providing informative liner notes and photos and promoting radio play and sales across the country and in Europe all helping make Bird and others well known jazz celebrities and romantic heroes in the new world of jazz music.

A Diary of the Underdogs

Brilliant pianist, Bud Powell deserves his rightful place among these heroes. His contribution has always been tainted with accounts of his social instability, although he was revered by his peers and rightly so. The story of Bud Powell is one worth the effort to understand as described here in living detail by writer Francis Davis with reference to his greatest works. This vivid account of the life and artistry of Powell is vital to the story of jazz music and the difficulty in which it has been forced to survive. Still, the joyful power of the music tends to drive one to whatever territory may exist to accomplish its desired expression and be born into society. This account is reprinted here with the permission of the author.

In a January 1996 interview with Atlantic Monthly, music critic and writer Francis Davis, discussing "Bud's Bubble," his critical essay on Bud Powell from the same issue, explained that bebop, or bop, is no longer a sub-genre within jazz, but rather a style that "has become jazz in a sense." That sense, he went on to explain, is the way in which jazz is no longer music to dance to- it's a music to listen to, an art as opposed to a form of entertainment. There are a handful of players generally credited with inventing bebop, and with a few exceptions (one of them obviously being Duke Ellington) these creators are largely responsible for the artistic respectability of the genre.

Bud Powell

Bud Powell is often called the father of the bebop piano, and credited with translating Charlie Parker's innovations to fit the keyboard. In essence, he reconfigured the instrument and influenced every jazz pianist that followed. It's interesting to note however that Powell developed his style on the piano as a contemporary and a peer of Parker's and not a student or disciple. Both were accomplished musicians at an early age, both began their careers in big bands; Parker in Jay McShann's band and Powell in Cootie Williams'. There is recorded evidence with those bands of both men's musical progression that indicates concurrent development. It's also interesting to note that both men were plagued by similar self-destructive tendencies, physical and mental health problems and both underwent electroshock treatments, at roughly the same time, which possibly suggests a concentric basis for a style of music that so accurately expresses conflicting emotion and internal (as well as external) struggle.

At the same time, as Davis explained in the essay, "the question of how much Powell owed Parker also ignores his arguably greater debt to two fellow pianists, Art Tatum and Thelonius Monk." But I think, more to the point, the pursuit of influences and mentors ignores the significant contributions Powell made to bebop through his own style and approach, and perhaps more significantly his original compositions - which show him to be, when at the height of creative powers, simultaneously on the brink of complete chaos, capable of a frightening level of introspection and intricately wired to the world he lived in.

Bud Powell was born in Harlem in 1924, the son of a building superintendent, who was reportedly a proficient stride pianist. Powell himself was a prodigy, classically trained and able by age ten to play in the style of Art Tatum and Fats Waller. By 1940, he was taking part in informal jam sessions at Minton's

A Diary of the Underdogs

Play House and running with a coterie of NYC jazz musicians that included Thelonious Monk, Charlie Parker, and Dizzy Gillespie. He made his first recordings at age 19 with Cootie Williams' band. In addition to his skill and talent, Powell was also known for his erratic behavior. In 1945 he suffered a blow to the head that began a pattern of institutionalization and deterioration that would both shape and destroy his career. The circumstances of Powell's injury are uncertain. According to Thomas Fitterling, author of "Thelonious Monk: His life and Music," Powell was beaten while defending Monk from the police during a raid at the Savoy Ballroom. The police stormed the club and went after Monk. He refused to show his identification, and was forcibly arrested. A fan barred the door and challenged the officers. They tried to push him aside, but he wouldn't budge. "Stop," he yelled, "you don't know what you're doing. You're mistreating the greatest pianist in the world." At this point the nightstick came down on his head like a lightening bolt. The young fan was Monk's best friend, Bud Powell." Miles Davis, in his autobiography, "Miles," claimed that Bud was pistol whipped by a bouncer at the Savoy Ballroom for being cocky and refusing to pay the cover. (Miles), "Bud had gone up to the Savoy ballroom in Harlem dressed in his all-black outfit that he used to like to wear. He had his boys from the Bronx with him, who, he used to brag, "Would kick anybody's ass." So he goes up to the Savoy without any money in his pocket, and the bouncer, who knew him, told him who couldn't go in without any money. But he's saying this to Bud Powell, the greatest young piano player in the world, and Bud knew this. So Bud just walked right past the motherfucker. The bouncer did what he was being paid to do. He broke Bud's head all the way open, cracked him upside his head with a pistol."

Dexter Gordon, in an interview with jazz critic Ira Gitler, contended that Powell was arrested in a Philadelphia train station for drunk and disorderly conduct while on tour with Cootie Williams and was beaten while in custody. Concrete evidence withstanding, more Powell biographies prefer the romanticism of Monk's account, citing the composition "In Walked Bud" as evidence of Monk's gratitude. Miles Davis' version, although seemingly less sympathetic, paints Powell as a bad-ass, instead of a victim and allows him to retain a strange dignity. In reality the particulars matter less than the results, and even those are refutable.

By all recollections Powell was first hospitalized as a result of headaches that began shortly after he was beaten. It was around this time that his slip into substance abuse began. Miles Davis recalled that even Charlie Parker didn't want Powell around because he "got too high." Davis' version is the only account of Powell's heroin use; most biographies claim he was only a drinker, but a heavy drinker.

In 1947, during a stay in Bellevue, Powell was given ECT, or electroshock treatment for the first time. Four years later, while a patient at Pilgrim State hospital he received another. In typical display of necessary bitterness, Miles Davis speculated, "I sometimes wonder if those white doctors gave him shock treatments on purpose, to cut him off from himself, like they did to Bird."

It's true that Powell was entering a creative peak when the treatments began, and that all but one of his significant recordings was made in the years in between his two treatments. Furthermore, all of his important original compositions were solidified during this period.

In the sessions he recorded during those few years, Powell managed to create some of the most memorable jazz tracks of the era. In particular I would cite The Amazing Bud Powell sessions recorded for Blue Note in 1949 and Jazz Giant, consisting of two sessions recorded in 1949 and 1950 for Verve. A significant number of originals appear between the two sessions, six on the Blue Note, and another five on the Verve.

Still, it seems though that far too many people dismiss Powell's work as technically impressive but artistically lacking. This may have something to do with his incredible speed, and also the way in which he revolutionized the left hand's role in jazz piano playing. Previously, while the right hand established melody,

A Diary of the Underdogs

the left controlled the stride, even and rhythmic, as apparent in swing.

Powell used his left hand to accent off beats, and often he seemed to drum with the left rather than roll with it. The left hand produced dissonant chords that subverted the melody and sometimes the tempo, although most frequently everything in Powell's music was overpowered by timing, an idea worth examining in a figurative manner. To imply that this unique way of playing didn't convey meaning of any kind is unfair. Understandable perhaps that speed and dexterity are often considered the result of strenuous practice and natural talent, and used often to the effect of showboating, but what Powell was playing with his left hand, was often uncomfortable to hear, and seemed to be trying to communicate a chasm within himself, and between himself and his environment.

"Tempus Fugit," "Un Poco Loco" (literally, "time flies" and "a little crazy") as well as "Glass Enclosure" all suggest in some way being grounded amongst motion, being out of sync with ones' surroundings. Like many of Powell's recorded works these tracks teeter on the verge of dissipating into weak chaos. Even the most light hearted of his melodies, when juxtaposed with the left hand accents, indicate something jagged.

Going one step further, the dates of these recordings and the number of original compositions suggest the real tragedy and achievement of Powell's art. That he knew what was happening to him, and also knew that he wouldn't always be in command of his own mind, because he had experienced a glimpse of that day already. It's likely this produced an urgency in his work, and an anxiety that really meshed with some of the most progressive ideas of his time, a time that saw existentialism collide with post modern philosophy, a time that saw war, that saw a thick gloss coating over almost all social tragedies, in a way that he couldn't have done had he not felt so pressed and so close to the void.

One of the most striking of any Powell recording is his two minute 50 second version of Arlen and Koehler's "Get Happy" played at a compulsive speed, the music box melody is a mockery of the song's expressed notion. It becomes maniacal and irrational and yet persists, only to be dragged back by an irregularly spaced, low plod dish chord that barely has a chance to make its point. It's like the sound of being unwilling to fight.

Indeed it does seem that whether he gave in or ran out, Powell's career ended long before his life was over. His last significant album was the 1953 recording of his concert at Massey Hall in Toronto. He moved to Paris in the late fifties and returned to New York in 1964, two years later he died. The end of his life, much of which was spent sick, drunk and incoherent, was the inspiration for Dexter Gordon's role in the 1986 film Round Midnight. Even in Paris Powell's reputation was that of an afflicted man as much as it was one of a visionary. By the time he arrived to that sanctuary, he was far away, and surrounded by people, who as Davis recalled, "Thought he might have been just a drunken bum." But the legacy, carried out in his music, his style, is that of a man completely in step with a place in time that very few people, only the brightest and strangest, could ever measure out.

* * *

Jazz had taken firm root in the period of the late 1940's and early 50's but by the early 60's it became shaded, over shadowed by the current pop music of the day which has always been the case with art forms and art primarily. By the 1960's jazz was dominated by the power of the new Rock music. Jazz

A Diary of the Underdogs

didn't have the message in the lyrics, except in the "blues" and the "blues" was always about loss, about pain, burning love, and cheating, and about misery.

By the mid nineteen fifties and into the early nineteen sixties jazz had become a subculture in San Francisco, a solid strata of society near the bottom, near the earth, where the truth, a thing upon which jazz music is based, a constant from which to extract spirit and sophistication, continued to privately survive. It lived because of the very essence that formed it early on and the freedom that is its core.

The poets of the late 50's having made their stand toyed with jazz. It was hip, a neat backdrop for recital, and a mystic bleak cacophony for the sadness of phrases, for the rebellious phonetics of dramatic recitation. That is where jazz fit, as a dark reclusive element in black walled wine bars and cellars. That was only part of the story. Jazz had always had its own voice and during the 60's, after a brief setback from the dominance of popular music and a lack of viable clubs and performance venues, it began to shout again. The music of "Bird" re-surfaced. "Bird Lives," found scrawled on sleazy bathroom walls was one indication that "Bird" was unforgettable, almost as an ill defined call, a remote protest against the bludgeoning rock music, the undying love for "bebop" and that earlier time when Bird did live, evidence that the music was heard and those who heard it were still around, that the music was remembered and would never die.

Musicians were affected deeply with that current broil of the society of that time and drugs were a part of it. The music had been developing through that, through the mire of substance, through speed, psychedelics and "smack," through the political climate in San Francisco, from North Beach, the Coffee Gallery on Grant, and the poets tables, from the Café' Tri Este, from Jimbo's Bop City on Post street, from Parkers Soulville, on McAllister, from Jack's on Sutter and from little tucked away Cafe's like Jackson's Nook and the Bird Cage, the Jazz Cellar on Green street and a hundred little clubs and coffee houses throughout the city where jazz was the "*word*," the language.

But one of the real sources was the "Black Hawk," located at the corner of Turk and Hyde streets in what is called the Tenderloin district. There, within the din, the small tables packed you close to the bandstand to watch Miles Davis tongue his mouthpiece and scowl at Sonny Stitt, and Philly "Joe" Jones, playing the drums with one hand on the ride cymbal while changing his foot pedal during a blistering fast tempo, and watch the sweat stream down the placid face of Paul Chambers playing bravely through the wretch of fever.

Another venue was the "Trident" in Sausalito, a frequent home for the Vince Guaraldi trio and where Bill Evans played rare weekend gigs with drummer Larry Bunker and bassist Chuck Isreals. Those were memorable performances, thick with emotion. Seeing Bill with his head below the piano in that familiar hunch, alive with resonance, was intoxicating. You could feel his music enter your heart and touch every part of you. It was a special form of magic; it was Bill Evans' own brilliance.

* * *

Jazz music needed protection, a buffer to survive. It wasn't strong enough then for the revolution, the social and music revolution. There was a great need for festive music, music for large crowds of people, for celebration and to create unity. Introspection would come later, when they realized they wanted something more, when there had been time to think and after everyone had been very high, when there was a need for music within a capsule that could speak for the soul and satisfy the emotional hunger they were feeling and provide a thoroughly developed and firmly established musical art form. Jazz required listening-opening up. Once you let it in it would tear at you, invade, and make you feel. Jazz musicians

A Diary of the Underdogs

sweat with the power, their bodies hunched, driving at the beat, pushing the chords into the piano, setting melodies to fly above the room through a horn, concentrating on the synchronicity of a cymbal beat, or leaned back pulling at growling bass strings and spilling private joy from their faces. Those things were permanent. That eternal dedication carried a high price and if death be a part of it then let it come now, in the act, in performance, in the heart of the music. That same attitude still exists today.

A local pianist, one night while performing at "Pearl's" in San Francisco, was so exasperated with the noise from the audience he stood up from the piano and yelled into the room of busily taking customers, "If you want to talk, go somewhere else! This is a performance club. We're trying to perform." The rest of the audience applauded him, the noisy ones quickly filed out.

Jazz had become the favorite music to "talk over," and thank God it was the favorite something. Jazz has taken a lot of abuse, the players also. They're a humble lot, moved by a relentless spirit, a spirit ever present in the "Underdogs." Their life is something outside of that, often fraught with hardship and struggle, the clanging reality of survival. The music rewards the soul for its persistence. Jazz makes it worth while, a peace within the private society to which we belong where we compare our scars, our wrap sheets from a life of music, and our joys. Some fit in and some fit out, and that's how it remains, within its own song and tempo. And there are certain tempos reserved for jazz music, 90, 140, 250, and they are immediately identifiable from the first note. Anything that precise can stand the years even with a restricted audience. Conversely, the fact that jazz music is a minority gives it protection and worth, though not often "wealth." The wealth is in the enrichment of the soul where its value has no limits. Jazz has an incorruptible purity that has outlasted the trends. It has become its own persona; it represents a definitive priority, a special character and life style.

* * *

Celebration appeared in jazz unexpectedly with Cannonball Adderley and his brother Nat in "Dis Here," a tune written by pianist Bobby Timmons which actually "moved" people. At the Jazz Workshop on Broadway in North beach they were "dancing in the isles." This was new, jazz audiences had always been "listening" audiences, non- participating, but this music moved them. Jazz retro-files were quick to accuse Cannonball of "selling out," "going commercial." The message was there in the music, "celebration." It was pure "soul blues" in three quarter time, Gospel.

Gospel music had always moved people through the black churches where it began. When it was introduced to jazz audiences in the early sixties it went over immediately. It uniquely combined movement with jazz music. Others followed with great success. Charles Mingus came out with "Better Git it in Your Soul" and "Wednesday Night Prayer Meeting," an album that firmly established his music and gave focus to his very intense compositional talent. Les McCann and Eddie Harris followed the same venue with success. It was a split-off from the main tree of jazz. John Coltrane and the Miles Davis cadre set it straight and it stayed that way. Church music became "Soul Funk" with lyrics, and many artists moved it far ahead. Aretha Franklin took it from there to become the "Queen of Soul."

A Diary of the Underdogs

Chapter 4-Haight Ashbury, the LSD experience

The Haight street collective was gaining momentum. In November 1965 it was known as "Hashbury," the intersection of two streets, Haight and Ashbury. There was a new consciousness developing in the youth of America. It was stimulated by "Rock and Roll" and the poetry of the "Beats" and an excitement to the spiritual and intellectual awakening and body awareness promoted through the LSD experience. The substance, Lysergic Acid Diethylamide, was first synthesized in 1938 by Swiss chemist Albert Hoffman who was considered to be the first "tripper" on LSD. With the sixties there was a need to explain the complication of feelings, the complex sensations, the disappointment with the war in Viet Nam, the atrocities, the "six o'clock news," seeing the bombs and the napalm, the vicious ongoing war that killed brothers and uncles, one of the first wars that you could watch on television, plus the very real threat of a nuclear war due to the restricted communication with the Soviet Union and the fear of the "H Bomb" during the period known as the Cold War. All of this weighed heavily on the youth of America. They needed to find new hope, something to believe in other than the government and in the process to define love.

Allen Ginsberg and Timothy Leary

The Fillmore and Avalon Ballrooms were centers of expression where new bands screamed with sizzling guitars and the primal beat of the drums, light shows flashed paisley psychedelic images over walls and floors combining with the music to create a grand and free experience, and it had tremendous appeal. Rock and Roll was providing the venue of freedom and unity. It was building to a point where a grand celebration was needed, an event that could give way to the experiences and sensations of the new community, a demonstration of spiritual expression, love, and freedom.

Painter Michael Bowen's apartment at 1371 Haight Street, above the "head shop" on Haight and Masonic was a meeting place for poets, artists and gurus, and an early office for Allen Cohen's hippy newspaper, "The Oracle." Bowen was often visited by Allen Ginsberg, Gary Snyder, Timothy Leary, Richard Alpert, Yippie leader Jerry Rubin and others including Jerry Garcia and some of the Hell's Angles. Through these influences and the insights provided with frequent trips on LSD, he helped to create the "Human Be-In" and was lovingly known as the "Psychedelic Ranger." His "cause" was to "turn on as many of certain people as possible to LSD for the enlightenment of humankind and produce a greater psychic awareness in the world." This was also Timothy Leary's quest and he voiced it in his statement to the press, "Tune in, Turn on, and Drop Out," which established him as a "Hippy" star. He advocated taking doses of LSD and dropping out of society, regarding LSD as a liberator of social hang-ups. Michael Bowen never did anything without consulting his guru John Cooke who lived in Cuernavaca, Mexico. He was often on the phone to him. The party in the Haight got into full swing, everyone was invited.

A Diary of the Underdogs

Chapter 5-The Both/And, National and Local bands

       Delano Dean opened the "Both/And" on Divisadero and he booked national artists. Vibraphonist Bobby Hutcherson lived in San Francisco and was always part of the lineup which included some great dates with Harold Land; also John Handy's Band with Michael White, Terry Clarke, Don Thompson, Jerry Hahn and later Mike Nock. Ornette Coleman came to town in a fantastic series of performances playing both trumpet and violin. Archie Shepp appeared there as did Bill Evans. Miles Davis came with his new band with Herbie Hancock, Ron Carter, Wayne Shorter, and the brilliant young drummer, Tony Williams, who was under age at the time. That same year the "Half Note," down the street presented pianist George Duke who eventually went with Frank Zappa. Organist Richard "Groove" Holmes found a long steady gig there and a popular recording of the Erroll Garner song "Misty" moved his career along. Over in North Beach things continued to develop. The Jazz Workshop was open and all the "greats" were coming in. The long list included; Cannonball Adderley, with his brother Nat on trumpet, Sam Jones on bass, Louis Hayes

on drums and Joe Zawinul on piano. Yusef Lateef, with pianist Elmo Hope; Horace Silver, with Blue Mitchell on trumpet and Junior Cook playing tenor, Eugene Taylor, bass, and Roy Brookes on drums, Charles Mingus, with John Handy and Jane Getz who one night was verbally assailed by Mingus on the bandstand for some unknown reason. Jane continued quite embarrassed as her mother and sister had come that night to hear her. John Coltrane appeared with the now famous group including, McCoy Tyner, piano, Jimmy Garrison, bass, and Elvin Jones, drums. Rashaan Roland Kirk appeared with Harold Maybern on piano. Thelonius Monk came with tenor man, Charles Rouse. Barry Harris, in 1961 recorded an album at the Jazz Workshop in live performance with Sam Jones and Louis Hayes. Miles Davis appeared in San Francisco many times beginning in the nineteen fifties, first with a quartet at Fack's on Market street when he was still quite young and later famous and well documented gigs at the Black Hawk. There was significant jazz history made then resulting in legendary recordings; "Miles Davis-In Person-

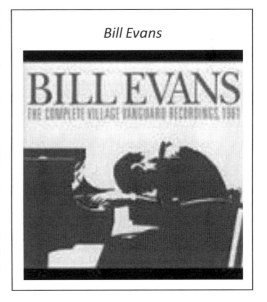

Bill Evans

Saturday Night at the Black Hawk." The group then consisted of Red Garland, piano, Paul Chambers, bass, Philly Joe Jones, drums and Sonny Stitt on Saxophones. That same group also played the Jazz Workshop on Broadway. Miles appeared there later with his new band that included Cannonball Adderley. Miles came later with a new ensemble including Herbie Hancock, Wayne Shorter, Bassist Ron Carter, and Tony Williams. Stan Getz appeared at the Jazz Workshop following the hit record, "Girl from Impanema" with Astrud Gilberto, a more commercial venture that netted millions of record sales. But Stan was burning in those early days at the Black Hawk with his own quartets. Les McCann's band had bassist Leroy Vinnegar. "The Master Sounds," Richie Crabtree, piano, Monk Montgomery, bass, Benny Barth, drums and Buddy Montgomery on vibes, were a solid San Francisco group that held strong on the scene for quite some time. Charles Lloyd had young pianist Keith Jarrett, with Jack Dejohnette on drums and Ron McClure on bass. Bill Evans appeared with the notorious trio from the Vanguard recordings consisting of Scott LaFaro on bass and Paul Motion on drums. Evans appeared again in the later 60s in San Francisco with drummer Tom Reynolds and Paul Warburton on bass.

A Diary of the Underdogs

Chapter 6-The Press, Ralph Gleason, Strip Clubs, Hungry I

There were Monday night bands where the local musicians got to play. Energetic writer-Ralph Gleason- of the San Francisco Chronicle, although writing about the Rock scene and the Jefferson Airplane, also wrote about jazz in his column "The Lively Arts" and was becoming more and more enamored with the sound of jazz music, with the intellectual content and the passion. Jazz at last would have a voice, a good and eventually, a well informed prolific voice. It would survive. Ralph came to love the music and the musicians, especially Miles Davis. Miles dedicated a tune to him entitled "R.J," written by Miles' bassist, Ron Carter.

The following is from an article by Joel Selvin, SF Chronicle December 24th 2004

Don't let the tweed jackets, trench coat and pipe fool you -- Ralph J. Gleason was an apostle of jazz and rock with few peers. Ralph Gleason, one of the first writers to cover Miles Davis in his columns, "The Lively Arts" became good friends with him.

At The Chronicle, Gleason became the first daily newspaper critic in the country to cover jazz and pop music openings like theater or opera openings. Although his main topic was jazz, he was no snob. He picked up stories across the pop panorama. He interviewed Hank Williams and covered his show in 1952 at San Pablo Hall in the far reaches of the East Bay. Gleason gave early glowing reviews to Nat King Cole ("the top balladeer of his time") and Frank Sinatra ("far and above anybody by a country mile").

Ralph Gleason, Miles Davis and Tony Williams

He kept an ear cocked toward other sounds and frequently lectured his readers on the musical qualities of rock 'n' roll and rhythm and blues. He interviewed Elvis Presley, Fats Domino, Louis Jordan, Ivory Joe Hunter, Big Joe Turner and Ray Charles in The Chronicle. He even paused to scorch the unspeakably square Pat Boone ("pretentious and a bit of a phony").

From the pulpit of the daily newspaper, Gleason's jazz criticism penetrated mainstream culture. He gave early coverage to Miles Davis and described Louis Armstrong in 1954 as "one of the most important people alive Today." Gleason and Davis became close friends. Gleason once returned from visiting the trumpeter during a nightclub engagement where the diabetic Gleason discovered that he and Davis used the same-sized hypodermic needles. Davis was not diabetic.

But Gleason never limited his contributions to the printed page. He played a crucial role in founding the Monterey Jazz Festival. It was Gleason's idea to take the music out of the dark, smoky, smelly nightclubs and into the fresh air and sunshine. Disc jockey Jimmy Lyons, who ran the festival for the first 34 years, located the horse show arena on the Monterey County Fairgrounds. "Ralph was essential to the festival," said the late Grover Sales, publicist on the first festival. He suggested the whole concept of the festival."

They certainly got the cast they wanted for that 1958 weekend -- Louis Armstrong, Dizzy Gillespie, Billie Holiday, Dave Brubeck, Modern Jazz Quartet, and Sonny Rollins. But serving the festival behind the scenes made little difference to his coverage. He was equally capable of cheering or criticizing

A Diary of the Underdogs

the event in the paper the next day. When Los Angeles Times jazz critic Leonard Feather complained about Gleason having better seats, Feather was informed that Gleason had paid for his tickets.

On The Town

A Prize Insult to Duke Ellington

Taken from a column by Ralph J. Gleason
San Francisco Chronicle about 1965

The Pulitzer Prize Committee last week, in case you missed the story, rather than accept the unanimous recommendation of its music advisers, decided to give no award at all this year in the music category. The unanimous recommendation of the Pulitzer Prize Committee music advisers was Edward Kennedy "Duke" Ellington. If you think there is any connection between this disgraceful action and the fact that Ellington is generally classified as a jazz musician (though HE maintains music is music) and that his skin is black, you got it, baby. That's where it's at.

At this point I would like to see some recipient of a Pulitzer Prize in the arts refuses to accept it on the basis of the appalling insult to Duke Ellington. Are there any volunteers? Has any Pulitzer winner the guts to stand up and tell these people off?

Dizzy Gillespie once said that jazz is too good for America. This is a perfect example of what he means. There are more than a couple of jazz musicians who are worthy of the Pulitzer or any other prize (just as there is more than one worthy of the Presidential Medal, beginning with Louis Armstrong).

It would be too much to expect that the cultural apparatus of the U.S.A., in agony of guilt, would make up for its years of ignorance and Jim Crow in one gesture and name Ellington, Armstrong, Gillespie, Davis, Mingus, Coltrane and Monk for high honors. Just let's take it in order of seniority, that'll be good enough.

The trouble is, you see, that the cultural apparatus does not know the names of America's greatest artists. It's as simple as that.

It strikes me that, at this point, Ellington would possibly refuse a Pulitzer Prize even if they changed their minds and accepted the recommendation of the music committee and offered it to him. He is more important than they are and, frankly, he would do them more honor than they would do him. Who remembers the previous winners of the Pulitzer music Prize, yet I'll wager Duke Ellington will be remembered.

The whole thing is absurd and an indication of the way in which the entire society basically rests on a segregated set of assumptions. I know of no jazz musician who is not widely acquainted with classical music (especially if he is a young composer-player) and yet the ignorance of jazz that is prevalent in classical circles is appalling.

Thelonious Monk, Duke Ellington and the others, are cultural heroes around the world, yet Monk could stand for an hour Friday night leaning on a parking meter and smoking a cigarette on Broadway without being recognized by anybody but the stone hipsters.

One of the reasons jazz has had to fight the battle against being categorized as a second class music is that from the beginning, it was not a matter of sound or music at all but the fact that jazz is Negro music and the Negro cannot he accepted as equal. Thus jazz cannot be as good as the so-called classical music.

The machine has even brainwashed Negroes so that Whitney Young of the Urban League obviously sets more status value on a beginning symphony musician than a creative jazz artist.

A Diary of the Underdogs

It is an absurdity but it is only symptomatic of the absurdities that run through everything nowadays. But somehow it is a particular galling absurdity when a committee which deals with the arts should be so blindly stupid. If the Pulitzer Prize committee has an office anywhere I hope CORE and SNCC picket them.

Ad Libs

The Sonny Simmons Quintet opened last night at the Both/And for two weeks. The Byrds, The Vegetables, The Ratz all will be with the Rolling Stones Friday night at the Civic Auditorium. The Stones play the San Jose Civic Auditorium May 21. Wayne Newton opens Friday at the Safari in San Jose and Johnny Rivers plays there beginning June 25. Roger Miller ("King of the Road") plays the Masonic Auditorium May 26. The Contemporary Jazz Quartet with Ron Smith, bass: Steve Gunda, saxophone: Legrand Rogers, drums and Herman Perez, piano, plays weekends at the Gilded Cage in Sacramento. Dolores Valez is now singing at the Chi Chi.

On and Off the Record

This World April 8, 1962 Chronicle by Ralph J. Gleason

Erroll Garner's first local appearances in almost two years take place April 6 at the Berkley Community Theater and April 7 at the Masonic Memorial when he gives concerts there. On April 9th he'll be at the Sacramento Auditorium. . .
Fantasy has signed folk singer Stan Wilson. . .
Tenor saxophonist Chuck Travis is now operating the Trio Room in Willow Glenn with sports figures Bill Leonard and Duane Pillette. Travis' group plays weekends. There are visiting groups on Thursdays. On April 4 and 11, the Vince Guaraldi Trio will be there. . .
Gerry Mulligan's Quartet opens July 2 at the Blackhawk.
The Larry Vuckovich Quintet plays this afternoon at 3 at the Cable Car Gallery. . .
Joe Venuti, the violinist and bandleader of the '30s, is currently living in Seattle and playing there.
Terry Gibbs is recording another big band LP, this time for Mercury, with arrangements by Al Cohn, Bill Holman and Manny Albam.
Slim Gaillard is set for a return to the Bay Area after several years in Los Angeles.
Thelonious Monk will have bassist John Orr, tenor saxophonist Charlie Rouse, and drummer Frankie Dunlop when he opens at the Jazz Workshop Tuesday night. —R.J.G.

Jazz Listings
Ah San Pan–Fred Gambrell Trio Wednesday and Saturday, 4562 Geary.
Alaska Club–Dottie Ivory, 628 Divisadero.
Black Sheep–Earl "Fatha" Hines with Wilber Stump on intermission piano, 465 Geary.
Black Hawk–Carman McRae closes tonight. George Shearing opens Tuesday 200 Hyde.
Bop City–After hours sitting in.1690 Post.
Boule Noire (Black Ball)–Fred Washington Quartet. Wednesday-Sunday. Mambo night Tuesday, Closed Monday. 238 Columbus.
Burp Hollow–Frank Goulette Original Inferior Jazz Band. Friday, Saturday. 487 Broadway.
Coffee Gallery–We Four Quartet Thursday-Saturday. Concert pianist Barry Heim Monday-Wednesday. 1353 Grant
Condor–Trudy Butchart Quartet. 300 Columbus.

A Diary of the Underdogs

Earthquake McGoon's–San Francisco Revival's Turk Murphy blows hot with Clancy Hayes, Pat Yankee. 99 Broadway.

Executive Suite–Chris Ibanez. 153 California.

Jazz Workshop–Sonny Rollins, Larry Vuckovich Quintet, Monday. 473 Broadway.

Hangover–Mugsy Spanier Quintet with Ralph Sutton. 7829 Bush St.

Harrah's–Red Norvo, Sam Butera at Reno. Kingston Trio opens at South Shore Room, Tahoe, Tuesday.

Little Chef, San Jose–Larry Vuckovich Quintet.

Park wood Lounge–Fred Gambrell Trio, Saturday. 2000 Irving.

Palate, Mill Valley–Bryce Rhode Trio

Piano Bar–Symphony in Sound and Skins. Tuesday-Saturday. 5420 Geary.

Gold Coast Singers. Joy Marshall. 140 Columbus.

Pier 23–Burt Bales, Ragtime, Embarcadero.

Redwood Room–Chris Mitchell Duo, 89th and Junipero Serra. Daly City.

RSVP–Johnny Whalen, pianist, 531 Commercial.

Sugar Hill–Mose Allison with blues and a far out piano. 430 Broadway.

Trois Couleur, Oakland–Maher-Bowman Quintet, Sunday-Tuesday; Glass Group, Wednesday-Thursday, Francis Quintet, Friday-Saturday. Sunday session, after hours.

Tsubo, Berkley–The Group. No Booze. Fine Jazz.

University Hide-A-Way –Jimmy Parker Trio, Thursday-Saturday, 2225 Fillmore.

Trident, Sausalito–Vince Guaraldi Trio, Friday-Saturday, Denny Zeitlin on Mondays

Zack's, Sausalito–Jim Purcell Trio.

The Rhythm Section

The Bob Clark Trio (Clark, drums; Larry Vuckovich, piano; Fred Marshall, bass) is now at Mr. Otis on weekends.

Benny Velarde has recorded an LP for Fantasy with his big band.

Chris Ibanez Trio with Harold Wiley added on tenor will play a concert at 5 this afternoon at the Claremont Hotel. . .

Anita O'Day cut an LP with Cal Tjader. It is mainly Latin numbers. .

A mid-July concert with Miles Davis and Dick Gregory is now being planned for San Francisco. .Duke Ellington's trumpet section now consists of Cat Anderson, Harold Baker, Ray Nance and a young Bostonian, Bill Barry who last played here with Woody Herman. . .

Odetta has taped two television shows for the BBC. They were done in Germany and in England on her recent tour and may eventually be shown here. . .

Miriam Makeba will appear at New Fack's in July . . .

Singer John Hawkins, who was a familiar figure on local stages some years ago, is now with the Ink Spots on a tour of Japan. –R.J.G.

On and Off the Record

This World, February 18th 1962
San Francisco Chronicle, By Ralph J. Gleason

The Jazz Messengers with Art Blakey opens Tuesday at the Black Hawk. This is their first San Francisco appearance in several years . . .

Sunday night sessions have begun at a new club out in the avenues. The Zanzibar on Ocean near

A Diary of the Underdogs

Keystone now has a group with Harold Wiley, tenor; Larry Vuckovich, piano Dick Fudge, drums; and Al Obidinski, bass . . .

There's a strong possibility that The Montgomery Brothers may break up their group, with guitarist Wes Montgomery joining either the John Coltrane of the Miles Davis Groups. Curiously, the Montgomery Brothers have not been a financial success despite all the publicity and the poll-winning achievements of Wes. Ironically, Buddy and Monk Montgomery dissolved The Master sounds, which were a financial success, to join with Wes in their own group a couple years ago . . .

The Concert Jazz Quintet, a Sacramento modern jazz group, is currently giving a series of Sunday afternoon concerts at the Jay-Rob Playhouse in Sacramento from 3 to 5 o'clock . . .

The Musical score to "A Thurber Carnival," which opens at the Geary Feb. 27 is by Don Elliott who will lead his own group (Tom Stewart, alto; Gary Elpern, Guitar; John Lee, drums; Whitey Cronan, bass) in the show . . .

British composer Robert Farnon will finally record his "Suite for Trumpet" which was written for Dizzy Gillespie. He is flying to New York to cut it this month. Farnon will also make LPs with Lena Horne and the Hi-Lo's. Erroll Garner, April 6, at the Berkley Community Theater and April 7, Masonic Memorial; the Weavers, April 15, Berkley Community Theater . . .

Pianist Dave Hoffman, bassist Bill Vavar and drummer Ed Sweeney are now playing week ends at Fairway Lodge in Hayward . . . R.J.G.

Some Clubs and Stories

Across Broadway from the Workshop was the "El Matador" where Vince Guaraldi and his trio were a steady format with John Mosher on bass and Colin Bailey on drums and Brazilian guitarist Bolo Sete and later the home of Sergio Mendez and "Brazil 66." The club's history establishes it well as a famous bistro as the publisher describes. When El Matador opened in 1958, Bennett Cerf called it "the most attractive room in America." Part saloon, part salon, Barnaby Conrad's nightclub was nestled in the heart of North Beach on Broadway, San Francisco's cabaret and nightlife district. On any given night, one might find Noel Coward, Marilyn Monroe, Truman Capote, Frank Sinatra, Ava Gardner, or Tyrone Power in the club, or might hear Duke Ellington, Art Tatum, Eva Gabor, George Shearing, or André Previn take over the piano. In his book, "Name Dropping," Barnaby Conrad vibrantly evokes this bygone era as charming, personable, and witty, the author is both celebrity and fan as he shares vivid, hilarious, and surprising anecdotes. ©1997 Barnaby Conrad; Blackstone Audio Inc.

Up the street on the corner of Broadway and Montgomery was Basin Street West. There you could hear big bands like Duke Ellington, Count Basie with Joe Williams, Otis Redding, Ike Turner, The Temptations and Anita O'Day, and many others, even Hampton Hawes on intermission piano.

Around the corner on Kearny there was a place called the "Off Broadway." The Stan Kenton Band of the 60's, (Cuban Fire) and Lenny Bruce in some of his most arresting monologues, arresting because the recordings by Everett Hill in the basement studio were the vary ones needed in the famous trial. Lenny made some classic recording at the Jazz Workshop that are collector's items now. His many North Beach antics helped to add to his mystique, like being arrested for obscenity, swear words on stage during his performance, the noted "obscenity" trial in 1963 where he was charged with obscenity and later vanquished. The court decision defined the idea of obscenity, or being "obscene," as being in the mind of the beholder, a personal freedom to choose. Lenny went on. One of his most outrageous incidents was falling out of the window of the Swiss American Hotel, above the Condor on Broadway. He landed in the alley below unharmed. The story on the street was that he "hit" a big load of speed, (Methadrine) and it blew him out the window. In a different version of the same story Lenny was on acid, a large dose, given to him by Wavy Gravy who was with him in the hotel room at the time.

A Diary of the Underdogs

Enrico Banducci's sidewalk café' was a unique spot to watch the action on the street and drink espresso as the cars came and went in front of the "Chi Chi Club" and "Finocchio's," the female impersonator show upstairs over Enrico's.

Up the street on Broadway, past the "El Cid," a dance spot across from the Condor was "The Committee," at 627 Broadway. A long running attraction of improvisational comedy that included Michael McClure, Howard Hesseman, Larry Harkin, Gary Goodrow, Mimi Farina, Wavy Gravy, Nancy Fish, and a revolving cast of others, many now well known celebrities.

The Committee was founded by a handful of ex-Second City writer/director/actors in San Francisco in the '60s. It was risk-taking, political comedy group. They were definitely the hippest comedy theater on the West Coast, attracting such future stars as Richard Dreyfus and Rob Reiner, as teens, to their shows. The more famous alumni include Peter Bonerz (from "The Bob Newhart Show," now a busy TV director of such shows as "Friends"), Howard Hesseman, as Don Sturdy, (Dr. Johnny Fever from "WKRP In Cincinnati," "Head of the Class," "Soap"), Carl Gottlieb (wrote "Jaws" and co-wrote and appeared in "The Jerk"), Avery Schreiber (the comedy team "Burns & Schreiber," "My Mother the Car"), Garry Goodrow ("Bob & Carol & Ted & Alice," "National Lampoon's Lemmings," "The National Lampoon Radio Hour"), Larry Harkin (the Trucker in "The Sure Thing," a grumpy neighbor on "Friends"), John Brent ("Catch 22," "Bob & Carol & Ted & Alice"), and *improv* guru Del Close (taught John Belushi, Chris Farley, & others at Improv Olympic & Second City). The troupe also commonly appeared on the famed "Smothers Brothers Comedy Hour" and had parts in the cult classic "Billie Jack." The show made reference to pot smoking cops. Creech & Chong apparently stole much of the Committee's then-outrageous drug humor to form the basis of their act.

Chapter 7-Who's playing where? (Districts)

North Beach:
Up on Green street pianist Bill Wejohn with Sonny Wayne opened the "Jazz Cellar" in the basement of a building that is now, Little Caesar's, a house trio format that featured soloists Brew Moore, Pony Poindexter, Leo Wright, Harold Wiley and sit ins; Eric Dolphy, Lenny McBrowne, Charlie Haden, plus live recordings of Jazz Poetry with Brew Moore.

The following is a list of more San Francisco clubs and musicians of the period.

12 Adler Place, located in the alley behind Pearl's on Columbus, later became "Spec's" featured bassist Vernon Alley duos with Shelly Robbins.

Copa Cabana located on Broadway and Tunnel featured the Duran Brothers, Benny Velarde, and Armando Peraza.

Hungry I, original Jackson street location musicians; Vince Lateano, Eddie Duran, Dean Reilly, last SF appearance of Lambert Hendricks and Ross, Virgil Gonsalves, Mel Torme, Jon Hendricks

Jazz Workshop, Broadway, North Beach; George Coleman, Red Garland Trio with Doug Watkins, Sonny Rollins, Elmo Hope, Lenny McBrowne, Wes Montgomery, John Coltrane, Eric Dolphy, Stan Getz, Gary Burton, Miles Davis, Tony Williams (at 17), Bobby Hutcherson (as a teen) Curtis Amy.

El Matador, Broadway, North Beach: John Cooper, Vernon Alley, Joao Gilberto, Cal Tjader, Martial Solal, Gabor Szabo, Vince Guaraldi, Bola Sete, Brazil 66.

Basin Street West. Broadway, North Beach, Hampton Hawes, Philly Joe Jones, Thelonious Monk, Big bands; Duke Ellington, Woody Herman, Thad Jones-Mel Lewis, (with Chick Corea, Richard Davis, Lew Tabackin, Joe Farrell, Anita O'Day.)

Sugar Hill, Broadway, North Beach, Redd Foxx, Lambert, Hendricks- and Bevan, Joe Williams, Shirley

A Diary of the Underdogs

Horn, Carman McRae, (recording made there)

Off Broadway, Kearney street, North Beach, Jerry Granelli, John Mosher, Mel Torme, Brew Moore, Lenny Bruce, Stan Kenton's "Cuban Fire."

The Place, North Beach, Political satire, and improv; Dave Van Kreidt, Jerry Good.

Coffee Gallery, Grant street, North Beach, Pony Poindexter, Nancy King, Sonny King, Beverly Kelly, Norman Williams, Don Alberts, Ben Doris, Max Hartstein, Little Rock.

Kewpie Doll, Broadway and Columbus, Marty Marcellus, Cuz Cousineau, Vince Cattolica. Tipsy's, Billie Bosier, Everett Hill, Bob Stock, Mal Sharpe. Gigi's, Big Boy Frank Goudie.

China Town:

Ross Alley: Mister Lucky's, The Rickshaw.

China Smith's: Washington and Grant.

Macumba: Grant near California featured- Carman McRae, Cal Tjader, Stan Kenton band with Pepper Adams, Mel Lewis, Bill Holman, and arranger Johnny Richards. The Stan Kenton "Cuban Fire" band, also Count Basie.

Forbidden City, 363 Sutter at Union Square: Larry Ching, the Chinese Frank Sinatra, Kathy de la Luz, Queen of Filipino Jazz.

Eddie Pond's Supper Club, Grant and Bush: Jack Teagarden, Jerry Dodgion, Jerome Richardson, Chuck Travis, Cedric Heywood.

The Tenderloin:

Streets of Paris; Sammy Simpson, Red Garland, Philly Joe Jones, also Si Perkoff.

Coffee Don's (after hours 2-6) Tommy Lokey, Mike Montano, Don Alberts.

Breakfast Clubs (6-10) Sonny Clark, Jerry Good.

Diamond Knee, on Mason Street; across from Streets of Paris; Big Bands-Les Brown.

Black Hawk, Turk and Hyde; late 1940's to 1960s; Vernon Alley, radio broadcasts, "Vernon's Alley," Early days, Wardell Gray, Jerome Richardson, Richard Wyands, Pony Poindexter, Chuck Travis, Dave Brubeck, Cal Tjader, Miles Davis, (Quintet of '57), the original MJQ with Kenny Clark, live recordings, Vince Guaraldi, Shelly Manne.

Market Street:

Downbeat Club: Louis Armstrong, Duke Ellington, Count Basie, Artie Shaw, Woody Herman, Buddy De Franco. This was later owned by Art Aurbach before the Workshop. Master Sounds first gig, also Woody Herman.

Fack's, lower Market (now Hyatt) featured the original Hi-Lo's, Anita O'Day, Georgie Auld, Vernon Alley.

Fack's 2: same format

San Francisco Big Bands:

Palace Hotel: Boyd Raeburn, (influenced by Stravinsky) Davis Allyn, Dizzy Gillespie, Stan Levy, Conte Condoli.

Theaters:

There were also Theater Music Formats, The Fox Theater, Paramount, Golden Gate, the El Patio, and Sweet's Ballroom in Oakland with Lionel Hampton, Duke Ellington, Harry James, Woody Herman, Les Brown, and Stan Kenton.

Nob Hill:

Other large hotels like the Mark Hopkins and the Fairmont had name bands for 2-6 weeks run. There could

A Diary of the Underdogs

be 8 bands coming through San Francisco at one time.
San Francisco Big Bands: Rudy Salvini, Gerald Wilson, Eddie Walker, Frank Leal, Don Piestrup, Full Faith and Credit (Dr Herb Wong)

Bush Street:
Club Hangover, 1949 -1960, Vince Cattolica, opened it. Louis Armstrong, Kid Ory, Earl "Fatha" Hines, Pops Foster, Earl Watkins.
The Tin Angel: Kid Ory Dixieland Jazz Band
Say When; Charlie Parker, 1952, Eddie Duran
Club Neve (Owned by Du Pont) booked name acts; Duke Ellington, Brew Moore Trio, Lambert Hendricks and Ross, Carman McRae
Boarding House (Neve)
Coast Recorders, Fantasy: Cal Tjader, Billie Higgins Nate Cole's last album, "Love" with Alan Smith on Trumpet.

Financial District:
Fred's, a place in the financial district; Hampton Hawes and John Heard played.

Fillmore District:
Bop City, at Post and Buchanan Streets; Started by Slim Gaillard in the late 1940's. It was later operated by Jimbo Edwards. There were house trios with guests sitting in. Norman Williams, house trio with Si Perkoff, Flip Nunez, Freddy Redd, Johnny Baker, Don Alberts, Eddie Kahn, Kermit Scott, John Handy. Many famous guests; Bird, Chet Baker, Duke Ellington, Jimmy Garrison, Philly Joe Jones, John Coltrane, Pony Poindexter, Billie Holiday, Alan Smith, Benny Wilson. Original club had Dexter Gordon while in town rehearsing a big band and Frank Foster sitting in while stationed in San Francisco in the Army.
Booker T. Washington Hotel; Ben Webster.
Blue Mirror, Fillmore Street; Virgil Gonsalves.
New Orleans Swing Club, on Sutter Street; Paul Desmond, Big Band with Chuck Travis.
Jackson's Nook, Post Street, late night sessions near Bop City.
Café' Society; Billie Holiday.
Jack's of Sutter, Organ soul blues and Jazz. Later moved to Fillmore and Geary.
Club Alabam, Fillmore; Saunders King, Vernon Alley.
Half Note, Divisadero; George Duke, Richard Groove Holmes.

Geary Street:
Geary Cellar; Dave Brubeck, Jack Sheedy (trombonist) recorded Brubeck, Cal Tjader, Ron Crotty on his own label "Coronet" and sold the masters to Fantasy records, nothing happened.
Ciro's, on Geary; Sarah Vaughan, Art Tatum, Charlie Ventura, Woody Herman small band.
The Tropics; Brew Moore, Harold Wiley, Cedric Heywood, Alan Smith, Bud Glen, Dean Reilly, John Mosher, Dizzy Gillespie, Lou Levy.

Fisherman's Wharf and the Waterfront. Traditional Jazz music clubs
Easy Street, (early '60s): Louis Jordan, Count Basie, Red Norvo, Turk Murphy, Mel Torme, Louis Armstrong.
Dawn Club, (in the 40s, Cherry's, later Redante's, then the Maltese Grill: Lu Waters "Yerba Buena Jazz Band," Clancy Hayes.

A Diary of the Underdogs

Pier 23, Embarcadero, Vince Cattolica, Burt Bales.
The Mission:
The It Club, Frank Esposito
2 C's, 30th and Mission; Benny Barth Quintet, Larry Vuckovich Quintet.

Oakland and the East Bay:
Jazz Showcase, Telegraph Avenue; Don Barksdale (DJ KDIA)
Golden Nugget, Telegraph Avenue; Don Mupo, (Stan Kenton alumni concept) John Coppola, Fred Murgy Band with soloists: Al Porcino, Conte Condoli, Frank Rosolino, Zoot Sims, and Mel Lewis. Guests, Dexter Gordon.
Martini Club, Nat Cole Trio
Slim Jenkins, (Seventh Street): Lionel Hampton
Club Algiers, Sonny Clark, and Jerry Good- recording there.
Paradise Club, Dave Brubeck
New Lincoln Theater, downtown Oakland- Chuck Travis.
Tsubo, "Full House," live recording with Wes Montgomery, Johnny Griffin and Miles Davis' rhythm section on Riverside L.P. First location of the KJAZ studio.

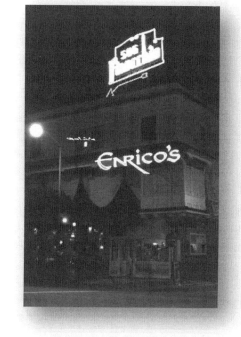

Peninsula and South Bay:
Band Box, Redwood City, Chuck Travis, Vernon Alley, Jerome Richardson, Sweetie Mitchell, Tin Pan Alley, Bernie Kahn, Duke Ellington, Count Basie, Woody Herman, Mambo Gardens, Santa Cruz, Oscar Peterson, Gerald Wilson, Frank Morgan, Chuck Travis.
Outside at the Inside, Palo Alto, Vince Cattolica, Ben Webster, David Allyn, Larry Vuckovich, Irene Krall, Jackie and Roy Krall, Leroy Vinnegar.

Fugazi Hall, across Columbus at 678 Green Street, was the site of abstract beatnik film showings in the early 60's and later for concerts like the Grateful Dead on March 20, 1967. It is now the home of "Beach Blanket Babylon, "a variety show created by the late Steve Silver and a popular tourist attraction.

Cal Tjader's Latin ensemble played at the Macumba up on Grant Street in Chinatown. Carman McRae also sang there in the early days of her career when she was quite successful singing popular music and before she crossed over to singing jazz exclusively.

One very famous place was the "Hungry I", operated by notorious North Beach "bon vivant" Enrico Banducci. Though previously located in the basement of the Columbus Towers, a landmark building now owned by Francis Coppola and his Zoetrope Film Company, the "Hungry I" ultimately found a home at 599 Jackson Street, just off Columbus, from 1960 to 1967. There the glib political comic Mort Sahl made his stand often with others, Jack Burns, Avery Schreiber, Lainie Kazan, (May, 1965) Shelly Berman, Jonathan Winters, Tom Lehrer, Dick Gregory, Bob Newhart, Mike Nichols and Elaine May, and Bill Cosby.

A Diary of the Underdogs

Woody Allen opened there for Barbara Streisand in 1963 to a cool audience. Lenny Bruce played there also. Some of the mainstays included the "Limelighters," "The Kingston Trio," "Peter Paul and Mary," all riding on the popularity of folk music of which they were undisputed kings, also singer Helen Humes, guitarist-composer, Tim Hardin, and a long list of fine pianists including, Don Asher, Clyde Pound, Vince Guaraldi, Shelly Robbins, Richie Crabtree, Buddy Mottsinger and singer Faith Winthrop.

The biggest draw eventually became the "Kingston Trio" as they swept the nation in undisputed popularity until the club closed in 1968.

San Francisco comic Phyllis Diller appeared at a little place on Columbus across the street from the Hungry I known as the "Purple Onion" at 140 Columbus. It was downstairs, a small theater stage where café jazz acts like "Jackie and Roy" often performed. The Kingston Trio, The Smothers Brothers, Maya Angelou and Vickie Carr also appeared.

Chapter 8-Carol Doda and the Condor Club

The most prominent attraction of North Beach in the 60's was Carol Doda at the "Condor," the corner of Broadway and Columbus, a topless act performed on the piano and rivaled by none. Carol was aided by the unique process of cosmetic breast enlargement. This was the real beginning of the topless era and it signaled the exit of the "Beats" as the North beach tourist trade became a frenzied to the topless attraction.

There were others, the "Moulin Rouge," 412 Broadway with stripper Marta Dane, and the Chi-Chi Club maintained a solid cast of strippers, but in 1965 Carol Doda was the undisputed Topless Queen of San Francisco.

Carol Doda

Carol Doda was a stripper in San Francisco in the 1960s. In 1964 Doda, still in her teens, made international news when a gynecologist injected silicone into her size 34 breasts adding 10 inches to what would become known as Carol Doda's "twin 44s" and the new "Twin Peaks" of San Francisco. Doda's enhancements were direct silicone injections rather than filled prosthesis, a procedure not practiced today due to concerns about silicone migration within the body although Doda has not reported experiencing significant side effects due to the injections. She worked as a topless waitress at the North Beach night club located on the corner of Broadway and Columbus. The large lit sign in front of the club featured a cartoon of her. But her premiere topless dance came on the night of June 19, 1964. Her act began with a white grand piano lowered from the ceiling by hydraulic motors. As it descended Carol would be atop the piano dancing. She danced the go-go and the Swim to a rock and roll combo headed by musician Bobby Freeman as her piano settled on the stage. From the waist up Doda emulated aquatic movements like the Australian crawl. She also did the Twist, the Frug, and the Watusi. She wore the bottom half of a black bikini and a net top which was soon discarded, to the delight of the crowd, as the dance progressed.

"Killer Piano Attacks in San Francisco"-The after hours piano incident.

After closing one night in November 1983, Condor dancer Theresa Hill and bouncer Jimmy Ferrazzo decided to "make love" atop the piano. The hydraulic system that raises and lowers the piano

A Diary of the Underdogs

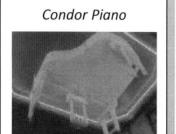

Condor Piano

during performances was accidentally activated and the piano rose to the ceiling and the couple were pinned there. The bouncer Jimmy Ferrazzo was crushed to death while Theresa Hill lay trapped beneath him until the pair was discovered by a janitor several hours later. The dancer, Theresa Hill survived.

Doda performed 12 shows nightly so that management could keep crowds moving in and out. She was 19 or 20 when she first danced at the Condor. Two months after she started the rest of San Francisco's Broadway went topless, followed soon after by the rest of America.

Carol Doda became a cultural icon of the 1960s. She was profiled in author Tom Wolfe's 1968 book, "The Pump House Gang" and appeared that same year as "Sally Silicone" in "Head," the 1968 film created by Jack Nicholson and Bob Rafelson, and featuring The Monkeys. The movie was produced by Columbia Pictures. She appeared in a "Golden Boy" parody with Annette Funicello, Sonny Liston, and Davy Jones. On April 22, 1965 Doda was arrested with Gino Del Prete, owner of the Condor Club but were cleared when two judges instructed the jury to return "innocent" verdicts. Judge Friedman's memorandum to opposing attorneys read; "Whether acts are lewd and dissolute depends not on any individual's interpretation or personal opinion, but on the consensus of the entire community." Peter Mattioli owned the Condor Club by 1967 and Doda still appeared in shows there. As of 2007, Carol Doda has been singing in several San Francisco North Beach clubs, including Amante's and Enrico's Supper Club.
From Wikipedia 2009

A Diary of the Underdogs

Chet Helms

Chapter 9-Chet Helms and the Family Dog, Bill Graham and the Fillmore

So, "that's great," one might say, "everybody's working and making money, except us, the guys who live here, the musicians who practice and strive and try to find a place to perform. Those rock and roll clubs won't hire us. They're making all the money, they're not friends of jazz; they're enemies of jazz. They're all happy taking their acid, making love to the young wide eyed girls who are far from home filled with hope and adventure, so high they have forgotten about everything back home. They are swept into an endless foray of music and freedom, glitter and intoxicating light shows, and the powerful pounding of the drums of dance and the festival of abandon cloaked in the sweetness of a ring of flowers and the celebration of life." The rock bands, as enigmatic and magnificent as they were, held no alms for jazz. They had become a powerful and effective device in the movement of democracy in the 60's and they garnered large crowds of followers. The bands were not intentionally political but they seemed to generate

Original home of Chet Helms' Family Dog at 1836 Pine Street

opinion, to speak to the issues becoming a voice of the people. They were originally folk musicians organized in basements, experimenting with amplified guitars, by discovery, being catapulted into prominence with the advent of music performance venues, gaining recognition, creating interest and attention and being offered recording contracts, becoming significant, even famous, often to their own amazement. The attempts at crossover were common among jazz bands and some had minimal success. "The Flower," a band from San Jose organized by alto saxophonist Paul Robertson and bassist Gordon Stevens (who later joined Moby Grape) wrote crossover songs, songs that assailed that bludgeoning rock market where a tiny crack, a variation in the venue existed, but there was only mild success. It seems that it would be more natural to incorporate jazz influences into rock music than it would be to try to infuse rock elements into jazz. No matter how it was presented the intrusion of the rock genres into a jazz format always left a bad taste in the mouth of jazz. Later, in the '70s period, jazz would have a chance in the advent of "fusion" music, but in the 1960's it would not fly. But there were specific bands that were easily accommodated into the popular rock venues without diluting their sound. Alto saxophonist John Handy and his group with

A Diary of the Underdogs

Michael White, Jerry Hahn, Don Thompson, and Terry Clark, were included in Bill Graham's early venues providing a cultural contrast that was welcome and compatible to the audiences. Charles Lloyd was also a sought after sound, by strange coincidence, in the early 1960s. So it could be done, but few other artists at the time were able to pull it off. Chet Helms arrived in the "Haight" with his girlfriend after fifty hours hitchhiking on the road from Austin Texas. The girl, little known Janis Joplin, had dropped out of summer classes at college and together they had rushed to the music scene in San Francisco. Chet wanted to play his guitar and become part of the new music scene but he soon found his talent in promotion by default. Chet Helms and Luria Castell produced the first of what would become a dizzying series of dance concerts and events and founded the original "Family Dog" at a rooming house at 1836 Pine Street where everyone owned a dog. The first concert was billed as a Rock 'n' Roll Dance Concert at Longshoreman's Hall on North Point Street near the Fisherman's Wharf area of San Francisco. The Jefferson Airplane, The Marbles, and The Great Society were the attraction, also The Charlatan's in their "full gear," as it was billed. It was October 16, 1965. Chet Helms subsequently went on to promote the weekly gigs at the -Avalon Ballroom- on Sutter Street in what is now the Regency Theater, and later the Carousel Ballroom at Van Ness and Market streets, upstairs over the S & C Ford dealership. But early on he used the Fillmore Auditorium.

Chet Helms' antithesis, Bill Graham, had not surfaced until the fall of 1965 when he produced his first event; "Appeal I," as a fund-raiser for the San Francisco Mime Troupe. It was staged in an old hotel, "The Calliope Warehouse." It had previously been used as a horse stable and was located on Fifth Street, south of the San Francisco Chronicle building. The "Jefferson Airplane" had just formed in August of that same year, 1965. The final bill, with the help of Chet Helms, was for November 6th, 1965 and it read: "APPEAL 1" "For the continued artistic freedom in the arts." The billing included: The Jefferson Airplane, The Fugs, Sandy Bull, The John Handy Quintet, The Committee Actors, poet Lawrence Ferlinghetti, The Family Dog, and The Warlocks, (an early name for the Grateful Dead). The crowd was lined up around the block.

Bill Graham

Graham moved from New York to San Francisco in the early 1960s to be closer to his sister, Rita. He was invited to attend a free concert in Golden Gate Park, where he made contact with the San Francisco Mime Troupe, a radical theater group. He gave up a promising business career to manage the troupe in 1965. After Mime Troupe leader Ronny Davis was arrested on obscenity charges during an outdoor performance, Graham organized a benefit concert to cover the troupe's legal fees. The concert was a success, and Graham saw a business opportunity. He began promoting more concerts to raise funds for the Mime Troupe, and eventually left the troupe to promote concerts full time.

One of the first concerts Graham promoted was in partnership with Chet Helms of the Family Dog organization and featured the Paul Butterfield Blues Band. The concert was an overwhelming success and Graham saw an opportunity with the band. Early the next morning, Graham called the band's manager, Albert Grossman, and obtained exclusive rights to promote them. Shortly thereafter, Chet Helms arrived at Graham's office, asking how Graham could have cut him out of the deal. Graham pointed out that Helms would not have known about it unless he had tried to do the same thing to Graham and advised him to "get up early" in the future.

A Diary of the Underdogs

Bill Graham was born in Berlin, Germany January 8, 1931. A charismatic but often difficult personality, Graham's shows attracted elements of America's now legendary counterculture such as Jefferson Airplane, Janis Joplin, Country Joe and The Fish, Lawrence Ferlinghetti, The Committee, The Fugs, Allen Ginsberg, and a particular favorite of Graham's, The Grateful Dead. He was the manager of Jefferson Airplane during 1967 and 1968. His successes and popularity allowed him to become the top concert promoter in rock music. He operated the famous venues the Fillmore West and Winterland (both in San Francisco) and the Fillmore East (in New York City), where the best up-and-coming acts would come to play. Also in New York City, he formed a booking agency called The Millard Agency which organized the booking of bands into various venues across the US. Because his music venue was the Fillmore, it seemed obvious to call the booking agency Millard after Millard Fillmore, the thirteenth president of the United States. Graham's music venues were open certain weekday nights for unknown bands like Santana to get exposure. Graham promoted the West-Coast leg of the legendary Rolling Stones American Tour 1972, also known as S.T.P. Tour (for Stones Touring Party), as well as parts of the Rolling Stones 1975 and 1978 tours. He would then promote the entire Rolling Stones American Tour 1981 and Rolling Stones European Tour 1982. When the Stones returned to touring in 1989 with the Steel Wheels tour, Mick Jagger took the offer of Michael Cohl's The BCL Group (Ballard Cohl Labatt). Cohl made his reputation (and his fortune) in 1989 by buying the concert, sponsorship, merchandising, radio, television, and film rights to The Rolling Stones' Steel Wheels Tour. The tour became the most financially successful in history. Graham later discovered that Cohl had only offered slightly more money. Graham took Jagger's repudiation as a personal defeat, writing, "Losing the Stones was like watching my favorite lover become a whore." Bill Graham was killed in a helicopter accident on October 25, 1991 while returning to San Francisco from the Concord Pavilion in California. .

Fillmore Auditorium

Chet Helms was born in Santa Maria, California, Helms was the oldest of three boys. Chet's father died, when Helms was nine. The family moved to Texas. Helms remained in Texas for the next decade, enrolling in and dropping out of the University of Texas before moving to San

A Diary of the Underdogs

Janis Joplin

Francisco in 1962. His beginnings as a music promoter were modest, as Helms served as a host of jam sessions in his Haight-Ashbury district home. Big Brother and the Holding Company was one of the groups that played, and while serving as their manager, Helms dramatically altered the course of the band by recruiting an old college acquaintance by the name of Janis Joplin to be their singer.

Helms was an early partner of legendary promoter Bill Graham, with the two putting on several shows at the Fillmore before parting ways. While Graham continued to promote shows at the Fillmore, Helms and his Family Dog production company moved to the Avalon Ballroom, with the Grateful Dead a mainstay, and everyone from the Doors to Bo Diddley passing through. Country Joe and the Fish honed their chops underneath the Avalon's psychedelic light shows, and the band's guitarist Barry Melton credits Helms with fostering the kind of nurturing environment that helped bands progress. "There was an ethic unique to the time and place of San Francisco in the Sixties, an extraordinary ethic of tolerance and acceptance, Chet was the living embodiment of that tolerance and acceptance and openness that made it all happen. That element was very much a reflection of who he was." Chet Helms was a rock promoter and manager and a key figure in 1967's Summer of Love. Helms died in 2004 of complications from a stroke at age sixty-two.

A Diary of the Underdogs

Chapter 10-Black Hawk

The Black Hawk Jazz club, located at Turk and Hyde streets, was one of the best known of all San Francisco jazz spots. They featured the most famous jazz stars of the time. Local jazz aficionados, many of whom were growing up with the music, following religiously after Miles Davis, the MJQ, Stan Getz, Chet Baker and others, were allowed in the club behind the wire to listen, more appropriately to feed their artistic hunger.

The Black Hawk, a San Francisco Jazz Club.
History: from Wikipedia

The site of the Black Hawk is now a parking lot, the club closed in 1963. The building next door on Hyde Street (now housing the 222 Club), where the tape recorders were set up to record the Miles Davis album, still stands, and where the engineer noticed the hole where the money was passed up from the club to the apartment above. (See interview John Handy/Don Alberts) The Black Hawk was a San Francisco jazz club whose intimate atmosphere was ideal for small jazz groups. In 1959 the fees that the club was able to pay for its jazz acts rose from less than $300 to more than $3,000 a week. For fourteen years, the best and the brightest in the world of jazz passed through the Black Hawk portals. A number of musicians recorded albums at the club, including Cal Tjader, Miles Davis, Thelonious Monk, Shelly Manne, and Mongo Santamaria. Billie Holiday and Lester Young played their last West Coast club dates there and the Modern Jazz Quartet played its first. When Charlie Parker was supposed to be opening across town at the "Say When" club he could be found instead jamming at the Hawk. Other notable musicians who appeared there include

Black Hawk-corner of Turk and Hyde

Dave Brubeck, John Coltrane, Dizzy Gillespie, Stan Getz, Mary Stallings, Johnny Mathis, Art Blakey, Shorty Rogers, Art Pepper, Jeanne Hoffman, Art Farmer, Gerry Mulligan, Horace Parlan, and Russ Freeman. Arthur "Art" Tatum, in the last 18 months of his life, mainly did concert work. He played the Black Hawk Club in San Francisco in 1955.

Sunday afternoon sessions at the Black Hawk offered blowing time to young musicians. A young sextet who was working at the Black Hawk nightclub brought Johnny Mathis in for a Sunday afternoon jam session. It was at the Black Hawk that Helen Noga, co-owner of the club, first heard him sing and decided she wanted to manage his career. In early September 1955, Johnny landed a job singing weekends at Ann Dee's 440 Club. After repeated attempts, Helen Noga convinced George Avakian, then head of Jazz A&R at Columbia Records, to see him. Avakian came to the club, heard Johnny sing, and sent the now famous telegram to his record company, "Have found phenomenal 19 year old boy who could go all the way."
Billie Holiday's old friend Dr. Herbert Henderson visited Billie when she played dates at the Black Hawk

A Diary of the Underdogs

Club in San Francisco during September 1958. Immediately after the Black Hawk booking Billie took part in the first Monterey Jazz Festival's final evening on Sunday October 5, 1958. For several months each year, Dave Brubeck, who got his real start at the Black Hawk, returned to the Hawk for an extended series of appearances playing for consecutive weekends, sometimes for three months at a time. Cal Tjader's "Jazz at the Black Hawk"1959 recording was part of a long holiday season gig at the Black Hawk club. Tjader patched together a superb program split between straight-ahead jazz and Afro-Cuban works. At the time, Tjader had both Willie Bobo and Mongo Santamaria in his rhythm section. Bobo handled the trap drums during the bop numbers while the Latin tunes found Willie and Mongo creating even more heat on the timbales and congas. Pianist Vince Guaraldi swings like a madman on "A Night in Tunisia." Other tracks include "I Hadn't Anyone Till You," "Blue and Sentimental," Bill B.," "Stompin' at the Savoy," and "I Love Paris." The Black Hawk was breaking in some excellent new stereo recording equipment at the time of this gig; hence the clear, sharp sound. Shelly Manne's Quintet, At the Black Hawk, Vol. 1 - 4, was recorded extensively at San Francisco's Black Hawk club for three nights in 1959, four live albums were recorded and now documented on five CDs with trumpeter Joe Gordon, tenor saxophonist Richie Kamuca, pianist Victor Feldman, and bassist Monty Budwig, the band was certainly capable of playing high-quality bebop. Highlights include "Step Lightly," "What's New," and "Vamp's Blues." These were lengthy performances; "Vamp's Blues" is over 19 minutes long. The third volume adds a long version of "Whisper Not" to the original rendition as well as Cole Porter's, "I Am in Love" and the spontaneous 18-minute "Black Hawk Blues." As with the first three sets, the fourth volume adds an alternate take of "Cabu" to the original program, "Just Squeeze Me," "Nightingale," and a full-length version of their theme, "A Gem from Tiffany."The lengthy solos are consistently excellent, making this entire series recommended to straight-ahead jazz fans.

"Thelonious Monk Quartet at the Black Hawk,"1960, also includes tenor saxophonist Charlie Rouse, bassist John Ore and drummer Billie Higgins and is augmented for a brief period on this live session by two guests: trumpeter Joe Gordon and the tenor saxophonist Harold Land. The extra horns uplift the date and add some surprising moments to what otherwise might have been a conventional, but still spirited live session. Highlights include "Let's Call This," "Four in One," and a swinging version of "I'm Getting Sentimental over You." Miles Davis In Person Friday Night at the Black Hawk," Complete Volume I.. This was to be the first recording of a Davis band live in concert for an official album release, with tenor saxophone Hank Mobley, drums Jimmy Cobb, bass Paul Chambers, and Wynton Kelly on piano for two nights in 1961 at the Black Hawk. Some of this music had been previously released in varying configurations. Tracks included are "Oleo," "No Blues," "Bye Bye," "If I Were a Bell," "Fran Dance," "On Green Dolphin Street," "The Theme," "All Of You," "Neo," "I Thought About You," "Bye Bye Blackbird," "Walkin',"and "Love, I've Found You."

"Miles Davis In Person Saturday Night at the Black Hawk," complete Volume II. Tracks include, "If I Were a Bell," "So What," "On Green Dolphin Street," "Walkin'," "Round Midnight," "Well You Needn't," "Autumn Leaves," "Neo (Teo)," "Two Bass Hit," "Love, I've Found You," "I Thought About You," "Someday My Prince Will Come," "Softly As In a Morning Sunrise."

Mongo Santamaria At The Black Hawk, in 1962, brought his recently-formed band to the legendary Black Hawk club showing how an international cast of top flight musicians could be true to both Latin roots and jazz's spirit of adventure. Cuba was well represented by tenor saxophonist José "Chombo" Silva, who also played violin on the mellower charanga tracks, and Rolando Lozano, an incredible master of the wooden flute. Another key contributor is the Brazilian João Donato, who is heard on trombone as well as his more familiar piano, while jazz great Laurdine "Pat" Patrick, another of Mongo's favorites, also put in a guest appearance.

A Diary of the Underdogs

In a time of the clamor for new freedoms set forth by Jack Kerouac and Allen Ginsberg and the cadre of those in creativity and expression and the push for cultural re-evaluation, jazz music seemed important. Jack Kerouac had in fact been dubbed the creator of jazz prose in that his writing at times represented the improvisational flow of playing jazz. Many of the "Beat" poets possessed similar rhythms. Ultimately "jazz and poetry" was born. Kenneth Patchin had a gig at the Black Hawk where he read with the "Chamber Jazz Sextet," a group of musicians from San Jose that included- Tom Reynolds, Freddy Dutton, Allyn Ferguson, Bob Wilson, Frank Leal, and young Modesto Breseno. That was a formal setting, but there were others, coffee houses where they tried their creations on each other, jammed informally, espoused freely the music and word all completely spontaneous. Earlier in 1957, at the Jazz Cellar, Kenneth Rexroth and Lawrence Ferlinghetti had recited with a live jazz trio. The night was recorded by Fantasy Records and titled, "Poetry Readings at the Cellar."

Jazz continued to be the cry of freedom spawned in the city sprawl. It was not unlikely that poetry and jazz music would often share the same venue. Those who were not poets played music and those who were not musicians wrote poetry about music and the life. The word was desperate and virile, cutting over hard lines, crying freedom in crude elegance, often like jazz improvisation, set in the very heart of expression. That attitude touched every endeavor and the mix, the composite, was inevitable. San Francisco was fertile for just such a garden of colorful expansion.

* * *

But, there had been problems, there would always be problems. Early in 1957 the Dizzy Gillespie Orchestra was engaged to play a concert at the San Francisco Opera House, an orchestra endowed by the Federal Government. Dizzy was now a world emissary and the orchestra was to tour the world as Ambassadors of Good Will. Mayor George Christopher denied the use of the Opera House and its grand opulence for the occasion and the band was sent to the Fillmore Auditorium. Not surprising, as the political establishment had always been rather "cool" to jazz. However, jazz was not to go away, not even later when in 1965 the Haight Ashbury rose with rebellion and celebration and the mighty bludgeoning fist of Rock and Roll sprang from the "Panhandle" with organized fervor and set the music world afire. The "Panhandle" is an extended strip of Golden Gate Park that reaches up from Stanyan Street between Oak and Fell to Masonic. It was a perfect location for Chet Helms to "air" his "Family Dogs," the budding rock bands formed out of jam sessions in his basement in the mid sixties and presented to the crowds on flatbed trucks in the park on Sunday afternoons.

Ken Kesey and the Magic Bus

The "Acid Generation" had come. The news of the Swedish Pharmaceutical Company, "Sandoz", and their product, "LSD 25," intended for treatment of extreme cases of psychosis, was a monumental event. Psychologists Timothy Leary and Richard Alpert (Ram Dass) conducted –psilocybin- experiments at the Harvard Drug Research Project, and later at the Millbrook Estate in

A Diary of the Underdogs

New York assisted by graduate student Ralph Metzner, on volunteer students. They also published the scientific journal, "Psychedelic Review." This pamphlet was readily available in the Haight Ashbury neighborhood. The news spread quickly and Sandoz doses began to turn up locally on the streets in the Haight Ashbury.

Novelist Ken Kesey first ingested LSD when a Stanford grad student working at the Veteran's Hospital in Menlo Park on a project funded by the CIA named MKULTRA in 1959. He later wrote the novel, "One Flew over the Cuckoo's Nest," which soon after set off the notorious adventures of "The Merry Pranksters." Kesey, with an intrepid crew including, Ken Babs, Hugh Romney (Wavy Gravy), Neal Cassady, Stanley Owsley, and members of the Grateful Dead, traveled around the country in the famous "Joy Bus" immortalized by author Thomas Wolfe in his book, "The Electric Kool Aid Acid Test." In 1965 "The Warlocks," an early name for "The Grateful Dead," came to Ken Kesey's Perry Lane home near Stanford where Kesey introduced them to LSD. Their first appearance following that experience was at Magoo's Pizza Parlor in Menlo Park. Kesey soon dubbed them the official band for the Merry Pranksters' Acid Tests, a series of psychedelic events which began in Soquel, San Jose, Muir Beach, and Watts.

The Charlatans, considered to be the seminal Rock band of the Haight Ashbury and the beginning of it all, appeared at the Red Dog Saloon in Virginia City, Nevada at the request of Chandler Laughlin, a music agent working as bartender. The request was for the summer of 1965 beginning in June. Strange things began to happen from the first night. There was surprising attendance. The Charlatans, not particularly proficient in music as much as in costume, felt set upon to deliver. To ensure their mystic quality and performance the entire band took doses of acid before appearing on stage. The result was a comic intellectual foray where they could not play their instruments individually or together as a band. As was typical of the Charlatans and their personal brand of magic benevolence, they were instant heroes. They continued to play through the summer at a hundred a week for five nights. That summer had given followers of the Charlatans in the Haight time to flock to Virginia City and invade the small town with drugs and costumed hippie types to the shock of local residents. On the final night in September, 1965, rivaled by none, Ken Kesey and the "Bus" with Neal Cassady and others arrived.

Other sources of LSD were soon discovered; the peyote cactus contained Mescaline, a very similar drug in natural form found also in the Psilocybin mushrooms. Another surprising source was Morning Glory seed, the heavenly blue variety. Soon the substance was synthesized by a brilliant clandestine chemist in San Francisco, Augustus Stanley Owsley III who dubbed it "White Lightning," the prize of both the initiate and the experienced "tripper."

The desire to experience this grand exotic mind extension and expand the known consciousness was amazing. It was an alternative to the familiar drugs heroin, marijuana and speed (methamphetamine). They took acid to see, to perceive more, to experience the "truth," and to open one's self to inspiration and creativity. The "psychedelic experience" as described in clinical terms would produce, "manifestations of hallucinations of the interior emotions and anxiety." Well, we knew that.

So why didn't everyone that took acid have the awakenings others had, like Allen Cohen's dream of the idea for the Haight Ashbury newspaper, the "Oracle"? They took it to get "high," to have great sex and love, and to be distorted, to expand or animate their reality. Some of those conceptions have been carried on having obvious effects on cinema, art and literature. These may have provided incentives for current computer imagery and the sensory experiences in what is now known as "Virtual Reality."

Other manifestations of those early psychedelic excursions, now a common and well known experience, though scantily documented, will continue to emerge throughout the evolution of future society and the sensory expansions provided in those root forms will continue to have their effect. Many of that prime generation and their children are now in positions that shape our current society and values. Those effects are also seen in the current generation of computer geniuses, some of whom may have regarded LSD as a necessary experience in expansion and awareness for the sake of conceptualization. LSD has had a profound influence on the perceptive abilities of man, although as previously thought, it did not provide the miracle of complete spiritual awakening, and the panacea for all. As a society we are still dependent on ourselves. But society is more aware of itself and that influence has advanced the world in ways yet to unfold. The influence is obvious, and it all began in the 60's in San Francisco following the "beat" movement which is well known as a period of creativity in poetry, literature, art, and music. This "hyper-awareness" has also had an effect on our conceptualization and the creative forces that have shaped our technology in the later

Allen Ginsberg

twentieth century. So it wasn't all bad. Ken Kesey called it the "500 year window," meaning an opportunity that comes once in 500 years like the "Enlightenment" (1650-1800) and Thomas Hobbs, Rousseau, Descartes, Immanuel Kant, and others, concerning ideals, freedoms, and individual rights, that influenced the writers of the American Constitution.

Chapter 11-The Response

It is interesting to note that as jazz was resurgent in the fifties, the poets of North Beach were gaining momentum. Though both are artistic pursuits, there was political conflict. This is important because it illustrates once again the alliance of conflict and creativity. It seems that creativity is born of frustration, the idea to push new ideas in the face of social turmoil or dissatisfaction as a cry to be heard, a sense that, "this must be done before something happens," that art survives the bickering and strife of everyday life and yet portrays that very thing, life itself, as seen through the eyes of the artist. Though many academic artists work from a long well thought out plan, others are spontaneous, responding directly to the world around them, usually in a critical interpretation. If an artist creates to define his environment and it is one of political conflict or human injustice, then this is exactly true. The parallel of events in the fifties, the conflicts and the artistic response, is uncanny. The poetic and literary response of the early nineteen fifties came on the heels of the Korean War, (1950-1953). As poet Allen Ginsberg reveals unwittingly in the opening passages of his work, "Howl," in 1955. The drug addiction and dereliction that followed the end of the war in Korea was brought about by the exposure to addictive substances by military personnel on duty in Korea and transferred home when they returned. This is really when America's drug problems began. Ginsberg simply described his environment and when he did, he was successful. It had been in the hearts of the people waiting to be addressed. Not so surprising, it was the same earlier with Kerouac, a social distaste that finds voice in wild abandon and becomes treasured and heroic at a time when the issues of a society are being ignored, creating his own voice and a radical new prosaic form.

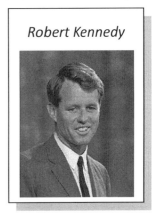

Robert Kennedy

A Diary of the Underdogs

A correlation with the actions of the Robert Kennedy investigations into the Teamsters Labor Unions in 1967 and '68, and specifically his ire with teamster boss Jimmy Hoffa, represents a conflict begging answers, and in many ways these and other similar conflicts were answered throughout the artistic environment. But a particular response might be the products of the Miles Davis quintets of the time and the radical new direction his music had taken with the release of "Snows of Kilimanjaro" followed by "Bitches Brew." These were hard edge advances to the jury of jazz, where earlier, "Kind of Blue," the classic group of 1959 possessed tenacity, a clarity and unification of sound that was unassailable, a music that was direct and powerful and yet sympathetic. It was an answer to the transformation of the time. Although Miles has always had a racial agenda it was as though his statement would seem a solid strata, a web of sound that would stand, a texture that could not be unraveled. This would change, as is the very essence of the jazz art, and especially with Miles Davis. He was at a point of leadership. He had the ear of the jazz world and he now had innovative saxophonist John Coltrane next to him in the front line of his band and bright alto saxophonist Cannonball Adderley. Change again ensued, the late nineteen fifties. Miles' new compositions begged for peace; "Freddy the Freeloader," "All Blues," "Blue and Green," and "So What," all set in thoughtful long time meters. It was a time of reflection and quiet, a time for lyrical singing phrases, musical lullabies. The album was "Kind of Blue." Miles was singing to us. America was entering the fledgling period of the 1960's and John F. Kennedy had been elected President.

Miles Davis

During Kennedy's early administration he had sent troops to Mississippi to enforce integration. The Cuban Missile Crisis followed, "The Bay Of Pigs." Political tension again was on the rise. Coltrane stepped out on his own. The statement was monumental! His early recordings stood pale by the intensity of his "Giant Steps," a truly powerful expression of emotion and unrest. John Coltrane was passionately sensitive to the world around him and it couldn't be contained. His composition, "Alabama" testified to his compassion for the victims of Selma, Alabama and the racial melee.

In 1963 the assassination of Kennedy, sent a shock through the country as if it had been hit by high voltage electric current, by lightning. Again, disarray, confusion. The Miles Davis exponent; cerebral, fleeting, erratic, ungrounded, fresh and original fly-away compositions and dynamic execution with an all new band. Young drummer Tony Williams was explosive, fiery and innovative. Brilliant pianist Herbie Hancock sensing a new urgency stretched the music from the piano in a desperate new direction. Miles had decided not to trust his own writing when saxophonist Wayne Shorter provided musical compositions that could carve a fresh path for the band and provide a solo style that would fill the void left by Coltrane leading the expressions of the saxophone and the band on a previously uncharted course. This music first appeared on the record "Miles Smiles" and included "Orbits," "Footprints," "Dolores," "Freedom Jazz Dance," a composition by Eddie Harris, and "Ginger Bread Boy," by Jimmy Heath. Miles contributed only one composition, "Circle."

It was 1964, the Viet Nam War, Haight Ashbury, Lyndon Johnson, and the Nation embroiled in a tough mix. San Francisco bore down as though blowing hot breath on a coal, a heat that fired jazz white-hot into the hearts of the "underground."

A Diary of the Underdogs

Chapter 12-The Neighborhood

The black musicians of the Haight and Fillmore barely survived on music. The spirit was in the bone and the blood, indestructible and resilient. They found places to play in the neighborhood, on Haight, on Divisadero, places like the "Bird Cage," "Jack's," "Sheldon's Blue Mirror," on Fillmore, "Parker's Soulville," on McAllister, "Van's Nook," around the corner from Bop City, "Jackson's Nook," upstairs on Post street. These were home-boy hangouts. If people came in they might make some money. The Fillmore was rough then. Everybody knew everyone that played. It was like family. There was an inner web of connection to each other and within that web were bands that were as important as any band has ever been even though they never "played out." When you played with a certain group of players you belonged. Every protocol applied. You could not be late regardless of the situation, whether for money or for rehearsal or even a jam session. The problems of one were known by all. Within that circle great musicians found shelter among those who understood the life.

The people of the neighborhoods were distinct individuals, players of specific character that set them apart in the dog mix of the "underground." The styles alone would define them, but the personalities they displayed in daily life were colorful and unique.

Jesse Hawkins had a place behind a storefront on lower Haight Street and a piano. It was a jazz den, four am sessions that went into noon. Jesse Hawkins seldom played outside his own house. He was a mentor for young players, a patient methodical teacher who taught by example, by gentleness and persistence, by magic.

Jimmy Lovelace was one who played within the ghetto and also outside of it with some of the national traveling bands. He was an incredibly inventive and fiery drummer who sparked the local sessions when he was in town and available, and was a regular drummer in the Monty Waters' Big Band. Monty played alto and

The original Bop City building moved from Post Street-now Marcus Books on Fillmore- a block and a half away

most of the good players from the Fillmore played in his band. From time to time they got gigs at the Both/And, a club on Divisadero between Oak and Haight streets, one of the few places where local bands could play for money in between the appearances of national acts.

Cowboy Noyd lived deep within the "underground" between the Haight and the Fillmore and was a legendary trumpet player. Although no one had ever heard him play, still all believed him to have once been a great musician. His warm beaming smile was seductive. The inspiration for the character "Cowboy" in the Jack Gelber play, "The Connection," may have come from local San Francisco character and musician Cowboy Noyd, who lived in the Fillmore district in the1960's.
See interview: BJ Papa with Don Alberts

Bishop Norman Williams was a young Be-bop alto player who was found regularly at the Coffee Gallery on upper Grant Street on Sunday afternoons. Williams could burn like "Bird" and he was at his

A Diary of the Underdogs

peak in blistering fast tempos. (1961)
See interview: Bishop Norman Williams with Don Alberts and Eric Whittington

Jack's on Sutter was a dim brown room, just off Webster on Sutter Street in the Fillmore district that had jazz music that went to two a.m. and sometimes after hours. The house band was an organ trio with Richard "Groove," Holmes on the Hammond, guitarist Saunders King, and various drummers, and you could sit in. It had a feel like home, small yellow lights and some red neon. The sound felt padded, insulated and soft.

The Bird Cage was upstairs on Divisadero just past Fulton where saxophonist Vi Redd held down the gig. Sheldon's Blue Mirror was a drinking bar on Fillmore between Fulton and McAllister. It was always full of action and not always the best kind. Theirs was a mean crowd, a working man's bar where tensions were high and on the edge, where people sometimes got out of control and things happened, but there was a jazz there, and blues guitar. Everyone in the Fillmore knew about it and the young jazz cats all played there.

Parker's Soulville, on McAllister was a strictly after hours spot. You entered through a narrow counter passage where you paid the five dollar admission and proceeded past the black curtain. Once inside it was very dark. The only light came from dim blue bulbs tucked away near the ceiling and a small white light on the bandstand. It was a hardwood floor for dancing that was crowded with groups of people standing and talking. The tables spread to the side and back. It was Israfel's gig. Israfel Ural played trombone with drummer, Joe Taylor and bassist Benny Wilson. Don Alberts played piano. The gig paid six dollars a night, from two a.m. to six.

Jimbo's Bop City-Alan Smith, Pony Poindexter and others

Jackson's Nook was upstairs on Post Street not far from Bop City. It was operated by a Jackson and his wife and they did all the food themselves with no other employees. The Nook had a small bandstand near the street window with white Venetian blinds and a spinet piano. The room was bright with white neon lights like a coffee shop with vinyl booths and linoleum floor. The sound was hard and loud but Jackson and his wife was sweet people, and it was a pleasure to find warmth and hospitality there and play jazz music on a cold San Francisco night. Jackson paid if he made money, otherwise you played for free, but he would feed you and that was often the main reason you came.

Most everyone worked for Jimbo at Bop City at one time or another. He opened at two a.m. and stood at the door collecting the cover charge. The place was magical. Somehow it always seemed very important to be there. You never knew who was going to come in that night. If you knew who was in town you could expect any of them to take a seat in front of the piano while you played, or maybe sit in. Johnny Baker was the best be-bop piano player the place had ever seen. When he came in the place romped. When he put his head down and got into the piano you'd think there was a war on. See interview: Vince Lateano, Mel Martin.

John Handy came in almost every night playing alto saxophone. Some of those sessions got real hot and one tune would last on hour or more without stopping. Other horn players would jump up on the

A Diary of the Underdogs

bandstand and blow awhile and sit down when another player came up. There would be ten or more people playing on one jam, and half of them would be in the audience. See interview: John Handy, Sonny Buxton. The picture of Billie Holiday dominated the entrance to Bop City. It was next to a picture of Bird with his arm around Jimbo. That picture of Billie Holiday always made the place feel like hallowed ground when you were at Bop City, like you could do no wrong because her spirit watched over the place. Many people felt that way about Billie, like she was a Saint, a Mother Protector. She was someone you could cry to, someone who would listen to your troubles, like she could get you back on track again when you were off. Young trumpeter Webster Young loved Billie Holiday. He knew all her tunes and he could sing the lyrics. Once in Los Gatos at Lorraine Miller's house, Webster was invited into the peyote experience. He was curious and he accepted. The hallucinogenic qualities of peyote cactus are legendary and the comfort mode can go either way. With Webster it may have been disquieting and he became immediately silent, he said nothing to anyone. He listened to Billie's records over and over all that night without moving from a cocoon position in front of the stereo. Billie's voice seemed to give him peace, help him hold on to reality.

A Diary of the Underdogs

Chapter 13-Diversification, Ethnic Roots

Suppose there was a plan to infiltrate the white community with blues and jazz inoffensively. The natural paranoia of the White is to think that way. The music has a lulling affect, a creeping satisfaction, and they like the feeling. It is not an imperial idea or a forced expression but one of invitation to an ethnic music, that which flows from the soul of the Negro as naturally as conversation. That "naturalism" is the key factor in our liberation. The dichotomy is promoted by the Blacks. Oppressed cultures cry their insistence on happiness from within. Their song is just that, one of joy and common understanding, religious. The imitation of that by the White is clumsy and awkward due to the neo-European nature and can be militaristic. There is no tenderness within a pounding insensitive drumbeat and metallic trombones, those rudiments were ingrained in the traditional melodies of the marching bands of 1944 Germany and the Prussians before them. There had been little advancement in jazz and popular music in the European countries since the turn of the century. American jazz and Ragtime was misunderstood and in fact it was considered illegitimate and foreign. The Black American music came from participation in an unequal society and was based in the blues, sung and played with guitar and harmonica and words of faith, in the churches of people believing in a better life in spite of disappointment and unfairness. From that premise it eventually became a commodity to the rest of the world because of its strong validity. It was not meant as a seduction. The appeal was only present because of its seemingly effortless form of expression, the will of that expression to soar, to reach the level to which it should naturally arise, no more different than works of artist and oil painters of the early Europeans had eventually become treasures, created either by high commission or through depravity and frustration. The expression of the soul remains, the story of the heart cannot be challenged, it lives for others to admire, to emulate and follow.

In describing a musical art form the source is paramount. Music comes from a central place in the mind and soul that screams to be recognized for various reasons, often the least of which is money. Reward and success are never in step with need and dedication, but the artist often has no choice, the creative impetus is visceral and inborn and the creator will often stretch himself to the thinnest means of depravity, even death, in his attempt to follow it.

Diversification in jazz has always proved essential to its growth as a product of its society. The mix is the secret. Originally, music was separated by races, by religions, by economic and demographic models. The mix has provided the strength of character needed and the current generation provides the agenda.

The effect of various ethnic influences is worthy of note. For example: Jewish musicians appear to be capable of consuming great amounts of musical material in a very commanding way and their creativity seems endless. However, it differs from the ethnicity of the Blacks. Klezmer music, having basis in European Arabic, is more concise and compact in nature where the African is a broader melodic mantra. An interesting contrast to this comparison is the Germanic-European, the structural classic influence, the romantic, the soaring melodies, the passionate "Wagner-esque," the lilting Mozart, and the indelible impressionist's tag that immediately recalls Debussy and "Ravelian" romanticism. As for the Italian jazz musician's influence, it remains always robust, proficient, energetic, and somewhat impatient, though dramatic and fetching. Italians will always command the strong center of attention within a jazz band and their contributions will be thoughtful, humorous, aggressive and grand.

The Latin influence is Indian by nature, born in ritual and festivity. It defines itself as passion, bringing force and mobility to the music through rhythmic intention. It affords a dedication, a reverence, and a trance-like commitment to the music allowing the player to be consumed by it as in a religious proceeding or even a chant.

The French, again European, are demonstrative and romantic, vigorously concerned and constantly

A Diary of the Underdogs

aware of performance. The European awareness of American jazz music is best served in the French. Their audiences are the most appreciative. There is uniqueness though. Jazz musicians have found refuge in the French communities where typically there is no racism, where art is held high, where creativity is regarded as a gift to be treasured and those possessing it to be respected. Thus a French counterpart in an American jazz band will be a treasure, however, most suitably as a melodic instrumentalist. Drummers are best reserved for Blacks, Latinos, and Italians.

The Asian influence has been mild until recently. There are many reasons. Typically, Asians have the ability to emulate at a fantastic level of accuracy. This may have contributed to the comparatively gradual raise of prominent Asian jazz personalities. There have been exceptions, Toshiko Akioshi, Kazu Matsui, and others, but over all, the American jazz format is intimidating. Approaching from outside the element can be difficult. However, the appreciation of the American jazz musician in Japan has reached an all time high currently. There are formats dedicated to the pure jazz art and the resident Japanese musicians are playing at a high level and becoming international by reputation.

Russia offers a mystic contribution. The ethnic resources are deep and rich. Just think of the many passionate Russian composers through time; Prokofiev, Shostakovich, Tchaikovsky, Khachaturian, Stravinsky, and there are more, of course. Musicians schooled in these classics and passions will be powerful jazz music practitioners once the proper insight is achieved. The music is bright, melodic and forceful, with strong discipline, a control not common in American jazz players where the attitude is more loose, open, discovered and implied moment to moment.

Often adding one ethnicity to a group changes it completely. In this sense it can be likened to combining spice elements to food preparation. Each delicate addition changes the flavor and brings new possibilities to the sensation and range of enjoyment. A balanced combination always propels the music. However, there have never existed pre-conditions for the enthusiastic jazz performance and inspiration. The spirit serves all. Currently the new generations of jazz musicians in America often have combined racial elements.

Fortunately, the flame has been passed; the legend re-told again and again, the story of jazz lives on by the passion with which it was born. But it has taken time and toll and also lives. Peer group pressure has been so strong upon young players in former times that many great artists have been lost to drugs, alcohol, or intentional dissipation and accident. (Albert Stinson) It was absolutely imperative to belong, as one musician states, "I would have done anything to avoid being rejected from my group of players, (my friends). If I had to wear a ring in my nose to belong I would have done it. It was that important!" That kind of peer pressure exists in sports and in many other walks of life especially in the young, the early teens and young adult years, and it needs to be understood before things get too out of control and irreversible mistakes are made and damage done.

Art as value has been recognized. One great redeeming factor of the "age of greed" and the class separation that characterizes the 1990's, is that things have value, even art, even music, and people have potential, there is money to be made; marketing! No matter how ugly that may sound depending on what it is applied to, it is a fact of valued property and motivation. Though music, jazz music, has always come from the heart it has had fringes of commercialism, it seems by its very nature it is required to be at a poverty level to retain its truth and validity. That is changing. Musicians of the nineties have done better than in any previous period over all. There are great young players performing on record and on concert tours who are getting the proper reward without sacrificing the slightest integrity. It would follow that success, reasonable and rewarding success is attainable, that diligence pays. Perhaps at last the balance of jazz music and value has been modeled, though it will take some time to reach the underdogs.

The sophistication of jazz music has always applied. Even in the early Miles Davis periods the precise placement of one note in a composition would influence the attitude of the improvisation and affect

A Diary of the Underdogs

the soloist toward their approach to the entire work. With the appearance of pianist Bill Evans through the resourceful efforts of Miles Davis in 1963, one incontrovertible essence emerged, *"romanticism."* Evans ability had been recognized by composer George Russell, one whom Davis consulted often. Davis complained he needed a new piano player and Russell had said he knew someone, to which Miles asked, "Is he black?" Russell replied, "No, but he can play his *can* off!" "Have him come by the Colony Club," Miles replied. Bill Evans met with Miles Davis at the Colony Club and became a part of the Miles Davis sextet. At a time when there was not yet peace, American military personnel were still dying in the war in Viet Nam, and there wouldn't be peace within that decade, Evans brought that quest for peace to the band and later to the jazz world through his own recordings. His influence deepened the music with a tonal richness and harmonic resolution, a pristine and delicate resonance through the piano that had not been present before in the language of jazz. "It bugs me when people try to analyze jazz as an intellectual theorem. It's not, it is feeling."- Bill Evans.

Language is the incomplete form of communication we depend on to define ourselves. There are many voices, and words are not present in most of them. These languages are hard amounts of information that come from both the dead and the living and occupy their natural space within the mind. Jazz, poetry, art, painting, dance, film, expression in all forms, is the vital language of personal struggle encompassing the past and foretelling the future in a voice of humility. It is sparked by the present or past society and environments, by the oppression or comfort of the giver, and by their level of personal peace.

There were many factors that influenced the idea of "Free Love." Not only because the idea was tantalizing, but also because it was within the life-style of communal living, the convenient opportunities for experimentation, for "wife swapping," the trading of mates within the friendship of two couples. There were accounts of permanent relationships developing through this idea and quick divorces to re-marry not only in communes but in established societies in San Francisco and Marin.

The influence of the "Tropic of Cancer," a controversial work of author Henry Miller was not to be ignored. It was a sexual work, pornographic by some definitions, obscene to others, however, in defining the more explicit activities of sexual behavior among adults it propelled the society in a new way, and in a time of search for new heroes after Kerouac and the "poets-elite" of the fifties, Miller became, unwittingly, a sexual guru.

Lenny Bruce, the prolific comic satirist dwelled in the intrigue of common human activities and his wit was quick and biting. Profanity was part of his technique and he used it easily as a weapon for shock, something that seemed to touch the pent up society with a release, a catharsis. Audiences found themselves enjoying the profane onslaught. He performed for them what they could not do for themselves;

release their feelings, calling things exactly what they were, feelings, putting words, by dialogue and example to their emotions. But he was too soon, too fast, a hot burning star surviving frequently on drugs and hounded by police. He died in Los Angeles of an overdose. (In 1966)

Chapter 14-Kerouac and Cassady

As far as anyone can tell, Jack Kerouac, Allen Ginsberg, William Burroughs, Gregory Corso, Harry the Hipster, and Lenny Bruce defined the generation of the "beats." This; according to Eric Anderson in an article for a Rolling Stone publication entitled-"Book of the Beats. "Anderson, along with others of that edition, maintains Kerouac, Ginsberg, Burroughs, Gregory Corso, and Lenny Bruce became America's new language models. "The Beat writer's language mixed shocking directness with sweet ingenuity providing a fresh, new literary landscape." But the ultimate demise of Kerouac as the hero and leading character of all this is somewhat unsettling. According to an article by Jack Boulware for the SF weekly, July 29-Aug 4th, 1998, Jack Kerouac spent the last few years of his life in St. Petersburg Florida with his wife Stella and his Mother where he watched TV, read books, and drank himself to death. On October 20, 1969 he wrote to nephew Paul Blake Jr., "I just wanted to leave my estate (which is what it really is) to someone directly connected with the last remaining drop of my direct blood line, which is my sister Carolyn, your Mom, and not leave a ding-blasted fucking goddamn thing to my wife's one hundred Greek relatives. I also plan to divorce or have her marriage to me annulled. Just telling you the facts of how it is." Gerald Nicosia says that this letter is proof that Kerouac didn't love Stella Sampas. The Sampas family and their attorney maintain this letter is a forgery. The letter was dated one day before Jack Kerouac died of an alcohol-related hemorrhage. Although married to Stella, his will excluded her completely and left everything to his mother Gabrielle. When Gabrielle died in 1973 her will left everything back

Jack Kerouac

to Stella ignoring her two grandchildren, Jan Kerouac, Jack's daughter and Paul Blake Jr., the only son of Jack's deceased sister. Wife Stella obtained one third of his estate under legal entitlement extended to widows by Florida law.

Jack Kerouac's second wife, Joan Haverty conceived their only child in 1951 when Jack was in New York writing the early pages of what would become the novel "On the Road". Jack left six months later for San Francisco and never returned.

Jan Kerouac met her father for the first time in 1962 when her mother's efforts to gain child support finally forced Kerouac to take a blood test which was positive. At nine years old she nervously accompanied him to the liquor store for a bottle of Harvey's Bristol Cream Sherry saving the cork as a reminder she did indeed have a father. Jan and her father Jack met once more in 1966 when she was a pregnant teenager on her way to Mexico. Kerouac turned from an episode of Beverly Hillbillies and said, "Use my name, write a book." Jan hit the road to become a writer and lived a similar life to her father's, working odd jobs sometimes prostitution to support her heroin habit. Jan's ex-husband John Lash, as her

A Diary of the Underdogs

personal representative filed to dismiss the Florida probate litigation and has reached a confidential agreement with the Sampas family to settle the suit. In January 1997 the New Mexico District Court ruled in favor of John Lash. Jan had died in Albuquerque, New Mexico in 1997 of complications of kidney failure. Gerald Nicosia appealed the decision and is pending a decision on August of 1998. If he wins he can pursue the Florida probate case where the letter is considered a forgery, in favor of Jan Kerouac even after her death as her literary representative and heir. Jan contested her grandmother's will and the Florida probate ruling concerning the estate of Kerouac going to the third wife, Stella Sampas. Remember John Lash, ex-husband of Jan, had made a deal with the Sampas family over the estate of Jack Kerouac. A Florida judge has put that probate contest on hold due to Jan's heirs (ex-husband, John Lash and her half brother have protested Nicosia's involvement. Lash has filed to dismiss the Florida probate in favor of his agreement with the Sampas family in which he would profit.

Neal Cassady

     Jan wrote two autobiographical novels; "Baby Driver" in 1981 and "Train Song" in 1988. A young heir of John Steinbach told her that being a direct blood heir to her father she was entitled to 50% of all royalties of her father's books as they came up for copyright renewal. She found she was to be involved with the ongoing business relationship with Stella Sampas. The value of the estate is estimated at between 10 and 20 million. Kerouac's raincoat went to Johnny Depp for $15,000.

As Jan's health worsened in 1991 and she was on dialysis Nicosia staged three sanding room only events for her in San Francisco. Entertainment ; Ken Kesey, Pranksters, Ramblin' Jack Elliot, Big brother, documentary film by Mill Valley film maker John Antonelli. Nicosia says to pay for medical bills and finance her legal efforts. Gerald Nicosia wrote "Memory Babe" autobiography and lives in Corte Madera. Kerouac's grave is in Lowell Mass. is often strewn with beer bottles. People are seen there quietly reciting poetry.

Notes form SF weekly July 29-aug4th, 1998 by Jack Boulware- website reference PEN-Oakland International writer's organization

Neal Cassady died Feb 5th, 1968 at Salia, Mexico,1½ miles from San Miguel de Allende, thirteen hours from Laredo. He took about seven Seconal and drank a bottle of muddy tequila called "pulque." He walked off down the train tracks and died there. In Aptos, Cathedral Drive is known to some as "The Neal Cassady Memorial Highway."

29 Russell Street, off Hyde, between Union and Green, is where Neal and Carolyn Cassady lived and Jack Kerouac lived upstairs in the attic during the winter of 1951-52. Kerouac and Cassady worked on the Southern Pacific Railroad. Kerouac wrote portions of "Visions of Cody," "Doctor Sax," and "On the Road" there. This period is romanticized in film "Heart Beat." ("Pagans on the Beach" at Lime Kiln Creek in Big Sur.) Neal Cassady is immortalized as "Dean Moriarty" in Kerouac's book "On the Road" and also as the infamous driver of the "Magic Bus" with Ken Kesey and the "Merry Pranksters."

A Diary of the Underdogs

The Chicago Seven

The "Chicago Seven" first appeared at the Democratic National Convention in Chicago during the week of August 21st to the 26th in 1968. The group included; David Dellinger, Tom Hayden, Rennie Davis, Abbie Hoffman, Jerry Rubin (Youth International Party-YIP leader), John Froines, Lee Weiner, and other local Chicago organizers plus Bobby Seal, co-founder of the Black Panther Party. They were all arrested for conspiring to incite rioting. They had planned massive demonstrations for the week of the convention under the title, "Days of Rage." Mayor Richard Daily stepped in to control the action and all members of the group were taken into custody. Although apprehended, the group had made their point, to discourage Lyndon Johnson from seeking re-election. After the arrests William Kunstler became lawyer for defendant Bobby Seal. Seal was vehement in the courtroom during the proceedings. Prosecutor Thomas Foran convinced Judge Julius Hoffman to have Seal bound and gagged in the courtroom. The trial continued for three days. It was finally declared a mistrial and Seal received four years for contempt of court. The Chicago Eight thus became the "Chicago Seven." In 1970 five of the seven were found guilty, but appeals overturned the decision in 1972 citing the Judge's procedural errors due to his hostility toward the defendants.

Chicago Seven

In the 1968 election Republican Candidate Richard Nixon with Vice President Spiro T. Agnew won the election over Hubert H. Humphrey and Richard Nixon become the next President.

Nixon's presidency had its hard times as Nixon inherited the conflicted drama of the Viet Nam war begun under Lyndon Johnson and Nixon continued in his own way to advance what he felt were the American positions in the war. In 1969-1970 he ordered the bombing of Hanoi and in 1972 underwater mining of Haiphong Harbor.

Nixon's Watergate scandal was his final undoing. The scandal implicated members of the Nixon White House staff in the break in of the Republican National Committee Headquarters at Watergate on June 17, 1972. The trail of evidence ultimately led to the president's knowing or possibly authorizing the break in of the Watergate facility. Plans for his impeachment were underway and rather than face a congressional committee requesting clandestine White House meeting tapes from the Oval office, Nixon chose to resign from the presidency and avoid being impeached or possibly convicted of crimes. Most of the prominent members of his staff had been convicted and were seeking presidential pardons in the Watergate case. It was over for Nixon. On August 9, 1974 at noon, President Richard Nixon resigned. By 1974 the US was in a financial recession.

A Diary of the Underdogs

Chapter 15-Interviews

BJ Papa- jazz pianist- with Don Alberts-September 4, 1997 in San Francisco

BJ Papa

Don: You knew Benny Wilson, the bass player?
BJ: I've been with Benny many times, through the years, you know. Oh, man, Benny! You know Benny was a good cook; cooked his ass off.
Don: Oh, yeah? I didn't know that.
BJ: Yeah. When we were roommates, all the cats who came to town, pretty much, especially Junior Cook and Blue Mitchell came by the house.
Don: Well, everybody, it seems like.
BJ: Yeah, pretty much. You know, to be able to put the spices on for them, like a gathering. You know, Junior's from Pensacola, I'm from Mobile, so you know. He's a home boy of mine, a player, and terrific saxophonist-a musician! I mean, you know, so...
BJ: So when they came to town, we always blew it. Junior always hung out; Roy, Roy Brooks and Eugene Taylor. So we'd put the pots on. These guys are on the road. We had a piano we could play, that way we could jam too, man.
Don: I knew Benny. He was cool.
BJ: Oh, man, he's cool. In them days, you know, everybody's bumming. That's the pattern; Cowboys, whatever. (People who understood the life)
Don: Cowboys?
BJ: Cowboys and girls, casseroled together. We could take seven dollars and make it work.
Don: The whole thing?
BJ: The whole thing, a whole bunch of people. I've always been impressed, you know, and it wasn't no great thing, you know, just the basic shit, like a casserole.
BJ: Yeah, remember Al Harewood? You know, there were always a bunch of women. There were the jazz girls. Cowboys have always been going to adapt 'em. Man, you now....
He was always a hero. You're old enough to know. He taught me & Les. He's a natural in fact...You remember Les?
Don: Tell me about Les.
BJ: Les played the saxophone.
BJ: Les is my age too. Me, him, Art Lewis, we were all 1930s class babies.
Don: Yeah. Pick him out.
BJ: Yeah, there's a few left. See, I went shopping' and I knew Cowboy's work before. I was married, you know. He had a rough take...Right?
Don: I know where he's coming' from. Yeah. (Cowboy)
BJ: Les was blessed with being his nephew. (Cowboy's) We're the same age. I met all these people through Art Lewis. Art Lewis is the guy who really introduced me to the scene. I got a picture of him. You come to my house and I'll show you.
Don: I can't place his face. (Cowboy's)

A Diary of the Underdogs

BJ: I'm Cowboy's sister's son. I guess it's like anything else, when you start playing'. I started late so I was ...I was overplaying it...like everybody else 'trying' to catch up.

Don: Overdoing it, eh?

BJ: Yeah, man; hard. I do it all the same night. After that...I mean, you know...Remember Van's Nook?

Don: Yeah, Van's Nook. That's one I forgot...around the corner from Bop City, Indiana Street, around the corner from Bop City.

BJ: Remember Bobbie Van? Played the trumpet...Could have been a real... First time I ever played music in front of him was at his place. I was so scared.

Don: Happened to you too? Everything you know disappears.
You can play everybody's style and then there's a big rat hole and everything you know disappears.

BJ: Oh, Man! My legs got to shaking'. I mean both of them!

Don: Well you're playing' with your buddies.

BJ: Yeah...My legs got to shaking' I mean both of them...Later we played two choruses of the blues. I was wringing' wet. First of all I was wringing wet in sweat. I started to perspire immediately. I wet all my clothes soaking wet and my legs are shaking'. I pressed back against the wall and real hard against the piano. There were about 7 people in the joint, along with the musicians. Ben was playing' piano, along with C.L. Jones. Anyway; when my legs stopped shaking- I played about 12 bars, people in the joint going, bla, bla, bla, I was more scared than anything else, but I made it, you know. I finally pressed back against the wall and pressed real hard against the piano. I finally got one to quit shaking the other didn't quit, it kept on shaking. But I made it; I think I made it through 12 bars of "Now's the Time" or something like that. I was wringing wet. I was so shook up, man.

Don: Yeah, we were jazz musicians.

BJ: I was so messed up I couldn't believe it! It took me a long time to get over that.

Don: To play it again?

BJ: No, stage fright, man, you know, stomach pains; it took me a while to get past that shit. Man, I was always nervous, anticipation, or whatever you want to call it.

Don: It still happens. It's still there?

BJ: I don't get it anymore. I've gone through some shit. You know what I mean. I used to get it a lot, man. It took me a long time to not get it.

Don: Remember Soulville? Remember when we used to play down at Soulville?

BJ: I remember Soulville.

Don: It was a dope gig.

BJ: I remember Israfel. I'll tell you about Israfel. I've got a picture of me and Israfel, and Cowboy on my birthday, maybe 6 months later. He was sick even then, you know. Yeah, 1978, I think it was.

Don: Oh yeah. You're filling me in. I can't remember a lot of things.

BJ: The last time I really saw Bill Evans. I saw him again on the road. He'd stand out. Played in our ears! So I come by cause I didn't have anything to do.. I can see him now. He was a white boy, down on Fillmore Street.

Don: I'd park across from Bob City, and Nate Lewis would go in, and I'd have Bill Evans in the back seat.

BJ: I saw him in Seattle; I was up there in May.

Don: Was he doing okay?

BJ: Yeah.

Don: That's good.

BJ: I didn't realize it's been 5 years since I was up there. I'd never been to Seattle.

Don: In winter or summer?

BJ: In August, '92. It was beautiful while I was up there. We went one day to Mt. Rainier, and all that shit.

A Diary of the Underdogs

Don: Mt. Rainier is starting to kick up again. They're talking about it...

BJ: That's a hell of a mountain, Man. I was impressed. It's not like looking at Mt. Diablo.

Don: its 14,000 feet!

BJ: Yeah, well Mt. Diablo isn't any 14,000 feet!

Don: Yeah, Rainier's a little bit larger...

BJ: You see Mt. Diablo is my spiritual landmark. I love it, man, hear me? I was up there with the earthquake. Those roads were damaged. It had one lane that was only gone half way. So it means we move... I wanted to go to the summit. I said I want to go up and see it, and we did. We hiked... This was like, in '91, or something like that.. The road had been damaged from the earthquake so they weren't allowing cars and drivers up there, but you could walk up there. That's how we did it. Man, I always liked that. Like Mt. Tamalpais, man...

Don: It's a cool thing. I've never been up there, but Dana's really into Mt. Tamalpais!

BJ: Who's he?

Don: My son.

BJ: You know what got me interested? They say it's the second largest area of land mass...that you can see to Mt. Kilimanjaro. That really fascinated me.

Don: You can see the inner & outer valleys.

BJ: Everything! That fascinated me. When I saw the brochures of what it was.

Don: You can see the Coast and you can probably see the Rockies.

BJ: You can see everything! For visibility on a clear day you can see forever!

Don: What can you say!

BJ: That's true, that's true! You can go up there on a clear day you can see as far as the naked eye will let you see!

Don: Can you see Yosemite?

BJ: Yeah! You can see all the way to Reno.

Don: (About Mt. St. Helens) It's changed a lot now. It's only about 7,000 feet.

BJ: That's true; that's very true. That's why when I read the brochure that it was second to Kilimanjaro, I had to see it.

Don: From the pad I had in Portland, I could look out my apartment balcony window and see Mt. St. Helens, and Rainier, and I could see Mt. Adams, and over to the right I could see Mt. Hood. On a clear day you could see five mountains.

BJ: Did you know Rene Strain, the singer? You didn't know Rene?

Don: From here?

BJ: Well he's from Seattle, he's from Virginia. I mean, you know how I knew him?

Don: How? I know the name. I might have known him. I've got a pretty good memory, but I've got voids.

BJ: It's like a lot of other things. There's a lot I can't remember.. That's the thing about when somebody's been around, you know what they say. Man, I know a lot of young people, and people I grew up, like with you.. We, Man.

Don: We've been around, but in 1968 it went bad and that's when I left.

BJ: I met you in the '50s...

Don: The late '50s.

BJ: That's a long time ago!

Don: You aren't kidding' it is!

BJ: You did your thing!

Don: Right. It was a period when a lot of things were changing.

BJ: Well, we changed with 'em too.

A Diary of the Underdogs

Don: A lot of stuff happened then!

BJ: We changed with 'em, and the fact about it is, we is still alive!

Don: I know! It's a kind of puzzling discovery, isn't it?

BJ: I know, man, I'm just going to enjoy it! I'm alive!

Don: Hey! What am I supposed to do? Somebody saved me so I guess I must have something to do!

BJ: I got my younger brother telling' me how old I am! He tells me, hey, you're old enough to be a senior. So I look at this little fuck and say "Dude, I taught you everything I know." He's 18 years my junior. And eating' pizza, he would take the last piece off me, and I say No, No, No. But you know he would. Check this out! I was a good athlete.

Don: You were, like In high school and stuff?

BJ: On sand box shit I was good.

Don: Really? I never knew that about you.

BJ: Yeah! I was a second baseman; I'm a "righty". I can bat right. And you know who the first baseman was? Willie McCovey.

Don: Oh, yeah?

BJ: I'm from Mobile.

Don: Oh, I thought he was Cuban.

BJ: Willie McCovey? He's terrific. Maybe we're the same, pretty much.

Cuba, Cuba, and then there's Porto Rico!

Don: Not much difference to us, but to them...

BJ: Look alike too? But the, it's always...in the Spanish thing...The light

Spaniards are in control of the political, economically...

Don: Always, they owned the world; they had the strongest navy...

BJ: You see the thing about it, it was cool...but they didn't keep the people happy, then they lose power. The thing with Bautista in Cuba is that why Castro came into power, because Bautista with all those dances, Havana was wild like Las Vegas, you know he destroyed his people.

Don: He used them for his own greed.

BJ: If he bled the people...If you mess your people around enough, it's going to come back to haunt you! That's why Castro was able to come into power with the backing of this country. Now this country is so high-minded, you know the way we look at things, look at the Southern Baptists, we don't have high roll and this and that. Castro wasn't as good as we thought he was going to be.

Don: Look at Russia. Russia likes him.

BJ: Yeah, we don't want to go with Russia. You got to respect a person. You can't defy a country like the United States and survive!

Don: It's a matter of time!

BJ: He's almost 80 years old. Who cares now what the fuck happens?

Don: He isn't going to get anything.

BJ: If you're around good people, like Bill... A lot of our people are dying. You know what I'm talking about? Well...

Don: You don't smoke, eh?

BJ: No. This is what you need to smoke... It took me a long time to get over here, man. So... Me and you are hooked together for life...Whatever goes around...We're hooked together for life.

Don: Tell me about when Monk came to town, remember that? He came to the workshop and played the first set then, when he sat down to play the second set he nodded out at the piano right there on the bandstand in front of all those people. Monk didn't care, he was out! Charlie Rouse put him in a cab out front and sent him back to the hotel. The gig was over. I met up later with Charlie and Eric Miller at a hotel

A Diary of the Underdogs

down on Bush.

BJ: I know when Philly Jo Jones fell down at the Black Hawk. Right on a table, you know... every thing!

Don: Yeah, the table to the right of the drums?

BJ: That's right. He fell right on our table, 30 or 40 fans were there... You could see him there. He was yawning, too. All of a sudden he just went poof! And laid out on the table to the right, there...

Don: To his right?

BJ: Yeah! A famous party with Miles was there. When you look at the bandstand, I always saw him there, at that little table in that little cubby there. He fell right on it!

Don: Were you there the night that Sonny Stitt was playing'?

BJ: Miles and Sonny were having' an argument, they never did get along!
They loved each other, but they argued over everything! J. J. Johnson was the trombone player in that band. It was a class audience! Let me tell you something' about Sonny. Sonny is kind of new. I think he's weird just like me. He's an opulent person, I'll always loved Sonny. You know Sonny, you come in a job where he's playing at, and you've got to play. He holds his own.

Don: You mean like Bishop?

BJ: Yeah, Bishop, That's why I love Bishop. I've always loved Bishop, man. I'm talking about 1961, 1963. You know Bishop would get right up on stage in front of Sonny Stitt and he'd blow his ass off stage if he could. That was his thing. Bishop could hold his own at the Jazz Workshop and other places, you know? Remember Bop City with the restaurant?

Don: Right side or left side of door; still on Post?

BJ: Yeah, but not later on.

Don: I did play at the other place, but it wasn't....

BJ: I did too, I did too. When I say Bop City, I think across the street. I don't think Fillmore.

Don: Yeah, I can't think of that little restaurant. It was to the left.

BJ: All right, it was Strawberry. (A little place across the street from Bop City) Don't do like him though. (at Strawberry) You know to me, as a young person, I like Jimbo...

Don: Yeah! There would be a crowd of people at the door, he just figured they'd pay, and they always did.

BJ: He knew where to hit too. (Who to address about conduct) Don't fuck up there. Be cool. He loved me. Don't make any moves... I kidded him about it too. I have the utmost respect for class. When you come in there, there's a guy (bouncer type) always to the left. Louis Armstrong came in, and Monk too. I wanted to say something to let them know he was in the house at 4 a.m. It got their attention, man. Monk walked in and sat in that little booth. "Monk's in the house," I said. In fact he was mad, he didn't like it. I saw all the great musicians in the world come to Bop City, in my time. I saw Eddie Moore almost fall off the drums 'cause Monk was standing' up there looking' at him.

Don: He would do that too...Walk right over there and look at him.

BJ: As good as Eddie is...you know he really loves me... I like my friends.

Don: What about Donald Garret and Rafael?

BJ: Rafael was Donald Garret when I met him. I met him in Chicago in 1964. He told me about SunRa and Miles. He used to play with them. He's got a name, like Clarence or something. Yeah. Rafael could play the saxophone, sometimes. He really did a number on me. I didn't do it right, playing I mean. It took me a long time.

Don: He (Rafael) seemed like he was around with an old band...

BJ: In 1963 or 64. The band was happening when he came. Rafael was a teacher, by nature. He was so into it, the way he went about doing it, and I knew he was correct. He was the one who got me together. He made me do it. (Dana walks in)

BJ: Hello!

A Diary of the Underdogs

Don: This is my son, Dana.
Dana: Where's my dinner? This is the coolest Dad!
Don: We ate it! Sixty one is a good time, and then you need glasses!
End: BJ Papa

Interview: BOB RIDDLE: broadcaster, jazz historian- November 22nd 2008-Portland, Oregon-by mail.

BOB RIDDLE

Well Don, my first exposure to San Francisco jazz was in 1958. At age 14, I sat in the "minors" section behind chicken wire after paying, a then expensive two dollar cover and drinking ninety cent cokes to listen to Cal Tjader's Latin Sextet. Cal spent the entire break talking to us kids. He loved kids, and would talk about anything: 49ers, the Giants, sailing, the city, anything imaginable. And the music; Mongo Santamaria, Willie Bobo, Eddie Duran, Al McKibbon on bass and Vince Guaraldi on piano. Guaraldi, interestingly enough, despite later writing all the Charlie Brown music, didn't care for kids. He never came near us on those breaks, just went outside and smoked. Just by luck, I got to the Jazz Workshop the night Cannonball Adderley and his quintet recorded, "Dis Here" This became my favorite group to see live, and remains so to this day, with brother Nat on cornet, Bobby Timmons on piano, Sam Jones on bass, and Louis Hayes on drums. The crowd got into it, and vice versa. This group always swung. Those experiences came during visits to the City from my home in New York. When I moved to San Francisco in the fall of 1961 to attend San Francisco State, the first place I found was Jimbo's Bop City in the Western Edition, near Fillmore Street. A continuous after-hours jam session went on all night, every night, over breakfast. After the bar closed at 2 am, everyone

Nancy King, Clare and Bob Riddle

was welcome. Pony Poindexter was the first of scores of musicians I heard there. A beautiful blonde waitress with a gleam in her eye served me breakfast. Of course I had no idea who she was but later, seeing her pin-up photo and hearing her stories from that era, it must have been Nancy King. Nancy had gotten the call on her parent's farm near Eugene to come down to San Francisco and Bop City and sing. Her girlfriend who called said she'd met this neat guy named "Jonis" Poindexter. I didn't hear Nancy sing myself until my wife and I went to hear her at the Benson Hotel's Piccadilly Room in Portland in 1970. She was, and still is a "wow," and my all-time favorite female jazz singer. Once I discovered no one cared to see my I.D., I've had a 5 o'clock shadow since I was 14, I went back to the Jazz Workshop several times to see Cannonball Adderley and Mose Allison in 1962 and 1963 and to the Black Hawk to hear Tjader's jazz group, Guaraldi and Monk. Got to Oakland to hear Bobby "Blue" Bland and Little Junior Parker at the Showcase Lounge, went to hear Joe Williams at the Sportsman's Club in Oakland. The place was jammed, but they left the front door open and about twenty of us heard the whole show out on the sidewalk. After we were married in 1965, my wife Clare and I got out as often as we could to the El Matador to see Vince Guaraldi, Bola Sete,

A Diary of the Underdogs

and Jerry Dodgion, To Basin Street West to hear Jimmy Smith, to the Trident in Sausalito to hear Denny Zeitlin, to the Both/And on Divisadero to hear Bill Evans and Bobby Hutcherson, and the Off Plaza for George Duke, before he found Fusion. Outdoor concerts were another great scene. The lawn at the Claremont in the Oakland hills for the MJQ. Sigmund Stern Grove on Sloat Avenue also hosted many great outdoor sounds.

End: Bob Riddle

Interview- Si Perkoff; pianist, composer-October 1, 2008 with Don Alberts at Bird and Beckett-about: Bop City, Strip clubs, Streets of Paris, playing organ, Philly Joe Jones, Thelonious Monk, Monk's music, Chuck Bernstein, Roswell Rudd..

SI PERKOFF

SI: This is a book of my tunes that I self published back in 1995.

DON: Oh, I didn't know it existed.

SI: Yeah, most people don't, there is no reason for anyone to know that it existed, because it only comes through me. So, I would like you to have it, but also let me show you something about it, which is the second reason I am giving it to you, the fact that you are a musician and a friend. You will see in bold, intro interlude, coda, those are autobiographical short essays. They are text in other words and if you read them you might find that I have written about stuff that you are writing about. And I don't know what it would take, some kind of release form, but if you wanted to quote something from this, it's just like interviewing me in a way. It's just a textual resource based on what you are doing.   The intro the least the autobiographical, but the Bop City stuff and the Thelonious Monk stuff is good....

Si Perkoff

DON: Yeah, great, I didn't know this existed and we are going to get this going. We will use some stuff.

SI: I think I did some good writing, even though I am not a professional writer. There are a few stories in there about my past, and I would tell them anyway. I think there is some useable and interesting stuff. Even if you don't use anything directly, it's some good material for you and your research.

DON: Yeah, great. – (Reading) *and that from a white boy* - now there is something to go with right there.

SI: That's the punch line of a great story, that right there is the punch line of one of the things in my life. Actually, that is not the punch line: that is the set-up for the punch line. The story of it starts here: The other gift from Monk was a great personal memory and a nick-name. We were at his hotel room along with several others. Monk was sitting in an easy chair and I was sitting on the floor next to him. Monk was periodically throwing his right arm straight out in a suddenly seemingly meaningless gesture as I watched and became aware that he was doing it in time with the blinking sign outside the window. He saw me watching and after one gesture, said, "Perfect, huh?" I was thinking he might have been a little late, and I shrugged my shoulders doubtfully. "Mmmm," he sort of grunted. This behavior could be interpreted as

A Diary of the Underdogs

simply playful boredom. But to me it fit in with the individualism that Monk displayed when he would get up in the middle of a tune and dance around, which he did. It was Monk's willingness to follow a rhythmic impulse. The next time he threw out his arm he looked at me-eyebrows raised that said, "Perfect!" Then in a loud voice Monk announced, "– that from a white boy!" The whole room suddenly became silent. Monk waited with that perfect sense of timing that makes his music so unique, and finally he said, "An orange boy!"

SI: I just love that. I've thought of myself as orange boy in some dimension ever since.

DON: That's interesting. Well, you know those things stick with you. I was thinking of some things we might talk about and what kept coming back to me is the idea that music, jazz music that I laid everything on the line for. I really did. There were points in my life where I didn't care where it was going to take me I was always going to go. Because the music was that strong and I know it affects all of us, because we are all still doing it. And so you make sacrifices for that and I did and I made some wrong decisions but fortunately the music was strong enough and valid enough that it kept me focused on and I'm back on it and I'm doing what I am supposed to do and it is all powered by this music we call jazz. And these musicians you mentioned, Monk is a very powerful one of those motivators and yet a pretty innocent guy, just riding along with the music as we are. Just enjoying the connection to the bliss of the music as is close to him and he interprets it and he plays it and personality becomes part of the personality and the music becomes part of the music. And you know, I'm sure it's happened to you and I would be interested in hearing a little bit about that, if you want to talk about it. And I am also interested in the early days when you were playing on the streets of Paris and the after hours gigs and some of those guys you played with and I forgot who they were, I can't remember your bass player.

SI: Well, its funny, I have been trying to remember some of the players and a lot of the names I have forgotten. I believe that I genetically I don't have a great detailed memory. But on top of that I lived in a wonderful fog of marijuana in those years and I am sure that didn't help matters any so far as remembering details. I remember flavors. I remember the way it felt, I remember how I viewed the world, and how it felt to be there, which is very difficult to describe something like that. But I am not real good at details, however I remember some details and the Bop City thing is specifically about those years of after hours. And the streets of Paris for example, that was, I didn't work there very much. But I did play there and the thing that it was, I think I am remembering the right place; the Streets of Paris was also a strip club.

DON: I don't remember, I just remember I walked upstairs.

SI: Yeah, upstairs, that was it. Yeah, well, when I played there, the trumpet player was sometimes the leader of the band, an Italian guy whose father was the head of the union. His name will come to me..... Well, anyway, the drummer was the leader and the trumpet player was the main horn. And anyhow, for me it was a big deal because I had started working non-jazz commercial type gigs, this was one. And, in course of that I wound up accompanying fairly often, certain small groups of female impersonators. And this was my first show job where the dancers were women instead of men, and I felt like I had finally arrived. Yeah, yeah.... I really felt better. There was still one female impersonator. I didn't work in the big clubs like Pinocchio's, I didn't work there, but I worked in a lot of little gigs. There was one guy, Ronnie, who I worked with a lot. And he died very young. I have no idea what got him, but he was very talented and I will always remember him as one of the people that really had something special. So, you know, when you were working for female impersonators, didn't mean that it was all bad, but it was new for me, it was show stuff instead of jazz stuff. Anyway, so that's what I think of the streets of Paris, I moved up a notch. Then, after that I got the gig at the Chi Chi Club.

DON: Yeah, up on Broadway.

SI: I had the Chi Chi Club gig for three years and that gig paid better then any of the gigs I ever had and enabled me to get financially in a slightly better position. And also, it was that I was there for two years as

A Diary of the Underdogs

a side man, and the final year I was there I was the leader. The first two years Bobbie Ferrera was the leader on the tenor saxophone and then Bobbie left and I became leader and Mel Martin became the tenor sax. And the drummer through the whole thing was Shep Sheppard.

DON: There's a name that I didn't know about.

SI: Shep Sheppard was the drummer on Green Onions. And he was a black man, and is still alive and lives in Southern Californian now and is in his 80's and still plays a little- a wonderful drummer, one of the best drummers. Certainly, I mean, I learned a tremendous amount from playing with him, and it was just behind the screen and no bass...

DON: Never a bass on a strip gig.

SI: And so I got my first experience really being a leader and on that kind of a situation and was playing with really good musicians in a really screwball situation, – ya know, behind the curtain.

DON: So she, the stripper, can see through the screen.

SI: Right. Miss Kanko and whole bunch of the show people of that time and one little story that goes with that. At one point shortly before Bobbie Ferrera left, Meyer, Meyer, I think it was Meyer, Kanko's husband, Meyer or Myron, I've forgotten, anyway, the guy who owned the Chi Chi and some clubs in the Tenderloin also, he pulled Bobbie aside and said I'm going to bring in an organ

Former location of "El Cid" at Broadway and Columbus Streets in North Beach. Paintings on the building's façade show Benny Goodman and Teddy Wilson.

instead of the piano, I've got an old, I've got an organ that's out at one of my clubs and does Si play the organ or should I fire him and get somebody else? And Bobbie says, Oh, Si plays the organ. So I played...... I never played organ except for, I think, one tiny gig, so I immediately went to a music store and started boning up on the Hammond. And he brought in a Hammond 'A' which had been modified with the vibrato units, so they called it an 'AV' – so it was wide, almost like a B3 – so it was the model before the B series.

DON: Did it have the Leslie?

SI: We had the Leslie with the blowing thing and all of that. And I played not pedals but left hand bass, I played left hand bass on the piano, so I did it on the organ. And I got through a whole other year on organ.....

DON: Another year... Well, that's a learning period.

SI: Playing strip gigs, playing that strip gig and then finally, the Chi Chi Club.

DON: Yeah, the Chi Chi, go on.

SI: It was a very powerful experience in some ways, but a very depressing experience in other ways, but mainly, the main thing is – I'll tell you the extremity to which it got. By the time I had been doing it for almost – ya know, probably the third year, by the time I had been doing it that long, I knew the shows and the things so well that I was so terminally bored, I literally, literally, I can hardly believe that I did this, I brought books with me, put them up on the organ music rack and read while I was playing the shows. I read.

DON: I'll be dammed.

SI: And you know, and kept, you know, and didn't fall on my face. And I can't believe I did that, but shows you how divorced it was from true creative musicality, it would even be possible to do that.

DON: You learned how to separate that stuff.

SI: Yeah.

DON: Those boring gigs, man....

SI: It's so true. You talk about, I've always admired people like maybe yourself, I don't really know you, from those years, to know how you did it, I admired people that were jazz players and refused to take non-jazz gigs even if they literally starved, so that they could stay focused on the true path, which I knew, was the true path. Everyone knew it was the true path.

DON: Yeah, absolutely, but we had.....

SI: My choice was to make a living with my music and play as much jazz as humanly possible and that's what I did. It's all I really knew how to play, were the skills of Jazz – improvising, chord reading – you know, all of that. I felt that almost everything I did was Jazz in one form or another because I was using those skills to play, but obviously it wasn't always music that demanded that the soul of Si Perkoff shined through. You know, and so I...so... I.....feel that I been a working professional musician playing Jazz, but playing anything that I was able to play that fell even remotely within the umbrella of what those skills told me I could do.

Chi Chi Club on Broadway

DON: Well, you're a Jazz musician, Si.....

SI: You know, so that's what I did, and that's what I still do. That's how I do it.

DON: Yeah, that's how you do it.

SI: As a contrast though, somebody who did the absolute minimal of that, I think he certainly did some of it, he did a year with me at the Chi Chi Club, but Mel Martin has pretty much through most of his career stayed really focused on being a Jazz musician. As close to as a hundred percent as he could possibly make it happen, and he has really soared in the Jazz world and definitely deserves it, absolutely, but if it wasn't for his persistence, staying focused and dedication, I admire that tremendously. That is really, like Monk, and like those guys from that era – a person decided what's important, no matter what and has really stayed with that.

DON: Yeah. What year was that you're talking about, the Chi Chi and those years?

SI: That would have been 65 through 68.

DON: Ok, that's like mid 60's we're talking about, lot of things going on.

SI: I came to San Francisco at that stage in 1960. And, the first years I was playing a few casuals and whatever gigs I could come up with and little Jazz gigs and Cedric Heywood, got me, I once sat in with Brew Moore. Cedric Heywood was his piano player and then he gave me some gigs at Coffee Don's and I started playing there.

DON: I've played there, yeah.

SI: And, Cedric really opened up and whatever he could for me and I played Brew Moore and played for

A Diary of the Underdogs

Cedric occasionally. I was very young and pretty inexperienced. He put himself on the line for me, you know.

DON: Do you remember some of the people in the rhythm section?

SI: The woman drummer whose husband was also a musician, Dottie Dodgion, something.....

DON: Dodgion?

SI: Yeah! She played with him and I played with her, there. And a really good – several bass players, there was one guy who later went to play with Les McCann and I'm not sure if it was Leroy, I think it was Leroy, Leroy Vinnegar , he wasn't up here I don't think.

DON: He wasn't the first bass player.....

SI: No, but there was another bass player that went down there from here to play with him and that played, I played with quite a bit and I been trying to dredge his name up and this person and I haven't come up with it.

DON: There was a guy named Eddie Kahn used to hang out......

SI: Eddie Kahn, I think is – I think that's who I'm thinking of....

DON: He was around Bop City and then he went and played..... So, it's probably Eddie Kahn. So, how was Brew Moore in those days?

SI: Well, he was wonderful to play with, a great Lester Youngish sax player and I admired him and didn't play with him a whole lot, several times sitting in. And then doing the gig.....

DON: Where was his regular gig? Did he have....?

SI: Well, it was on Arguello, there was a club, it was on Arguello, but I don't remember the name of it. It was a Jazz club, and it was his gig. Off of Geary, somewhere in that neighborhood.

DON: And he got occasional gigs at the Black Hawk too?

SI: Yeah, he did other things, but that was his little steady thing, at least that I knew about.

DON: That would have been after the Chi Chi Club, around that period?

SI: No, this would have been before, I got here in 1960. So 61, 62, is when I started doing.....I mean, I played in the Cellars, a little bit.

DON: Oh, did you know Bill Wejohn?

SI: Yeah, not well, but I knew him.

DON: And you knew the club.

SI: And I played with Joe Carroll quite a bit. The first time I ever went anywhere to sit in was the Cellars and Joe Carroll was the first bass player I played with. And he and I wound up playing together fairly often.

DON: And who was the drummer down there that owned half of the club?

SI: I don't remember who the drummer was; I don't remember who I played with down there.

DON: Bill Wejohn was partner with a drummer....

SI: I don't remember that. I probably knew him, but I don't know who it was. I was on the Jazz scene but I quickly found my way into the after hours gigs and then I got the gig on week nights at Bop City. But Flip Nunez gave me that gig. I had been going there and sitting in. One story that is not in the book, which I can tell you about is – that I really like. Jimbo could be very intimidating at times. He was wonderful at other times and intimidating at times. And he laid a test on me, that thank God I passed. What is was – the very first time I played there, that I sat in there and got up the courage to go and play, and sat in... In the middle of my solo on *Round Midnight,* he jumped up on stage and changed the set. Stopped the music, changed the musicians; in the middle of the song. And of course I was, I'm sure, I don't remember how I felt, but I know I was devastated. And so, I considered the test was, that I went back there and kept going back and sitting in. I mean, I could have no screw this and not ever gone back and I would have missed one of the greatest experiences of my life. But I went back and I became one of the regular people sitting in and he never jumped up and changed the set on me again. And I don't know even know if it's because of me that he did it, it just happened in my solo. Then when Flip got the gig on the weekends, which, I don't remember if he got it from Freddie Gambrell is what he called himself at the time and became Federico Cervantes. Bass Player was Ben Tucker. He either had it before Flip or after, I don't remember which. But Flip got the weekends and gave me the week nights. Four or five nights a week, I played at Bop City for a couple of years. And the gig was 2-6 for $7. I quit when he lowered it to $5. He lowered it to $5 and I was working at Soulville too at that time. And Soulville, I think was paying $7. I stopped working because I got pissed, because he lowered it to $5.

DON: Well, you depend on that, I remember, when I worked I wanted my $6.

SI: Oh, yeah, I was living on it. Not only that, but that was some of my income. But it was also my education and my joy. It was so much. That was such a great gig. I got to play with people there that never in my life.....there is a story in the book, about my thing with Philly Joe Jones and you can read that and Wes Montgomery, those are a couple that I tell about.

DON: Just give me a little preview of some of that.

SI: Well, I.......I played with Philly and with Wes and with Roland Kirk and his rhythm section, Louis Hayes and I have forgotten who the bass player was, and Charlie Rouse on Tenor, who was with Monk.

DON: Ah, here it is – interlude – 1960- 1964 – Bop City. Where you say, "*Much of my musical life took place at 2am – 6am at a famous after hours club called Jimbo's Bop City.*

SI: So, that will have some names and some information that will be background for you. The story with Philly is that we – they called *Cherokee* and they played it so fast, that I couldn't play, it was faster then I could play. And I had, I had come to sort of an agreement with myself that I was working there by that time, I was the piano player, and my thing was – if things were beyond me, I would just lay out, until I could handle it again. I was not going to let it – make me get off stage. I was going to stay there and do what ever I could and be the piano player. When they called *Cherokee* and it was so fast I couldn't play, I decided to lay out and let the bass and drums carry it, after all it was Philly.... and Philly did something – I mean it was magic, I can hardly – it was one of those things I can hardly believe happened. So, I'm looking at him, he was over here – the piano was here, looking this way and he is over on my left side, looking back a little bit. So, I would have look over behind me to look at him. And I was just kind of waiting because it was too fast. And I got the information from what Philly was doing that he did not want me to lay out and that he was counting on the drums. He was showing me on the drums what I should be doing on the piano. It wasn't just that he was playing good; I mean I knew that he was telling me that. And I started to do what he was showing me. And by the time it got around to my solo. I took one chorus of solo on that sucker at that speed. And I never could have done it if it hadn't been for him. He laid it out for me. He absolutely laid it out for me and did it on a psychic and musical level, without any eye contact. It was just what was happening and even as I tell it to you I can hardly believe that – and I must have just thought that – you know it must have been me making that up, it almost doesn't matter, but I knew he was telling me and he was playing piano type rhythms in such a way, so clearly that I could tell and I started doing it.

DON: Did you get to talk afterwards?

SI: No, we didn't talk about stuff like that.

DON: Yeah, lot of those guys wouldn't talk; it was something that just happened.

SI: I'm trying to think, I think I played with Elvin Jones; I hung out with Elvin some. I think that I actually played with Elvin in Soulville. But I am more impressed with something else. My memory is on to something else. I am not sure if I played with Elvin. Elvin, he was hanging out with my sister in-law for awhile, while he was here. And she and my brother have long since broken up.

SI: Yeah, and she had a little upstairs attic and it had a drum set in it. I don't think it was Elvin's drum set, but I don't know whose it was. And Elvin played up there one night and we were all just hanging up there getting loaded. And he played there for a little while and then there was another drummer there, and

A Diary of the Underdogs

thankfully I don't remember his name. He was not a good musician. And he had the balls to get up and play for Elvin and Elvin's reaction was – I'll never forget it- he said, Man, you couldn't swat a fly with that stroke.

DON: Yeah, interesting stuff. That was all in the period of the 60's.

SI: Yeah, but that was probably during or after Bop City. So, during the 60's was a big time for me.

DON: Yeah, but this wasn't talked about enough, you know? It got overshadowed with a lot of other stuff.

SI: I always thought that between the music and what was happening on the social level, which I was partially a part of-going on the anti-war demonstrations – the marches... and stuff like that. I wasn't an activist but certainly that's where I was. I thought the 60's were going to transform America. And then when the flower power thing happened, I really thought that – that was going to be the future. So, when that all really fell apart, and the backlash started; that was quite an awakening of a negative sort for me. And I always felt like, the 60's should be the future; that they ought to be in front of us. That search for freedom and the search for expression. Lifestyle and I just had that we really had our hands on something and obviously it wasn't perfect, but it ought to be coming around again. I don't know if it ever will.

DON: Yeah, we are heading into a lot of more complicated things.

SI: Yeah. The country was on its way to become fascist and it was going in a strange direction.

DON: And I think what is important is how it feels to be in San Francisco at that time; musician or not. Just to be there and feel what's going on. People taking LSD and Allen Watts on TV saying how great it was, how it opened his eyes.

SI: Well I was very much a drug person, for many years. Not heavy drugs; just Pot, LSD and Uppers. I never rejected that in the sense of thinking that this is horrible and wrong – I never put it literally down. But rather I went through a whole lot of internal conflict whether or not I could survive without it, whether or not it was ruling me – whether or not I could be a happy person with out it. And I went through several years of being on the outside of a very happy musician drug user. And then on the inside going through six months of the year where I was totally fighting myself and then I would usually give up and say oh – fuck it. And just relax and forget about the struggle for awhile. And then I would start to struggle again and finally I was in one of my struggle periods and I heard something on the radio. And it clicked. It was on a Dr. Dean Edell show and he pointed out that because Pot was fat soluble and lodges in the fat in your body, which it takes 90 days before it gets out of your system, when you stop using it. And when I heard that, I said to myself. Oh, O.K. I'll give it 90 days and if I can't make it and if I don't like music and sex, those where the two things I was worried about. I was afraid I wouldn't feel about playing and fucking so.....then I had permission from myself – and I meant it – that I would smoke again. So 90 days later I was still able to play and make love and have a good time with life. And I realized that there is no reason to start smoking if you know you can do with out it. So, I didn't start.

DON: So, you kind of woke up yourself and took care of business.

SI: Yeah. And I have never put down other people for doing it. I never felt that I had to reject it in order to give it up. I just had to – it also was getting physically harder. My lungs were starting to get more resistant to it. It was a psychological and physical thing; on a personal – my body and my mind – not a kind of judgment.

DON: Were you married?

SI: Oh, yes. I got married to my first wife before we moved to San Francisco and married in '50 something.

DON: So, most of your musical career you had your mate and your family.

SI: Yes, and then I was with her through the late 60's. And then broke up and met my current wife and we have been together since.

DON: And who is that?

A Diary of the Underdogs

SI: Jane. And we have been together – we have had our 30th anniversary. We've been married for 30 years but we have been together for a few years before that.

DON: Tell me a little about your recent accomplishments with the Monk music.

SI: That's a very interesting story. I take very little credit for it. I don't deny that I have a certain feeling for it, and association with Monk that is valuable and really glad to have had a chance to explore it and people have – I know been actually turned on to Monk's music when they particularly weren't aware of it or interested in it because I did some of it or was interested in it. Because I did something they liked and they went and listened to the real thing. But it would have absolutely not have happened for except for Chuck. This was Chuck Bernstein's baby from the beginning, and Chuck's dream, and it still is.

DON: Yeah, a great moving force- he really is.

SI: He is the one who made it happen and keeps it happening. And it's because of him that I still go in there and play once a week and because of him I have learned way more Monk tunes then I ever used to know. And have become more associated with it and its done me a tremendous amount of good both personally and how other people see me.

DON: I think you have become a prominent voice in that music, an authentic interpretation of that music.

SI: Well, I just simply try – I feel like his tunes are so – they have so much integrity in the tune. The tune itself expresses in itself what he wanted to express so through and all you have to do is play the tune and play yourself relating to the tune. And you the tune makes you interpret Monk. I have never had to try – sometimes I feel like that in my less inspired moments I try and take to imitate Monk, I try to sort of sound like him. I will be playing along and maybe I'm pissed at what I am doing and I will do something "Monkish" and sometimes it works and sometimes it doesn't. But most of the time I just try and play the tune. And take a solo. And it's the tune and the way it's put together and just an emotional – on a sub-conscious level - Monk always symbolized freedom, determination to be free. And so when I play his music, I contact that emotional level. Its permission to do – the tune gives you permission and with his example gives you permission to play whatever is the right thing to play. It gives you permission for whatever you can come up with. And that's what I feel through playing his music so much now, that every once in awhile I go to the gig thinking - I don't want to do this – I've done this so often, and almost always, in the course of playing, is the challenge of doing it – because some of it never gets easy. But some of it I can not guarantee that I am going to do a good job on this tune.

DON: Yeah, because you know what is ahead of you?

SI: And so, almost always – I get turned on to it for the rest of the gig. Rarely do you have a whole gig that is simple pleasures. There are times when I am not interested and engaged deeply and sooner or later I get "turned on" in doing it – regardless in how I came to the gig. But it is true that I have played so much of that one particular persons music that now sometimes I have to make myself get there and start doing it and then.....Oh yeah, Oh yeah....

DON: Well, you have become kind of an authority, but you don't hold it over people. And people feel about Si Perkoff that you are pretty much a authentic voice of Monk's music and its obvious that you have given it a lot of dedication and that you search and really apply – and even when Chuck called me up and asked me to write some liner notes on that first CD you guys did together, all I could think of was – well what I know of Si Perkoff - I think I said something like – I have always felt that the door was ajar for Si to receive messages from Monk.

SI: That's a title from one of my tunes.

DON: Really!

SI: Message from Monk – I think is on page 30. And I will tell you the story. This tune – what happened was after he died – not to long after he died, I woke up from a dream. In the dream, in the middle of the night, Monk was playing and I was looking over his shoulder, watching his hands play – and he was playing a tune and I ran to the piano, jumped out of bed, ran to the piano and grabbed as much as I could remember of this tune which was disappearing by the seconds, like dreams do. I got as much as I could and this is it – and it's like a Monk tune, but it's not – but he didn't write it while he was alive. I wrote it – but in a sense he wrote it. So, I called it Message from Monk. So, this is a tune from a dream of him playing.

DON: In conclusion Si, tell me about some of the situation in recording Roswell Rudd encompassing the latest music on the CD you guys put out.

SI: Well, Roswell is another spirit of permission. And love. He really, really projects – I mean I was scared to play – I get nervous pretty easy and I have a big ego and when I think – when no demands are placed on me I can really be great. But when demands are placed on me, I hope I can be great, but I get nervous. So, here we are going to play Monk's music with Roswell and I was really wondering if I could come up to that. The band consisted of my son Max on trombone and me and Sam Bevan, Chuck Bernstein and Roswell Rudd-two trombones – my son on trombone. And in rehearsals, and just in talking to him, he totally lets you know that he loves you, you are the greatest, he thinks that music is wonderful and it's all beautiful.... and everything is really positive and then he gets up there and he plays totally far-out stuff that you would have never thought he was going to do. And it's funny and it's right and it's with the same kind of permission to just do whatever it seems the right thing and good thing to do this instant. And he love Monk and he just really – I am gaga about him and as a human being I totally loved playing with him and we did a really good piece of music on the CD. Max reached new heights and I did a really good thing and took some good solos and I really like my comping and I just really felt like – and Roswell is beautiful.

DON: And what is the title of the CD?

SI: It's called, Monk's Bones.

DON: Did you do some touring?

SI: No, we only had a gig – but no tour; a gig at Pearls and a gig over at The Throckmorton Theater. And he came out and played with us in Simple Pleasures during that time, he was getting ready for doing it and being here.

DON: What was the release date?

SI: I don't know – a couple of years ago.

End: Si Perkoff

Interview: Al Molina-jazz musician-trumpet player-bandleader- and Richard Brown-jazz bartender, music fan- October 8, 2008 with Don Alberts at Bird and Beckett, San Francisco-about: early big bands, San Mateo, Kent Glenn, Booker T. Hotel, Bop City, bartending at the Scene. Al Molina with Don Alberts-October 8th 2008 at Bird and Beckett, San Francisco re: Early Big Bands, Kent Glen, other musicians. Richard Brown with Don Alberts-October 8th 2008 at Bird and Beckett, San Francisco re: Bop City, Booker T. Washington Hotel, the Scene, Clubs, Ed Kelly.

AL MOLINA with RICHARD BROWN

DON: Good to have you here Al. I was going to ask you about the early big bands, because you started off mentioning something about that. Can you fill me in?

AL: Yeah, well it was the Kent Glenn Big Band which had no charts at all. We used to rehearse at some flute players house. Bill Atwood, Tom Harrell, Hart Smith. Guys like that. Vince Lateano, on drums and Bob Maize was the bass player. A lot of people would show up. It was on a second floor, you never knew who was going to be there. You would hear footsteps coming up the stairs and you never knew who was going to be coming. You said, "Hey, it's Bob Maize." You know....

A Diary of the Underdogs

DON: Yeah, that's the kind of information we need to bring up, because you know, because sometimes you can't remember who was sitting next to you.

AL: Cats would come to town and they would know somebody, come see some family or whatever, and they would come through town and hear about a rehearsal and just show up with their horn. Kent ran it very differently. It was like a head band, like a head chart band. That's how he auditioned you. You came up and said, "Hey, you know this tune? Okay, I'll teach it to you," and he would play the first line and then you would play that line. Then he would play – and if you made it the first time, then he goes on to the next part of the phrase and then he would play that. If you missed the first note or two, he would go back again, but usually not more then twice. Those cats all had good ears. Then he would teach you the head, and then you go through that - and he would say, "Okay, that's good," and then he would want to show you another tune or maybe two tunes. And then people started showing up. You couldn't wait or play along. Then he would teach the next cat. Everyone showed up, trombone, sax, trumpet, maybe a bass, drummer. Next thing you know we are running through the tune and then start playing on the head and then like that, and that's how rehearsals were. You never knew who was going to show up. Different cats all the time.

DON: Where there sections?

AL: Well, everyone just stood around.   Trumpet player next to sax, another trumpet player next to the trombone. And we all just played together. That's the way it was.

Al Molina

DON: A real spirit band?

AL: Yeah. So, the core of the band was three cats. Kent Glenn, Hart Smith, and Vince – The sax player was Vince Wallace. The three of them had all the heads already nailed.   And what happened was they would be the leader of each section. Trumpet players – Bill Attwood, he was a real kingpin, was for example, or myself would be the leaders. And then they would all play around the leader. When you had the core, you had a whole band like that. Maybe like twelve guys. You would count the tune off and play the tune and harmony would start to appear.

DON: Yeah, I was going to ask you - like if a guy was teaching you a second part?

AL: Yeah, like if he was teaching you a second part and you hear counter lines start to develop, and trombone or tenor may double on that line. And that is how the tunes were built.   There were no set endings. They were just like playing in a quintet. The music just evolves.

DON: So, where was this taking place?

AL: This was in San Francisco at a flute players house, can't remember his name. There was rehearsals everyday. The day was open everyday. Show up around 12pm 'till about 6 or 7. Sometimes play into the night. Playing, jamming, playing sometimes not rehearsing with the band, just cats playing.

DON: Not at the Union Hall, but someplace.....

AL: Yeah, it was somewhere near Mission High School.

DON: And when was that?

AL: Pretty much all through the 60's.....Some form of the band would be playing somewhere. The main quintet was Vince Wallace, Hart Smith, or Vince, Bill Atwood in the front section; Bob Maize, Vince Lateano and Kent Glenn. That was the nucleus. That was the main quintet – they were working coffee galleries and anywhere they could. But the big band got a gig, over on Divisadero – a couple clubs had opened up there and we would always end up playing there on a Sunday afternoon. The band would just kind of show up and stand around and play.

A Diary of the Underdogs

DON: Was it at the Both/And?

AL: Yeah, it was. I think we played there; yeah, when that place opened up. We played Divisadero too. We played the Coffee Gallery, on Grant, around the corner from Green.

DON: Yeah, it's still there.

AL: In those days, the Cellar Club was right around the corner   on Green Street, The Jazz Cellar. They didn't call it the Jazz Cellar in those days; they just called it the Cellar. It became known as the Jazz Cellar – later. And historically, people started naming it, I guess. That was a good scene, that was Bill Wejohn and Sonny, a drummer, can't remember his name. He was a partner with somebody...

DON: Yeah, nobody remembers that guy's name. Everyone remembers Bill Wejohn.

AL: Yeah, Sonny wouldn't play all the time, that's why. He would have to tend bar. And so Bill was always on the gig, you know. Various people went through there.

DON: Did Brew Moore ever play there?

AL: Brew Moore played there, Judy Tristano, a couple of other sax players, Harold Wiley, I think... a guy from Boston who came in who was a poet and a tenor sax player, Bruce Lippincott? Yeah, he was there. Guys would come and sit in – I sat in there frequently. Also, Dickie Mills, trumpet player. I took my first trumpet lesson from him. He came in when Brew was there. They played a lot together, they played there and they played another club – The Tropics, down on Arguello and Geary. That was a good little club – the Escovedo Brothers used to play there.

DON: This would be before the band, Azteca – the early years?

AL: Oh, yeah. This is when they went out –three brothers actually, the third brother played bass. I can't remember his name either. But I played with that band. What they would do is get a guitar player, a piano player and a horn player and they had a B flat book, and you would see different combinations, playing that B flat book, could be two trumpets, trumpet and trombone, two tenors or two trombones. Al Bent was involved with that – he did some writing for that band and stuff. It was a good little band. They played in clubs all over the back of the Mission. So, there were a lot of Latino's there. I remember I worked a gig there, myself and Tom Harrell and we had a guitar player and the Escovedo Brothers, the three of them. I can remember being in a back room, a back room that was separate from the bar area, it was like a little dining room or something. Nobody ever came back there, I mean the band was playing, we played in this room and some people would come around the corner and look in and see the band and snap their fingers a little bit. And then go back to the bar area. They could hear the music out in the bar area.

DON: What was the name of this place?

AL: Maria's or something like that. It was way out – like 22nd and Mission or toward South Van Ness.

DON: So, Tom Harrell was pretty young in those days?

AL: Yeah, he was only about 17 years old. Sounded good and getting a reputation around San Francisco. He played with Sonny Lewis and they did a lot of Coltrane stuff and that was considered pretty modern stuff. He played down on Haight Street and I was working at the Haight Levels with the quartet, and he was right across the street at the Jukebox.

DON: Yeah, I remember the Jukebox. Kent Glenn often played there.

AL: Yes, Kent Glenn, and this band was Bishop Norman Williams and Tom Harrell. They used different cats in there all the time. That was a good hot bebop band. Bishop taught a lot of us. He knew all the Charlie Parker heads; the intro, the endings, the shouts and stuff like that. And if we weren't in the band together, he would be in the back room running some jazz patterns, you know, some very hip stuff. And you know, like you, you would go over to Bishop and say, "Hey, Bishop – hey man, what is that? I need you to turn me onto that." And he would play it and play it and that's how everything was taught in those days – by rote. So, next time you see him, you are in the back room and you start playing – warming up – playing his stuff. Playing all his licks and patterns and he then he would have more. He would say, "Hey, man, have you heard this one?" And then he would give you another one. And they were very hip, get you through all the keys and stuff like that.

DON: Yeah, he was kind of alone, I think. He was the only guy who was doing that stuff. He was his own kind of separate sound. I remember coming to San Francisco in 1960 and going to the Coffee Gallery and playing with Norman-and he just played, any key, just played. He was the Charlie Parker clone at that time.

AL: Yeah, he was the guy who was heading up that school. As a matter of fact I did – later on I got involved with non-profit Jazz Society called Loft Jazz. We got together and went out and solicited, found places where we could put Jazz. And we told the owner, look, we will provide the band just let us have the door and we will charge $10 at the door. You can have all the booze, and all the other concessions. You don't have any business here anyway on Wednesday's so we will bring a band. And we set up these places all over. Pier 50 was a natural – right on the water. I did tribute to Charlie Parker; that was my gig. I got Bishop... and.....

DON: Who was playing in the rhythm section?

AL: Well, I called Larry Vuckovich for the gig but he then backed out, but came to the performance. And then I got Ed Kelly. I can't remember. The drummer I had played with Charlie Parker. It was a black rhythm section. I was the only white cat in the band. So, I had Bishop, Ed Kelly, and the bass player – oh, can't remember- it was the drummer who played with Charlie Parker. I can't remember his name either. It was my first gig with Ed. And we packed the room, man, we were sold out. Back to Bishop, Bishop taught us. I didn't know any of the Charlie Parker hits, I knew Au Privave or something like that but we had to do two shows – all Charlie Parker, two sets so that meant sixteen Charlie Parker tunes. He put me to work. And they were not very easy. I went over to rehearse with him and taught me by rote.

DON: So, when was that?

AL: Well, it was getting into the late 1960's into the 70's, then got aced out and had to go to Oakland. We got tied up with another non-profit, another dance troupe. We would be under their umbrella so they could get some gigs. Ken Shubert was the President of that whole thing. During the early 1960's I was going to San Mateo JC, in the music program. Coyote Point, that was were the old campus out on the water-really beautiful. There were Quonset huts out there like for merchant marines or something like that or maybe a school for merchant marines, or could have been for Coast Guard. And then when the war was over, after the war, then they converted it to or gave it back to San Mateo, San Mateo put a college out there. A really beautiful campus; a nice place to study man, go out and look at the Bay, see all the beautiful trees and squirrels running around. The program was great and I went because I heard it was the best Jazz school around. I think John Handy was starting the Jazz program at San Francisco State, but it wasn't a good program yet. Their performance situation was more about classical, they did have a Jazz band but it wasn't that sophisticated yet. We had the band, we had Elmer Bud Young. He was running the Jazz program down there. He had a big band. A fine arranger, a great tenor sax player and when I got there he was going to retire in two years. And that's one of the reasons I went there, because he was teaching the regular two year theory course. But he was cramming it in a year and a half and then giving us Twenty-century for the last six months, so we got more than our money's worth. And there was no one else around doing that kind of stuff.

DON: It was hard to find that kind of education.

AL: Yeah. So, I got in at the right time 1962 on the GI Bill. I was in Korea – I was a Korean Vet. But that was earlier – 1954 -1956. Got out and got married and in 1962 I went to school. It was a very cool thing to do, that was the thing to do.

DON: Yeah, I actually did a very similar thing.

AL: I was lucky that the GI Bill came along. And I really didn't know anything about and had to do some research on it. But the guys I went to school with, was Jerry Gilmore, Eugene Puzzie Firth; a great bass

A Diary of the Underdogs

player. But he wasn't playing bass at that time, he was a vibes player, but he knew how to play trombone, because he got into the big band. Big band didn't have a vibes player. They could have put him in front, but he didn't want to drag his vibes down there, so he took up trombone. He didn't have a good tone, but he had studied with Cal Tjader when he was a child, like seven or eight. Yeah, he was a child prodigy. He hooked up with him at Larooz Studio down on tenth and Market or so. Brew Moore was teaching there and Cal Tjader was teaching there. A lot of good drummers were teaching there. Cal produced a quintet with Daryl Hutchinson, Puzzie Firth, Gil Shockwell - sax player, Jack Ford – trumpet player. And they put together a sextet and played Jazz. They played Lullaby and Rhythm, they played How High the Moon, they played a bunch of stuff and I can still remember them. They were all arranged by Cal but he had these little shout chorus in the background – you know easy stuff that they could do. And Puzzie was like such a wiz, I remember going to see those guys play at Larooz Studio and Puzzie would have a comic book in his back pocket. He was only like eleven or twelve years old. And they would play the tune and while is everyone else is soloing he would be reading the comic book. And then when it was time take his out, he come back in and play.

DON: Yeah, very talented guy. He also became a bass player?

AL: Well what happened when he got into college, he found out that bass players were working and part of the rhythm section and he learned how to play bass. Well, Lenny Lasher was playing bass in a college band and the college band was terrific. The trumpet section was Buddy Powers, Larry Souza and Fred Radke, who later ran the Harry James Ghost Band. He was a trumpet player that played in the Harry James style. He was up in Washington somewhere. It was me Sir Gay Vanderwheel, who was a good little Jazz player and a trombone section with Puzzie, Don Schamber, the guy who ended up head of the music department down in Monterey, one of the colleges, junior college or something like that and was also a good arranger. He has charts that he had published that go out to all the schools all over the USA and stuff like that. He's in demand because his charts are at that level. They all sound good. He also studied arranging from Elmer Bud Young teacher there – San Mateo College. We all learned from there, everyone in that band became professional and they all went out and did things. Dick Leland, well he teaches in the area but he's Nelson Riddle's trombone player; whenever Nelson comes to town. So these guys – the sax section – Pat Britt, alto sax player, tenor too. And I think he was playing lead alto – a guy named Dave Misner who is teaching I think in the East Bay somewhere and is also a great player. And Jerry Gilmore, he played baritone in the band. Ed Wetland played piano. Lenny Lasher played bass. Louie Altemarano played drums and Len Alexander and Paul Distel. Three drummers, they all enrolled at the same time.

DON: They were in and out of the band?

AL: No, they were all in the band, they came to class, and everyone got a chance to play certain charts. They alternated. And Puzzie learned, because Lenny Lasher was playing bass, we didn't have any other bass players, and Lenny sometimes had to sub out and so Puzzie learned how to play. And he could read the charts because he played trombone and he would play. Plus he knew vibes and he knew theory from Cal, and he was way ahead of everyone in theory. Cal had taught him Jazz theory a long time ago when he was a kid. So he was able to arrange and write. He knew what flat 9's were and what raised 9's were, plus 5's and all that stuff.

DON: He was pretty young?

AL: Yeah, still when he was in college he was only in his 20's, a very talented guy. That band ended up playing in the Monterey Jazz Festival. We won the State competition and that was our reward, we got to play the Festival. And then they had the small band contest which Pat Britt and I did. Pat organized the band. I played baritone and I played trumpet. And I think Alexander was playing drums with us. We didn't win the small band, but we still played in the big band.

DON: Did that transfer to any gigs in the city?

A Diary of the Underdogs

Richard Brown

AL: Well, no, but Pat Henry was one of the Judges and I don't know at that time if he was doing KROW or he was doing KJAZ. It was probably KJAZ – this was before they moved out to Alameda.

DON: Speaking of Pat Henry, he was kind of the voice of Jazz in the Bay Area but there was KDIA who had Wally Ray and a couple of other people.

AL: Well earlier on in the 50's there was Don Barksdale. Jimmy Lyons had a show, and Vernon Alley.

DON: Yeah, it was an interesting time. Actually, Jimmy Lyons got Brubeck going and Tjader and all those guys.

AL: Yeah, Jimmy Lyons was a real west coast advocate before he started doing the Monterey Festival thing. Always had a good show, played a lot of Jerry Mulligan and Chet Baker.

DON: So, tell me what you think you have accomplished in Jazz and what do you think and where are we going with this and are we healthy.

AL: Sure, Jazz is – as far as musicians, the spirit is there, you can see it in young players and they are all playing real good and they are deep into the tradition, they are going back and playing some old stuff and playing some new stuff. Interested in education and interested in learning. You see them out and they are going to the sessions, and they are hanging out and playing. And they are respecting the older players too. And I think it's healthy, the only part that is not healthy is business, the clubs. Nobody is playing. They are paying the same that they were paying in 1950.

DON: Yeah, amazing, you get art for free. The necessary part of life and you get it for free. They don't want to pay for it.

AL: Yeah, they don't want to pay for it because it's not like pop music. You know you have somebody come in and play pop music and there is a forum for them. There is a full house or young people that identify with that music and they can dance to it or whatever. And they enjoy the rap or whatever and they will go to see it. What I am kind of seeing is the younger audiences don't seem to have the attention span.

DON: Little different society....

AL: Yeah, its like music is background stuff. Its basically stuff to talk over. It's not anything like a concert.

DON: Yeah, I am seeing that a lot. But, it doesn't affect our work. I'm noticing that your work still produces a high quality product; music of high quality. Hiring of the right kind of musicians and presenting it anyway. I think that; that is a true spirit. We grew up with it. We can't do it another way.

AL: Yeah, right, it's a dedication to the art form and we are going to take it all the way to the end, till we can't do it anymore. And then you will find some other way of appreciating it. (Richard Brown just walked in)

DON: Tell the people who you are.

RICH: Richard Brown.

DON: The resident bartender, at the Dog Patch Saloon. And Brown is down!

RICH: Yeah, the good old days.

A Diary of the Underdogs

DON: The other day you were talking about Booker T and the hotel. They used to go and hang out.

RICH: That was a weird thing in those days. Like now days you can go and check into any hotel, with a girl or something and nobody pays any attention. But in those days, you kind of got the feeling that you were doing something wrong. And then the people that work there were kind of staring at you, you know. You are signing in for the room and they are watching you go up the stairs and everyone knew what you were doing and you didn't even know them. But it was fun.

DON: But you used to go down to Bop City – that was one of the reasons you went down there. Like in the 60's or something like that?

RICH: Well it had to be - well, I was hanging around North Beach when all the clubs were on Broadway. The early 60's I would say. Late 50's early 60's. And nobody went to bed. I don't know how we survived. We had jobs. I remember going to work a lot of times having not slept. Listening to music.

DON: Yeah, you could do it on three or four hours sleep!

RICH: Yeah, but you were young and you could do that.

AL: Yeah, well my experience with Bop City was when I was in high school. I was in the band and the drummer who was in the band, he was 21 and still going to high school. Because he wanted to stay in the band. He didn't go to any other classes! He just only went to band- Connley Hall.

DON: Yeah, Connley Hall. Now you are talking about a real icon.

AL: So, he said hey, you wanna go play Friday night? Go with me to Bop City... and I said yeah, sure I do. So what I would do is go to bed, close the door, prop up the pillow in there so my father or mother would think I was in bed. And I would climb out the window and take my horn and jump into Connley's car and we would go down there. And hang around and try and sit in. And then I found out that when it was busy, when there were big crowds waiting to get in, maybe Miles was around or something. And so, we had no where to go. But Connley knew where to go and we would go across the street and this guy named Daddy Joe, he would open up his house and charge $5 to get in. And you would go around back and he had a piano in his kitchen and musicians would show up there and play. And every weekend, Friday night, Saturday night, Daddy Joes! Right across the street. He took all the spin-off. And make a little dough. $5 would buy you a cup of coffee..... and then he would come around and give you a little splash, you know....a little brandy....

RICH: Yeah, but that was a lot of money!

DON: Yeah, you still getting $5 at the Dog Patch...?

RICH: Yeah, still getting $5 at the Dog Patch, but because it was illegal, you had to pay that. And it had to be because when I was working at the hotel, not the hotel, but the Scene, upper Fillmore and when I went to work there drinks were 65 cents. This was 1962.

AL: Was Tommy there?

RICH: Tommy was there. I was the day bartender and drinks were 65 and 75 cents. And then of course when Tommy played on the weekend we would jack the price up and we had a cover charge and everything. And the regulars didn't like that but....you know....

DON: Now talk about Tommy, who was Tommy?

RICH: Tommy was an organ player. And I didn't know this, but I knew Tommy for five or six years and never knew what he did other then play there. He drove a Muni bus. A bus driver! But he was there quite a while and when he would take a vacation or something Ed Kelly would sit in for him. And then Eddie Henderson – his mother worked as the hostess of the Scene for a while. She really was a beautiful woman you know. She had been around the scenes of New York and all that stuff and she knew how to greet people. Now this just was a neighborhood bar but Ray the owner of the bar had Eddie's mother greeting people when they came in like it was some great big time casino or something. And then Eddie was going to Med school, I forgot where he was going to school, but it wasn't in California, some place back East or

A Diary of the Underdogs

something. But when school was out he would come in and sit in all the time with Tommy and you could tell then this guy was going to make it. He was a great trumpet player.

AL: Yeah, he had all the best teachers too, Miles Davis. He got lessons from Miles, from Clark Terry. His father was connected to all those people.

RICH: The other thing is that everyone knew that Eddie was a doctor and they knew he gave all that up for the Jazz. And you would say, gee, I wonder why this guy is doing this – it's tough making it as a Jazz musician, but he gave it up. He did practice at Langley Porter and the Haight Street Clinic. And he did graduate. And he handed in all the papers but he gave it up. It's something to have all that knowledge and then give it up for something you really love.

AL: Eddie used to come to the sessions in the 60's on Pierce Street; we used to have sessions over there. George DiQuattro.

RICH: I remember one time somebody asked Miles after he got done playing, some stupid girl – "Mr. Miles, do you ever play serious music?" Miles said, "what the fuck do you think this is?"

DON: Weren't you bartending at Both/And? You told me a funny story about that.

RICH: Oh yeah, well Miles was there, Lenny and the two guys that owned it, a black guy and a white guy.

DON: Delano and Lenny.

RICH: Yeah; which I found out years later, where I am living right now, I'm out there one day and the mailman came and it was Delano. It was him. He had been working for the post office all those years, I never knew he had a job. Anyway, I was working at the Scene and one of them, Lenny or Delano called me and asked me if I could work the bar that evening because Miles was going to be there. And I said, man, I'm working for nothing! And Claude Allen he would work there off and on if they would get stuck and we would work for no money because we didn't know how he kept that place open. But to have Miles there, so I go there when a underage Tony Williams was playing, he was like 19 or something, and I think it was like a 8pm show and so people started coming in and the place got packed and it was a funny thing because I wondered how they stayed open, because nobody drank. I'm standing behind the bar and they are sipping on a coke or whatever and I'm thinking how we going to pay Miles. I don't remember what the door was....but anyway, 8pm comes and Tony is there and I forget who was on bass, but no Miles. So it gets to be 8:30 and man, everyone is getting restless now and either Lenny or Delano got on the mic and said – we just got a call, Miles just arrived at the airport, he's been delayed or something. And everyone starts to clap. Good 15 minutes he is going to be here. Another half n hour, Miles still is not there. And the band is just waiting. So finally, the band, I think it was a quartet; they get up there and start playing. And all of a sudden Miles busts in the door with the trumpet, playing as he is going through the door! And everyone says, oh, fuck this is a set-up. He came in right on the same note that they were playing.

AL: Yeah, Charlie Mingus used to do that all the time. He would pull up in the back of the Jazz workshop in a limo and get out with a white mink coat on and walk around and then walk inside.

RICH: I remember I saw Monk at the workshop; I went for the first set. Right across the street was Enrico's, right, and I saw the first set and then I walked across the street to Enrico's. So I am sitting at an outside table and Monk came over there between the sets and Monk is out there and he is doing a little jig. So, Enrico's wife came out and said, hey, you got to get this guy out of here. They would usually run street people away from there; people eating and all that. And someone said, "Don't you know who that is? That is Thelonious Monk!" And she said, "I don't give a fuck what church he belongs to!" She thought he was crazy.

RICH: (about some guy in the bar) Yeah and I said man, you got some nice old stuff here and this was when I was transferring mine to CD and stuff... I will just give them to you man; I don't even have a turn table. There is a guy who comes in the Dog Patch and he said he has a friend.... I know you know this guy, but I can't think of his name. Big thick mustache....

A Diary of the Underdogs

DON: Don't know...

RICH: But he knows somebody who can find you any Jazz album that you name, if you got the right name. So he has found a couple for me that I couldn't find. One of them was by Sarah Vaughn and it's called "It's A Man's World," and he found it.

DON: So he will find vinyl or if it's been moved to CD.

RICH: Yes. And that's good because my favorites are all scratched up.

DON: Do you know about Tom Madden over there, he is on 20th Avenue off of Judah.

RICH: Yeah, somebody told me about that.

DON: That is a good place for people to go for local musicians who have made a CD. It will end up there and he will have it.

RICH: I told Sonny, I went to Borders and it was a couple weeks ago Sonny was playing a tune by Larry Coryell. "What's New" and man, that was so pretty; I've heard Larry in person but I ain't never heard anyone play it that pretty. And the piano player was Cedar Walton. So, I went to Borders out in Stones Town and they have a pretty nice selection of Jazz, and they used to have four or five aisles, but now there is one aisle. They are getting rid of it man, people downloading and stuff. They had one aisle and nothing really, though someone told me to go online to Amazon. I found the album, $14! Yeah, man, the record business is taking a beating, look at Tower. We had a softball team and Al Jarreau played on our team and he had a gig over in Sausalito, forgot the name of the place, we all knew he could sing because he would sit in with Tommy sometimes, but when he got a gig over there he slowly started packing them in there. And I thought, this guy is going to go somewhere, you know..... and well, he did. Local guy, married some rich woman, I heard, down in Carmel or something. Yeah, he married money. What was it, Miles or Dexter Gordon? I think it was Dexter that had some wealthy woman supporting him.

DON: Well, Monk had a patron too. She was a Baroness!

RICH: I wonder if it is the same woman.

DON: Well, she helped out Bird. Baroness -Nica Koenigswarter; that was her name.

RICH: Well, I don't know if it is the same woman, but even in the movie they made about Dexter they told how he ended up with some rich woman over in France-the movie "Round Midnight."

DON: Love that movie, Bobby Hutcherson was in that movie, and Herbie Hancock.

RICH: There are certain horn players that you can tell who it is just by them playing. Dexter is one of them and also Gene Ammons, you can tell- and Getz when you are hearing him. Yeah man, in those days you had Basin Street West, Jazz Workshop, the Matador and then there was one up the street there, the guy had owned the Half Note on Divisadero, ended up owning this club on Broadway because he met a rich woman. But he blew that. Did you ever go to the Half Note?

DON: No.

RICH: They didn't have Jazz. George Duke played there. But he wasn't playing any straight Jazz, for that crowd – it was a little soul and Jazz mixed in. Carman McRae used to come there all the time because she was a good friend of Warren's. Great places to hop around in go to different places.

DON: Oh, there was Sugar Hill.

RICH: Oh, yeah, that is what I am talking about. Carmen liked that place, she was in town here quite a number of years in the 60's.

DON: She started out as kind of a Pam Greer looking black lady with long hair, a very sexy looking woman.

RICH: When Miles was talking about Ella and somebody told him – well you know what they are calling her and he said, no, what? The first lady of song and Miles said – The first Lady of song, then what the fuck is Carmen? He was saying, wait – what about Carmen?

DON: Do you remember the Macumba Club? Wasn't that on Grant in Chinatown? Carman McRae did a lot of her gigs there.

RICH: I remember a club on Bush, Earl "Father" Hines was the regular pianist there.

DON: Was that 70's? He had some of his band there with him.

RICH: Late 60's...Maybe early 60's....

DON: There was a place where young Johnny Mathis used to sing up on Bush Street.

RICH: Can't remember the name. I remember the Black Hawk, but that was Turk and Hyde- a funky and funny joint. Nobody ever cleaned that place. I went by one day, and someone was in there cleaning and I walked in and man, that place was very dark, and they had all the lights on and the carpet was all beat up and dirty and the big old thick drapes were all dirty. Man, they should never turn the lights on. And he and his wife, Helen Noga, got a hold of Johnny Mathis and Helen became his manager until Capital Records got a hold of him. Yeah, she really is the one who picked him up. Johnny now is like, 70 or something and I saw him on TV not too long ago and he looks the same.

End: Al Molina and Richard Brown

Interview: Don Alberts-pianist, composer, author- with Eric Whittington-October 10, 2008 at Bird and Beckett-about: jazz and coming of age.

DON ALBERTS with ERIC WHITTINGTON

ERIC: Do you know what he did with him here in town? What he did with Charlie Parker?

DON: You mean played with Charlie Parker?

ERIC: Yeah, here at a club in town.

DON: Oh, we would have to reserve that for Eddie.

ERIC: Was there a club called Say When?

DON: Yeah, the Say When, but it was kind of a Dixieland club I think.

ERIC: Oh, maybe I'm wrong.

DON: It doesn't mean that they couldn't have stuff there. If Bird came to town and there wasn't a club that said Jazz, he would play wherever he could play. There was a place on Market Street, Lower Market; a long time ago called Fack's remember that?

ERIC: When you say Lower Market – do you mean down by the Ferry Building?

DON: Yeah, down in that area and it was a nightclub and actually Matt Dennis appeared there. The reason I mention it is because in those early days when Miles Davie had the quartet with Horace Silver and Art Blakey and Percy Heath – that beautiful little time there. Miles came out to San Francisco and he played this little club there called Fack's and then there was Fack's II. I don't know much about that one – lost track. I don't have any idea who owned it. Then there was an evolution of that club and Matt Dennis starting coming out and Ray Barretto came out. I saw both of those groups and then the High-Lows were hot which was probably just entering the 60's or something. Never been a vocal band like that. And they were really good. My wife Julie and I had to go see them because she is a singer. Then, anyway, who knows what happened, it just closed.

ERIC: Yeah, I wondered what the longevity of the clubs was. How many dozens and dozens turned over and how often?

DON: Yeah, well I'm hoping some of these musicians can tell me that.

ERIC: Do you have a feel like when the peak was?

DON: Well a lot of people say it was the 50's. Some of those classic Miles Davis records were early 50's. 52, 53. And then he had the other groups in 59 and by 1960 he had Tony Williams. So that was another evolution with Wayne Shorter; a different kind of band. It's all really the one thing. One thing I like to

A Diary of the Underdogs

talk about is what it is. One of the things that I was thinking about on the way over is this thing we call Jazz has a personal meaning to each of us depending on our era and the time we heard these certain things. And we tend to be critical of the new stuff because it doesn't have that quality.

ERIC: Well the best Jazz record ever made was probably when you were eighteen. Is that the kind of true?

DON: Yeah, well a little later; that's when I really started listening. Something happens to us and we can't be dissuaded, the music does something to us and we come away with something. And then we would go to a concert and hear these people live and be even more hooked.

ERIC: What would you say that hooked you?

DON: Oh, obviously Miles Davis and then later Bill Evans. It would have to be Miles; I was

Don Alberts

absolutely hypnotized by his sound and the guys who played with him. It was just so good. For one thing we didn't understand the music, we were young musicians. Everything they did was creative and new and wonderful. Now years later we have had a chance to look at the same chord changes we all played, it's the same stuff you know, but not with that artistic intent and those guys had it and Miles was a great leader even though he was little paranoid and withdrawn. He had a great way of directing musicians in his band to get the most out of them. And he really wasn't a great manager, he would say dumb stuff. And those poor bands would go on tour, Paul Chambers and Philly Joe Jones would have to go and play *Bye Bye Blackbird* everyplace they went. And after four or five years they get a little tired of that. But that was the venue and Miles made it work. He was a great leader; he was good even though he was very insecure with Bird. He admitted he was insecure with Bird, he couldn't do that stuff but he ended up doing his own thing. This developed his style.

ERIC: Yeah, well it seems in listening to him, that he really couldn't.

DON: Yeah, he couldn't but Diz could, Diz could do it and he knew that Diz could do it. In fact there is a section in this book and you have probably come across it – Miles was supposed to do a record with Bird and he did most of the record and it came time to record *Koko which* is very fast. So it was based on *Cherokee*. And Miles knew he couldn't do the job on that so he kind of bowed out by hiding. So, he just hid. And Bird got Dizzy to come in and do that track. And Miles was sleeping on the floor of the studio, just stabbing himself with arrows....

ERIC: Oh, yeah, it must have been torturous.

DON: But I was thinking, well what do you think of some of that stuff?

ERIC: How important is it to have the audience in sync? It's got to be good when the clubs are drawing people. It must be tough those long periods. You must get to play, intensely in an interior way when there is nobody in the house, but at the same time....

DON: I try and do it that way. I try and encourage the band to that, to play as if the house if full. It's important to do it every time. But it took a lot of years to get there; because for me it was a lot of years of being self-conscious. I mean, I am playing the piano and they are listening. And this little thing that I experience is too intrusive, I had to learn to believe in what I am doing and let them enjoy it and then I finally got to a more advance place. It takes time or it takes instruction. I think the instruction is coming along now in the younger musicians. They are getting all that bandstand behavior and posture and confidence in how they play and they are getting that now in classrooms, which took us years.

ERIC: Well, nobody must have had real schooling....

DON: Well, nobody talked about anything like that.

ERIC: Were there schools that were teaching all that Jazz performance? That was all in the 70's and 80's, so all that had to be learned on the bandstand.

DON: It had to be learned on the bandstand and we didn't give it to each other. Nobody gave much of anything. In fact if you ran into a musician that would talk about that stuff everyone would love that guy. No one gave away secrets, it was all private. Whatever you could manage to learn off the record or whatever, that was yours. You would only find out if it was wrong if you got into a situation - somebody would tell you, "that's the wrong chord man." Someone would tell you that. But they wouldn't tell you what the right chord was, they said – "hey that's wrong," but nothing about professionalism, nothing about presentation or behavior on the bandstand. I think a lot of it was because people were looking for a style of their own that was similar to what Miles had done. Or what Coltrane had done. And all those guys were of the cool idea of that you didn't really acknowledge the audience. Not really. You are into your own stuff. It's their privilege to come and hear you.

ERIC: How important was it to have Keystone Korner, was it really like, like through the 70's and 80's, when did Keystone start, in…?

DON: Well you will have to talk about that era because I was in Oregon at that time. I did come down a couple of times to San Francisco. I did see Bill Evans there and Stan Getz. But I knew it was there. Did you ever go?

ERIC: Yeah, several times because I used to live a few blocks from there in Chinatown. Mostly, well I couldn't afford to go in so mostly I would stand on the sidewalk because you could hear it all from the sidewalk. So I would go in a few times. It seemed like so many heavy people came through there all the time.

DON: Yeah, everyone. Todd Barkan bartended, I guess he was the manager.

ERIC: Yeah, I have a flyer somewhere that shows the line-up for a couple of months and Blakey is playing one week and God know who, it was just week after week.

DON: How long did that last?

ERIC: I don't really know; I would have to look at the dates. I got to San Francisco in 1974 or 1975, and it was running and I think it ran to 1981 or 1983.

DON: It was a very successful Jazz club. It was in the heart of North Beach on Vallejo and it was formally the cop shop, everyone called it the cop shop. And before that there was another club called Dino & Carlo's – it was a bar and it had an archway, it's a beauty salon now. We played there a long time ago with Virgil Gonsalves and Art Lewis and Benny Wilson, and actually, Dewey Redman. And so that bar was there and that band broke up in the 60's and everyone went there. But it was the one next door that became Keystone Korner.

ERIC: Okay, so it was Dino & Carlo's. Was it Dino & Carlo's or was it Gino & Carlo's, because there is a bar called Gino & Carlo's?

DON: Yeah, that's a separate thing. That's up on Green Street. Yeah, because I was up there, I went and talked to Carlo, Dino had died. It was a good bar. Bikers used to come in there because it had a mezzanine. They used to sit up there in the mezzanine and drink beer.

ERIC: Well, if you figure all this started in 1944 or 1945, everything started basically during the war. Be Bop and subsequent music.

DON: Well, Bird was 1946, 1947, 1948....

A Diary of the Underdogs

ERIC: Whenever that sort of recording band was. And it all got quickly perfected off the map and came out. So, that's sixty years. And the guys who are playing in here basically have fifty years under their belt playing. Several of them came out of San Francisco State and in 1964 or 1965 or something like that.

DON: BJ Papa said that he got here about that time. He was in the service. The army I guess. He was a medic and stationed at the Presidio. And I am trying to think of where Norman Williams came from.

ERIC: He was from Kansas City. I don't know whether he came straight out here or not.

DON: Well, I met him in 1960, so I don't know how long he had been here. He was an interesting person. And I hope he will be included in some of these interviews. Yeah, and so.... in a brief conversation with Eddie Duran – a brief conversation about what we are going to talk about – he kept going to the subject of that the young cats don't know what it is – in other words the legacy is in peril and he is concerned about that.

ERIC: What do you think he thinks is missing?

DON: He thinks the young guys don't get down with tradition and really learn that enough.

ERIC: But there are a lot of kids that are incredibly schooled.

DON: There are; which brings us to a broader concept which is what I was thinking about on the way over. We are not going to get to preserve our style of music. It's going to move on. And the people that write about that, critics that review those kinds of things are going to be influenced by what's new and what's fresh and not so much about traditions and what we lovingly call Be Bop in our time, you know?

ERIC: Yeah, but it seems that in the last twenty years there are a lot of young players who are really trying to work at it and do it. So, it's hard to tell if they are the last batch that is going to do that and the next batch is going to go on – that is pretty hard to tell.

DON: Well, Stephan Harris talked about a lot of interesting things and one of them was he is first generation, educated Jazz musician. Now that is quite a statement because an educated Jazz musician never existed before. So, it's academically educated in Jazz by Jazz masters and people who really know- which includes the whole thing that we were talking about which is stage presence, presentation, marketing, packaging, music, ability, the whole thing.

ERIC: How do young players around here come out of family's of musicians? Do you know a guy named David Foston? His mother was a singer.

DON: Oh, that's Rhoyal.

ERIC: Yeah, exactly.

DON: He is a very good friend of mine.

ERIC: Yeah, he used to play in here from time to time with Henry. And he comes from a family....

DON: His mother was a great singer-yes, Fran Foston; a great singer, just wonderful.

ERIC: So, I wonder, did the Alley's have kids; did Vernon? There are a lot of great musicians around.

DON: I don't know, as far as I know Vernon....

ERIC: I wonder if their nephews and grand kids are around playing.

DON: You never know, sometimes its one generation back. The grandchild will pick it up.

ERIC: Have you talked to anybody doing research on the Fillmore historical district and all that?

DON: You mean preserve it and document it?

ERIC: Yes, document it.

DON: Well, they are interested.

ERIC: So, they might know what families are long-time residents.

DON: I hadn't thought of that –

ERIC: Because it is one thing coming from school, like Peter Sparacino that plays in here on tenor sax.

DON: Peter! Yeah, a great player, love that kid.

ERIC: I'm sure these guys are getting a lot – playing with the older guys. But I don't know it also comes back to family, if there are older relatives that are starting it off.

DON: It's not a sure thing, but I do think there is a lot of it. Like Ron Marabuto. I hope I get to talk to him. Great musician, great player, John Marabuto was his father – piano player, composer, and arranger. He wrote for a lot of the big bands. Rudy Salvini was one of them.

ERIC: One thing that would be interesting to figure out is there is a lot of rehearsal bands around and nobody knows what they are doing and where they are playing except the guys involved.

DON: And then they loyally go there every Tuesday night.

ERIC: And there are still a lot of house concerts going on. And so there is a lot that is still percolating but not so many venues.

DON: You know its, funny those two clubs in North Beach closed where all the piano players were playing, I was one of them.

ERIC: You're talking about Pearl's

DON: Yeah, Pearl's and Moose's, and Washington Square changed ownership. I like to say to say all the piano players on the streets like rats. Basically that is what happened - everybody was scheduled at night – 7 nights a week – different piano players, so everybody had a job there. It was good. I miss that venue because it's a venue where you can play standards and you usually can play with a bass player and the art of Jazz piano has always been based on interpretation of standards and regard for melody and lyrics and those are the places you get to do it.

ERIC: A duo or trio format.

DON: Yeah, and do it the best you can. Really get into that format. Really make those melodies sing. It's very enjoyable.

ERIC: Stars used piano players.

DON: That was Billie Philadelphia and Mike Greensill's gig. That was the old Stars; they had a seven foot Baldwin. Beautiful piano – I got to play there a few times. Everything changes.....

ERIC: It's hard for a restaurant to make room for a band and to part with some of their money. At the prices they get you think that they could toss the band a little and keep it going.

DON: Well there are some courageous people out there. As much as a fan you and I are – a lot of people are like us and there are people in business willing to make room for that music because they love it as much as we do.

ERIC: The place on the corner is doing Jazz again - I think Friday nights, though maybe not every Friday – the restaurant on the corner. When it was a bar they did it every Friday and that was a great band. David Parker was the bass player that organizes it. There is a trumpet player named Mike Petri that plays with him and Jerry Logus on tenor sax. Keyboard player, Yamamoko, can't think of his first name. And they would fit into a very tiny part of the bar and it was just a bar and you can imagine how they could give up that much space. But now it's a restaurant that is impossible to get into and so crowded; so small and packed. And they have agreed to move a little space in there and keep some music going.

DON: Well, people still love music and sometimes they just want something to talk over. Though Miles Davis would have never stood for that! But we get to play music and we get to play Jazz and if they like our music to talk over then that's fine.

ERIC: I do like that people sit in the back and chatter, but a lot of people are sitting right there is front listening to every note.

DON: Yeah, people came just for that. It's an interesting format. It will be interesting to see how it keeps going on. We always had leaders, our Jazz favorites. Miles was always leading us onto something new. Even Coltrane and Monk and Horace Silver, they were always leading – they were leaders. And after all that kind of change, we are a bunch of musicians in an orchestra with no leader - everyone is trying to make a sound and carry on a tradition and do what they think is – what the music should be. And so you have all these little cells around you instead of unity. So, now the word Jazz is really a big umbrella.

ERIC: But you can manage to find some like minded musicians to stay together on it. It's hard to keep a band together for more then a few months – or a few years.

DON: We have been very successful with the Bad Boys.

ERIC: How far back to you go with Don. Do you go back to the 60's with him?

DON: Yeah, him and Art. Back when Virgil Gonsalves and Dino & Carlo and places like that and art galleries. But what makes the current band work is feeding it and keeping it alive. Try and bring something fresh all the time. So, we play some new stuff, but then we still play the old stuff.

ERIC: How many times did you bring in a horn front-line because you did a quintet?

DON: We've only done it once. We are doing it this Thursday and Friday- the De Anza on Thursday and Friday at an art gallery in Santa Cruz, with the same guys; Al Molina and Peter Graves. It's not a concert situation. The first one was in protest of the San Jose Jazz Festival, which totally ignored us. And we thought, well we will put this on.

ERIC: Don Prell runs around trying to get arrested just by playing obnoxious places in public. He says, *"They won't even arrest me. I'm going to walk across the Golden Gate Bridge and play on my bass and hold up traffic"*

DON: Oh, that funky bass too, that ugly one!

ERIC: And he's got that electric one too.

ERIC: So, yeah, how to keep these venues going.

DON: Well, I believe in this music and I've put everything on the line for it and made a lot of mistakes, but it's a strong enough force, even in writing books, it's a strong enough force – its really become, well not the only reason in my life, but one of the strongest reasons in my life and from that everything seems to grow out of and everything seems to work - friends and relations and where I live and what I do and what I think about and its all pretty much based on that.

ERIC: How important is it - like the writing is a different thing and that is very intense, but music is so – I mean you have a commonalty agreed on set of things to with, chord changes and tunes - some of which is composed, but a lot them aren't your standards and so forth and so how important is it that it is a non-verbal thing? That's his bass and you don't have to say anything except the basic key.

DON: This is the phenomenon – I have been trying to describe that - a few attempts at writing about that. I think you have to go into the realm of some kind of bliss which is some kind of connection with the universe in a way that allows you to be free in it. And everything seems to work you know, Like Joseph Campbell – that is the bliss of realizing that you are one with the universe instead of having to work for it so much and try to find convenient ways to find it. That could be one explanation for it. When you go to composing – which I have done a lot of – and I am absolutely amazed that complete composition will come to me. Absolutely complete, write it down in twenty minutes and its absolutely there. And sure some of it will be based on experience and what I've heard. But something absolutely something original coming out of nowhere and flooding to my piano – it's like something outside of me. And I know I am not the only one. And I think a little bit of that in the middle of the Jazz passion, Jazz bliss - it's so connected. If you don't play music it's hard to get it there but a good listener can get that too.

ERIC: Yeah, and it makes you realize how many times you have not been listening. Sometimes what you hear is just a fraction of what goes on; the same thing with records. You look at records and there are so many incredible recordings and you realize that those were just the tiny bits that got recorded even though it seems like an immense body of work. So you multiply that by how many times, a thousand times, ten thousand times.

DON: Yeah, you can't number them and you are always wishing that somewhere secretly the recorder was on for this thing that just happened because it was really great. You go in the studio and you get like a

A Diary of the Underdogs

portion of it.

ERIC: Yeah, and sometimes the band is like not there but somebody on the bandstand is doing something. You listen to the recordings of Lester Young with some pick-up band in a hotel somewhere. And the music is adequate until you hear him playing and you realize it doesn't really matter. It's him and the horn and notes. You are glad that other people were around to give him a bandstand to make it happen.

DON: Yeah, that magic, that magic thing. They didn't have big audiences back then. Those guys were really heroes. They were obviously moved by peer groups or by liberation or to get out of the ghetto. But those guys who stand out in our memories and made all those records, they are really special people. And yet, they didn't think they were so special. They were a pretty humble lot. But they were able to contribute a wonderful art-form that is still here.

ERIC: And it came out of – I mean it had historical roots but all that music came out of nowhere.

DON: Comes out of life and comes out of conversation with each other, desires... doesn't matter too much. That was it the music was their identity, it came out of them.

ERIC: Seems like there are still a lot of good players that have twenty or thirty years that were playing in the 50's. There are still guys that will go for another twenty years, easily. And then of course they have influenced about two or three generations of players since. So those guys are carrying it forward and there is always time for the young guys to be mature musicians while are still two or three generations coming up through them. So I think that it has potential to stay good for a long time. It can be self perpetuating, because the simpler forms will continue to drop away; every generation. You know, like a simpler drum beat or a funk kind of thing. Those things are wonderfully sweet in their way, but they are not quite as complex and they will give way to some other simpler form. The more complex stuff will keep percolating.

DON: I watched it go through the 70's and 80's – disco and what not and where the beat changed. And it went through its phase. And it came back to center. It came back to traditional Jazz based on Be-bop and Charlie Parker and Swing music.

ERIC: I think the drummers have a lot to do with keeping the knowledge of complex beats that stay alive. There are drummers that you just can't stop them. And as long as they do that everybody else has room.

DON: I think you are right. It goes back to the very primitive beginnings.

ERIC: Tony Williams must have been a hugely important figure in those early 60's.

DON: Yes, because he was so young and yet he had so much maturity and fire. He had to learn to be quiet. He played so loud. His cymbals were so loud.

ERIC: So can you name like a dozen drummers that you have played with – or a dozen bass players.

DON: Oh, I wish I could. Leroy Vinnegar, David Friesen, great bass player. Chuck Metcalf, John Wiitala- so many different guys. The thing with bass players; it's symbiotic – you agree to play with each other. If you don't it's just a piano and a bass. And you will get through the tunes, but it will be big and jagged and awkward. When things really start coming together is when you believe in each other. One of the greatest combinations is piano and bass. I've done it for years- over five years with David Friesen- and a lot of gigs with Leroy Vinnegar. We seem to have a sympathetic connection just because of the time period that was similar to us. He was so much aware of the Los Angeles music of the 50's and that really started moving me around. I outgrew it but it was the thing I got started with; Chet Baker and Hampton Hawes, Shorty Rodgers, Bud Shank and all those guys in Los Angeles. That was really the stuff. When I started listening to the New York music I outgrew that style really quick. It was musically correct and beautiful and based on very good intelligence, but it didn't have that passion or the color or primitive urgency.

ERIC: You are talking about later New York styles....

DON: Yeah, probably 60's. Well, 58, 59.... I would say mid 50's on through the 60's; Sonny Rollins and Horace Silver....

A Diary of the Underdogs

ERIC: So where they kind of like harkening back straight to the Bop guys without paying much attention to what was going on out here? Or did they take what was going on here and.....

DON: They had their own agenda, which the East Coast always has. They were dead on and strong. It wasn't that there wasn't any communication with the West Coast; in fact Horace Silver had a lot of that in him. And Stan Getz obviously did. And Getz influenced Coltrane and Coltrane admitted that. But that music just had – I mean Art Blakey – commitment. It was more than just tapping out time.

ERIC: Well, yeah, that was a more spiritual experience.

DON: Yeah, those guys were so strong, it was my transformation; to try and belong to this music, and I had no idea how far I would go with it. I definitely belonged to it and all the people I cared about belonged to it. We hope that it goes on. It will be different. But we will still have it – it's like trying to hold on to a Benny Goodman record. That doesn't apply now. Some of the lessons apply now, but we don't play those records anymore.

ERIC: But you can hear playing inside those records that's great. You can hear instrumentalists that are doing wonderful things. The structure is.....

DON: Well, yeah, it's changed because we allow creativity.

End: Don Alberts and Eric Whittington

Interview: Eddie Duran-guitarist- with Don Alberts, October 23, 2008-at home, San Francisco-about: Duran Brothers, Cal Tjader, George Shearing, Al McKibbon, Great Eastern, Pearl Wong

EDDIE DURAN

DON: We are talking with Eddie Duran today for "Diary of the Underdogs." This is a real privilege, Eddie. Thank you. I was talking with you on the phone the other day and you had real concerns about what the younger musicians are getting from the older guys.

EDDIE: Yeah, seems to me a lot of the   younger players are looking for instant recognition and instant fame. And that's fine, you know, but it seems that they forget where they got their inspirations. The way I look at it is that they are starting in the middle of the book. They are not going back to the musicians who came before them. Like Louie Armstrong and Teddy Wilson, Benny Goodman and all these cats. They might have heard of a few of them but that's cool and all. But they are starting with either Bird or Coltrane.

DON: Nothing before that?

EDDIE: No, not much before that. And t hey lack being able to play a good ballad. They are so into technique, getting their chops up fast. But when you get your technique up, you know, that's fine, it's flashy, and of course it is attention getting, but after awhile fast playing becomes a bit repetitive. Now there are a few good cats that can play fast, swing, but it's lacking something. Sure, great play all your notes fast but make it mean something. Make it swing, it's got to swing.

DON: Yeah, regardless of the time.

EDDIE: Yeah, regardless of the time and they seem to be focused on that which is fine, but they seem to forget they are also lacking in harmonies.

DON: Yeah, harmonies the sweet notes.

EDDIE: Yeah, the sweet notes and also the sound of a beautiful harmony. And they are just going for the straight out you know.

DON: Do you think they are moved by peer groups? They haven't matured enough to strike out their own-have their own opinion? I know that is what happened to me. When I decided, this is how I feel about the music everything settled down. I wasn't trying to please everybody else. I think some of the younger cats haven't gotten there yet.

EDDIE: No, not yet. They are trying to prove and please everybody at the same time. And they are striving for attention and the beauty of the music, either they haven't listened enough to it or they never heard it. Oh, if they have heard it, they say, OK, I've heard it now I am going to do my thing. In other words it's like trying to reinvent the wheel. It is fine when you are first listening to the music and you are impressed and you are inspired, but after awhile you have to let go and let's see what you sound like. And that is what I feel is missing in a lot of players. And as I said, to even play a beautiful ballad, for one thing they didn't grow up in the romantic era-and they didn't really listen to the great composers, the great lyricists and the great singers- Ella and before that – the 20's or the 30's. And so I look at it like they don't know what romance is. They don't know what love is. They don't have love songs.

DON: Yeah, I have noticed that, the popular music today.....the generation of today didn't grow up with love songs.

EDDIE: They grew up in the rock era. How can you make love listening to rock music?

DON: You have to have a big bed.

EDDIE: Yeah, where are those tender moments, and the romance? And it's not blaming them, but they grew up in a different era. However, there is no excuse for them not to be able to go back to that era and listen to the music and read about it. You know Ken Burns did a beautiful thing in doing his documentaries. It shows how things were then. You can go back in time. It's all there on film.

DON: Yeah, much more information than we had at our time. If we wanted to copy a song we had to take it off the record.

EDDIE: I remember you know, playing the record and listening to two bars and lifting up the arm of the turntable and letting the sound sink in and the phrases and being able to remember them. That was such a challenge. And nowadays you can slow down anything and keep it in the same key. Yeah, that's cool.

DON: Oh, yeah, I wish I could have done that.

EDDIE: I used to do it on my tape recorder. First I did it on my turntable because I was able to slow the record and the speed down to an octave below. And it doesn't get indistinguishable, but if you got good ears, that was another thing. And doing it that way was a good training for the ears. And that is another thing that they are still lacking in. Like I said, it's no excuse, it's all out there and it's all how you apply yourself.

DON: One thing I discovered and you probably did too was – I went crazy over some recordings and because it was complicated there was stuff that I could only hear parts of. I couldn't hear all of it. But later on as I matured, I could hear the rest of that music and I could go back to the original recording and hear the whole thing. And even understand it. And what I found out is the ear automatically blocks out what it doesn't understand. So you have to go back and what you are talking about is what these younger cats have to do. I heard a couple of tracks that Bud Powell said that's spicy that's fine and then go on and then later on learn a little more come back to Bud, and that's brilliant. So, it's a study like you say.

EDDIE: It's also a way to develop a good ear, because again, you have to listen to all of it, it's out there and there is no excuse. You can go to the library and take out the old recordings and its all there.

DON: Yeah, there are even transcriptions.

EDDIE: Yes. And also it helps you develop the ability to remember and play a lot of music. A lot of people these days – their vocabulary in music are pretty slim. I mean take you and myself for example, we can go on a gig and remember a lot of music but they have to bring along their book. But then there is no feeling in it. They can read a nice ballad in a fake book but they have no feeling for it because they have never heard an original version. They didn't hear the singer sing it and they never listened to the lyrics.

DON: And they never got it inside them.

A Diary of the Underdogs

EDDIE: I remember, Lou Levy once said, *when I am playing a ballad, I'm listening and reading and remembering the lyrics as I am playing it.* Because how can you play a ballad if you don't get the meaning of what this composer meant. And that's why you have to go back and study.

DON: And yeah, it's probably a good idea to get the recording of the one that really defined it.

EDDIE: Yeah, that's what I say. Listen to the music the way that it was originally composed and originally played. And you will get so much more out of it. You will get a meaning. And then if you want to use different changes. Good. But while you have been listening to your music, your mind automatically starts to hear different harmonies.

DON: Yeah, one of my complaints about singers is – especially singers who want to sing Jazz and

Eddie Duran

sing standards, and they will take that ending and resolve it to another note and you know there was a composer who sat there for a long time and decided what those notes should be and he wrote them down and it's not going to work unless you do that. That person spent hours, a lot of his heart and a lot of his energy doing it. You have to respect that. You can put a ninth on that, and that's OK, but the melody is the one. That's what he sweats over. You know, I mean I write music and you write music – I don't want a different note played there that is the one that I chose.

EDDIE: And if you do want to change it, it takes years to develop an ear that will at least complement what you the composer wrote originally. But first you have musical knowledge and the harmonic knowledge to know where to place it and to know where it won't work. And sometimes the best way to go is just to play it the way it was written.

DON: I think one of the things that we talked about was that the passion is missing, that's because of the love songs idea that we talked about earlier. I think some of the passion is gone; you have to have some passion. There is a time in your life when this music comes along and it's more important than anything. It moves into your life and creates its own energy, it's more important than anything and you make sacrifices for it.

EDDIE: Yes, and it tells a story of your life and everybody's life. The lyrics of songs tell you what it was and when it was and how people felt. It was really honest. It wasn't embellished with a lot of – how can I say, you weren't making things up or embellishing them. That was life as it was happening and the feelings that went with it.

DON: Yeah, I think when you look back on conversations in the 30's and 40's and even in the 50's people had trouble talking to each other. And I think that some of these songs helped them say what they couldn't say to each other.

EDDIE: Yeah, and maybe they didn't know how to put it. But in a lyric you hear it all.

DON: Yeah, you could sing it to your girlfriend and she would have it. But you probably couldn't say it you know.

EDDIE: You felt a little embarrassed or it was too awkward. And also, there was not a lot of anger expressed in those lyrics. But now you are finding a lot. Not just now but new generations have come and they have grown and they are showing a lot of their anger and irritation and dissatisfaction with the way

A Diary of the Underdogs

the world is. This is fine.

DON: Yeah, freedom, democracy of course.

EDDIE: Yes and my idea of rock and roll is that it was expressing the times, these generations were promised a lot of things and going back to the wars; the wars which promised a lot; the first war a new way of living and better way of life. Well, that didn't work; it lasted for maybe twenty years. And then here comes another one. That promised a lot too. And then these generations growing up, luckily most of those wars were in other countries, but still a lot of people did have to fight those wars. But the thing is the promise – you know, for a while it was great, but then here comes another one. It was disappointing. And one way to express their disappointments and anger is thru the lyrics. It seems that they needed to express themselves in a way that they would get attention. So, you make it louder and you let your anger out thru it and also it shows up in rap. And that is fine but we can still vote, we still have a say in government, but this is their way of expressing themselves. And after all everyone has something to say.

DON: And pretty soon that's how we say it.

EDDIE: Yes, but probably in that time, there was another way of learning and being aware and another way of saying it that works much better- voting, writing, expressing what you want in newspapers-having a voice in whatever situation. There is a gentleman who just wrote a book on radio, the history of radio and how it became a communicative instrument. But still, there were things that we did not have, when you turned down the radio you could hear what was happening. But you still couldn't respond to what you were hearing and still your voice could not be heard as much. But in this generation they can use technology, the internet, everyone can put their views on YouTube and everyone can hear it. So, that is more freedom of expression and technology is helping.

DON: It is helping and a lot of people have things to say that are not important, but some people do. But that is what I am saying, music is feeling and it comes to how you feel and if you get used to expressing yourself in any area, your music is going to get stronger.

EDDIE: And I always say, you can't do without music, if you can imagine a world without music – what would that be like?

DON: Oh, it would be chaos.

EDDIE: But I always say; when we get done playing gigs – anywhere – think about this: when we are playing music and people are up there and they are listening to music and for a two or three hour space – no one is mad at each other! The audience is sitting together, listening together and nobody is mad. They have left all their things behind and you have taken them on a journey. Which is always like an out of body experience and now you are operating in a non-physical environment. And that's great; they can take that home and look back on it.

DON: Yeah, they remember that night and the vision of you playing the guitar and the mandolin and whoever is in the band.

EDDIE: And just listening to the music and the arrangements and just the friendship, the hang, is beautiful. But music will not only live, but Jazz will live. Because think of Jazz, it is improvisational and it's speaking at the moment of what you feel and what you are feeling and it's free. Freedom of expression, but freedom of *musical* expression.

DON: With discipline and experience. I was reading some Joseph Campbell this morning and I came across something that you would probably agree with. With one brief sentence he said exactly what I was looking for. And he said that *music excites the basic human rhythms that are already inside of us – it turns those things on.* So, that is why people like it, it goes right to their basic make-up, it goes to the sound of nature and if we all shut up for a moment, maybe we can hear it.

EDDIE: It's the rhythm of a spiritual being.

DON: You know about that? I didn't know if you did.

A Diary of the Underdogs

EDDIE: Oh yeah, I feel it all the time; even more and more. And we need it. We need beautiful music and we are fortunate that we can get out there and play it.

DON: Yeah, I love it and it is not about the money as much as it used to be. The money was about respect. You pay me the money because it shows that you do respect me. But also we are more mature now and realize the value of music wherever is important and I will take less money.

EDDIE: And you can see it in the faces of the younger people, the young ladies and the little girls especially when they see Madeline (Duran) playing all these instruments and they are fascinated because now they are seeing a woman expressing themselves musically, which is different.

DON: Yeah, it's the half of the energy. I think you really got that, it's the other side, it's something we can't do, and it's always been a man's world.

EDDIE: Yes, but now women are being recognized. And in past history, there have been a lot of great women composers, singers, arrangers.

DON: Singers have been promising. I didn't realize that Billie Holiday was actually a horn. It was the sound of the horn that lead the band and it had content, and story and meaning. Meaning and feeling. And so the band kind of formed around them and I think improvisation guys were imitating Billie. Those ballads, if you could play it like she sang it. The phrasing! Even without the lyrics.

EDDIE: And yes, so I am glad that women have come about in music. And they have become important in the music. And even in the 20's and 30's it was hard for them to be recognized, but they did it. There were so many women composers and lyricists. There has been a book written about women musicians and composers.

DON: Yeah, I should look that up and insert that into this dialogue. Yeah, let's mention Melba Liston, Mary Lou Williams. There is a Mary Lou Williams Jazz Festival.

EDDIE: We were there in May, in Washington DC at Kennedy Center and they presented all women performers and players.

DON: Was that the Montclair Orchestra?

EDDIE: Montclair all Women's Jazz Orchestra and this was started by - oh, can't think of the name, a Dr. or Professor – they just had a thing about him on KCSM. It was very successful and all these women get out and these women playing instruments. And the young people, there are very few colleges that feature Jazz studies and there are a lot of women studying not just Jazz, but the history of Jazz.

DON: And playing instruments. I have noticed there are quite a few sax players in the last few years. Not a lot of trombone players though I did see one in the big band at Pearls. I forgot her name and she played great, she played lead.

EDDIE: And so, music is not about gender, but who can play.

DON: And I think women have a pretty big responsibility just being women and it's taken them a little time.

EDDIE: Yes. Marian McPartland had Ellen Sealy and Jean Fineberg– they appeared on the Marian McPartland piano show. And they talked about – of course Marian is very conscious about women in Jazz – and they talked about the difficulties of women being accepted as players. But it has and is coming around.

DON: And in Marian McPartland's case Dizzie really validated her. She probably had her own validation but signed Marian on. What a great complement.

EDDIE: She has been a true pioneer.

DON: At the Hickory House. And he tells a story that goes with that. It would be wonderful if we could talk to her but – she is so available, she does give a lot. She talks about history and pretty much everything. But, anyway, to get back, Madeline is really a big part of that. Her contribution and her association....and

EDDIE: And I am glad that KCSM does a women's month. So that is so great to honor the women in the area.

DON: The first one I ever heard of was Phil Spitalni first all girl orchestra! Which was probably in the 40's – mid to late 40's.

EDDIE: And there was Inna Ray Hutton. She was in the 40's.

DON: OK, so I want to ask you about the Duran Brothers.

EDDIE: Yeah, when we had started playing when we were kids, Manny and I and my brother Carlos and my sister was a singer – a fine singer. And she sang in a lot of nightclubs in that era – in the 40's. Her name was Celia: my older sister. But she was going by the name of Celia Mauna. Because my mother divorced and she remarried and we had a step-dad and she took his name. She sang in the clubs and my brother Carlos started playing with her because he was playing guitar at the time. So they were both working and Manny had already started playing piano. And that is how I got into guitar, because my brother Carlos was playing it. And I was fascinated by the guitar and started playing on it and finding my way through it. He my brother helped me through it. So, after I came out of the service, that was WWII and we formed a trio that was like – well we were impressed with Nat King Cole Trio and we did a thing like that. Yeah, we had a sound like that and Manny sang and block chords and unison guitars. We started playing and did a lot gigs in the city.

DON: That would be like you and Manny on piano and Carlos on bass?

EDDIE: Yes.

DON: So where did you play around here? Do you remember them?

EDDIE: Oh yeah, but there were a lot more clubs around to play in then. Television hadn't even been on the scene yet so people went out a lot.

DON: Yeah, like before the 50's- late 40's?

EDDIE: And people went out for their entertainment-as opposed to Today where they have television. Times are different.

DON: Can you remember names and neighborhoods that those places were in?

EDDIE: Well, there was one place; of course Manny was playing at a place called Copacabana when he first started playing Latin with his group. There were a lot of nightclubs that featured floor-shows. And my sister worked at those with Carlos and she sang and there were great dancers in the clubs and they put on amazing floor shows. Yeah, so that was the music scene in those days. So we started playing some trio and we started branching off and I started getting work in other places. And then Manny decided to put together a Latin group. And then in the space of that time he met Cal Tjader. And Cal put his group together after he left George Shearing. Yeah, Cal had been playing with George Shearing. And when he left he put his own group together and he was so enamored with Tito Puente and all these cats in New York. And he was so impressed when he heard the music in New York and came back and started his group. And so Manny and Carlos joined the group and they started recording for Fantasy. So that became a thing.

DON: So what year was that?

EDDIE: Well, had to be in the late 40's. I would say 47, 48 or maybe the early 50's. And I was working more gigs and doing more Jazz. And some groups that would come in out of town – see I had built a reputation and they would call me. So, I just started playing.

DON: So, they would need a guitar player and they would call you.

EDDIE: Yeah, I started getting a lot of work that way. I did do some recording with Cal and Cal was also playing Jazz in addition to the Latin stuff. So, I would join Cal with the Latin music.

DON: So Jazz and straight-a-head music too. I think I saw him at the Blackhawk playing straight ahead and Brew Moore was in the background once in awhile.

EDDIE: Yeah, and that was a great Jazz scene that was happening back then.

A Diary of the Underdogs

DON: Who was some of the guys that were in the band at that time?

EDDIE: Well Brew played and sometimes we would have Al McKibbon, bass player. And then Al played a lot on Cal's Latin stuff because he had worked with George Shearing. And then there was....what was his name?...

DON: Conga player? There was a couple, but the one I was thinking of is the guy who lived in the Peninsula. I can't remember either.

EDDIE: But Mongo played with Cal.

DON: And how about piano players?

EDDIE: Well, Manny played piano most of the time during that period. And Carlos played bass most of the time. Can't think of most of the names, but it was a going scene.

DON: So most of the gigs at that time, if you get into Blackhawk was it. But maybe not too much on North Beach at that time?

EDDIE: Well, let's see...some clubs did start to spring up in North Beach. Like the Jazz Workshop and The Matador and then there was Ann's 440.

DON: Yeah, Ann's 440, that later became a strip club-the Chi Chi. And then there was Basin Street West.

EDDIE: Yeah, Basin Street West, up on the corner. There was a lot of music happening there. Yeah, Ellington came out and the Count Basie and Stan Kenton. And Woody's band played there.

DON: And there was a place around the corner called Off Broadway and I saw Kenton's band in there so I know that they were there-the early 60's.

EDDIE: Yeah, that was a good scene.

DON: So, if you didn't play at Blackhawk or North Beach where else would play?

EDDIE: There was the Playboy Club. With Al Plank and he had a good trio going there.

DON: Tom Reynolds, Puzzie Firth?

EDDIE: And also at the "Hungry I" we were playing Jazz with the trio there. House trio and we have different piano players. And we did have Richie, can't think of his last name. Don Asher worked. The trio was a tenor bass guitar thing and sometimes we would have drums. Benny Barth played there.

DON: Do you remember a piano player named Shelly Robbins.

EDDIE: Yeah, Shelly played there. He was a very fine pianist. Jean Roderick also played. It was great, because Enrico was great, we used to call him..... When we talk about Enrico, he was the best boss I have ever had in working in clubs-because he was an artist himself. We would open the club with our Jazz set and then we would get through and he would bring other acts in. People like Bill Cosby and Woody Allen.

DON: Yeah, all the great comics like Phyllis Diller and Mort Sahl. Did you know Faith Winthrop?

EDDIE: Yes, I did, because I worked with her.

DON: I was going to ask Don Asher about her because I knew that he worked with her.

EDDIE: As a matter of fact I played there with Vince and Dean. We were playing with Faith in the outer lobby at the Hungry I. We played a lot with Faith.

DON: I wanted to ask you about the early Pearl's Jazz Club. I think that you were important in guiding her into that. And how did that happen?

EDDIE: Well, we talked about the idea of putting Jazz at Pearl's and that is when she was on Jackson Street. It was a restaurant at the top and then you would go downstairs and it was always the banquet room and she decided to use the banquet room as a Jazz club. And so, we started there as a trio.

DON: I thought the story was that you suggested that why don't you make it into a Jazz club.

EDDIE: Yeah, I did. And she went for it. And it ran for quite a while. I know that Lou Levy played with his trio. It was a great setting and turned out nicely. I say that Jazz belongs in the Jazz club. You can have festivals and whatever, like San Francisco Jazz Festival, but when it comes down to it Jazz belongs in the club because it is an intimate place. And you are closer to the music and the ambience is made for it.

A Diary of the Underdogs

That's the way that it started. You go back to the 20's…Louie Armstrong and all these players started in the clubs.

DON: So what was it called?

EDDIE: It was called Pearl's.

DON: Yeah, she just called me and I am going to talk to her. So, she left Jackson Street eventually ended up on Columbus. And I don't know that story. How long did that run over on Jackson?

EDDIE: Can't be for sure. But it ran a good long time; four or five years. Then she moved to Columbus. Then she got together with Sonny Buxton.

DON: I'm trying to think of side men. A sweet guy played with Cal.

EDDIE: Can't think of it either. When Cal left George Shearing, I took Cal's place. George had this idea of using two guitarists instead of vibes. Toots was on it and myself, and the bass player, Al McKibbon, and a drummer from New York, can't think of his name-and the Congo player, Armando Peraza. While we were in New York George decided to use the vibes at some point. It was a guy from New York and it was a sextet at this time, two guitars and vibes.

DON: Was that recorded?

EDDIE: I don't think it was recorded.

DON: So, there was a vibe player early on and it turned out to be Margie Hyams.

EDDIE: Margie was the first one. Then Chuck Wayne was the first guitarist. And the one who was playing bass was George's manager. And I don't know when Cal joined George. Cal was a new addition, and Armando was still playing.

DON: And Cal was really good about letting local guys play in the band. Vince was in the band and Robert Fisher was in the band and Lonnie Hewitt and Al Zulaica.

EDDIE: The albums I did with Cal were Jazz. It wasn't the Latin Jazz. Oh and when Stan Getz happened to be in town we used Stan's group and recorded an album-with Bill Evan's bass player, Scott LaFaro, and Billie Higgins.

End: Eddie Duran

Interview: Bishop Norman Williams-jazz musician-alto saxophonist-October 22, 2008 with Don Alberts and Eric Whittington, California Street Pizza-about: Coffee Gallery, Bird, New York. Bishop Norman Williams with Don Alberts and Eric Whittington-October 22nd 2008 at California Street Pizza, San Francisco re: Coffee Gallery, Bishop's beginning, Bird's influence.

BISHOP NORMAN WILLIAMS

DON: OK, you are on the spot, now! Hey, who was that drummer, I called him KC ?

BISHOP: KC? He was a sax player.

DON: I thought his name was Casey actually. I asked Art Lewis about that. He said, his name was Casey.

BISHOP: Art? I haven't seen that cat in years.

DON: Have you always been here?

BISHOP: No, I was in France, Nice; I played in New York. I did a dedication for Charlie Parker.

DON: What year was that?

BISHOP: That was in the 80's- in Small's Club- in the Village.

DON: Who did you play with?

A Diary of the Underdogs

BISHOP: Jimmy Lovelace was the drummer, and a New York sax player. You know Jimmy died?

DON: How was he when you saw him?

BISHOP: He was OK, he was playing OK, but you know, he was sick, man.

DON: Well the story I heard from Art was that Jimmy was downtown in Times Square, naked in the winter! And he had been taking acid. Jimmy loved that acid. Yeah, he was out there. Guess they took him to the hospital and he had some frostbite. He had gotten real cold. But anyway, he did a lot of playing in New York and Monty was there.

BISHOP: Yeah, Monty. Does he still live in New York?

DON: Yeah, I think he does. Those are the guys I knew, with you. I knew Monty and Sammy.

BISHOP: Sammy? Didn't Sammy die?

DON: He got hit by a car or something like that. Yeah, that's what BJ told me.

BISHOP: You know BJ is gone?

DON: Yeah, I know he is gone. That hurt. I didn't think I would fee it as much as I did. Lot of people came to the memorial. Lot of people loved him and they feel the same way about you. We have played for years. When I came back, see I went to Fort Worth…. You guys were playing at the Gathering. And I used to come in and sit in with you. Do you remember Carla? Carla was the bass player. Carla Kaufmann; she played with you at the Gathering, the place in North Beach. It's something else now. Who was the drummer? Because BJ was playing the piano and you on alto and Joel Ryan on trumpet.

Bishop Norman Williams

BISHOP: Joel Ryan sat in with us. That was years ago.

ERIC: Yeah, I saw you – you were playing with Joe and Jimmy and Bichu.

BISHOP: Yeah, I didn't know Bichu yet. I met him years later.

ERIC: He was playing in the bookstore with Joel and Bichu and Jimmy and you and Rick Elmore the trombone player.

DON: Well, he's talking about when he went back to New York for the tribute to Charlie Parker.

ERIC: Oh, there is a CD of that, yes?

BISHOP: Yeah, somewhere around.

ERIC: Did you know there was a CD of that?

DON: No.

ERIC: I used to have a copy of it and I might still.

DON: Oh, another guy I thought of – Ben Doris. Remember Ben Doris-piano player? Did he play in your band?

BISHOP: No, not that I remember. Don't remember that name.

DON: Remember Max Hartstein?

A Diary of the Underdogs

BISHOP: No...

DON: Max, Max the bass player?

BISHOP: Who played with him?

DON: Well, everyone, up at the Coffee Gallery; up on Grant. Yeah, Bishop was leading the gig there man. Lots of people came in later, but you were first. Then Pony Poindexter came next.

BISHOP: No, Pony was before me.

DON: And Little Rock, because he was from Little Rock, Arkansas. And Nancy King used to come in and sing.

BISHOP: Nancy King and Sonny King.

DON: Oh yeah, with Sonny King- alto player!

ERIC: They were a couple?

DON: Yeah, they got married. And they had kids and stuff.

ERIC: Where was Sonny from?

BISHOP: He was from L.A.

DON: I thought he was from Texas. Maybe grew up in L.A.-anyway; a great sax player.

ERIC: So who did he play with in L.A. before he got up here?

BISHOP: A lot of people.

DON: Maybe, Sonny Clark?

BISHOP: Yeah.

ERIC: What about Frank Butler?

BISHOP: Frank Butler – he was from Kansas City. He stole something from me man. But then he gave it back to me.

ERIC: Did you know him there?

BISHOP: No, I was too young. I had heard him but I didn't meet him until I went to L.A.

ERIC: So you lived in L.A. for awhile?

BISHOP: Yeah, before I came to San Francisco, 1961.

ERIC: Where did you play down there?

BISHOP: I mostly forget. Hermosa Beach?

ERIC: The Lighthouse?

BISHOP: Yeah. Howard Rumsey.

ERIC: Who played with you at the Lighthouse?

BISHOP: Don't know. That was back in 1961. Then I went to Vegas. Vegas was really slow man. Not a lot of work. People up there, they are sophisticated, you know. They didn't really like Jazz there.

ERIC: Who did you play with there?

BISHOP: I had my own band; mostly guys from there. Then I moved from Vegas to L.A. and then from L.A. to San Francisco. And I have been here ever since.

DON: That's all before I met you?

ERIC: So you went from Kansas City to Vegas?

BISHOP: No, Kansas City to L.A. and then Vegas.

DON: Where did you grow up, in Kansas City?

BISHOP: Yeah, me and Frank Butler.

ERIC: Did you first start playing in high school?

BISHOP: I started in grade school. I bought my first horn when I was fifteen years old. I had me a C Melody and all the kids used to make fun of me.

ERIC: They made fun of you because you had the C Melody set?

BISHOP: Yeah, all the kids used to make fun of me. But then they came and saw me at the best club in

91

A Diary of the Underdogs

Kansas City – the Mardi Gras. They said, oh yeah, we knew him when he wasn't nothing.

ERIC: Yeah, when he was playing that C Melody set.

DON: Did you ever go to the tenor? Ever play tenor for awhile?

BISHOP: No. Just went straight to alto. I started on C Melody. It's like a baby tenor. So after the kids started making fun of me, I started playing baritone. They had a cat named Richard Prank, he was my idol in high school. He is still living. He was my idol so I switched to baritone, then went to alto. He was a senior and I was in eighth grade.

DON: And you guys still hooked up? You connected with him now?

BISHOP: Yeah, when I go to Kansas City.

ERIC: So, did you play clubs in Kansas City before you moved to Las Vegas? Were you old enough?

BISHOP: Oh yeah, I been playing since I was fifteen. My first gig with a cat named Rudy Diamond I showed him how to play the piano; showed him how to play chords. He was a good hustler. He made a lot of money. He's dead now.

ERIC: So, piano, sax, bass and drums, or what?

BISHOP: Yeah. I'm sure he did. Everett Dobbs was a fan. And I was playing alto.

ERIC: Were you playing Be-bop tunes?

BISHOP: Yeah.

ERIC: And people liked that?

BISHOP: Yeah. You know everybody used to go to Kansas City. You know I got to see Count Basie, Lester Young, and all those kind of people you know?

DON: How did you get influenced by Bird? I mean everyone was. But you had a knack for it.

BISHOP: My mother introduced me to *Parker's Mood*. And so I started mimicking that sound on the alto.

DON: You had a knack for it that the other cats didn't have. You got that sound right away, you always had it. Not easy to do.

BISHOP: You got to be practicing. You got to study that stuff.

ERIC: Who was your best teacher?

BISHOP: Leo Davis. He used to teach Charlie Parker in high school. He said, *oh, yeah, I couldn't teach that boy nothing.* So, Leo was my teacher in high school. Charlie had a natural gift. He could read real good and he taught himself how to read. Good ear.

DON: Well, that's interesting. As long as I have known you, I didn't know all that history.

BISHOP: Jimmy Lovelace was a couple years behind me. Like, I was around fifteen or sixteen and he was about thirteen or fourteen, something like that. But I could tell he was going to be a great drummer. He was from Kansas City.

ERIC: Was he part of your band?

BISHOP: See, we played together in high school. He moved to New York. When I got the gig in New York, we played together in New York. But, yeah, I was a couple years older then him.

DON: But he was around here. Remember that band with Monty Waters? He played in that band. Monty was an alto player.

ERIC: And so Jimmy Lovelace eventually came out here? And that's where this band was – Monty Waters?

BISHOP: Well, we all came out here together.

DON: Well, Jimmy played with various cats. But Jimmy was the better of the musicians of the lot because he was a fiery drummer. He was in demand and out on the road. And when he was in town we would get to play with him. But in the Fillmore there was that group of people.

BISHOP: Oh yeah, all kinds of people. We would play all night and the next day; and everyone who came to town and to do Bop City and I was the leader. That was my band for a stretch.

A Diary of the Underdogs

ERIC: And Don, did you play on the bandstand?

DON: Well, I would just sit in. I mainly played with Bishop at the Coffee Gallery. But it was always Norman Williams. I was going to ask you who called you Bishop.

BISHOP: Franzo Keene at the One Man Temple; Coltrane Church, he is the one who made me the Bishop. But I taught him how to play music and that's how he got the church.

DON: It's still going.

BISHOP: Down on Fillmore and Eddy. That's where Yoshi's is.

DON: Yeah, that's where it is. The first time I saw the Coltrane Church was across from the Both/And, on Divisadero.

ERIC: That was later then this?

DON: No, the first time.

ERIC: I think it was on Fillmore first and then went to Divisadero; because I saw it there.

DON: Do you remember Jack's on Sutter?

BISHOP: Yeah man!

DON: And there was an organ player who played there and a guitar player. And it was kind of a happy hour joint. I can't think of those guys names.

ERIC: Organ player? Like a B3 or something?

DON: Yeah. And then we had Soulville. Remember Soulville?

BISHOP: Yeah, Soulville, that was my first job!

DON: Down on McAllister?

BISHOP: Yeah. 1961.

ERIC: So who would play at Soulville? Touring bands, or locals?

DON: Mostly local cats.

BISHOP: Remember Wilber Brown-baldheaded cat? He played so good man, he played so long, would make people mad. Yeah, I will never forget him. He was from L.A.

DON: Yeah, I was working that gig too.

BISHOP: You remember Wilber don't you?

DON: Yeah, I was working Soulville with Joe and Benny Wilson. One night Milt Jackson comes in and he doesn't want to play vibes. He wants to play piano with his fingers like mallets. Played the hell out of the piano-just like it was vibes, it sounded like vibes.

BISHOP: I wasn't there that night. I must have missed it.

DON: Yeah, I think they were playing the Blackhawk. Yeah, he came around and would snoop around. You never saw John Lewis. John Lewis never came out.

BISHOP: He was a teacher.

ERIC: He was in his hotel getting his tie on straight....

BISHOP: He used to be the leader......

ERIC: Yeah, sophisticated cat.

DON: Yeah, it was good. We got to see all those cats. Yeah, just go into Blackhawk and get to see everybody.

ERIC: So what year did Blackhawk operate from?

DON: Oh man when I discover it – it was already going....

BISHOP: Oh, what year you come?

DON: Oh, I started coming to the city in 1960...

BISHOP: You beat me out here. I came in 1961.

DON: Well, that's when we started.

ERIC: We got Bishop at the beginning of the San Francisco circuit.

A Diary of the Underdogs

DON: Well, that's when I started. I was living in San Jose, married guy with kids; crazy about Jazz. I had to come to the city. And I ran into Norman and he said – *you got the gig!*

BISHOP: You remember Hadley Caliman?

DON: Yeah, I do.

BISHOP: Yeah, from L.A. played tenor.

DON: He lives in Washington now.

ERIC: Did you use to see him when you were living up there?

DON: Yeah. And Julian Priester lives up there too.

BISHOP: And what's his name that used to sit in?

ERIC: In Seattle?

BISHOP: Yeah, Seattle; yeah, Vancouver. You go across the bridge and you're in Vancouver. I used to live there....

DON: Well, just had the name, but anyway, it's an organization that promotes Jazz. And that is where this radio station KPLU comes from. And they broadcast just like KCSM does.

ERIC: Was KPOO important in Jazz early?

BISHOP: That was in....

ERIC: KPOO, it's still operating. Did they do a lot of Jazz?

BISHOP/DON: Yeah!

ERIC: Just DJ's, they do any live days?

BISHOP: Maybe, I can't remember, and it wasn't all Jazz, they would mix it up.

DON: The one I remember was KDIA. Do you remember?

BISHOP: KDIA came out later.

DON: Wally Ray?

BISHOP: Yeah, Wally Ray.

DON: Wally Ray, DJ. He used to play a lot of Horace Silver. That probably is the first time I ever heard Horace Silver. That was really great stuff. KDIA and then we had...

ERIC: There was a guy named Kelsey that was involved in KPOO?

BISHOP: I don't remember.

ERIC: I might check on that because I know a woman who was married to him. He is gone now. But he was one of the founders. See what they know. They should have a good history.

DON: Yeah, the media stuff is pretty easy to get. What we can't get is information that Norman can offer.

ERIC: Yeah, some people involved probably know about what was happening. Especially anything that was broadcast live.

DON: Do you remember Brew Moore? Did you ever work with Brew Moore?

BISHOP: From L.A.?

DON: He was around here for awhile.

BISHOP: He was way older then me.

DON: Yeah, he was an older guy. He had a gig out there at the Tropics.

BISHOP: I heard him when I was a kid.

ERIC: Was there a club around here called the Tropicana, on Masonic or Arguello?

DON: Yeah.

ERIC: I think it might be where the Indian Consulate is now. Chuck talks about playing with an Italian tenor player, named, maybe Frank Muzone, or something like that; or Vito Musso?

BISHOP: He played, man.

ERIC: Did he play around here?

BISHOP: And if he did, I wasn't here. I was young; I wasn't but twenty-three. I'm seventy now.

A Diary of the Underdogs

DON: Yeah, but you are sharp man, you still got the Be-bop Soul! Just like all of us, can't get rid of it.

BISHOP: Did we talk about Monty Waters?

DON: Yeah. He was kind of a leader guy. He organized people and he had a band.

ERIC: And he was a tenor player or what?

BISHOP: Alto. I don't know if he is still living or not.

DON: I heard he was in New York, but I don't know if he is living. Art will know.

BISHOP: They were tight!

ERIC: So you remember Art?

BISHOP: Oh, yeah!

DON: How about Smiley Winters?

BISHOP: Yeah, man, Smiley Winters. I think he died.

DON: Yeah, I think he died. I had a gig with him at the Blackhawk; Sunday Jam sessions. He had really happy feet! He was a great drummer.

BISHOP: And left handed!

ERIC: So is he older then you or about the same?

BISHOP: Older.

DON: Got any Philly Joe stories?

BISHOP: No, I never met him. I've seen him with Miles Davis.

DON: Yeah, well he was around here for a little bit.

BISHOP: Yeah, he used to be around here!

DON: He would stay out here. Not sure who he stayed with. He had a lady.

ERIC: What about Miles, did he spend anytime visibly or did he just come and play in the spirit?

BISHOP: He would just come.

ERIC: Come and do his gigs and go back East?

BISHOP: Yeah.

DON: Well, yeah, there are a lot of stories about Miles. He left his trumpet at the Jazz workshop and left early, left town and everything. They had to mail his trumpet back to him. Gig was over for him, you know. And the band played without him.

BISHOP: I met Miles. .... I told you.

ERIC: I remember. It was a dream.

DON: What was that about?

BISHOP: I forgot...

DON: You playing on the bandstand with him?

BISHOP: No, I never did play with him.

ERIC: But in the dream?

DON: What was the dream?

BISHOP: I forgot, man. In the dream he said he was alright. He said everything was fine. When he died that's what he told me.

ERIC: Well, he was probably right. And who is going to question him now.

BISHOP: Like I said, I ain't ever played with him.

ERIC: Did Art Pepper come through here?

BISHOP: Art Pepper come through here.

ERIC: Did you know him in L.A.?

BISHOP: No.

DON: Well, you got a pretty good memory; you got a lot of stuff.

BISHOP: Yeah, I'm seventy!

A Diary of the Underdogs

DON: I can't remember half the stuff – somebody will be talking about something and then just fill it in for me. Yeah, man you are sharp, you got it! Did you ever see Bird?

BISHOP: No.

DON: Never saw him play? I never did either.

BISHOP: I was too young.

DON: Yeah, I knew some people who did. When he came to the West Coast he played L.A. He wouldn't come to San Francisco.

BISHOP: You ever hear John Jackson?

DON: No, John Jackson?

ERIC: Him and Bird were raised up together.

BISHOP: Bird played alto. Bird was in Earl Hines Big Band; and in all the big bands, you know?

ERIC: So you heard him play?

BISHOP: Yeah, I knew John Jackson. I didn't know Bird. We had the same teacher. See I was too young. I wasn't but fifteen.

DON: So, what do you think about where Jazz is today after we have dedicated our lives to it?

BISHOP: Straight out; got a lot of good players.

DON: Yeah, they have learned from us; and from you particularly. You have been a mentor to a lot of cats and an inspiration.

BISHOP: Yeah, well you too! You always have been top man.

DON: Well, thank you! But I knew what you and BJ were doing was a real community thing, you know; at the Gathering, you set up a situation; you played the music, but you invited young cats to understand the music and take away that fear and get them to play and get them to go and love the music and communicate.

BISHOP: Yeah, innovators.

DON: Yeah, you and BJ were really something.

ERIC: Some of those kids are playing a lot now. Like, you mentioned Joel Ryan, yeah?

BISHOP: Yeah.

ERIC: Who else?

BISHOP: Some of those kids are dead, or I haven't seen them.

ERIC: And Ed Kelly use to...

BISHOP: Yeah, Ed Kelly.

ERIC: Ed Kelly used to teach those kids too, right? Like Robert Stewart learned from Ed Kelly.

BISHOP: Yeah, see Robert Stewart was teacher, Laney College.

ERIC: Right, so a lot of them were students not so much on the bandstand.

BISHOP: Yeah.

ERIC: But they took people on the bandstand too.

DON: Well what advice do you have and we will wrap it up.

BISHOP: Study your music.

DON: Study your music, yeah.

BISHOP: Whatever you do, study your music. Put all your effort in it. Got to love what you are doing.

DON: Yeah, that's it, got to love what you do.

BISHOP: Allen Pittman was in my band. And he said, man I'm going to get a record label. So he got me and got Pharaoh Sanders and a whole lot of other people and formed a record company, Teresa Records.

DON: Teresa Records, John Hicks was on that.

BISHOP: Yeah, John Hicks.

ERIC: Yeah, that's right, John Hicks.

A Diary of the Underdogs

DON: That was a San Francisco Record Label.

ERIC: So, Allen comes to the bookstore once in awhile, you can talk to him. So, you put out records out on your own name…

BISHOP: That came later.

ERIC: Pharaoh Sanders, there was a lot of Pharaoh Sanders on his label. And Ed Kelly had a record on his label, and John Hicks. So they played on more than just your record, they played on other…

BISHOP: No, just my record. See they had their own band and I had my band and I used people in my band.

ERIC: Who was in your band? Who was on your record?

BISHOP: Pepper Adams.

ERIC: Baritone sax?

DON/ BISHOP: Yeah.

ERIC: Oh, man! Was he around here?

BISHOP: No, New York, but he came out here for this. They flew him out here and we did a lot of songs.

ERIC: Do you remember the tunes on that record?

BISHOP: Humming….we did *Cherokee*, I think.

ERIC: I got it back at the store. How many records did you press? I mean how many different records did you record? Were there others?

BISHOP: Just that one, Teresa.

ERIC: You do anything for any other labels?

BISHOP: No, I don't think so..

ERIC: But there are tapes around?

BISHOP: Yeah, probably some tapes around.

DON: Well, yeah, that's what they did in those days, tapes and cassette recorders.

BISHOP: See they made tapes; then they would take it and make records off of that.

ERIC: Sort of bootleg stuff?

BISHOP: Yeah, bootleg.

ERIC: You ever get any money off of anything like that?

BISHOP: Yeah, he paid me good. When I needed money all I had to do is call him up and he would always make good.

DON: Is he still around?

ERIC/BISHOP: Oh yeah.

BISHOP: He's back with Betty. Remember Betty?

DON: No, no I don't.

BISHOP: Well Betty and him are together now. That was his first old lady. Now they are back together. He and Betty broke up and then he had a girl named Lois – remember Lois?

ERIC: Yeah, Lois… Lois Kantor - yeah she still comes around.

BISHOP: I think that it is a different Lois.

ERIC: Was she a piano player?

BISHOP: No, she didn't play. So, now he back with Betty.

ERIC: So, he was there for that?

BISHOP: Yeah. Like I said, when I need money, he would come right over and give me some money. He was always good to me like that.

ERIC: So you recorded a lot of Pharaoh Sanders. Pharaoh Sanders was pretty….?

DON: Yeah, from Little Rock.

BISHOP: Yeah, he would come in from Little Rock and then he got the name Pharaoh Sanders.

A Diary of the Underdogs

ERIC: Who gave him that name?

BISHOP: Don't know. He might have given himself that name.

ERIC: We got Duke, we got Prez, we got the Count, we got Lady Day, we got a Bishop, and we need a Pharaoh. That was a good choice.

DON: Yeah. Pharaoh is still going…

BISHOP: But Pharaoh got a chance to work with Duke.

ERIC: Do you remember where that was?

BISHOP: No, that was so many years…

ERIC: Here in town though?

BISHOP: In San Francisco somewhere. He said, hey man, I will never forget, you gave me my first gig.

ERIC: You gave Pharaoh his first real gig?

BISHOP: Yeah. Yeah, his name was Little Rock.

ERIC: So where did he play with you, at Jimbo's?

BISHOP: No, he didn't play with me……I think he… I don't remember.

ERIC: Did you have a tour out here?

BISHOP: No.

ERIC: Always stayed rooted.

DON: That's funny. I never would have figured you came from Vegas to L.A. I never would have figured that!

End: Bishop Norman Williams

Interview: Sonny Buxton-musician, jazz historian, author, broadcaster-jazz club owner-and Pearl Wong-jazz club owner and operator- with Don Alberts and Don Russo, October 28, 2008, San Francisco-about: Pearl's beginnings, Jazz at Pearl's, the Great Eastern, Sonny's Club, Milestones-about: Peter Washington, Chris Conner, Albert Stinson.

SONNY BUXTON and PEARL WONG

DON: I was going to ask you Pearl about the early day of Jazz experience in San Francisco, I think you started out in Chinatown. I was talking to Eddie Duran the other day, and he was the one who convinced you to get started in Jazz.

PEARL: Yeah, he used to come in after the gig and have supper. And so, being in the restaurant business, I would go around the tables and socialize a lot! And I would sit down you know and I got to know Eddie. And so every time he would come in we would talk. And so it happened that the Jazz club on Vallejo Street, Keystone Korner was available. And downstairs in my banquet room nothing was going on because of the economy.

DON: What year was that?

PEARL: 1978, no 1980 or 1982.

DON: Was that on Jackson?

PEARL: 649 Jackson – between Kearny and Grant.

DON: So, was that meant to be a restaurant?

PEARL: Well, downstairs was the banquet room.
I turned that into a Jazz club.

DON: What was the name of it?

A Diary of the Underdogs

PEARL: Jazz at Pearl's!

DON: The original Jazz at Pearl's?

PEARL: That's right!

DON: That was the first one. So did you have an after hours license at that time?

PEARL: Yes, I did.

DON: So you were open late.

PEARL: Yes, we were open till 6am

DON: Do you remember some of the bands that used to come in?

PEARL: Babatundi Lee, Gaylord Birch, Donny Schwekendick, a piano player who went to Japan and got married. He married a Japanese girl.

DON: Okay, I didn't know him.

DON: So, what where the hours, 2am to 6am?

PEARL: Yes. I had an earlier show of course. 8 pm or 9 to about 2am.

DON: So, two bands a night?

PEARL: Yes, two bands; weekends were just after-hours, every Friday and Saturday. Flip Nunez talked me into it. He gave me the idea and so he said go ahead and do it. And so, I did it.

DON: So, at the same time this is going on, Keystone Korner is going on, and so there are some other places in town?

PEARL: We had Kimball's.

DON: That was on Franklin and Gough, that brick building?

SONNY: When did Basin Street close?

DON: 68 or 69, something like that.

PEARL: Yeah, I was at the Great Eastern from 1963 until 1986 with my father. It was on Jackson Street in Chinatown. Then in 1982 I started the Jazz there between Grant and Kearny.

DON: So, how did that evolve into the place on Columbus?

PEARL: Well, I sold the Great Eastern in 86 and I was too young to retire. And I just kept looking and looking for a Jazz club – a real place; and not real food like I had done before at the Great Eastern. I didn't want to do food anymore; previously I had a large banquet menu....

DON: Yeah, that's hard work. But you liked the music?

PEARL: Yeah, I liked the music and I like to do the bar.

DON: Yeah, you made it work and few people can. How did you come upon the place on Columbus?

PEARL: I just found it. I liked the area and I liked the size of the place. But I did not get it right away. Northern Nights got it first. And I was so disappointed when they got it.

DON: What were they?

SONNY: They were a couple of guys who actually didn't know anything about the business. I was really sick at that time and I would walk by there after my treatment, I had cancer, and I would go down to this place called Captain Video, in fact I was with Pearl the first week there – right?

PEARL: Yeah.

Pearl Wong

A Diary of the Underdogs

SONNY: Those guys outbid you – I called you a couple of times and told you that I met those guys and they were two of the biggest fools I ever met in my life. I give them a max of six months.

PEARL: Yeah, they were there only six months. They didn't make it – they were out. They said it was too hard.

DON: What was their venue?

SONNY: They were there to party. They opened it for a Jazz Venue.

PEARL: They did jazz.

DON: Who were some of the acts you had in there?

SONNY: Bruce Forman was one of the acts. And they had a brick wall behind the stage, it looked good. Same look as a matter of fact, Pearl didn't change anything to speak of. They were some minor changes, but basically the same look. But these guys, one of the guys recognized me, I would go walking down the hill to Captain Video, Coppola's building. I'd go down there and get a movie or something and I'd trudge back up the hill and it was all I could do to get back up the hill. So, I started talking to these guys and they really were the two biggest fools I ever met in my life.

Great Eastern

PEARL: When I first saw it, it was dark, there were benches, all this wood, water had leaked into the basement and it was all flooded down there. And I thought, this is going to cost me too much money to remodel the whole place, so I didn't take it – that was one of the reasons why I didn't take it. Then, when Northern Night's came in they remodeled it all themselves. They bought new chairs and tables and things like that. And they didn't last after five or six months and I went and claimed it you know. And I did a little bit, put in new drapes and new stools, and padding over the brick backdrop.

DON: And there was no piano at that time right?

PEARL: No. I got that too. That came later. I had an old piano...and old Steinway that had been in Cookies place. And Sonny went with me to get another piano. We went to Yamaha.

DON: I noticed that you got that piano, didn't you Sonny, and did you have Al Plank pick it out for you or did you pick it out?

SONNY: No, I picked it out and then confirmed the selection with Al Plank. And we were lucky because there had been a convention down in L.A. - a Yamaha convention and they shipped pianos down there and then they shipped them back and had ones that had only been used for an hour, so it was a used piano. So, the salesman was discounting and he was going down the aisle and he would sit and play one and then move to another spot and he would play a little bit. And so I heard that one and it had a rich, deep sound others were a lot brighter. And so I said to the guy, go back to that one over there and he did and it sounded great! And he said do you want to play it and I said I don't play but I can hear! So then we had Al Plank come and play and he said great, great piano! It was different then all the other ones that he had in that size.

DON: So it's a model C5, right?

SONNY: Yeah. It's still there in the place.

A Diary of the Underdogs

DON: So, you guys then became partners?

PEARL: Well, I had two other ladies that were partners. But I was on the lease. They were there to help in case I needed any or got into a pinch. They were wonderful. Sometimes on New Years Eve they would come and help.

DON: So, you were kind of on your own?

PEARL: Well, Sonny helped.

SONNY: Well, we had met at the Great Eastern. And she ran the downstairs.

PEARL: Yeah, I had downstairs.

SONNY: Yeah, you were doing downstairs and I had gone in there because I was hired by the San Francisco Jazz Society to do a Billie Strayhorn night and the place was packed and they had people lined up. So Pearl wanted to know who this guy was. So we sat and talked and she invited me back for lunch. I was working for the U.S. Olympics back then and I said first of all I don't have a lot of time and I don't think you would be willing to pay what I would charge. So, here I am walking back to my car and I'm thinking here are two Chinese women trying to do jazz and they don't know much about it and yet they are still willing to do it. So, I thought it was pretty cool and I called Pearl and said, listen I'll help you and do what ever I can, take care of my parking. I remember I parked down in this little lot, I think it was like $15 or something. And give me a lunch here and there and that's how we started.

DON: Yeah, well it certainly worked out. You guys are really great together.

SONNY: Yeah, that was after the original Great Eastern. Then opened Milestones I would go down there quite a bit and it wound up being a pretty good thing and most of the people that I brought into Milestones…we would close and leave and go over to Pearl's place. So, it was a good profile and as word got out and so and so and Teddy Edwards is going to be over at Pearl's and so on.

DON: Yeah, that worked well. And actually you have quite a story about setting up that place don't you? That's kind of a hard thing to do. I have heard you talk about it before. And then the whole thing came down in an earthquake – right?

SONNY: Yeah, in 1989. That was on 6th Street, there was a lot of rattling in that area. That whole building went down about 6 or 9 inches something like that. So, they red-tagged it which meant you couldn't do anything with it.

PEARL: You guys used to have floods too – down there in the basement….

SONNY: Yeah, when we first opened. We had twin sump-pumps down there and the tide would come in and actually we were pumping for the whole block and I didn't know that but that's what we were doing. Yeah, it was a low spot and the contractors who put the place together, their office was just up on the corner, so like a block n half away, and I used to go up and see the guys for one thing or another, there was always some kind of construction going on, and I went up one time to talk to the principal of the contracting outfit and his partner said – "Oh he is downstairs." "Downstairs?" I knew their downstairs was always in about 6 inches of water, so I went downstairs and it was all dry and the guy had his drafting table set up and everything! I said – hey! And he said, well you guys are doing this – oh, so I found out that we were pumping for the whole damn block! Yeah and so when we first opened we had a flood, I think it was the second night and we had John Handy playing and I had my suit on – my blue suit and tie and everything. Fortunately a fisherman had left some hip boots down there and I put those hip boots on and went down there and turned the pumps on and was trying to get them going and it was hot down there and awful!

DON: So, it was hard to get all that cleared up and get the fire approval and the city's final clean bill of health and get up and running. You started booking name acts right away?

SONNY: Well yeah, but we were taking a lot of heat. It took nineteen months to get the place open. We had one delay after another. The liquor control people stiffed us and put us through a lot of changes. And then the fire marshal made us change the whole design. And then we were open and doing business finally. And then one night, the fire marshals came in – right in the middle of the show – and they are checking for the fire extinguishers which was fine, but the guy calls me over right by the stage area saying one of the extinguishers was in the wrong spot as far as he was concerned, and I said wait a minute – what are you doing here? You want to shut the place down? Then go ahead and do that I'm going to call my attorney, you know, don't come in here harassing me about this. Then he told me that he had heard that there was four-hundred people in there two nights before that. I said look around you – how could I possibly get that many people in here? I said you know people would have been about six deep, nobody would have seen anything, come on, I wouldn't have done anything like that. I asked him who told him that, he said – oh, I don't have to tell you that. So, needless to say we got into a big blowout right in front of everybody – right in front of the stage. So, anyway, he went to talk to Pearl.

PEARL: Yeah, he came to talk to me and I tried to charm him you know…and well, I did it!

DON: Good for you Pearl! Well, you charmed him and you were well established in the city and it made a difference.

SONNY: Yeah, they were being real ass holes about it. There was somebody really out to try and not let that thing happen. Somebody wanted that spot.

DON: Somebody on the street?

SONNY: Well, let me give you an example. After the first delay from the liquor control board, they initially said that we posted to low. The funny thing that was happening was the building was being painted and we had the scaffolding and we posted too high, not too low. And so we did the posting six feet from the level of the sidewalk. And you know you have to post your desire to serve liquor and etc. and so we waited ninety days, you know you have to wait ninety days, and we didn't hear anything from the liquor control board. Didn't hear a word and I am thinking everything is fine. No one had said anything. So we went down to check and they said, well – you are going to have to re-post. I said what do you mean re-post? He said well, you posted too high, has to be eyesight level. And I said, the place is being painted, the city had something to with the painting and everything else and in fact I measured – six feet – anybody can see that! He said, well its got to be eye level. I said, what is eye level? Four feet or what? Anyway, they made us re-post. So, that was a big delay. So, after the next waiting period, a similar thing was happening. Didn't hear anything from them, went to check and they said you got two grievances posted against you. So, there will have to be a hearing and blah, blah, blah…and so I was trying to find out what the grievances and they said well, we don't have to tell you that. And I asked – can you tell me who filed the grievances? Can't tell you that…so, it was at that stage that we went out and hired an attorney, Phil Ryan who was partnering with Willie Brown at the time. So, Phil started getting on the case and then eventually through a bunch of changes…..we got going. But it all caused a big delay and we still didn't have a liquor license. And in my view, construction is going on and money is going out and nothing is coming in. And you are beyond being nervous. I was just sick. Phil had to pull a lot of political strings and apply some pressure and we found out finally that it was some cop who had filed a grievance. So here is what we were told to do – 1. I had to go and canvas the neighborhood within two and half square blocks. To let everybody know what I intended to do – if anybody had a grievance. But first they had to sign this document, well most of the residents around there were Chinese, can you imagine that? All these little apartments…a lot of Chinese! I'm going around knocking on doors and trying to get people to sign. And during the day, of course nobody was there most of the time and so I would go in the evenings and I had to get a couple of friends to go out with me. Nobody wanted to talk, you know.

DON: Wow, this is the story nobody knows. All they know is Sonny had a Jazz club.

SONNY: So finally, Phil finds out….we were told that there were two grievances…one backs out – whoever the hell that one was, never found out who that was – the other one who was adamant about the noise level. So in the meantime, I have a bunch of signatures and I submit the signatures and then we find out that this principal grievance is from a San Francisco police officer. So, then we said, can we talk to this guy. Well they said, not unless he wants to talk to you because he has requested a hearing and the hearing is not scheduled, found out it wasn't scheduled at all. Then we wanted to know when it might be scheduled, well they said, it could be scheduled between now and the next six months. And then I think Phil got to Willie and all of a sudden the name comes out of the officer, he worked in communications and he didn't even live there! He lived in San Mateo. He had a P.O. Box some where under the Bay Bridge. Never found out why he did that and then we went down to have a meeting with the Chief and is this grievance going to be that he is going to drive by and be insulted by the sound or what? So, everyone started backing off and then we got past that roadblock. But Phil was saying, we pulled off some political stuff and now someone is really going to be upset, whoever it is they are trying to prevent you from opening. And so now we get right down to the grand opening and in the meantime the city planning came back in and made us change the whole configuration of the front as we didn't have proper wheelchair access.

DON: Wow, they were really after you!

SONNY: Yeah, so that cost us quite a bit. Then we were going to have restrooms downstairs and they said with proper wheelchair access you are going to have to have an elevator. So then we went out and priced the elevators, the cheapest one I could get was $125,000, so we weren't about to that, so we had to put the restrooms upstairs which eats right into your space. We had nice restrooms and that was a good third of the original space. So that was major. We still had restrooms downstairs for the musicians – not for public. So, the next thing that happens is we are just about ready to open and this is state of the art – acoustic work and all and the sound had to be just right. So we go in for the final license hearing which is at the police department. So, we are waiting and the cop, a sergeant who was in charge of noise abatement comes in, and I'm not giving this a second thought, you know, we had done it all and spent a lot of money, everything was just right and we the acoustic tile up there. And so this guys says in all my years, and I have been a noise abatement officer for twelve years, I have never seen such a poor job of acoustic sound…..and I hadn't slept for two nights trying to get the joint open – it was supposed to open that day! And then Phil said, okay, it's time to call Willie and it's getting close to noon and Phil asked for a continuance for that afternoon. They were just going to shut us down and not let us open and if they said denied then you have to go through the whole process again. So, we requested a continuation for that afternoon and meantime Phil went down the hall to use a pay phone to call Willie and I am standing out there and I saw that cop, a group of cops, standing outside the hearing room and I was crazy and I have just gone nuts. I'm thinking, all this money…might as well just torch it! So, I walked over to the cop and said what the hell is this all about? And he said, I don't have to talk to you, and I said, yeah you do! I was mad! And all these cops they turn and look at me and fortunately the conversation between Phil and Willie was pretty short and there was a hand on my shoulder and it was Phil he was whispering, now don't say anymore! They are getting ready to put you chains man! So, he called Willie and he got it and it just shows you how insidious this stuff is. So we go out and have lunch and come back for the afternoon hearing and its like 1pm or something and we got a couple of massage parlors ahead of us and Phil says hey, look at this, we got the deputy chief standing there and police legal and all these people standing behind us. And this same sergeant gets up before the Board and says, well I can see that Mr. Buxton has put a lot of effort and money into this and he says, wonderful job, wonderful job! Yeah, a little downtown grease! All of a sudden they like me. And the President of the Board says, well, when is it that you intend to open? And we said, well, today, this evening. Oh, this evening? And we said, well, this has been planned for a long time and there have been a number of delays including this morning. So, then they said go downstairs to room, whatever it was, and we got this temporary permit which was good for sixty days so we could open that night. And I told Phil as we were walking from there back to the club, don't you think someone would say, hey, wait a minute – two hours ago you said that it was the worst job you had ever seen in your whole career and now you are saying its wonderful and not one word….

DON: Yeah, they were looking for grease. Willie helped out on that one though. He overrode that – it takes that kind of power sometimes.

SONNY: Then we get back and of course everything is upside down - we don't have all the carpeting down yet and we needed to open that night. We don't have the bar together; the shelves aren't in for the bottles. And its 3pm! So, the guy who is supposed to sign off from planning walks over to me and says this is going to be quite the operation but I can't sign off today. And I said what! What do you mean? I'm off at 3pm and the guy looks at his watch and says, you don't have the downstairs completed. And I said, we were told by the City that we don't have to have that phase done because the customers are not going to be down there besides the rooms are there we just don't have the finishing up. And the guy says well, somebody could go down there and they could get hurt and… and I said, that could happen in any place! Somebody could go out on the fire escape! You can't control that. So, the guy said, well I am off for the day and if I can get back here tomorrow I'll sign this off. And I said, no man, we plan to open tonight. And he said, I can't sign off and you can't legally open. And he's gone! He walks away. And we have all these workmen out there and people are standing around. So, Phil goes inside and calls Willie. About fifteen minutes later this same guy comes back and says, "Mr. Buxton what do you need?" I said, "Just sign those papers; that's what I need." Yeah, so there was this attorney, who had parked his car around there and came in and asked for the owner, and I introduced myself and he said, "When do you plan to open?" I said, "We are opening tonight!" And he said, "I bet you $50 you are not opening tonight." And I said, "Oh, no – we ARE opening tonight! This joint is opening tonight! Come 9pm we are open!" He said, "It will never happen," he said, "You don't even have all the carpeting down yet." And I said, "Come on back," I said, "I will be here for a while, so bring your $50!" We were just barely ready. We had just put the third coat of shellac on the bar the night before and you know it takes a couple of days to dry and you could smell it. I looked at one guy down at the end of bar and he was dressed really sharp and he had his elbow on the bar! Ripped the material off his sleeve! Talk about first night jitters. Yeah, we put shelves in at the last minute behind the bar. Two of the shelves collapsed! We didn't have the rubber runners yet behind the bar yet and bottles of beer on the floor. We opened though, and we opened with Joe Henderson – he played that night.

RUSSO: That was five years before the quake.

PEARL: I told you not to open that night because of the Chinese calendar. I told you when to open.

SONNY: Yeah, you did. We had already missed one opening, so I didn't want to do that again. We had sent invitations out and everything. We had missed the first opening which had been ten days before and I just couldn't do it again.

RUSSO: Did anything happen to Pearl's during the earthquake?

PEARL: No, not really. North Beach is pretty stable. All my bottles stayed on the shelf.

DON: Yeah, its solid rock.

SONNY: Yeah, where Milestones was, that's all landfill. A lot of the City is on landfill. Moscone Center is on landfill. And they have had numerous problems there.

PEARL: I wasn't open then. I was negotiating at that time. I opened New Years Eve 1989.

SONNY: But you had the old place…

PEARL: No….

SONNY: When I had Milestones you still had the old place.

PEARL: Oh yeah.

SONNY: Yeah, because all of us used to come over there.

A Diary of the Underdogs

DON: So, it was working together…

SONNY: Yeah. Both of us fed off of each other.

DON: You had a lot of great acts there, Sonny. And you had a lot of local guys work there to that you mentioned – like Meryle Hoover. Wasn't he was there a lot?

SONNY: Meryle Hoover had Monday nights for a while. John Handy was the house band, after the first six weeks or so, he became the house band. Then Peter Washington developed out of that place. He had only been playing bass for eighteen months.

DON: Yeah, he was the young bass player that came out here and you kind of groomed him.

SONNY: Yeah, he was a student out of UC Berkley and he started playing there. And I was told about this kid by someone and I said, oh no, eighteen months. I'm not going to do that kind of thing. He was adequate. He would come and fill in here and there. And I thought, damn, he's really raw and there were so many tunes he didn't know. But you would keep hearing this steady groove. And all of a sudden he became the regular bass player. I was scared to death and angry about it too, I though that it was really crummy sending this kid in here. I mean he was a nice guy and so I didn't want to just break it off. He started getting grounded and you started to hear a change every night. Every night! He was moving that fast. That was one of the most amazing things I have ever witnessed and in fact I don't think I will ever witness that again. In fact I brought Chris Connor in one time and he had really progressed enough to the point where I thought he could work the gig with her. She needed a bass player and drummer. And I went to Peter and said, look I got Chris Connor coming in the next couple of weeks and you think that you will be ready to handle that? She will do a lot of standards and probably be relatively short in length and so on. And he said, yeah if you have confidence in me. And I said, yeah I'm thinking about hiring Eddie Marshall and you, so I contacted Eddie and he was set for it. So, I was still reluctant. Peter didn't seem to be that sure of him self. And I wasn't sure, you need some arrangement for the singer, you know. So, she comes and we have a rehearsal. And he couldn't have been much worse. He just didn't know the tunes. And so it was my worst fear. And she is gay and her partner who is also her manager from New Jersey, and this woman was in my face – wanting to know what had I done and what did I have against Chris and etc. and I better get another bass player. She was right in my face, like six inches away. And I really wanted to smack her, but then I was thinking, well, I was wrong. It's really my fault and I am the one who did this. So, I said, it's not likely that I will be able to get another bass player for tonight, but I will get somebody for tomorrow. And she said, yeah YOU BETTER – Chris is upset and you can't do this and he doesn't know anything! I hear he has only been playing the bass for a couple of years. Oh, man, I'm thinking, great somebody told her. And that made me really sound silly that I would do something like that.

DON: Did you have a pretty good crowd out there?

SONNY: Yeah, I brought her in two or three times and she was the most lucrative act that I brought in. She attracted a lot of those limousine type gays so you had a mixed bag. You had old fans of Christy, Chris Connor and then you the upper level gays. I've never had so many limos as I did when I had her in the club. So, after rehearsal I told Peter I'm sorry but I am going to have to get somebody else. And then I said, do you have the music? He said he did. I said, look man, go home and do the best you can. Come back tonight. She won't make it hard on you, she has to get through the night too, so lets pull it together, but I am going to have to get someone else. So, he comes back that night, and I said hey Peter, what did you do when you got home? And he says, well, I took a nap…. I mean he was a real innocent young kid…. And I looked at him and I was getting pissed. And I said yeah, and then what? He said, well, I took a nap and took a shower and came here. And I said, "That's it? What was the nap all about?" And he said, "Doug Watkins (now deceased) came to me in my nap. And I looked at him and he's looking at me very straight and I didn't see any strangeness in his eyes or anything and then…" I said, "And then what?" And

A Diary of the Underdogs

he said, "Well he told me how to do it!" And I said, "You feel like you can carry on his instructions and everything is ok?" And he said, "Yeah I think so."

PEARL: I saved all of Sonny's Milestones calendars…

DON: So, tell me how Peter did…

SONNY: So, we get to the show and this woman runs over to me of course what's going on. And I said, yeah I made a couple of calls and I have a couple people on stand-by and it's going to be ok. So, they start and I don't hear anything funny, I'm listening and seemed to be coming along all right. And Chris was very tense when they first started but she seemed ok and it looked like a regular show to me. I didn't see anything strange and I didn't hear anything strange. And I am listening as hard as I can. And then about three-quarters thru the

Sonny Buxton, Pearl Wong, and Vernon Alley at Jazz at Pearl's on Columbus Street, North Beach

first set I see Chris turned in and she was red you know and I'm thinking – what's that? So they get thru the set, no glitches. And then Chris is really relaxed and she is talking to people. So it seems fine, otherwise she would have had him over at the table and they would have been going over stuff. And so they get to the second set and she introduces him and the band, you know the trio backing her and she describes him as darling and she would like to adopt him, I'm going to take him back with me. He rose to the challenge and went right thru all the music. I and I thought, man, I don't know what the hell that was all about. I told him later, I said, are you serious about the Doug Watkins thing. And he said, oh yeah! I said is this the first time he's come to you. And Peter said, oh no, I have called on him a few times; he comes to me and shows me how to do it.

DON: A real spiritual connection!

SONNY: Yeah! And he was dead serious. And I said, Okay Peter, look you are still on the gig, so go on!" (Photo: Sonny Buxton, Pearl Wong and Vernon Alley at Pearl's on Columbus, SF)

DON: Okay, I am looking at a Jazz calendar from Jazz at Pearl's. Saturday, November 10, 1984. Bob Parlocha MC, host Babatundi on drums, Mark Levine on piano and Scott Steed on bass, Wayne Wallace on trombone, plus invited artist Lori Antonelli and Babatundi, Jules Broussard, George Cables, Jeff Carney, Pete Escavedo, John Handy, Eddie Henderson, Vince Lateano, Tricky Loften, Bobby McFerrin, Eddie Marshall, Mel Martin, Eddie Moore, Russell Sedick, Tuck & Patti, Frank Tusa, Don Weed, Cookie Wong and Martha Young. Eddie Moore was this that great big guy, played great drums and really warm….

SONNY: Just before he died, he lost about 150 pounds. He used to come into the club and I said, "Eddie, looks like you are losing that weight way too fast." And he said, "No, I feel good." I said, "Eddie, you can't lose weight that fast." Yeah; and so he died on the bandstand at the old Yoshi's over in Oakland.

PEARL: He played after hours at the club on Columbus.

A Diary of the Underdogs

SONNY: Yeah, he did. So anyway, one night at the club a lady walked up to me and said, "Sonny, did you hear about Eddie Moore?" And I said, "Yeah, he's gone. He was working with John Handy when he died." And she said, "Do you know what tune they were playing when he died?" I said, "Well, NO!" So, anyway I am at the Eddie Moore funeral, there were a lot of people there, it was off of Fillmore in the Haight, so after, everyone goes downstairs, we got a lot of chicken and etc. and Handy is there and I am talking to him and I said, "By the way John, just the other night some lady walked up to me and wanted to know….and this may be a little off, but now I want to know… she wanted to know what tune you guys were playing. And he had this little plate of food in his hand and he started laughing, he was bent over laughing… and he said, "Man, it was the last tune, and we were playing Dizzy's *"Ow,"* and then he falls on the floor! He said, "I looked at him and he was going in sort of slow motion and I thought it was part of the act!"

McCoy Tyner and Pearl Wong

DON: So he actually fell off the drum stool and onto the stage?

SONNY: Yeah, he fell to the side. And he was going over slow! And then there was this crash and John said, "I realized then that this was no act."

DON: What a strange thing, in a Jazz club playing music, what a way to go!

PEARL: Is that the Jazz Society's News?

DON: Yeah. *"Bay Area Jazz Society – Jazz Society at Pearl's will present a Monday night showcase every week. Join us in our new home for some great sounds at Pearl's"* November 15th – Brenda Boykin and the Swiss Movement – Kent Cohea Group with Steve Ture, Carl Garrett Quartet with Pony Poindexter, Sonny Buxton and the Bay Area Jazz Society presents a birthday tribute to Billie Strayhorn, who collaborated with Duke Ellington and composer and artist in his own right. Here is another line-up for December, Jazz At Pearl's – Bobbe Norris, Larry Dunlap Trio, Benny Barth Trio, with Paul Breslin, Larry Vuckovich and Benny on drums. Eddie Duran Quartet; with Al Plank, Dean Reilly, Benny Barth, special guest vocalist Cookie Wong and Sharman Duran. Then we had Nina Cozi and Company, Lane Aires Kurt Fineberg Duo. Then we had Jim Grantham Quartet and Jerry Dodgion and Quartet, with Johnny Markham and John Mosher on bass and John Marabuto on piano. Then Friday the 14th, Eddie Duran Quartet and then Eddie Duran Quartet with Sharman Duran, which is Eddie's daughter.

PEARL: $2 cover!

DON: Here is a calendar for Jazz at Pearls – January 1985. Battle of the tenor sax; with Chuck Clark, Laura Dryer with Jeff Carney, Vince Lateano, Eddie Duran Quartet with Cookie Wong, and special guest, Jerry Dodgion. Sunday jam session with Mark Levine, Hal Stein, Larry Grenadier and Smiley Winters on drums. Farewell to Larry Vuckovich as he leaves for New York, Larry appears with Paul Breslin, Gaylord Burch in a tribute to Sonny Clark. Smith and Gayle Dobson are a extraordinary vocal musical team with

A Diary of the Underdogs

Seward McCain and Vince Lateano, Eddie Duran Quartet again, Lou Levy Trio, wonderful pianist up from L.A. Jam session with Mark Levine, Steve Heckman, Jeff Carney, Ron Marabuto. The Cobb Complex Quintet. This exceptional quintet returns by popular demand with Harvey Wainapel, Phil and Larry Grenadier, Smith Dobson. Jam session with Mark Levine, Larry Douglas Quintet, Martha Young Trio and their All-stars – Scott Steed on bass, Babatundi on drums. Denise Perrier returns from Japan.

RUSSO: Steed worked a lot.

DON: Yeah, he did. It says: Jam Session with Harvey Wainapel, Steve Grenadier and Jeff Carney. Also: George Cables, Bobby Hutcherson Duo, David Friesen Duo with John Stoll on guitar. Then: David Peterson on piano. Bassist Dave Friesen presents a true musical experience in a exclusive San Francisco appearance here at Pearl's. January 1985. Here are some clubs in a Phil Elwood article of 1985, its Kimball's, Bajones, Pearl's, The Great American Music Hall, BIS Concepts, Garden City, Bach Dancing and Dynamite, Wolfgang's and the Kabuki, The Warfield and The Stone among others are now presenting Jazz. It was really going on! *And of course the traditional New Orleans Jazz fans continue to be strong, loyal bunch. Turk Murphy's move to the Fairmont New Orleans Room for instance has proven to be an overwhelming success. And our Royal Society Jazz Orchestra recreating pop jazz of the late twenties and the best such band in the country.* That's a lot of stuff for 1985!

PEARL: I had people trying to tell me to put in rock music but I didn't want to hassle with all the fighting. I don't like that. People tried and tell me to put in Chinese music which I really like but there is all kinds. I didn't want that. So, I figured Jazz would be the nicer way to go. And that is one of the reasons I went into Jazz. And besides, Eddie Duran had helped me with it.

DON: And you had heard from Eddie Duran too that it was good music.

PEARL: And Cookie.

DON: Yeah, it's interesting how you go that way. I was talking with Eric Whittington who owns a bookstore and he said well, people get hooked on Jazz at a particular time in their life. They hear it and they make a decision and it goes into them and that's what they like. When you are growing up and you are a kid and you hear a tune, you figure you are about nineteen years old when you hear it, when you recognize something and you decide that you really like it. But with you – you had other kind of options.

PEARL: Yeah, I had lots of options. My main thing is Chinese music. I like Chinese music.

DON: But you made a life and career in Jazz! And you became important to a lot of other people because of it. You gave a hang out and a place to play. And it was tough.

PEARL. Its tough, but a lot of fun too and I enjoy it, I enjoy every minute of it-operating the restaurant, operating the Jazz club.

DON: You are one of the few people who can operate a Jazz club and make it pay. I can tell you that. We have seen a lot of people try. Okay, we were talking about Albert Stinson he was a great bass player in the area for a while and he ended up with Chico Hamilton.

RUSSO: That's when I met him, he was with Chico, he was in his late twenties, and we were about the same age. The last time I saw him play was with Herbie. That must have been 1966 maybe 1967.

DON: I used to rave about how well he played for how young he was.

RUSSO: Yeah, but age was… now there is sixteen, seventeen year olds, in those days twenty, twenty-one you were considered a young player.

DON: Did he ever play with John Handy?

SONNY: Yeah, he played with John Handy, Bobby Hutcherson, which was all a band. Andy and Bobby Hutcherson – that was in the 60's. Bobby and John fell out during that period and haven't gotten back together yet. They had a falling out. I never knew what that was about. I think it was John's band and Albert Stinson was the bass player. Albert was working with Charles and we were all back in New York and I met up with him at the Apollo Theater. And he was dating Mary Wells, the singer – you know the

A Diary of the Underdogs

Motown girl. He loved Sisters, and every time I saw him he was with some Sister and it usually was some woman living the fast track, you know. Mary Wells used to wear something like three wigs and so we were all standing in the doorway and Albert had this Russian fur on, hat and everything – all bundled up. And it actually was kind of warm. I kept looking at him and he had all that wool on, all that heavy stuff. And Mary is sitting at the dressing table in front of the mirror and she was tucking these wigs in – pushing one side up and pulling the other side up and everything. So, it was a Motown All-star Review and she started whining about it. She said, this is the last R & B gig I do, I'm not singing any more blues! And somebody said, "Well, what you gonna do?" And she said, "I'm singing Jazz!" All of a sudden Albert says, "You know *My Ship*?" And she's tucking her wigs in and she says, "What?" And he says, "You know *My Ship*?" And he says, "Bitch, you can't sing no Jazz if you don't know *My Ship*!" We almost died!

DON: So, Albert was kind of a funny guy too?

SONNY: Yeah, he had a good sense of humor. And anytime I see that tune anywhere, I always remember that.

RUSSO: Herbie came to town with his quartet without a bass player. And Albert happened to be in town. This was 1960's. Anyway, Herbie is throwing this sheet music at Albert and Albert's got this little rickety ass music stand – he was having a rough time with that. But he sounded great. He was a funny guy- kind of sad the way he died. He overdosed on a stairway in New York. I heard in died in Manhattan.

SONNY: I think it was upstate, like Rochester.

End: Sonny Buxton, Pearl Wong, Don Russo

Interview: Larry Vuckovich-jazz musician, pianist, educator-with Don Alberts-November 11, 2008-San Francisco-about: SF State, John Handy, Jon Hendricks, Danny Patiris, Brew Moore, the Tropics, Virgil Gonsalves, Alan Smith.

LARRY VUCKOVICH

LARRY: Bill Perkins, he was part of Benny Barth quintet. Have you ever heard of a trombone player, Fred Murgy? He was one of the greats anywhere! He was not recorded, this guy! He played like JJ. He played so good; it was just one of those things. He and Bill Perkins were the front line. Steve Sidom was very close to Fred. Steve is a winemaker and he sings real nice, he is from days when they sang in the old Sinatra style. Chuck Peterson, you probably know.

DON: He plays at the bookstore.

LARRY: Yeah- and John Coppola who headed the band at the Gold Nugget in the East Bay when they presented the Stan Kenton Alumni. You know Rosolino, Wardell Grey would go there.

DON: Yeah, I know Coppola played with Kenton.

LARRY: Yeah, but the club was run by a guy named Don Rupal. And every Sunday Coppola had Danny Patiris, John Marabuto, Johnny Markham, Al Obidinski, and they would have a special guest either Frank Rosolino or Bob Cooper or Conte Condoli. So what I have here is my history but it covers San Francisco days from the years of the clubs. I have highlighted some stuff for you.

DON: Larry is a long-time musician of the art of Jazz in San Francisco way back into the 60's and even before then. So, you have wanted to talk about the concert at San Francisco State. Was this during the time of the demonstrations?

LARRY: No, it probably was earlier. There was no date. The first time I heard of you was at San Francisco State and with the San Jose band that was a really strong band.

A Diary of the Underdogs

DON: What happened down there was this: Tom Reynolds, Sammy Bobo and Frank Leal had a pretty good quintet and they were getting all the gigs at the college down there in San Jose and we decided we would put our own band together. I think originally it was Gordon Stevens, Tom Kronser, Harvey Leventhal, and Buddy Barnhill and things evolved out of that. And we developed a pretty strong band because of that competition. And so things happened and I think that's how this concert at SF State came about, it was some of those guys and some of that music that we had written for those guys. I was writing a lot then. The instructor, Clifford Hansen didn't know much about Jazz. He would take you up through Classical and then his information just kind of ran out. And so he said, "Just do what you want." So, I just started writing and I was the only one around that was composing.

LARRY: Was this in San Jose?

DON: Yeah, that's how that started. And you knew about Tom Kronser probably before you ever heard him. He was a very brilliant young trumpet player.

LARRY: He became a member of the quintet you could see on Monday's at the Workshop. He and Danny Patiris were the horns.

DON: Who was in the rhythm section?

LARRY: Buddy Barnhill and most of the time it was Monk Montgomery on bass, he lived here, he switched to regular bass. And sometimes it was Eddie Coleman on bass. But most of the time it was Monk. So that was the group. Tom and Danny had their lines down because they lived in the same building on Fulton Street. So, they had their lines down and they sounded great! That was early 1960's or 61. So, let me show you here, Jazz Workshop, Sonny Rollins during the week, Larry Vuckovich Quintet on Mondays. That was 1962. I would do that for a few months and then it would change. It was the kind of things where the bands would come in

Larry Vuckovich

early, like one time Red Garland came as a trio and so we were like, come on... and so I go off and Danny and Tom stayed and the trio accompanied them and that was great. And another time George Coleman was in town early and so he played with them. But I was lucky to get the gig with Tom, believe me. We rehearsed every Saturday. We had some gigs here and there, but the union, you know, every Saturday.

DON: Well, that was San Jose's band, right?

LARRY: Correct, but they would rehearse at San Francisco Union Hall.

DON: I wrote some charts for that band. I wrote two charts, *Moments Notice* and *Minority*.

LARRY: Oh, you did... those guys, the level of playing of those guys was, like my reading was ok to get by, but those guys would bring a huge chart, first time, knock it down.

DON: Yeah, Harvey Leventhal was in that band.

LARRY: Yeah, Harvey was there. They got Danny in the band and Danny and Modesto were the tenors. Frank was on alto and another cat, maybe Rich Henry, trumpets were Coppola, Tom Kroner, the guy who

A Diary of the Underdogs

was at Stanford, and I forgot…he was teaching at Stanford, but he was a trumpet player and then Forrest Becktell was a trumpet player too. And Carl Ladley was in the trumpet section. The band was real strong. In fact when I was working for Mel Torme he needed something to be heard because he wrote for big bands so he came to our Saturday rehearsal and Wally Hyder recorded the rehearsal and so the band played these charts easy.

DON: So, this band you are talking about started in San Jose as a rehearsal band at the rehearsal hall in San Jose, because that's were I first found them- local 153.

LARRY: Yes. Monty Budwig was the bass player because he played with Vince; (Guaraldi) he was living here so he and Tom Reynolds was the rhythm section. And Tom Reynolds, and that cat, he liked to live in style! He would go into a gig with a big band. So we were in a car and Tom and I were in the back seat and Tom wanted to drink champagne and so we went to a liquor store and Tom said…no paper cups or plastic, I want a real glass. So they gave him real glass and at the same time he had eye drops to clear his eyes, you know he was smoking shit and drinking and putting these eye drops in his eyes… And we also had Chuck on tenor too…Chuck and Danny. So the band was really exciting.

DON: So, they started rehearsing at….

LARRY: Local 6. Because a lot of guys lived here, it was a combination of San Jose and San Francisco.

DON: Wasn't Dent Hand in that band or was that later?

LARRY: Yeah, I think Dent also played in that band.

DON: So, Dent played with Paul Robertson probably…

LARRY: Yeah, I think he did.

DON: So, this band, it was a great band but didn't have many gigs.

LARRY: Here and there. You know, because like Today, who is going to hire a big band for decent money. One time we played a dance at Jack Tarr Hotel. And John Coppola was playing at these regular gigs at Moulin Rouge on Broadway, a strip place. That was the only one of its kind on Broadway, not like Today, garbage. People would dress up in suits and they had an MC and all the ladies were beautiful. So anyway, Coppola couldn't leave and so Alan Smith comes, without a rehearsal and he just…BOOM…shit, just cuts it. So anyway that was one gig and some of the other gigs I forgot, some big convention or some shit. That was early 60's.

DON: So, how did that evolve through the Jazz Workshop? What was going on there?

LARRY: Well, lot of local guys were involved and what happened was the owner, Art Aurbach who was our attorney, opened a place on Market called Jazz Showcase, it might have been the Down Beat or one of the Jazz Showcase and it had some big bands playing there. But somehow he got this place on Broadway, the Workshop and he moved there.

DON: So, before the Jazz Workshop?

LARRY: The place on Market….

DON: But wasn't there a place down there called Fack's?

LARRY: Oh yeah that was separate. OK, let's go through this. Some of the clubs I didn't highlight are from the 40's or 50's. But I highlighted the 60's. Bop City was still going and the Blue Mirror on Fillmore, New Orleans was an older place. And then Jackson's Nook was still happening and then Jack's on Sutter then the Black Hawk in the Tenderloin and then on Broadway you had the El Matador across from the Workshop, Basin Street West on the corner. Across from Basin Street West was Sugar Hill. Sugar Hill was mostly a vocal place, with Joe Williams and even Redd Foxx, Shirley Horn, Carman McRae. And then on Kearny, before going to Broadway in the middle of the block you had a small supper club, next to Tomaso's. Jerry Granelli had a trio. I was working with him and John Mosher and then Mel Torme opened the place and soon after Jerry joined Vince Guaraldi and they were playing on Broadway at a club and it might have been Ann's 440 and Jerry came back and said that Miles walked in and he needed

A Diary of the Underdogs

a piano player and he asked Vince and Vince turned him down. And whatever the reason was – he was getting going with his own trio…or didn't want to deal with Miles. I don't know.

DON: Yeah, that's a wild story. Same thing happened to me. I turned down Cal Tjader.

LARRY: Wow, well talk about lessons. After I worked with Mel Torme, we had a good relationship we played in San Jose too, at the Safari. So he calls and along the 280 there, Seramonte, there is a place, it's still there, I got my first gig as a leader, trio with Bob Steel – Do you remember Dick Fudge? A drummer, he got killed. So, I got the trio and Mel Torme calls, come back to town, he's got some good gigs, and I didn't know what it means to set this up in those days, for my gig. I was afraid to lose the gig and I blew the connection. But I learned the lesson later. Anyway, you turn a corner and you go to Grant, Coffee Gallery was there. And a place called The Place. That was a little place where Dave Van Crete the tenor player, Jerry Goode played, they had a Jazz. Remember the Jazz Cellar?

DON: Yeah, Jazz Cellar, Bill Wejohn …

LARRY: Bill Wejohn and Sonny Wayne and they had a concert which was every month, they would feature a guy. Harold Wiley, Brew Moore, Pony Poindexter. But one night I walk in there and they asked me to play, I was just learning stuff and so I go to play there is Lenny McBrowne on drums and Eric Dolphy and I was studying with Vince and Vince just showed me the alternate changes, the Cycle of Fourths, Cycle of Fifths and F Sharp and B, E…so, Eric Dolphy starts playing and I pick that up, and if he hadn't shown me I wouldn't have known.

DON: So, that's interesting, that happened at the Cellar? And the house trio was Bill Wejohn, Sonny Wayne and Max Hartstein. Yeah, Bishop Norman Williams talked about Max.

LARRY: He was a swinging bass player man; he recorded with Brew on another album.

DON: So, we have Brew Moore, Pony Poindexter, Leo Wright, Harold Wiley the great tenor sax player.

LARRY: These guys sat in and the same night, Charlie Haden and Scott LaFaro are sitting in the audience.

DON: Those were the days when San Francisco was just like New York and they came looking for cats, they came looking for us, they were like, "Where do you guys play man, where do you play?"

LARRY: Philly Joe needed a trumpet player and he hired Mike Downs.

DON: That's a sad story; Mike didn't make it back from New York.

LARRY: Yeah, sad story. And then the Copa Cabana was a Latin club on Broadway. And then I mention here somehow, Black Hawk Jazz and poetry, Chambers Jazz Sextet, Allen Ferguson. I was listening to the poetry and I didn't know what the fuck they were talking about. And then the Cellar had poetry too, then the Hungry I of course. And Danny Patiris told me that Enrico booked Virgil once because he knew theater. So everything was done like a real show. They would do *Senor Blues*. So, everything was dark, the lights go on the bass and the hands of Eddie Kahn. So, anyway, Virgil played there too and Eddie Duran and Vince, they had a trio there. And of course, besides all the singers, you know Steve Sidon, the singer, what he told me, he was there, when Jonathan Winters kind of flipped over there and went down the street to direct the traffic – he said what happened was amazing and I never knew, was that Banducci took a violin and played the most beautiful violin and everything got calm. Winters might have been on the street but the audience was all tense, but he played violin solo and just calmed everyone down.

DON: Ok, so moving on. That is a great list. Chinatown- Jon Hendricks?

LARRY: Jon Hendricks, they all played there, besides all the singers and all the comics who came through there. Then in Chinatown…Remember Ross Alley, off Washington? Mr. Lucky's, Flip Nunez and Mike Montana used to play there. I would stop sometimes. And Buddy Rich was across the street Dick Vartanian played there. Then China Smiths had the father of the piano players, Leonard Thompson, Rex Thompson, that's where he would play. Then there was the Macumba, remember that?

DON: I remember the Macumba. I can't get anybody to talk about the Macumba.

LARRY: I was there several times. Kenton's Band was there…..

A Diary of the Underdogs

DON: I saw Carman McRae there.

LARRY: Yeah, they had all the great Jazz. Tjader was there, Basie. Kenton came, remember the Contemporary Concepts Band? Pepper Adams, first time he came that's where they played. The whole band, the big band, Mel Lewis and I had never heard of Pepper Adams, he was ripping all that East Coast shit, you know, so anyway that was Macumba. And then the Tenderloin, Streets of Paris, Coffee Dons. I played there.

DON: Don't know that.

LARRY: Don't know it either but I knew of it. That's where Harry James and Mel Torme big bands used to play.

DON: Across from the Streets of Paris?

LARRY: It was in that area, the Tenderloin. I don't remember. Some of the older guys might know the address. These are the 40's and 50's. OK, now, there was a place... the DuPont's son, have you ever heard of a place in Palo Alto called the Outside at the Inside? Well the son, Michael DuPont, he liked Jazz he opened that place first. You go inside; you go to the roof and its outside. So there is Jazz mainly in the summer. When I was studying with Vince, in 1960 or late 50's actually, Vince Guaraldi, he was showing me a lot of stuff on the records, so I was learning you know and he went out of town, so he sends me to sub, remember vocalist, David Alley? He was mostly a ballad singer, and Irene Krall...a beautiful singer. So I go there and I guess I go through it.

DON: Irene Krall?

LARRY: Yeah. She sang there. We did a week with her and a week with David Allyn.

DON: Wow, so you played with Irene. She was one of the most outstanding singers.

LARRY: She was! And she said, man, you learn fast but one thing I didn't know, she finishes the set, Jerry Goode, Hank Uribe and I are sitting there and she goes off to her dressing room – *"those stupid mother fuckers! They didn't play the chaser."* I didn't know what a chaser was. Well that's how you learn. Then the Tropics; that was on Arguello and Geary.

DON: That got advertised a lot by Pat Henry, he pumped that up pretty good on the radio at that time. So what about the Tropics, tell me who played at the Tropics.

LARRY: The house band was usually John Marabuto used to play but then they changed and they had Cedric Heywood who became a regular guy. He was a regular but Glenn played drums and then on bass they would have John Mosher or Jerry Goode. But then Harold Wiley and Brew, the two tenors were there. They played really well together, just swinging. But what was so great about it was that any great guys in town would look to go there. Dizzy would come. Lou Levy would sit in; different instrumentalists. They had a good reputation. One time I am there, Ornette Coleman and Don Cherry come in, they didn't know who they were so they said go ahead and play. They kicked off a blues, they played a line grouped together and they got into a little shit, you know, and I didn't know what was going on and I could tell that they knew what they were doing you know. But I wasn't quite clear on the concept as I am now. After one tune they told them to get off. That was a traditional swinging place.

DON: Yeah, well Eric Dolphy fit in ok and he wasn't quite that far out.

LARRY: No not quite, because Eric Dolphy could play Charlie Parker. He could really get down, studied and stuff. So that was the Tropics.

DON: In the late 50's early 60's we got one called Easy Street.

LARRY: Easy Street was in Fisherman's Wharf. They had shows like Louie Jordan and Basie and Red Norvo Louie Armstrong and Mel Torme. They had a lot of shows. And then Pier 43 had the traditional music going. And this was earlier then the one I was saying, Jazz Showcase, there was one in Oakland too. But I am sure the one on Market was also called a Showcase, somebody will remember. Then Gold Nugget was the place; that was Oakland, that was Don Rupal who liked Kenton and then he would have guests. Kenton Alumni, Al Porcino, Conte Condoli, Zoot Sims, Mel Lewis, they would be the guests. In the Mission there were two clubs, The It Club and then I had the same quintet I was playing with, the two owners were called Charlie, two Charlies. The Two C's. Benny Barth played there...30th and Mission. It was a listening room. Remember a trumpet player, Tommy Loki? He was there and then he left. He was on the scene then, really nice trumpet player. Then there was Tin Pan Alley with Bernie Kahn. He played with Connley Hall. Tommy Beason was the rhythm section.

DON: Yeah, lots of people talking about Connley Hall, lots of stories. I talked to Frank Passantino the other night and he said, oh yeah! Connley Hall, I should tell you some stories about him. Like the night we went to the gig and he left his bass drum on the sidewalk!

LARRY: He would follow Art Blakey. Art Blakey was this guy with the big high hat.

DON: Remember Mambo Gardens?

LARRY: That one I don't remember.

DON: We used to play Santa Cruz in the summertime. Connley Hall had that gig too. Frank Morgan.

LARRY: Yeah that was the early days, Frank Morgan played there – that was early 50's.

DON: Palo Alto – you talked about that.

LARRY: Yeah, Vince had a trio there and they would have Spoon (Jimmy Witherspoon) and Ben Webster there. The same DuPont, the old man, never came around, it was on Bush. In the old days, above it was the Coast Recorders, later it became the Boarding House. John Mosher had a trio gig – they would book Duke's band, Carman McRae, different things, John Mosher had a trio gig to play in the Mission, opposite Duke Ellington so he hired me and that was the first time I heard the band up close. I liked Basie, but I could hear all the colors of Duke. And listening to that for two weeks, man, shit! It will change your style. On the opening night Brew Moore was with us, they played *a Blues* in C and so I am playing a solo and the trumpet starts rifting behind me, so Duke comes in after and he said, *"Well, if you haven't noticed I have a swinging piano player and my guys drowned him out."*

DON: Did you catch Duke at Basin Street West?

LARRY: I didn't hear him there but they have videos of those shows.

DON: I see you have Fack's listed here, do you know anything about Fack's?

LARRY: Well there is Fack's One and Two. The Fack's on lower Market, the High Lows were there and Vernon used to play there plus the bass player Jack Weeks who was a good arranger. You know the record Cal Tjader has with strings? Jack Weeks arranged that. He accompanied the High Lows. Then there was Fack's Two, which was on Bush, I think. Remember Gus Gustavson, the big drummer? The story that Danny told me was that Gus played with Stan Getz in the 50's at the Black Hawk. Getz got him for $200. You know when guys were famous – younger guys would be foolish enough to loan them money. So, Gus kept after him for years and he saw him at The Trident, in Sausalito, ten years later. So he said Stan, what about my $200? And Stan says, oh, you're the idiot that gave me the money! And Gus picks him up like a sack of potatoes and throws him in the Bay! Yeah, that's Gus. I liked playing with him.

DON: I played with Gus because I had a little gig in San Jose. I called John Handy to come down but he wouldn't come down, he couldn't believe there was anybody in San Jose playing Jazz. He would not come down, he said, I am a Jazz player, do you realize who you are talking to? But I did get Gus and I said, I did get Gus, he's going to play with us. But John wouldn't come down, he didn't know any of us, we were young guys. Of course later on we got together with John.

LARRY: Well John was upstate when I was there. We were going to school at the same time. He knew all the guys from New York. Milt Jackson would come. I would pick up the other guys....Willie Bobo and Larry Gales were playing at the Black Hawk with Herbie Mann so I would pick them up and we would go and play. They had a gig at night and they would go and play during the day! Another time I went to pick up Mickey Roker, and Bob Cranshaw who were playing with Joe Williams. So Handy would organize all this stuff you know. Because they knew John they would come to the school.

DON: Is this before John went with Mingus or after?

LARRY: After. John came back from New York and wanted to finish his degree.

DON: Yeah, that was a great time. Who were some of the instructors at that time?

LARRY: Well, there was no Jazz, really man. The only cat that was teaching Jazz History was Wayne Peterson. I studied classical piano from him. He used to play with Ray Anthony's big band. There was no jazz theory or anything. Handy took over the big band and as far as I know that was it. Later, Bennett Friedman was given the gig too, to teach arranging. Handy was the guy who got things going. Now they have Andrew Speight. It's a very good program now. One time Handy and I are in one of the practice rooms and the trying to work some stuff out and the head of the instrumental department, he was like a Nazi tyrant, he comes in and he said, *"This is reserved for serious music!"* And John said, "W*e ARE serious!"* What an asshole man, but that is how it was.

DON: Yeah, that was similar to schools in San Jose.

LARRY: What the other guy did is because he played clarinet, he brought in Buddy DeFranco because DeFranco played so good.

LARRY: Bill Perkins, sax:….

DON: Is that the Bill Perkins that was in L.A. all those years?

LARRY: No, the L.A. Bill Perkins is called L.A. Bill Perkins. This one is called Denver Bill Perkins. The poor guy has Parkinson's. He played really good, man. Anyway; Bill Perkins in the East Bay, the tenor player who played with Benny Barth and Fred Murgy.

DON: Yeah, I called Virgil a couple of years ago and told him I was back in the Bay Area and we talked briefly. In fact all of us called, Art Lewis and Don Russo. Because we had all played together in Monterey, we had that quartet for a long time. And so we were all surprised to hear this.

LARRY: How did he sound?

DON: He sounded a little weak and a little spacey. One of the things he said was that he did the final tour with Cream. Even though it was no connection to what we did, it was big stuff and he was very proud of it. I got the impression that he wasn't doing too well and maybe in a wheelchair or something. I didn't ask.

LARRY: I heard that too. He was what in his 80's when he died?

DON: Yeah, he was a little older then us – probably five or six years older. But I had a good time with him. He's is in this book, but I published this with the real names and then I realized that was not the thing to do. So, I changed all the names. It's a fictional story based on reality. Did you know Eve Jackson in Carmel? We all stayed at her house…

LARRY: I didn't know her.

DON: Yeah, it was quite a scene there. Stan Getz, Chico Hamilton.

LARRY: Was she like a patron of the arts?

DON: Yeah. She was divorced from a Navy Captain. She loved Jazz and she loved musicians.

LARRY: Brings back a lot of memories. With Jon Hendricks, while on one of the East Coast tours in 68, the band was; myself, Benny Wilson, Art Lewis and Monty Waters. So we played in Boston and then we were going to New York and we were on the Pennsylvania Turnpike, this fucking racist cop stops the car and sees all the black guys and me. They had to go pay a fine, the last of the money they had. What a motherfucker man!

LARRY: All the guys you mention, when we used to hear them in the clubs, they played with such feeling and soul. Today, you have a lot of good players too; the only difference is that it is a little too clinical.

DON: That's what I hear and think too.

LARRY: See, those guys didn't come from that shit. They could hear it, but they rely on clinical knowledge and not music knowledge.

A Diary of the Underdogs

DON: Yeah, if you could get a book of chords you were lucky. There were no voicings, nobody showed you anything.

LARRY: Yeah, you just had to listen. In the old days I had a turntable that could play 33 and 16, so I would slow it down to 16 speed and learn stuff that way. And that is what a lot of people did.

DON: Yeah, well we took things off the record... that is what we had to do. And that was the only way we got it. And you go to the jam sessions and some guys ears are a little better then yours and he already has it figured out and you haven't got it yet. You gotta go back to the record and come back and you're playing a new Miles Davis tune! We really valued that because we worked so hard to get it. It was communication; you could talk to a musician about the tune and not know anything about him or not talk about any other thing about life except the song and the guy give you everything he's got.

LARRY: When I first met Red Garland before he came to play on a Monday night, he had brought his trio and later I got to know him a little bit and I said Red, how do you voice your chords? He said, *Well the left hand you have E Flat, F sharp, A and D. With the right hand you have F, B, D and F.* I came home and I said oh shit, that is a little bit slicker then a regular voicing. I remember I was so excited, I had figured it out on my own, those changes and voicings on *So What*. I used to live here, that was my small room there. My father and mother were there and my brother downstairs. So I figured those fourth chords and some shit was so exciting to figure out by yourself! When Danny and I were playing with the band, Coltrane is playing during the week, so we see McCoy sitting on a break and we say, McCoy what are those changes to *Body and Soul*? Those alternate changes. He takes a napkin, breaks it out. Very down to earth guy; he just wrote it down. It was a very exciting time. There were so many interesting events and nights. The Tropics had those guys playing, mostly on Sunday afternoons, then the owner said, I want to get that band here on weekends, Friday and Saturday and bring dancing, so expand it. And so the place is doing pretty good and so I called Ralph Gleason of the Chronicle to help the place, he said there is Jazz and dancing at the Tropics. They didn't have a license and the IRS jumps on them and the guy had to stop and it killed the dancers, they wouldn't come. So, I had the last trio gig there on Sunday, Eddie Coleman, myself and Bob Gland and no more dancers so the business went down and on a Monday night we came to play also and there is a padlock on the door. But anyway, one Sunday afternoon we are playing there was Wes Montgomery sitting there. We said, hey Wes you got your guitar? He said yeah, it's in the car. So talk about hearing, we do a medley... and I said ok, we are going to do *Autumn Nocturne*, not a typical tune. And Wes never played it before, or not much. Man, he played all the right shit behind me. Like Monk Montgomery would be playing Monday nights, Danny would bring the changes, like Sonny Rollins recorded that piece, you know *My River* and so he brings the changes and the Montgomery brothers didn't read, they didn't want to see nothing man, so Monk says just play it once, he played it once and he got it. In the record studio, Jon Hendricks was saying when Montgomery Brothers played they didn't want to see no music. Gleason mentions in his column that Miles asked him to go with him or Coltrane and that he didn't know where to go so he formed his own thing. I heard Wes Montgomery sit in with Coltrane, they were playing *My Favorite Things*, in either E Minor or E Major, so Coltrane and McCoy all the pentatonic and polytonal all over the place and Wes is not doing that, he's playing in just one key but he is playing all this beautiful shit. It was such a contrast to what they were playing. Jon Hendricks said that Miles, none of those guys liked to fly, they were scared to death of airplanes, so Miles hires Buddy Montgomery to go to Europe to play vibes. He is on the plane and the plane is getting ready to take off and he looks out as he is taking off and there is Buddy running down the runway! He just couldn't get on the plane. So Miles had to go without him.

DON: Well, Miles came to San Jose for a rare concert and Buddy Montgomery was with him and he was playing vibes. And Keith Jarrett was playing piano. And Coltrane was there of course, but Coltrane was still trying get those dual harmonic notes and so all he did was that all night, screech..... And San Jose was

A Diary of the Underdogs

looking like a bunch of bumpkins because nobody turned out to see Miles. I paid $25 for a reserved seat in the front row and there is a bunch of kids sitting there with their feet up. Miles still played.

LARRY: Coltrane liked to experiment, that probably was his later period, probably a lot of LSD and shit.

DON: Tell me about Black Hawk – I've seen Miles at the Black Hawk a number of times.

LARRY: Well, the Black Hawk was….. I came to San Francisco in 51, and then I was in school and I lived in the Haight, and then in 53 I think we moved to this house and so Lincoln High School is right up the hill. So Vince Guaraldi was there before me, it was the late 40's…it was an artistic school. The other people who went there were Abe Battat and then the actors like Barbara Eden and my classmate was Joan Blackman, the one who was with Elvis in the films, but she sang, her father was a union musician. You might have seen her in Blue Hawaii, she was in other films as well, she was very pretty and she sang good. She is still around. Then, this is before your time, I don't know if you have ever heard of Bruce Tennet, bass, he was in the same class. He had a great ear. He was studying with Jerry Coker.

DON: Yeah, Jerry was doing a lot of teaching in those days, Jerry was giving up a lot of the information.

LARRY: So, Bruce was learning all this shit from him. We had a quintet, vibes, guitar, piano, bass and drums. So, later, we didn't have a Jazz program but because of an instructor, Dr. Gordon, who had a classical string quartet, but also loved Jazz, he made practice and everything. So that is where I went to school. So I started going to the Black Hawk in 53, 54 and I heard the original MJQ with Kenny Clarke on drums. I got to play with him in Europe, great drummer. Back to the Black Hawk, Dizzy was there, Oscar Peterson Trio and then I would be listening to Cal Tjader with Vince and the great Latin players. And there was a hell of a Cuban tenor player, Chobo Silva. I never heard a Cuban play Jazz like that. This guy played like Lester

Larry Vuckovich

Young, Stan Getz. He was great, he is on a record called *Black Hawk Nights*. And then there was Miles, the first Miles I heard was with him and Coltrane. But what stayed with me the most was the rhythm section. Coltrane I didn't remember much, I wasn't quite opened up yet. And then when Miles came with those live albums he did with Hank Mobley, I got to hear more. And Miles would come with Victor Feldman and then with George Coleman and it was all exciting. Another interesting thing is Stan Getz would come to town before he had his own group, later, like when *Bossa nova* hit he could have a steady band, and then he would have Gary Burton and whatever the band was. But at the Black Hawk he would come with L.A. guys, Leroy Vinnegar and Carl Perkins. And another time he came with Roy Haynes and Scott LaFaro, and then the Jazz Workshop would feature horns before Sonny Rollins with Jim Hall, he came solo. One time I am listening to him with Scott LaFaro on bass, the drummer, Lenny McBrowne and Elmo Hope. What a band, that's how it was man! And then Johnny Griffin would come with a mix of guys, before he had the band with Lockjaw. And then one time Buddy DeFranco came as a single and he had Lonnie Hewitt, wonderful piano player. And later Cannonball had his band with his brother.

DON: I always liked those early Stan Getz records. He was so swinging; Jimmy Raney on guitar, Al Haig on piano. One time I went to the Black Hawk and saw Sonny Stitt with Miles.

LARRY: That's the band I heard too! J.J. Johnson was playing with that band.

DON: And Miles had some kind of conflict going with Sonny, probably something over a lifetime. It was always there and you could feel it. So, I happened to go to the bar and there was a spot at the bar and Miles jumps off the stage and elbows his way into the bar next to me, and I said, hey Miles, sounds good. And he says, listen to that shit! Listen to that shit, that motherfucker does that shit all the time! And I thought it sounded beautiful.

LARRY: Miles wanted to hear some new shit. That's the way he was. From what I heard Miles was always into something new. And you would play something old and he would be like, what the fuck, man! In the 60's I lived in Calistoga near Cobb Mountain and I played at some of the resorts up there. I played at Forest Lake Resort with Bob Steele and Billie. Cedar Springs had a traditional Dixie Band that was very good. Yeah, so we would be playing there in the summertime.

LARRY: Yeah, so we played summers there and one summer, I did a different gig. Remember Russian River, Rio Nido, Dick Crest used to be there, so you mentioned Al Molina, Al Molina and Bob Dominguez had a gig across from Rio Nido at the River Club. The Armenian Family owned it. Bob Steel and I and Bob Dominguez and Al Molina are renting a house we played there for a month, in this place, real nice. And Mike Downs came back from Philly with Philly Joe, East Coast, so he meets this chick in Russian River and Bob Dominguez had this old Plymouth and loans it to him. And Mike Downs crashes it, stoned. And he comes back all bandaged to the club, we are playing, and he was in the emergency and he says to Al can I borrow your trumpet and can we play a tune? And he played *I Thought About You*, and he played so beautiful that tears are coming down Bob Dominguez's face. He forgot all about the car, he had played so beautifully.

End: Larry Vuckovich

Interview: Donald Duck Bailey-musician, legendary drummer- with Don Alberts-November 19, 2008-at Bird and Beckett about: Philly, Bud Powell, Max Roach, Un Poco Loco, Bebop, Jimmy Smith, Peggy Lee, Jimmy Rowles.

DONALD DUCK BAILEY

DONALD: I am supposed to be a so-called visionary.

DON: Well, you are man.

DONALD: I haven't had one thing that I can remember that supports that in a way, say we are talking about Max Roach, say we are talking about people that have money, do they say, hey, how is Max doing? Is he ok? Is there anything we can do to help- make sure he is not suffering? And the cats that got money, they should support him. That's the way I feel.

DON: They are starting to do that in a little bit in New York, I hear. They are providing housing and concern for musicians.

DONALD: I have been here for like twenty-seven years and I have received some support by people I know, but I haven't go nearly the amount of support that I feel like I should have if I had been another person on the same planet. I don't get any gigs and I don't go after gigs but I said well, what's the use of being famous? I never went after being famous. Well, what good is it-I'm walking around like the every day cat?

A Diary of the Underdogs

DON: Yeah, but you deserve a lot more then you ever got. And I know what you are saying and it's not a complaint it's just the way it is.

DONALD: Yeah, just the way it is and cats need to be ready for that. People might think the best of you but you might not get any material benefit. You might get respect and that means a lot to be respected.

DON: It does, to be respected and accepted.

DONALD: Being respected and accepted means a lot to me. It really is a great feeling to walk in some place and be respected.

DON: Well, I have gotten over the feeling that there is going to be a bunch of money. I let that one go, because it's not going to happen. It's not going to happen, even selling CDs and stuff. But it's just not the reason anymore, the money. I just want respect like you want respect and respect is to give me some money for my work.

DONALD: I think too that a lot of producers and whatever, they pay you as much as they can because they don't get anything from it. Like several club owners I know now that keep the club open and still pay the musicians some money, like every night. And there is like nobody who comes in this club. I been in this

Donald "Duck" Bailey

club, playing in this club like twenty times and I have never seen anymore then two or three people in there. I don't see how he keeps the club open. But he does because he has the passion. The passion is to keep the club open and to keep it nice and it's available. There is a guy who wrote me from Germany, his name is Alan Blairman. He is a drummer that I met when I was with Jimmy Smith. This would have been about fifty years ago man! I met him when he was about fifteen in Pittsburgh. And he came in with his father to the Hurricane Club. He was just little guy and his father said he had been playing drums. So I let him sit in with Jimmy Smith. He was like a young Tony Williams I would say. I hadn't heard anybody play like that. So, when Tony Williams came up with Miles, I thought that was him! And I wondered if that was him, because I didn't recognize him and I had forgotten his name. And so, he called me up about six months ago and we been having these great conversations and he never forgot the fact I let him sit in with Jimmy Smith and he remembered all this stuff that me and Jimmy was playing together. You know, rhythmically and stuff and he said he never forgot it. And that it inspired him to play and I am his mentor like Max is mine. I have heard a lot of great drummers. But Max Roach for me....is like it. First it was Gene Krupa. I bought my set of drums and then when I heard Max Roach, I said man, I really wanna play the drums! I mean we hear it now, but there was nothing like it. It was so modern. Lot of bass drum and straight ahead and it was great! He was such a great drummer. It was Cozy Cole, Big Sid Catlett, and all those cats. I had seen all of them. I had seen them on the stage of the Earl Theater in Philly. But for some reason it was Gene Krupa that made me say I wanna get some drums. I was about maybe twelve years old. I went to Junior high school and me and my wife at that time, which we were married for twenty-five years, and I quit school and I been playing music ever since. This was in Philly. I used to go to a day job and then go to the gig, day after day. And then when Jimmy Smith got me, we were together for about fifteen years or something like that. And I have been on the road going from country to country ever since. It's amazing and it's amazing I never made a lot of money! It was just week-by-week. It wasn't like you had a big bank account where you could say, I can take off for a month and lay back and rest with my family. It wasn't like that. Because I never signed any papers that would take care of the business that I would get a percentage. So, I was a sideman and I never had enough brains to do that. I would tell musicians Today – try and write a song or music, get your name on it and get yourself a lawyer. Just to have it so you have some kind of back-up money so when you get older that will come in and support you. All the records I made, I don't have anything coming in from all those records. No money, no residuals.

DON: They didn't do that – that way.

DONALD: They did it. But Jimmy had an agent. At that time they had agents. And an agent would sign with the leader and the agent would take over all the responsibility of that and there was no conversation about the sidemen. Jimmy Smith signed with an agent and he had a lawyer and he got whatever. There was nothing malicious about it, that's just the way it was.

DON: Do you remember who the first guitar player was when you joined the band?

DONALD: Thornell Schwartz, a little known guy; big heavyset black guy from West Philly. There is West Philly, South Philly and North Philly, and the musicians who came from each of those areas played a certain way. Like McCoy Tyner from West Philly, the Heath Brothers are from South Philly. I'm from Germantown, which is between North Philly and South Philly. And Bud Powell is in the woods, he was like from Willow Grove, which is considered the country; the country part of Philly. There was a piano player and his name was Eddie Green, him and Richard Powell, I would work gigs with Richard Powell and Eddie Green who were living in Willow Grove. We would go up and play at Bud's house! I was the first drummer who played Un Poco Loco. He was getting it together like in his house. And he said, I want you to play this beat for me. And I tried to play the beat and I didn't know what he was talking about man! He would say, get up from those drums! And he would sit down and he would try to play the beat but he couldn't get it himself. And he threw the sticks on the floor and he said *man, I am going to get Max Roach. He will know how to do this!* And then he would say, get back on those drums!! He wasn't malicious; it's just that I didn't know what he was doing. But he knew what he wanted in his head. And so when they came out with the record, I already knew the tune. Because I had been with Bud! We used to drive Bud Powell around in our car, like he would come home, Eddie Green had the car and if Bud wanted to go to the store and we would drive him around to get whatever, cigarettes or candy. We were driving around with him! We didn't even know that he was going to be this great cat.

DON: Well, you must have known that he could play. Even early on did he have that technique down?

DONALD: Yeah, we knew he could play, and yeah it was there and it was magical. It was already there. There was a guy in Philly and nobody knew this guy and he was a friend of Bud Powell and he was in with Thelonious Monk. And who was Monk's idol? Hasaan Ibn Ali. Nobody knows that! And Monk liked him; he liked Art Tatum and Hasaan Ibn Ali. And so did Coltrane and Jimmy Heath and all the rest of those guys. He was a different kind of cat man. He would play; he sounded like an advanced bebopper playing like Art Tatum and Bud Powell and Monk, but advanced. Like nobody knew what he was doing.

DON: So do you think Monk got a lot of stuff from him?

DONALD: I would say that he did. I mean they all influenced each other.

DON: So, Bud seemed so schooled and so controlled – I always had a hard time linking him with Monk. Because Monk was so much the opposite of the way Bud played. But they did influence each other.

DONALD: I think they did have a big influence on each other. I think that probably, Monk was such an individual that he probably didn't listen too much to these cats. I think he was too much of an individualist himself. When I played with Bud Powell and practice with Monk, I would get a different experience of

A Diary of the Underdogs

what I could do rhythmically. There is Monk, Bud Powell, and Art Tatum, three different styles and each one of them had so much there.

DON: What were your earlier experiences about Art Tatum?

DONALD: I think my father played with Noble Sisell's band as the drummer and I didn't know the importance of Noble because my Uncle Duke Johnson played with Freddie Cole, Nat King Cole's brother, he was a bass player. And so he would come home off the road and my father.....well, my brother brought home records all the time of Art Tatum and of Bud and everything and Monk and I remember my father saying, yeah, yeah, play that Monk guy, whatever that is. My father loved Monk. He told my brother, yeah, play that Monkey guy. So, this is a true story: I'm playing in the house and just like we are sitting here, my father is sitting in the chair and he comes home every day from work and smoked a pipe, read a paper and I am crashing away on these drums and he never said a word to me, like nothing- about music, about nothing! I never even knew, he would go outside and smoke the pipe, him and his friend up the street, Daddy Joe, he used to be an iceman – he used to carry ice for the refrigerators. They would go outside together and start bull shitting about whatever they were talking about. My father liked to drink beer and whiskey and one day he got to feeling good, this was like after three years, get up from those drums I wanna show you something! And I thought he was just drunk or something and I said man, what and he got up there and played them drums! And he was twirling all the sticks around, you know, like they used to do. He did all the stuff! And I was surprised! I didn't know he could do that! I didn't know he was a musician, he didn't say anything. And so he took us upstairs and he opened up a trunk and he showed us a picture of him all dressed up in Richmond, Virginia. He was in a group called Happy Pals and he was behind a big bass drum, and he showed me the picture and he said- that's me right there. And he closed the trunk up and never said another word about nothing. Didn't talk music, didn't say nothing. So, my brother and I made the assumption that his grandmother probably told him to stop playing drums because it was considered to be devils music at the time, like Jazz. Can you imagine saying that Jazz is devils music? This was the late 40's or early 50's. My Uncle used to come off the road from playing with Freddie Cole and all the Cole family and I remember him having on this long, long coat and I remember getting a long coat like that. I always liked long coats because of my Uncle and I thought it looked real hip because you couldn't see the legs. My legs were like toothpicks and I could hide them! And when the ride cymbals came out, he hated those ride cymbals, he liked the sock cymbal – that was the thing. He would smack the bass with the string, you know, he knew how to do that stuff. There were two bass players that lived right around the corner from us, him and Henry Patrick. They were great musicians! It was considered Jazz and Two Beat.

DON: And what, music of Louis Armstrong at that period?

DONALD: Probably Louis or whatever went down.

DON: Red Allen and all that....

DONALD: Fats Waller, Jimmy Lunceford's first band; and Duke.

DON: Those were the swinging bands, so they were getting into 4/4.

DONALD: My father had records by Jimmy Lunceford. They were little vinyl records before they made the LPs they were the wax records. Then they made them out of durable plastic. But they didn't sound like the ones we had. You could hear the difference in the sound quality. And so when they went into the LPs you could hear the quality of the recordings, these records are not as good as those. I loved hearing those scratches.

DON: I think they used to pick up a lot of good mid-range. I don't know what it was. I love my records!

DONALD: And that is probably something magical and unexplainable why we like that. I'm looking at a picture right now of Bird and Miles and I remember them being like that, see how clean they are with their clothes like that. I remember them coming to Philly the first time, they were clean like that. Bird looked

A Diary of the Underdogs

young and healthy looking. Yeah! And look at Miles. People misunderstood Miles.

DON: He found a way to be with Bird though he couldn't play Bird's music.

DONALD: Because he was an introvert, people misunderstood him. There was a story one time and I think Freddie Hubbard told it, where Freddie was coming up and Miles would Miles would come in the club and like stare at him and glare at him. And Freddie was really scared; people were scared of Miles Davis. I remember the first time I played the Apollo Theater and all the cats from Philly would bring boxing gloves. We would box each other. And so we would beat each other upside the head because if a guy from North Philly found you in his territory, he would beat you up. So you had to take care of yourself. So I am the first time in the Apollo Theater and I'm sitting there and Miles comes running back there, *get em up motherfucker, get em up!* And he threw his hands up, you know.... and I was like, ok, man, let's get it on! And he ran out the door! And I faced up with Miles Davis, I did man! I'm telling you the truth, because I could box. And in fact, I didn't care; I used to get knocked down a lot of times.

DON: I went to Richmond High School, same thing.

DONALD: I was like if you want to get with me, I'm right there in with you, because of Sugar Ray Robinson and all those cats. Miles ran out that room and ever since then we were buddies. He used to come behind the bandstand, we would be playing....they had little stages that they rolled us out on, and he would be like down and we were playing, opposite Miles with Jimmy (Jimmy Smith) Miles would say, "get um up here, Duck," and we was joking around and we were buddies you know; and it was fun man.

DON: Well traveling you ran into everybody right – double bills....you meet everybody.

DONALD: And we were like buddies, he was the same age. He never screwed around with ever since. And he would say, hey how ya doing Duck? He'd be joking around and say what's that funny shit you be playing up there, and I'd say, I don't know, man it's just me and Jimmy playing.

DON: That's respect man. But he knew that you had some shit that other guys didn't have.

DONALD: They let me know that I was different then the others, even Max and Art Blakey and other cats came to me and said… what are you playing?

DON: So you did get your voice with Max and let him know that he was your great idol.

DONALD: Oh yeah.

DON: And what was that like? And he already knew about you by then probably?

DONALD: He saw me, they all saw Jimmy Smith. Everybody came to see Jimmy. Just like when everyone saw Miles, they saw Tony Williams. Witnessed the same kind of thing, he was so different…Max was my mentor but I didn't sound like him. I wanted to sound like him but it didn't come out that way.

DONALD: Its funny, like I heard a record recently where Ray Brown was on the bandstand with another young up and coming bass player and they were recording and he told the bass player, *you got to do more then that man, you gotta do more then that, wait on the record.* But at that time it wasn't malicious, it was like fun and helpful. If you say something like that to a guy nowadays they take it personally. You can't say, hey man, you didn't do well right there. And we took that like… well we got to go home and practice. We would joke around with each other. We would say, man, that's sad. We would do like this, put our hat over our heart! And we would laugh, we would say, we know you trying to make it, but you sound bad. Why don't you go back home and practice! People are so defensive now, you can hardly say anything. They take it the wrong way. I don't know why that changed, but all I know is when society changes, music changes.

DON: The music that you have inside you is such a big part of your identity. That is one of the most vulnerable parts of you. You can be hurt by it, you can be elated by it. And I know I worked with David Friesen and although he was giving me good information, he knew that music was my softest spot, he knew he could get in there. And sometimes he was a little hurtful. And I would say, David, I'm open to you, and you know I can be wounded and that's right where you go. And he did teach me a lot, but eventually I had to get away from him. He'd say now Don, just stop for a minute, let's think about this, don't play. And there's people in the audience, and he'd say, now we're just going to take it easy, we're just going to play... so finally I'd say, Come on David, look I'm just going to play and if you find a note you'd like to play with me, just join in, because I'm going to play this gig and get paid, okay? So by then he was around behind me where I couldn't see him because by then I was threatening him. But, that's music and that's how it gets sometimes. The point is- that it's the softest spot we have and we can be easily hurt. I think people like us who have been through a lot of it, it's a little easier to take and we understand it more. But for young musicians, they need to be encouraged...by peers on their level, man that was battleground.

DONALD: That was part of your growth, Like when you go to school and the teacher says two and two is not 6, two and two is 4, and so I'm not getting it, so why are you saying it in front of these students so they'll think I'm dumb. But somebody has to say it in order for you to get the message that two and two is not six. There has to be a teacher. There should be a teacher to tell you what bebop is all about. What is the difference between bebop and swing? And there's a big difference between bebop and swing music. But a lot of people don't realize it. And you may not be able to explain it to them unless you play with them, and then it might not get through.

DON: Well, in teaching, especially in class, it has to be so academic, and it does not have emotion. The beats on paper go here and here and it has no meaning unless it becomes emotion. You have to play it, and you have to prefer it and want to hear it, that sound and that feeling. Like when you listen to a tune, you listen to the parts you like and some parts get ignored, the parts you don't listen to are the parts you don't understand. So we have to open up our ears, you have to be educated. There's more there than you have been hearing. You have to listen harder. You have to learn how to listen.

DONALD: Well we can say, it wouldn't be right to keep our mouth closed, a lot of times you have to be careful what you say to people because they might think you're trying to be boastful or trying to show off, it's not like that, it's just that we are trying to explain to them that this is what we learned and a lot of times I use the wrong words when I try to explain something to people because I quit school when I was in junior high school so I don't have an education of words and what they really mean, I assume that what I say is... I met some one the other day and they said... no, you can't use that word or you are going to offend a lot of people, and I didn't really know, I didn't realize it. I might tell a person in a way that they consider is horrid. Like if a musician comes to me and he don't do anything that I think is cool, for me I see he is trying to learn, I'll tell him, you know. I try to tell people and they are offended. I don't want to have to talk about someone coming to me and want to talk about another person, I would rather talk to them face to face, instead of , Hey, man I didn't like what some other cat did, wow-and then somebody says, Well, you know, Duck said that about you. I'd rather tell him to his face and you know sometimes I use the wrong words.

DON: Well, that's ongoing, that's forever. I'm still trying to learn. But what I know about you is that you'll tell a person what you think right away. And I think that's right, good or bad, take it or leave it-at least it promotes conversation and maybe you can get to something.

DONALD: I do it in a sense that somebody is trying to learn. If you don't get instruction on how to get the ball to the basket, it's not going to get there. "If you take this road here rhythmically you have a better change of doing what you are trying to do." But what happens is, everybody is an individual and they are going to do it their way. There was some evidence used in a crime investigation with cat hair and they found that every cat hair was a little bit different and so that means that we are all a little bit different and in music that's a big thing so we have to account for that.

A Diary of the Underdogs

DON: I was going to ask you – all the great drummers eventually come to you because of some stuff you have – it's like the cat hair you were talking about, its different, its Jazz, but it is different. You have a specific individual ability that other people can't match, you know? And great drummer, I've seen it, they come to you, man.

DONALD: Yeah, I know it. I don't know why it is, I just consider that I am blessed. I thank God everyday that I am blessed because I don't even know myself why. I can play the sax, the piano, the trumpet, various types of harmonicas and the banjo to a degree that I can get on the bandstand and play any song I want and I don't know why. Its not perfect playing but it seems to work out, it seems to make people happy. But I just keep doing it but I don't want to be considered as a

Donald Bailey

show off. Right now I want to study how to play the sax so I am at jam sessions trying to learn just like a beginner.

DON: Yeah, there is something unique about your playing, Billie Hart and other cats, it goes around the conversation about drummers. And you are definitely included as someone who has something special. Its not a stroke, its not a lick, I think it goes back to our beginning conversation, comes from Philly and being inspired early on and some great people around you that gave you some great stuff.

DONALD: Yeah, there were great drummers around Philly! There was Earl Curry, Bubbles Ross, Bubbles Frasier and there was a drummer that gave me a gig with Jimmy Smith. I was working in a brass factory at the time and I think I had about two kids and a drummer called up the guy who was running the brass factory and said he wanted to speak with me and that there was a guy named Jimmy Smith that needed a drummer and he said that he thought I was the guy that he could play with. And that's how I got the gig with Jimmy Smith… he was getting ready to go to Pittsburgh. And I quit my job because it paid more money. And I never rehearsed with him, I went from the factory to the bandstand! And Jimmy never even kicked the song off! And he never said nothing! It was like a miracle! Jimmy never said nothing to the musicians or tells them how to play. It's just like Sachmo. Sachmo could switch into anything. He could fit into Be Bop, Jazz, Classical, anything! That's how Jimmy was. Jimmy was actually very humorous, he was like a comedian.

DON: Well, later on he traveled around in a hearse – didn't he? He would drive around in a hearse to keep the organ in there?

DONALD: Yeah, the organ goes in the hearse with a set of drums and our baggage. And we sat in the front seat which is three feet across. It was the most comfortable ride in the world! And he drove, he liked to drive. I remember we were coming from somewhere and we were trying to make this jam session in Bloomington, Delaware where Clifford Brown was from. And this guy pulled Jimmy over and he said, *wow! You guys in the hearse, why you guys in a hearse going so fast?!!* And Jimmy said, *we are going to a gig! We are musicians!* And the guy took us directly to jail because we were speeding! We were late for the gig!

A Diary of the Underdogs

DONALD DUCK BAILEY – PART TWO

DON: Did you have a story about Jimmy Rowles?

DONALD: When I moved to the West Coast I had to change my way of…..from the East Coast and the West Coast….I really experienced a difference in how the West Coast music is different from the East Coast. When I moved here I had to play differently. Anyway I ended up playing with Bill Hampton and all the West Coast musicians you can think of, I played with them: Frank Rosolino and all the cats. I ended up having hits with these guys. I recorded with them also. One thing I will never forget though is when I had a gig with Jimmy Rowles and he said he was playing with Peggy Lee. I said Peggy Lee! And he said I'm going to introduce you and we are going to go play with Peggy Lee. I was like, frightened. He took me and introduced me to Peggy Lee and we made one rehearsal and she said oh, this sounds great and everything. I was subbing for her regular drummer. He was a big band type of a drummer. I think he was her boyfriend. So we are at the gig and I'm playing and on this song I was playing real soft and she came back to me and said *No! I want you to hit em! Hit em hard!* She said she wanted me to kick her in her butt! And I learned from there. That's what most of the singers wanted. Like, Sarah Vaughn and Carman McRae, what made them perform was a drummer that had confidence and boost them. But you have to have confidence in yourself because here you are playing with these great singers. And I also learned there is a difference between rehearsal and when you get to the bandstand. You have to have knowledge for rehearsal but also have knowledge that when you get on the bandstand you got to boost this stuff up. And I learned that way from her. And I learned it in a hard way. And Jimmy said nothing. He was interesting, he didn't care how you played, he was an individualist. And nobody played piano like him. He had an identifying sound. All those guys had an identifying sound. You could tell the difference between Max Roach, Roy Haynes and Art Blakey. And so when you hear that little difference, you say, no, that's Art. And so on. That's how individualistic it is. But when the corporations get a hold of you – you think that it is only that way. That's why Sachmo said, *it don't mean a thing if it don't have THAT swing.* Everybody can swing, but to get to *that* swing, that's where we are all headed. And we never seem to get there. And like every time you get on an instrument it keeps you aware to the fact, that man, you didn't get there yet.

DON: Yeah, but we have been to that swing and we couldn't talk about it. We know what it is.

DONALD: Yeah, we know what it is! And even though we got there, we just about made it, you know what I mean. We didn't really get there which is what kept us going back night after night trying to get it. There was no end to it.

DON: Yeah, it's just like what we are doing right now, talking about this thing that is still growing. And we are talking about what keeps it alive and what it needs, like sunlight and water. But it needs our input and our opinion of it in a reverent way.

DONALD: Yeah, its sort of like Dixieland music swings, Swing music swings, and Be Bop music swings and Rock music swings. That determines whether it's good or bad. All God's children got rhythm. Just like the song says. Those are true words. But the thing is – is who is going to be the lucky ones to get it recorded, who is going to be the lucky ones to make the money and stuff. I never go out for that, for me man, I just want to play.

End: Donald Duck Bailey

Interview: Mark Levine-pianist, composer, author, educator- with Don Alberts-November 24, 2008-at Bird and Beckett, San Francisco-about: Cal Tjader, Keystone Korner, Jackie Byard, singers

A Diary of the Underdogs

MARK LEVINE

DON: Did you get here in 66?

MARK: No, I got here in '74. I got to California in '66, I was down in L.A.

DON: What was it like to be in the band with Cal Tjader? What period was that?

MARK: I was with Cal right before he passed away, roughly 80 to 82 – with Vince Lateano on drums, Poncho Sanchez on congas, Rob Fisher on bass. There was some movement in the other positions. Roger Glenn was with the band for awhile, playing flute, percussion and vibes. Also, Noel Jewkes was in the band.

DON: Didn't Cal have a Jazz band and a Latin band?

MARK: No, he was just doing one band. He would start a set and play a couple of tunes

Mark Levine

straight ahead, and then he would bring the percussionist up. For a long while there the sax player was a guy from L.A. named Dick Mitchell who I haven't heard anything about since then. He went back to L.A. so we kind of lost touch. Willie Colon, local conga player was always Poncho's sub when Poncho couldn't make it.

DON: Was Armando Paraza around then, had he retired from the band?

MARK: Yeah, Armando played with Cal maybe five years or more before I got there. Clare Fisher was in band then.

DON: Clare preceded you?

MARK: No, I think right before me was Al Zulaica. But I am not sure, that was thirty years ago. Either Zulaica or Clare Fisher preceded me, but both those guys were in and out of the band for decades. Zulaica I think was the last pianist that he used. He joined the band just as they left for the Philippines. And Cal died as soon as they got off the plane. I think it was 82 or 83.

DON: He just collapsed, right? Heart attack and that was it.

MARK: Yes. He had one previous heart attack about two years before after we finished *Longa Babien* which was the recording that won him a Grammy. When he won the Grammy, he still wasn't playing, he was recuperating. We were about to get back together again. I remember calling Cal the morning after he won the Grammy to congratulate him and Cal was a guy with a great sense of humor and I said, Cal does this mean we are going to be making more money? He said, *no, it means I'm going to be making more money!* But Cal was a generous man, he was just being funny. But Rob is still around, Vince is still around and so is Poncho.

DON: Did you get to know John Rae?

MARK: I got to know John pretty well because anything that had to do with the union you had to go through John Rae. He was the phone operator for years. He was in the office. And he was a great musician. But I pretty much knew him thru the union. I may have played with him once or twice, but the last fifteen or twenty years I knew him as the union officer. And if things were slow, I would call him up and he would throw something my way a trust fund gig or something.

DON: He was a vibes player mostly, but he doubled on something?

MARK: Drums. He was actually Cal's first drummer. In fact there was a TV show I just saw. Someone

A Diary of the Underdogs

put together a compilation of Latin music videos. There was a section in it – *Cal & the Oscar Brown Jazz Show*. Remember that show? It was in the 60's. And John Rae was the drummer. Freddie Schriber was the bass player; Lonnie Hewitt was the piano player. Bill Fitch, a legendary guy was the conga player. We all wore those suits with the little thin ties, big horn rimmed glasses. That was the style for the late 50's early 60's.

DON: I remember that, in fact at the Savanna Club they have some videos playing and they had these little thin ties. As I was talking to Donald Bailey about that – he said, yeah, we used to all dress up, all the bebop players dressed. Anyway, how about Richie Goldberg, did you get to know him?

MARK: Yeah, I knew Richie. In fact one of my most memorable moments.....well, first of all Richie was a very unusual guy. He was a Black Jewish cowboy – Jazz drummer. He used to take part in rodeos, especially black rodeos. Fly off to Oklahoma or some place like that and come back with bruises all over – he was a tough guy and a Jazz drummer. And I had a gig with him and a bass player- I can't mention his name because at the time he was known as the worst bass player in the Bay Area. Later on he moved to New York and I heard him when he came back from New York and he was much worse! He had this Wednesday afternoon gig with Richie and I and I think Graham Bruce was playing trumpet, and it was at some restaurant in the Embarcadero Center and it was like 5-7pm. And I went into the gig one day and Philly Joe was visiting town and since he was an old friend of Richie's he was hanging out at the gig. So, here we are at this gig with the worse bass player in town and Richie says to Philly Joe, you wanna sit in? And Philly Joe says, sure. So I got a chance to play with Philly Joe! And I got the chance to play one set with the greatest drummer in the world and the worst bass player in the world! And in all fairness to the bass player, later on he sounded much better. Sometimes you hear everything backwards and you go to the center of the universe and you suddenly realize that you have been hearing everything backwards! And you turn it back around and then you have it!

DON: So Richie Goldberg....we know of course that he passed away....but he played the local scenes, he played Pearl's...

MARK: He played the local scene and he was one of the best brush players around. You didn't have to tell him, he took out his brushes a lot of the time.

DON: Was he the kind of guy who would put a band together or was he a sideman only.

MARK: I think of him as a sideman. He might have been a leader at times but every time I worked with him it was because he was in someone else's band. He was a session guy too.

DON: Speaking of that, was there anything going on late night at that time...after hours?

MARK: There was one place in the early 80's, I can't remember the name of it. It was somewhere south of Market. A drummer was running it and I can't remember his name. But everyone used to show up there. There was always a big pot of chili and it was free. I wish I could remember his name, the drummer. For awhile he had this strange thing hooked up to....he had pneumatic tubes hooked up to his drums and he would stick one end of the tube in his mouth and by blowing in it he would be able to change the pitch of the drums. Someone might be able to remember that and identify this guy. And he used to have a lot of gigs in Emeryville. He had some connection with the casinos in Emeryville. And there was quite a bit of Jazz happening around there at that time too, late 70's early 80's.

DON: Was it Club Albatross in Berkley?

MARK: That rings a bell but I can't place it. Bill Douglas was going to put a calendar together, each month would have a before and after picture of Keystone Korner. And as he started researching and putting photos together he realized that twelve photos were not going to be enough – so he expanded it to three-hundred and sixty-five; every single day of the year, before and after pictures. And then it just became an overwhelming project and he never finished it. But I hope he has the photos and everything and donates them to the Smithsonian or something. That would be a history of Jazz clubs.

A Diary of the Underdogs

DON: And speaking of the Keystone – did you play there?

MARK: I played Keystone a few times; once or twice with my band when Todd was feeling magnanimous, and once in awhile with someone fairly well known. But I wasn't. I was never in the position of being the house piano player there.

DON: Did you ever catch any of the last Bill Evans concerts?

MARK: I think just once – shortly before he passed away. The people I use to see where my heroes – Joe Henderson, Freddie Hubbard, Woody Shaw – those Christmas and New Years concerts. Todd would put those together – it would be two weeks straight – sometimes it would be Woody Shaw, Freddie Hubbard, Joe Henderson, Bobby Hutcherson, Cedar Walton, Billie Higgins and usually a local bass player; usually Herbie Lewis. And I have tapes of some of those concerts. And I think this is ok to say now, because the guy is dead – but do you remember the guy who was the sound man at Keystone Korner? Well, maybe I shouldn't mention his name. The guy who was the sound man all those years at Keystone Korner, he used to tape every single night. And you would get to be friendly with him and I got to hang with him and he would pass out these tapes. And he laid one on my one time and it was December 28th and I looked at who was playing and it would be Woody, Freddie, Joe, Hutch, Cedar, and Billie Higgins! So I have some of these bootlegs. I will burn them for you if you want. Well, Todd will probably be a little pissed off.

DON: Wasn't he responsible for making some of those bootlegs copies himself?

MARK: He might have been.

DON: I think he got credit for a Bill Evans album called *Consecration* or something like that. It was totally a bootleg and I'm not sure that the last week that Bill played there, that Bill was aware anyone was taping.

MARK: Some of the best recordings I have in my collection are bootlegs. I think the best bootleg I have – you would like this – especially since McCoy was in town – just after McCoy left Coltrane, he came to Boston with his first trio as a leader. Eighteen years old, Jack Dejohnette, a good bass player that has since disappeared from the scene – Scotty Holt. And it was a live TV show WGBH an NPR station in Boston. And he did not tape it – it was just a live show. And I hooked up my tape recorder to alligator clips; I took the back of the TV off and attached them to my speaker wires. And I got a remarkably good recording of a half an hour of the McCoy Trio playing a burning version of *Green Dolphin Street*, and *Summertime*. It was the best McCoy I had ever heard. I will burn them for you – remind me.

DON: You did mention Woody Shaw a few times. You did play with him?

MARK: I played with him when he lived out here and he had a band. And the band lasted roughly a year – a little less, a little more. on bass, who now lives, like myself, up in Idaho. Clarence Becton, a wonderful drummer. He went to the Netherlands or Amsterdam. He's been there for twenty years or more.

DON: Yeah, Woody, a strong influence on trumpet players and also on piano players. Onaje Gumbs- that was his name?

MARK: Onaje Gumbs…and then later Mulgrew Miller.

DON: Back when I first met Mulgrew he said, you ever meet Woody Shaw? He was very impressive, that guy. That was a big gig for him.

MARK: Oh, I think it was his most important gig at the time. It was a real break out for him. When he came to New York I think he was a member of the Ellington Orchestra, you know, Duke had since passed. It was with Mercer Ellington. And then I think he was a member of that band and then I think the first big gig he got was with Woody…several years and lot of good records.

DON: What do you think of him these days?

MARK: He still is just about my favorite pianist. I just got Dave Holland's new record because he's on it. I was kind of surprised. He sounds wonderful. I run into him every once in awhile. Beautiful guy; another Memphis piano player. That town just breeds piano players. James Williams, Donald Brown, Tony

A Diary of the Underdogs

Reedus– I think he was James Morgan's nephew. I liked James Morgan, he passed away way too young.

DON: Yeah, makes you think and be thankful.

MARK: I've been talking a lot with Bud Spangler and exchanging emails with Eddie Marshall and we are all the same age! 70! And we are still doing it. No body hires us anymore, but we are still doing it. I think we need to pass 70 and turn from being a veteran into a legend.

DON: I was going to ask you about Jacki Byard how that came about?

MARK: I was lucky; I had some really good teachers when I first start playing this music. Jacki was probably the most influential. And I have a bunch of bootlegs of his too, if you want them. I studied with him in Boston for a couple of years and he moved to New York. He had an unusual way of teaching. I will never forget my first lesson with him. I had met him before, I had actually sat in on a jam session when he was playing alto sax. So we had some little bit of a connection. And I came to the lesson and he sat behind the drums because he played about six different instruments, and he said *ok, let me hear you play, what do you want to play?* And I didn't know and he suggested *I Got Rhythm.* And he told me to run a cycle – one chorus each. B-Flat was ok, E-Flat was not quite as good, A-Flat was a little sloppy, D-Flat was a struggle and G-Flat, I just had to stop. And he said, *ok, I will see you next week.* So, my lesson was ten minutes. But I had to pay him for the full hour. But it was at that time like only $10. But that was a very valuable lesson – practice to what your weaknesses are. Identify your weaknesses and practice them. He would make suggestions, but he would never actually show me anything like a regular piano teacher would. He concentrated more on concepts. On the other hand, he had a gig at the time, four nights a week at a club in Boston that is still there, still a Jazz club – Wally's Paradise- just a funky local Jazz club. But it was on a stage and there was a curtain right behind it, the band was in front of the curtain and the back part of the stage was behind the curtain and if you went right to the middle of the curtain where it parted, and if you peaked through, you could see the keyboard, it was right there. So there would always be like four or five of us pianists leaning at a 45 degree angle peaking through this tiny little crack in the curtain just watching his hands while he played. And sometimes we were able to find out some of the stuff he was playing even though he wouldn't show us. He had a tremendous sound and he was really outstanding. There is an influence from him in my playing. Every once in awhile if I listen to something that I have recorded, there will be this little fragment of something and- oh yeah, I got that from Jacki.

DON: What year was that?

MARK: I was in Boston 56 – 60 and then again 62 – 66. It was the earlier time, probably around 58 or 59. And he used to let people sit in on that gig at Wally's Paradise. But he didn't like singers to sit in. But he would let anybody sit in, but he didn't like singers to sit in unless they sang songs in the original key. He used to do this thing; it was very cruel – even though we got a lot of laughs out of it. A singer came in one night, this guy, and Jacki said- *what do you want to sing?* And the guy said, *Lush Life.* Okay, Jacki knew *Lush Life.* And Jacki asked him, *what key* and the guy said something like A. And he said *ok, what do you want - four bars in front?* And they guy said, *yeah fine.* He would play the B-Flat chord and the bass and drummer would come in – in tempo. Then an A-Major chord and then he would modulate away from that in the slickest way possible thru several different keys within four bars. And then finally end up on an A-Flat 7 chord. And the singer would be trying to find his range, and the singer would turn around and whisper, *Key of A!* And Jacki would say, *yeah, man Key of A!* I have a bad rep among singers and it all stems from this incident, of course I won't mention the singer – it's a pretty well known Jazz singer in the Bay Area. We were doing a gig at Auberge de Soleil, fancy restaurant up in the wine country. This was a Jazz gig with three different bands at a party, lasting six or seven hours- invited guests and everything. And after the first couple sets we just started switching musicians back and forth. And I ended up playing for this singer and she was singing *Wave.* And we got to end of the tune and it was in original key too, and it was D minor 7 and she is scatting on top of it and I am playing the fail safe chord for D minor 7 and she

129

A Diary of the Underdogs

turns around and frowns at me and says, *Change that chord Mark!* And I am not going to say what the two words were that I said, but you know what they are. But I said it with a smile on my face. And she hasn't spoken to me since and I found out that she called every singer in town the next day and told them don't ever hire Mark Levine. But there have been some singers that I really enjoy, Kellye Grey. Kellye Grey was a musician's singer. She heard the changes and soon as she was done doing her thing, she would get off the stage and let the band take solos and play as long as they wanted. And when she scatted, it fit the chords. It wasn't overdone.

DON: Yeah, I enjoyed her too. There was a couple up in Portland that were pretty good too. Kelly Broadway was a one.

MARK: I wanted to tell you I was emailing Graham Bruce last week and we were reminiscing about a gig we had in Fresno and my car broke down in Los Banos, right off the freeway and we had to sit the shade next to this gas station, grocery store and Quick Stop, it was the only thing around. We had to sit there for six or seven hours for someone to bring a part. And while we were there we wrote a song about the girl who worked behind the counter. This was twenty years ago. I asked him if he remembered that song. He remembered the name and the lyrics.

MARK LEVINE – PART 2

DON: We are talking about Bud Spangler. Did you use to do a lot of live recordings?

MARK: Well, he used to do those at Yoshi's, but he's in the studio too, obviously. He has produced the last four CDs I have done and two new ones I have coming up in the coming year. He is still playing drums too. He is producing an album now with a wonderful singer named Challani Rose, I see her around the Jazz school, I'm not sure if she is teaching there or not. She has a partner singer and the two of them are completely singing an album of songs by Eva Cassidy. She came up in the late 80's early 90's and died very young. She died of breast cancer, she was 33 – check out her album with Chuck Brown – *The Other Side*. I like living in Idaho, it's peaceful. I'm away from everyone and everything and I get a lot done. The day belongs to me and I write music and practice and sit out on the deck and look at the mountains, drink a beer. It's relaxing yet I get much more done then I do here. Then I fly back down here and teach Friday's and Saturday's and if there are any gigs I stay around a day or two extra. I have lots of frequent flyer miles.

DON: Have you been composing at all?

MARK: I haven't been doing any composing or arranging. I'm doing an album in April – all the music of Moacir Santos, Brazilian songwriter and composer who is very famous in his country but pretty unknown here even though he has spent the last thirty years around. He was partially retired. He wrote some really big hits back in the 50's and 60's and his influence actually extends beyond his composition as a teacher. Everybody studied with him, Antonio Carlos Jobim. Everyone studied his composition and his harmony. His harmony and his theory were way ahead of anybody else. I am transcribing his songs now, some of them from the 1950's and they have chords that really didn't come into Jazz until the 60's. Like, Major 7th plus 5 chords and sus flat 9 chords, stuff that you associate with early Herbie Hancock or Wayne Shorter; he was doing this stuff way before. And I had the good fortune of working with him for a short period in L.A. in the 70's and was on one of his albums, *Sodaji*, which came out on Blue Note, three albums came out on Blue Note. Blue Note didn't know what to do with him. Somebody said, sign this guy! And they thought they were getting another Sergio Mendez, but he didn't like commercial music like Sergio Mendez did- even though his music is pretty and sing-able and every thing else. So, I have always wanted to do an album of his music, so that is basically what I am working on.

DON: Does this follow *Isla,* or am I way behind here?

A Diary of the Underdogs

MARK: No, its pretty much the same band – the Latin – Paul Van Wageningen on drums, Michael Spiro on congas, a different bass player, Peter Barshay did all those early records, but John Wiitala is my bass player now- and Mary Fettig on flute.

DON: I don't know Mary Fettig…

MARK: Mary Fettig is a little off the central Jazz scene, so you might not have run into her. But she is a wonderful reed player. When Joe Henderson used to put his big band together for gigs at Yoshi's, which maybe he did three times in the 90's, she was always his lead alto player. And I think she is just about first call in the Bay Area as far as record dates, shows, very busy woman.

DON: So, how are you integrating her into the band?

MARK: Just flute, the lead voice – flute. Those albums that Moacir did for Blue Note were not typical Brazilian Albums. First of all everyone on them was a Jazz musician. Frank Rosolino, Clare Fisher, George Bohannan, Don Menza, Ray Pizzi, some of the best Jazz musicians around. So, it was Brazilian music but with a Jazz edge. It wasn't your typical Brazilian band. It was Jazz but not Brazilian Jazz; it was like Jazz playing Brazilian music. But all these musicians were picked specifically by Moacir. He was hip enough to know what was going on.

DON: So is this project viable enough in name recognition that you should go into the Latin market?

MARK: I don't know. The marketing aspect of it I leave to Dr. Jazz. He is a radio promo guy, radio print promo. And I attribute what little success I have with my last three albums, which the last one got a Grammy nomination; I attribute it largely to him- because he knows the radio and print media more than anybody else. He knows everybody in it and he's friendly with everybody. I remember the first time I met him was at an IAJE convention in New York and he said lets go have lunch and we went down to the hotel dining room to have lunch and three people walked in the door and immediately saw him and came over and gave him a big hug and sat down and talked. Winton Marsalis and the guy who was president of Blue Note Records – Bruce Lundval and I can't remember who the third was, but I was very impressed, not only did he know these people but they loved him and they were friendly with him. So, he's doing the promo or at least that part of the promo. His name actually is Bob Cohen, I think, but he is known as Dr. Jazz.

DON: Dr. Jazz has been around for a long time, I remember his name when I lived in Portland. He would do a three to six week promo for a certain price.

MARK: Yeah, actually I think he does it now for twelve weeks. The last CD I put out was six or seven years ago and the world has changed since then. The record business has changed. I hear more and more that the only way you can make money on records now is single, 99 cent downloads. So, everything is changing. I wonder sometimes as a teacher, the one aspect of Jazz that is booming is Jazz education. Schools are opening up all over the place. The Jazz School in Berkley is expanding, they are going to open up a San Francisco campus and start a new school – a degree program – the Jazz School Institute. So, we are teaching all these tens of thousands of kids how to do something for which there is no work.

DON: So, are they getting it?

MARK: Well actually I brought this up – the ethics of it – I brought it up to the Dean, just in a passing conversation with the Dean and I said, I teach there too, she started the Jazz program at the Conservatory and she said don't worry about it, the classical music scene is the same way. We are training thousands of pianists and violinists and cello every year and do you think there are any gigs for them? To get into the Symphony Orchestra these days you have to wait for someone to die or retire.

DON: So what is the answer to that?

MARK: There is no answer. But there is no doubt that music education makes you a better person.

DON: It does, it's kind of like a psychological grounding.

MARK: Yeah, they have done endless tests to prove that kids get better grades when they do music. I thought it was very instructive of a school district in, I think it is Vallejo, went bankrupt a few years ago and in order to survive they cut music, athletics and closed the library. But then the message got through to the town itself - hey – what's going on here? So the banks and the real estate companies and all the people with money got together and had these huge fund raisers to save the school programs. And they raised millions of dollars and they restored the athletic program and they opened the library and not a penny for music. So I think a lot of people haven't got the message yet.

DON: Anything you want to throw in at the end here – got any words of wisdom?

MARK: Not really. I think now that Obama is President I think that everything is going to be all right.

DON: Well there will be more Jazz clubs.

MARK: Right! Well, I did hear one piece of good news. I was in Nashville a couple of weeks ago and I had dinner one night with a couple that run a Jazz school there, very similar to the Jazz school in Berkley. And I was just asking them- *what's country music?* They said there was a guy who was the head of NPR for a couple of years and he was promoting Jazz and he has just been named to Obama's transition team so that is good news. I have to say that I have not read either of Obama's books, I just ordered them from Amazon, but I heard about that in one of his books he expresses admiration for John Coltrane.

DON: See, there is going to be more Jazz clubs!

MARK: There is going to be more Jazz clubs!

DON: Do you want to let people know about your books? There are three books?

MARK: Three books, yes.

DON: They are available through Sher Music.

MARK: They are available through Sher Music. They are available in music stores; Amazon, used copies on E Bay.

DON: What are the titles? The first one was?

MARK: *The Jazz Piano Book*.

DON: Which by the way is groundbreaking?

MARK: Thank you very much! The second one was *The Jazz Theory Book*. And the last one is kind of a niche book that is about a particular type of voicing technique and arranging technique called *Drop Two*. It's about block chords.

DON: All great books! You know you kind of broke through there, there were some complaints about giving away secrets. We never did give away secrets for years.

MARK: My teachers did, except for Jacki. My first teacher was a guy in Florida, Joe Bates, he showed me everything and I studied with Hal Overton in New York, he showed me everything. Barry Harris, one of the greatest teachers in Jazz, he shows you everything. Those techniques are just the ABCs. The music is gonna come from inside you or you won't get that book. I say that on page one – you do not learn how to play Jazz from this book. It just shows you some techniques. You got to listen to the records and it's got to come from inside you.

End: Mark Levine

Interview: Sharky-Art Lewis-jazz musician, drummer-with Don Alberts-November 25, 2008-at Seven Mile House, San Francisco-about: BJ Papa, Dewey Redman, Andrew Hill, Jon Hendricks, Sonny Simmons, Sonny Rollins, Virgil Gonsalves

A Diary of the Underdogs

ART LEWIS

DON: We are at Seven Mile House and tonight Art is playing with the Al Molina Quartet. Larry Chinn on piano, Frank Passantino on the bass and Art is playing on the drums. I was going to ask you about BJ Papa, you brought BJ to San Francisco and got him going?

ART: I met BJ I think in the early 60's, maybe 59 or 60. And at the time I was working around San Francisco and BJ would come by at the jam sessions and he would carry a tenor sax case with him. At first I didn't know what was going on. Well, he would carry this case around but I never seen him take out a horn, right? I said, "*What you got in that case, a ham sandwiches or something?*" There used to be a Tamale lady that would come around and she would bring hot Tamales and she had this case right, but her case was more like a metal box strapped to a bicycle. So, it was a standing joke, you have somebody with a case that never opened it up you wondered what was in there – what you got in there man, ham sandwiches?

DON: His name was BJ Papa?

ART: His name wasn't BJ Papa at the time it was Bill Jackson. And he did have a sax in there but he said he was just learning how to play and he was afraid to get up and try in out in a jam session. Eventually we coaxed him, with some help of some others to take it out and play. We will play some blues. So, he started learning how to play some blues on the sax. And that's the most I remember about him because I was hanging in another circle. I moved out of the area about 67 or 68, I started going out on the road with different people. And one of the gigs was with Jon Hendricks and his quartet, after his adventures with the.....

Art "Sharky" Lewis

DON: Lambert Hendricks and Ross?

ART: Yeah, Moulin Rouge also, then it became Mr. D's, we did Motown shows there. So, I just hung out and did that. Then in the 70's these rock bands started calling me up, people I knew in college.

ART: Yeah, he (Hendricks) started doing the solo thing and he moved to Mill Valley because his wife's sister lived over there. I think he bought a house over there and anyway, we became friends. I was working with a piano player at the time, Flip Nunez and he got wind of Flip, Flip was a great accompanist for vocalists and a good Jazz piano player. So, I worked with Flip off and on. Flip pulled me on the gig.

DON: Yeah, nobody's talked about Flip; he was a pretty impressive piano player.

ART: Oh yeah, he was a ground breaker. We all lived in the house together; it was called the Happy House. It was on Oak, right off of Fillmore.

DON: Wasn't that the place where Dewey lived too?

ART: Yeah, it was run by some people that were patrons of the arts and they had a Jazz club in Sacramento, on the outskirts of Sacramento, The Swinging Lantern. So I had worked up there with Buddy Montgomery and Wes Montgomery and Monk Montgomery. So, it turned out that they had bought a house in San Francisco and so when they moved there they started renting rooms to musicians. So I was one of the musicians fortunate enough to get a space in there. And I shared a room with Dewey Redman for a long time. We shared a spot up there and different people would come in. I was there for a while.

A Diary of the Underdogs

Virgil Gonsalves

Wes Montgomery stayed there. It was that kind of a scene at that time. So, that was my experience with BJ, I didn't see BJ for many moons, I started working with Jon Hendricks and I went back East a couple of times. And I was living in Mill Valley and I got married and my first child was a son. So, I started working around and in those days, horn players and piano players and band leaders, they would come out here and they would get a local rhythm section, so I was lucky enough to get some of those gigs thanks to Monk Montgomery and a lot of other people.

DON: How did you run into Virgil Gonsalves?

ART: I ran into Virgil, a friend of mine, Chuck Carter, drummer, was working with Virgil and Chuck was a friend of mine. Chuck got out there a little bit and I worked in Chucks place a couple of times when Chuck couldn't make it. So, Virgil hired me to do some more work with him. And that's when I ran into you. And Virgil was a guy, you know he always had a roaster of musicians on hand that he could put together a band. And he was a guy that could hustle the gigs and he had some contacts and I did a lot of good work. I got introduced to Bob Dorough, he was working with Virgil.

DON: Everyone seemed to know Virgil!

ART: Bob knew him and Lenny Bruce knew him and Al Shackman, the guitarist. He was Nina Simone's musical arranger too. So, I got a chance to work with Al. There were a lot of different people, man. I worked with Bud Shank, working with Virgil.

DON: Tell me about Andrew Hill.

ART: After I moved back....I met Andrew when he was coming through San Francisco and he played at the Both/And after a bad gig in L.A. So I met him here and he stayed here for awhile because he was having a court case down in L.A. So, he was running around here for awhile and that's when I initially met him here. And then later on when I eventually moved to New York, I went back to New York a couple of times with Jon Hendricks and then I moved there. And that's where I connected with Andrew Hill. He was living on the Lower East Side and we knew some of the same people we had met out here. So, I kind of hooked him up. He is a really friendly guy. He loves people to come over – warm guy – come on over, lets play something. He had a great loft on the ground floor in the East Village. So not only did he play great piano and he composed, but his wife Lorraine played the keyboard and the organ. So, I would play with her sometimes. And she would dress very mysterious. Remember an organ player named Corla Pandit, she used to have a TV show, right, and she played that kind of music, mysterious, spacey....

DON: Yeah, and dress up like .....

ART: She had candles on the piano. Lorraine Hill! I worked with her in New York at the Bottom Line and the Bitter End and Top of The Gate and all those big plushy kind of clubs. She would get those kinds of gigs, just me and her – just drums and organ.

DON: Did she play foot bass?

ART: Yeah, she played foot bass. She would play some blues things, she wasn't a Jazz pianist. She would play some Gospel.

DON: Yeah, I heard a lot of Gospel in Andrew Hill too. He had those Gospel roots. There was something about his playing that was really warm. What year was this; late 50's or early 60's?

ART: Well, Andrew had been around for years, he used to work with Dinah Washington when he was about nineteen years old. He was around in the 50's, maybe late 40's.

DON: Yeah, when he made his first Blue Note he was pretty young....

A Diary of the Underdogs

ART: Yeah, he was pretty young. When I met him it was in the 70's; late 70's, early 80's. When I started working with him. We became friends and then we started doing gigs. He would call me up just to run over somebody's music. And I would just bring my snare drum over – he would say, *all you need is a cymbal and a snare drum – that's all you need – I just want you to hear this.*

DON: Who were some of the other guys he used in the rhythm section?

ART: He used Chris White for a long time and then he used Richard Davis. I worked with him in the trio and I recorded with him. I recorded with him with the trio – Chris White on bass, I think on Steeple Chase Records, maybe it was something else. Two labels, one was produced by Michael Cuscuna, that was Steeple Chase. He produced for a lot of labels. He used Lee Konitz on it, and that one had Cecil McBee too – on bass. He had Ted Curson on trumpet and Lee Konitz. I think I did a gig with him with Ricky Ford too; a tenor player.

DON: How did you run into Sonny Simmons?

ART: I knew Sonny Simmons from around here, from Oakland. He was an Oakland guy and he and these other guys were like five or six years older then us. So we used to go and listen to those guys, they were the cats. That's where I knew Sonny from. Over the years I did about five albums with Sonny. And I didn't know there were albums until I went to his website! We did one up in Montreal, this was in 2006, I think, or maybe it was 2004 or 2005, with Charnett Moffett on bass, just me and Charnett trio. It was pretty hot! And then I did this tour with him in 2006, but Sonny and I go way back. I remember Sonny

Flip Nunez, Scott Steed and Vince Lateano at Pearl's

A Diary of the Underdogs

when he came to New York and I told him that he should stay in New York. But Sonny is the type of guy that likes to go everywhere. He could never stay in one spot. But he was in New York for a few years. Sonny Rollins used to go out and pick him up and he would go practice with Sonny. Sonny Simmons had such a great sound. In the early days he was on that Ornette Coleman trip with Eric Dolphy, Sonny was in that mix.
End: Art Lewis

Interview: Dick Conte-musician, pianist, educator, broadcaster- with Don Alberts-November 29, 2008-at Bird and Beckett, San Francisco-about: Bill Evans, Freddie Redd, Max Hartstein, Marafio, Mexico, psychedelic mushrooms, Keystone Korner, Conrad Mendenhall, Todd Barkan, Farwell Taylor, Kenny Elmore, Bill Evans last interview.

DICK CONTE

DON: Do you happen to remember the last concerts of Bill Evans at Keystone Korner?
DICK: Yeah, I was there. I interviewed him on Friday, saw him on Sunday and then he died the next week. So, that is the last interview on tape and I have it. I interviewed him on KJAZ. He looked like he was already dead when he walked into the studio.
DON: I saw him a month before. I saw him in August and he was at Keystone in September. I saw him exactly thirty days before. He did a concert in Portland and he remembered me from the old days in the Fillmore. He said, "Come on up to the hotel room." We talked and he gave me a back stage pass – Don Alberts and guest! My son was with me and Nancy King was there. We talked to Bill and he was very forthcoming. He talked to my son. My son had listened to all those records growing up. We all went to breakfast later, then he called me and asked me to take him to the airport. I took him the next day and said goodbye and that was it!
DICK: That interview was at the old KJAZ on Webster Street and he walked up the stairs and he was huffing and puffing – just one flight of stairs. He was all yellow and looked terrible.
DON: Yeah, he had jaundice.
DICK: I said, "What the hell is going on?" He laughed and said, "Oh, I'm gonna die!" The doctor at Keystone, remember the partner there was actually a doctor? He was one of Todd's last partners, I don't remember his name. He told Bill that he needed to go to the hospital and Bill said, "Screw it!" He told Bill that he should stop everything that he was doing right then or he wouldn't last. And Bill was just like – fuck it. He was injecting, you know. He played his ass off that night though!
DON: I have every one of those recordings. I got the whole week; I got every night. It was a box set, I don't know who produced it. There was some talk that Todd secretly recorded.
DICK: He sounded great that night! Yeah, I saw him and then I think he died like that Tuesday.
DON: There was one night when he couldn't play.
DICK: Well, he played that Sunday night because I was there. He looked okay that night. Like I said, when he came to the studio, he was huffing and puffing and took out a cigarette and a coke. Once he got settled in he was fine. His mind was just as alert as ever but his body was falling apart. I was on the air the day he died and I got a call from Todd. He told me what happened – that he had died. I had something on the turntable and I went into the library to pull out a bunch of his records so I could get a number going. And it was the weirdest thing, I bent down and pulled them out and it suddenly hit me that he was dead. It started down and then came up through my whole body and I let out this animal scream – I have never done this before or since. It was unbelievable! The woman from the office came running out and I was crying!

A Diary of the Underdogs

Dick Conte

The scream was very weird! It was very emotional. We had hung out and I had just seen him a few days ago and now he was dead. I started playing his records but I wasn't able to go on the air for at least half an hour before I could get control of myself. Then I went on the air and announced what happened. It was so strange and that emotion went through me. It started at my toes.

DON: Because you picked it up?

DICK: Yeah, I was bending down and there is was – this uncontrollable force that went through my whole body. That sound! It scared me! Yeah, you know he lived five doors away from me in Larkspur. I lived in a houseboat.

DON: That was the period he was going through withdrawals.

DICK: Right, that's when I met him, 1965.

DON: Did you know my friend Conrad?

DICK: Conrad! He was living on Conrad's boat! I was living on a boat, five berths down. I remember while I was there *Trio 65* came out while he was staying at Conrad's. I went over there and he didn't like the album and he didn't like the bass player.

DON: Yeah, he wasn't feeling very good.

DICK: Then his wife came out from New York, his first wife, the one who jumped in front of the subway and killed herself in New York. I can't think of her name. I have an album that he gave me, signed Bill, Conrad and her name. It was a box set that he gave me for my birthday. Elaine!

DON: Elaine! *B Minor Waltz for Elaine*!

DICK: That's her. That was his first wife. She was a total junkie. When he was staying at Conrad's she came out and stayed with him. He had been in Marin General Hospital, had fallen out at The Trident and ended up in Marin General. The houseboats were across from the hospital. They are gone now. So, Conrad had gone to visit Bill when he was at the hospital and Bill was looking out the window and said, "Boy, those houseboats are really nice out there!" And Conrad said, "That's where I live!" Bill needed someplace to stay and Conrad asked him if he wanted to stay with him so that is how that happened. When Bill got out of the hospital he went and stayed with Conrad. It was like six weeks or something and we got to be really good friends. He didn't play the whole time he was there but he did gig at the Jazz Workshop with Tom Reynolds, the drummer. The bass player was from Colorado, Paul Warburton. He brought him in from Denver because they had worked together. They did either a week or two at the Workshop. That was the only time he played. He came to my house. I had a piano on my houseboat, and he came over and Don Thompson and Terry Clarke, the guys from Canada, they were playing in John Handy's band. They came over because they knew Bill was staying there. Max Hartstein was my roommate at the time. We were all there in my room having a party. Bill spent the time in the corner but he did play one tune. And I actually got on the drums! I was playing drums! I don't remember what the tune was – the year was 1965 though. Max had just come back from New York and then he split and moved down to Palo Alto. He met a chick

A Diary of the Underdogs

and moved down there. Then Freddie Redd became my roommate, piano player. I was tending bar at the No Name Bar in Sausalito at that time and Freddie Redd came in one night and introduced himself. I had seen Freddie perform in New York at the Connection. I moved out in '59 or '60. So anyway I knew who he was.

DON: Yeah, I met him at Bop City.

DICK: He was living somewhere in the City and looking for a place to live and I said, "Well, I've got this houseboat and I have an extra bedroom." So, he moved in and moved in his grand piano and I got a little bread out of him and that was it. From then on he would borrow shirts and go away for three days, then come back and I would be asking for my shirts and he would be like, "Oh, I don't know where it is, I left it somewhere." But the piano was there. The only thing I had was the piano. Finally, after about maybe two or three months, he always came up short with the rent and I was basically carrying him. He was a good guy but totally off the wall, could not keep anything together at all.

DON: He had some pretty good little songs.

DICK: Oh, yeah, he would be playing, banging on the piano. So that was a good thing, I had his piano. Then he decided that he was going to split. He had a gig at the Committee Theater. Remember, with all the comics?

DON: Howard Hesseman and...

DICK: Right, Howard was a good friend of mine too. Then Freddie decided he was going to go to Europe. They had a big party for him at the Committee, a fund raiser, because he had no money. Then he came back to my place. He had bought some cheap fucking car and got his stuff together and gave me a little bit of money. He left owing me money but I just wanted him out of my house because it had turned into a real drag.

DON: Was he bringing people over and stuff?

DICK: He was doing all kinds of crazy stuff. He would go away, borrowing my shirt and never bringing it back and so on. It was just too much. So, I was really glad that he was splitting. About two hours later he called me from San Jose and said that his car broke down and he wanted help. I said, "Freddie, we said goodbye, right? You are in San Jose and I am in Larkspur, so, I'll see ya." And he said, *"Okay,"* and he hung up. I know he went to the next number because that is the way he lived. I didn't see him again until years after that. He was gone. But he didn't go to Europe, he went to Mexico instead. Then I heard he was in L.A. and he was here and there. In the 80's I was playing and booking Lascaux. Do you remember Lascaux, downtown on Sutter Street? Did you go in there?

DON: Yeah, I remember I came back to town and you told me what to do and I ended up playing there.

DICK: I booked him a couple of times and then the last time I get a phone call and they said, where is Freddie and I was like, what do you mean? They said, he didn't show. The last gig he was supposed to play he didn't show up; didn't call me, didn't tell me. And then he left town again. That was the last time I saw him and that was back in the 80's.

DON: Do you think he went to New York?

DICK: Well, I have heard different things; like he was in L.A., he was in New York. What he does is burn all his bridges and then he splits, owing everybody money. He is real slick and people love him. He makes you think he is your best friend. But the Bill Evans thing, that was special.

DON: I think it was very special that you got to know him. I got to know him through my connection at Bop City with Virgil.

DICK: That was earlier, right?

DON: Yeah, I think it was a little earlier because he would come to town and then he would leave. He would always stay at the El Cortez down on Geary. That was his favorite hotel.

DICK: He was in real bad shape when he was staying on the boat. He did that gig at the Workshop because he needed the money. Helen Keane was calling him back and forth to try and get him to come back. His wife, whew! All her front teeth were rotten. It was hard to look at. She was real skinny. After she died he got straight. The one he married, that wasn't Lori that was...?

DON: Annette? Nanette?

DICK: I think so, and then he remarried and she freaked out and the story was that she jumped in front of a subway train. (This was Elaine)

DON: So, a tragic demise of his first wife. Bill was carrying around a whole lot of guilt and his music was affected by that. Not many people know about that story.

DICK: After that he got married and got all straightened out. That's when he looked good for a long time. He stayed clean for quite a few years, but she wasn't part of that life. Then it went downhill from there.

DON: Who was the one who bore the son, Evan? Elaine?

DICK: No, not Elaine, he didn't have any children with her.

DON: Nanette? Annette?

DICK: Is it Annette? The one he married, the second one, the straight one.

DON: I hope I am right about that.

DICK: Evan came later. I hear he is a composer.

DON: I have no idea what he has done lately.

DICK: I heard he is a composer of serious music.

DON: Well, that would be interesting. There was probably a lot of that around the house because Bill did master a lot of that music.

DICK: But he had him late because he was still on that second marriage. Now I never knew Lori, was she in between the two of them?

DON: I met Lori on that last trip, he wrote a song for her so I know she was significant. So we are talking August 1980, he died in September. He was traveling with Joe La Barbera and Mark Johnson. I knew they were going to play and I rushed down there in the afternoon. I thought I could catch them in a rehearsal, but when I got there they had just left. Joe La Barbera was there and I said I am an old friend of Bill's and I would like to catch him. Joe asked who I was and he called Bill and Bill said, "Send him up!" So when I went up to see him, Lori was there. But Lori was a traveling companion and it was very obvious that she was.

DICK: Yeah and when he got back into it again, that's when the wife said it was over.

DON: Did you hear him much in the 70's when he was very clean and very healthy, robust with long hair, which was a great period?

DICK: Yeah, he was real healthy then.

DON: Yeah, did a lot of European tours.

DICK: Compared to the way he was in '65. But it was great to see him.

DON: He had great respect for friends along the way, musicians, especially piano players. I had no trouble getting to know him. It was very easy.

DICK: Yes. I have a picture somewhere among my souvenirs, he was real loaded staying on the Boardwalk and they were taking Darvon by the handful, he and his ex-wife Elaine, because they were both kicking and they were both in really bad shape. He would take a huge handful at a time to kill the pain. They didn't sleep; they were up for days and days at a time. I had to get up and leave. I thought, this is the icon that I have treasured since 1958. I had him on a pedestal and then to watch him falling apart like that, I just couldn't stand it.

DON: Well, that is part of the temptation. I somehow used his lifestyle as an endorsement for what I wanted to do. If that's what it took to play with that much emotion, I wanted to at least experience it. I wanted to know about it, which led me on a road that took a long time to come back from. And it turns out that it isn't necessarily true.

DICK: Bill told me he never got high when he was with Miles. It was after he left Miles.

DON: It must have been right after, when he did *Everybody Digs Bill Evans*.

DICK: Yeah, that's when he started.

DON: Yeah, it was there. It probably was Philly Joe.

DICK: It was Philly Joe. He told me that. Yeah, and he said the whole time he was with Miles he was totally straight and when he formed the trio he said, "This may sound like a cliché, but the first time I got high, it was the best I felt in my whole life." And he knew at that moment that he was hooked for life. It was total surrender; he said he never felt so good. He was a very inward cat and he was shy and quiet and all that.

DON: And he was sophisticated as hell.

DICK: Yeah, and smart too. He was into deep breathing and even during that period in '65 when he was falling apart he was constantly reading big heavy intellectual kind of books. He was very well read.

DON: Oh yeah, and music and the current stage shows. He would memorize all those orchestrations, all those overtures!

DICK: Yeah, he also said the reason he knew he was hooked was not only did he feel better then he ever had but also, he had always been uncomfortable in his skin. And this changed that. When I was talking about the Darvon, I came over one day and he had this whole thing that he had written out for me. He wrote out the tune, *My Bells*. Then he had a list of stuff that I should listen to and try to play – sheet music. It was all this classical music. He thought I should look into it. My reading is terrible, but the fact that he did it, and the music paper was all like scratches, you could barely read it. He did it when he was totally loaded and had been up all night. I have to find that. I have it somewhere and I should take it out and frame it. The fact that he sat up all night – for hours – trying to think of stuff that would help me is humbling.

DON: When I heard about his death I was living in Portland and it was tragic for me too. I don't think I broke down but a local newspaper asked me to do an interview. This guy came out to talk to me and that's when I lost it; talking about it, talking about him meeting my son, talking about knowing him in San Francisco and talking about the music.

DICK: The first thing I bought of his was *Portrait of Jazz* which is still one of my very favorite albums of all time. I have listened to that album a million times and I have gone through several copies of it.

DON: You and I both know that we can't go to the piano and press those keys and get the same sound that he had. It was his touch. My wife Julie was a singer and she was totally in love with him and all of her girlfriends were totally in love with him. Later on, after we were divorced, they went to the Trident to meet him and couldn't believe it when they did. He was very friendly. He became friends with one of her girlfriends. Her name was Annette. She lived in San Jose and when he came to town he would contact her.

DICK: He had friends everywhere. You probably would dig hearing these interviews that I have, especially the last one. I came out here in '61 from New York and that's where I met my first wife and we decided to go to Europe for a few months. We said let's get out of here and packed up our station wagon and came to San Francisco not knowing one person. I just wanted to get away from the East Coast and we had no idea what it would turn out to be. I got out here and realized after a few days, I'm never going back. We found a pad the first day we were here; $75 for an apartment in the Castro on Henry Street, an old building. Three months later we moved to Sausalito in a big house for $135 a month! It was like eight rooms looking out at Tiburon. I rented a piano. I had lessons when I was a kid, classical music, and then I had a jazz teacher who showed me some stuff. Do you remember Kenny Elmore?

DON: Yes!

DICK: He was the guy who opened me up. He was a very good player, he died fairly early.

A Diary of the Underdogs

DON: I met him through Virgil.

DICK: I met him through Lee Konitz; he was playing in Mill Valley at the Palette which was Farwell Taylor's restaurant. *Farwell's Mill Valley*, which is a Mingus tune. He and Mingus go back. It burned down. A beautiful piano was in there, an English import that he brought in. I was living in Sausalito and I had just started working at KJAZ a couple of shifts a week. The very first interview I ever did was with Lee Konitz and Kenny Elmore, Monk Montgomery and Jimmy Lovelace. They were playing at the Palette in Mill Valley. This was 1962. I was new here, we had just moved to Sausalito and I didn't know anybody and I started meeting Marin County people through that scene. Bryce Rhode was playing week nights, actually he took the gig after Kenny, or maybe he was first. Konitz played; he was living up in Fairfax somewhere with Judy Tristano.

DON: She was a tenor saxophonist.

DICK: Exactly, Lennie's ex-wife. Lee was living with her in Fairfax and he wanted to get away from New York and he was just kind of cooling it and he started playing weekends at the Palette. He had that group I just mentioned so I went to hear them and after the gig one night, after they were done, I went over to the piano just to try it out and I started playing something. Monk picked up the bass and Jimmy Lovelace sat at the drums and they joined me and I played a tune. I think it was *Yesterdays*, one of my favorite tunes. I was just learning to stretch a little bit and I was learning on my own, mainly by ear.

DON: I remember that period. I met you around that time.

DICK: When I met you I was just getting into it. You were way far ahead of me. I was very impressed; you were one of the cats as far as I was concerned. After I got through, Lee came over and said, "Hey man, how long you been playing?" and I told him and he said you got soul man. He said, "You are doing some interesting things and I think I can help you." And he started giving me lessons. I took maybe a dozen lessons from him. He would come to my place, smoke weed, drink coffee and he would hang around for three or four hours. I think I paid him $5 or $10, something like that. We would sit in my little pad in Mill Valley. Dean Reilly was living near by in Mill Valley. Dean started coming over after that period, while I was studying with Kenny, and he would play the thing and to this day I thank him because he was really brave to come over and put up with my shit. He was showing me voicings and things that I was not aware of. So, I had a chance to practice and Dean was very patient with me. He would say try this and that. That was the last time I studied, that was like 1964! And then I met you when I was just starting around 1965.

DON: It seems that you were on the radio already.

DICK: Oh yeah, I started at KJAZ in '62, so there was a lot of music in my head. I was just trying to figure out what to do and Kenny opened it up for me. I could read the chord changes but I didn't quite know what to do with them. He showed me Bill Evans voicings and that kind of stuff. And I was like, WOW! I can do that! That was the beginning.

DON: Look what happened to you – you got a life! And you are a piano player and well respected and you play and you have a great band. Those guys are loyal; they have been with you a long time.

DICK: Yeah, this trio? Yeah, we've been playing since '99 or 2000.

DON: I met Steve Webber once, I don't know Bill, but I know of him.

DICK: Chris Amburger and I played together for years before that.

DON: That's right; I was going to ask you about Chris.

DICK: Yeah, we played together for a long time and finally I couldn't put up with his crap anymore. He's a great bass player, but just out there. He called me one day and cancelled four gigs! That was it. That was too much.

DON: Yeah, I had my times with Chris Amburger. He was referred to me by Francis Vanek when I lived in Portland.

DICK: Yeah, we played some gigs together.

A Diary of the Underdogs

DON: You knew Francis?

DICK: Sure. I played gigs with him and Chris. Chris turned me on to him. We did some casuals together. In fact, he came and played at Lascaux with us a couple of times. And then we did a gig at one of the hotels in the City.

DON: So you spent some years with him?

DICK: Yes. Then he moved back up North somewhere. I think he went to the Reno area and then up to Fort Bragg.

DON: He was in Santa Barbara for awhile. Good player.

DICK: I remember a couple times we played together, it really came together.

DON: What else do you want to share?

DICK: When I first got here I was working for the Examiner selling advertising on the street! It was classified; I was calling businesses trying to get them to by ads. It was great because it was salary plus commission. It was like $125 a week at that time and that was good money. That was 1961. We were living on Henry Street and then Sausalito and I was still working there. I did it for one year and during that year my territory was from Market Street up to North Point, so all of North Beach. I would leave in the morning, go have coffee with the guys, then I would take off on my territory and make three or four calls so I could write them down and then go hang out at Coffee Gallery where Howard Hesseman was the bartender. After he got a job at The Committee, as a back stage guy then he became Don Sturdy.

DON: You remember the guys in The Committee?

DICK: Yeah. Larry Harkin was there.

DON: Was Robin Williams there?

DICK: Later, Gary Goodrow, Hesseman, a whole bunch of them who went on to be movie stars. Then there was this guy, Danny Benson, the black guy, he was some kind of stage manager. He passed a few years ago. He used to call me at KJAZ all the time so I could get into The Committee for free whenever I wanted to. He was at the door and I used to go there a lot. I think that was around '64. But Howard, he was the bartender at that time at the Coffee Gallery. That's where I met Max Hartstein, he had a one man show of paintings and he was doing a play that he wrote and he was playing bass with a group, sort of like The Connection in New York, that idea. I met him there one afternoon and Howard was bartending. In fact, I even worked there for a little bit as a doorman and they were supposed to have Tiny Tim but he didn't make it and they brought out this old banjo player. They had this show and Hugh Romney, who later became Wavy Gravy, did a show there.

DON: Yeah, good times. I played there with Norman Williams. And that's where I met Max Hartstein because he played bass once in awhile.

DICK: So Max I got to meet there, that was '62. In '63 my wife and I bought a van and went to Mexico for a year. We went into this little town of Juanajito and we are coming out of the movies and there are two or three hip Americans and I look over and I recognize Max Hartstein! I said, "Max?" And he said, "Who's that?" I said, "Dick Conte." He came over and said hello and you know we had only met briefly before, he knew I did radio and played piano, and he said, "Come up to my pad, man, we are going to go and hang out." We followed him out to this little town, Marafio. He was living in this great pad that belonged to his aunt. He was staying there for months and months. He had his bass and he was doing painting and there were two or three people hanging out. In fact a chick that was there was Bob Dylan's manager's wife eventually can't think of her name. Dylan's manager's name was Albert Grossman.

DON: Also Janis Joplin's manager.

DICK: You ever see Dylan's album cover? He's standing there and there is a chick in a red dress, in front of a fireplace, it was one of his earlier ones, *Bringing It All Back Home*. Well, the chick in the red dress is the girl whose name I am trying to think of now. She was with Tom Law who was the brother of the actor,

A Diary of the Underdogs

Law, what was his first name? He died, John Phillip Law. She was traveling with this guy who was a road manager for Peter, Paul and Mary and they were all staying there at Max's place. We ended up staying there for a week or two. Tom Newman was also there, that's when I met him. Tom had just been living in Mexico for years. Did you know Bryce Wilson? He had spent a lot of time in a Mexican jail for dealing and he and Tom were real good friends. Anyway, Tom was this older cat, he was in his fifties, long gray goatee, a super hipster, and he was like this guru type. John Law split and it was Tom and the girl that I still can't think of her name. They went up to this mushroom country in the mountains of Oaxaca, to this magic mushroom place.

DON: Did you take the mushrooms?

DICK: Oh, yeah! It was 1963. We drove up there on this mountain road and got stuck over night. Indians were walking around with machetes and shit and we finally got to the town the next day. Wapa; which was the place of the magic mushrooms. At that time it was relatively unknown. Bunch of hippies knew of it and the locals knew of it; it was their religion. They were very down on gringos coming there because for the locals it was a sacrament. We went up there and ended up spending a whole month there! We couldn't get out, the rain wiped out the roads. I did mushrooms maybe three different times. The first time was quite amazing. I had my wife with me, Margie and we had a little shack up there for like $5. My wife was from Brooklyn. We met in New York, at Pan Am when we were both working there. We took our airline tickets, then quit and went to Europe and spent three months all over the Middle East and Europe. And let's see, after Max left my place, he went down to Palo Alto for awhile and then he went back to New York and got a studio there down in the Bowery. In '65 we took a road trip and drove back cross country and visited my folks and he said come and see me at my place. So we went and stayed overnight. He had been in touch with the woman whose name I still can't think of, she was living in Woodstock and was married to Albert Grossman. She was like twenty-five or thirty years younger than Albert, a flower child. She invited us to come up to Woodstock, so the three of us drove to Woodstock to this big house and Grossman was there and so was Bob Dylan! He was staying there. That album with her on the cover just came out and he had broken through really big time. It was a big old house and they gave us a wonderful bedroom and Max got really crazy that night. He was drinking and smoking and carrying on. And you know, he liked to challenge people and he was challenging everyone in the house. There was also a bunch of other people staying there. He made such a ruckus that the next day they said we had to leave. It was weird because the next morning we were sitting at this table having breakfast and I was sitting next to this guy, but I thought it was a woman, had this cap pulled down and I see this stubble and I had thought it was a chick. I am looking and looking and it turned out to be Bob Dylan! But he never talked to anybody. The previous night he had been playing that Chinese game, Go, with a couple of people, but he wouldn't talk to anybody. He would just sit in the corner. He was constantly writing. But we had to leave because of Max.

DON: Yeah, I remember that about him. But I got along with him and he was an outstanding bass player. He made more music than anybody.

DICK: I know, he and I would jam all the time. Then when he met this chick who lived in Palo Alto he split. And even though at the time in Mexico I didn't know who Dylan was, he later became like a staple to me. I followed and listened to all his stuff. I was totally apolitical until I met Max. He was totally political. He would go to Berkley, that's when they were having the big protests and all that. He would take me with him. I was there when they were throwing tear gas bombs and shit. Prior to that, I had never paid much attention to politics.

DON: I remember Jerry Rubin was a very active guy, did a lot of those speeches, flatbed trucks, the Hells Angels were there. I played a gig over there, Vince Guaraldi's trio played and I played with Virgil Gonsalves. That was over in Berkley, in the park somewhere.

DICK: I was at Golden Gate Park. Prior to that there was the thing in the Panhandle, which started it.

A Diary of the Underdogs

DON: Well, that was ongoing.

DICK: And up at Muir Beach they had scenes going on. I was there, I was living in Marin. It was a very inside thing. It wasn't advertised. It was word of mouth and hundreds of people would show up and there would be a rock band.

DON: Those were really exciting times.

DICK: They sure were. We got our minds blown!

DON: Yeah, you wonder if jazz music got affected by it all or if it was a secret recluse we went to. I mean we were a small percentage of what was going on. But still, we were considered part of it. They loved John Handy. They loved Charles Lloyd. All those rock concerts and all those people, even Bill Graham. They recognized it as a really valuable from of music.

DICK: Were you here when the Both/And opened?

DON: I was here when it was open.

DICK: That was around '65. I went in there because I was working at KJAZ and I met Delano Dean and his partner, Lenny. We became really close, in fact Delano and I were roommates for a time later on. Delano died a couple of years ago.

DON: Yeah, Delano was going to offer me his booking ledger and I was going to reprint it in a book.

DICK: We had a tribute to him out at Muir Beach. Bobby Hutcherson was there, they had been good friends. But anyway, that was the mid 60's and I fell into that scene. In fact, they were building the Both/And club. It wasn't even open yet, they were just getting it open. I got to be friendly with them. I was working part-time and all I had was playing music and I was just piecing it all together. I was on unemployment and I used to get by on practically nothing. In fact, when I met you down there I had just got my unemployment and then came down there! So I started working there as a bartender because I had been working at the No Name Bar in Sausalito. This is when they first opened the Both/And and Hampton Hawes was playing solo piano during the week. They tried to have a cocktail hour in there from like 5-7pm or something like that and Hamp would be playing piano and drinking and he was going downhill and there might only be four people in there. Then I got to see all the people. When Miles came, he was there two weeks in a row with that band, with Herbie and Ron and Tony. They were paying him something like $5,000 a week, which I thought was incredibly expensive. Imagine Miles for a week for $5,000! So I got to hear them, night after night. It was amazing; Ornette Coleman, Chick Corea, Circle, and all these out bands and Sam Rivers and Rashaan (Roland Kirk) and John Handy when they got a great band together, before the Monterey Band. So I got to be part of that scene.

DON: That was a great place to be.

DICK: They used to have Sunday afternoon jams. One time I went in and Milt Jackson was playing there at night. They booked Bobby Hutcherson and Milt together so it was like a rhythm section, the two of them. They had two sets of vibes or marimba and vibes or something like that, and so I'm sitting there and they started the session. Ed Kelly was the piano player but he didn't show up. I'm sitting in the front row and they started the set and Bobby looks down at me and gestures to me to go to the piano. I was like, oh shit! Fortunately they were playing something I knew, I don't remember what it was. So, I jumped up and started playing and we went through the tune and I thought they were going to kick me off the bandstand by then, but they didn't and here I was playing with them, I couldn't fucking believe it! So, I got to play another tune. I saw Monk there. He played like a week and half at a time and he didn't show up. But I remember my wife had become a jeweler and had made me this beautiful ring and they had the Sunday afternoon sessions so I went and sat in and played a few tunes, took the ring off and put it on the piano and I walked out and left it. I came back later and Monk was playing and I thought, I wonder if Monk got it? But I was bummed that I lost it.

DON: Did you see Stanley Willits there?

A Diary of the Underdogs

DICK: Yeah! And he covered his hands up.

DON: Yeah, I saw him one time at an upright piano and he had put a little mirror on top of the piano so he could see behind him! Anyway, let's wrap it up. You got a new CD called *Autumn Leaves* and you got your regular guys on it.

DICK: Recently at Yoshi's. Peter called me up and I had hit on him that maybe we could do a CD release. He said, "Oh man, I am booked months in advance!" If something should happen, he said he would let me know. Well sure enough, he called me up and said that he had a group cancel three nights and he had a Monday and Tuesday. So I think I took the Tuesday. It was only a few days in advance and we did the thing for free but he charged a $3 fee for tickets over the web and both shows sold out in a few hours; our show and the other guys' show. And what a gorgeous piano! It's a Hamburg Steinway; they brought it in when they opened the club. We had two shows and it wasn't anybody I knew but they came just because they wanted to see the club. I got full pay and they made money because people were buying drinks and food. I can't think of the tenor player who played the other night, a white, local cat. Anyway, that was a high point.

End: Dick Conte

Interview: Ron Marabuto-jazz musician, drummer- with Don Alberts and Chuck Peterson-jazz musician, saxophonist-December 3, 2008-at Bird and Beckett Books, San Francisco-about: John Marabuto, John Coppola, Rudy Salvini, Pepper Adams, Fred Murgy, The Golden Nugget, Zoot Sims, Virgil Gonsalves, Johnny Baker, Jerry Cournoyer, Jerry Coker, John Markham, Al Obidinski, Earl Hines, Tommy Flanagan, Barry Harris.

RON MARABUTO-CHUCK PETERSON

DON: Clarence Becton?

RON: Yeah, ever hear of him? He has been in Europe for years now.

DON: I think Sharky mentioned that guy.

RON: Yeah, I remember how hot they were. When I saw them it was Art playing. Yeah, they were hot - a hot rhythm section. I always remember them; it was one of the few things I had seen that really woke me up. They sounded like Horace Silver's band or something. I hadn't heard anyone around here play like that.

DON: Yeah, Art was playing pretty hard then.

RON: Yeah!

DON: I didn't know that about Art.

RON: Well that's what I always remember about him.

DON: Well, I played with him early on in the 60's and he was ok, it was controlled, he played a room, played the size of the band. I mean that's kind of what he does now. We all took a trip to New York a couple of years ago and he wanted to go jam at this place in Harlem, a little place in a bottom apartment and they asked him to sit and in man, I never heard him play like that! He was turning the sticks around and whacking them and those guys were playing hard, they were playing John Coltrane!

RON: Yeah, that's how I remember him. Yeah, and it's surprising to see him play now and he doesn't really play like that now – they were slamming!

DON: What band was this?

A Diary of the Underdogs

RON: I think it was Larry Vuckovich– I think he had the rhythm section, I don't remember who the bass player was – I was like ten or twelve!

DON: So, I was going to ask you – your musical career is pretty well respected and what I always got from you was a really good sense of time that was natural – and so, I was going to ask you if you really had to work hard at that or if it just came to you and you knew what it was? Was that a rocky road?

RON: It's still rocky! Just coming up with that music, I know what it is and I have a good idea of what I want the time to feel like.

DON: Was that always good?

RON: In my head it was – you know I was getting it out in my chops. To learn how to play hard and keep in time was not easy. I spent a lot of time on the metronome otherwise it was going to be a fight between me and the bass player. So, if I know I am right….

DON: Well, at some point you know you are right and that's a big day when that happens!

RON: Yeah, you start to trust yourself.

DON: Yeah, when you are playing and if anybody moves, you know it immediately.

RON: Yeah, if I am right, I can kind of see it around me. And that's been challenging for me because I have different feel then most people.

Ron Marabuto

DON: Do you know when that was?

RON: When I came back from New York.

DON: So, you learned a lot in New York?

RON: Oh, I learned a ton there, that's where I learned how to play.

DON: What period of your life was that?

RON: I was about twenty-five, twenty-seven. I spent about ten years there.

DON: You grew up in San Francisco?

RON: Well, the East Bay, El Cerrito mostly.

DON: Yeah, I know your Dad was a famous musician; I wanna talk about him in a minute. So, at some point you said, I gotta go to New York because that's where the cats are playing, right?

RON: That's what my ex-wife said, we are going to New York, and I said, uh…ok….I kind of got dragged. I knew that it was the right thing to do.

DON: So, where did you land?

RON: We lived more or less in mid-town. We had a loft there. The marriage didn't last all that long but the loft did. I got to play there a lot.

DON: So, where did you play?

RON: Oh, there were all kinds of places to play. There was my house for one. And then I had a bunch of friends out in Queens and people all over town who were playing. So I met a lot of people – all my friends. Everyday!

DON: So, who were some of the impressive people that used to come over?

RON: I worked with Pepper Adams a lot. That was really the best for me. There was something about my playing he liked. The rhythm sections were always these friends from Detroit guys from the 50's. Tommy

A Diary of the Underdogs

Flanagan a lot, Walter Bishop, Barry Harris. I had a car so I had to drive the guys to the gig. That was a big plus for me. Pick up Barry Harris in front of the Port Authority, a big bus station. He would take the bus in from Jersey.

DON: Who were some of the bass players?

RON: Ray a fair amount. I did a few things with George Mraz but not nearly enough. Everyone wanted him in those days. You know, these little things that I was doing he couldn't do.....

DON: Oh, there wasn't enough money.

RON: Yeah. And a lot of times, its funny, there would be a great piano player but not a real good bass player and that was on me. He definitely made it real clear.

DON: Oh yeah, because you got to keep it together.

RON: Yeah. Anyway, he was just brilliant, all the time, (Pepper Adams)

DON: Yeah, he was brilliant. Nobody surpassed him really.

RON: A couple times someone was sitting in and I was out front, probably had a few beers, but it just hit me how close to Bird it was. I was like this is it, that's Bird's phrasing and time, that's it.

DON: You mean Baritone sax?

Chuck Peterson

RON: Yeah, he was just playing a couple octaves lower but it was Bird and it just blew me away.

DON: Well he was one of those guys who must have absorbed it.

RON: Well, yeah, he knew Bird. He said he knew Bird not so much as a musician, they would just hang out, he was really young and Charlie Parker would go to Detroit and they would go to the movies and have dinner at his Mom's house and Pepper was an intellectual and Bird was really bright so he really appreciated it. The philosophical things they would get in to. He didn't want anything from him.

DON: Was Pepper Adams well documented?

RON: Well, not so much. There is this guy who has been writing his biography for twenty-five years. He called me about three or four years ago and said I have the discography finished! He's been working over twenty years!

DON: Sounds like Lewis Porter trying to write the Encyclopedia of Jazz. And he's been writing it for twenty years. So, who is writing Pepper's biography?

RON: Gary... (Chuck Peterson walks in) Hey, Chuck!

DON: So, we were talking about Pepper.

RON: Whenever Pepper played here, Chuck was there. We played a few times here with Pepper and my Dad and Chuck was always there.

CHUCK: I was surprised one time, I played with the Oakland Symphony, David Amran had written a piece for Jazz quintet and I played baritone and all I knew was written for alto sax, baritone sax and the rhythm section. Then we rehearsed, we did a full weekend concert. The first night out on stage I looked in the front row and there were your Mom & Dad in the front row. Then I found out he had written it for Jerry Dodgion and Pepper Adams.

DON: He was in Europe, Ron's Dad's generation John Marabuto...

A Diary of the Underdogs

CHUCK: He was a little older, yeah, I knew John from the 50's. I could talk about him for hours; I love him and miss him.

DON: Yeah, right; a pianist, writer, composer, arranger.

CHUCK: Great arranger and piano player. I took a boat cruise with him once to Alaska with John Markham and John Marabuto and me. I don't know if it was once week or two that we all spent in this one cabin and it was interesting.

RON: My Dad never got over that!

CHUCK: I have tapes of your Dad snoring. Markham used to set up a tape recorder.

RON: You didn't tell me that!

CHUCK: I had received a phone call from this cruise ship; Danny Patiris somehow was involved in hiring. It was the last cruise of the summer. I asked Markham, do you want to do this? And he said that he would do it only if Marabuto came also. So, he called John and John was reluctant….

RON: My Dad hated to leave home.

CHUCK: Yeah, but once he got out there, he had the best time of all three of us! But I learned so much from that because the three of us spent so much time together.

DON: How would you describe John Marabuto's style – his piano playing?

CHUCK: Extremely thoughtful. He would put down the pipe and think for a moment and would think it over about what he was going to play. He didn't believe in playing notes just to fill up the space.

RON: My Dad never did anything very quickly.

CHUCK: Yeah, but it was great, he was thinking it over. It wasn't like, ok, I will just play eight bars and a bunch of notes- he was going to play four or eight bars that were meaningful.

DON: How was he influenced? What kind of styles motivated him at that time?

CHUCK: Markham brought a tape player along and…..

RON: Do you have that? That was a good band.

CHUCK: No, we didn't tape the band; we listened to tapes of people like Art Tatum and Fats Waller late at night. We didn't play till 10pm. And he was the last one in, he was the social butterfly. Yeah, so, we would listen to Teddy Wilson and talk about Fats Waller.

DON: Would it be fair to say that he was a good stride player?

CHUCK: When he wanted to, yeah.

RON: He said his hands weren't big enough, you know? And he listened to Fats Waller and mainly Art Tatum was going in the background all the time. He said he couldn't really do stride because his hands weren't big, so he had to sort of work around it.

DON: So, modified stride?

RON: Yeah.

CHUCK: Well, like I said, John played thoughtful. Your Dad played behind the beat, right?

RON: Yeah.

DON: On purpose or is that how he felt it?

CHUCK: He had a plan and he was executing and not dragging, he was thinking and executing a thought out melodic line. But some drummers, I won't say who, made it difficult – that he was dragging the tempo. But show you how wrong they were – Markham would only go on this cruise if John went. Markham had no problem at all, he kept the time and had the attitude that Marabuto will be there when he gets there.

RON: Yeah, John was strong enough to do that.

CHUCK: Yeah, John loved that.

DON: Now there is one more joining us – Allison.

CHUCK: So, on this cruise, we stopped in Vancouver and Markham was still drinking in those days and he was hung over and didn't want to do anything – he just wanted to recover. So Marabuto and I walked into town and he wanted to go this music store because they sold Bosendorff pianos, which are the ones with the extra keys. Anyway, we had time to kill in Vancouver and he knew where this music store was and we walked there and he asked permission if he could play on this Bosendorff, and I decided to take a walk and come back in fifteen minutes or so. And I came back in fifteen minutes and he had a crowd! And he was just playing away!

DON: This stop in Vancouver was that part of the cruise?

CHUCK: Yeah. We were headed to Alaska; people came to see the glaciers. It was pretty exciting.

RON: Yeah, I did that thirteen times! I did it out of New York, yeah, it was that trip. I know more about Alaska then anybody needs to know.

DON: Was it an obligation of three or four months at a time like it is now?

RON: No, they just kept adding weeks.

CHUCK: You left from the East Coast?

RON: Well, they flew us to Seattle and started from there. And then we did like twelve trips, up and down and then back Ft. Lauderdale, so I went through the Panama Canal, saw Mexico a little bit. We went through the Caribbean also. There was this trumpet player – a nice guy but he was really – all these Lester Lannin guys. So, I learned that style.

DON: Which is kind of square right?

RON: It's not kind of square – it's horrible square. I really learned a lot actually because they played these odd dance tempos and they have to stay the same or the old people on the boat will get up and start yelling at you! So, you just had to stay the same and these guys had it down to an art, I really respected them. The music was awful but they could really do that – you know they ad-lib everything and second trumpet players making up parts all the time. They are amazing what they do! It's just terrible though!

DON: Yeah, they really got it down; they have been doing it for years. Yeah, a couple guys I ran into, they had been on the ship for eight years and I was thinking what kind of life do they have?

RON: They are secure out there.

DON: Yeah, they have been on there long enough they have their own TV in their own cabin. I actually wanted off as soon as I could get off.

CHUCK: I remember when we got on – and I was the leader – I got the trio together and so when we boarded the ship and instead of the leader having his own cabin all three of us in this tiny cabin – below the water line! No portholes; the absolute minimum.

DON: Tell me a little bit more about John – when he got into arranging. He had a talent for band arranging too?

CHUCK: He wrote some for Rudy Salvini's band.

RON: That was one of the first things I remember was going to Rudy's rehearsals, because my Mom worked on Saturday, so my Dad was babysitting me. So I would go to the Union Hall to the rehearsals every Saturday.

DON: How old where you?

RON: I was like five or six. And watching Markham……

CHUCK: He arranged like he played the piano. Late in his life he was still writing octet arrangements for Rudy had an octet right up until, well, a couple of months ago when he had his……but John's arrangements were incredible. Rudy would ask John to write an arrangement but John wouldn't write it until he was ready to write it.

DON: So, what came first the rehearsal or the arrangement? Sounds like the rehearsal came first.

CHUCK: Well, we used to rehearse once a month. And when Marabuto had an arrangement ready, Rudy would go get it. They were great arrangements.

DON: What was his instrumentation – four or five trumpets?

A Diary of the Underdogs

CHUCK: Well, the big band was the regular four trumpets, four trombones, five Saxes. The octet was alto, tenor and baritone, trumpet, trombone.

DON: Do you remember some of the tunes?

CHUCK: Well, there were standards...I'm having a hard time thinking of titles. I remember one – *If Dreams Come True*. By himself, which is to this day......Bill Perkins went out to see your Dad because he knew he had written this arrangement with the Lester Young intro. He had written it for the octet with that Lester Young saxophone, playing the Lester Young intro. It was a great arrangement, we couldn't play it...

DON: Do you remember some of the guys in the band, maybe in the sax section or something...the big band?

CHUCK: Well, Jerry Dodgion was there. Danny Patiris. It's a little confusing because when it first started out it was a regular standard two altos, two tenors and baritones. Then we switched to three tenors – Harold Wiley, Danny Patiris and myself – early in the band I was the last tenor. The reason I was there was because they knew it was those other guys that were going to solo my job, they knew that I wasn't going to play over solos – I was just happy to be there.

DON: You mentioned Bill Perkins – was he in that band?

CHUCK: He came in later. There were a whole lot of guys, Jerry Dodgion went on the road with Norvo-different guys played – I left the band when Jerry Coker came to town. We already had to tenors in the band. Jerry Coker was interested, he had already wrote several arrangements for the band and he would come to the rehearsals and he would be standing in front of the band and there were two other jazz tenors and me. I'm thinking Rudy is too polite – he had only fired one person whom I won't name. But anyway, I had an opportunity to play a Latin dance on Sunday afternoons and they were working the Sands Ballroom in Oakland and I said, well, I knew that Coker belonged in that band, it was silly for him to show up with his arrangements and have nothing to do, and he should have been in the band. So, I smoothly withdrew and let Coker come in. Ben Hughes was in band, he still is in the band. Trumpet player was Alan Smith; he was in there almost all the time. Jerry Cournoyer was the main arranger. Dean Reilly was there too – bass player.

DON: John Markham on drums?

CHUCK: No, he wasn't there yet – the guys that were there twenty years later were: Dean Reilly, Alan Smith, Harvey, me and Rudy. Other guys came in and dropped out....

DON: So, the full band would be late 50's?

CHUCK: We started in the mid 50's – 56, something like that.

DON: Then the octet was the later era?

CHUCK: No, it went at the same time. As a matter of fact, it might have preceded the big band because I was sort of new in town and I discovered the octet, he called me at the last minute because somebody couldn't make it.

RON: Were you the one who sent my Dad the tape of you guys at Monterey? The first Monterey Jazz Festival.

DON: Were you in that band? The Virgil Gonsalves Big Band – no trombones.

CHUCK: Yeah.

DON: Five saxophones, five trumpets.

CHUCK: I don't know who was first. I know going down with Rudy once when we played – it was the big band– behind Earl Hines and Billie Eckstine was the same band but with different leaders, different drummers. Charlie Persip. Then when we played the Earl Hines music – Earl rehearsed the band....

DON: He was in San Francisco for a time, in fact in died here.

CHUCK: That's true. Well, Earl stayed in town for years. Your Dad used to tune his piano.

RON: Yeah, they were in the right arrangements for him. Oh, yeah, they would hang out all day. He loved

A Diary of the Underdogs

Earl. The gold teeth and the smoky voice – I had never seen anybody like him.

DON: Big hands too…big guy.

CHUCK: It was basically Rudy's band and we played a couple of gigs – or at least one – Earl Hines at the Cannery – they had a big grand piano in there and a big view. I think he wrote a tune called the *Cannery Walk* or something like that. We played there – it was basically Rudy's band. One thing I will always remember about Earl Hines is that if he played an eight bar intro – you better pay attention because you never knew where he started! He may have been starting on the third beat of the second bar or something. But it was great!

DON: Now what about the guy that got fired from Rudy's band, you said he never fired anybody?

RON: Its not that big of a story, he was expecting Rudy…..

CHUCK: Well, you weren't there….

RON: No, I wasn't. Was this not that long ago or this was a long time ago?

CHUCK: No, it was quite awhile ago. I was working with David Winn and that band was rehearsing on Wednesday afternoons, I would stop by sometimes on my way to a matinee and I walked by – it was at the Union on Jones Street – and I walked in – just killing time and I saw this episode unfold and I thought it was a joke. I thought they can't be serious! A couple of the trumpet players got fed up with one of the other members of the rhythm section. One guy had a very deep powerful voice and he was about 6'5 and he was very threatening. And that basically was it. I don't want to bad mouth this drummer. I already have revealed that it was a drummer that's as far as I go! It didn't have anything to do with the quality of the guys playing; he was suggesting different tunes and etc. And these trumpet players got up and were standing behind him - it was funny!

DON: But anyway, it was the end of it?

CHUCK: Yeah.

RON: In regards to my Dad's writing, his favorite thing was this twelve piece band. That was his favorite ensemble.

CHUCK: Did you tell him about the Golden Nugget band?

RON: Oh, man! That was serious 60's!

DON: That was a club called Golden Nugget?

CHUCK: Yeah.

RON: Yeah, it was in North Oakland.

CHUCK: Just a corner neighborhood bar. Did you go there?

RON: I was too young. The guy who owned it was a Woody Herman freak – Stan Kenton, and he loved big bands.

CHUCK: The co-leaders were John Coppola; he was a driving force behind the band. But his co-leader was Fred Murgy who played trombone with a bunch of people. I have a picture of them. They called it the John Coppola/Fred Murgy band. And your Dad wrote a bunch of arrangements.

RON: I was like, nine or something.

CHUCK: That's why you can't pin down the number because Coppola being a trumpet player and having been on the road a long time and he loved playing with other trumpet players. One time – the book was written for two trumpets, one trombone, tenor sax and baritone – I played baritone. I was not a featured soloist- I was the anchor of the band. I was only there…..anyway, Coppola loved to have trumpet players. He would bring up Al Porcino on a regular basis.

RON: There were a lot of great players featured.

CHUCK: One time it was at least three and I think we got it up to four and they were all talented. It was Porcino, Coppola, and Condoli…and at one point someone brought up that the brass section was getting a little lopsided. And of course John Marabuto was the piano player and wrote some great arrangements.

A Diary of the Underdogs

DON: This is the band at the Golden Nugget that we are talking about?

RON: Yeah.

CHUCK: There would be guest artists all the time. Frank Rosolino came up regularly. Conte Condoli came up often. And Al Porcino was around more often then not.

DON: Did he ever bring the Woody Herman Band in?

CHUCK: No, the bandstand was not built to accommodate a big band.

RON: It was a small place.

CHUCK: Yeah, just a corner saloon. We moved a couple of times…. But I am proud to say some of the guys they brought back twice. I remember when Zoot Sims was one of the first. And I think he came in thinking it would be like the Jerry Mulligan concert band where you would come out and be featured. That was not the case. Coppola had to calm him down and say that there wasn't room for him to get on and off the stand. It was kind of a homemade bandstand. I wasn't in on it, but I am sure he had to tell him – you get on the bandstand and you don't have to play all the parts, you can just solo when you want to – and so forth. But he came back! Rosolino came several times and Ray Brown once.

DON: What period was this?

CHUCK: Middle 60's.

RON: Yeah, Dad would come home so happy!

CHUCK: Well, yeah! It was fun! Yeah, and you know Coppola had a humorous side to him.

DON: Yeah. He was a tricky little guy. He would throw you a chart looks like its simple and has a little tricky thing in it.

CHUCK: It was a good little band, all these great guests. It's hard to say how big the band was because it was always changing. The core of it was three brass and two reeds.

DON: And core rhythm section – did that stay the same?

CHUCK: Yeah, there was John Markham, Al Obidinski.

DON: Yeah, I will be talking to Al, so I will ask him about that.

CHUCK: Ask him about a rumor – or maybe it isn't a rumor – Coppola told me that the first time Zoot had played he was reluctant to get on the stand because he wanted to spend an evening playing strange arrangements And they made it clear, Danny Patiris plays the parts and you play anytime you want. And I mean, Zoot was an idol of mine, and I am watching him getting on the stand kind of reluctantly and I thought oh, I hope he isn't going to be sulking all night. He made early contact with the bartenders and so they would bring him drinks to the stand and everybody knew that Zoot was a pretty serious drinker. But the funny thing is at the end of the night when the club owner announces who will be the featured guests next time, and he's trying to do this and empty the club by 2am and so it's like 1:30am and its time to quit. He is in the middle of this speech about future featured artists on such and such a date and Zoot went right into *Good Night Sweetheart* all by himself. And of course the rhythm section jumped right in! And they were getting into it and they poor guy was trying to close the place down. It was hard to get him on the stand and it was hard to get him off the stand.

RON: A lot of musicians like that.

DON: And a lot of those people liked coming to San Francisco. I am finding out more and more that a lot of those people from New York liked to come here. And people from L.A. as well. They liked it out here and they found good rhythm sections and comfortable ways to play, and a good reception.

RON: Yeah, that was pretty much it. Everyone was happy.

DON: Well, yeah, and San Francisco has always had a pretty high level of musicianship and integrity and it's an interesting attitude too. San Francisco does claim its own, I used to love that sign up there that Sonny had in the bar that said – We don't care what they think in the "Apple," or something like that. I always felt that San Francisco had its own style. Anyway, did you happen to come up in that early San Mateo band? It

A Diary of the Underdogs

was a bunch of volunteers, Al Molina talked about that, I think Kent Glenn had a bunch of arrangements and no sheet music it was taught all by rote. And eventually it became charts. Kent was interesting because he would show you your part, even if it was the harmony part, and he was pretty emphatic about it, he wanted you to learn your part. Al used to go to this thing and he told me that's how it was.

CHUCK: I got to know Kent later on. He stayed at our house a lot, he was homeless, and we had an extra room. Really didn't get to know him that well, he and his career were kind of mysterious.

DON: Yeah, I met him during the days of Haight/Ashbury. We were playing the same club.

CHUCK: Was that during the Vince Wallace days?

DON: Yeah, playing Bop City.

CHUCK: Vince Lateano?

DON: Vince wasn't here then, that was too early for Vince. Philly Joe Jones he came to town. It was this place called the Haight Levels. So, he played there and so did I- and through Jimmy Ryan later on I found out that he and Jimmy Ryan were great buddies most of his life. He was always hanging around Jimmy and his family. I didn't know much about his career and he didn't make many records. He was responsible for getting Johnny Baker recorded with Vince. And there was one record and it's on vinyl and Kent Glenn is responsible for that.

RON: My Dad was with Johnny Baker the night I was born! My Mom was looking for him. They were real buddies and they were hanging out. He really liked Johnny Baker.

DON: Yeah, I used to hang out with him too, we got along good.

RON: He is a nice guy.

DON: Yeah, and what a player, no preparation, he would just go to the piano and start burning it out!

CHUCK: I never got to know him, we met but I never played with him, when the Cellar was happening and Brew Moore was playing and I think Bill Wejohn and John Baker came in and sat in. Brew played entirely different. I spent a lot of time hanging with Brew. But I really could tell the difference in their playing. John copied Brew and Brew altered his style a bit, but wasn't totally going to change his style.

DON: You probably knew Harold Wiley?

CHUCK: Oh, sure. Harold and Brew had a band together. They used to play the Tropics. It was on Geary and Arguello.

RON: That is the one place I could get in! When I was six and seven – that's where we were on Sundays.

DON: So, we are talking about Cedric Heywood. Was Cedric from here?

CHUCK: Hard to say, I think he was from Houston. He had played with Lionel Hampton and he even played with Kid Ory.

DON: Well known piano player.

CHUCK: And a very good arranger. He was fun to play with and he was the kind of guy when you sat in and if he felt that you were uncertain about a change or something he would lead you. He was a very sensitive accompanist.

DON: Anything quirky about him?

CHUCK: Nope! He worked after hours.

DON: Did he ever work a place called The Scene on upper Fillmore?

CHUCK: He played everywhere. I played with him on some place on Bush Street – the place in the 900 block that changed names a lot, it was owned by Michael DuPont, from the DuPont family. Anyway, we were there and there was a comic on and Cedric fell asleep at the keyboard.

DON: Who was the comic?

CHUCK: Buddy Lester. And he made a semi-racist comment and I looked over at Cedric and there he was sleeping away! Wonderful guy!

DON: Yeah, I haven't heard much about him, you are the first to talk about him. Richard Brown who is a

A Diary of the Underdogs

bartender at Dog Patch had a lot of good stories about the early Fillmore. For awhile he was a bartender at a place called The Scene on upper Fillmore above California and I played there, a lot of people played there on and off. But I think that he mentioned that Cedric came in and played piano there. I don't know if you remember that?

CHUCK: No, I just remember the Tropics. I was allowed to sit in because I knew the tunes and Brew had a pretty set repertoire – that was on Sundays, and I would sit in late for a couple of tunes. And so I am on the bandstand and in walks Milt Jackson. And Cedric knew him and said, *Hey! Come on up and play!* So, Milt is like two feet away from me at the piano and I'm thinking Oh, My God! I can't play with Milt Jackson, are you kidding! And sure enough they played *Bags Groove,* which is not difficult except that nobody plays slow blues like Milt Jackson and Brew Moore was my mentor – and when you play slow blues you don't double time, its like playing a ballad, and when you play slow blues, you play slow blues and two feet away from me is the greatest slow blues player in the Western World!

DON: Yeah, he is pretty impressive. One night I was working at a place called Soulville on McAllister, one of those six nights a week after hours jobs, and the place was really dark and you couldn't really see anything at all. And all of a sudden Milt Jackson is there! And he didn't know if he was going to play or not, he was interested in us and likes what were doing. And so, he sat down and played piano with two fingers! And it really was him; it was crisp and brittle, but still sounded like him! It was great, just great. He was just hanging, a very friendly guy.

RON: Yeah, and most swinging-est and funky-est guys around, any of those guys.

CHUCK: I was near out of my mind trying to remember what Brew Moore had taught me about slow blues, but with Milt Jackson....

DON: Yeah, he liked coming in. We used to see him a lot at the Black Hawk. He had beautiful sounds. Do you remember a place called Fack's on Market Street?

CHUCK: Sure. That was one of those places…See, I came to town in '51 and it was going…..

DON: There were two, Fack's One, and Fack's II later on. The reason I remember it is because I saw the Miles Davis Quartet there. They came to town, Miles' first quartet. He just came out with Percy Heath, Horace Silver and Art Blakey and they came to town. And actually I have that record on ten inch vinyl! Yeah, and Miles didn't come back for awhile so it had to be 58 or something like that.

RON: That late?

DON: Might have been sooner…..

RON: Yeah, I think so……I think that was early mid 50's.

DON: Well, anything you have to say guys? Do you want to give advice to the Jazz world?

RON: Jeez……

CHUCK: He is half my age, but he has been to New York, he knows what it is like.

DON: Yeah, he was telling me about New York, very interesting and he got to play with the masters, he knew a lot of those guys.

CHUCK: Didn't you say that Jerry Dodgion and Pepper Adams were pretty tight. Jerry had a place in New Jersey or something like that.

RON: Yeah, I was telling Allison that…….

CHUCK: Your Dad went and tuned his piano…..

RON: Well, he rebuilt this Steinway, Jerry and he was married to Dottie at the time, they were house sitting this Steinway, someone couldn't have it in their house, and it was a good one so they called my Dad (John Marabuto) and said come and rebuild this thing, we will pay you for the trip. They were there for like three weeks or a month and Dad worked on it. Our family was pretty close. And when they got it together they had a piano party, it was December and they just invited all the piano players they knew. We had to invite everybody, it was Christmas and it was snowy and was hard to get out there and they all showed up!

A Diary of the Underdogs

DON: Was Tommy Flanagan there?

RON: Well, they said they couldn't get Tommy off of the piano! They mentioned a whole lot of other players; I don't remember all of them. Certainly Roland Hanna, a lot of great players with all kinds of styles. Jerry was into different styles, so there were some older styles, my Dad liked kind of in between the boppers and the Teddy Wilson thing. So there was a bunch of guys like that; maybe, Sal Mosca. Can't remember all of them, just a bunch of guys and they don't have names; great players, maybe not household names. John Bunch, people like that. Anyway, all these people showed up with different styles and they all liked each other. And then there was my Dad, Mr. Social! So, this was like an all nighter, you know.

CHUCK: Yeah, we all loved John Marabuto. I can't think of anybody in my fifty year career that was deeper into music then John Marabuto; his whole concept, not just flying fingers, life changing arrangements. Everything was just top of the line. He knew so much!

RON: My Dad would teach, he had students and he would tell his stories and they would just last hours and hours. No set lessons, turned out to be a hang. And he also tuned pianos for a lot of musicians and that would turn into an all day thing. After he died all these musicians have told me all this stuff about him! Like, this one woman was taking lessons from him and it was like the third hour and she said, *John! I gotta go home!* They were people he was teaching on the piano – he had the same clients for like thirty-five years or something. Jeff Neighbors told me that, *every time I call your Dad I block out the afternoon and get a six-pack!* They would do the thing in a hour and half and then they would end up playing all day.

ALLISON: He tuned my piano!

CHUCK: I had a friend who was a piano player, very fine ear and when he found out that your Dad was tuning pianos over at UC right?

RON: I don't know if he did those.

CHUCK: Somewhere over at Berkley on the Campus…..and John could tune a piano that would hold.

RON: Yeah, my Dad would sometimes have to tune it and then it sometimes it wouldn't hold and he would have to tune it again. He sometimes would have to go over it a few times and he hated that! But once he got started he couldn't stop.

DON: Yeah, he was smart enough to put a bigger pin in it if it was slipping. They don't bother to do that these days.

End: Ron Marabuto, Chuck Peterson

Interview: Dean Reilly-jazz musician, bassist-with Don Alberts, December 10, 2008-San Francisco-about: Vince Guaraldi, Kingston Trio, Shelly Robbins, Hungry I, Buddy Mottsinger, Don Asher, Al Plank, Jeannie Hoffman, Black Hawk, Art Pepper, Brew Moore, Earl Hines, Benny Goodman, Anita O'Day, Vernon Alley, Bill Young, Chet Baker, the "Say When," John Rae, Jerry Spain, Local 6, the Trident, Frank Werber, Tom Reynolds, Steve Atkins, Noel Jewkes, Lou Levy, Eddie Duran, Ornette Coleman, Jackie and Roy, Enrico Banducci, Buddy Barnhill, Zoot Sims, Al Cohn, Vince Lateano, Moose's.

DEAN REILLY

DON: We lost two last week and then we lost Jeannie.

DEAN: Yeah, it just goes on and on!

DON: And Omar Clay and Henry Irvin. I didn't know him, did you?

DEAN: No. And I just got an email from Carlos about……can't remember.

DON: Yeah, Carlos is becoming the old bitch guy! Bob Riddle wanted a San Francisco obituary before his

A Diary of the Underdogs

Wednesday show, which is today. I didn't find one so far, I don't know if anybody has found one. Okay, so looking at your bio. Your father was James C. Reilly. Do you still play the pocket trumpet?

DEAN: Yeah. Daily!

DON: Really! No shit!

DEAN: Yeah, even if its five minutes. Just to play everyday and I play it on gigs too.

DON: There is a guy I met in Portland that plays one and he is pretty good too.

DEAN: It wasn't Don Smith was it?

DON: No.

DEAN: That is who I bought my horn from.

DON: I know you played a lot with Vince Guaraldi.

DEAN: Yeah. That was one of the first things I did here.

DON: Who was the drummer?

DEAN: In the early days it was Eddie Duran. We were the house trio at the Hungry I. And we did two LPs that were made into CDs. And they still sound pretty good.

Dean Reilly

DON: I talked to Eddie a few weeks ago and he really liked Enrico Banducci; a guy who really represented the artist.

DEAN: Yeah. He wasn't in it for the money. And it made happenings and it made money. They were lined up.

DON: So, at the Hungry I, did you run into those piano players that played the early sessions with Clyde Pound, Don Asher, Buddy Mottsinger, did you know him?

DEAN: Yeah! Buddy and I were house duo at the Black Hawk.

DON: What kind of guy was he?

DEAN: He was like a little old lady! He was so finicky, so precious. And he played wonderfully and we got along good musically. He had perfect pitch though and he would come over to my place and wouldn't let me put on any records on my stereo because the pitch wasn't exact. He would be like, *take that off!* Let's see, I have my scrapbook here, maybe I will get some ideas out of that.

DON: So, Vince Guaraldi...Is that when you went with the Kingston Trio?

DEAN: No! That was much later. Here is a picture of me and Buddy Mottsinger and Lloyd Davis at the Black Hawk. It must have been Red Norvo. We were playing his intermissions. Yeah, there's Red, Monty Budwig and Tal Farlow.

DON: Yeah, Tal, great man. Did you know Monty?

DEAN: Oh, sure. Monty and I hung a lot!

DON: Was he around here for awhile?

DEAN: Yeah. He had a pad here. I would go up there after a gig and play duets and laugh ourselves silly till the wee small hours.

DON: How about Shelly Robbins, did you know that guy?

A Diary of the Underdogs

DEAN: Oh yeah. I lived in the same building as he did.

DON: What kind of piano player was he? Was he a stride player?

DEAN: No! He played real pretty. Couldn't play the blues to save his ass but knew a lot of tunes. He made good changes. His favorite tune was *Putting on the Ritz*. And he was very tricky. He had show tunes down pretty well and he was a Hungry I piano player.

DON: You know Don Asher right?

DEAN: Yeah.

DON: And was Clyde part of that?

DEAN: Yeah, seems like it.

DON: I remember seeing you with Lou Levy and Vince Guaraldi….

DEAN: Did you now?

DON: Yeah, it was upstairs I think somewhere on Sutter – I can't remember…..

DEAN: Oh, where the hell was that?

DON: I think it was around 1993.

DEAN: I have a tape of that. That sounds about right.

DON: Where else did you play?

DEAN: I played at Moose's and the Wash bag.

DON: Oh, Lou Levy played the Wash bag?

DEAN: Oh yeah, maybe four or five times; once with Al Cohn, I remember on a Sunday afternoon, and Vince Lateano. That was one of my highlights. I love Al Cohn!

DON: And Zoot came out here at one time – in the old……

DEAN: Great American Music Hall, I saw him there with Al and Jimmy Rowles.

DON: How about the Golden Nugget in the East Bay; big bands, with John Marabuto and maybe John Markham?

DEAN: Well, the Golden Nugget I did that with Piestrup Band. Don Piestrup. I am still on that band. In fact I just got an email today that since Art Dorty died, Dave LeFever is taking over the band and we have our first rehearsal in the New Year – January 5th. It is going to be renewed. Jim Rothermel is playing in Art Dorty's place. But that was the Golden Nugget with John Rae on drums.

DON: You used to have to call Johnny at the Union Hall right to find out about a gig?

DEAN: Yeah! He had some official capacity there.

DON: Switchboard.

DEAN: Yeah, you had to have some time on your hands to ask him what's doing. He would be like well, I'm here at this gig tonight and then I'm over there tomorrow night and he would go on for like ten minutes.

DON: (looking at pictures) Man, you have some good stuff here! Who is that?

DEAN: That's Jimmy Lunceford, Illinois Jaquette. And that's Paul Webster, Jimmy Lunceford's high note trumpet player. He was a trumpet freak in those days. I have a lot of autographs…..

DON: What about Tom Reynolds and Al Plank – did you know those guys?

DEAN: Oh yeah!

DON: Did you do the Playboy gig with those guys?

DEAN: I subbed for John Mosher in that trio maybe six times. John was the regular bass player. And then Plank and I had the gig at the Hyatt Regency from '79 I think until '83.

DON: Duo?

DEAN: It started out as a duo, the room manager used to walk through and he would say, *play a samba!* And so we would struggle with a samba, and one day he said, *wouldn't it be easier if you had drums?* And we said, *yeah!* And he said, *I will see what I can do.* So, Scott Morris came in. So, we became a trio. And then Vince Lateano became available when Cal died so we switched drummers and Vince came in and

A Diary of the Underdogs

somehow we were able to add a fourth guy. We had Noel Jewkes. That was the sweetest job in the world; Monday – Thursday from 4pm – 8pm.

DON: Great gig! So, what were you playing – what was it like?

DEAN: Oh, I have a lot of cassettes of that. We played whatever tunes we felt like and there was no pressure. No one told us when to take a break or anything. We were on our own and it was union sanctions. Oh, look, I have Fats Waller's autograph!

DON: How did you get that?

DEAN: Oh, I used to go check out bands…..

DON: WOW! You had to be very young…

DEAN: Yeah, I was in high school.

DON: When did this music bug really bite you? When did you realize that it was really important to your life?

DEAN: Well, I took piano lessons because my Dad, my Dad played almost every night. I would hide under the piano with my soldiers or whatever. He played a lot of light classical things. He had been a bassoonist in a Navy band. So, he got me playing bassoon in junior high school. And it seems like we never really talked much – but he exposed me to it. Got piano lessons, but he really didn't help me there. Once in awhile if I was struggling with something he would show me how it went. He was good, he didn't ride me. So, I liked it.

DON: Yeah, something happens to us when we play Jazz, most everybody.

DEAN: Yeah.

DON: And something happens at a particular time and then you become really responsible to the music. For me it was Benny Goodman and Teddy Wilson, what they did just really stuck.

DEAN: Here is Teddy's autograph. I got Benny Goodman……

DON: What is this? A check? It says, $154 to Dean Reilly from Park Recording Company – 200 East 64th Street, New York.

DEAN: Yeah, that was a paycheck. $154! Thanks a lot Benny. I had to go to Chicago for that.

DON: Benny was notoriously cheap!

DEAN: Oh, Jesus! Yes he was. Here is the Black Hawk, look what it says,

DON: BLACKHAWK – TURK & HYDE – SAN FRANCISCO CALIFORNIA – CENTER OF WEST COAST JAZZ. On the back - COMING IN 1960 & 1961: CAL TJADER, AMAD JAMAL, MILES DAVIS, SHELLY MANN, JERRY MULLIGAN. Says, MINORS ALLOWED. And so these guys did come, in fact I saw most all of them.

DEAN: Yeah, they would come in for a week, maybe two weeks.

DON: It also says: GOOD ONLY ON TUESDAY, WEDNESDAY, THURSDAY AND SUNDAY, SUNDAY JAM SESSION FROM 3-7PM.

DEAN: What is this a pass or something?

DON: Yeah, ADMIT ONE.

DEAN: So, anyway, you asked how the bug bit me – I was in high school and in the class ahead of me was a very good friend who played tenor sax and so once in awhile we used to skip school and go into Tacoma and there was a music store there and in the back room guys would go and jam. That was heaven for me, hearing guys make up music on the spot.

DON: What kind of music?

DEAN: Standards. I remember playing *How High the Moon.* That was the anthem. Yeah, so one night, I was either a freshmen or sophomore, and they said, lets go out and hear this Duke Ellington guy out at the dance hall. So, we went and got a ride with some guys out to the dance hall. We got there early and watched them set up, and we were like WOW- fascinating! We watched them tune up, and then the band – Jimmy Blanton on bass, I was right in front and six feet from him! And my hair went straight up! It was like an eight mile ride out to the dance hall with these guys and then they said, well we are going to go home now, after the gig was over, and we were like, we will walk! So, we could get it out of our system. We were really fired up. We wanted to linger. Sonny Greer – this was the original band. Ben Webster Band. Rex Stewart, Cootie Williams, so it was even before Ray Nance, you know.

DON: (Looking at stuff) What about this?

DEAN: That's a little foggy for me; I think I played the Trident maybe just one night, I think I subbed for somebody. Rob Denato who I played with quite a bit around here – Brazilian piano player, do you know about him?

DON: No.

DEAN: Oh, he could really play that Brazilian stuff on piano. We played three weeks at the El Matador with Bud Shank, Denato and Tom Albering on drums. And then Denato played with Chet at the Trident and it seems like only one night. But then I remember I asked Denato and Chet, they both came over - I was living in San Anselmo – and they came over after the gig and we had a little tea party or something in the middle of the night.

DON: Some great things happened at the Trident– I heard that was the place then in the 60's – 70's. Bill Evans was there early on, and Cal Tjader was there.

DEAN: Yeah, and Brazil 65 right?

DON: Yeah, when they hit. What was the owner's name?

DEAN: Frank Werber?

DON: Yeah!

DEAN: Yeah, he was the manager of the Kingston Trio, that's how I got on the Kingston Trio. I did Kingston Trio – 62 to 67, five or six years.

DON: All over the world?

DEAN: Yeah, Folk music. I was on salary. It was nice. Good set up and really nice guys.

DON: Yeah, I talked to Frank Passantino and Frank always talked about that. And Frank got a lot of his connections and establishment through working with those guys.

DEAN: Yeah, he was Bob Shayne's bass player for most of the time.

DON: So when you were home you'd play the Hungry I?

DEAN: Yeah…….well no….

DON: That was the biggest venue – or was it the Trident?

DEAN: Yeah, Trident, mostly. We would go out for two weeks and come home for two weeks. Yeah, we were out half the time, but I was on salary which was neat, yeah, I come home and I am still getting paid!

DON: Did you know Tim Hardin during those days?

DEAN: No.

DON: Tim Hardin was around at the same time you were. I only knew him because he played with John Briani.

DEAN: Mmmm, is that right, well that was after me then.

DON: Yeah, might have been later on. Got anything about Flip Nunez– he was mid career for you I guess?

DEAN: Well, I had a gig in San Rafael for a year – a place called the Executive Lounge and Flip was the first piano player – it was a trio job. Buddy Barnhill on drums. And Louise, she was on the gig. We had a four-piece thing. I got my piano moved to the gig. That assured the gig for quite awhile.

DON: Didn't George Muribus follow Flip Nunez in there? Or was that a sub situation?

DEAN: No, Flip played it for about two or three months and then Steve Atkins came in. That would have been about 69. I think I was split up by then with my wife at the time.

DON: What about Smith Dobson? Did you get together with him?

DEAN: Just occasionally on informal things, I don't know if we ever worked a gig. He would sit in or I would sit in – so we knew each other.

A Diary of the Underdogs

DON: What about Vince Cattolica?

DEAN: Yeah.

DON: George Cerutti.

DEAN: Yeah. George played accordion and piano. We were house trio, with Paul Miller on guitar, George, me – Channel 7 TV – we did The Jack La Lane Show. I think it was once a week – I forget now. We did exercise music.

DON: That's a sweet gig – TV – Union and all that?

DEAN: I guess so; I don't remember anything about wages.

DON: Do you remember Jerry Spain?

DEAN: Yes. Sure.

DON: He helped me out – getting paid. He was using the arm and getting it done.

DEAN: Yeah, he was a forthright guy.

DON: TV gig or something I did and they transferred to another TV station and didn't let me know. So, I didn't get my residuals and I said, hey, Jerry…. And he was like come on; we will go down and talk to them. I watched the guy write the check on the spot.

DEAN: He was very convincing. Good old Jerry Spain!

DON: Yeah, Union Secretary. I think it was mid 60's. Did you ever know Ernie Droid?

DEAN: Oh yeah, sure. Saw Ernie when he was in Hospice care.

DON: Yeah, he was old around that time I guess.

DEAN: We all played with Jimmy Diamond, you know kind of the Dixie thing.

DON: I didn't know Jimmy Diamond.

DEAN: He was a piano player and we played the New Orleans Room at the Fairmont. I was pretty much regular bass player on that. That was Vince Cattolica and Jerry Dodgion, Buddy Powers and John Markham. This was around in the 70's.

DON: How about Richie Goldberg?

DEAN: Never knew Ritchie Goldberg. I knew a Specs Goldberg, drummer from New York that I was on the road with for a year.

DON: One more thing on Jeannie Hoffman, my first recollection is – you guys with the trio at the Black Hawk when Jeannie was singing.

DEAN: That was the last gig. That was after six months or so. We started at the Jazz Workshop, that's where the trio started. I wasn't the bass player – Dick Knudsen was the bass player. Boy, I used to go in there, in fact I would take my Dad in there, he was living with me at the time, and we would kick back and listen to The Jeannie Hoffman Trio, I loved it! They were having such fun! Bill Young, he was my favorite. But then Knudsen had a falling out with Jeannie and she asked me to join and I said what do you want me for – you are perfect without me. And we went back East and played the Village Vanguard and played Chicago at The Cloisters Inn and the Southerland Lounge.

DON: Yeah, she was hot; I thought that was really going to go. Good band, she sings well and plays good.

DEAN: We had two weeks at the Village Vanguard opposite Ruby Braff and Peewee Russell with Walter Page on bass. I got to hang with Walter Page.

DON: Did you play with the Sal Carson Band?

DEAN: No, never did, maybe a casual or something.

DON: What about Rudy, you must have played with Rudy.

DEAN: Yeah, lots. I called a couple of days ago and got the machine. I don't know if he is feeling so good. I think he is back from the hospital.

DON: Everybody talks about Rudy. He was like the validation of the big band school. Everybody went through his band; everyone who played around here went through his band.

A Diary of the Underdogs

DEAN: We made a recording in 1955, a LP – with Alan Smith.

DON: John Marabuto?

DEAN: Yeah.

DON: And was John writing at that time?

DEAN: Yes, right. We played some of his stuff; Jerry Cournoyer arrangements. Jerry Coker is on the band and Jerry Dodgion.

DON: Did you ever run into Virgil Gonsalves or work with him?

DEAN: Oh, yeah sure. I played the Black Hawk with him.

DON: He had a little sextet, or quintet?

DEAN: Yeah.

DON: Sextet. He had a trombone. Was that Fred Murgy?

DEAN: No, can't think of his name – remember he got busted…..

DON: Danny Patiris?

DEAN: Yeah, Danny. Howard Dedune. Howie is playing the Bookstore with us when I play there on Fridays. We do the 5th Friday of every month that there is five Fridays. I love playing there and I like Eric a lot. I like the acoustics there.

DON: He has non-profit status there, he can receive donations. Anyway, did you ever work with Azteca?

DEAN: No, I never even heard of Azteca, I don't think.

DON: Did you know a guy named Connley Hall?

DEAN: Connley Hall, drummer?

DON: Drummer, kind of wild guy.

DEAN: Kind of – yeah. In fact he lived over in 19th Avenue.

DON: How about Brew Moore?

DEAN: Brew, sure, played a lot with Brew.

DON: Who was the rhythm section with those guys besides you?

DEAN: Gus Gusterson on drums. John Marabuto played a lot with Brew. I played quite a bit with Brew. In fact he lived in the same apartment that Shelly Robbins and I lived in.

DON: Was Brew a San Francisco native?

DEAN: No, he is from Louisiana, well that area, the next state over, Mississippi. I will never forget his interview on KJAZ - Pat Henry – supposed to interview Brew. So, it was a Monday night and Brew stayed sober all day and went down to meet his ride over to the KJAZ studio and got a message its not tonight, its tomorrow. So, tomorrow comes and Brew does his usual thing, beer for breakfast! And we were listening to the radio, Brew's wife, Shelly Robbins and two or three others and he said, *Well tell me Brew, what brings you to the West Coast?* And Brew says, *I think it was a 1951 Buick.* And then he says, *well when did you do most of your big band work Brew?* And Brew says, *uh, lets see, 43/44.* And Pat says, *Oh, during the war huh?* And Brew says, *I worked a lot then, when are going to have another one?* And Pat says, *What's your overall plans?* And Brew says, *I haven't worn overalls since I was a kid.* And he was really putting Pat on.

DON: Yeah, and Pat is kind of a serious guy.

DEAN: And Brew's wife was saying, *I'm going to kill him, I'm going to kill him.*

DON: One of the horns that played was Harold Wiley I understand. He and Harold had a good sound together.

DEAN: Yeah, he and Harold. They recorded a couple of things.

DON: In the vinyl days?

DEAN: Yeah.

DON: So, Brew Moore and Harold Wiley. Were you around for Bajone's? Do you remember that club?

A Diary of the Underdogs

DEAN: No. Not really.

DON: That was later on, maybe in the 80's. I think it was on Valencia. Also, I wanted to ask you about Frank Tusa.

DEAN: I never knew Frank to well. Saw him with Jimmy Rowles at the old Kimball's.

DON: Didn't you do something with Jimmy Rowles?

DEAN: No, darn it!

DON: But I do know the guy you worked with, Earl Hines. Fill me in on Earl Hines a little bit.

DEAN: Mostly, just a recording, we did an LP that was also a CD, *Father Plays Fats*- All Fats Waller tunes.

DON: Earl Watkins, and Eddie Duran.

DEAN: So, we rehearsed a couple of times for that and then recorded. And then I think I played two out of town gigs with Earl. We went to Fresno on a train.

DON: Didn't you have a gig on Bush Street – somebody told me.

DEAN: Oh, yeah, it was at The Hangover.

DON: You had a little larger ensemble too?

DEAN: Yeah. We had Darnell Howard on clarinet and Jackie Coons on cornet, Earl Watkins was on drums.

DON: Was young Modesto in that band?

DEAN: No, he was with the Chamber Jazz Sextet though. That was at the Black Hawk with Kenneth Patchin and I was with Jeannie Hoffman playing there intermissions with Art Pepper. It was like a three ring circus.

DON: Tell me about Art.

DEAN: So, we were a trio, playing intermissions, Jeannie, Bill Young and me. Then Art would join us halfway thru the set and he would play. And one of the first things he said was *lay out Jeannie*. And so we would play bass and drums and after the second night, Jeannie didn't even come up! We would do our trio thing and she would get off and Art Pepper and Billie Young and I would play.

DON: How was it that Art was around so much?

DEAN: He was booked for gig. That was a month long gig. We played two of those weeks with the Chamber Jazz Sextet and Ken Patchin. That's when they used to have the entertainment tax – ten percent if there was singing or dancing you had to pay Federal tax. So the third and fourth week was just Jeannie Hoffman and Art Pepper. And the first night of the third week the owner came up and said, *now Jeannie, don't sing because we don't want to pay that tax, just instrumental music.* And Bill Young said, *oh she will never make it!* But we tried. About the third tune she starts singing. And the guy comes up, *no singing!* And she went on singing and he came back up and unplugged the amplifier and she stood up and kept singing! He said, YOU'RE FIRED!! And Bill Young was so paranoid, he said, *what have I done?* And Jeannie walked out and slammed the door of the Black Hawk. We didn't even get paid for the night! And that's when Jeannie and I parted company.

DON: Great story and knowing Jeannie, I can totally see it. She was a great player – kind of amazing.

DEAN: Yeah, she had a lot of charm. You know who got us all those gigs was Martha Glazier. Earl Gardner's manager. She got us all those back East gigs and didn't ask for any compensation, did it as a favor. She loved the music and loved Jeannie. I am sorry to hear she left us. I haven't seen her in fifteen years probably.

DON: I haven't seen her either. I just talked to her about this project a few years ago and she said she would help out. She kind of stopped playing and she wasn't on the scene too much. For awhile she was right next door to the No Name, she brought her own piano in.

DEAN: Really, she played the No Name too right?

DON: Yeah, and she played Christopher's or whatever – down the street- so she created this gig and I said, *how ya doing Jeannie?* And she says, *I'm doing fine man!* And she said she was living down there on a houseboat. Yeah, she was doing great.

DEAN: When we went back East, she was playing that little Wurlitzer, the first one that came out and it was terrible, out of tune.

DON: Well, they would bend, you play them hard and those little things go out and then you have to wait for a while and it comes back.

DEAN: Sounded like a mouth organ or something, funny sound. She would go back and forth from that to acoustic piano. It was a dinky thing, probably weighed forty pounds.

DON: I was going to ask you about Ornette Coleman, that probably was at the Both/And or something?

DEAN: No, this was way back. I went out on the road when I got out of college, got married and my friends in Tacoma, Washington went on the road with this band, Daryl Harper and made a request that I go on the band, so I joined the band in Fort Worth, Texas and that's where Ornette Coleman was. I had only been playing bass a couple of years. Never with a drummer, it was just piano and guitar. And Specs Goldberg was this drummer. We did our opening day, the afternoon of the night we were opening in this hotel, we had a jam session where Ornette Coleman was there and I played with Ornette but I had never played drums before. I got such blisters and I had to play that night, the opening and my hand was so sore and blistered! I tried to play and I looked down and my hand was bloody and I fainted on the bandstand! The leader played a little bass, he took over. I went and lay down. I did that band for a year and boy that was a panic band. The music was great, it was a great library, and it was like a seven or eight piece band; wonderful arrangements. And that is why everyone stayed on the band because it was such great music. We played a lot of Latin stuff, a lot of Mambos.

DON: How about Jackie and Roy, did you spend some time with them? When I was married they were our favorites. My wife and I used to mimic them, she would sing her part and I would sing his part and we would sing at parties.

DEAN: That was my first big name gig, the Purple Onion. For a couple of weeks, they came back and used me again.

DEAN: I should mention George Barnes. We rehearsed here every Monday for a year. He played guitar and he was fantastic. He smoked cigars and the place still stinks. Benny Barth and me and Douglas and Duncan James, we were a quartet. We recorded; we got a couple nice albums. George past in 77, so it was up till then that we were a quartet.

DON: How is Benny?

DEAN: Yeah, we talk, he is still around. We talk once a month or so. He lives up in Guerneville – Monte Rio actually.

DON: I always liked that group.

DEAN: Yeah, Master Sounds.

DON: I always like that – Ritchie Crabtree, Monk Montgomery.

DEAN: Ritchie and I were roommates.

DON: And Buddy, right, both Montgomery's?

DEAN: Yeah, and with Wes occasionally.

DON: How about Anita O'Day?

DEAN: I had one night with her with Plank.

DON: Oh, how did that go, because she is famous for trashing somebody in the band in front of the audience?

DEAN: Yeah, it was me. She says, *ok, Tea for Two in E Flat – ready, you got it, 1, 2- 123.* And I was like, what, huh? What do you mean I got it? I survived I guess, but what *Tea for Two* in a new key? Don Manning just sent me a CD of Anita, Plank, John Pool and Al Obidinski. I never knew John Pool, but he is Manning's right hand man. John's not still around. Don is writing a book and he has a lot to say. I would say he is the purest of them all. He doesn't really care for Sonny Rollins. Don, I don't think you have seen the *Jazz Icon* series of Sonny Rollins, it is really wonderful. Have you seen it?

DON: This is recent?

DEAN: Yeah.

DON: Because he recorded with Branford Marsalis. Oh, this period.

DEAN: Oh, is that good!

DON: These are concerts that somehow got filmed?

DEAN: It's all European stuff. I have twelve of them, I think there are fifteen.

DON: Yeah, okay, Sonny has these; I will borrow them from Sonny. Yes, this is outstanding. Is there an Anita O'Day in this series? I think Sonny showed me one.

DEAN: I don't know about that.

DON: Yeah, I watched one with him one night and she was at her prime and very sassy.

DEAN: There is a Sarah Vaughn and Nina Simone. I don't see Anita on here. She has her own video thing out that is supposed to be very good. This is all European stuff. European TV – all in black and white.

DON: I was going to ask you about John True, he was a piano player and also Nico Bunick.

DEAN: Oh yeah, Nico! Nico passed recently.

DON: He went back to New York, right?

DEAN: Yeah.

DON: He was from Hungary?

DEAN: No, he was Dutch. Netherlands.

DON: Did you know Count Dutch?

DEAN: No.

DON: Did you ever get to work with George Cables?

DEAN: No.

DON: And Vernon Alley?

DEAN: He got me the Black Hawk; he was the house bass player there. But he couldn't handle all the work. I owe Vernon a lot.

DON: And there was a radio broadcast on Saturday's or something?

DEAN: Yeah, "Vernon's Alley" on Saturdays, KSFO in San Francisco.

End: Dean Reilly

Interview: Mel Martin-jazz musician-saxophonist- with Don Alberts-December 16, 2008-Novato, Ca. About Johnny Baker, Bop City, Jack's, the Blue Mirror, Bennie Carter, John Handy, Vince Lateano, Rufus Reid, Sacramento clubs

MEL MARTIN

MEL: There was a whole community of musicians a lot of them from the Bay Area, Flip Nunez used to be up there a lot. Flip played piano. George Walker, the drummer that used to play Bop City.

DON: I don't remember that guy at all.

MEL: He was actually around a lot; he played a lot like Art Blakey. I started working gigs with him. An organ player up in Sacramento named Jimmy Smith, back in the 60's; I would be the only white face in the club. Played thirty blues a night! Every one was always like – how come you play blues so good? Because

A Diary of the Underdogs

I played thirty blues a night for years!

DON: I wanted to talk about Bop City but before you got to Bop City you played a lot in Sacramento.

MEL: Well, I am from Sacramento. I went to Sacramento High. And Vince and I used to come down, when we were still in high school, and we would just sort of approach Bob City, just go in and hang out.

DON: Vince Lateano?

MEL: Yeah.

DON: Did you go to high school together?

MEL: Yeah, we graduated same year. Rufus Reid I think was a year behind us. He was a trumpet player. He was like the

Mel Martin

third trumpet player. And he would stand up and play these really cool solos once in awhile. And then I remember he went into the service and he came down – he was up in Seattle I guess – and he came down and bought his first bass from a high school friend of ours, we were all living in San Francisco in this apartment – there was this guy named Malcolm and he bought his first bass from Malcolm. I remember he came and took one look at all of us – and said, hey man – I gotta go back. But he was in the service and stuff and we were like at the height of going crazy over everything; trying to stay out the draft and all that.

DON: What was it a plywood bass?

MEL: No, it was a very good bass. He eventually moved to Chicago and started studying from the symphony guys. And he would do some gigs with Buddy Montgomery actually before he left. He started to play…..we didn't know that.

DON: He was playing with Buddy?

MEL: Yeah. Well, Buddy would be around, the Montgomery Brothers were around; I used to sit in with them a little bit.

DON: Yeah, Ritchie Crabtree and those guys…

MEL: No, no not the Master Sounds, the Masters Sounds broke up – Benny Barth, Ritchie Crabtree, Monk and Buddy was the Master Sounds and sometimes with Wes. Then they broke up and the brothers all decided to put a band together – the Montgomery Brothers Band – they actually did record around that time. They made that record with Johnny Griffin, Paul Chambers and Jimmy Cobb. But they were in Sacramento, in fact Wes went and recorded that album – he said that he had to go East – some guy had a record date for him. And then the incredible Jazz guitar – Wes Montgomery turned the guitar world on it literal ear. And from then on he became much more famous. Unfortunately I saw him a number years later at the Jazz Workshop with his own group – Wynton Kelly, Ron McClure and Jimmy Cobb, but he wasn't the same guy – he was just in this mill. He had about eight kids – Wes – and he had to leave Indianapolis – they were after him for a lot of money! He was a steel worker or something.

A Diary of the Underdogs

DON: Did he have a number of wives?

MEL: He had a number of kids!

DON: Different wives?

MEL: I don't know, maybe girlfriends. So, anyway, they all jumped in Monk's big pink Cadillac convertible and drove out, they really didn't want to fly. Wes told me once that Miles wanted him to go with him and he said he just couldn't deal with the pressure and he would have had to fly. Buddy got to play a little with Miles too

DON: I saw that band.

MEL: With Buddy? Wow!

DON: Yeah, that was a rare thing. It was the period where Coltrane was still screeching and trying to do Harmelodics with a couple of notes in between.

MEL: Well, I think he succeeded actually. Later on I did hear Wes play, I think it was 1960 at the Monterey festival with Coltrane. It was Coltrane's band. It was perfect, because he had that same kind of power. He would build solos like with single lines; go to octaves and then chords. It wasn't just the octaves, he would build it like a big band. He would play these wonderfully hip lines and then he would do the octaves and then block chords. By the time he got to the block chords the whole momentum of his solos would just knock you off your chair. But he was the sweetest guy. I was a kid and I asked him, *hey man, can you give me the changes to West Coast Blues, I just love those changes!* He wrote them out a napkin for me which I probably have. I think it is buried at the bottom of some box in my closet. So, it was a good Jazz town – it was a good environment. There was a lot of music that came through. We heard the Master Sounds; we heard Benny Goodman, Woody Herman, and Duke Ellington. I went to a dance in 58 with Count Basie's band with Joe Williams and the two Franks and Marshall Royal. Sonny Paine threw his drumstick up, you know, and it finally came down, Sonny wasn't there, he fell off the bandstand!

DON: Sonny was kind of a notorious waster…..

MEL: Yeah, I'm sure all those cats were whatever they were. That's kind of why I never wanted to go with the big bands because I saw what those guys looked like coming off the bus. You'd bee seeing Sal Nistico with Woody Herman's band and those guys were like, oh, where is the stand?!

DON: Yeah, they were out there.

MEL: A lot of the guys wanted to go – you know the late Joe Ellis – Joe Ellis just passed away….

DON: Yeah, I know, he was going to do an interview with me.

MEL: He was in our high school too. And he went with Stan Kenton; his big thing was Kenton and all those screeching trumpets. And several trumpet players wanted to go with Stan Kenton. Me? No. I would have loved to go with Duke Ellington or Count Basie, but not Stan Kenton; it just wasn't going to be my thing.

DON: Why was that?

MEL: We came up with big bands but I just really didn't like what I saw in big bands. First of all you just solo a little bit unless you are a featured guy.

DON: Yeah, and all the guys looked pretty wasted too.

MEL: Yeah, the guys would come off the bus and be a wreck - alcoholics, junkies, you name it; just terrible.

DON: Yeah, Vince mentioned something about that.

MEL: Eventually we did some stuff with Woody. Its horrible man, you ride on a bus for hours….those were the days for some people. I actually started touring with the rock bands. I was married by the time I was twenty-two, twenty-three.

DON: Did you have kids?

MEL: We had kids by 1965. And I worked as a journey-men musician in San Francisco because I could come down and get gigs and once we settled in this apartment in North Beach – we settled in. That

A Diary of the Underdogs

apartment was $75 a month! I could walk to Broadway where there were several places of employment – strip clubs. And they all needed sax players.

DON: Danny Patiris was there.

MEL: Yeah, Danny was there, I met a lot of people there. I met Si Perkoff, Shep Sheppard, used to play the Chi Chi Club, Bob Ferraro was up there.

DON: Moulin Rouge?

MEL: Yeah, Moulin Rouge also, then it became Mr. D's, we did Motown shows there. So, I just hung out and did that. Then in the 70's these rock bands started calling me up, people I knew in college.

DON: Yeah, making money.

MEL: Well, I didn't know about that, to me money was a $125 a week you know with taxes and that was enough to pay the $75 a month rent and have a little groceries, cheap little car.

DON: Yeah, right, steady gig.

MEL: And the rest was like, oh, play Jazz – yeah, well you can make a dollar doing that and I definitely did a little of that and certainly jammed with people all the time – you know, because I am a Jazz musician. But these rock bands kept calling and eventually I went with a band called the Loading Zone, which George Marsh played and Pat O'Hara, the trombonist. And that led me going eventually with Cold Blood finally because I knew Raul Matutay from college and Tom Harrell and I both played with them for about six months and then we formed Azteca, which was more to my liking, Jazz, Rock, Funk and Latin. Juggernaut Band, George DiQuattro was in it Flip was in it, George Muribus – for some reason we thought we needed three keyboard players to do the job of one – I am not quite sure why….

DON: That was Pete and Coke? Were they fronting the band?

MEL: Well, Pete was. Well. Coke was actually running the band and Pete was more like just a vocalist. He didn't even play percussion. There were four vocalists – Wendy Haas, Earl Knowles, Rico Reyes – a lot of it was Santana spin-offs. Originally it was like Michael Shreve – Carlos was supposed to play with and never did, Mongo played with us. And the horns were originally Jules Rowel, Bob Ferraro, Tom Harrell and I, four horns and I doubled on tenor, baritone and soprano. And our first gig was at San Diego stadium for twenty-five thousand people because they all thought Carlos was going to show up. And the buzz was out and the next day Clive Davis flies out from New York and signs us to Columbia. That was what was happening in those days, you could literally form a thing that would be a totally new – see Columbia had a policy, if they had Blood, Sweat and Tears, they had to have Chicago, if they had Miles they had to have Freddie; they had two of everything. They had Santana so we came along and they said, we need them too, in case one goes, then you are hedging your bets, a very corporate idea. And it resulted in a lot of great music.

DON: Weren't there big advances in those days too?

MEL: For those days, yeah; $50,000 recording budgets and $50,000 advances. You would do two albums. And so it put us in business and we actually got out on the road and did a lot of gigs. We opened for Stevie Wonder-Yeah, a bunch of acts.

DON: This would be late 60's early 70's?

MEL: Early 70's. But first I went with Boz Scaggs actually. I was with him for about three years, from 72 to 75 and then Azteca came about after that.

DON: Yeah, he was popular.

MEL: Yeah, for sure at that time. We did all the Fillmore stuff and we were in the movie – The Last Days of the Fillmore, which I understand is just coming out on DVD.

DON: Let me step back just for a minute to Sacramento because there was a guy from Sacramento that was a great piano player – John Baker. Do you know anything about him?

MEL: Vince gave me this picture.

A Diary of the Underdogs

DON: What a great picture!!

MEL: I will scan that for you and send it to you. I don't know where that was taken exactly. I used to hang out at his house.

DON: Yeah, well he was a house and be-bop piano player, crazy, I knew him.

MEL: I did a lot of gigs with this guy. It was Vince and me and Bob Maize and Johnny Baker playing at some hall over in San Rafael.

DON: Oh, that's an old one, a snapshot picture. Is that Vince?

MEL: Yeah.

DON: Wow! That was before his hair turned white.

MEL: Before all of our hairs turned white. I think that is before he became Jimmy Stick – the one armed drummer.

DON: WOW! Look at that – look at the hair!

MEL: Yeah, I had hair! I don't know what year that was....

DON: How did Johnny Baker end up being such a notorious character?

MEL: (laughing) How did he end up? He didn't "end" up, he always was! Because I talk to guys in Chicago and they said they used to have to pick him up out of the gutter. He was a terrible junkie, wino, and then he became a speed freak, they were making speed in his bathroom. You didn't want to use the toilet because you were liable to get really fucked up; there was shit that came out of that door that you didn't want to know about! But I met guys like Hank Crawford – Hank Crawford's band came into town and they all went to like this after hours place – and Donald Garrett lived out there – I hung out a lot with those two guys – I played a lot and I was just a kid,

Johnny Baker

because I could just go out there and play. I wasn't into all the drugs, I hardly even did pot. Eventually I did, but mostly I was just a straight kid learning how to play Jazz saxophone and these guys would get me in there and start putting me through bebop changes galore!

DON: How did this guy get there? How did he do it?

MEL: Well, he left Chicago, that's how Rafael Garrett knew him, Donald Garrett knew him because he was from Chicago, he came out- he wanted to clean up basically. Then later on he moved down to San Francisco, I used to hang out at his house, we used to practice marches– out of March books – John Phillip Souza and long-tones and....Dewey Redman was there! So, there was always some kind of hangin' going on. So, I would see those guys and we would hang out and play some. My first gig in San Francisco was in the 60's at the Both/And on Sunday afternoon, $5 for the jam session.

DON: And Donald Garrett was around...

MEL: And he would be playing sometimes. So, we would all see each other and hang out. So those are the kind of guys I came up with from Sacramento to San Francisco. Flip would be there, go down to Bop City

A Diary of the Underdogs

and Monte Waters, The Bishop was down there.

DON: What about Kermit Scott?

MEL: Kermit Scott, I got to meet later on, but the guys in Sacramento told me a zillion stories about Kermit Scott. He was like a fucking genius at the saxophone because he was playing Coltrane long before Coltrane. He used to play at the Reunion Club with Martha Young. Martha Young was Lester Young's niece and played great piano. She also used to play at Johnny Bajones; she used to have a night down there. But Kermit used to play down there and that is where I got to know him. But in Sacramento this guy said, man, you got to check this guy out in San Francisco – every time Jazz at the Fillmore would come down, he would get up in the balcony and start playing back at those cats and he knew them all. He knew Lester Young and Coleman Hawkins and those guys, he was from that school. And he would just be blowing back at them – he would just get his horn out up there in the balcony and I thought, oh, my God, who is this guy? Eventually Dizzy Gillespie played the Monterey Festival and he just walked out on stage and started playing with him! Dizzy knew him, I talked with Dizzy about him. He knew Shep Sheppard really well too from Philadelphia.

DON: How can a guy be so famous and yet not famous?

MEL: Some guys are known to the musicians.

DON: Well, yeah, the inside line is much better then any other.

MEL: I mean a few guys get through and become really famous – that's the difference. That's why there are legends and famous legends.

DON: Yeah, there are legends and there are famous people who got signed.

MEL: Well, who just got out there for various reasons were marketable.

DON: This is great – you got a lot of information.

MEL: Well, I was there and I remember a lot, but don't ask me so much about the 70's because its over my head – gone.

DON: There was some reason that Sacramento was important, because there were venues.

MEL: Well, people would go up….I got to take lessons from Lee Konitz because he lived in Mill Valley for awhile. For some reason he wanted to come to California, it wasn't happening for him in New York and he was kind of a quirky dude….

DON: I ran into him about that period too, I spent some time with him.

MEL: Right and he would play pizza parlors and all kinds of oddball shit and he came up and somebody said well, I can get you some saxophone students up here, so he would go up there and there was a cool little club in the guy's basement and – Johnny Mantabow. I think was his name and he had a little basement gig and I used to play down there with Flip and different guys and so he would line up several of us students – seventeen year old or eighteen year old students – and we would go in and hang. So, I did take three lessons from him and he showed me his method of slowing a song like *All the Things You Are* down to sixty on the metronome and playing ten choruses of melody. Each chorus you add a little variation to it. You don't try and play the changes because you wouldn't them anyway if it bit you in the nose – being that slow. But it's from like *theme and development* which is a very valid and serious approach.

DON: Yeah, a lot of guys use it.

MEL: Right, a lot of guys use it but he made a very serious art out of it. And he still plays that way. But that really turned me around and made me realize how deep you can get into a song as a saxophonist. Before it was like, well yeah, I know this song….

DON: Well, right, plus it makes you play long-tones.

MEL: Well, if you put an hour into a tune, if it is sixty on the metronome you are going to know that tune and you are going to find out real quick what you don't know in that tune in terms of melodics and intervals. And he would tell me - go out and get Frank Sinatra records and play along with them because

A Diary of the Underdogs

Frank Sinatra had perfect phrasing for Jazz. He would learn it all from Tommy Dorsey how to breathe and stuff. He said learn it and learn the lyrics to the songs. Old school guys, Ben Webster and those guys would play. Even Sonny Rollins, they need to know the lyrics to a song before they even attempt to play it. So he gave me some stuff that nobody in that town would even talk to me about. Vince and I were both in the Union by the time we were sixteen, so we played with professional Jazz musicians up there all the time. In fact, I even got to play with Sinatra when I was seventeen because the President of the Union put together, well there was a show, when Frank Sinatra was still a Democrat he came up and played for Pat Brown's inauguration in 1960. He was still a Democrat and he brought his whole rat pack up and they did this whole show – all these acts.

DON: Where was that?

MEL: In Sacramento, at the Memorial Auditorium. And they brought an L.A. band; they had a lot of famous L.A. musicians.

DON: The Condoli brothers?

MEL: I don't remember the Condoli's but I remember Zeek Zargen, Milt Burnhart, Dave Grusin. So, there were a lot of famous musicians so they needed to fill in some of the tiers. So, this other alto player that I was in high school with, myself and a trombone player and some other people that were involved, we filled in the tiers. So, there I was on stage with Frank Sinatra! And he comes out and the lights go down and it was pure magic, I have never experienced anything like that in my life. You could just tell, he would put the audience in a spell like immediately. And he would sing these songs and bring them to life in such a way – it was just like magic. And it was just like how he was in the movies. He would walk in and he had his hat on and he would be like – *Hey Baby! How you doing?* And he would have his coat over his shoulder; it was like really funny if you think about it. And that's who he was – all tanned out and everything. And I loved it, because there was Frank Sinatra!

DON: Yeah, you mentioned the age of sixteen – it seems that all the people I have talked to that the age of sixteen and nineteen years old something clicked in and this is the music......

MEL: It really clicked for me at fourteen for me. My father got me my first job on the back of a flatbed truck – he was a food salesman – so these supermarkets openings would have little celebrations for their openings. So, we got five bucks a piece and had a little combo with accordion and drums and we played Benny Goodman charts. And then we would go down and play at Mel's Drive-In in Sacramento for tips. We would play a dance and then go to Mel's; that was our hang afterwards.

DON: Sounds like you had a really good time.

MEL: Sacramento was a great town to come up with as a young musician. And there was the State Fair. I walked in the State Fair one afternoon – there was Duke Ellington's Orchestra playing! Woody Herman was there and different people would play the Fair, would see all kinds of people. And I walked in and there was Duke Ellington and I was like right up close! Willie Smith was playing alto and Dave Black was playing drums.

DON: Wow, Dave Black, which was a long time ago.

MEL: Right! And he was playing two bass drums, and doing all those Louie Bellson things.

DON: Yeah, before Louie?

MEL: No, after. I believe he came after Louie. But he was in there in between that and Rufus – Speedy Jones or somebody. But for awhile he played with the Duke. Willie Smith.....

DON: Willie the Lion?

MEL: No, not Willie the Lion, Willie Smith the alto player. Willie the Lion was an older, like ragtime piano player. Willie Smith was a hell of an alto player who also played with Harry James. Vince and I would get in the car, when we were old enough, drive to Lake Tahoe and go stand in the back of Harrah's Club and listen to the Harry James Band with Buddy Rich on drums and Willie Smith on alto; and Red Callender on bass. And we would go hang out with Red Callender and get high and stuff.

DON: Was Ernie Figueroa in the band?

MEL: I don't remember Ernie being there, could be. I don't think so. I just remember those guys, Corky Cocoran the tenor player.

DON: Corky! He was the best Jazz player in the band!

MEL: And Jack Percival the piano player. It was a great band, they were playing Basie charts and a lot of Thad Jones and Bill Holmen and Basie and all kinds of stuff.

DON: Thad was writing early then?

MEL: Yeah. And Buddy Rich was the highest paid side-men at that time in anybody's band. I think he was making somewhere around $50,000 a year playing with Harry James because they played nine months a year in Vegas. Now take Buddy Rich and those guys, they were dropping big bottles of Brandy and Cognac and stuff and yet played their asses off! Buddy Rich was like just amazing and another jaw dropping player and so we came up in an era of jaw dropping – literally! And of course you remember 1958 was a hell of a year for Jazz just on records and stuff. Here I was listening to Coltrane and he was coming out with a record every six months, Sonny Rollins was coming out with stuff, all the Blue Note stuff. We used to just sit around and listen to those records and just go nuts. And that music just kept growing. And what kids Today don't get is what an impact that had on us as youths. Because we were like, yeah, what's next, come on, bring it on! So, now its like, oh, I gotta go to Berkley, what do I do when I graduate high school? We were like; I don't know what the hell we are going to do when we graduate high school! Get me to the city man, get me to some sessions. You didn't even think about making money at Jazz, who ever even dreamed of it. And look who the giants were; the people that were at the top of their profession. I wasn't going to go even near that. I was sitting listening to Art Blakey with Lee Morgan and Curtis Fuller and Lee walks up – I had my horn – I am at the old Jazz Workshop right, and he says, *Hey man, you wanna play a little?* And I said, *NO!! Thank you very much Mr. Morgan!* He said, *Well, Wayne is playing an old Bundy and would you mind if he played?* And Art comes over to me, and says, *Wayne is on an old Bundy, would you mind if he played your horn?* So, I said, *No, man!* So, Wayne played my Selmer because he was playing this horn and he had just come over from somewhere and his horn was in the shop and he had a really bad horn with rubber bands and chewing gum holding it together! So, he played my horn and I got to listen to Wayne Shorter play my horn with Art Blakey. But I wasn't going to sit in man, are you kidding! But those were the kind of things....make money at Jazz? Well, eventually I went out and did some little gigs in San Francisco and stuff but there was no money in it. There were the Union gigs and stuff when we actually had a Union. So, those early days in the scene, we were young and newlyweds and it was a great time. I was living in the neighborhood and if I wasn't working I would come down and hear music. And if I was working the intermissions were unbelievable! You had the Jazz Workshop here, Basin Street West here, the El Matador here, Moody, Dizzy, all these cats are walking up and down the street, *Hey man, how you been?* And they were all friendly. And so I go and there is Coltrane, and across the street, Sonny Rollins, I go in with Sonny one night after my gig and who walks in but Elvin Jones, a drummer just gets off the bandstand sits down in front of his bass drum because Elvin was going to kick it through the door and then.....*ladies and gentlemen we have a great dinosaur in the house and this is what Jazz is all about!* Here is Elvin Jones and they played for three hours! I mean, starting at 1:30 in the morning!

DON: Where was this?

MEL: The Jazz Workshop, they closed the doors and they kept playing! We just sat there and witnessed this shit, like oh, my God! Elvin Jones and Roland Kirk just went off. Totally into it! Elvin was up there all bleary-eyed, bashing and playing and swinging. And the Coltrane Quartet with McCoy and Jimmy Garrison and I hear Sonny Rollins up at Basin Street West with Freddie Redd. I eventually got to know him a little bit and played with him some.

A Diary of the Underdogs

DON: Yeah, he was out here for a little while…

MEL: Yeah. He still is in L.A. I think.

DON: I saw The Connection, the black and white version - that one apartment in New York. I had to watch the whole thing. Jackie MacLean and Freddie Redd. And I can't remember – Matos was the bass player? And the drummer I can't remember his name. I wrote all of this down because it was all so fantastic. Freddie was somebody you could hang out with at Bop City.

MEL: That was the other thing at Bop City there were all these things going on during regular hours…and me and Eddie Henderson by the way, when I went to San Francisco State, Henderson lived right around the block with his Mom, he was doing med-school, pre-med, and so, he had a car and he would pick me up and we would just go to the sessions at Bop City and Soulville every weekend. So it would start on Friday, you would sit in from 9-1, this is before I got married and was actually a working dude, but we would start out on Friday sit in somewhere, and then to sessions from 2-6 and you could go back and forth and there was Shelton's Blue Mirror and Jazz on Sutter Street from 6-11 and then you crash, maybe unless had Benzedrine or whatever and then you would go all over again the next day and by Sunday night I was in such a blur I could hardly make it back to the school. Which it was, what it was, and I learned some stuff there but I learned a whole lot more on the streets. Because at the after hours clubs, you would run into Horace's band and all the New York musicians would come down and hang out afterwards. Sometimes you would find yourself on the bandstand with some pretty bad guys.

DON: Did you run into Freddie Gambrell?

MEL: Well I heard Freddie Gambrell up in Sacramento actually at some concerts; he came up there and played. He was pretty amazing. Cal Tjader's band was around, with Willie Bobo and Armando Peraza.

DON: And there were times when Cal was playing Jazz with Brew Moore, right?

MEL: I met Brew Moore in Sacramento at a private session at a house. He just came up and played and he hated me because I was young and full of piss and vinegar and he was old and tired, I guess.

DON: He had an attitude huh?

MEL: Oh, big time!

DON: Did you know Harold Wiley? Harold Wiley and Brew got along pretty good.

MEL: I sort of knew Harold Wiley, but not real well. The guys from the 50's I didn't get to know that much. But Johnny Baker knew Brew Moore; I think he was at that session too. So now and then you would run into some pretty outlandish kind of people. Just as a kid, I'm just a kid, man! Running around with a horn trying to show up and play.

DON: So, I heard that Art Pepper used to come in and play with Jeannie Hoffman's Trio at the Black Hawk. She would sing and there was a vocal tax if you had a singer.

MEL: Ah, right. Well Max Roach told me that's how Bebop kind of got started because there were these heavy entertainment taxes. You couldn't have vocalists, you couldn't have a big band in there, and you couldn't have dance bands. You just had to have people sit and listen. So they would just bring in quartets, and quintets. So, that was going on in San Francisco too?

DON: Yeah.

MEL: I remember we would come down to the Black Hawk and sit in the chicken coop and hear the bands. I remember hearing Miles with Hank Mobley and Wynton Kelly. And JJ was there. I heard Dizzy's band with Leo Wright.

DON: Did you get hooked up with Smiley Winters?

MEL: Eventually, yeah, I did get to know Smiley. And I got to know the Oakland crew – Ed Kelly. Those guys would come up to Sacramento now and then too. See, there were clubs up there like coffee houses. Iron Sandal was a famous one. Right on Broadway, right across – that club that is there now – 21st and Broadway.

A Diary of the Underdogs

DON: Was Flip part of that Sacramento thing?

MEL: Yes, he lived up there a lot. And Wilma Reeves. He was a pretty well known guy that played both up there and down here. He played a thing called the Organo. And he and Wes Montgomery and George Walker would play gigs up there.

DON: What about Stanley Willits?

MEL: I got to know him in the early days.

DON: He wasn't a Sacramento guy was he?

MEL: No, but I got to know him in the 60's in San Francisco. He would teach me tunes like, *I Want to Be in Pictures* – in B! Benny Harris used to wander into Bop City now and then. Yeah, there were all kinds of weird bebop guys.

DON: Yeah, Stanley Willlits would cover his hands because he didn't want anyone to see his tricks.

MEL: Yeah, and he was genius. He really could play all kinds of stuff.

DON: Yeah, but he was not negotiable. (Lots of laughter)

MEL: I remember playing at Soulville one night with Phineas Newborn Junior and Reggie Workman. Yeah, there were all kinds of cats you would run into. And it was a great education. This is what made me a Jazz musician. I didn't go to Jazz school – although our high school was so advanced. We had music theory, composition, four-part dictation, orchestration, wrote music for plays, we played dances all the time. We went to the earliest Stan Kenton clinics. And so we had a Jazz education that the kids in high school Today don't know anything about. Most kids in high school are just starting because they didn't have anything in junior high. And they are not getting much in high school. The stuff we got in high school, they may get in college. And it turned out real pros because besides Vince, Rufus and myself, we had a lot of people….

DON: Well, not only that but there was some good motivation to continue…

MEL: Well we were highly motivated and organized and there was this environment of really good Jazz going both here and in San Francisco and it kind of spilled over, obviously from the Bay Area because it would be a touring spot on the way. I heard Cannonball Adderley at the State Fair. There was a lot happening! And there were after hours joints there too. As a matter of fact, my parents got nuts when I turned sixteen and I would stay out all night playing a place called the Orange Villa – out in the boonies somewhere with whores, pimps, junkies and Jazz musicians.

DON: Your parents thought you were going to get in trouble?

MEL: Well, somehow I managed to not get in serious trouble but I learned how to play some music. And maybe got into a few fender benders! So we came up in a great time. And I am sure Vince will vouch for a lot of these stories because he and I did a lot of this together.

DON: Yeah, I am going to meet with Vince and he wants to talk about Johnny Baker.

MEL: Yeah, we did gigs with Johnny. And Bob Maize was up there. Bob was in my wedding party; Bill Douglas, Bob Maize and Hart Smith.

DON: Three bass players?

MEL: No, Hart Smith is a trombone player. Bill Douglas and Bob Maize were bass players. They all kind of lived in the Haight Ashbury. Max Hartstein was around. Si Perkoff was around. He lived up on Montgomery Street in North Beach, played gigs down the street. He played organ at the Macumba Club and Shep Sheppard was like the original drummer in Honky Tonk.

DON: Honky Tonk?

MEL: The hit, Honky Tonk. Bill Doggit. And so he taught us all how to play shuffles to the enth degree – women taking there clothes off and stuff - six nights a week. I did that stuff in Sacramento, we used to play at a club, both Vince and I played a lot of these clubs – not together – he would play with one group of Black musicians and I would play with the guys the other guy fired. There was a saxophone player up there named Gene Morris who I eventually met down in Fresno at the end of his life. He had all this cancer and was dying. And he was like one of those Lionel Hampton Flying Home dudes, he played with Hampton and did all that shit. Man, he could play, big tone and he was very influential to my sound. You'd hear a guy play the tenor sax with a real manly sound; a big sound, the R & B sound. And he had that and I used to hear him on the radio, follow him around and listen to him. Then I got old enough, and he was kind of temperamental, so he would fire the rhythm sections – like Sacramento Jimmy Smith and George Walker and they would hire me! So, we would go into the same clubs he just left and we would go around and around these little clubs. Play the shows, strippers and all kinds of stuff.

DON: I think R & B helped us out.

MEL: It was an important part of the music. What people don't realize well, actually some people don't realize, came out of that. Lionel Hampton was a first to start putting crowds into pandemonium.

DON: Yeah, he taught people how to play time.

MEL: Well, it was part of that back-beat that is part of Rock-n-Roll to this day. And there were hit records, as you may remember in the 50's there were hit R & B records and Jazz records.

DON: Yeah, Earl Bostic.

MEL: Yeah, Earl Bostic was a wonderful sax player. And there was Jazz on television! Where do you get that now; Dave Garaway, Steve Allen, the Timex Jazz Specials; all kinds of shows? And there were only a few TV stations so we are talking like not a widespread thing, so all the major networks had Jazz on TV. They had house bands and all kinds of stuff. And so, this is stuff we grew up with. Jazz was in the environment. I mean it's in the environment in this day and age but it is like such a much larger environment that kids have to search it out more; it's not right in their face.

DON: I think that a lot of them are not getting it.

MEL: But some do.

DON: What I mean is the passion and the fascination....

MEL: Yeah, that's what I am saying – they can't get that impact. There is no way they can duplicate that. All they can do is go back and try and trace the history through the CDs and recordings and lots of books. But none of that is the same as witnessing that growth and being impacted by it. I mean walk in and hear Duke Ellington's Orchestra with Harry Carney and these guys. Cootie Williams and they are playing *Mood Indigo* and *Take the A Train.* We heard Benny Goodman and Leroy Vinnegar was playing bass with Benny Goodman. Bud Johnson was on tenor with Benny Goodman! I heard Stan Getz and JJ Johnson at Jazz at the Fillmore. The auditorium would have regular Jazz concerts. There were regular Jazz concerts at the Senator Hotel in Sacramento; and the State Fair. So there was Jazz all the time if you really think about it, and the Monterey Festival the first time we ever went to we took a camper and went down to the 1960 Monterey Festival and heard amazing stuff; J.J. Johnson with the Modern Jazz Quartet.

DON: Do you remember Virgil Gonsalves with no trombones, do you remember that band?

MEL: I remember hearing them because Ralph Gleason's show would also be on TV, we would see a lot of Bay Area musicians from era. That's how we got to know about that. So, if you had antenna, you were picking stuff up all over the place.

DON: Plus, it was hip and your friends knew about it.

MEL: I had a little one-two pilot FM tuner – I used to build HI FI sets, I could build my own amplifier and speakers and stuff – so I had this tuner and I would tune in – well, there were Jazz shows on the radio up there – Glen Church had a show called Jazz, Rhythm and Blues, which played all sorts of stuff. Phil Elwood was on every Sunday then, so I could get this on this FM radio on KPFA and he would start with this old Dixie Land stuff and I would be like why does he want to play this stuff, I mean I was this modern swing guy, but he would progress thru his program and he would go thru his swing era and then play some Be-bop and then play some Brubeck or some modern... and he would take all the era's... and later on I got to know him quite well and just said, man, you were part of my important musical education because he played shit that I didn't even want to listen to. But then he played some shit that I really wanted to listen to. And I would hang and listen to. And then what became KRE over in the East Bay - in Oakland or the transmitters to Berkley and they used to have all kinds of R & B and Jazz stuff…

DON: You mean KDIA?

MEL: Yeah, that's what I was thinking of…so, Jazz radio was big….

DON: Ok. Here is one for you – how about the guy from Salt Lake City?

MEL: Don't know that. But I was a radio nut. I remember stereo radio, you get two FM radios and they would multi-plex two different stations and you would tune them in and they would sync up and put one by one ear and I would lay on the floor….ah yes, I was an audio addict for sure. I built that shit, I was nuts, I took that shit and took all my radios apart and drove my parents nuts. I was a tinker right off of the bat. I wanted to know how that shit worked.

DON: Did you ever have short wave?

MEL: I didn't care about short wave; I just wanted to hear music on the radio.

DON: OK, so you want to talk about some of your accomplishments, how about that Grammy you got?

MEL: Well, that was in the 70's that was with a band called Listen. Just released the original record company inner city actually, just put out both volumes.

DON: Is this from 77?

MEL: That's the first one, yeah; with Andy Lovell and George Marsh and Dave Dunaway and Dave Creamer. And that's after Azteca and that's when I first started composing music and it was original music and it was a very innovative band. Because that was the other thing that was happening – Jazz Fusion in a very innovative sense before it became commercialized; before Jeff Lorber put out his albums. And that was the same label by the way. It took this guy thirty one years and he is just finally available on…

DON: Oh, Inner City.

MEL: Yeah. He offered me the masters a long time ago, and I thought man, I don't play this…

DON: Same price?

MEL: Yeah, more then he put in. And I said I will give you a thousand dollars for both of them. He wanted seven or eight. I said, you didn't put in that much. And he is like this shrewd dude and so I said screw it, and I am not going to go back and play that music. That was a very popular album. Some tunes are mine and some are others.

DON: (reading the album) *Mosquito Steps Out, A Tribute to Clark Kent, Egg Rouge….*

MEL: Which is George spelled backwards; George Marsh is an expert on *Odd Times;* so we practice *Odd Times* for hours on end till we found some grooves.

DON: *At the Mountains of Madness….*

MEL: Yeah, Andy Narell was probably going crazy. This is a beautiful record. I was actually pleased; I think I will send a copy over to KCSM because they tell me to this day they get requests for this. I don't want it to get widespread airplay; I don't want it to get widespread distribution because the guy is not going to pay me. I sell them at my gigs, it's a little on the high side to buy my own copies. This is the album that came out in 94, and its mostly a studio session of a quartet of myself, Kenny Barron, Victor Lewis and Rufus Reid. But there are three tracks from a live session in which Bud Spangler helped record it at Yoshi's out here with Harold Jones and Jeff Chambers and Roger Kellaway and me and Benny Carter. There are only three tunes that I used on here, there is a whole evenings worth of material. This album I put out for his 100th birthday last year.

DON: It's great that you acknowledge Benny Carter this way.

MEL: This is one I did….this is my music. I recorded Dizzy's music, Monk's music and Benny's music and so I wanted to do mine. I had a pretty good band in New York.

DON: Sonny Buxton said he just saw you in New York.

A Diary of the Underdogs

MEL: He saw me? No, he might have seen that I was playing, but he didn't come to the gig. Yeah, Taylor played with me there, it was quite good actually; a wonderful player, really deep especially for twenty-four. Two hand player too!

DON: Yeah, he has a great understanding of the media. (Reading the album) Winard Harper, Billie Hart. A nice group of people.

MEL: That was actually my last studio recording which was like 2001.

DON: Yeah. Bobby Watson, Jack Walrath.

MEL: And now I have completed a new studio recording. Its not a *Be-bop and Beyond* record per se. And I am going to put that out in May.

DON: Mel Martin plays Benny Carter....Mel Martin/Benny Carter Quintet - *Just Friends.* And Mel Martin *Be-bop and Beyond- Friends and Mentors.*

MEL: Yeah the Dizzy and the Monk records that we did in the 90's are no longer available except on oddball websites.

DON: Were they small groups?

MEL: Yeah, augmented with other people. Joe Henderson and Howard Johnson played on the Monk record with Dizzy and John Santos and Vince actually played on some of the tracks. George Cables is on all of those. And then there is the original Concord record done in 84 and somebody just reminded me Today, that it has been twenty-five years. And am I going to do anything about that.

DON: Are your copyrights secured?

MEL: Oh, no, Concord owns that one, everything else I own, I have the rights to. It was in the contracts, or I leased them or some situation that once they are out of distribution with the record company – they are mine. I own my records except that Concord one. And I have asked them to re-release it or at least to consider giving it to me. They just ignore me because they are going through all their changes. Now they are very corporate.

DON: Who bought them out by the way?

MEL: Some big company. That band actually took off like a rocket; John Handy, Warren Gale, me, George Cables, Frank Tusa and Eddie Marshall. It was a great band! And it was fresh and we were doing new stuff and some old stuff. I wrote some and arranged a lot of it. Eventually *Be-bop and Beyond* became a 501(C3) a non-profit which allowed me to get grant money to do other projects. There is some available grant money, I put in NEA grant for a Joe Henderson project that I want to do. But right now I don't know what the government is going to come up with. If the budget is secure maybe we will get that money. They funded the Benny Carter one. One of my grant writers reminded me about doing something for my 25th anniversary. I didn't know I had a 25th anniversary. My, how time flies. However, *Be-bop and Beyond* was an excellent Jazz group of people and the people are still playing – John is still playing. George Cables has a new kidney or got his liver now and is in New York. Anyway.....Rob Fisher has been playing bass with me for a long time.

DON: Yeah, I heard that.

MEL: And I much prefer him to just about anybody.

DON: Yeah, I heard those samples; Rob Fisher and Jeff Mars. It's very thick harmonic sound.

MEL: Yeah, its busy, it's thick and it's rich. Don Freidman and John Santos played on some of this.

DON: Are you writing new stuff?

MEL: Well, I am recycling! I have taken some of my old tunes and re-done them. I would love to write something new – I can't seem to get it out. You get to a certain age and you are happy just to make lunch!

DON: OK, so, just in closing, I want you to tell me about *Rumple Fish* and some of the stuff you might have done....

MEL: Well, I did a ton of studio work.

A Diary of the Underdogs

DON: What was it like working around Francis Coppola?

MEL: Well, I actually used to see him in his studio because we used to do Sesame Street and jingles down at his studio in North Beach. Richard Beggs became his main engineer and ran that studio and he used to wander in there and wander out. I didn't really know him. He wasn't around. I did that score with Stewart Copeland. We actually did it in San Rafael at the old Tres Virgos and they needed some scoring because Stewart Copeland knew nothing about writing music and they wanted to add different instruments. I played some and wrote a lot of stuff out and he was just getting started as a film scorer, which was his first one. They say that movie is Coppola's most artistic achievement because it is really inspired by Ingmar Bergman; a very deep movie. He did shit in there that he hardly ever did in any other movie. It shows up on TV and I still get little checks for it. I did a lot of *Charlie Brown*. I did some with Vince on *Charlie Brown* but eventually Ed Bogus and Lee Mendleson did a lot of *Charlie Brown* down the road after Bruce past away. Tom Harrell and I did a session with Vince for *Charlie Brown*. I used to play with Vince down at the Matrix on Lombard right across from the old Reunion. Yeah, I did a lot of studio and a lot of film work.

DON: Tell me about Keystone Korner.

MEL: Oh, man, I practically lived there. We got to eventually play there as much as a week at a time with *Listen*. And there were always benefits; I remember playing so many benefits trying to keep the club open. I still see Todd Barkan and occasionally play for him at Dizzy's in New York. But I remember all the bands that came through and I would hang out. Dexter Gordon, George Cables, I mean who didn't play there! Freddie was there a lot. Stan Getz. Getz I hung out with a lot and I got to know him fairly well. I interviewed him. There is an interview on my website. I used to write for the Saxophone Journal for about ten years. He was very friendly to me, but I didn't work for him, everybody said he's a whole different fellow to work for.

Mel Martin

DON: Did you ever see a video of him and Chet Baker on tour?

MEL: No.

DON: Some concert they did and they were not getting along. And Chet would take over the stage and sit down there and sing. And Getz would go way back to the end of the stage.

MEL: I loved Stan though. I'll tell you what- you didn't want to follow Stan if you did a ballad. I never got to play with him. Standard Oil used to make educational records and there is a record on Reeds, Woodwinds and both Stan Getz and me and Jean Pierre Rampal and some others being interviewed and playing with their own bands and stuff. So that's the closest – I am on a record with Stan Getz. But I got to know him and hang out and he would always ask me what's going on and we talked and taught together down at the Stanford Jazz Workshop a couple of years. He would take me outside and he would want to go get a beer. And he would say, *I don't know what it is with these little fucks, they can't play shit!*

End: Mel Martin

Interview: Mal Sharpe-"Man on the Street"-musician-bandleader-trombonist-broadcaster- with Don Alberts-January 28, 2009-at Bird and Beckett Books San Francisco-about- Trad bands, North Beach clubs; Tin Angel, Say When, Hangover, Burp Hollow, Gigi's, Tipsy's Kewpie Doll, Amelio's, and musicians..

A Diary of the Underdogs

MAL SHARPE

DON: So, Mal, tell me about the Man On The Street – just say that once for me.

MAL: "HI, THIS IS MAL SHARPE – MAN ON THE STREET."

DON: That thing with the pajamas was funny.

MAL: Oh, yeah, I did that so long ago I forgot about it. I think it was about four years ago, I should go out. I got to get some new equipment.

DON: You probably are very knowledgeable about the Trad bands. And the ones that got advertised in the 60's are all the very famous ones– Turk Murphy, Earthquake McGoon's and Clancy Hayes. I wonder if you knew any of those guys or knew about those places and clubs.

MAL: Well, there are people who know much more than I do. But I will say this, one of the reasons I came to San Francisco was that I had a Turk Murphy record; I think it was on Columbia or RCA. And it had a picture of Turk's band, playing and it was in a club, I found out later it was the Tin Angel opposite of Pier 23, or around there. I don't even know if Turk's band was playing there but they shot the picture there. And they were standing on the floor in the middle of the club and there were all these interesting Bohemian people there, weird sideburns and weird amulets on and the light was all dim. I was into Turk's music, most people my age were – I lived back East – there was other music of that era I liked but I knew about Turk's music. And I think that album cover just evoked something – these Bohemian people, the band standing there, Turk with his trombone and the trumpets and this dimly lit place. That cover is still around the record store. That's the thing that made me say, San Francisco looks interesting. San Francisco was in the air then, anyway; the beat-nick thing and all that.

DON: What part of back East?

MAL: I am from Boston. And, you know, I started listening to Jazz back there. I had six months to kill before I went into the Army and I think because of this cover – I knew nothing else about San Francisco and it wasn't even that I wanted to come out and see Turk, I just – the cover evoked something to me. Of course, years later, I found out, all these Bohemian's on the cover – they were all gay! We didn't know anybody who was gay then. It was a whole bunch of gay women and gay guys, they were known people. There was a woman, Peggy Toke Watkins; I think her name was; it was her whole crowd. I didn't know that then. And so I came out here, sort of because of Turk, and his band was his band, and it kind of evoked San Francisco - nationally. People don't realize it but they were like the Rolling Stones. They were big stuff. This was the music that went out throughout America and people all over the country came out to San Francisco to see his band. But right around the corner from Turk's place, up on the corner of Broadway and Columbus, kitty-corner to Carol Doda's, there was a place called the Kewpie Doll. There is like a Chinese restaurant there now, it's a long thin place. And of course I am from the East Coast and my music orientation was a little different and I was kind of a Eddie Condon and East Coast, Chicago and New York…..anyway, but up at the Kewpie Doll was a band with a guy, Marty Marsalis trumpet player, Cuz Cousineau the drummer, a guy named Tiny something, he was the piano player. But the guy who made my jaw drop there was Vince Cattolica, the clarinet player, the blind clarinet player. This band was hot! Turk's band was a band and had this full San Francisco sound, but these guys were hot! They were traditional swing musicians.

DON: What kind of tunes?

MAL: Oh, they were playing all those tunes. They were playing *All of Me, Fidgety Feet, Tin Roof Blues*, you know, all that stuff and stuff they still play today. Murphy's repertoire was kind of different, all the new artists, but this was all the tunes; *Rosetta, Rose Room, Beale Street Blues*. And it was that four-beat and I sat there and was just captured.

A Diary of the Underdogs

DON: Four beat?

MAL: Yeah, just that swinging, good bass player. Cuz Cousineau. Did you know him?

DON: I didn't but Dean Reilly spoke of him.

MAL: Yeah, Dean would know.

DON: So you got thrown out of the place in Pacific Heights, huh?

MAL: Yeah, but the point is then I was living up on the corner of Greenwich and Grant and I just starting walking down Grant Avenue and around Broadway and that's when I started walking by the Jazz Workshop and El Matador and all those clubs. Plus kind of the beat-nick Jazz scene that was down on Green Street.

DON: What year is this?

MAL: This is like 1961. I came back here like in 61. So, I was walking around and I would walk by the Jazz Workshop and look in. I didn't have any money; I couldn't go in to El Matador and etc.

DON: Yeah, I did the same thing; I went up and down North Beach. I was playing the Coffee Gallery in 1960 with Bishop Norman Williams.

MAL: OK, yeah, I was in there at the Coffee Gallery. There was another guy, who was it Red Fred, he played there, like a piano player or something.

Mal Sharpe

DON: Yeah, there was a bunch of them, like Ben Doris, did you know him?

MAL: No. Did you know Walter Roberts, Black bass player?

DON: No, I didn't. How about Max Hartstein?

MAL: No, I didn't know him. That was the scene down at the Cellar, right?

DON: Yeah, he was in the Cellar, but he would come up to the Coffee Gallery.

MAL: There was a guy named Indian something that played valve trombone….

DON: Indian Joe Lavato?

MAL: I don't know, he was Indian Joe and he played valve trombone.

DON: If it's the same guy, I met him up in Portland. But there was another guy around called Omar and he played valve trombone. Omar and Indian Joe were buddies. And they were kind of a sinister pair.

MAL: Yeah, Indian Joe was always in some kind of trouble or something. Yeah, but they were around, they were really the troops in North Beach; Red Fred. I would hang out at a bar called Mr. Otis' on Green Street. And that's where Walter Roberts, the bass player, played. He was from Kansas City and Walter would sing *I Want A Little Girl*. That's the first time I ever heard anybody sing that. I loved it when Walter would sing that. And that was a really nice scene there. Nice little trio. Brew Moore played at Otis', and Bill Young, a drummer.

DON: Yeah, Bill Young was a drummer with that little trio with Dean Reilly and Jeannie Hoffman.

A Diary of the Underdogs

MAL: Bill Young was kind of crazy and Walter Roberts and I wish I could remember the name of the piano player, but I have seen pictures of street fairs on Grant Avenue with Walter Roberts picture in it and it was unidentified, nobody knew who he was. And he was such a sweet guy. And years later, maybe twenty-five years later when I was doing radio commercials, he went back to Kansas City. I did a lot of commercials in Kansas City and I would look in the phone book for the name, Walter Roberts, and there was a number, an about every two years I would call it and no one would ever pick up. And I am talking like ten years I was going to Kansas City. I always tried to find him and I never stopped and then I swear, probably fifteen years later, this woman picks up the phone and I said, *I'm looking for Walter Roberts.* And she said, *I'm his daughter and he is in the hospital now and frankly he is dying of diabetes and you can go over there.* And the hospital was right near where I was staying. And this is like twenty-five years later that I have been in North Beach, and man, I go to the hospital and I walk in this room and there is this scrawny thin guy in bed with tubes and he looks up and he says, *Mal, how ya doing?* We had that kind of connection. We didn't spend a lot of time together, but we had a connection. So, that was real sweet and he died after that. Jim Lowe; that was the piano player.

DON: OK, that's one for the list; no one has spoken about him.

MAL: Yeah, he was a good piano player – The Jim Lowe Trio. They played at Otis'; Bill Young and Walter.

DON: What kind of music were they playing?

MAL: It was kind of bebop stuff. It wasn't far out, it was nice. It was kind of a dull place to hang out, I thought the whole beat-nick thing was kind of dull.

DON: Yeah, they weren't sociable people.

MAL: Yeah, I know, I had come from New York and lived in the Village and it w, as a lot more intriguing, not that I met that many people there. But looking back on it – it was kind of sweet.

DON: Yeah, well the earth was beginning to move. It was an important thing, a little glimpse of the enlightenment that was to come later with the LSD.

MAL: Yeah, a little crack was starting to open. Lenny Bruce was playing down the street and that guy I never liked very much – Lord Buckley, he played the Coffee Gallery. And so anyway, I would hang out in this place and next door to Otis' was this place called the Anxious Asp. It was a little thin bar and it was run by these two gay women, which was pretty exotic then, maybe it was a mostly gay bar, I don't know. It was in North Beach, this woman Arlene and her partner. One night this poet, Bob Stock, he was a local beat kind of poet, he had a trumpet or something and he and this drug addict, Billie Bosier who was this methadrine addict. Bob and Billie and this guy, Everett Hill, he had been fired from KSFO as an audio engineer, because he too had gotten into methadrine and stuff. So, they were playing at the Anxious Asp, and I am just sitting there and they were playing one of those simple songs and I said, *Hey, I have a trombone.* And they said, *well, get it.* I went up the street to my pad and got it and I had never played any place and I brought it down and they were playing *Bye Bye Blackbird*, something like that and I could kind of play that melody. So, suddenly I was in this band, you know, Everett played the spoons- that was the rhythm section. Bob played the trumpet and Billie played a metal clarinet and they were all really awful, including me. But somehow people liked it, it was ok. We would go there once a week, and then I got a job down at Broadway at Tipsy's for that band. And then that's where I kind of folded into the more traditional scene in North Beach. Broadway had some interesting people. And next door to Tipsy's was a place called Gigi's and a guy named Big Boy Frank Goodie played there, a tall Black man with a beret. And Frank Goodie was from New Orleans I believe, he had been in Paris, he played in the original Hot Club of France, he was an ex-patriot and Frank played there and then he went to Brazil and led big bands. He played clarinet and tenor. He led big bands in Brazil during the war and stuff. And then he kind of settled here for some reason, I think he had some day job. But he played at this place called Gigi's and he would come into Tipsy's, which was just this Italian neighborhood bar and that's where we were making $7. And Richard

A Diary of the Underdogs

Hadlock said to me one day, I am not going to play for $7 anymore, either I get $9 or quit. He drew the line. And Frank was next door and we didn't know who he was. And I just read this book on Django and Frank Goodie was on one of the original recordings. He was around and he played Pier 23 and stuff. And down the street on the other side of the street next to the Jazz Workshop was Dixieland place called....oh, I can't think of the name of it. It was an X-Rated store, you know that....

DON: Yeah, its still there.

MAL: Yeah, that's there, but that's what this place before that had been. And it was traditional Jazz club and a lot of the traditional musicians like Bob Mielke and Bill Mayphere and people like that, they played in there and they had pretty good bands. And it was run by this guy Amelio, he was in a wheelchair. A really mean guy and to this day, I didn't play in there but I watched them and would yell at the band, in a gruff voice-"*SHOWTIME!-SHOWTIME!*"

DON: Was it Amelio's?

MAL: No, it wasn't. I am just blanking out, it will come to me. But the big thing that Amelio had in there at the bar was this Female mannequin sitting there in a coat. It was sitting there looking down at the bar holding a drink. And it was a dimly lit place, these sailors would walk by and look in and see this woman sitting there and they would come in and sit down at the bar and they would buy a drink. Amelio used this and then they would start talking to her and then realize that it was a dummy and people would get really pissed at Amelio. He was this tough guy, he carried a gun and I think he had been shot in the spine that's what had happened to him. And so there was this whole scene in their right next to the workshop and I think that Hadlock can tell you....in fact the guy who was playing there, the guy who played three horns, Roland Kirk came in and sat in with them. He liked that music. I remember some musician or some girl I knew, Miles was playing at the workshop, she took me across the street, he was staying at some flea bag hotel, I remember sitting up in a room with him, he was sitting on the bed in these pink, silk underwear and this chick and I were shooting the breeze with him, I can't remember what the conversation was but it was just up the street over by the Matador.

DON: Not, the Swiss American?

MAL: No. Did you know Joe Alias, black guy, with missing teeth?

DON: No.

MAL: He was hanging around there. So, we were playing in this place and the band changed because Billie Bosier, the clarinet player, he didn't even have any shoes after awhile and he sort of drifted off into the drug world, and we got better bands. The bands got better.

DON: The gig held up, you stayed there for awhile.

MAL: Yeah, we were there for about two years. And some of the people who later played with Turk Murphy, a guy named Bob Neighbors came in and would play with us. Dick Laney who also was in the Turk Murphy band who was playing up the street, there was a banjo place up the street. Laney would come in; these were all big figures that made recordings with Turk. This guy, Allen Hoff played piano. Hadlock played in that band. He plays piano and clarinet – he is a reed guy. You know, he was the guy; he was the critic at the Examiner. He gave his job to Phil Elwood. You should talk to him also. He has a scrapbook of all his reviews. He was out reviewing in these clubs. He didn't give such a great review to Charles Mingus and Mingus threatened to kill him.

DON: Yeah, I heard a story last night from Frank Passantino, that the pimp was sitting there with a couple of these girls watching Mingus in the workshop and I guess they were cutting up and making noise or something, and Frank said that Mingus put the bass down and went over and smacked the guy! These things kind of follow Mingus around.

MAL: There was actually somebody here in town that stored Mingus' bass for awhile. We have this film that we did and you could look at this rough cut because Vernon and Earl Watkins talk about a lot of the stuff you are interested in. This is all on tape. So, that was kind of our scene. I don't know if you know this but Everett Hill, the spoon player, he was still playing with us on spoons, but one night he couldn't play the gig because he was a recording engineer and Lenny Bruce asked him to go over to the Jazz Workshop and record his act. So, Everett was down in the basement recording his act at night when he got busted and that tape became a big thing in Lenny's trial, they refer to that tape a lot, you know all the swear words and all that stuff. That was Everett's night off, that band was called the Mal Sharpe and his Modern Regressive Jazz Band. But that was interesting, Everett sitting down there in the basement.

DON: Was this off Broadway or at the Workshop?

MAL: At the Workshop. It was fun being down there on Broadway. It stayed with me my whole life. It was happening, most certainly, Grant Avenue because of the beat-nick thing. And this photographer Jerry Stoll, Jerry has some great photos. He shot a lot of stuff during those days, in the Coffee Gallery and in the Cellar. He has a ton of stuff. His son, I think is Casey Stoll has his archives now. And I will tell you why he has a lot on the Cellar, because we did that movie –the spaghetti factory movie and we used a lot of Jerry's photographs in there. And Jerry bugged us after that to do a book on the Cellar.

DON: And what about this Spaghetti Factory movie, is this something that is available to people?

MAL: Oh, yeah, mostly through me.

DON: What is the title of it?

MAL: *The Old Spaghetti Factory.* I will get you a copy of it. It's about the Spaghetti Factory that was up where the Bocci Café is now. That was the old Spaghetti Factory, the original. Freddie Coo owned it, there wasn't much Jazz up there, but it was a real scene. And there was Flamenco dancing. The soundtrack on the tape is all Johnny Coppola, it's a Brew Moore record that Brew made with a tune called *Edison's Light On* that Johnny Coppola wrote, the whole soundtrack is just one tune. Johnny Markham is on there too; all San Francisco people. I was doing my hidden mike stuff at that time, that's what I was mostly doing. And Jim Coil and I ultimately got a job at KGO but Tennessee Ernie Ford was doing a TV show and people like Johnny Coppola and all those people, they played that show; all these hip guys. And years later, Jim and I went on that show and Johnny said, *I remember you guys going on the show.* It was all very hip and these guys were like flies on the wall with all this history.

I wrote a song this summer at Jazz Camp, it was based on the fact that we were playing at the Savoy Tivoli and there was one of these guys at the bar there, and you don't know if he is drunk, or nasty or crazy, you know all those kind of guys, they are like yelling at the band and you don't know whether they are having a good time with you or what. And they guy came up to me and we were setting up for the next set and he said, *you guys you are almost as old as the Count Basie Band.* And I blurted out- *I used to be the youngest guy in the band!* And so, I wrote a whole song about that – I used to be the youngest guy in the band. IT WAS 1962 (singing) AND I WORE A WING TIP SHOE, I USE TO BE THE YOUNGEST GUY IN THE STAND. And I wrote a whole picture about that time in my life. I should give you that. It was a portrait of people I was playing with and stuff.

DON: You were all about thirty?

MAL: No, I was about twenty-two.

DON: I tried to fit in, Corduroy coat – green.

MAL: Everybody looked the same then – in all the pictures, they all looked like JFK. Grey suit and little thin ties.

DON: Yeah, until the Beatles hit.

MAL: Yeah.

DON: Everybody had those boots!

MAL: Back to Everett, my wife and I moved to L.A. around 64 or 65, her mother lived up on Grant Avenue and we would come back and I saw Everett just walking up and down the street, he had some metal

A Diary of the Underdogs

sculpture thing – he was totally gone. About ten years ago, the phone rang one night on the show, I could do phone calls then, and this guy called and said, *Mal, It's me!* And I said, *what do you mean, it's me? Who is me?* And he said, *me, the spoon player.* I said, *Everett?* And he said, *don't say my name.* And I told him to come and see me; and I gave him my address and then Everett later re-appeared like ten years later, he had been in jail. He was living in a halfway house; he had a different name because he was wanted all over the place. And he survived. He would call up and play the spoons on the radio. He was all right. But it was so uncanny. And he was like, don't mention my name, I don't go by that name anymore. And he was around for a few months and I haven't seen him since.

DON: This is ten years ago?

MAL: Yeah, maybe less. He came to my house, met my wife. He was like from another planet. I was a suburban Boston guy and I just never got into speed and stuff like that. I had this whole other career going on and I didn't really sink into music. We left Tipsy's and got a gig over at La Belles and then we started playing with Pops Foster and Darnell Howard and there was this whole other scene of New Orleans and New York musicians that came out here and lived and played in the 50's in places like the Hangover, this is parallel to Turk Murphy, Earl Hines and Pops Foster.

DON: Did you have some interaction with those folks?

MAL: Oh, yeah. Pops played with us and Darnell played with us over at La Belles in Berkley. One night I was driving Pops, seventy-five years old, from New Orleans, Darnell Howard played with Jelly Roll Morton. And Amos White, who was living in Oakland, he played with Faith Merabil on the Riverboats – these three guys were all over seventy. And they were coming to the gig with me at La Belles and this is when I was doing my thing with Jim Coil and I had my tape recorder and I put it on the floor of my car. And we pulled up in the back parking lot behind La Belles, and I told them that we had to perform an experiment that night – this UC Professor had asked me to do this   I had jars of insects in the trunk of the car – we were going to bring these jars of insects in the trunk of the car and set them next to the band. And while they were playing take the tops off and let the insects kind of roam through the club. And see what reaction people had to the insects. And I wanted them to bring the jars in. I asked them if they would mind doing it. And they freaked out, you know what I mean? Darnell was like; *I ain't messin with that shit!* I got all of this on the tape. And this guy Amos was like, *yeah, man, I'll do it.* And Pops didn't care about anything but the bass. And it was going to be all these spiders and stuff crawling all over the place. It was a funny scene and they played with us over there in Berkley. That was a whole scene that happened around the Hangover which was over on Bush Street and it is a male dance club, a gay place now. Harley…do you know Harley White?

DON: Yeah.

MAL: Harley ended up playing with Earl Hines; he ended up doing some tours in Europe and stuff. Harley would know a lot about Earl.

DON: Did Earl come over with you to La Belles?

MAL: No, Earl was I think the great "Earl Hines" then. Lots of guys- Pops, Hadlock, Darnell-Tony Lamphier- he got drunk and crashed.

DON: How about Frank Goulette?

MAL: Oh, yeah, Frank, he played at that club next to the Workshop.

DON: Burp Hollow?

MAL: That's it! The guy in the wheelchair, Amelio, he is the one who owned Burp Hollow. Frank Goulette, Bob Mielke, old guy, still alive, he knows tons of shit too. They all played in there; this whole other scene that was going on half a block away from Miles Davis at the Workshop and Sonny Rollins. I talked with Hadlock a lot and he knows a lot about Amelio and Burp Hollow.

DON: So, why was there this separation between Trad players and Jazz players; this barrier that seems to be

A Diary of the Underdogs

there?

MAL: Yeah, there were the bebop players in general – in the history of Jazz, the bebop players had left the traditional players behind. You know, like Dizzy. But when you really get into those guys Dizzy and Charlie Parker, they had great respect for traditional Jazz and Swing. Mostly, like your generation, kind of bebop hip guys, that Louie and all this stuff was kind of Uncle Tom. And some of the guys like Miles would put them down as being Uncle Tom. But in San Francisco, there was more of a, I can't say there was a big crossover then, but as the history of San Francisco has gone on…you have people like Johnny Coppola, who was in the Woody Herman band that probably thought Turk Murphy was a bunch of shit. But I think it has come full circle and there is more respect. And I think the musicians in San Francisco honor the interconnectedness of it all. The traditional guys, they didn't want a sax in the band. And some of them felt a little inferior to bebop music. I am still grappling with the chords. We could play a lot of traditional Jazz without a lot of knowledge, but you couldn't play bebop without knowing unless you were a genius. Right now I am studying with a guitar player. The Swing players, the players I like, you really find out that a lot of those Swing guys, they knew exactly what they were doing, with Plaz Johnson and others like that. Vic Dickenson is my favorite trombone player. He was the guy that trapped me in Boston. I saw him when I was in high school and I was like, wow, that's interesting. And I'm still gone on Vic Dickenson, and I'm still studying one of his solos just the other day. And Danny, the speaker said to me, and he studied with Plaz Johnson and he said to me, *those guys knew. He's doing a melodic minor here and knows that it's resolving in this C minor thing, so instead of playing the B flat he's playing the G seven,* and he knew that-these guys knew all of that stuff. So we, the traditional players, could only get so far, like I did, just on guts of some sort. But yeah, there was a big division and the bebop guys were heading off. Miles would be playing next door at the Workshop but they never came by to hear us. Roland Kirk did.

End: Mal Sharpe

Interview: John Handy-jazz musician-educator-saxophonist-with Don Alberts-February 12, 2009 in Oakland-about: Oakland, Richmond, Dallas, childhood, SF State, Bill Graham, Appeal III, Charles Mingus, Jane Getz, Virgil Gonsalves, Don Thompson, Terry Clarke, Michael White, Jerry Hahn, Bobby Hutcherson, Both/And, Kermit Scott, Rafael Donald Garrett, Bop City, Art Tatum, Skip Warren, Freddie Redd, Eddie Kahn, Randy Weston, Bishop Norman Williams, BJ Papa, Vince Wallace, Teaching, Nancy King, Sonny King, Saunders King, Jack's on Sutter, Jackson's Nook, Record companies, Larry Carlton, Cal UC Berkley Concert, New York, The Five Spot, Abdul Malik, Sam Jones, Clifford Jarvis, Mal Waldron, Mike Nock, John Handy Scholarship.

JOHN HANDY

JOHN: Bobby's sick, Bobby Hutcherson, he has emphysema.
DON: I didn't know he was sick, I was hoping to talk to him.
JOHN: He still is doing some gigs.
DON: He was sitting down last time I saw him.
JOHN: He was?
DON: He was sitting on a stool. I saw him at that last Freddie Hubbard concert, did you see that?
JOHN: No.
DON: With the guys at Yoshi's. It wasn't a pleasant thing; I took Sonny with me because I knew he wanted to see it.

A Diary of the Underdogs

JOHN: Buxton?

DON: Yeah.

JOHN: Yeah, has been sick a long time.

DON: Well, he's in great shape now.

JOHN: Yeah, he looks great!

DON: He does his walks and his exercises and he really watches what he eats, I go and see him a lot. Because you know once an awhile something goes wrong over there and I said, Pearl, I am not that far away, you call me. And I did take him one time and it really is a good thing I did because he was bleeding internally and didn't know it. He was feeling faint and stuff. I am not that far away, they live in Westlake.

JOHN: Who is George DiQuattro?

DON: Piano player that used to be around here.

JOHN: I remember his name, but I don't remember who he is.

John Handy

DON: I know he played at Pearl's a lot. I don't know if I will be able to talk to him, he doesn't play anymore.

JOHN: But he is here?

DON: Yeah, he is down somewhere around Los Altos, or something.

JOHN: Did you miss BJ Papa?

DON: Well, fortunately, I talked to BJ in 1997. When I started this whole thing! (WOW!!) But one day I had BJ over and cooked dinner for him and I had a nice interview with him, so that worked out. And he was a little wasted; he had a little bottle of Crown Royal in his back pocket. I cooked a really nice dinner for him and we talked about all kinds of things. Norman Spiller, Bobby Van, Julius Ellerbe.

JOHN: Norman Spiller? He's gone isn't he?

DON: Yeah, all those guys are gone. And BJ talked about standing up there trying sit in and his knees are shaking, he couldn't stop them from shaking, he had to lean against the wall to get one of those legs to stop shaking so he could stand up there! He was so nervous!

JOHN: Is this when he was trying to play the tenor?

DON: Yeah.

JOHN: I remember him coming around. I have known him pretty much since he got here. But we never hung out, I know a lot of his people, but I never hung out with him. I played with Sonny on gigs that he had. And Vince, he always played like he… well, you always think Vince is going to collapse like a…..a powder! And he keeps playing his butt off!

DON: Yeah, he is still playing. I talked to him yesterday and I am going to interview him.

JOHN: Yeah, I remember when he came around, he is younger than BJ. He was a teen and I was just out of my teens.

DON: Yeah, you were pretty young, you got here in 48?

JOHN: Yeah, I was fifteen.

DON: I got here a couple of years before you, I lived in Richmond.

A Diary of the Underdogs

JOHN: Did you go to Richmond High?

DON: I did go to Richmond High. I graduated in 1950.

JOHN: Did you know some first cousins; there were about four or five. The Gosses- Earl Goss, Raymond Goss, Howard Goss. Raymond should be around your age. And then the Smiths, they were all first cousins. And I am first cousin to the Smiths. Roy Smith, Marvin Smith, Ernest Smith, they all went to school out there.

DON: Where they musicians?

JOHN: No. The Smith brothers became ministers.

DON: So, did you stay in touch in those days?

JOHN: Oh, yeah. We stayed with the Smiths when we moved here.

DON: You know Richmond wasn't a very good place in those days, and what has changed?

JOHN: I didn't know.

DON: North Richmond, over there?

JOHN: Well, that part I got to know later.

DON: I used to go out to the plunge out there. I was fine. I got along great a school. The problems at school were the people from Dust Bowl, you know, from Arkansas, Nebraska, Oklahoma, Texas people that came out here to work in the shipyards and they send their kids to school. That's the problem! That was the conflict, because the Oakies and the Arkies and the Blacks couldn't get along with the Mexicans! So, it was tough to go to school. There were times when I just didn't go to school for a couple of weeks.

JOHN: Is that right? I didn't go with them to school and they never talked about it. We didn't see each other a lot, but we did stay with them, but only for about three weeks and then we moved to Oakland. I never even went to school there. I was a tenth grader. I started in Dallas and then I went to private school almost five years that we were there. So we came out here and school starts in September and you are a tenth grader and you end up going to school in November out here and so anyway, I never enrolled in Richmond and never knew anything about it. I heard that it was tough. Yeah, its strange, I moved from Dallas to L.A. as a younger kid and the Zoot Suiters were older than I. You heard about that thing where the sailors followed each other? Pachucos. They were wearing the Zoot Suits.

DON: Yeah, young Mexican guys. They were rough.

JOHN: Yeah, there were several killings on both sides. The sailors were bad too. The cops eventually sided with the Mexicans and by the time I was there, 43, 44, just leaving L.A. back to Dallas, I just missed it but they were still doing the Pompadour and the Duck Tail. And those built up shoes.

DON: Oh, I had those too! All steel on the bottom. You had to take your Levis and take all the belt loops out and roll the waistband over, so it was only so thick. And you couldn't have the red Levi tag on your pocket. If you did, somebody would rip it off!

JOHN: Come on man, that's what was going on out here? When I went to MacArthur, which was considered a tough school – the toughest school in Oakland in the system and they had a reputation of – if they lost the game, they won the fight.

DON: And that's what we said in Richmond too! If we lost the game, we would win the fight. Richmond, El Cerrito.

JOHN: Yeah, MAC was tough. And the first day I was there and gym was one of the last classes and they must have had fifteen or sixteen pairs of boxing gloves and you know its dress up clothes, the first day and they were pushing me and I was a skinny guy, I didn't really know want to box, I really didn't. But, they kept pushing me and I ended up knocking this guy down and I really didn't want to because he was a really popular guy and then there was this big guy and we got into it and I bloodied his nose and he said, "motherfucker!" And just the way he said it and everybody started laughing, just the way he said it and he became my best friend and he was a sax player. And he ended up marrying my sister! We became best friends that

A Diary of the Underdogs

day. He was a kid who weighed 185lbs and all muscle; he looked like a black Charles Atlas. And I weighed like 135lbs and that's why he was surprised. I was quick! I should never have boxed, but I did.

DON: How did you get trained in that? Was that something that just came along?

JOHN: Yeah, basically. I was in St. Peters Academy, which was all-academic until like I was fourteen. And it was a small school but it ran from Kindergarten through the Twelfth Grade and we never had more then 500 kids. And so you knew faces even if you didn't know their names. And I remember in the Ninth Grade guys just playing their asses off! Jazz! And they were juniors and seniors and by the time I got there, like I was fourteen, all those guys were gone. And so, they started athletics. And I got into football and my mother never wanted me to play and my younger sister would always tell on me. My Mom didn't want me to play football, but she let me box. I shouldn't have boxed; I was already blind in one eye. I only had one eye!

DON: WOW! Really, very few people know that John.

JOHN: So, I got into it and I ended up being the champion. And I really didn't like it but I got into it only because we didn't have anything else to do. And we started baseball.

DON: Well, there is something about getting hit man; it will wake you up real quick.

JOHN: And strange enough, I got hit more in training than I did in sparring and I finally got hit, that last fight, in this eye. And that did hurt, but I was never really hurt at all. And I was seldom hit. My first fight was the hardest. I fought a kid that I had fought in the preliminaries.

DON: How many rounds?

JOHN: Three; and he was pretty mean; every time he hit me I could really feel it. But luckily, he never really got to me. And I beat him and I was never afraid of anybody.

DON: I was going to ask you about Jane Getz, did you know her? She played with Mingus, and there is a famous story about her at the workshop and that Mingus actually closed the piano on her hands…did he actually do that?

JOHN: I didn't see that. Somebody said that happened. I was there almost every night. I was there the last night they played and I sat in – I am on that album. I did hear him really put her down. When I came back out here in 62, I was living officially in New York….and I came back because I hadn't gotten my degree from SF State. And so I was back in school. I should have had my degree sooner. There was one main person that kept me from graduating; he was over all the instrumental music, Ed Couch, And so just recently, just last week, we went to something for SF State and somebody's wife, Karma and she said they saw Ed Couch and they talked about half an hour about me. And, I won't see him, I won't talk to him.

DON: He was standing in the way of your success over there?

JOHN: Yeah. And he knows that I know it and he told her that he was going to be 89 this year and he wants me to come by and I can't push myself to do it because I had to come back out here, I would have stayed in New York. I would not have been here then. And the wife that I had at the time, we had known each other; we had lived together in New York. And we were married out here and we had just bought a house, that big old house that we were in. You came to my house.

DON: The one on Baker Street?

JOHN: Yeah-that big house. It had fourteen rooms!

DON: That was a great old house; big Victorian.

JOHN: Yeah, we bought that house in November of '63 and she and I broke up around less than a year around the time you came by.

DON: Yeah, I am thinking 63, 64.

JOHN: 64. I had that Freedom Band.

DON: Yeah, the Freedom Band. You talked about a tune…..I think I wrote one or two charts for that band. I don't know where they are and I don't remember the tune.

A Diary of the Underdogs

JOHN: Red Eye. I know it. It was a good arrangement. And then I didn't see you again.

DON: Yeah, well, I got mixed up there. My story is just too strong to be told!

JOHN: Were you here?

DON: No, 1969 I left and went to Portland. Actually I went to Eugene for a gig which is what I needed. I needed to get out of town. Things were not working out.

JOHN: How long were you there?

DON: I played that gig for five nights a week, for a month. And then the gig was over and I had a little money and I didn't want to come back to California so I went onto Portland. And it was a very, very rainy day and I arrived there and couldn't get anything going and ended up sleeping in my car. And it took me awhile and so that whole trip ended up being twenty years.

JOHN: So, you must know Ed Coleman – the bass player.

DON: No.

JOHN: He might have come up later. He is an African American who looks Jewish. Very Jewish looking. Not quite as tall as I am and played very good bass. He also taught up there. He must have come up there after. He retired in Eugene. We went to school together, as we used to say, the old campus, SF State was on Haight Street.

DON: Yeah, that was a long time ago!

JOHN: …….I spent two days up there…

DON: Well, you came up, we talked really briefly, you were on a tour and you were playing tenor then and you were playing a little club in what we call the South East part of Portland. You came up and played with the local rhythm section; probably Mel Brown.

JOHN: No, it was Ron Steen. And was Nancy on that gig?

DON: She might have been because she lived there, she was there. I don't know if she did the gig or not.

JOHN: So, that's where we saw each other, and that was the last time, that's been a few years too.

DON: Yeah, I don't know what year, must have been 1980 something.

JOHN: Yeah, 86, 87. A long time ago, and Sonny King was there.

DON: Sonny King was still alive – he died there you know? He was alive and he and Nancy weren't living together, they were separated.

JOHN: He had just gotten married, to that young woman to whom he was married when he died. I remember her, I met her.

DON: Oh, I didn't meet her…I didn't know here. I knew about him and Nancy.

JOHN: He used to lend me his horn, here, when we were kids and I didn't have one. We went to school together; he was almost two years ahead.

DON: He was a terrific player! He would say, *I love the way you guys play, but nobody comes in to listen to us.* He would play that wild stuff. He was pretty free and abandoned. But he was very sincere about his music. It was the real thing.

JOHN: His Dad was a blues guitarist from San Francisco. Did you know that?

DON: No, not Saunders King?

JOHN: Yeah!

DON: Saunders King was his Dad?

JOHN: Yeah, he was Saunders King, Jr.

DON: Saunders King played at Jack's at Sutter.

JOHN: I knew later, but I knew about the records. His blues, Saunders King Blues I guess. He was famous in my hometown when I was like thirteen, fourteen before I even moved out here knew about him. Yeah, those records came out just after WWII.

DON: Saunders King! I didn't get to know him, but I think I have seen him.

A Diary of the Underdogs

JOHN: Yeah, he was one of those good looking little cats!

DON: Wasn't it a guitar, organ trio at Jacks?

JOHN: These are cats that are ahead of us.

DON: I think they were still around when Bop City was around.

JOHN: Yeah, Bop City, I was going over there, I was sneaking over there. When I was under age. I was over there when it was "Vout City." Slim Gaillard owned it.

DON: Yeah, Slim started the whole thing and Jimbo got it someway, I don't know how he got it.

JOHN: Who was the guy who used to run the Fillmore – oh, Sullivan was his name.

DON: Sullivan, yeah, from the earlier time, from the 40's.

JOHN: Sullivan had it and I just talked to his nephew, who used to be my sons roommate for awhile. My son lived with me for almost a year and this kid; well he is about 30 years younger…. I just talked to him about three weeks ago. He said that Mr. Sullivan owned that building.

DON: Sullivan got bumped off, didn't he, mysteriously…?

JOHN: Yeah, mysteriously and Bill Graham took over. He was renting that place from Sullivan.

DON: Yeah, I got a lot of info from Chet Helms.

JOHN: Yeah, I liked Chet.

DON: Yeah, he was a nice guy, I was going to ask you about that –

JOHN: He hired me.

DON: What was it about that you did that fit with what they did?

JOHN: I was the first headliner. I didn't know Bill Graham. But, I didn't do those benefits for him. I did it because….

DON: But you are on the bill.

JOHN: Well, I was the first headliner. But he had come out and hung out like you and I are talking for about three hours. He was talking about the holocaust and his experience.

DON: Yeah, he was very heavy into that.

JOHN: Yeah, and I had a lot of compassion, he and I were close to the same age. I agreed to do the Fillmore – the third benefit – and some of the players – other musicians lived on my street, so we were all politically involved. That's why I did it, I didn't know Bill. He was like their fundraiser and that's when he came to me to do the headlining. And so I agreed and his wife brought the contract over couple of days later. I signed it. It was nothing. I mean, I had a Columbia Records contract and a fantastic band and we had a steady gig whenever we were in town at the Both/And, six nights a week or whatever we wanted to do. And we traveled to all western states. So, anyway, he told me that I could be there between 9 and 4.

DON: AM?

JOHN: And I showed up at 1. And he didn't let us play. He didn't swear at me, but close. And I couldn't believe it, here is a guy that I was doing a favor, I was the headliner, and we just walked right out. And the place was packed. And so, I just never did the gig. And we didn't speak for twenty-three years.

DON: So, you were on the bill, but never did the gig.

JOHN: Right, I was the headliner. And it was because of what he said – and I will save that for my book.

DON: Yeah, ok. But the thing is – is you did it for Chet. Because Chet…

JOHN: No, no, I didn't even know Chet. I did it for the Mime Troupe.

DON: Oh, because it was a benefit for those cats.

JOHN: I went there, but I didn't take the band. I was working a gig and somebody came to the gig at the Both/And and asked me if I would play and you know I didn't want to take the whole band, I had cats from Canada and all that.

DON: Yeah, yeah, you had those guys; you got them right here, Don Thompson, Terry Clarke, Michael White and Jerry Hahn.

A Diary of the Underdogs

JOHN: And originally, instead of Jerry Hahn I had Freddie Redd. He was the first guy I ever fired.

DON: I remember him from Bop City. He ended up doing the Connection.

JOHN: That's right; I remember seeing him in New York with that. So, anyway… I didn't play –

DON: Yeah, well people who went there would have remembered that, but people who didn't go there have no idea you didn't play.

JOHN: Yeah. I didn't deal with him again until years later and I played a gig at CAL that he had…well this is even maybe before that….I played at CAL with Larry….he did a lot of sessions with my wife….he got his degree….Larry Carlton.

DON: He ended up with the Jazz Crusaders.

JOHN: Crusaders, yeah and after that he became his own star. He was on some recordings, sessions and I got to hear and know him a little bit. So he was headlining and we both were headlining at CAL – UC Berkley, and when we had the big earthquake that's when he and I talked. And then he asked me to do the benefit. And I did it for the victims but I wanted to meet Taj Mahal because I was a fan and I got a chance to meet the younger brother.

DON: Taj Mahal borrowed my piano in Portland one time. And somebody said, you better follow that piano, man, because he is going to leave town after the gig. So I talked to Taj and he was like, don't worry man.

JOHN: Nancy King. I thought Nancy was very talented by the way.

DON: She was a wonderful person.

JOHN: I didn't know her, I met her when she and Sonny were together and I came out for vacation and my first time coming back after I went to New York, like nineteen months or so and we had a son here, my wife and I- first wife- and we had met Nancy and they both were young.

DON: She was quite beautiful.

JOHN: Yeah, well she was a beauty queen. And she was very talented. I don't think people realized how talented she was.

DON: Yeah, that finally came out later and once she got to Portland, she was revered. Finally! She was considered a vocalist that was a Jazz saxophonist, because she could play with the horn.

JOHN: Yeah, and she could really hold her own, she was a good player. And I wouldn't be surprised if that was a problem for her and Sonny King, and you know, they had three boys.

DON: Yeah, I met one of them.

JOHN: One just died in recent years; accidentally, a motorcycle or something. But I got to know Nancy years and years later when she was in her early forties. And she came down here and I don't know how we met….and very interesting….oh, I have to tell you something about Sonny. Sonny was a couple years ahead of me in school and we almost got into a fight the first time we met.

DON: Sonny was a little aggressive as I remember.

JOHN: Sonny was a lot bigger – tall. They had us running in gym class and there were two guys ahead of me and I must have run in front of them and didn't notice it. And he grabbed me from behind and said….you know… what..? And I didn't know why this guy was grabbing me and then I pushed him away and we kind of looked and each other and we didn't do it but we got very close. And I found out later that Sonny was an animal and he could really bring you down. But somehow we didn't fight and I ended up like a day or two…..

DON: Did you know he was a musician?

JOHN: No. And so we were in class on the campus and I don't know how we got…he invited me to his house and second time I ever played with him for a half day. And I went over and he played Charlie Parker records. His Mom was home and we were very close to school, and we went back to the second and only did that twice. And since then we were very close friends. And he used to lend me his horn, I didn't have

A Diary of the Underdogs

one.

DON: Do you remember the days at the Coffee Gallery? He used to come in and play there and Nancy did too.

JOHN: That's when I saw them....

DON: That's when I kind of hooked up with all of them.

JOHN: .....in 69. Sorry, 59.

DON: Yeah, 59, 60, 61.....That's when it was happening. Norman Bishop had the gig most of the time and Pony Poindexter was there.

JOHN: Well, I was in New York and I came here for like just two weeks and that's where I met... well, I knew Sonny... and I think Pony was there. And Pony and I knew each other since I was about sixteen, seventeen....

DON: I was going to say you probably were buddies in school....

JOHN: No. He was older. I found out many years later that he went to Mac Clements also. And he was never very nice to me. We played the same instrument. He was....well... see... Bishop came later. Bishop is almost five years and a few months younger than I. But he wasn't here when I left; I went to New York in 58.

DON: Yeah, that's early. I started coming to the City in 1960 and sitting in at the Coffee Gallery.

JOHN: Oh, yeah, ok, well you were coming in when I was out. I was living in New York at the time.

DON: And then you were back for awhile in the sixties, I used to see you....at Bop City.

JOHN: Well, I came back and stayed....I came back in 62 to stay three weeks and I never went back to New York. That's how that happened. Bop City.... I have to tell you youngsters...and here is what happened. Bop City started to go down hill as far as I was concerned, musically as early as 54. And it was still there in what...61, 62 when I came back....

DON: Yeah, even longer than that.

JOHN: Yeah, and they moved it. They moved it over on Fillmore.

DON: That must have been late 60's...

JOHN: And it was not happening. And I am talking about when the bands used to come in like, Duke's band and Ella and Harry Bellefonte, Sammy Davis....

DON: The glory days.

JOHN: Oh, yeah, and I was lucky enough to be there- and Art Tatum, even Art. He's walked on the bandstand and I didn't see him and he was playing behind me and when I discovered it I almost had a heart attack!

DON: He doesn't do background – does he?

JOHN: Well, he did! I mean, he was sitting there. But he was not the background. We were playing a song I didn't know very well and we were in the bridge – a ballad – thank god it was a slow song. And I heard....brrrrrrritttt...and it sounded like somebody opening a zipper and I looked over there and I realized....and I didn't have to see his face, I saw the diamond ring, the glitter on the ring and I saw those hands and I wouldn't look back up. And I started to walk off, but I finished the melody and got off the stand like everybody else.

DON: Did he end up playing solo or...

JOHN: He used the bassist and drummer. I don't remember the drummer, but the bassist was Skippy Warren. Did you know him?

DON: Skip Warren....I didn't know him personally but....

JOHN: Well, he died in 59 or 60. And he had gone to MAC and I used to come to Bop City with him because I didn't have a car in the early days. I lived on this side. And so anyway, I was gone until 62 in New York and had a great time there. New York was very good to me. I never...I hooked up with...

A Diary of the Underdogs

actually I played with Randy Weston, it's never on the recording…you know in the book set. We actually played more than I did with Charles. But we didn't record. We spend like four months at The Five Spot and never recorded. We were opposite Mal Waldron's trio and we backed bands that came in and he was there for eight months straight. So we would…we often played at….we had a spot…. It was like in front and the tenor player and Clifford Jarvis was seventeen and came and copped the gig like that…right out of Boston, Springfield or wherever he was from in Massachusetts and he uses our bass and drummer. And we had Sam Jones or Abdul Malik. It was either he or Sam Jones. And Cannonball formed this band after Miles, he went with Miles, Sam Jones went with Cannonball. I opened there with Mingus earlier, Christmas week of 58. With his quintet and opposite one of my heroes, Sonny Rollins; and I had met Sonny and talked and sat and talked to him like we are doing now for about two hours. You know he was a wonderful person as well as a fantastic musician.

DON: Yeah, he was a nice guy to get along with.

JOHN: I played with somebody whom I had known here – met – here just briefly, Kenny Dorham. We did a big band gig dance with him.

DON: Kenny Dorham?

JOHN: …..before I played with Mingus and Idris Sulliman…..

DON: Oh, yeah, the trumpet player.

JOHN: He was a guy I played with in New York before I played with Charles. And after Charles I was able to get my own recording dates.

DON: Let's see, Charles was on Atlantic or something and you ended up with Columbia right?

JOHN: Yeah. Charles was with a number of places, people because when I was with him we did…..we auditioned for about three record companies in his living room and we ended up on Colombia. Before that we were at United Artists. We did the first album there and then….see…Columbia and then Atlantic.

DON: Yeah, Atlantic. That was a strong one there.

JOHN: I hated that album though. I didn't like the music

DON: No?

JOHN: No, it was confusing. And I hadn't been with them very long but I could see that it was too much craziness.

DON: Jeez, in 67 you were on Roulette.

JOHN: No, no, it was much earlier than that. 59 was Roulette.

DON: Oh, yeah, 1960 Roulette…..

JOHN: Well, yeah, the recordings came out in 1960 but I recorded them in 59, released in 60.

DON: Great stuff John. Few musicians get to accomplish this. So, I was going to ask you about Judy Tristano. Did you ever hook up with her? She was Tristano's wife….

JOHN: Oh, the saxophone player?

DON: Right.

JOHN: No, I never played with them. I don't think we ever even met. But I believe I walked into a club where she was playing, but I don't remember hearing her playing.

DON: Yeah, she was around; but back to the Jane Getz thing. He didn't close that piano on her hands? They just had a conflict?

JOHN: Quick story about Jane. When I moved back out here, Jane, Achutan…

DON: The drummer?

JOHN: Yeah... and Marvin Patillo. And….I don't remember the bassist, but I used tell Jane, she was very young then, learn to use your left hand. She was almost all right in the middle…kind of a McCoy, inspired influence and she never used her left hand other than to play chords. And of course she was young and didn't listen and she left eventually, this was 62 when I cam back and she came back in 64, that was the next time I saw her, she was with Mingus! I happened to go to the matinee at the Jazz Workshop and Cliff Jarvis was playing, had been…..was a tenor player, the saxophone player had a quartet but he didn't show up and I took my horn…. And I heard them the like the Wednesday before….and I memorized the tune and I had it….just an affinity…. and I just knew his style and I went in and played the song …and it impressed him although and it had been a few years since we played together. And he asked me to show up that night, and I said I had a gig and he said come after the gig. I had a big band thing downtown in Union Square. And so, I went there and they were recording and as soon as I walked in Mingus was like….*hey man, get your horn!* And so that's where I start to see the fireworks with Jane. He wanted something played in the bass and she just couldn't get it and Mingus would never, you know... First of all her Mom was there, she was so proud she had come up from L.A. with a friend of hers. And she was walking around like you know; a proud parent. And Mingus said, she couldn't play the tune without her left hand, which was actually, the one thing he wanted and poor Jane really started to really bury her head, the more he would yell at her. And I think at one point, I think he called her bitch. And Mom was a little woman and her girlfriend was there and she was so shocked and embarrassed and I was too and I remember I leaned over and said *Jane, remember I told you to start to use your left hand.* She was hurting. So, no he didn't do that, he just yelled at her.

DON: But she went on as far as my research shows, she still is playing, she calls herself, Mother Hen. I think she is in L.A. somewhere.

JOHN: We played a gig, about…. oh, I played at the Catalina….something like that…

DON: Yeah, the Catalina, in L.A.

JOHN: Yeah. And she was on the gig. And that was like ten or twelve years ago. And she was playing…I have her number somewhere. She got a divorce……came out with the house.

DON: You knew Monty, Monty Waters and Jimmy Lovelace?

JOHN: He just died.

DON: Smiley Winters.

JOHN: Monty just passed.

DON: I know he did. I went out the little memorial. Art Lewis played out there.

JOHN: Where was it?

DON: It was out in the East Bay, here, somewhere.

JOHN: I actually thought…I knew Monty had been sick for a long time but I hadn't seen him for years and years.

DON: Yeah, Monty and Sammy the baritone player.

JOHN: I think Sammy died in the earthquake.

DON: Well I have heard a number of stories. BJ told me that he got hit by a car, that he was out in the street and a car came by and hit him.

JOHN: Oh no. Sammy something, I knew him, but….

DON: Did you know Donald Garrett?

JOHN: Oh yeah. Rafael, after he went with Trane…. And Little Rock changed his name to Pharaoh Sanders and Don decided to be Rafael Garrett.

DON: Yeah, Rafael Donald Garrett. Who also did flutes, recorders and….

JOHN: He picked them up… he didn't play…

DON: Now see, completely different opinions; because, I didn't get any of that out of him. He was a very strong bass player.

JOHN: Yes.

DON: But he was a little bit unreliable.

JOHN: He was nuts as far as I was concerned. He was very nasty to me and my band. I hired him for a gig and he got on the gig and did all he could to ruin it. And it was the meanest gesture between him and

A Diary of the Underdogs

Charlie Persip. I have never had a musician just purposely try and ruin the music. And he did this is Carnegie Recital Hall; not the big one, but the one next door.

DON: Yeah, I remember he wasn't very popular. And the reason I mention him is because he was a big presence for some reason. He was loud.

JOHN: Yeah, he was loud. At first I considered us friends, we didn't hang out but….we were very amiable until he did that gig. And he was showing off in front of Mike Nock and Mike White who laughed and he said something to me that I won't repeat because I tried to help him and his family with money and that's why I hired him. And I let him play those stupid flutes that he couldn't play that he had made. And I even bought some trying to help him. And what he said to me was like….and then I never had anything to do with him after that.

DON: Well, he left the Bay Area shortly after that. He wasn't doing very well, I don't know where he went – he was from back East somewhere.

JOHN: And actually, I did hire him at CAL State Hayward when I was teaching out there. I kind of hired him to show them…what….I can…you know…how crazy some of the so-called vanguard was. I had one-hundred and twenty-five students there in that class. Ed Kelly was in that class. You know- the late pianist. We were going to high school….he was a very well know pianist, especially here. And a guy, George Spencer and his wife were in my class and John Faddis' sister who was a very fine piano player was in my class. So, I had all these performing musicians; professionals in there amongst all the others. And so I brought Don out and he brought all this crap out here to get audience participation. Sheets of metal, where you can go whrrrrrrr….you know, but everybody was having fun and it wasn't hurting anybody, but one of my students freaked. And they called security, I didn't know it. And by the time they got there… it only lasted for maybe twenty minutes….and I remember I was on the piano….and you know I was not going to let anybody ruin anything….I am not crazy…and didn't even like the music…as far as….but we were having fun. We stopped and I was lecturing and all of a sudden security came in and it was almost like Keystone Cops! They had everything going except drawn guns. And everybody looked at them and it got totally quiet and peaceful. And the class just started applauding, you know and those poor guys, their faces changed. The color of one brother and a white guy, and even on the brother, he got darker, he was so embarrassed. So, they just walked on out!

DON: So, do you want to tell me about some of that unfair treatment by these record companies and then give me a little wrap up on what you would like to see in the future.

JOHN: The record companies were business, but some of them were gangster business, business. They were doing what they were doing like so many people are doing now – with the property – homeowners.

DON: Re-selling their…

JOHN: They never gave you royalties. You got a little bit of money up front and they took everything and all your charges were charged against your little three or four percent and they were just…..and you never saw a royalty. Hardly anybody did.

DON: Back in those days didn't you get an air play check?

JOHN: You might have gotten that. But, I am talking about the actual recording itself from the company. You got this BMI or one of those kinds of agencies; one of those that are ASCAP but nothing from the record companies, generally nothing. You are always in debt to them no matter how long they had the recordings and re-issued them. I finally got some money from the owner, who owned this record company, from his benefactors, I think he was gone. I finally got a check from…a nice check…after some forty years! No, they are really awful, really terrible.

DON: So basically they take a guy who is ambitious and wants a record contract and they get him while they are anxious, he signs it, they give him a little money in advance and they say you are going to sell a million records and don't worry you can pay me back with the royalties.

A Diary of the Underdogs

JOHN: They don't even mention that. They don't tell you that. Most of the time you never saw the owners, you just saw what they call the A & R man. When my wife at the time was my manager and she did the preliminary work. They didn't cooperate and after awhile I didn't either. I stopped recording.

DON: Now, they are re-issuing your stuff. And you can make some more money on it.

JOHN: Yeah, well…you know for five years you are under these…most of the time…under those contracts and they expect at least two albums. And so that's a total of ten albums. I only did three with that first company and the second one I only did four. And so I should have had twenty albums …and then I went with….I got a million dollar contract. But then in 79, the record industry went belly up. And so, they gave me a little bit of something and my masters. So it was nice. I wasn't hurting for money and that gave me peace of mind. When they wouldn't treat me right and I wouldn't record, I would just go back to school. And I would just take more courses in college.

DON: Yeah, you can teach now and lecture.

JOHN: Well, yes, and I did that for twelve years. I was mainly at SF State but I was also at Stanford and CAL State. Actually there have been seven different institutions in the Bay Area and internationally. And really in eight and half years, I just did a few classes and I never did the classes because I really wanted to, I made my living as a musician and performer. I never did a little bit more than part-time and it was never enough to make a living unless you wanted to be a professor and I didn't. I only wanted to put the music there. My living has come from playing. Knock on wood; and buying a little stuff early like property.

DON: Yeah, you were smart like that, I always envied you, not only were you smart, but you also always kept your music. I have always admired you for your larger vision.

JOHN: Well, I'll tell you what basically happened there. I was married to a Caucasian woman and we had trouble getting…we came out here and stayed three weeks and I ended up moving here, right and we couldn't get any nice apartments and she would go in and they would say yes, and then….then there was a problem. And she found this deal on this house and we had not planned to stay here, we were in New York living there, we still had a place there. And we didn't cut that loose for ten years or so. Paul Winter lived there for a while. And so that is how I ended up with the house. And we hadn't planned to buy a house, but it was a bargain, my money and her face got the house. Yeah, and I got it at thirty years old and it was great. And we both went on to buy stuff and we are still friends.

DON: OK. So just give me a little forecast of where you are going, what do you see in the future?

JOHN: You know at this age….I just had another blessed birthday at seventy-six. I just had it on the third. My wife and I…my wife is retired from…City College, she was President. And we love where we are and we are very happy in our lives and comfortable.

JOHN: You were talking about Marcus Book Store and how small Bop City really was. Did you used to hang out at Jackson's Nook?

DON: Oh, yes.

JOHN: So, you have been most of the time in San Francisco?

DON: Yeah, I got back in like 92. Early 92 and I started living with my daughter and John and picked up some gigs and finally got some stuff rolling.

JOHN: I would see your name around several times and just never got around….

DON: Well, I was at a place called Cypress Club for about six years – that was on Jackson Street, right around the corner from Bix.

JOHN: That's an area, even when the beatniks, you know, our group? I was so busy in school – sometimes from 8am to 10pm. I did that for about two or three years. And then I was drafted and I went into the Army.

DON: Yeah, I got drafted and joined the Navy Reserves so I wouldn't have to go into the army; probably happened about the same time as the Korean War, right?

A Diary of the Underdogs

JOHN: Yeah. I was drafted actually on my 20th birthday but I went in six months later, and then I was in the Army. Joe Wilson, Teddy Edwards, all those guys were living here. And then I hooked up with them. Frank Morgan, Sonny Clarke, Kenny Drew, they were all living here.

DON: I love those guys!

JOHN: Yeah! Me too! Addison Farmer lived right down the street. He was in residence for years.

DON: Art's bass player, yeah.

JOHN: And then you know; Richard Wyands was from here. Jerome Richardson, we rented from the same landlord, he lived across the street in their house and I lived…you know…Elman Wright was one of the brothers and fathers that were trumpet players and he had played First Chair in Dizzy's big band. And then we were in Gerald's band, originally I played baritone for awhile. Then I switched to alto. And I was the only one drafted so….we rehearsed till the first till the first until we got the first gig and I was drafted on Monday and the gig was Friday. And Art…no, Oscar Pettiford was living here playing cello. Addison played the bass. And he was taking solos….

DON: The cello? Is that when he was doing the cello?

JOHN: Yes.

DON: And he tuned it in fourths, he cheated! That is a big question; we've been talking about that for years.

JOHN: I guess. Oscar was only thirty years old and I was twenty and he took me with him to go to… the first time I was up in a studio, radio, where they broadcast and I think he was interviewed by Pat Henry, it might have been Ralph Gleason, but I think it was Pat – in some little alley in San Francisco and he was going to give me a gig with him but it was going to be two weeks after I was drafted and I couldn't take it of course.

DON: The Army blew that one for you.

JOHN: Yeah, and I really didn't want to go, but I was the only one out of all those young guys.

DON: Do you remember Kermit Scott?

JOHN: Of course, he gave me my first. He used to let me sit in when I was a kid. Kermit and my Dad were about the same age, my Dad was young, you know. Yeah, Kermit and my Dad were born around a year or two of each other.

DON: Yeah, I remember him from Bop City.

JOHN: He used to let me sit in with him when I was sixteen. First time I went over there – over there, because I was here, that's when they had two black hotels, The Booker T and the Manor Plaza. And I came over with them and he had this trumpet player that was from my high school but he was like five or six years ahead, Burnett Sutton, played kind of like Miles, and he was about that age.

DON: Do you remember Webster Young?

JOHN: He was here for awhile, but he came later. He came in the early 60's. He was good, I enjoyed him.

End: John Handy

Interview: Dick Fregulia-pianist-and Don Alberts-March 19, 2009 at Mario's Cigar Bar, San Francisco-about: Washington Square Bar and Grill-piano players-owners-pianos-evolution

DICK FREGULIA

DICK: Some things shifted in the owner's tastes and what they like to have and I was the last to know. And I kept hustling and then I gave up on ever getting back in there, but I used to like to play there at that place. You ever been there, the place in Sausalito?

A Diary of the Underdogs

DON: Yeah.

DICK: It has a nice baby grand piano. It pays nothing.

DON: Well, it pays something.

DICK: We used to get a $100 for three ways and a dinner, which was a salad, pasta and a glass of wine. And in the old days you would have gone home with some hot thirty-year old Sausalito chick, because they are all over the place. And yet, it still beats the nursing home circuit even at $150 a man or whatever. I brought two things for you –the thing I marketed around and never got published, but people love it. It's my memories of thirty-three years of Washington Square. I actually managed to get this on to CD baby.com for one of my albums, I sort of attached that to one of my albums. And

Dick Fregulia with Don Alberts

this is my Palo Alto Memoir– it's another thing I tried to sell, once in awhile I will get into freelance, journalistic mode, and we tried to sell it but nobody is buying now. But that is my memories of Palo Alto as a spawning ground for Jazz players, mid 1950 to mid 1960. In fact, I could re-write a paragraph and work your name in there. But there is no market for it other than the people I trade manuscripts with.

DON: Can I include some of this – would that be possible?

DICK: Absolutely. You can quote me or you can summarize the information and use it. It's funny; half the time when I started doing independently produced records and then CD's it was because I wanted to write the liner notes. Or I wanted to package something with photographs. It was an eternal project. The music became secondary. Yeah, so you are a few years ahead of me. You were already in the mainstream while I was still the kid looking in the candy store window. Well, sort of. I remember hearing you at various places on the Peninsula. Anyway, you will get a lot of stuff out of what I gave you and it will be easy and you won't have to take notes. You will have it right there.

DON: Yeah, so what you can really help me with is the history of The Washington Square Bar and Grill and some of those piano players in there – because you were there.

DICK: When I went in there the re-opening Sunday when Mike Greensill was there. Well, it had been open for a week – the day after you had played when Mike Greensill was playing Sunday Brunch. First people I run in to- Ed Moose and Marietta. The first thing they say is, "we just read your article about the square and we loved it." And then I was talking to Ron Fimrite about it and I gave him a copy and he sent a nice note saying how much he liked it. So, you write something like that and you send it in to the Chronicle – you send it in to – well who else do you send it in to but the Chronicle? And they are cutting back, this is about nine months ago, and then you put it on your website, or in my case on cdbaby.com.

DON: When did you first arrive over there, at Washington Square?

DICK: It was the fall of 1974. They had been open for most of the year and they were just one room at the time. And I heard on KJAZ that Jim Lowe was playing piano there, he was with Cleveland Wrecking Company but he was also a Jazz piano player. And my thought was cynically enough, if they are listing a Jazz piano player that means two things: it means that they like Jazz piano and it means that the guy no longer has the gig. Because that is how it goes, you get the gig, you get some publicity out about it and then

197

you lose the gig. And then the publicity is still out. And he had been playing on an electric grand piano in the alcove window for three weeks or something like that and they knew him and they liked Jazz. Then they bought a new little Yamaha piano. Not that one, the one before it. And they had it up against the wall to the left when you walk in. And so I got the gig playing there. And that lasted for about three or four weeks, it was just for one or two nights a week.

DON: Who were you dealing with there?

DICK: It was Ed and Sam. Ed was hiring, Sam was the partner. And I get a call – this is all in what I have written here – and I get a call during one of my breaks, the bartender says, come over and get the phone, Ed would like to talk to you. So Ed fires me! He said that they were going to do something a little different. They wanted to bring Ken Fishler who is available five nights a week. And Ken was kind of up and coming and he had a good name, he had a record out and he wasn't a Tim Hockenberry but he was definitely one of us who had a little bit of a name going for himself and a draw. So, I lost the gig, but I knew that Ken was working five nights a week over at the Hungry Tiger and so I went over and got his gig! So I had that five nights a week at the Hungry Tiger, three of them solo and two with a trio and that lasted a year. And then I had to go back East to teach one summer so I got Gini Wilson to sub for me and of course everybody loved Gini so I was out of that gig. But then I went back to the square and by that time Fishler was no longer playing or maybe he was playing the weekends, they had different people every night and Thursday night was open. Thursday night was the audition night they called it. And so I started just sitting there playing for free on Thursday nights for two or three weeks. And then Sam took an interest in me and by that time Sam was the one who was doing the hiring and Ed was doing the politicking. And Sam said to come in and watch Norma and see how she plays the room.

DON: Oh, Norma was there by then?

DICK: Yeah.

DON: Tell me about Norma Teagarden. Is she a direct relative of Jack Teagarden?

DICK: She is one of his sisters.

DON: Oh, I see, same generation?

DICK: Yeah.

DON: Do you know anything about how she learned to play piano?

DICK: They probably all learned by ear because Jack learned that way.

DON: Yeah, so in the family probably was music.

DICK: Yeah, and she was already in her sixties there. She was like eighty-five or something when she last played the square. The piano player that I loved that was there, was John Horton Cooper. John was about my age now; he was a gentlemen piano player that sort of slid through a lot of things. And he used to be a real swinger with Vernon Alley. But I never heard him as a swinger, I heard him play solo piano. He would play *Try A Little Tenderness*. He had a nice touch and a perfect feel for the place, and I used to go and listen to the bridge here and chat a bit. Cooper was there on Friday nights, Norma was there on Wednesday and she had her entourage of people that were coming in to sit in with her. Burt Bales was there on Monday. This all happened between 1974 and 1975. When I lost the gig it was probably November 74 and by early 75 they had knocked into the other room and expanded the two rooms and then they had worked out what they were going to do with their music. They would experiment. They had Eddie Duran in there, Jerry Good playing bass. No piano, just guitar and bass. And so they experimented with things that weren't necessarily piano.

DON: Was Vernon in there a lot?

DICK: He was always a customer and he was playing various times; sometimes he would play with John Cooper. It took them a while before they settled back on it just being a solo piano place, or being piano only and without a non-piano group.

A Diary of the Underdogs

DON: What is the evolution of that first piano?

DICK: Ed claims that the first piano I played on when I was first there, he bought for, I think it was for a $1,000 and he got it for $800 or something like that and he said that was not the first piano to be played on, so I think within a year of fairly soon they got a new Yamaha Studio and that Yamaha Studio lasted for over twenty years or twenty-three years or so and then they replaced with the same model which is what they have now. The one they have now they got when Peter took over – that's in there (the book) too. Basically, there has been two generations, two different Yamaha uprights that were the same model essentially.

DON: Norma Teagarden, did she play stride and then her style? Was it like Teddy Wilson?

DICK: Yeah, more like Teddy Wilson, more eclectic than Mike Lipskin who was also in there. And then she would have trombone, clarinet, various guys who would come in who were sort of on the edge Dixieland, Swing contemporary guys. I used to play those gigs with some of those guys like Ev Ferray, Bob Schultz and there were all these Berkeley guys that were in that Dixieland thing but they also had an ear for early Miles or Chet Baker. So I would play these gigs and one chorus would be like 1938 and the next chorus would be like 1952 and so on and of course as a piano player you would sort of comp accordingly whether you play more modern chords or sort of do Basie.

DON: All in one song?

DICK: Yeah. And all the bankers and businessmen loved the Dixieland stuff and they had all the money. They were the bread and butter. That scene had an automatic financial base to it. And Norma was a darling of that crowd. She was a little above it too but she had all those festivals that we never know about, because we were always pursuing the cutting edge.

DON: So, she would be doing Earthquake McGoon's and place like that and the Say When club?

DICK: Right. That would be her circle. I am not exactly sure when she came to town. She was married to a guy and they were married for a long time. That may have been why she settled in San Francisco.

DON: I don't know where her roots were. Do you know where the family grew up?

DICK: I want to say Oklahoma but I am not sure. That rings a bell because my first wife was from Oklahoma and usually when somebody, like Don Bennett is from Oklahoma, I remember.

DON: Don Bennett, the bass player, is from Oklahoma?

DICK: Yeah.

DON: Would have never thought that. He played with Jeannie Hoffman for years.

DICK: Where is Jeannie, have you heard anything about her – is she still alive?

DON: She passed away maybe four or five months ago. She was living in Sausalito.

DICK: She didn't have a great past few years.

DON: No, she wasn't feeling that great.

DICK: Yeah, I never knew if she wasn't feeling great because she couldn't get off drinking or if she was drinking because she didn't feel great.

DON: I don't know. She liked her wine. I knew her in Portland. There is some interesting history there, she played at the Blackhawk with her trio with Dean Reilly, and she would sing and Art Pepper was around and Art Pepper would come in and play with her but they would tell her not to sing and she would always sing in the middle of his tune. And so they would play the trio without her because she would sing. Plus there was a tax problem because if you sang, they had to charge more money.

DICK: Well, last time she was at the square, when Guy was the owner and Guy just couldn't deal with her, she was drinking too much. We tried to set her up for lunch, because the alkies were in there drinking but that didn't work out.

DON: OK, so we are up to Burt Bales and some other guys, Vernon Alley and you were in the mix all this time.

DICK: I was the youngest and I was the modernist.

A Diary of the Underdogs

DON: So, you were pushing the envelope?

DICK: Well, what happened right there, 1975, I mean between 1970 and 1975 it probably was the case for you, and certainly for me, the bottom just dropped out of trios, I mean I was basically a trio, Rick Garland, Bill Evans, Oscar Peterson piano player and the bottom just fell out. And right around 73, 74, I started listening to Art Tatum and Dave McKenna and I started learning how to comp and play walking bass and I learned how to walk through the tempos and get that ear for that Tatum kind of stuff where you are playing one hand against the other. And playing restaurant gigs was a good way to practice that stuff. But the other side of me that loved modern would go more to the Ellis Larkin direction. And I loved that John Wasserman would go to New York and he would write a couple of paragraphs about hearing Ellis Larkin. He was such a gentle piano player. And such taste! So I would sort of play that gig half way between Ellis Larkin and a little bit of Tatum and a little McKenna.

DON: Ellis Larkin was Chris Connors pianist; and probably a lot of others.

DICK: I used to hear him at a little joint that was like the square, in New York when I would go; just very quiet. They (the square) recognized the quality of having a different stylist every night, still under the umbrella of Jazz but not having an Earthquake McGoon kind of thing; but different individual styles. They also recognized that in the way they employed their entire staff, they had such an oddball collection of characters as bartenders and as wait people. And in many cases they were people who wouldn't have been hired like by places like Moose's when it was under that other ownership. Or DiMaggio's or something like that. But as long as they could do their job, their character didn't matter, in fact that was an asset because that's what people were drawn to that place for.

DON: Yeah, that lunch crowd and the long martini lunches…and not too many noon time piano player though. I did it at Moose's. In fact, it was one of the best things I ever did was to talk Ed into playing lunches. Okay can you give me some more piano players?

DICK: I have listed a bunch of them in there (the book) already, so we are ahead of the game.

DON: So, this is still under Ed Moose's control – Ed and Sam were running the place?

DICK: Yeah. Mike Greensill would come in and he would play clarinet. And he would sit in with Norma playing clarinet before he even met me. There was also Federico Cervantes (Freddie Gambrell). I heard Freddie when he played at a little funky place in Palo Alto in 1959 and he had an Atlantic Records album out. And that was big time!

DON: Yeah, and he used to play with Ben Tucker, the bass player.

DICK: And so, Federico had a stint there and I don't remember whether it was six months or six years. Ray Skjelbred, do you know him, he is a stride piano player who flirts with Monk. And so he would play ¾ of Mike Lipskin stuff and ¼ Monk. He was my age and also a darling of the Berkeley traditional Jazz crowd. He also is a poet and an English teacher, he taught at the same high school I taught at. One year we both taught in the same classroom, this was 1972 or 1973, we both taught a Jazz workshop class. (That was before Proposition 13), and end of the school year he got a gig out at Port Costa at something like the Big Bear Inn or whatever and within two weeks I got a call from the place across the street to play a gig and so we both had gigs in Port Costa. And that's how I got those gigs with the traditional guys, Ray would trade gigs with me. But he played at the square. It was never a comfortable place for black musicians, although we did have black musicians. There was a guy named Will Hammond that I hired last time around to do some subbing and he was good, he was from the East Bay. But one of the ironies of the place it never attracted a black crowd. It was Irish, English, Anglo bar and grill crowd.

DON: So this is all under Ed and Sam?

DICK: Oh yeah, they had a long run. Twenty years! It was 74 until about 92 or something like that. DON: And then they went across the street, is that when Peter took over?

DICK: The first person to take over was Peter Lomax. He was older, older meaning our age restaurateur

A Diary of the Underdogs

who had owned places like Monroe's on Lombard or the Coachmen, do you remember a place called the Coachmen up on Nob Hill? He was a real restaurateur. But he was getting on in years and when I first met him when he was refereeing high school soccer matches. That is when I was teaching. And he had a couple of sons that he had envisioned setting up in the business, but the sons never really took to it. And he was sort of losing his energy. His wife was a former Miss San Francisco from the 40's or something like that. But the place went downhill for about two years when he owned it. And just to make things worse, Ed opened up Moose's two and a half years after he sold – and the agreement was that he wouldn't open up a competing place for at least three years and he jumped the gun and did it anyway. Lomax sold it to Peter Osborne. And Peter Osborne brought some life back to it and Peter was like a young Moose. He was a bear-hug kind of guy with personality and he brought it back and brought people in "Boom Boom!"

DON: And so Peter Osborne took it over and he was clearly a very good businessman.

DICK: Yeah, and he had a presence that people liked. You know, certain restaurant owners like to go and chat with people and say hello. Yeah, he was very good. But he was moving in another direction, and he opened up Mo Mo's while he still owned the Square, but he couldn't handle both. And so the Square went up for sale. And then Guy Ferri came in, but Guy didn't have the money. Guy and his wife bought it. But they were basically underfunded.

End: Dick Fregulia

Interview: Mike Lipskin-pianist-and Don Alberts, June 10, 2009, San Francisco-about Willie the Lion Smith, stride piano, RCA studios, New York, Brecker Brothers, Moose's, Washington Square Bar, Hyde Street studios, Jefferson Airplane, Grace Slick, recording engineering, NY and SF club scene, customers comments, bar crowds, SF characters, Art Tatum, Earl Hines, Teddy Wilson, Burt Bales, Trad Bands, Clancy Hayes, Pat Yankee, Earthquake McGoon's, Waldo Carter..

MIKE LIPSKIN

DON: But anyway, yeah, tell me about that, you got here in '70 or something...

MIKE: I came in '71 and I was working. I was stupid and headstrong and I was used to the old way of producing records. And they want to spend 9 months in the studio, just floating around...

DON: Well you were at the Golden Gate Recorders?

MIKE: No, RCA.

(Continued)

A Diary of the Underdogs

MIKE: Yes.

DON: They had the studio here in town?

MIKE: No, oh the studio I was working at was on Hyde St... Most days Columbia had their own beautiful studio too. It was in the big days when there was money in the record businesses. There was Golden Gate, there was Fantasy.

DON: I remember Golden Gate 'cause I saw Janice there and she was a friend of mine and she was so excited that she got a record deal with Columbia...

MIKE: I have an 8 millimeter film I took of her. I wanted to sign her for RCA...Combining R'n B with Stride piano and I didn't think it would work at all because...

Mike Lipskin

DON: Sounds good to me!

MIKE: Yeah, but we never got to it because, uh, most of the people were stoned all the time and...You know, and I'm from New York and I'm used to, well, "a week's vacation, now let's get to work!" and they want to sit and dope... So it was my, I didn't adapt well

DON: Well let me get this clear, Mike, you had the skills already though because you had spent a lot of time in New York in the studios, according to your bio you dealt with a lot of...

MIKE: Oh sure!

DON: That was prior to coming here, though.

MIKE: Yeah but rock people think they know everything...and uh...

DON: Yeah I know, they're stoned all the time and...

MIKE: The easiest thing is Grace Slick. She was the smartest, most down to earth.

DON: Most direct?

MIKE: Yeah. I remember one time we were in the studio, and Paul Cantner was sitting right there. I and the engineer had our hands like this and he says, "What did you do? You screwed up the sound!" and we hadn't done anything. But I was lucky to start at RCA when it was still a family. I mean, people had been there for 40 years. I got, I learned recording from the engineers. In the old days, you had to mix on the spot. Because it was just wax recording, mono, no echo, no overdub

DON: So you're not gonna change a damn thing, it is what it is, right?

MIKE: Well you can't. There was no technology...

DON: Right.

MIKE: Tape only came in, in '48

DON: Well, went direct to cutting, right?

MIKE: That's right. I like these older engineers because they could tell me great stories. If you could mix in those days, if you could mix a big band and get a good sound, know what you have to do. Then when you would get new recording equipment you could even make it better. And the young Rock n' Roll engineers didn't really know how to do acoustic that much. They just weren't used to it. They were used to just plugging in, you know, plugging in. You have a direct guitar and you have isolation both with a singer. I mean how hard is that? You don't have any leakage; you have 600 different types of microphone.

DON: Wow. So you come in as a sound tester with headphones, do a mix, do a balance and then you say "Ok I got it. You guys can go".

MIKE: They had speakers. They didn't use headphones. They had RCA speakers, monitors.

DON: Oh I see.

MIKE: But anyway, so, I was lucky to learn from these guys and the first thing I started doing was reissuing all the records because at that point I thought... I had a lot of '78's by then... At the age of 13 I started going up to Harlem and studying with the old pianists there.

DON: I like that part of your bio. Very interesting, because I think what you brought here was a lot of skill and it didn't, I mean it doesn't follow you around. You have to know you to find out. I mean you have to get to know, you have to listen, and then you realize the stuff you've been through.

MIKE: Well I think it is part of maturing, to be more interested in what other people do

DON: A little selfless, considering your skills, Mike!

DON: There's no body that can do what you do. There are a few guys, you know.

MIKE: Are you talking about the Stride piano style? There are some good ones...

DON: Yeah, I'm talking about that classic, that classic art form, you know. I don't know about young kids getting interested in that.

MIKE: Because most young kids, unless you start early with parents that whip them into shape, everything is instant gratification; synthesizer, sampling. They now think that a tune or composition is just sampling other people's work.

DON: Right, so it's ok to take part in somebody's...

MIKE: So that's why Stride was taken not too long. I have some students once in a while but they usually give up because it takes so long. You have to be relaxed in that idiom enough so that you don't have to think about it. Tension, being up tight is the enemy in that style.

DON: I bet.

MIKE: If you have to look at your hands while you're doing it then you're not really talking about Stride. And there are a lot of people that say "Oh I play a little bit of Stride." and you don't, you're not really playing stride. It's a whole style that you play.

DON: Well, the right hand is pretty interesting.

MIKE: The right hand is more of a problem in most people.

DON: You know there are some classic sounds that I hear there. Some is totally yours but some of it is right in the genre.

MIKE: It's a language, you know?

DON: It's a language. You gotta think. It's the same in modern Jazz piano

MIKE: Oh sure, little riffs. I think the better modern Jazz pianists are self-taught, not coming out of a Jazz school. You play different then Greensill, or some others.

DON: Oh yeah.

MIKE: Dick Conte and I think that's great, you know?

DON: Yeah

MIKE: But if you all went to the same Jazz school, you'd probably come in here sounding like, you know...

DON: Certain things would be irreversible among us and even in the university in particular. But it's outside of that, you know. What I found about jazz piano and you have obviously learned early on, is a sense of time. Not only a sense of time but knowing that you have a sense of time and that it's reliable.

MIKE: Well before, I speed up, I say let's erase the whole thing. I mean I really think I'm not doing well. When I was younger can you believe that I had a duet with Duke Ellington? He had just started on our label, and I became friends with him.

DON: No kidding!

A Diary of the Underdogs

MIKE: And I was studying piano, and I listened to the recording and I was rushing...

DON: I think when you're confident, if it moves, you know it. If it speeds up, you know it. If it slows down, you know it instantly.

MIKE: Yeah.

DON: You know, and that's a sense of time.

MIKE: Well you know the worst thing that concert players do, is they put the bass on one side of the stage, and they put the piano on the other and the drums in the middle. The first thing I do is complain that we won't be able to hear each other-We have 3 different tempos going on. You know the joke about... a true story about some pianist in Vegas at a fancy place, and he was telling the owner that George Shearing was gonna be there next week. The owner didn't know anything about jazz, so he told him what a wonderful experience it will be and what a starred figure. So Shearing comes in next week and the owner says "I heard of what a great pianist you are. I had the piano painted for you!"

DON: Yeah, White! Well there's that old story about Stevie Wonder who came into Shanghai 1930 when they had the bad piano down there for years. He was in town, he comes in; "Oh Stevie!" they say, how about playing a tune for us? Stevie sit's down, puts his hands on the piano and plays a chord and says, "Ah, Young Chang."

MIKE: Well you know, part of the fun, the wonderful thing which I'm missing out here, is hanging out with these guys in Harlem, and actually because I knew their story so much, they started talking to me as though I was there. They'd say "Well you remember so-and-so" ... And Eubie Blake, He starts talking. Then suddenly he looks, he's standing there after he starts telling me "Remember that bar and this-and-that"!

DON: How about Willie the Lion Smith?

MIKE: Oh, Willie...

DON: Didn't you study with him?

MIKE: I couldn't study with him because he was intimidating. So I'd play some things and he's "That's not the way you do it!" He'd be in his pajamas in his apartment. He'd have a cigar and his derby on. He'd play very fast. And uh, I learned, I think, you really learned osmotic ally. You absorb.

DON: Any others?

MIKE: Well Dick Hyman taught me how to do Tatum runs. If you hear it on the record, you have no idea how his fingers are. He only uses 3 fingers on a descending run.

DON: Yeah, only 3? Sounds like a full hand to me.

MIKE: I know!

DON: Sounds like Fats Waller, like he's using 5 fingers or something. It's a streaming series of notes with power and everything! Is that the same kind of thing?

MIKE: Well, I don't know about Waller's fingers. Waller first started on the pipe organ when he was 16, playing to silent movies. And so, have you ever played a pipe organ? I studied, I could play organ about a tenth of what Fats Waller does. It's like the difference between a clerical typewriter and an electric type writer. If you just hit a key this much, it won't sound but the organ; it's sensitive, so what ever you do it's coming right out. You're dead if you make a mistake! That's how he developed an incredible, classical touch.

DON: Oh, you mean because it's light?

MIKE: Because they came from a time when you would listen to classical music. They absorbed essentially classical dynamics, tension and release. There are so many people that are playing at this level all the time, so they know how to think, so it's very important. And it's very important in Stride. If you could play, you have to add devices to be coloring everything. Otherwise it's just boring.

DON: Well I was gonna ask you, Willie the Lion Smith is probably your strongest early on influence.

MIKE: Um, no; James P. Johnson and Fats Waller. They died when I was 10. It used to annoy me.

DON: You didn't like talking about that?

A Diary of the Underdogs

MIKE: Well he would, James P. would, every once in a while he'd say "Aren't you interested in beautification? ...I did learn a lot by listening to some of them for so long.

DON: You were only 19.

MIKE: 13, when I started with him. (James P.) My parents would get scared.

DON: But what brought you to that point? Your parents gave you lessons early on?

MIKE: No. My father grew up in the 30's on Fats Waller. So he had the 78s. By the time I was 4 I could play them. Those were my kiddy records.

DON: Ok, I see where it comes from.

MIKE: Yeah.

DON: There had to be some place for piano tutoring, right?

MIKE: Well, tremendous to my detriment, I was lazy and I'm self-taught. I've only really learned how to use proper fingering techniques in the last 30 years. In my first 33 years, I didn't pay attention. I tell everybody "When you're young, get some classical technique, then you can do what you want".

DON: There are ways to get around the mechanics of the instrument, I'm still learning.

MIKE: Me too. I'm taking lessons from a guy, a wonderful player. I said "I'm having trouble with this run." So he figured out immediately how to show me how to do it without running out of fingers.

DON: Right, right. I just hear the great George Cables at Yoshi's with Bobby Hutcherson and Charlie Haden. It was wonderful and I happened to get a seat right up in front. But here's a guy that's been playing for years- pretty much sounds the same. Except that the brilliance in his later years is coming through without any emotional distractions or struggle, all that stuff is all gone. He's just a piano player and he's confident and he's very skilled. He just does his great skill. Not looking for any accolades, not looking to knock anybody out, just playing! Which is wonderful about taking the name out of the center, so it's just a person and the music, you know? Which I think is the ultimate. It's just not practical when you have talk to people. If you can remove yourself from there, it's just you and the music! It's a complete human experience and the music is free to evolve, you know?

MIKE: Well I agree, and one thing I notice; a lot of the post-pop sax players, when they're recording, the one's who didn't die young... It was almost as though they were really trying to prove something when they were younger. When they got older, they'd listen to the song when they'd mellow out; Zoot Sims, Stan Getz, Al Cohn. I'm a tenor head, I like, Chu Berry, Don Byas, Lester Young. And then later on, what the hell was it? Can you imagine this? I was lucky enough...When I came back to RCA, there was an old friend, John Hammond Sr. I don't know if you remember him, a very close friend of mine. He got me a job back at RCA with a guy names Ken Gillespie. And before that, the people that ran RCA were shoe salesmen. They wouldn't know the difference between Louie Armstrong and Neil Young.

DON: Why would they be able to work in a studio?

MIKE: RCA was a studio, a big corporation. They way you got up to the top was by politics or through personnel, knifing somebody. But I came into the office for an interview. I mentioned Fats Waller and he could tell me all the side men. I almost fell out of my chair. Here's the guy who actually liked music! He liked it so well he asked Vladimir Horowitz to come back.

DON: Wow.

MIKE: He was very, very good with the artists.

DON: So is this Hammond?

MIKE: No, this is his buddy, Ken Gillespie. So they both worked at Columbia Records. In the '50 and '60s Columbia Records hired more Jazz artists and they had good pianos.

DON: Talk about the pianos.

MIKE: Yeah, they were all Steinways. Are you talking about in the studios?

DON: Yeah.

MIKE: RCA and Columbia both had very good pianos, not all of them great. And when we would record

A Diary of the Underdogs

classical people, they'd usually go to the Steinway basement, pick up a piano, one of the best, and ship to the studio to record.

DON: Oh, ok.

MIKE: The pianos, the house pianos were good. In fact, can you believe that we had 3 floors of studios and maybe we had 6 or 7 pianos; Steinways. The tuner that did the work all the time, he wasn't a good regulator, he wasn't good at voicing. He was a good tuner though, but he was blind. He knew his way around the whole place.

DON: He had a personal relationship with his pianos.

MIKE: Now, one piano that RCA- I don't know if it's still there…There is no RCA anymore- was Rachmaninov's piano that he recorded on. It was a 9 foot and I loved practicing on that.

DON: I bet!

MIKE: Right, when they kept it in shape.

DON: Well it used to go, they didn't go by model numbers but I think they were 'B'?

MIKE: Well those were smaller.

DON: Yeah.

MIKE: In the studio like Columbia or RCA or Decca you'd have a 'C' and a 'D'. A 'C' I think was 6.9 or 7 feet; that was the smallest one you'd have.

DON: Yeah, ok.

MIKE: But I'll tell ya, I learned to tune pianos once when I was out of work. I don't do it well but it's helpful. I can do octaves and unisons. There's an art to it. You have to do it all the time to do it well. It's like playing Basketball. I think 60% of piano tuners here, in New York and in Europe don't know the right temperament. You could tell it's off.

DON: Yeah?

MIKE: So now there's a big recording session, Dick Hyman and some other really great pianists in New York and they brought in a Beckstein and a Steinway piano. So before the session, by myself I went in and the temperament was off. I didn't say anything- it wasn't my session but I'd say, ya know "God damn it, you get a piano tuner!"…But see, people wouldn't know.

DON: Well, of course! If you knew, someone else would know…You can't allow that to go on unless.....

MIKE: Well first of all, the politics in the record industry, if I came in and said something, the producer would get furious.

DON: Yeah, ok.

MIKE: I'm coming into your session and I'm saying your piano's not tuned properly? You didn't give me permission to come in there. You're not interested in my opinion. Suppose you're on a budget. If I say that in front of the artist, then you have an artist problem because then they look at you and they think; "Schmuck, why didn't you get the piano tuned?"…

MIKE: So you can't…I'll tell you another-

DON: No, tell me about the session. It's a good story. What happened?

MIKE: Oh, it turned out to be a very good record because most people can't hear, including a lot of pianists, cannot hear when the tempo cuts out.

DON: Well I don't think a Beckstein and a Steinway go together at all.

MIKE: Well the old Bechsteins were good. I mean, this is 30 years ago.

DON: Yeah.

MIKE: And it was an older piano. No Bechsteins were very…Now they're terrible.

DON: So the record came out in-

MIKE: There were very many funny stories. The engineers in New York, because they were union, you couldn't fire them. And they had that thick New York sense of humor. They were so funny. They'd play jokes and uh…The funniest story involves Sonny Rollins and this engineer, I think his name was Paul

A Diary of the Underdogs

Goodman. He was in the Village Vanguard recording Sonny Rollins.

DON: Yeah.

MIKE: So he's in this little ante room, he's got his headphones on.

DON: Right.

MIKE: And he's looking…you have to look at the VU meters; he's in this little anti room.

DON: Right. You don't want it to go down to red…The needle going into the red.

MIKE: So he said "This is something I've never heard of in my life". The sound got louder but the VU meter kept going down. What had happened was, Rollins had a habit of wandering. He'd start a solo and then he'd leave the mike, he'd go around, go out of the studio, he'd leave the studio and start playing out in the hall!

DON: A real live situation.

MIKE: Yeah, in a studio, that's what had happened.

DON: Oh yeah. Who were the sidemen; predictable? Bob Crenshaw and the guys he played with all the time.

MIKE: Well, I don't know. I had forgotten who was with Sonny Rollins. We had Charlie Mingus on there too. He was on the label.

DON: Any interesting recordings about Charles Mingus?

MIKE: Uh, I'm trying to think because that was just before I came. His contract ran out. There was a guy, he's probably 85 or 90, George Avakian. You've seen his name on the label. He did a lot of stuff…

DON: Oh yeah, sure, a very famous guy.

MIKE: Teo Macero. You remember him, his name?

DON: Teo Macero yeah, he was Miles Davis's A and R man.

MIKE: That's right, yeah. No, he was a producer.

DON: Oh. Anyway, he produced a lot of Miles Davis and he wrote a song after him.

MIKE: Yup.

DON: That was on Columbia!

MIKE: That's right.

DON: Well that's pretty interesting that Rudy Van Gelder worked at Hyde Street Studios. Do you know what year that was in San Francisco?

MIKE: He probably was imported. Rudy had his own studio.

DON: Yeah, in Englewood Cliffs.

MIKE: Yeah, and he was really…

DON: In demand at that time.

MIKE: He was very in demand. I thought he had a very good sound but I didn't think he had a much better sound than anybody else did.

DON: Well, all his records are pretty much classics, ya know?

MIKE: Oh, they are!

DON: He managed to get the artists. The company was feeding him the artists, so he got, ya know…

MIKE: Well that was pre-tailored. Rudy was the engineer.

DON: Yeah, yeah. McCoy Tyner, early trios.

MIKE: That was- those were the producers. They liked his studio.

DON: So they used his studio.

MIKE: He wouldn't allow any smoking there.

DON: Yeah.

MIKE: No booze and no smoking. He's right because cigarette smoke does leave a film on your equipment…It gets into the deposits on the microphone…So anyway…

DON: That's pretty interesting stuff but why did he come out with a special project in the 60's, Rudy Van

A Diary of the Underdogs

Gelder, to work at Hyde Studios on a project...

MIKE: I assume that's what happened because I don't think he was living here. He was making too much money on his own studio.

DON: Yeah. So if I could bring some of this to 1960, just to connect some of that-

MIKE: Sure, to here, yeah. Well, I first came out here in 1968, the Monterrey Jazz Festival.

DON: Uh huh, yeah!

MIKE: You're gonna laugh; the most exciting act to me in the Monterrey Jazz Festival was Janice and Big Brother!

DON: Well, I bet!

MIKE: And I don't know why they put them in the Jazz festival because they had a pot festival too but I was just very glad they did! Those were beautiful days...

DON: Weren't those beautiful days?

MIKE: Did you ever meet Dizzy Gillespie?

DON: No, I never met Dizzy- Oh I did meet him once! Leroy introduced me...

MIKE: I got to know him. He was funny! He was funny all the time. Ya know he was on; he was a comedian, very smart. We're jumping around but, Willie the Lion, he was, see those guys were from another generation than Dizzy and Willie was born before the turn of the last century. So he had these funny ideas about- his own ideas about religion. He never went to church but he kept talking about being spiritual, and God and all that. One day he said to me, "You know, I must have been 15 or 16." He said; "You know why the water disappears from the bays?" "Why?"He said, "The spirits come and drink it." And I said "Don't you mean evaporation?" He said, "That's it!"

And when he would introduce me to somebody, he would be very short, in fact he was... Duke Ellington had a bass player who was, I don't know how he did it; he got one of the best recording sounds from a standup bass. This was in the 20's and 30's, when it was hard to record bass. His name was Wellman Braud.

DON: The bass player...

MIKE: Yeah. Eventually Blanton replaced him. He was well known of being modern and stuff like that.

DON: Yeah.

MIKE: But the sound that Broad got was wonderful. This is the way Willie introduced him. He said "That's Braud. He was accused of bigamy years ago!"

DON: Ah, so he put something on everybody, huh?

MIKE: Oh, he would, uh...

DON: So he's kind of a character?

MIKE: Oh yeah. I used to tape these guys. I taped them arguing with his wife. It was the funniest thing in the world.

DON: Yeah

MIKE: And it was so amusing because they loved Amos and Andy, which I loved them too and I'm not embarrassed...

DON: Oh I like them too, I think they're great

MIKE: Yeah, it was good writing. I'd be taking them in the car, and they'd see another Black person in a car or something and they'd go; "Jiggaboo! Spook!"

DON: But not for you to say.

MIKE: Oh no, I'd never-

DON: You can't say it!

MIKE: No, I wouldn't.

DON: It's kind of an ethnic thing.

MIKE: Well yeah, sure. Ya know, with Jews, we...If a Christian calls us a "kyke" or something that would be offensive...And I'd never use the n-word...Well, I've been drunk, close enough with a Black guy and

we'd do it because then I'd immediately say something derogatory about Jews.

DON: Yeah.

MIKE: Because that's one thing I miss out here. There were no holds bar, and everybody loved each other.

DON: Yeah, yeah.

MIKE: And they were just kidding around, ya know.

DON: It's a little more difficult here but it still exists.

MIKE: Yeah.

DON: I think the bar culture here is so terrific, ya know? I'm starting to see it tone down a little bit because there was so much creativity, so much conversation-

MIKE: I agree with you.

DON: Communication, and so much hustle. All of these things that go with music actually, you know? Our lives, you know, all these years, it goes with the music.

MIKE: So anyway, you wanted me to bring it up to being here in San Francisco.

DON: Yeah, well…

MIKE: Go ahead; just tell me what you want to talk about-

DON: I just don't want to stop you as long as it's feeling good. But the thing is, your talent, your experience evolves through San Francisco.

MIKE: Yeah I came out here on business and then I fell in love with San Francisco because everything was easier than New York. I miss New York now for many cultural and professional reasons but I can't afford to go back.

DON: Right, right.

MIKE: You need $400,000-

DON: To live in a box.

MIKE: You know they even pay less for casuals. Can you believe that? The rent is more expensive there but they pay less for casuals.

DON: Sonny Buxton told me a story after he gets back from New York. He says "The parking meter is in front of the club and you have to stop in the middle of a tune to go out and plug your parking meter!"

MIKE: When I was a kid I would do that.

DON: That's terrible!

MIKE: There was a place called the Metropol and they had the older Jazz musicians pre-bop; Big Chief Russell Moore, who played the trombone. He was really big! They had a Console piano, Cozy Cole on drums-

DON: Cozy Cole, yeah.

MIKE: And Red Allen-

DON: Henry Red Allen, a trumpet player, yeah.

MIKE: And he came. And you know I'm standing there, and he says, "Will you put a quarter in the meter for me?" he said "That's the car." And so I would do that for him!

DON: The parking meters ran all night; or into the evening anyway?

MIKE: No, this was an afternoon session.

DON: Oh, I see. Well I guessed the situation changed in New York where they at least run until midnight of something.

MIKE: I have no idea.

DON: Anyway, that's a different situation.

MIKE: But, uh-

DON: Well a lot of what I try to set up in this book, in this project is the effects of politics and what was going on; how it felt to live in San Francisco in the 1960's-

MIKE: Well I didn't come here until '71. But still, what was beautiful about San Francisco-

A Diary of the Underdogs

DON: Yeah, what kind of impression did you get when you got here?

MIKE: It was more social than just the music. The music was good and there was great attitude. In fact, Burt Bales, the pianist who is now dead, he was a saloon pianist. He said "There was so much business when I was first in San Francisco that I got fired from 2 jobs in 1 day!"

DON: That was kind of a badge of honor, wasn't it?

MIKE: Yeah, yeah!

DON: But Burt Bales, he played at the Wash bag, he played at Pier 23…

MIKE: That's right.

DON: Would you consider him a Stride player?

MIKE: Yeah, he could play Stride. He wasn't- he had his own style that Stride influenced but he wasn't- I don't know if you'd call it "west coast saloon piano player". That's very inaccurate, derogatory because he was a good pianist, wonderful guy…

DON: A Honky Tonk?

MIKE: Well Honky Tonk unfortunately takes in everything from Knuckles O'Toole to Ragtime. Same thing with barrel house or whore house pianos-

DON: Right.

MIKE: And the worst thing you could say to someone who is playing pre-Bop is, "Oh that must sound so great on an out of tune piano!"

DON: That's a hell of a comment, isn't it?

MIKE: When I came to San Francisco, it was very clean, it was quiet, there were no traffic jams, there were 10 times as many piano places as there are now. In fact I heard the term "Hollywood" from this guy who taught me how to tune pianos. He was the funniest drunk in the world, but he's a good classical pianist. But when he'd drink, he'd play all night on the tuning pedal and we'd call it "The B Minor Mess"!

DON: Is this guy, you got a name?

MIKE: Faye McNally.

DON: Faye McNally.

MIKE: Rafael McNally.

DON: Rafael McNally.

MIKE: He was the funniest drunk…He was a fast reader. He would read fly specks on the staff.

DON: Oh yeah.

MIKE: He taught me the term Hollywood because…Piano tuners would have their rule. Every week, or every month they'd tune various pianos in the bars… and in the Geary Theater and all those places. So they'd do what was called a Hollywood. So they tuned it and didn't have to go through the whole piano temperament. They'd just fix up the unisons and the octaves that had come away, that had drifted. Because when you learn to tune pianos, you learn that as soon as you finish tuning, it's going out slowly…

DON: Yeah, it's slipping, every note.

MIKE: But one of the funny things about temperament; for years- remember the Yamaha Clavinova?

DON: Yeah!

MIKE: Which is sampling; it's a sampling, it's not like the old Fenders that you could tune.

DON: Yeah.

MIKE: It's sketchy, but they used the wrong model. Every Clavinova was slightly out of tune and had its own temperament.

DON: Because they didn't start with a good source!

MIKE: They didn't, that's right, they didn't know. So I told the head of Yamaha in New York…I said "I'm not dumping on you, I just want you to know that all the Clavinova's I've ever played, no matter what; whether it's just a keyboard or ones with the stand and the speakers; they're all not tuned properly!" And you know what happened? Years later, they fixed it. In other words, if you buy a Clavinova now, the

A Diary of the Underdogs

temperament is corrected.

DON: It's better?

MIKE: Yeah. Anyway, about here… My first job was- so anyway…I didn't get along well with Yamaha people for many reasons. I mean they were nice to me. I was just headstrong and blah-blah-blah…

DON: Were you playing their book? Playing their library?

MIKE: No, I did play on 1 album with Papa John Creech …a violin player, a wonderful guy-

DON: Yeah, yeah!

MIKE: I played with him because he knew the old songs. He was twice their age. They didn't know any of the standard American song book.

DON: They wrote their own music.

MIKE: Sure. Yeah he was a very nice man. I was unemployed, I was broke, so that's when I decided to go back to New York in '73. I missed it out here. I rejoined RCA and I was fired along with 200 other people at the end of '77. So I came back out here. Ed Moose gave me my first steady job on Sunday night of 1978.

DON: Yeah.

MIKE: So I'd been at the square for what was it? 31 years.

DON: Yeah, Ed Moose, I just ran into him at Yoshi's the other night because he came out to see George Cables-

MIKE: Oh good!

DON: And I told him I was meeting with you and about the book. He said "Oh you're writing a book?" I said "Yeah, I'm writing a book and you should be a part of it!" And he was excited about it!

MIKE: So you're gonna interview him?

DON: Yeah!

MIKE: You know why you should? He and Sam …they were the only guys who loved Jazz enough, that they would…bring in someone like the great Dave McKenna.

DON: Oh! Dave McKenna! He did bring him in; and Stan Levy.

MIKE: Levy. And one or two others…Stan Getz!

DON: He brought in Stan Getz?

MIKE: Yes.

DON: Oh! Who'd he play with?

MIKE: I don't remember, I think…I can't remember who he had. One of my favorites of all time is now gone; Vernon Alley.

DON: Oh, Vernon, yeah.

MIKE: He and I had so much fun because he was older. He'd play with Tatum. He knew how to play the pre Bop.

DON: Like Teddy Wilson.

MIKE: Yeah

DON: Some of my favorites too…So then that became the situation.

MIKE: There was so much noise there. That's how I learned to play in every key, because I'd start playing and, ya know, I'd play lousy. I'd go into B or E…

DON: Yeah?

MIKE: But there was so much noise, nobody could hear me.
Oh! One night at the Square, Bill Evans was there.

DON: Oh really!

MIKE: Yeah!

DON: Now that would be interesting-

MIKE: Now that guy, I think he was there with Don Asher and Hampton Hawes. So Bill Evans, I'm not sure whether he was there with them, but he was there with some good people and it was great to meet him and talk to him. So he said "You know maybe I'd like a job like this!" I think I was playing that night. I said "it'd be an honor. The piano is yours if you want it". So he comes up and plays for a while. Nobody's listening to him! Ya know, he's just like us, they don't know who he is!

DON: Yeah!

MIKE: So he says "I don't think I'd like to do this."!

DON: But he did play a couple of songs?

MIKE: Yeah. But they talked, you know, when I was younger. Only when they ask me to do a very difficult James P. Johnson piece and then they talk all the way through it.

DON: They talk a lot.

MIKE: So what I do is I go into feelings or some piece of shit like that.

DON: Yeah!

MIKE: It's like "You're not listening so why should I care?"

DON: So what about Hampton? Did Hampton Hawes sit in?

MIKE: No he didn't, he was more shy.

DON: Yeah.

MIKE: I admired him. As soon as I got back to RCA in '73, I hired him to play in a Blue Mitchell session. I signed Cedar Walton, I got...You remember Harold Land?

DON: Yeah!

MIKE: Wonderful sax player. We got him on the date. Cedar Walton is still playing his ass off.

DON: Oh he plays great, yeah!

MIKE: He could write stuff-

DON: I see him whenever I get a chance, whenever he's around.

MIKE: And he's a nice person.

DON: Yeah! He calls me Albertson!

DON: He thinks I own the Albertson's stores...But yeah, he's a great guy and he's still producing and sounding good, new records...

MIKE: He used to play with Billie Higgins all the time

DON: How about bass players? Did you ever-

MIKE: Vernon Alley! He was the best. There is who I really like and he doesn't play that much. He lives downtown. I really like him. He's got a good tone. And you know, for my style, he's nice and legato. And then there's one, a great guitar player, Duncan James.

DON: Duncan James! Yeah!

MIKE: I think Jim Nichols is one of the most impressive. Have you played with him?

DON: Yeah and he played bass mostly when I played with him.

MIKE: That was his brother.

DON: Oh, ok.

MIKE: Jim Nichols-

DON: He was the guitarist...

MIKE: He's an old timer, he knows the Bop tunes. He was friends with Chet Atkins. He would go to the Atkins festival because he could play a certain style of guitar which is a little bit different. I don't know very much about guitar...Chet Atkins, I was thinking the other day... He and I were close friends and we worshiped a guy named Steve Sholes who had signed him, took him out of the bars... He was my boss, my manager. Steve was a wonderful guy. He'd recorded Fats Waller's last recordings, he did lots of big bands, he had 30,000,000 sellers...He also did all the country field recordings. He'd go to Crystal, Tennessee with the waxed masters...

DON: The whole thing, huh?

MIKE: Yeah.

A Diary of the Underdogs

DON: What was his name again?

MIKE: Steve Sholes…Yeah and he signed Elvis Presley and did his first big hit…if you Google him you'll see all sorts of stuff on him, and I was lucky enough to have worked with him. I was doing a book on him when he died. He said "Well, there's this group called Willis Brothers". A lot of these groups you had to give them some "Hooch," or get of them some marijuana.

DON: Do what needs to be done!

MIKE: I'll tell you a story…I hired the Brecker Brothers. You remember them?

DON: Yeah! Of course!

MIKE: They had me do the fusion records. I'd get a Motown type rhythm section…Gordon Edwards, Steve Gadd. They were the Atlantic rhythm section. They were on a lot of Aretha's things…So I do the basic track, and then I'd hire reeds and horns to come in and go over…I'd give them the chord charts and say "I just need this, you don't have to play all that, just do a solo here!"…So they're coming in and I made some charts for them; simple sweetening.

DON: Yeah.

MIKE: And Phil Wagner was with us. And they say "You mind if we light up?" And I'm not gonna tell a musician of their stature "No, you can't" you know? But as soon as they did their playing fell off. They could play it but the articulation and the edge was gone.

DON: Oh they were really great in their hay day.

MIKE: Oh, wonderful!

DON: They were undisputed.

MIKE: And Ernie Watts, I used to use him.

DON: Ernie Watts, a tenor player!

MIKE: Yeah. He'd come in and…You'd never want to book these guys in the morning but the evening because in those days it was so hot. They were doing 3 or 4 sessions; you'd book them in the afternoon…because in the morning they were hung over, or tired. In the evening they had their energy, so if you want them to do solos…

DON: So you figured it out! So top it off with something for me. What have you got?

MIKE: One thing about out here is there are little known, wonderful characters from Jazz like Waldo Carter. In fact, you've got to interview him because he was with Ellington, Harry James…He has more funny stories of –

DON: Yeah, Waldo played with me at Moose's; we got to be good friends. And he knows about Ernie Figeroa!

MIKE: Of course! They were friends! I donated some legal services to Figeroa when he was sick. You know, made up his will and everything because everyone wanted Waldo to have everything. He didn't have a lot of money.

DON: His horn went to Waldo.

MIKE: That's right. You really have to interview him.

DON: Yeah, I'll get him… I'll definitely do that.

MIKE: What else do you want me to say?

DON: We don't need anything. I'm just glad that you're here, Mike, and you tell me of your San Francisco times because I think that's really important for readers.

MIKE: Well you know the thing about San Francisco...

DON: It's a philosophical impression…

MIKE: Well, it's sort of a warm place with generous people and really good fans too. And then you have some really great critics like Phil Elwood. He really knew his stuff. Jesse Hamlin is great too. We had some good people, Ralph Gleason-

DON: Ralph Gleason, yeah!

A Diary of the Underdogs

MIKE: -Who was great, I got to know him…

DON: Sullivan, did you know Sullivan? The guy that went off the freeway on the wrong ramp and-?

MIKE: John Wasserman?

DON: Yes!

MIKE: He was a very close friend of mine. He helped my career, he and his family. But this to me, having grown up in New York, has a small town warmth, especially amongst musicians. We know everybody, you know?

DON: I think you're right, I feel the same thing.

MIKE: And I don't think any of us would steal a gig from the other one, you know? I usually say I'm not available that night. If they want to replace me with someone else, I mean, if they fire somebody else and then next week they ask me, that's different, you know? But I'm not gonna… You know, if I come into a sit in and you're not available, I think that's the honor-

DON: There is an honor system and people pay attention. The ones that don't, they're just not in that circle, you just can't include them.

MIKE: That's right.

DON: Because you can't trust them.

MIKE: No

DON: But it's wonderful to belong, I'm telling' you. What you're talking about is respect and quality reputation.

MIKE: Well yeah because what comes around goes around. If you screw somebody, water seeps in. This one guy, again I'm not going to mention his name; I had a gig at the House of Shields. He tried to get me and the vocalist fired so that he could get the gig. The owner immediately told me about it. And I told him, I said "you that's really a low thing to do." I said "I wouldn't do that to you."

DON: Yeah, that's totally unethical! So there are some ethics here. You know, San Francisco has a bawdy reputation and it's not like it was but there's still-

MIKE: Well look at the people we've had here. The thing I miss is I wish I was here in the '50's when Art Tatum was here. That's what I was gonna tell you. The reason no pianist should get upset when people are talking while he's playing is because they did that to Art Tatum too. So if he could put up with it, we could put up with it!

DON: Yeah, That's a good philosophical note!

MIKE: Well did you hear the story; Vladimir Horowitz loved him so when he was playing at the Cookery in New York, Horowitz and some other classical pianists would go down and listen to Art Tatum. And usually the assholes are talking. But Horowitz stands up on the table and he says "Will you shut up, you idiots! The genius is playing!"

DON: Referring to Art Tatum?

MIKE: Yes.

DON: Yeah, that's wonderful!

MIKE: One thing about San Francisco and its uniqueness is, you know…New York is a melting pot for Stride piano or 30's and probably was the biggest city for elevation. San Francisco has one thing that New York doesn't have; it had its own style of Dixie land music, Clancy Hayes style …from the 50's and it's unique. New York, because it had such a melting pot, it never developed…Sure you had a New York-Ellington kind of sound. You had Kansas City, Chicago, and you had New Orleans and San Francisco. There was no specific New York Dixie land style because the musicians grew up on so much diverse music. I've never developed a real dialogue. There were too many musical melting pots, so I think that's unique.

DON: So San Francisco actually had a sound.

MIKE: Yeah, that's right.

DON: Who do you think was mostly responsible? Who contributed?

A Diary of the Underdogs

MIKE: Well, it's not one person but I would say that Clancy Hayes and his band in the 50's. Turk Murphy is also like that. The problem with Turk's band is that, I could say it now; it's that, after a while, some of these bands got tired because they were playing the same notes all the time, playing the same heads. But in Turk Murphy's hay day, he was great too. He had a San Francisco sound as well

DON: Yeah.

MIKE: But at the same time, you had bop here, bebop. …You could tell me this because you know more about modern stuff than I do. There was a west coast mellow and cool sound-

DON: In Los Angeles basically.

MIKE: New York had more of an edge to it.

DON: In fact, that's a good way to describe it. That was coming through Shorty Rogers and..

MIKE: Didn't they come up and work here too, those guys?

DON: Yeah.

MIKE: A lot of them were LA based but then we had a lot of our own people …And then of course, one of the most important Jazz pianists of the 1920's was James P. Johnson, and he was the dean of that time. The first one to branch off was Earl Hines.

DON: I was going to mention Earl Hines

MIKE: I got to know him…A wonderful guy!

DON: Right after you talked about the San Francisco sound, Earl Hines arrived on the scene in February.

MIKE: That's right.

DON: And here's where he died.

MIKE: That late? I thought he came in here earlier, didn't he?

DON: Well I'm sure. I think it was some time in the 70's.

MIKE: He was a very modest person.

DON: So what did you think of his playing in comparison to Stride style?

MIKE: It's very different. He's not a Stride pianist at all. But he is one of the most important, significant Jazz figures because without him, Teddy Wilson, Joe Sullivan, Jess Stacey Joey Bushkin, all the other pianists that fit; Errol Garner…You know the other thing? Tatum had structured his solos. He'd do Stride, he'd do Fats Waller, he'd do his runs, he'd do his beautiful harmonies and his transpositions…His greatest genius was his break-out harmonics; the circle of fifths starting on a minor third of the key that he's in. Or going up a half step, modulating in that, and coming back. Beautiful! But he'd go into his Earl Hines section…

DON: So he was influenced by him too.

MIKE: Oh, tremendously!

DON: Even though he was before Earl…

MIKE: No, he wasn't. He was a little younger.

DON: Oh, ok.

MIKE: He was just such a prodigy.

DON: He absorbed his environment.

MIKE: He terrorized everybody when he came to New York! Johnny Guarneri, who played here, he was a wonderful Stride pianist.

DON: I haven't heard his name in a long time! He had a radio show.

MIKE: He played with Benny Goodman's quartet, with Arty Shaw's quartet. He played- this is how they treat us…He played for 10 years at a restaurant on Ventura boulevard in Hollywood. In the end they fired him after 10 years because they wanted a sing-a-long.

DON: No accounting for people!

MIKE: I used to go, when I was in Hollywood looking for a job I'd go there and he was wonderful! He'd let me play. We'd become very, very good friends. The people like Art Carney would come in and play. He

A Diary of the Underdogs

could play a little piano. So these movies stars, the nice ones, the ones that weren't stuck up, we got a lot of animators from the Warner's Studio.

DON: So they would draw picture and put you on there?

MIKE: Anyway, back to San Francisco… New York has 2 or 3 Jazz stations, but for our size- we used to have 2 or 3…

DON: Yeah we've had quite a few for a while.

MIKE: The other thing about San Francisco is that we almost do treasure our Jazz. I mean we all want to keep in alive.

DON: I think everybody treasures that, yeah!

MIKE: But there's a special meaning for San Franciscans…Don't forget the other thing, because of its social [make up] you could do experimental things here too. You could be really weird, nobody would bother you.

DON: That's why we love the city; because it's weird and it's kooky and it's ok!

MIKE: When I first came here there was a bar called Mooney's Irish Pub. It was on Grant St. Mooney was from New York, I saw the yellow pages. He exaggerated his Irish accent and the Irish would come into the bar. He wasn't making any money. They put dry ice in the toilets…But in his bar, this was San Francisco. You have a dope dealer; you have a Jim Dunbar who was a radio/TV personality. You'd have a hooker; you'd have a college professor-

DON: And a cop!

MIKE: That's right! And you know- you'd have gay people. But they'd all be at the same bar, and they'd all be at the same level. There was no snootiness. Or you'd have a rich person. Or a journalist! Plenty of journalists! And that was a beautiful thing about Washington Square and Moose's and places like that.

DON: Well I think the press has really kept every art form alive, you know, and they're very vital.

MIKE: What used to be the press. I hate to see the newspapers now-

DON: Any writer, any art form, as long as you have a writer, he's carrying the ball for you, ya know? And we miss those guys and there aren't enough of them…

MIKE: Time marches on. I just think we were lucky enough to be alive and young at a time when our heroes were around.

DON: And they didn't even know they were heroes.

MIKE: No! Can you imagine this? I once saw Thelonious Monk …Really I couldn't say anything because it's none of my business and I'm not the right color to step in and say something. It was at the 5 Spot.

DON: What was it about?

MIKE: He didn't like the notes he was playing.

DON: Oh.

MIKE: I think he was trying to do some sort of head.

DON: We went through all of that.

MIKE: The other thing I think is great is Denny Zeitlin-

DON: Yeah I was hoping to get to talk with Denny Zeitlin. I don't know if I'll be able to.

MIKE: Well, uh…

DON: I hope so.

MIKE: Well if you have any trouble, it's just a matter of time to make contact. Have you had trouble reaching him?

DON: I haven't tried.

MIKE: I can put you in with him if you want. He's very nice.

DON: Oh good!

MIKE: I'm very envious of his technique. I mean, his runs are "WOW!" He must have had some classical training.

A Diary of the Underdogs

DON: I'm sure; a studious kind of guy-PhD.

MIKE: The other thing we used to have, I don't think they have anymore, was a union rehearsal band. Waldo would run it and he'd have everybody in there... When did you get here?

DON: 1960.

MIKE: Oh boy!

DON: Played up on Grant St. with Norman Bishop on Sundays with Max Hartstein, Nancy King and people like that. I can't even remember all of them. That's how it started. Pretty soon I had a steady Sunday gig; I couldn't wait to get here! I got to play here on Sundays with Bishop Norman Williams!

MIKE: That's great!

DON: And eat chocolate bars and drink muscatel! You just had to be there, you know?

MIKE: Ok, I just have to ask you; what's the weirdest story with the customers?

DON: I did have a lady come by and say "Thanks for playing 'Easy Living'" with her husband. And then she come up later and kisses my ear and puts her tongue in my ear!

"I just love you!" in a big whisper and then she goes back with her husband and they walk out and leave a $20 bill on the piano!

MIKE: That's happened to me. They can flirt because they're protected and they're loaded. They don't do that when they're sober.

DON: Yeah!

MIKE: 2 things happened to me when I first started playing here. I was wondering why people liked my music about 2 hours later. I finally realized it's because they were drunk!

DON: Well, they gotta be a little drunk!

MIKE: Otherwise you're not making any money! The funniest thing that ever happened happened twice. I playing piano and this guy comes up and says "Do you now where we can hear any live music?"...While I'm playing!

DON: While you're playing!

MIKE: So I say "Well I'll let you know as soon as I'm finished typing this letter!"

DON: Great response!

Would you mind turning the page on New York Times?

MIKE: I got fired from a gig reading the Wall Street Journal.

DON: You watch in the mirror to see who's behind you.

MIKE: Yeah.

DON: That's the old Wash bag, right?

MIKE: Yeah. But I did that at Lascaux. Ever get to play at Lascaux?

DON: Yeah, I did; the downstairs place.

MIKE: Yeah. So the waiter came up, "How come you're reading the newspaper?" I said, "If people are gonna talk while I'm playing, I can read the newspaper"

End: Mike Lipskin

Interview: George DiQuattro-jazz musician, pianist- with Don Alberts-April 22, 2009-San Francisco-about Azteca, Cameo Club, Tom Harrell, George Muribus, Lenny White, Paul Jackson, Coke Escavedo, Flip Nunez, London, Vince Lateano, Frank Passantino, Jerry Gilmore, Colin Bailey, Joe Ellis

GEORGE DIQUATTRO

DON: So Vince was talking about going on the road with Woody Herman, the right hand was screwed up

A Diary of the Underdogs

and he had to play with that band with his left hand!

GEORGE: You know when I was with Azteca, we had a great drummer; Lenny White.

DON: Lenny White, yeah! He played with Chic! (Corea)

GEORGE: And I took Lenny to the Great American Music Hall to hear Vince play with...I forgot who he was playing with...A big band I think, with one hand! And we're sitting there and I go, "What do you think of the drummer there, Lenny?" Lenny goes, "Man, he's a good drummer!" I go, "Man, he's only playing with one fuckin' hand, man!"

DON: And he's left handed!

GEORGE: And he's left handed! He said "What?! Holy shit!" and they

George DiQuattro

became good friends after that! I think that all 3 of them lived together for a while. Him, Lenny White and Paul Jackson, a bass player...I could tell you the funniest story about Paul Jackson; Bare-ass naked, sitting on the pot, reading a book and eating a sandwich!

DON: That's a strange combination of activities!

GEORGE: That's some real old shit, man, ya know? I mean that's some real funky shit, boy! He's eating a sandwich! Taking' a shit, reading a book, bare-ass naked! I mean goddamn, boy!

DON: That wasn't at the happy house was it?

GEORGE: That was down at the Marina, I don't know where but down at the Marina somewhere. What was the Happy House? Refresh me.

DON: Well it's a place where a lot of cats lived. It's on Oak and Fillmore, a 3 story house. Dewey Redman lived there and Art Lewis "Sharky"... in fact, Flip Nunez met his wife, this girl there, and married her!

GEORGE: Oh yeah, I remember now! I remember that place!

DON: Yes, it was called the Happy House, and these people from Sacramento had a club there called the Swingin' Lantern, where everybody used to go up there to Sacramento and play. The owners bought the place on Fell and Oak streets and turned it into the Happy House. Many musicians stayed there.

GEORGE: A lot of guys from Sacramento, man!

DON: Yeah, Vince, Joe Ellis, Mel Martin...

GEORGE: Rufus Reid...A lot of Cats, man.

DON: I had a nice talk with Mel Martin...

GEORGE: You know, Vince and Joe grew up together. You know, it killed him, man, when Joe had passed.

DON: I know, yeah, it was sad.

GEORGE: It killed him, man. But you know, you fuck with those ancient spirits when you're 60 years old, it's gonna get you, man.

DON: That's right, man. They're bigger than we are!

GEORGE: Shit!...You know, we start thinking about all the shit we did...How did we make it here, man?

DON: Yes. Well, it's like you say, ancient spirits, man. You finally realize that you're messing with things that are much bigger than you are! And they have been bigger than we are for centuries, and we're gonna

A Diary of the Underdogs

walk around with some ego and think that we're gonna dominate and control this stuff...You know, you just can't, you can't do that. But after a while you start getting a sense of things, you know? Things start to get a little clearer...

GEORGE: Yeah, but how come it took us this long, man, you know?

DON: You have to go the wall, man. You have to hit the wall…

DON: How about some talk about the band, Azteca, from 1972...?

GEORGE: A good band, man!

DON: Now there were 3 piano players, right?

GEORGE: Me, Flip Nunez, and George Muribus!

DON: Yeah, I mean those are the hottest guys in town, man! Those are the Cats! And you too!

GEORGE: I was actually just learning how to play then. I wasn't near George or Flip.

DON: Well you obviously were, you wouldn't be in that band, man, don't cut yourself down there, don't shorten yourself.

GEORGE: No, but I was! I had the least experience of everyone in the band.

DON: Yeah, buy you had something.

GEORGE: Yeah, well my time. I've always had great time.

DON: Yeah you had good time. That's what it was, you could swing. That's what everybody says about you, George, just for your own archives. That's what they say about you.

GEORGE: And don't forget my name, George DiQuattro.

DON: George DiQuattro; George DiFour. You changed your name, right? It was George DiFour?

GEORGE: Yeah it was for a while, when I worked in Sausalito. Here's the movie we made.

DON: You made a movie, ok! (reading off cover) Pete Escovedo, Wendy Haas…This is about Azteca, ok! So there's a DVD of Azteca that exists and you can buy it on…?

GEORGE: It just came out. You can buy it on Amazon.

DON: We can do a little commercial here; 17 musicians, 2 albums, 1 band; Azteca. La Piedra del Sol is the story of the world's first super group. A group which pushed the very boundaries of Soul, R and B, Rock, Funk, Jazz and Latin rhythms…Cool and you're in here!

GEORGE: Oh yeah!

DON: And this isn't all the personnel, or is it?

GEORGE: No.

DON: Pete Escovedo, Wendy Haas, Earl Knowles, Lenny White, Paul Jackson, Bill…?

GEORGE: Bill Courtial, yeah, a guitar player.

DON: (reading) Victor Pantoja, Jules Rowell, I know Jules. And George DiQuattro! Well Who's Wendy Haas?

GEORGE: Wendy Haas is a singer. She's married to uh…I can't remember his name, man. Well she was a vocalist anyway. There were 4 vocalists, 3 keyboards, 4 horns, a conga player, timbales, drums, and guitar.

DON: Who played timbales?

GEORGE: Timbales player was Coke Escovedo.

DON: Oh, it was Coke, Coke was around then?

GEORGE: Yeah, actually it was his idea, his band.

DON: He started it?

GEORGE: Oh yeah.

DON: And actually Pete was a singer at that time, right?

GEORGE: Pete was a singer in the band, yeah!

DON: At that time, and then he started playing timbales later?

GEORGE: Yeah, when Coke died, passed, and then he…

DON: And when was that, mid '70?

A Diary of the Underdogs

GEORGE: I don't know but it should be in there.

DON: Ok. So, Earl Knowles, I never met this guy.

GEORGE: He's another singer, a good singer, he was one of the good singers and uh...

DON: Was he Latin?

GEORGE: No, no, black cat...He's at the American School of Jazz in Japan now. He married a Japanese girl.

DON: He's Denise Perrier's brother? No, wait; Paul Jackson is Denise Perrier's brother

GEORGE: You know- I'm not sure. It might be! .

DON: Now tell me about these guys one at a time.

GEORGE: This is San Francisco in the 70's. I mean, here is the horn section. Goddamn what a horn section! First of all, it wasn't Jules, it was Pat O'Hara. I don't know if you remember Pat. He overdosed. He was the trombone player. The saxophone players were Mel Martin, Bobby Ferrera, who's a great player, man. The trumpet player was, Tom Harrell.

DON: Tom Harrell and that was it?

GEORGE: Well, fuckin' 4 great horn players, man, and geez! When Pat died, Jules came on the band...But Tom Harrell and Mel Martin, you know, Jesus Christ! Tom Harrell arranged everything-

DON: He did? 'Cause he's a bright kid, huh? What was he, mid 20's then?

GEORGE: Yeah.

DON: So smart...

GEORGE: He couldn't talk. He was like, so introverted, really introverted. Like, I'd give him "Peace Everybody" which is like a 2 chord tune. He fuckin' made it sound gorgeous. After I heard him, "Did I write that? Shit!" You know?

DON: So he turned it into something-?

GEORGE: Oh he turned everything! Anybody give him anything, he turned them all into great songs, great back rounds, great everything, man, a wonderful arranger.

DON: I ran into him at the Mt. Hood Jazz Festival. He was playing with Phil Woods. I had a backstage pass because I had to go and see him, man. And he was writing a chart to the Star Wars theme!

GEORGE: Was he?!

DON: Yeah, for the band! On the spot! Creating a chart!

GEORGE: Yeah, he did that a lot!

DON: And they played it the next set!

GEORGE: I know. Tom Harrell, a genius, man.

DON: Yeah!

GEORGE: One of the greater trumpet players the world has ever known. I really believe it, man.

DON: Yeah. Well tell me about Lenny White, why was he around here? I thought he was an LA guy?

GEORGE: He was a New York boy.

DON: What brought him out here? How did he get up here? Do you know anything about him?

GEORGE: Sure, I keep in touch with Lenny all the time, man. We hung out a lot when I was with the band. Coke called him. Coke knew him when he was on the road with Chick Corea and Al Di Meola...What the hell was the name of that band?

DON: Light as a Feather? Return to Forever.

GEORGE: Yeah. They came back together again. And he was playing with everybody by that time; Freddie Hubbard. Paul Jackson was the bass player for the Headhunters.

DON: I thought so, it was the same guy!

GEORGE: With Mike Clark.

DON: Yeah, Herbie Hancock, the original Headhunters.

GEORGE: Mmmm, boy that was a funky band, man!

A Diary of the Underdogs

DON: It was something' huh?

GEORGE: Mike Clark and Paul Jackson; Very funky players, man very funky. We even had Neil Schon play on this album. They guy from Journey.

DON: Oh, I don't know those guys. Journey, eh?

GEORGE: Carlos Santana was an original member of the band (Azteca) but Columbia wouldn't let him do it. He came and rehearsed with us and everything, but Columbia wouldn't let him get on stage with us.

DON: Not ever get on stage?

GEORGE: Nope.

DON: Well who…Tell me about this idea, how did this happen? This is a great thing.

GEORGE: This is Coke! If you wanna know, man, I'll lay this DVD on you; just make sure you get it back to me.

DON: Yeah, I wanna read it, but I want it on your interview. Now how did this happen? Coke Escovedo comes along, and he already knows Santana, right?

GEORGE: Yeah, he's already been with Santana. He wrote a song for Santana, a big hit for Santana. (sings melody) *"I ain't got nobody, that I can depend on,"* You know, that one.

DON: Oh, that one!

GEORGE: And that was a big fuckin' song. And that was Coke's song. He got tired of it, playing with Santana, and he wanted his own band. Ha had his idea. He says "I want this band that can play everything!"

DON: Jazz and everything…

GEORGE: "I want a big band that can play everything!" That was his idea and he put it together. He came and talked to me. He came and heard everybody play first, you know.

DON: So who were you playing with at the time that he came around?

GEORGE: I was in Sausalito playing at Gatsby's. We used to pack that joint, man!... Right down the block from the cop station... Who in the hell did I have in that band? Everybody in that band went through that band.

DON: You know, Frank, obviously…

GEORGE: Frank wasn't on that band. I had Nat Johnson, played bass originally; and then, Puzzie Firth, Vince Lateano, me, and Francisco Obligacion, a conga player.

DON: So what were you doing there? Were you playing Jazz with a Latin flavor, or…?

GEORGE: We were playing Latin Jazz!

DON: 'Cause there's a little thing here about this over here with Tjader?

GEORGE: Well that was my last band, you know.

DON: Oh, ok. I thought maybe this was early.

GEORGE: No, no. This is right before he died. I mean, I was supposed to go on a Philippine trip with him… But I couldn't do it. So I called him and I said "I can't make this, Cal, I'm sorry". So he got Mark Levine…They went to the Philippines, he died there. That was the last I saw or talked to him.

DON: But you didn't get with him early in his career?

GEORGE: I knew him! I used to go down to the Black Hawk and sit in when he was there. He used to have sit-ins on Sunday afternoons. I used to go down there with Puzzie and play with him. He knew me for a long time. I knew his wife, Pat Tjader- a wonderful piano player. And so I've know him for a long time, you know. We were both die-hard 49er fans! Die-hard! Like my first gig at the Great American Music Hall with him. Was the year the 49ers won their first super bowl. We had a uniform to wear, but I put my…And he didn't mind, he said "Alright, man!" But I put my 49er thing on, ya know? So yeah, he liked that… He was a good guy man. Cal was a good guy, a wonderful player…

DON: Yeah he was a good guy and he had a nice tone. You hear the other vibes players and they plank and plank and plank, that sound is just consistent…

GEORGE: There were no other vibes players that knew Latin music like Cal. Cal could play all the Latin

A Diary of the Underdogs

percussion.

DON: Oh, he could do that! He could do the drums and…

GEORGE: He could do all of that. He knew all the claves for all the music, everything about Latin music. He taught Vince when Vince went with him, Poncho Sanchez; that was a great band! Vince learned a lot about playing Latin music.

DON: And the bass player?

GEORGE: That was Rob Fisher.

DON: And then, on piano, Mark Levine?

GEORGE: Yeah, Mark Levine…He was the piano player. Vince and…Poncho!

DON: Yeah Poncho, and then later on it was that other guy?

GEORGE: No, Poncho was the last guy.

DON: Oh, he was. I'm thinking of the guy before, Armando Peraza..

GEORGE: Oh yeah that was a long time ago. There were a bunch of conga players after Armando; Bill Fitch, I can't remember the other Cats…But with Armando, that was Al McKibbon.

DON: So then the guitar player was in there…

GEORGE: Eddie Duran?

DON: Eddie Duran!

GEORGE: No, no. It was his two brothers! Carlos on bass and Manny on piano. That was the earliest Cal Tjader band… Real, real early! They did some funny shit, man!

DON: But you were around then, you could sit in. You knew those guys.

GEORGE: Oh, yeah. I knew all those guys… There was a club on Broadway St., a friend of mine wrote me an e-mail and wanted to remember the name and I can't remember the name of the fuckin' place where I learned all-

DON: Broadway North Beach?

GEORGE: Coming out of the tunnel, coming out of North Beach on the side of the tunnel.

DON: There's Alfred's Steak House over on the left…

GEORGE: No, it was on the other side…What was it, the Copa Cabana?

DON: No, it was something like that. Benny Velarde played there.

GEORGE: Yes, that's where I learned how to play Latin music!

DON: Ok!

GEORGE: He would let me sit in with the band and every time I'd get off he'd say, "Man, it's good, but you sound like "Git-that-brotha-brown"! He used to crack me up. He said, "I'll tell ya what; you learn how to dance to this music, and then you can play it" Son-of-a-bitch, man, I did!

DON: That's absolutely true.

GEORGE: I love to dance anyway so I started to learn how to play the Mambos and Cha Chas, and I felt the clave. And it wasn't at a dance studio or some place, you know. It was different than that shit. These were real Cubans and Puerto Ricans, man. So I learned that, the next time I sit in, he goes, "That's the shit, that's the shit."

DON: That's it, yeah. So did you end up playing with Benny at all?

GEORGE: No. We played a couple of times together but never…We tried to get a band together with Francisco Aguabella but that didn't work out. But I like Benny a lot, man. Good guy.

DON: Yeah, I like him too. I remember going in to hear him with Virgil…But you don't need to talk about that. I'm interested in what you're saying, in where it goes. Like, you were a Jazz player, I met you years ago down in the Peninsula.

GEORGE: Yeah.

DON: And we did the Cameo Club. I was all messed up, I took off. But you inherited the gig, right?

GEORGE: Yeah.

A Diary of the Underdogs

DON: And wasn't it Buddy?

GEORGE: You know, I think Buddy came along after…Geez I had another drummer, I had this guy, Ronnie Scott. Robbie Ogborn is his real name, but anyway, Ronnie Scott is his stage name. He came in and he says, "You know, you only have a drum, piano and tenor sax, no bass. You want one?" I says, "Yeah, but you know, I can't afford another guy." He says, "I play drums and bass at the same time." I go, "what the fuck?" He says, "I'll show you, man." So I had him come in early one night before Forest came in. He sat down, he started playing. He had an electric bass in his left hand and with his right hand and feet he played drums. He played tremendous sound, tremendous time, the notes were right, he cooked! I mean, me and Jerry, we went, "What the fuck? Where'd this guy- what the?" Later on in the gig after I hired him, it filled up the whole band ya know? Now we got bass now!

DON: Yeah, you need it. You and Jerry Gilmore

GEORGE: Yeah. So now he plays one night, he puts his sticks down, he's still playing the bass and he's playing the drum and high hat with his feet and he picks up a valve trombone and plays valve trombone with his right hand!

DON: Some kind of brain here! What kind of brain's it take to do that, huh?

GEORGE: You know, if he was playing just bass, or trombone, he'd always pick something else up like a tambourine, anything!

DON: What's this guys name again?

GEORGE: Ronnie Scott.

DON: Ronnie Scott…Where's he from? Did he just appear out of the-

GEORGE: Yeah I don't even remember where he was from, man. He stayed with me for quite a while. And then he went down to San Diego and hooked up with 2 brothers who played all these instruments at one time. So now you'd open up the stage and 3 guys would walk out and there'd be like 30 instruments behind them!

The guys are playing 2 horns at one time, he's playing drums and bass…It was fantastic!

DON: It sounds like a carnival!

GEORGE: It was! Then we got a little gig together at a little place in Mountain View, I don't remember the name of the place, where I met John Brody by the way. Me and Ronnie Scott, just the 2 of us. I played organ, he played bass and drums, and we stay there for quite a while too. It was fun, man. …I love Buddy, man, great drummer! I loved his time, I love everything about him. He liked the juice, ya know!

DON: Oh yeah.

GEORGE: So when the check came and you pay your tab, he'd have to pay more than what the check was!

DON: Oh yeah? He'd owe them money!

GEORGE: He'd be so pissed off at them. One night, on our breaks we'd go out to the parking lot and fuck around, and Buddy wanted to show us how he was a hop-skip-jump champion in high school. "Watch this!" so he went hop! Skip! Break! He broke his fucking leg! I had to take him to the Stanford hospital, man! I had to hire another fuckin' drummer.

DON: So Buddy never wanted to talk about that!

GEORGE: He didn't say anything about that when you talk to him?

DON: I talk to him all the time but he don't wanna…

GEORGE: Oh, he'll remember that…I guarantee you that, man! Gerry and I just fell on the floor laughing. Alright let me tell you a couple of things about Cameo. We had some of the weirdest fuckin' acts because we had strippers, but they would always either be a singer or magician or a chameleon; that would be the guy that would bring everybody out, the MC! We had this guy who was a magician…Nothing ever fuckin' worked! I ain't shittin' ya, man. He had a thing where during a rehearsal, we'd play a thing, and he'd go in his coat and bring out 2 live doves. The first fucking night, he goes like this and he pulls out the doves, Jerry starts to play the horn and they're both dead. Right there in his hand, they're both… Jerry blew his horn,

223

almost passed out…2 dead doves, man, both of them, just hanging there.

GEORGE: Then there was another one where he had 15 minutes. He'd do this elaborate thing, setting up a table with all kinds of pagodas, shit from China, with a big blanket put over it and a cape. He'd pull that cape off and everything would come out. One night he pulled the cape off and everything just fell; crash! Everything fell to the floor. This guy couldn't do anything right.

DON: Maybe that was part of his act! Well you had strippers too?

GEORGE: Well it was a strip club, that's what it was, you know. A "burlesque house" that's what they called it but it was a strip joint, man. We had some funky chicks. We had this Chick one time with a… The owner told one time, he said "When she's dancing and she shows her anus, you can't do that, it's against the law". So I went into the dressing room, I said, I think her name was Holly. "Holly" I said, she goes "What?" I said "The boss told me to tell you that you're showing your anus and you can't do that, it's against the law". And she goes "Is that the front or the back?"

GEORGE: I mean, I remember that shit like it was yesterday. I looked at her and I went "That's the back" geez.

DON: Well I remember one called Wendy Night, a little blonde chick. You remember Wendy Night?

GEORGE: Wendy? Sure, man.

DON: Wendy Night would give the band a good show.

GEORGE: Oh yeah, absolutely.

DON: And then she'd turn, 'cause she had a little carpet she'd put on the floor and spin around, and she'd always stop for the band, she'd stop at the guy she was going out with a little longer than the other guys.

GEORGE: I even had Noel Jukes play there. You know Noel played with me for a long time there. He was madly in love with this Holly chick that had a snake.

DON: She had a snake, a stripper with a snake?

GEORGE: Yeah, a big Boa.

DON: See, it's funny stuff, people don't know anything about that, I mean, these days you don't see that kind of stuff.

GEORGE: You don't, man.

DON: There's always some restriction. You can never do it.

GEORGE: Here's Noel Jukes playing a strip joint.

DON: Yeah, Noel Jukes, a great Jazz player, man.

GEORGE: Gerry Gilmore's another one. And the drummers, I went through Vince, Buddy, you know, Forrest Ellige, who taught drums in San Jose.

DON: Yeah, Forrest. Tell me a little about him. Where did he come from?

GEORGE: Oh, Forrest. He was a very weird, kind of insane kind of a guy. His old lady broke up with him. He came home one night after the gig and knocked on the door. She wouldn't let him into the house. So he got into his car. He drove his fucking car right into the front door into the living room! I get a call the next day "I can't make the gig, I'm in jail"… I think that's the night I got Vince! I called Drumland and go "Kenny, you got any drummers?" "Yeah, there's a kid from Sacramento." I go, "Send him"!

DON: Right. So Vince showed up to the gig.

GEORGE: Yes. I looked at him, this little guy. I go "Can you play this kind of gig?" He says "I just got off this gig in Sacramento". I found out later it was a Black club with 2 Black players.

DON: So he was kicking' butt.

GEORGE: And Vince sat down and boy! He- whew! His time was right where my time was and I go "Could you stay with me for a while?"

DON: Yeah, he has wonderful time.

GEORGE: I think he stayed with me for a while, I don't remember how long.

DON: So how about, Jerry Gilmore is a big part of your playing life. How did that happen? Where is Jerry

A Diary of the Underdogs

from?

GEORGE: Jerry's from here.

DON: 'Cause he can't speak for himself too much. I wish we could talk to him.

GEORGE: I don't even know if he's alive anymore, man.

DON: I heard he was in real bad shape.

GEORGE: He lost both his legs to diabetes.

DON: But where did he start out? Did he grow up in San Jose, San Francisco?

GEORGE: San Francisco.

DON: Did he study at San Francisco State or something?

GEORGE: I don't know what schools he went to.

DON: But he was a really good player right away, right?

GEORGE: Excellent player. I liked him a lot.

DON: Great sense of humor and everything.

GEORGE: We drove to work every night, you know. Smoked a joint, and then go to work every night. I love Jerry a lot, man.

DON: Of course!

GEORGE: it's just; the ancient spirits really got him, really got him, real bad.

DON: Sometimes you don't get back.

GEORGE: He didn't get back, you know. So, Jerry's hard to talk about, 'cause I loved him, man.

DON: Yeah, I know, George. But I just want to gloss over him. He's too important.

GEORGE: No, no. You know, great player, great guy, you know, wonderful guy, man.

DON: Yeah, he worked with you there then he migrated up to the city and played there. Did he play the Playboy club?

GEORGE: I played the Playboy club, I don't know if Jerry did. I'm not sure. I remember one night when George Muribus was playing downstairs in the Playboy club, and I'd always go in and he'd let me sit in, you know? I sat in one night and I was playing. I don't remember the name of the song I was playing. I think it was "Shadow of your Smile" I was playing, I had my eyes closed, and I felt some body sit down next to me and some hands playing down below me. And I looked. First thing was, it was a Black hand, and it was like, 10 ft. long! It was the biggest fuckin' hand I ever saw. He looked like Oscar Peterson.

DON: Really? He came up and put his hand on the piano while you were playing?

GEORGE: He sat down, he played a little piano next to me, I got up and said "What the fuck, Oscar Peterson?" He was my idol at that time.

DON: Of course, yeah!

GEORGE: He just burned the whole night. He played like about, 10 songs, man! He was just...

DON: He liked to come in and mix it up, be friendly and stuff. Not a stand-off guy at all.

GEORGE: Oh no. He was a real nice guy. I met him again at the Fairmont one time. He remembered that time when we played before and that was like, 7 years ago so...

DON: Right, yeah that's cool. Well tell me a little bit about George Muribus. No one ever talks about George because he was in that time period where he was kind of covered up in a way, you know?

GEORGE: Gerry introduced me to George. From then on, I was at George's house every night. For years.

DON: It's rare for piano players to get together.

GEORGE: We'd play games, we'd bullshit, and we'd play piano together. Gerry would be there every night. But we'd usually play games like Dealer McDope and shit like that. George had some real far out games... To explain George is real hard. He was a child prodigy.

DON: Yeah, classically trained.

GEORGE: Yeah, classical music. He traveled the whole world with his mom. He had built up pedals for his piano so he could hook them up to any piano, so that his feet could reach the pedals.

A Diary of the Underdogs

DON: Did he have short legs?

GEORGE: No, when he was only 5 years old!

DON: Oh! When he was young!

GEORGE: Yeah, 7 or 8 years old. He liked Jazz a lot and he started to play Jazz. He taught me a lot too. He was just a beautiful, fluid player...

DON: And warm, beautiful chords...

GEORGE: He introduced me to Flip Nunez, and Flip had all the shit up here, he could play you know? He could play all that and they were 2 kind of opposites but not really.

DON: But you guys were all friends! That's what's amazing!

GEORGE: Yeah, 3 piano players on a gig!

DON: Piano players usually don't get that because they're never on a gig with each other.

GEORGE: I was friends with Al Plank. I loved Al; he was a friend of mine. George and Flip; Flip and I roomed together on the road; we were roomies, ya know? When I was in Azteca, we went to London to sign our contract.

DON: Let's hear about that.

GEORGE: That was insane, man! We got there and first of all, we were told by Columbia, "Don't bring any dope, don't bring any weed, nothing! You're gonna go through customs"! Everybody in the band did something, in Azteca! Except for Wendy and Lenny, you know, a couple of clean kids that didn't do shit. Anyway, we get to London; we have to go through customs. Go through customs, and we're ready to go and all of a sudden we see a guy who Columbia put on us to handle us, take care of us! He went-"Come over!" So we go to the gate and there was an officer there, he opened the gate and said "Go on". We went through and everybody went "Fuck! We didn't bring shit! We could have brought everything! So we're there. We're stay at the great hotel, right across the street from Hyde Park; I forget the name of it. A beautiful fuckin' old

DON: Well, I don't mean to distract you but what happened at the London concert? It was an English hotel, probably $1,000 a night. Anyway, everybody stayed there, all the bands that were there, stayed there. The 3 bands that signed that day were Azteca, Earth Wind and Fire, and the Doobie Brothers! And you see where they went and you see where we went.

DON: Well why didn't you guys get bigger? What happened to Azteca?

GEORGE: What happened to Azteca was, after Coke died... Coke fucked up. Ancient spirits again, man. And uh, he took all the money. We'd go and play a gig, there'd be 50,000 people. 50,000! And we'd get $50 each!

DON: Oh, no way!

GEORGE: In New York or something!

DON: So how long did that last, do you think?

GEORGE: Through the second album, for 2 or 3 years at the most. That's about it. Well, I told you we didn't have anything with us.

DON: Yeah.

GEORGE: We had met a guy that I met in San Francisco and he was an Englishman. He was a good guy, liked to smoke weed. I said, "When I get to London, I'll give you a call" So I remembered, I had his name. His name was Carl. I called him, he said "Yeah, come on up." I met him at some house. It was down under a house up top, you know like a basement thing...

DON: Yeah, basement apartment.

GEORGE: So I knocked on the door, he opened the door and it was like hippie heaven. Everybody was in white robes. Shit, there was incense going on, real far out music playing, and the smell was just unbelievable. Anyway, I scored for the whole band! I scored like, 5 bags of weed, and...

DON: Hash?

GEORGE: About 3 big temple balls of hash! The whole thing cost me about $40.

A Diary of the Underdogs

DON: Ha! Unbelievable!

GEORGE: Honest to God! I brought it back and Flip and I were in one room together and that room became the most popular fuckin' room in the hotel let me tell ya! Everybody came! That was a great time. We had a great time there.

DON: You didn't play around at Ronnie Scott's right? You played a larger venue?

GEORGE: We played that hotel, downstairs. Clive Davis from Columbia…

DON: Was he there?

GEORGE: Oh yeah! He booked all these bands to be there to play.

DON: So was the deal to showcase you guys, The Doobie Brothers, and Earth Wind and Fire?

GEORGE: Yeah, and we all went downstairs after the concert, this big beautiful hall with big chandeliers and all the waiters wee in tuxedos, and they brought us this gold scroll thing for all of us to sign our contracts, with champagne. It was fantastic, man! That was a good time. Then it got worse. When we got back to San Francisco…

DON: What kind of venues did you do with Azteca in San Francisco?

GEORGE: We played the Cow Palace.

DON: Yeah, big places, right?

GEORGE: We played Winterland…We played a lot of places, man.

DON: Fillmore?

GEORGE: Yeah, but the Kabuki Theater is where we rehearsed. There was a beautiful rehearsal hall down stairs. We rehearsed 7 days a week.

DON: Every day.

GEORGE: And they gave us $50,000. So everybody got about $150 a week for 6 months or something. Then it ran out. Then all the money we got for concerts…We went to New York and we killed them in New York on Roberto Clemente Day in Madison Square Garden.

DON: Ah man. That's gotta be a high point in your life.

GEORGE: I want to tell you something about the 3 piano players; me, Flip and George. They have us listed playing this and that on the thing.

DON: Yeah, I noticed that.

GEORGE: Whoever got to the fucking gig first got their pick! So I'm going-"Madison Square Garden!" I got there real early so I could play the Steinway. I knew they had a big fuckin' 6 ft. Steinway, man, so I just sat there, "No body gets it"! Flip came in; "Son of a bitch!" So he had to play organ and George came late, he fucked up, man. He played electric piano.

DON: So how was that gig?

GEORGE: 15-20 of the top Latin bands; Tipica '73, El Gran Combo, Tito Puente, La Lupe, Celia Cruz, everybody you can think of was there. Every great band in New York was there and we closed the first half of the show and we got the best ovation than everybody. We got a standing ovation. We killed it! Then we were supposed to play The Cheetah. It was a big fuckin' venue in New York. If you played at Cheetah, you made it. Fucking Coke got the money and split back to San Francisco.

DON: He left you guys?

GEORGE: And we never got to play. And they were after him to get, you know…

DON: Yeah, he owed money and stuff. So Pete couldn't take over?

GEORGE: We heard there were lines 2 blocks over to get in that night to see us.

DON: At the Cheetah and you couldn't do it, huh?

GEORGE: You know, fuck!

DON: Well you could have played, maybe but…

GEORGE: No, they didn't want us after that. Coke took the money and took off, they said "Fuck you guys."

DON: And it was over.

A Diary of the Underdogs

GEORGE: And that was the end of that.

DON: That's a hell of a story, George.

GEORGE: Yeah it's a good story, man.

DON: Jesus. That band could have really gone somewhere, huh?

GEORGE: Well we could have gone it's just-

DON: As big as Earth Wind and Fire, look what they did!

GEORGE: The problem was, in our band you couldn't hear anything! I remember playing in Sacramento and I had my Peavey amp right behind me, and I was play clavinet, electric clavinet. I had the peavey amp sittin' right behind me and I'm playin', I can't hear shit! I turn around, I turn it up; it's all the way up to 10!

DON: You can't hear nothin'!"

GEORGE: I can't hear shit! Nobody could hear anything until finally we got stereo monitors around the band and that helped a lot.

DON: Yeah but your ears are taking a beating! Back then we didn't realize. You know I got hit real hard with a Fender twin amp turned up when I plugged in.

GEORGE: Me too, me too.

DON: Now they ware sponge plugs in their ears, people don't even take a chance!

GEORGE: Yeah that band was so loud sometimes, it was just ridiculous. And trying to tell the rhythm section-

DON: To cool it?

GEORGE: You can't tell them that!

DON: "Turn up"

GEORGE: Yeah, and I'd get it up to 10! Geez! Everybody's up, man. Wow!
I want to tell you about my first trio. The first trio I ever played with, other than that I was playing solo piano. I didn't know much about Jazz or anything. I had a feeling for it, I didn't know much about it. So I got a gig at this place called Titone's in Redwood City. Right next door was a bait shop and cigar shop run by this Sicilian mob from New York. Tony Titone was a Sicilian mob guy from New York. He opened this bar. Him and his nephew ran it; guns all over the place. Anyway, he had 2 bands playing and he liked me but he didn't like the 2 guys who were with me, I don't remember who they were. He liked the bass player and the drummer who played with the other band. He said, "Fuck, I'm gonna fire those guys, I'm gonna hire you and the other guys. That's gonna be the trio that's gonna play". I won't argue with the guy.

DON: Who were they?

GEORGE: Paul Distel and this guy named Bill Gage, I don't know if you remember him, a bass player.

DON: Bill Gage, I don't know, but Paul, yeah!

GEORGE: It was my first fucking trio, man! And then Puzzie came in and played bass. Then Jerry Gilmore came in and started playing. Then Al Molina started playing, everybody came in and started playing and pretty soon that place was packed! There was gunfire like, every other night, there was fights-

DON: Was that, the piano sat down, by the little bar?

GEORGE: Yes! That's the place!

DON: I came in there, I saw you in there!

GEORGE: Yup, that was Titone's!

DON: Tony Titone, huh?

GEORGE: Yeah, Tony, he was the owner. He loved me 'cause I was a Dago. First of all I was Sicilian, he loved that! But he liked the way I played and he liked the way Paul played but he didn't like the other piano player, I don't remember who it was, I don't remember who the first 2 guys were on the scene.

DON: It doesn't matter, you got the swing.

GEORGE: Yeah I got the gig. That was the first time I had a trio and it was fun, man! You know who else came in? Pharaoh Sanders! We used to call him "Little Rock."

A Diary of the Underdogs

DON: He was little.

GEORGE: He came in and played with us all the time.

DON: And his real name, I forgot his real name.

GEORGE: Pharaoh Sanders.

DON: No, that's later, but originally?

GEORGE: Oh, I don't know his original name, I thought that was it.

DON: But you know who gave him that name, Nancy King!

GEORGE: Oh she did?

DON: It was Nancy King. Did you ever get up there? 'Cause I started playing in San Francisco in 1960 with Norman Williams and all those guys.

GEORGE: No, I never did. It was fun in those days. I played an after hours club; Streets of Paris. I don't remember the black tenor player's name who used to jump- Sammy? He used to jump up on the table and play. He was a good player too.

DON: Sammy. He didn't play baritone?

GEORGE: I just remember we used to play from 2:30 to 5:30, made $5 and a spaghetti dinner. And I'd do it every weekend.

DON: Yeah I did it too; I did it at Bop City. $6!

GEORGE: This is like 5:30 in the morning, who eats spaghetti, ya know?!

DON: What was the place across the street?

GEORGE: I don't know. I remember Paul Distel told me a story when he was playing there with the guy from Duke Ellington's band, he played tenor saxophone.

DON: Yeah, Paul Gonzalves.

GEORGE: Paul Gonzalves! He said after he'd take a solo he'd run to the bathroom, come back, play another 45 minutes, solo, all in one song.

DON: Well that's what they did in Dukes band, you know, Duke would put them out for 20 minutes.

GEORGE: As soon as the solo's over, he'd go to the bathroom. Anyway, Paul said, "The gig is over". He's still playin'! Paul, and probably Puzzie, packing up and he's still playing. They left, he was still playing.

DON: This is Paul Gonzalves.

GEORGE: Yeah, he'd be playing his ass off.

DON: We were playing somewhere in the Castro. Me and Virgil had a gig, and Paul came in, did the same thing; played all night!

GEORGE: Another gig I had was Al Obidinski on bass, Pepi Watson, pretty good little drummer, we played at the Condor. Gino the owner says "I'm gonna bring in this trumpet player from back east. Can you play with him? He's a jazz trumpet player!" we said "Yeah we can play with him!" Al said "Who is it?" His name was Red Rodney. Red Rodney is gonna play at the Condor? He did! Came in and played 2 weekends with us, Fridays and Saturdays.

DON: He's on all the classic Bird records, all the Charlie Parker…

GEORGE: Al and I said "Holy shit, it is Red Rodney!" He's a beautiful player.

DON: So the Condor does have a history of Jazz.

GEORGE: Oh yeah, it did.

DON: 'Cause it's always been identified as just a strip club.

GEORGE: Oh no, before that, they had a lot of Jazz players play there before, man.

DON: And you know the story about the piano, we don't have to go into that- the piano squashed the waiter, the waitress and the doorman.

GEORGE: They were screwing', they were fuckin' and the piano came down. I heard that story. I don't know if it's true, was it true?

DON: It's been written a lot. In fact I included it in this book. I got the names, Ferrazzo, was his name and

229

A Diary of the Underdogs

Virginia Hill or something was the waitress.

GEORGE: Get the fuck out of here, you got their names too?

DON: I got their names

GEORGE: Do you remember what year?

DON: I don't remember the year.

GEORGE: It must have been the 60's?

DON: It's in my notes, it's in the books.

GEORGE: "Diary of the Under Dogs" great title, man!

DON: I wrote all this stuff 12 years ago.

GEORGE: What made you want to do this, man? Good for you!

DON: I just want to record it, man. So much happened in the 60's and I was here. Hanging out with Chet and playing Roland's and too messed up to continue, busted, going to jail-

GEORGE: I remember...

DON: Jumped bail and left.

GEORGE: I remember all that shit about you. I remember you were here, you were gone.

DON: I had to be gone.

GEORGE: That's what I remember...I used to love to come hear you play. Next thing I know "He's gone". Never heard from you again, never saw you in 20 years. Wow!

DON: I was gone 20 years, but I had to. I couldn't do what I needed to do.

GEORGE: Then there was the Jazz workshop.

DON: The workshop! Yeah! Anything you got, tell me about it. You got any pictures? I need pictures, man.

GEORGE: You gonna put pictures in the book?.The only thing I got pictures of is Azteca in rehearsals, that's about it.

DON: Anything you got, because I'm gonna have to put out a bulletin on KCSM and try and get some photos...

GEORGE: I'll send you the pictures of Azteca and you can have them, do whatever the fuck you want with them... I didn't know you were into this, I'm proud of you for doing this, man. Nobody has done this for San Francisco.

DON: It's a lot of work, but I did it out of love, you know. I got interviews with Leroy Vinnegar. Fortunately I interviewed B.J. Papa in 1997, had him over for dinner.

GEORGE: Oh yeah? How was that?

DON: Oh you know, he was out, talking about all kinds of stuff. But he gave me the inside on the Fillmore. I knew all those guys 'cause we all used to get high together, but he remembered everybody and he had these little stories about Norman Spiller and all that inside stuff.

GEORGE: That's great man, that's great... That was the 60's huh?

DON: Yeah, that was.

GEORGE: In the 60's I was living in LA and I had that cock-stretcher business.

DON: A what?

GEORGE: A cock-stretcher business.

DON: Oh, that's right! Early male enhancement!

GEORGE: I got busted for it on a felony. And now-

DON: It's everywhere!

GEORGE: It was called the Hyper-Reminator.

DON: That's the shit, George!

GEORGE: I played a little bit down there. Two weird guys who called me for a gig, very popular, I can't remember their names. Very outside players and I was just inside. They were so far outside, I was so far inside, it worked! I don't know why!... I gave them my address and I never should have done that...At that

A Diary of the Underdogs

time I met Victor Feldman. I went to his house, took some lessons and he said "I can't teach you shit! You're a trip player just like I am"! That made me feel god. He had great bands, he had Monty Budwig, Colin Bailey, and Victor Feldman. And Victor was a drummer and a vibe player also. So he would go home and play, and record a vibe solo, then he'd bring it to the club. It was absolutely fantastic, he'd do it so good, you'd be looking for the vibe player! It was so good, I couldn't believe it!

DON: He'd just play it back, huh?

GEORGE: Yeah. You should interview Colin; he's got millions of stories.

DON: And he's got that great English humor.

GEORGE: I keep in touch with him too a lot because he was my last drummer. In my last trio I had Colin Bailey and...What the fuck's his name? See? My memory, man! Scott Steed!

DON: Oh yeah, Scott, he's in Oregon.

GEORGE: Playing with Diane Schuur. I loved that trio man. Colin and Scott...

DON: I love the way Colin just lays it down!

GEORGE: He was part of Red Garland's trio! And he said one night; he played in Austin, Texas. He played "Funny Valentine" so fuckin' slow! He finished the chorus, he looked and Colin and said "You got it"! Colin had to play a drum solo at that tempo! Are you kidding me, man?! He told me that, I fuckin' fell out, I couldn't believe it. It was so fuckin' slow, he could hardly even play it in time and then turns around and said "You got it"!

DON: But he did it?

GEORGE: Yeah, he did it. And he's a wonderful player. Colin Bailey, his time for trio playing...If you wanna hire someone for a trio, Colin Bailey's the guy!

DON: I've heard him play a lot, we're friends. I've had shingles and he's had shingles and we talked about "acyclovir" which is the cure for shingles. He says "Yeah, that's the stuff"!

GEORGE: Are you gonna interview him?

DON: Yeah, I hope so!

GEORGE: I hope so too, man. He's just a...

DON: I want to talk to him and Al Obidinski-

GEORGE: Al Obidinski, what's his nick name, do you know?

DON: Only-have-eye-for-you.

GEORGE: "One Eyed Jack"

DON: Ok! I thought it was "I only-have-eye-for-you."

GEORGE: Well that's another one...He was part of my trio too for a long time. Both of us played with so many bass players and drummers, man!

DON: I love those guys man.

GEORGE: Every one of them!

DON: Every one of them, you know! Jesus, I've been playing with Frank Passantino for years.

GEORGE: Me too, me too.

DON: And Frank, you know, if you're playing with Frank, you're in Frank's life! He'll tell you what he had for lunch! He'll tell you what he had yesterday for breakfast!

GEORGE: That's correct! When his mom passed, I called him right away, 'cause I know how empty the house can be.

DON: He said he hadn't been in the room yet.

GEORGE: I believe it. When my sister goes, this house is gonna be, awfully big, man.

DON: Well you got friends, George. You know, it's hard not to play anymore, I mean, it must be a different life for you.

GEORGE: I mean, it's hard for me to listen to music.

DON: 'Cause it moves you too much.

A Diary of the Underdogs

GEORGE: And look at my fuckin' hands now, man.

DON: Have you had an operation?

GEORGE: No, my hands are just always swollen. The only thing they can do is just fuse my wrists. What the fuck, then I can't do anything! How am I gonna play? It hurts a lot, there's always cysts.

DON: Well technology moves ahead, you know.

GEORGE: Well technology is ahead, man, it just pisses me off that the doctors tell me they can't fix this! They attach hands and fingers! The tendons separated and so now the bone has moved over. The bones are against each other, there's nothing in between them.

DON: So you have a lot of pain?

GEORGE: A lot of pain. I have no more cartilage. But that's my fault. It's not playing piano. I fucked it up by playing pinball. My nick name was Pinball George!

DON: Oh, that's right!

GEORGE: I made so much money playing pinball machines, more money than I did playing music! You know, but it fucked my hands up.

DON: Yeah Vince said something; "I got a feeling this pinball fucked up George."

GEORGE: That's exactly what did it. I will admit it.

DON: Well you verified it. He wasn't really sure.

GEORGE: I mean, pinball and piano playing too because I'm hammer-hands, I play hard.

DON: Me too, I'm feeling it back here.

GEORGE: That's neither here nor there now. I am what I am now.

End: George DiQuattro

A Diary of the Underdogs

Interview: Vince Lateano-jazz musician, drummer- with Don Alberts-February 18, 2009- in San Francisco-about: Bop City, Groove Holmes, Bishop, Both/And, Kent Glenn, Haight Levels, Jazz Workshop, El Matador, Montgomery Brothers, Wes, Billie Hart, Eddie Duran, Bill Douglas, Vince Guaraldi, George DiQuattro, Burt Bales, Ernie Figueroa, Marty Marsalis, Cuz Cousineau, Pat Henry, Bennie Barth, John Markham, Steve Atkins, Al Obidinski, Don Piestrup, John Mosher, Playboy Club, George Muribus, John Rae, Lenny Lasher, Purple Onion, Hungry I, Clyde Pound, Scrooge's Bar, Johnny Baker, Gene Warren, Los Lobos Lodge, Richie Goldberg, Jules B., Bajones, Eddie Marshall, Mike Nock, Ron McClure, Keystone Korner, Deno and Carlo's, Virgil Gonsalves, Dewey Redman, Bill Atwood, Pianos, Drive by gigs, Wash bag, Dick Fregulia, Johnny Baker recording, Bob Maize, Tom Madden, Record Plant, Dick Whittington, Dexter Gordon, New Orleans Bar, Frank Tusa, Chet Baker, Richie Cole, Al Cohen, Jack Sheldon, Woody Herman, Hair Musical, Julius Simmons, Tom Ruderic, Vaughn Aubrey, Ben Vereen, Bob Burgess, Sal Nistico, Frank Tibeiri, Alan Broadbent, one hand drumming, Kenny Williams Drum shop, Jerry Gilmore, Cameo Club, Roland's, George's cigar store, pinball, music business, players attitude, Happy house, Flip Nunez, Noel Jukes, Clarence Beckton, Larry Vuckovich, Marian and Dick Richards, Lawrence Marable, Ole Kalmire, Iron Sandal, Ronnie Ennis, Swinging Lantern, Orange Villa...Sacramento..

VINCE LATEANO

DON: Did you know anything about those guys there?

VINCE: Well, I went to Bop City once, Mel Martin and I came up from Sacramento.

DON: Yeah, Mel Martin talked about that, you guys used to go to Bop City and then you would go to Jack's

(continued)

and then you would go to the Blue Mirror.

VINCE: I remember Bop City, I don't remember going to Jack's with Mel. I remember we came up from Sacramento and we were both about nineteen.

DON: Yeah, you are both kind of the same age?

VINCE: Yeah we are.

DON: And Joe?

VINCE: Well, Joe is a year older then us. Anyway, Mel and I came and Flip was playing at Bop City with Jimmy Lovelace and I think Monty Waters. I remember we gave Flip and Jimmy a ride home, and we knew Flip from Sacramento, he used to come to Sacramento to play. And actually I met "Lace" in Sacramento. I was home on leave from the Army and he was playing with Groove Holmes in Sacramento, they had some gigs....

DON: I can't remember who Groove Holmes was, was he a Sacramento guy?

Vince Lateano

VINCE: No, Groove was from New Jersey somewhere. And he lived in L.A. for several years but he was getting ready to leave. Anyway he was doing this gig in Sacramento and Lace was playing and he couldn't make it and Mel and I were hanging out one afternoon and we ran into the guitar player, Gene Edwards. He was in the neighborhood and was just walking around. And so Mel stopped and started talking to him (Groove) and said, yeah, we need a drummer, Lace is hung up in the Bay Area and we need a drummer, and so I ended up working two days with Groove Holmes!

DON: Was that before he had a record?

VINCE: Oh, no. He had already been in L.A. for years. And he was bugged, he didn't like L.A. In fact, one time we were talking and he asked me what I was going to do when I got out of the service. And I said I didn't know and I said that I was thinking about going to L.A. and he said, *no, man, don't go to L.A. – if you want to play Jazz – go to Oakland – you will play more Jazz in Oakland then in L.A.* This was 1965 or 1964 or whatever it was. And that was just because he was bugged about L.A.

DON: Well, he played the Half Note down there on Divisadero didn't he?

VINCE: Well, I don't know. I don't know what he did around here because I wasn't here until 66, until the fall of 66. And I knew Kent Glenn.

DON: I was going to ask you about Kent.

VINCE: Yeah, Kent......I have a cousin that is a year younger then me- Tony, and he lived here before I did, he was a drummer also. He turned me onto Kent Glenn and Bill Douglas and Bill Atwood and Vince Wallace. You know all those guys, and Bishop. And I used to come down here and hang. I spend a year in Sacramento when I got out of the service in 65 because my Father was ill and then he passed away and then I moved up here. So, I already knew those guys, but I didn't know, there was a whole scene here I didn't know about – you know? The music business I didn't know about because Kent and Bishop and Vince were all playing on Haight Street at the Jukebox and that was my entry into San Francisco. Started playing there and hanging out at the Both/And and the Workshop was just running out and I think the Blackhawk might have been over by then.

A Diary of the Underdogs

DON: Blackhawk was over in 63.

VINCE: But the Haight Levels was a good scene and of course the Both/And that is where you saw everybody. And the Workshop was still going – oh yeah – I saw Trane there and Cannonball and British Moon.

DON: Yeah, I started coming to the City in 1960 to play with Norman – Bishop – that was at the Coffee Gallery.

VINCE: Oh you were way ahead of me. Uh, the Matador was gone.

DON: Yeah, I would like to find a picture of that somewhere. Who was there when you were there?

VINCE: Well, Vince and Cal played there a lot. I saw the Montgomery Brothers there; Wes and Buddy and Monk.

DON: Before Wes had taken off?

VINCE: Well, I think he had already done something – this was 66 or 67, I think he was already on the map wasn't he?

DON: I don't remember what year. He left the Montgomery Brothers.

VINCE: Well, I think he left, but then I think they re-formed. But anyway, Billie Hart was playing drums; I remember that, that is where I met him. He was playing at the Matador and I was playing across the street at the Workshop with Eddie Duran. And you know, you cross the street, you go see each other, that's how I met him. Eddie was the first guy I played with that had some recognition. I remember playing a lot with Kent and Vince Wallace and Bill Atwood and those guys. I think Bill Douglas was playing with Eddie every once in awhile and he introduced us and I started playing with Eddie. And then I started playing with Vince….

DON: Yeah, Vince and John Mosher?

VINCE: Yeah, and then I started working with George DiQuattro.

DON: Vince Guaraldi we are talking about right?

VINCE: Yeah.

DON: Because there is another Vince – Vince Cattolica.

VINCE: Right! And I played with him too! I played with him at Pier 23 with Burt Bales. Yeah. And I knew Jerry Butson. Did you know who Jerry Butson was?

DON: No.

VINCE: He was a trombone player. Jerry Butson was in on that – I don't want to say Dixieland scene, a better word – Traditional, Swing; good players, but anyway- Burt Bales and Ernie Figueroa.

DON: He was around then? I need to talk to Waldo Carter about that.

VINCE: Yeah, Figueroa.

DON: But he was always a Big Band guy wasn't he?

VINCE: No, no.

DON: Did he go around and play small groups?

VINCE: Oh yeah. There was a band that came – I remember when I was still in high school – there was a band that came from the Bay Area – I think it was Marty Marsalis. What the hell did he play? I think he might have been a piano player. But anyway, they came to Sacramento and Vince Cattolica was in the group and I had a connection – my Aunt worked with his sister in Sacramento and my Aunt…

DON: Musician?

VINCE: No, my Aunt worked at a department store. And she asked me about him and I said I had heard him and she told me that she worked with his sister and that he was coming to town and he is going to stay with her if you want to meet him. So me, and another buddy of mine went over to meet him. And we went to hear him play; he was playing at a pizzeria in Sacramento. And Figueroa was on the gig and Jerry Butson, which is when I met those guys; this was maybe 58 or something. And Cuz Cousineau was playing

drums.
DON: Yeah, Cuz Cousineau, you know who talked about him was Dean Reilly.
VINCE: Oh yeah. Did you know Cuz?
DON: No.
VINCE: He was a pretty cool guy.
DON: Yeah, colorful guy right?
VINCE: Yeah and he had that radio show – he was on KJAZ.
DON: So that was Pat Henry and Cuz and some other guy?
VINCE: Yeah. And Cuz got a rehearsal band here that used to meet every Monday or Tuesday night – at that park on Duboce – do you know what park I am talking about? Duboce and Market there is a park up there. And there is a recreation center and the band would meet there. And the band was so loose, oh, my God! People just wander in and everyone was smoking shit and you're talking, and every now and then you would play a tune and take a break and smoke some more shit. And everyone just ended up playing three tunes; it was just a great hang.
DON: So was Fred Murgy in the band?
VINCE: No, Murgy was already established, the established guys - established meaning that they stopped doing rehearsal bands and all that stuff, they were actually working gigs. Bennie Barth, Dean and Eddie Duran, Murgy and John Coppola, Bill Perkins and Chuck Petersen and all those guys they were already doing some of the work around here. John Markham was across the street at Bimbos.
DON: And who was the piano player? George DiQuattro was too young for that?
VINCE: Yeah, George was.
DON: Had to be John Marabuto or somebody…
VINCE: Marabuto, John Price, Steve Atkins. Those guys were doing all that stuff, Mosher, Obidinski, all those guys.
DON: This is just in rehearsal band….
VINCE: Yeah I was just getting acclimated with meeting guys and going from one scene to the other. Speaking of rehearsal bands, I started doing Don Piestrup Monday night band, over in the East Bay.
DON: Yeah, that was a good band.
VINCE: Yeah, a very good band. Bill Atwood and I and I remember we use to pick up Jules Broussard and he used to go over there all the time, someplace over in Oakland. And when I was doing that band I met a bunch of guys, that's when I met Markham. Markham would do that once in awhile. John Markham. He had everything sowed up around here!
DON: Yeah! He was the guy on the gig!
VINCE: Couple of live TV shows he and Vinnie did. He did theater work, he worked with Sinatra. I met him, I was doing a gig with the Piestrup band and we started hanging out and talking and he started using me as a sub and that opened a lot of doors around here for me. Yeah, he was doing all this stuff. And he would go out for weeks at a time with Sinatra and I would sub for him over there and play all these shows and do all this stuff and then I just started meeting those guys, Steve Atkins, Mosher and all those guys. And it was a great circle to be in. And I was just moving around and trying to keep playing. And Steve Atkins and John Mosher and I got this gig – or Steve got the gig and hired me – to do this gig at the Playboy Club. That's where I met Al Plank.
DON: Was he already there?
VINCE: Yeah, Plank was there - he was there from the beginning.
DON: And didn't he have Tom Reynolds and Puzzie?
VINCE: Tom Reynolds and Puzzie, yeah. That's where they played the shows, the showroom and then they had – downstairs in the living room – they had a trio. And so, Steve and John and I started playing there.

A Diary of the Underdogs

And so I started hanging out with Puzzie and Reynolds and Plank. There's like a whole different group. And then I met a lot of guys who were working around here. George Muribus – I started working with George…

DON: Was George in the Playboy Club?

VINCE: Yeah, he would do some of it too. He would sub. You know, we were all kind of subs. And George was doing the Purple Onion. John Rae was playing the drums…

DON: Vibes too?

VINCE: No, just drums on this show. Lenny Lasher was playing bass. And I started subbing on that gig!

DON: Did the Purple Onion have a Jazz group or was it like a back-up a show?

VINCE: They were all, well not all, but even with Steve at the Playboy, we had to back a singer.

DON: Not of your choice.

VINCE: No, whoever was working the showroom would come down and we would play. We would play trio stuff until the singer came down.

DON: Who would the singer be-somebody we know, or locals?

VINCE: I can't think… like no name people; no, not the big names. Anyway, the same with the Purple Onion, usually there was a singer and a comedian. And they would bring in bus tours and the trio would play and they would start the show and all that stuff. The Hungry I was going. Bennie was playing over there with Clyde Pound, the piano player. Bennie and Dean and maybe Mickey McPhillips might have been playing over there. But there were all these little scenes. And then there was a great hang, because there were so many musicians in that neighborhood in North Beach….did you ever go to Scrooge's?

DON: No.

VINCE: A great little bar on Columbus and right there almost at Jackson, right there on the same side of the street as the Purple Onion, just down the street, towards Clown Alley.

DON: Was Clown Alley there?

VINCE: Yes it was the original one. And everyone would got to Scrooge's, this funky little bar, it was great! And it would just be wall to wall musicians at 1am and then they would throw us out and then we would be on the street carrying on… you know?

DON: It was a good time!

VINCE: Yes, very much so.

DON: That was the old Hungry I on Jackson?

VINCE: Yes.

DON: And then, the Hungry I had shows in the main room and they had a lobby trio didn't they?

VINCE: It might have been more like a piano bar, outside the main room. I don't think it was a trio.

DON: Buddy Mottsinger, Don Asher?

VINCE: Yeah, something like that. Yeah, so I met a lot of guys and I continued to play with Kent and Johnny Baker. That's when I first met Johnny Baker when I first got here.

DON: Was that more like the Fillmore or the Haight?

VINCE: Well, yeah, he was never in the mainstream of players, you know? In fact I went back to Sacramento…

DON: Wasn't that where Johnny was from?

VINCE: No, Johnny was from here. But I remember I moved here in 66 and when I went back I was here about a year, maybe, and then I got this gig in Sacramento and I went back for three or four months. Well, wait, maybe it was before I moved here, I was working in Sacramento…yeah, that's what it was, the year I got out of the service I was working in Sacramento with this tenor player, Gene Morris, great tenor player. He used to play with Lionel Hampton's band, he was a fixture in Sacramento. And he always had a gig at a strip joint or something. Anyway, I ended up playing with him before I moved here. And somehow, I met

A Diary of the Underdogs

Johnny Baker. Right, I met him in Sacramento; he had a friend there that he would hang with, this bass player. And I got him on this gig with Gene Morris. It was a trio gig, no bass, just piano, drums tenor.

DON: Strip gig?

VINCE: No, it was a motel/restaurant called Los Robles Lodge and it was great, it was right on the highway there. Great scene and great hang there in Sacramento. And so, Johnny did that and I used to pick him up every night. Sometimes he would be ready, sometimes he wouldn't. Johnny, man…he was with Cheryl, did you meet Cheryl?

DON: Yeah.

VINCE: And you know, it would be….deep, man, deep. Anyway, that was probably the longest gig he did, he was there for months. And I was picking him up and taking him home….and he was great. Gene Morris loved him.

DON: He was a very strong player.

VINCE: Oh, yeah. He would eat the piano. It was just a little spinet and he would just gobble it up.

DON: He was from San Francisco, huh?

VINCE: As far as I know, he was a native. His name was (I'm not even trying this one 19:48).

DON: He was Greek.

VINCE: Armenian. He was my favorite! But nobody really liked him.

DON: He could really swing!

VINCE: Oh boy! He was really something else. He was like a wild horse. There was no taming him either, he would come in and his eyes would be blazing and he would just sit down and eat it up.

DON: Yeah, I met him because I was hanging out at Bop City, I think I was playing there. And he would always come in and sit in.

VINCE: He played vibes!

DON: I never heard him play vibes. Now was Richie Goldberg around at all?

VINCE: Yeah, Richie was around. When I first ran into him he was playing with Jules Broussard at Storyville. But before it was Storyville it was called…..can't think of it. Anyway, Jules and Richie were playing there. I would see Richie around once in awhile and I got to know him better later, when we were both hanging out at Bajones.

DON: That was on Valencia? Was that 70's?

VINCE: Yes to both. Richie and of course Eddie Marshall…

DON: When did Eddie get started around here?

VINCE: Well, Eddie came I think, after me, in the late 60's. He moved out here. I think he was on the road with Dionne Warwick and he came here and liked it and stayed. And you know, he played with everybody. He played in that band that he and Mike Nock and I think Ron McClure and…can't think of the fourth guy, they were called The Fourth Way, with violinist Mike White.

DON: Oh, that was a good band, they played the Both/And.

VINCE: Yeah. Anyway, Eddie, you know and Keystone Korner, I got to see Eddie a lot because he was playing there. He was the house guy.

DON: Did that start in the late 70's?

VINCE: No. Not sure.

DON: I know I was out of town then. But before Keystone Korner there was a little joint there called Deno & Carlos. Did you know Deno?

VINCE: Yes. I met Deno probably in the early 70's because my ex-wife, who I wasn't married to yet, worked just down the street here on Stockton and Filbert. There was a little office that was the West Coast office for McGraw, Hill Publishing. And they had a film outlet there: "West Coast Films." And my ex-wife, Vicki, was a secretary/receptionist there and the woman who ran it had been married to Deno. Her name is Barbara Taylor. And that's how I met Deno, they were divorced but they were still friends and he would come around and I got to see him once in awhile. Nice cat.

DON: Yeah, that is interesting. There was a place called Deno and Carlo's over on Vallejo in north beach. That was a small venue and the Hells Angels liked to hang out there, they had a little upstairs and they would go up there and get drunk and they liked the Jazz and everything. It was one of their hangs. I went to the gig one night and Russo had the gig, it was a duo on a Sunday and he sent somebody else to play, and the guy got there early before I did. And I drive up there and the ambulance is driving away and I said, what the hell happened? He had said something wrong to the Hells Angels and they got him good and the ambulance took him away! And they said, "That's your bass player!"

VINCE: You know what? I bet I have been in there, I was in there. You know, I did go in there, because Kent Glenn and Bill Atwood and I and I guess it was Bill Douglas, I'm trying to think who the bass player was…we used to play everyday at somebody's house. I rented a piano wherever I lived so we could play. I didn't play, but I had it in the house. Just a little spinet, you know. And we used to go and make auditions and it would be like a hit and run – we would drive up to a bar and we would go in and I had this little set of drums, this little tiny thing I could carry with two hands. Snare drum and a little tom-tom for bass drum and a ride cymbal and we would go in and we would set up and we would play and try and get a gig. And I know we went into that joint. I know it! It was great; it was like a drive-by man! Those guys would be in there sitting and drinking and they would be like – what the hell is that? And then we would be gone.

DON: Yeah, Virgil would do the same thing, he would go in and bring a baritone, very impressive, and then Virgil would go over and talk to the guys and pretty soon Deno & Carlo are old friends with Virgil! He had that way of doing that. And that's how we got in and we were all messed up and none of us were responsible.

VINCE: You know what's different is that all the bars had pianos. There were a lot of pianos. They weren't always in very good shape, but all the joints, there was a piano somewhere.

DON: Mike's Pool Hall had a piano! Of all places!

VINCE: Yeah, and now nobody has a piano! You know going back to the time when there was a piano player in the joint, even a bar!

DON: Yeah, like the Wash bag, been doing it for years. I just talked to Dick Fregulia, he said, *thirty-three years at the Wash bag, I can't believe anybody can be playing piano that long in one place.*

VINCE: Yeah, and Mike Lipskin. You knew about the Johnny Baker recording right?

DON: Oh, I know about the vinyl, you and….

VINCE: Bob Maize.

DON: Oh yeah, Bob Maize, and Kent Glenn produced it, yeah?

VINCE: Yeah, Kent Glenn took it from an old cassette tape that I had of it, I couldn't get the…well, here is how it went down: I had been doing a little bit of jingle work at this one studio, I got to know this engineer and it was the Record Plant over in Sausalito and especially in those days that was a big deal – you know first class studio, rock and roll and all that. And so I got to know this engineer and I asked him if he ever recorded Jazz and he hadn't but he really wanted to. And I asked him if I could get some studio time, you know, I would pay for it and he agreed. And so, a window opened up and I got John and Bob and we went over to the studio and we started playing. And it was the same thing, the guy futzing around and futzing around and by the time he would get ready to do something, we had already been playing. And Johnny was starting to get real antsy because he had to go and cop and he couldn't stand the earphones and he threw them down, he hated the earphones, *I can't play with these!!* And anyway, that recording was like that and Johnny was just getting real….but the fact is if the guy had it ready when we sat down to play, we would have got a lot more.

DON: Right, but you ended up doing about ten or twelve tunes?

A Diary of the Underdogs

VINCE: I don't think we had that many....

DON: I had a copy of that. You know who has it know, is Tom Madden.

VINCE: Yeah, I think I have one copy of it. I had a couple but gave them away.

DON: Well that's pretty interesting, that became a real thing, huh? And that's probably the only surviving recording?

VINCE: I know. And I couldn't get the master because I didn't have the money, he wouldn't give it to me.

DON: Does it exist somewhere – somebody else?

VINCE: If anybody had it, it would be the Record Plant and at that time they wanted $1,200 or $1,500 or something.

DON: So, back to names – did you ever get together with Sal Mosca or Dodo Marmarosa?

VINCE: No, missed them. Dick Whittington. I still play with him once an awhile.

DON: But he was here, he was in the City for a long time.

VINCE: Yeah, I met him, like late 70's, he had been around, he came up here from L.A. with Dexter Gordon and liked it and stayed. And then he got his teaching credential. I met him...I'm trying to think what gigs we did together. We did a couple of gigs together. And then he got the gig in at that place in Montclair, New Orleans Bar & Grill. You ever know about that?

DON: No. In Oakland?

VINCE: Well, Montclair, yeah, Oakland, way out Park Blvd., a real nice part of the area. And he was living up there in what I think is called Skyline.

DON: Was that the place on Euclid in Berkley that he finally turned into a performance space and produced all those recording, the Maybeck?

VINCE: No, that came later. That was Maybeck. No, he was living up on; I think it was called Skyline, beautiful neighborhood up on the top of this hill. He got this gig at this place called the New Orleans Bar & Grill, he knew this family, basically it was like this fish house that sold fish and it was just this little restaurant. And at that time Cajun cooking became the rage, spicy flavors and all that, blackened red fish and that sort of thing. So they started this restaurant, this family. The sons ran it and Dick had done something for them, played a gig or something and they asked him to put some music in there and so he and I and Frank Tusa played there. And then he would bring in Bruce Forman and then he would bring in Chet Baker or Richie Cole, Al Cohn was in town, I played there with Al. That was a very nice gig and that lasted about three or four years. Jack Sheldon came in. But I had already played with Jack a few times.

DON: That reminds me, how did it work out with Woody Herman's band?

VINCE: The guys in the band recommended me. They were looking for a drummer and I was here playing the musical HAIR. It had just ended.

DON: Was that at the Curran?

VINCE: Well, we did six months at the Geary and then a year at the Orpheum, year and a half.

DON: Pit band kind of thing?

VINCE: Yeah. We were on stage, parked in a truck in the dark. It was great. It was fun! We had a ball. That's where I got tight with Coppola, Chuck Peterson and Julius Simmons was on it, did you know Julius?

DON: No.

VINCE: Guitar player. He was on it, two guitars, Tyrone Schmedlin, changed his name to Tyrone Dorian a few years later. Those were the two guitar players. Tom Roderick, bass player, young bass player who moved here right after that, he's in Idaho somewhere now. Anyway, Vaughn Aubrey, piano player, he was from Reno. Anyway, we did that show, Bill Atwood and it was such a great gig, just sat up in the dark and we just played the music and when it ended it sounded like Duke Ellington plays HAIR. We had our own way of doing it.

DON: How big of a band was it?

A Diary of the Underdogs

VINCE: Two trumpets, trombone, saxophone, drums, percussion, bass, two guitars and piano, an electric band of course. And as you looked at the stage to the right, there was a flatbed truck parked there and the band would sit in the flatbed and we had the music memorized and we just sat in the dark and played.

DON: Was Don Haas or somebody like that in there?

VINCE: No, Vaughn Aubrey. They had a book, you know, we had to play the HAIR show.

DON: Yeah, and the show was pretty interesting itself, especially from backstage.

VINCE: Oh yeah! It was crazy, all these hippies and young kids and some good actors, Ben Vereen did it for awhile with us, a great singer and dancer. And some other less known people, but good. And then there was always the hang, you know. And everyone liked to come into the band room because we always had a card game going. Before the show there was a card game and there were breaks in the show and we would go downstairs and play cards and we could hear the show in the monitors and we had a cue and then we would have to get back. And then after the show we would hang and it was so cool. And then that ended and I got this trumpet player from Woody's band that was from San Francisco recommended me and so I joined the band outside of Chicago, that lasted about three months and a summer and I was really struggling, I had gone through this thing with tendinitis in my right forearm, I was playing hard and a lot and doing some things wrong and I thought I would play through it but I started having these problems and it just got worse and worse and when I was with Woody's band it really got bad and it was just a miserable time, struggling.

DON: Did the band record while you were with them?

VINCE: No. I waited till the band got back out here and then I quit because you know wherever you quit, you got to pay your own way home. So, I had to hold on and we were you know, in New York, Philadelphia, Detroit, all over the place, but not out here.

DON: So what version of the band was that? Woody's band?

VINCE: Well, it was 71, I guess. Sal Nistico was in the band and Bobby Burgess, trombone player. And Frank Tibeiri of course, he was in the band forever. Alan Broadbent was doing like right and left stuff; so, I got tight with Sal. Sal was great. I saw him a few times after that, whenever he came to town we would hang and he would stay with me. He was just beautiful besides being a great player.

DON: Was Virgil on the band at that time; because he did something with Woody?

VINCE: No he wasn't. I think he did something with Woody before. And so anyway, when I finished with that, I came back to San Francisco and I could hardly play. I couldn't work my right arm; it just didn't want to respond. So, I stopped playing and I just couldn't do it.

DON: Did you think it was over?

VINCE: Yeah! I started going to doctors and wondered what the hell was going on. I was getting all these opinions and I didn't let anybody cut me, I am glad of that. And they would be like, *well, we could...* and I didn't like the *well, we could,* sounds like in the end, maybe we could or maybe we couldn't. In the meantime I would be stuck with their handiwork. And so, I just stopped playing and I will never forget George Muribus got this gig at the Holiday Inn over in Richmond and he wanted me to play this gig with him. And I said, *man, I can't do it, I can't play.* And he says, *well, just play with one hand!* I swear to God that's what I did! I laughed and I said, *you got to be kidding!*

DON: Which hand?

VINCE: Basically my left...my right arm was screwed up. And he said, *can you play with your left hand?* I said yes. And he said, *well, just play with that!* And I thought he was completely nuts, but I said I would try it. So, we were at his house and I got my high hat and my ride cymbal and my snare drum and my bass drum and I put the ride cymbal over by my high hat, by my left hand, and I started playing. And it was weird, you know, at first, but pretty soon I realized that I could play time and I could get things going with the feet and I could play little fills and before I knew it I realized I could play a gig. Conceptually I could play and once I started getting comfortable playing with my left hand and the more I did it the more I got comfortable with it and I started gigging again! With just my left hand!

DON: So this was the opposite set up!

VINCE: Yeah, and I could play! I could play fills and stuff! I could play gigs! I could play different grooves and keep time.

DON: And you could still get your famous swing on the cymbal!

VINCE: Yeah! And the only thing I couldn't do was roll!

DON: Yeah, how are you going to roll with one hand!

VINCE: Well, Buddy Rich could roll with one hand! Yeah, the rolls were funny, but I started gigging man! And I started getting confident and people started calling me for gigs. And I would just rest my right hand on my leg or I would put it on my tom-tom or something. And I would play with one hand and I did it for over a year. And regarding my right arm, I didn't know what was going to happen and gradually it started coming back and I think it was because I laid off. And I figured I got myself into it by playing badly or incorrectly and too hard and everything and I just let it take its course.

DON: Do you still have to favor it a little bit now?

VINCE: It still reminds me that I did something to it. Sometimes when I start playing before I am warmed up it won't respond very well so I have to just hang in there until it starts to respond and just keep stuff going.

DON: Yeah, some of that physical stuff with playing music.

VINCE: Yeah!

DON: So do you think it happened because of Woody's band?

VINCE: No, no, it happened before that. I think doing HAIR, it was pretty physical, playing hard and loud and playing a lot, the show was two hours. Really, it was just playing wrong. And when I wasn't gigging I was jamming. And so I was playing ALL the time. And every moment that I was awake I was playing. I just wore it out.

DON: So, I guess that is what happened to George DiQuattro he got carpal tunnel?

VINCE: I met George in an interesting way, when I first moved here there was a drum shop around the corner from the musicians union in the Tenderloin, called Drum Land, Kenny Williams. He had that for years and years. Great place! Great hang for drummers. I make rehearsal bands all the time at the union and then I would go in and hang with Kenny in the late afternoon, go in and have a beer with him, he always had a little beer in the fridge and we would sit and bullshit. And I am in there afternoon and I was just starting to meet guys, I was kind of brand new, and the phone rings and Kenny is talking to this guy and he says, *well there is a guy right here, new guy.* And Kenny says, *you ever play for strippers?* And I said, *Yeah!* And so he had me talk to the guy on the phone and it was Forest Ellige, Forest was a drummer from San Jose, or from that area. And he was playing this gig in Palo Alto at a card room, the Cameo Club.

DON: Yeah, I played the Cameo, many, many times.

VINCE: Well, George DiQuattro was playing there.

DON: Well, he got the gig from me!

VINCE: Yeah, I'm sure. George and Jerry Gilmore were playing there. And so Forest was the drummer and he was sick and couldn't make it, and this was like 5pm and the gig was at 8 or 9pm. So, he was in a panic and he didn't have time to go through my resume. Can he do it, yeah! I can do it! And so I show up and there is George. I had never met George. And you know George, he is very animated, smoking and talking, you know, very friendly and very nice and he made me feel comfortable right away. He was like, *wanna a drink? Yeah, come here!* I played the gig and we hooked up-musically and otherwise. (Mmmm) And we started playing together a lot, he would get a gig and he would call me and we did a lot, Roland's, the Weekender, the place on Hardy Street, and we played Holiday Inns. Yeah, George got around pretty

A Diary of the Underdogs

good and I always liked playing with George, great swinger, great feel. And he played good Latin. His Father had a little cigar store, right up here on Columbus, where that alley runs into Columbus at an angle. George's Cigar Store, his father was named George too! And George used to work there during the day sometimes and help his father out. And so, I would go by there and hang out and see George. And he had an old style beer case, where you get the beers out, icebox, and a couple of magazine racks and cigars and a pinball machine! And George played that pinball machine for years, and I think that is what screwed his hands up. I mean George was heavy-handed anyway and he hit the piano pretty good, but I think all those years at the pinball machine took its toll on his hands.

DON: He doesn't want to play anymore…

VINCE: No. He had to make a decision. But after all that I went through to learn to play with one hand…..I kept going, I really like to play! And the guys I play with are like that, that's why we play together. I like guys who wanna play. And think of all the gigs we have played sick as a dog or whatever, and we just do it. And the music transcends all of that. And you don't think about it and then when you are not playing, you're sick. I am glad I didn't get discouraged with this arm thing, and also I didn't want to miss the scene and the so-called music business. But I am not in the "music business", I mean I play. And all these guys that play Yoshi's and the so-called "main" clubs, how do they exist? Because there are so few of those and they don't play nickel/dime gigs. But one thing about doing nickel/dime gigs as I call them, but regular gigs, is that they keep you in gas and groceries.

DON: Oh yeah, well you always come to a gig in a very positive manner. That's what I try and do. And guys who think like you do, music happens and it works. Now days these cats are having music wars with each other. They try and out do each other. It was kind of like that at Bop City, it became an athletic event.

VINCE: Yeah, I think as you get older you distance yourself from that athletic event syndrome where you have to prove something. And the longer I played I figured out what my part was in making this thing happen.

DON: Yeah, it cooperation.

VINCE: Yeah, and when you play in a rhythm section-that is your section! Those are your boys and girls. And you wanna hook up and you psych each other out and then you meet somewhere. So- it's a matter of how are we going to make this happen. And then there are the horn players or the soloists and how are we going to make them sound good. I think you learn this stuff as you go along. And so in the beginning you are just going along trying to figure stuff out and you hear somebody play and you say, why can't I do that or how did they do that, or how can I make mine do that.

DON: You know they are writing about you on the internet.

VINCE: That's what you said.

DON: Yeah, it's a nice thing; it's about the Dog Patch. And everybody's getting their shot; Michael and Rich and you- they just kind of hit on everybody; the doorman, the doorman's girlfriend. Actually I was on the internet looking for your bio. I got a short one off of there. OK, got anything you want to add? The Happy House we talked about a little bit.

VINCE: Well, I got there towards the end of all that, I knew it existed from Flip, Flipper talked about it all the time. I knew Flip – in and out of Sacramento-and Noel, Noel lived downstairs there; and Clarence Becton, real good drummer. Clarence played with Larry Vuckovich and Bob Maize when they left Jon Hendricks. And Clarence lived under there too and everybody used to stay there and hang there. And then I got to know Marian and Dick Richards, the owners. They had a place in Sacramento….

DON: The Swinging Lantern.

VINCE: Yeah! Did you play there?

DON: No, I just knew about it.

VINCE: I went there, I was still in high school, and maybe I was in junior high…..anyway. I saw the

A Diary of the Underdogs

Montgomery Brothers there; the first version of the Montgomery Brothers.

DON: Ole Kalmire?

VINCE: No, well, it might have been. When I heard them, Flip was playing with them at the Swinging Lantern and Lawrence Marable. Ole Kalmire, there was a place in Sacramento also called the.....

DON: Iron Saddle.

VINCE: Oh, you know about all this! Did you play there?

DON: No, I have been doing this for awhile!

VINCE: Yeah, the Iron Saddle. That is the first time I saw Flip and met Flip.

DON: Yeah, I think Mel Martin told me about that.

VINCE: And Ole Kalmire was there with somebody. And Dave Pike used to play there. He had a house gig there with a local drummer too, Ronnie Ennis, good drummer.

DON: So, Richards had that club first....

VINCE: They had the Swingin' Lantern; I don't know what they had before that.

DON: They had the Swinging Lantern and then they got the Happy House.

VINCE: Yeah, and then they moved to the Bay Area. Did you talk to Noel? He will fill you in on that one.

DON: I heard one story that Wes Montgomery was staying there because he liked Marian. I think Art Lewis told me about that. Anyway, I didn't know Flip was interested in their daughter and they got married.

VINCE: Yeah!

DON: And so that was it and Art said something about Flip used to have hives and stuff and he would scratch them out and this girl would come down and give him massages.

VINCE: Yeah, he was great. I miss him.

DON: There was a place in Sacramento called the Orange Villa?

VINCE: That was an after-hours place way South of Sacramento, Southern end of town. When I was in high school it was hard to hang out at some of these places because I was under age.

End: Vince Lateano

Interview: Terry Hilliard-bassist, and Dick Saltzman-vibist- with Don Alberts-July 13, 2009-Bird and Beckett Books-San Francisco-about; the Jazz Workshop, Art Aurbach, John Coltrane, Monday night jam sessions run by Dick Saltzman, Dave Pike, Fred Murgy, Bobby Maize, Chuck Travis, Red Rodney, Bob Cedar, Max Hartstein, Gary Miller, Brew Moore, Dottie Dodgion, Arthur Fletcher, Solomon Grundy, Stan Popper, Pony Poindexter, Ernie Hood, Buzz Eatry, Bill Hood, Kenny Dorham, Wardell Grey, Bob Skinner, Vernon Alley, Back Stage on Powell, Earl Watkins, Blue Mirror, Johnny Mathis, Jerome Richardson, Ernie Royal, Elsie's Breakfast Club, Sammy Simpson, Richard Wyands, Tin Pan Alley, Lawrence Kato, Paul Desmond, Chez Perez', Eddie Duran, Strip clubs, Virgil Gonsalves, Meryle Hoover, Mike Downs, Red Mitchell, Jerry Coker, Rudy Salvini, Benny Barth, Playboy Club, Al Plank, Tommy Reynolds, Beatles, Bartender Jimmy, Miles Davis, Black Hawk, Helen Noga, Guido Ginatolli (Black Hawk) Teddy Noga, Brew Moore, Cal Tjader, Al Zulaica, Coke-Pete Escovedo, John Rae, Dave Brubeck, Burma Lounge, Eddie Coleman, Sonny King, Vince Guaraldi, Lonnie Hewitt, Al McKibbon, Mongo Santamaria, Willie Bobo, Al Torre, Don Manning, John Handy, Dick Berk, Federico Cervantes, Smiley Winters, Palladium, Skippy Warren, Richard (notes) Williams, Leo Wright, Union-local 6, Eddie Burns, Pop Kennedy, Black Union, April 1967 (end of black union), Saltzman on Ecuador.

After interview: Story about Miles Davis at the Workshop: Art Aurbach dies, his wife calls Dick Saltzman, what do I do, Miles Davis Trumpet is here, I want to return it? Miles is at the Crown hotel down Columbus Street. Dick takes here there. She finds his door, calls Miles and says, "My husband has died, I have your

A Diary of the Underdogs

trumpet, I don't know what to do." Miles opens the door and says, "Get in bed with me!" She returns to the car and says to Dick, white faced and humiliated, "That son of a bitch!"

TERRY HILLIARD and DICK SALTZMAN

TERRY: I had the Jazz Workshop. I was working with Cal Tjader in the 60's. And I was with Cal and our home base was the Matador.
DICK: You were on the road.
TERRY: I was on the road most of the 60's.
DICK: Ah, that you were. Because I missed you and at that time I had a band with my ex-wife who was a singer in, Tom Hart was the saxophone player. And it was Chuck Travis for a while. And I had the Monday nights at the Jazz Workshop. I ran the jam session. I was barely, as a drummer I could have done it but I was playing vibes at the time and my boss was Art Aurbach.
DON: Yeah, he owned it then. What year was that; early 60's?
TERRY: It was early 60's, yeah.
DICK: We used to have jam sessions every Monday night. And guys would come in – it was a cutting session.
DON: Yeah, they all were. Just like Bop City.
DICK: And my boss trusted me, Art Aurbach, he said, *Dick, I don't care who comes in, if you don't think they should play with a guy they want to play with don't let them do it. And I will back you up.* And I would say, like you would come in and you would be perfect with him on bass and so I would wait and orchestrate it. Guys used to come in and I was telling him about Dave Pike, he used to walk in and just destroy me, just destroy me.
DON: Dave Pike the vibes player?
DICK: Yes.
DON: Was he from L.A.?
DICK: Yes. He was quite a fine musician boy! He wiped me out. But I heard Coltrane the first time, the first time he played San Francisco, at the Workshop; he played one tune for forty-five minutes.
DON: I think I was there.
DICK I was on the bandstand and I didn't play a note! This was on a Monday night.
DON: Oh, so he came into the session. Oh, ok. I heard the performance, not the session. That is phenomenal. What kind of guys were in their rhythm section there?
DICK: At that session?
DON: Yeah, who were your regular guys?
DICK: Well, I had Red Rodney for a while. Trumpet player. Somehow he matriculated to town. I had a guy named Bob Cedar; he was a very strange saxophone player. Fred Murgy, Trombone player, but he was playing piano. He played very good piano. I am trying to think of the bass player's name –
DON: Norm McKay – was he in there? Max Hartstein?
DICK: Max Hartstein, some of the time on Monday nights. Who in the hell played bass…
DON: Bob Maize?
DICK: Yes; we had Bobby Maize, and also Gary Miller, a very good bass player. Anyway, those were the Monday night sessions. And they went on for about two years. And we had Terry, but he was traveling, but when he would come back he would play with my little Mickey Mouse dance band. He would play with my little band that I had doing casuals.
TERRY: But I worked there with Brew Moore during that period.

A Diary of the Underdogs

DON: OK, who would be in that band?

TERRY: Dottie Dodgion played drums.

DON: Was she married to Jerry Dodgion at the time?

TERRY: They may have been. I met her originally at the Cellar on Green Street. Wejohn was it?

DON: Yeah, Wejohn. And what was his partner's name? Sonny?

DICK: Sonny something.

DON: Drummer?

TERRY: Don't know. He did some playing at the Workshop, can't remember who was on piano.

TERRY: Might have been Arthur Fletcher.

DICK: Vince Guaraldi played with Brew Moore some of the time.

TERRY: It might have been Arthur. But

Dick Saltzman

we used to play a lot together during that period of time. And we used to play at Solomon Grundy's in the East Bay. And then we played a lot of gigs in San Francisco.

DICK: He has played more gigs then exist in the world.

DON: Dick you were on a lot as I remember it.

DICK: I was, but not anywhere near as much as he was.

TERRY: I was thinking about Stan Popper and Pony Poindexter.

DON: Was Pony around here for a couple of years?

TERRY: Yeah, for a couple of years.

DON: That was up at the Coffee Gallery, he was up there a lot. And Nancy King was there. I'm going to Portland to interview Nancy King. And Sonny King was up there, Sonny passed away up there.

DICK: Were you from there?

DON: No, I was from here, but I escaped to up there for twenty years and had a whole different life.

DICK: Was the Hood Brothers there then?

DON: Ernie Hood and Bill Hood were up there.

DICK: Ernie Hood was a guitar player who played with Charlie Barnett, Buzz Eatry was the name of the guitar player with Charlie Barnett's band, he got killed in an automobile crash and they had the chair on the stand with Barnett's band for two years with no guitar player. And they mourned his death and they hired a guy named Ernie Hood who played with a wild band, a genius.....

DON: He was a good arranger too.

DICK: Oh, a good arranger, he could beat you at pool and write an arrangement at the same time. I knew him. Anyway, he got polio. And I remember a picture of him, where he was all twisted from Polio. And he had a rubber hose around him and it was a Christmas card - Merry Christmas from Ernie Hood. And his brother's name was Bill Hood. Bill could write two arrangements one with each hand; and a hell of a saxophone player.

DON: Yeah, Bill would come in. He wasn't playing a lot; he was kind of taking care of his brother. His brother was in kind of bad shape. There were a lot of people that really knew about Ernie Hood. When Ernie Hood came to town the news spread pretty fast.

A Diary of the Underdogs

DICK: Oh, tell me about it he was...I heard a tape, well you know Dean Reilly, the bass player, he has a tape that Ernie Hood has something to do with Charlie Parker, I believe, Something about Ernie Hood being in L.A. when Charlie Parker came to L.A. and the people were putting him down.   You know natural resistance to something new. And Bill Hood or one of the Hood brothers on the TV said, hey, you people are idiots. He was saying it to some big shot. He was saying, what's wrong with you! I remember listening to that – Dean Reilly's got that. Dean Reilly has a lot of stuff.

DON: Yeah, he gave me a great interview. I need to go back and see him because I failed to get one of the most interesting things he offered me, a picture of a check from Benny Goodman! So, tell me a little bit about the Tjader band.

TERRY: We had a lot of fun!

DON: Who was in that band at that time?

TERRY: Lonnie Hewitt was on piano, Armando Paraza on percussion, John Rae on vibes. The Matador was on Broadway.

DON: What year was this?

TERRY: Mid 60's, 63 to 66.

DON: Where you ever in the band with Al Torre?

TERRY: No. But I played with Al. We used to work with and piano player, Dick Whittington- Plaz Johnson group. We had a little group for a while. That was a good group. But that is as much playing I did with Al. But Al was in the band before I was in the band.

DON: So, that band was traveling in and out of town a lot?

TERRY: Yeah, we spent, as a matter of fact I moved to New York for about a year or two during that period.

DICK: Yeah, that's right, I remember that.

TERRY: Cal didn't care where I lived because we played half our jobs on the East Coast. So I just moved to New York. I lived on 125th -down in Harlem. I knew I had a lot of friends in New York. It was great. That place is just the place to be, especially in the 60's. You just heard everybody.

DON: Yeah, and there was a general attitude of New York musicians to help each other too.

TERRY: Yeah, they were very helpful. You had guys like Bob Brookmeyer hanging out there. Clarke Terry.

DICK: Yeah, you are younger then me.

TERRY: Yeah. It was sure an interesting time. It's hard to talk about because there was so much going on. We were doing so much traveling and we had that Soul Sauce album was kind of on the charts.

DON: Yeah, there was another one too.

TERRY: Soul Berg. We did both of those albums in New York. Creed Taylor was the engineer for those.

DON: Who later got his own label, right?

TERRY: Yeah.

DON: So how much older are you Dick than Terry?

TERRY: I am seventy-three.

DICK: I am eighty-three. I got to play with Kenny Dorham, you know what I mean-and the guys before him; Wardell Grey. They were all passed away by the time you were a baby.

DON: Yeah, ten years makes a lot of difference.

DICK: I remember I was in a band with Vernon Alley; Bob Skinner on piano. I was playing drums. Jerome Richardson was the alto player.

TERRY: Bob Skinner was wonderful to play with. He was fun to play with, a fun guy.

DICK: He was – I can't explain it to you – those days – we rehearsed at Vern and Ali's place on Post. He had a one of those Brownstones. We rehearsed in the living room.

DON: Yeah, talk about Vernon. We lost him you know.

A Diary of the Underdogs

DICK: Yeah, I know. But how can I explain it to you, it was the first mixed band in San Francisco; more or less. I was telling him they picked me out of a jam session at the – it was called The Backstage right on Powell Street. It was all sofas facing the bandstand. Anyway, Vernon decided to use me on drums and I took Earl Watkins place. And Earl Watkins called me up on the phone and I had told him about it and he said he was glad that I was going to take his place, a real nice guy. It was a different attitude in those days, that ten years really made a difference. The Fillmore used to be like a microcosm of New York.

TERRY: Yeah. I used to work at Blue Mirror, the lobby show. We did those shows with Johnny Mathis at the Blue Mirror, with Virgil and that band.

DICK: Well, right, and back to Vernon. It was kind of tenor, bari and alto. It was Jerome, and Ernie Royal was the trumpet player. Wardell Grey was the saxophone player.

DON: What were those guys doing in town? Just passing though?

DICK: He was just passing though. He was a remarkable guy. Do you know the Breakfast Club? That was before Bop City.

DON: Was that down on...?

DICK: Fillmore and Sutter, up three flights. I was just a kid. I used to play there. And then downstairs was the fighter, Harold Blackshire had a club downstairs and this is before, I guess this is before; it was a two to six in the morning club. Beautiful, red and blue and Harold Blackshire was a fighter who looked like Joe Lewis. And he wasn't too good of a fighter but they used his name to open it and man it was a disaster financially. But it was the hippest club probably any where. All the big stars would come. I saw Billie Holiday there and they would come in an sit in.

DON: Would you say this is mid 50's?

DICK: I guess it was late 50's. And I used to go up to Harold and take the money out of his hand to pay the band. Richard Wyands, he was in town.

DON: He was San Francisco guy before he left to go to New York.

DICK: Lawrence Kato was the bass player. Qudelis Martin had the band. Paul Desmond was the alto player. And I was the drummer.

DON: How many nights a week was this?

DICK: Five nights a week!

DON: A real gig!

DICK: Yeah, a real gig- 2 to 6 in the morning.

DON: What kind of money did you get- seven or eight dollars?

DICK: Financially it was kind of a disaster.

DON: Yeah, because Jimbo was paying six bucks. And Soulville was another place that we played. And that was six bucks and that was it.

TERRY: Yeah, that was it. That was the going rate.

DON: But the thing about it – you could work another gig.

DICK: Well, you would have to you – exactly!

TERRY: Dick, did you ever play the Streets of Paris?

DICK: Oh, yeah, I played the Streets of Paris.

TERRY: That was a real nice club.

DON: Yeah, Si talked about that. Si had a gig there.

DICK: This was before all those guys.

TERRY: I used to play there with Sammy Simpson.

DICK: Yeah, but this is even before that! I worked for a guy named Sid Wolfe who looked like Edward G. Robinson and he was a gangster and he owned all the clubs in the Tenderloin. And one of the Clubs was the Tin Pan Alley, on Eddie around the corner. Then I worked at the Streets of Paris. At the Tin Pan Alley one

A Diary of the Underdogs

Terry Hilliard

night he comes up and walks in and he has a bag full of money and he throws the money in the bag – six cash registers, three times a night, whatever falls on the ground he doesn't even bother to pick that up! And he looks up at me and Paul Desmond was – we were over the stage you know, and he says, *Get those brushes away from those drums!* He pulled them out of my hand, he stood up on a chair – and said, *Play the sticks!* And he walked out of the club. Desmond was playing alto at that time and we worked there for a long time playing Jazz. It was before the Blackhawk or any of that stuff. That was a long time ago.

DON: Wasn't there a place across the street was a strip joint?

DICK: Not across the street from the Streets of Paris but across from Chez Paris it was called. That is where I first heard Eddie Duran he was playing, he was sixteen years old he was playing in this strip band sounded beautiful! So he was playing up the street and I was playing the Streets of Paris

TERRY: We all played those gigs, we played behind the curtain.

DON: Well, you were lucky to do that because usually the strip bands does not include bass players

TERRY: No, no, I was playing guitar. Guitar and drums that's all we had.

DON: No sax even! You could see the others? You could see the dancers but you always had the scrim.

TERRY: Yeah, the scrim, you could always see the silhouette.

DICK: Oh, I can't tell you, I played six nights a week, 8 – 2 in the morning, if the comedian wasn't playing you didn't get an intermission. Three shows a night. One singer, I will never forget her, very sultry like Marylyn Monroe, that kind of thing, she kissed me one New Years Eve and I fainted! I was just a child and she grabbed me and kissed me! We used to work so hard, my hands used to be sore from playing. The strippers would get mad at you, don't blow the whistle at the right time or hit the cymbal they would stop dancing and come after you!

TERRY: We worked a lot. Weekends we worked almost around the clock and played those things and then played the after hours things. And then go play a breakfast gig.

DON: Any breakfast clubs that you can remember?

DICK: Don's something, Don's? Coffee Don's-it was a breakfast club.

DON: I worked Coffee Don's, I worked 2-6.

TERRY: You played Jazz on Sutter, right?

DON: I never played there, I went in a lot.

DICK: There was one on Geary; I don't know what the name of it was. Too bad, those places were good music.

A Diary of the Underdogs

DON: We used to party all night, there were no restrictions. No curfews and the cops didn't role up the streets and we just kept going.

TERRY: We would take our breaks and go down to the Streets of Paris and hang out.

DON: Tell me about the Virgil band.

TERRY: The Virgil band was a great band. I met them at San Francisco State. I was going to San Francisco State and I ran into Virgil and Meryl Hoover was playing piano, and Danny Patiris and Bobby Poolrod. That was a good band. And Mike Downs was playing. Trumpet player. Meryl was on the road with Anita. And Arthur Fletcher took Meryl's place in the band. Then we started playing in L.A. so Art and I drove to L.A., Warren Mitchell had a flophouse down there for musicians and we stayed at his place. It was down, just down wherever it was in L.A. We were playing like the Hollywood and Western somewhere in that area.

DON: Who was booking the band – Virgil?

TERRY: Yeah. And then we would play all these parties that would hire us up in Beverly Hills. Art and I would do duets and we would play all these parties. So we stayed around L.A. for a good year.

DICK: Virgil was remarkable.

TERRY: It was a lot of fun. Virgil was from Monterey. His family was from there.

DICK: People loved him. When his band played a gig, everything was right. It was nice.

TERRY: And then Jerry Coker came into town and started teaching at Monterey Peninsula College. So we all went back up there to play in his big band. So, Virgil and all of us were playing in Jerry Coker's big band at Peninsula College.

DON: Yeah, Jerry was writing right?

TERRY: Yeah.

DON: And then he had his teaching method.

TERRY: Right. That was fun. So we did that for a little bit and then ended up in Santa Cruz area in the summer, playing resorts. We just stayed around and played around all summer. And in the fall, we played the Monterey Jazz Festival.

DON: Wasn't Virgil included in the very first one?

TERRY: It was 1958 when we were there. I don't know if they started in 1958. I still have a recording of it; the sessions of the Rudy Salvini Big Band with John Marabuto and all those guys and the Masters Sounds with Buddy Montgomery.

DON: And Benny Barth and Richie Crabtree.

TERRY: Right. And we hung down there for a good week. Just hanging and Diz was down there and we had jam sessions. Folks were just jamming; it was a big music scene, all over town, nothing but music.

DON: Yeah, downtown they had a comedy club.

TERRY: All these clubs and there was music everywhere.

DON: What do you think happened in the late 60's?

TERRY: Well, late 60's I was playing with the Playboy Club.

DICK: Yeah, there was a carry-over of the Hungry I and the Playboy....

TERRY: Yeah, and we were doing that, and Al Plank and Tommy Reynolds were around.

DON: Took Puzzie's place?

TERRY: Yeah. That was a good period of time. That was the later part of the 60's.

DICK: That's when, well, my two daughters announced to me that the Beatles were the greatest thing in the world! Nothing against them but it was like a curtain came down, I can't remember the day, I can remember the frame of mind. And when they announced to me that Chuck Berry was now number one, I couldn't believe it.

TERRY: We got a lot of commercial gigs. I remember the Happy Day Choir at the Love Center (yeah, I

A Diary of the Underdogs

sang a lot with the Gospel Choir at Love Center and the Hawkins Family) we played with them and we did shows with Credence Clearwater and Jefferson Airplane. So that was all happening in the late 60's. So we started doing commercial gigs.

DON: Well, yeah that's when things changed, Bill Graham and Chet Helms. And I think the influx of Acid changed people's minds. And the Haight became a real destination. It had an effect on things. But during that period, Blue Note was still sending guys out to the Workshop and Mingus was around and Miles was coming to town.

DICK: It was amazing that they made money because the Workshop…I was kind of close to them, I ended up selling furniture to Art Aurbach and his wife. He was a lawyer, he wasn't a musician. He had two things – he knew exactly what to do with the musicians, and how to treat them otherwise they would have run his place into the ground. And he had a bartender named Jimmy who could hold a bottle of whisky up high and the glass down low and pour exactly one quarter of an ounce. It looked like Niagara Falls. They sold drinks for 50 cents; they used to have Miles there for $25,000! For the big names they would pay a huge amount of money. Where did they get all that money?

DON: Yeah, well the strip clubs were doing ok too.

DICK: Yeah, they were doing ok.

DON: There were people on the street and it wasn't dangerous.

TERRY: No it wasn't and everyone was happy.

DICK: Yeah, at 2am you would be in front of the Workshop with fifty people, just standing there talking and having a good time.

TERRY: Yeah, you didn't get hassled by the police.

DON: Mike's Pool Hall down the street, everyone would go down there and eat.

TERRY: Yeah.

DON: I guess Vanessi's wasn't there?

DICK: Yeah, it was – for awhile.

DON: So we had the Matador, we had Jazz Workshop, we had Basin Street West. That's Broadway pretty much.

DICK: It was starting to wane even then though. The strip type of thing, Go-Go dancer, it was encroaching on that scene. But the Workshop really held the door.

DON: Yeah, and then we had the Black Hawk down there for a while.

DICK: Yeah, that of course was a major thing.

DON: Yeah, I am still trying to get pictures of the interior of the Blackhawk. I have talked to Helen Nova's daughter, she is in L.A.

DICK: I remember the night Helen Nova discovered Johnny Mathis.

DON: She became his manager…

DICK: She got on the stand, he sang two tunes, Helen Nova came from behind, she was the cash register lady. She got up from the cash register, closed the cash register, walked over and grabbed him, I don't remember if they signed something, but they hugged and she walked out the door, the next thing you know there was an article in the paper – Washington High School track star something – and she built him into a million dollars inside of about two or three years. I remember the night it happened. It was amazing. Those two guys, they weren't really Jazz club owners. Guido and…what was his name?

DON: Guido's partner? I thought his wife was his partner.

DICK: Well, but there was another guy with Guido. He was something that Guido…

DON: So Guido wasn't a Noga?

DICK: No, he wasn't a Noga. Guido Ginatolli was his name. No wait, I think Ginatolli was the guy who used to own the 365 Club, Bimbo's. But Guido's last name began with a G, and Teddy Noga was his

A Diary of the Underdogs

partner.

DON: John Handy told me something about they had a hole where they passed the money up to the upper apartments. They were very successful.

DICK: Yes, they knew how to merchandise our music to make it – to get it off the hook of having to fend for itself. Those guys were terrific.

DON: Well, I am thinking of a little place where Brew Moore used to play out on Taravel or something like that.

DICK: Yeah, I can't remember that place. He used to play a place on Arguello, right across from Roosevelt High School; he and Vince Guaraldi. It's a veterinarian place now. But it was a bar then. Brew would blow! Yeah, he did a little sideways thing. He was a very nice person.

DON: Well, Eddie Duran mentioned that he played with all those guys in various combinations.

DICK: Yes, true.

DON: And I ran into a girl named Linda Zulaica who is Al Zulaica's daughter. She comes around to the gigs once an awhile and sings.

TERRY: Yeah, I brought Al into the Tjader band. We had a little Salsa group with the Escovedo Brothers. Al, Coke, and Pete and I, and Lonnie left the band and I recommended Al. I stayed with them for another six months or so.

DON: Where you with that last band when they were in the Philippines?

TERRY: No, I left the band in 67. And Al was still with the band, he stayed right until the end.

DON: So is the story that Tjader had a heart attack in his hotel room…

TERRY: Yeah, that's what I heard, in the Philippines.

DICK: They probably could have saved him if he had been here. He had problems, cigarettes and whisky.

TERRY: Yeah- Whiskey, yeah.

DICK: Had nothing to do with drugs. He called me up one time for a little advice or something in those days, and he had it all backwards. Unfortunately then, which means use more cigarettes and whisky. And that's what killed him. He would go into the Matador and he would sit in the corner of the bar and before that band started he had four double shots of Scotch! To get up to play the first set!

TERRY: Oh, it would get so bad sometimes he couldn't stand up anymore. So John Rae would play vibes and put him on the drums. Cal on the drums!!

DON: Tell me a little bit about John Rae.

TERRY: John Rae was just a monster! His mind was amazing. He could remember all these details of all these people, phone numbers, so he managed the band because he could keep info in his head. Anytime we went anywhere he would call ahead and have everything set up, everything organized, he knew where to stay in every town. And he would drive that van across country all by himself. And he would stop off in all these towns; he had friends all over and would hang out. He knew everybody across the United States.

DON: Wasn't he the guy who answered the phone for Local 6.

TERRY: Yeah. That was later on.

DICK: I used to say, *Hi Johnny, how's it doing?* And he would say, *Well, Monday I am at the Curran, and Tuesday I am at Golden Gate……* He was working all the time.

TERRY: He was a great manager.

DICK: He was hell of a good musician.

TERRY: When we did Be-bop, I read a play with John rather than Cal. John could kick it, oh, those Be-bop tunes.

DON: And he was a drummer too…so he could do Latin and all that stuff?

TERRY: Oh yeah!

DICK: Went I went with Cal, he went into a place on Fillmore Street, the Blue Mirror, and he was playing

A Diary of the Underdogs

vibes and bass and piano or something. And I used to come in and sit in and this is before he became famous, and I used to come sit in on drums so he would have a rhythm section. So we played there a lot. And then that Latin thing happened and he turned it right into an instant hit. And then one night, Brubeck called me up, I played with Brubeck in the beginning, and I told him that he should try Cal Tjader and he went over to the Burma Lounge in Oakland, right by the Grand, and next Jimmy Lyons heard him and two weeks later his face was all over. He went right from unknown San Francisco musician to world famous. Then Cal went with Brubeck and then he went with Shearing and then he got his own band with Armando and then Terry got in the band.

DON: So you were in one of the early bands?

TERRY: No, Al Torre was before me. And guys like Eddie Coleman. He was a bass player and used to play a lot with Sonny King. They had a group in Eugene.

DICK: Well I guess he had gotten into the Soul Sauce thing when Vince Guaraldi was a piano player. That band was kicking!

TERRY: That band just went to another level with Lonnie Hewitt and Verve was really promoting us. And we started seeing the tunes on the charts.

DON: Yeah, Lonnie Hewitt was the match.

TERRY: Yeah, that was it. It got a little soulful and it was interesting.

DON: So, early on was probably Al McKibbon?

TERRY: Yes. All those guys played with Cal. Mongo played with Cal; Willie Bobo, and of course the Duran's. The Duran's played with Cal.

DON: Carlos and Manny…

TERRY: Yes, all of them. Cal had a lot of bands and a lot of gigs. Al McKibbon sounded great with him.

DICK: You were talking about somebody, Spider? That played bass with Cal? Can't think of his name. He had a lot of great and quality players.

TERRY: Yeah, it was there. But when he got John Rae to manage that band it really tightened up. We had so much work it was ridiculous, we couldn't play all the gigs. We just couldn't do them all, we were doing promotional gigs with General Motors. Advertising the Mustang and we would hook up with acts out of Vegas and play those. John Rae, just had it hooked up.

DON: Did he have any problems?

TERRY: No, just women. He had women everywhere.

DICK: He had one family with four or five kids and another family with six kids, that's what I heard.

DON: I returned from Oregon in 92 and one of the first things that happened was there was a funeral for John Rae. At St. Peter and Paul and I ran into Al Obidinski, who I didn't know, I knew he was a musician and I said what's going on and it was John Rae.

DICK: Was Portland a good Jazz town?

DON: Very good.

DICK: I played at a place called Jantzen Beach.

DON: Oh yeah, the big band used to go there.

TERRY: Yeah, Leroy Vinnegar was up there quite a bit. I ran into him a lot. He loved to play.

DON: Yes he did love to play. And he loved to play the real stuff. And Leroy could play ballads. And he would play that note that you didn't think anybody knew about. He had a great musical attitude.

DICK: Dean Reilly said that there was disc jockey up there in Portland that loved Charlie Parker…

DON: Don Manning.

DICK: Don Manning! That's the guy! One of the most progressive disc jockeys ever!

DON: He is still on the radio, little tiny station called KBOO.

DICK: No kidding!

A Diary of the Underdogs

DON: Another friend of mine has a show up there, I just talked to him recently, Bob Riddle. The last I heard the local drummer Ron Steen has jam sessions six nights a week at a different place. And Dick Berk, do you know Dick Berk?

DICK: I was thinking of him, is he still around?

DON: I got an email from him.

DICK: Would you tell him hello from me?

DON: I would be glad to. I told him I wanted an interview with him.

DICK: Is he still heavy?

DON: Yes.

DICK: My family was in the furniture business, and through the business the Berk's were a middle class couple who played Bridge with the groups, some rich some poor and their son was Dick Berk. So when I was at the Jazz Workshop, my father said to me, Dick Berk's parents said for me to help him out, he wanted to become a drummer. So he came into the Jazz Workshop, a little kid, and I remember helping him a little to play and I tried to help him. Two years later he was playing the best drums I had ever heard in my life.

DON: And he got the gig at Bop City.

TERRY: Yeah, there is a nice video out on that. Check it out; a bunch of guys on it, Eddie Kahn.

DON: And did you know Federico Cervantes?

TERRY: Oh yeah. I used to work with him.

DICK: I saw him one night at Bop City they were playing *Cherokee*. And he would change keys every eight bars. He had the sax player's hair turning white!

TERRY: Yeah, he would drive people crazy. He had Smiley Winters on drums. We were just wailing. We would run the horn players off the bandstand! That was the thing to do. That was so fun, we would change keys and go faster and faster.

DON: Yeah, it was an athletic event; you had to be in shape.

TERRY: Yeah, true. We also did clubs in the East Bay, the Palladium and places like that. Good players- Skippy Warren, and Smiley Winters- played there a lot and Richard Williams, "Notes" Williams. They would run everybody off the bandstand, those guys would get up there and shoot.....And that's when Les McCann was in the navy and Les would try and get behind the piano and he wasn't that good. He was trying, but just no good!

DICK: Yeah, the Cellars, Richard Williams, Leo Wright was the saxophone player. He went to Germany and Richard Williams became a famous trumpet player.

TERRY: Yeah, "Notes" Williams.

DICK: I was learning to play the vibes then, I was on the floor, and they were on the stage, so they would blow their spit valves all over me. I would spend all day in the furniture store, drive back to Marin County, pick up my vibes and walk down those stairs so I could play eight chorus' a night, maybe. Depending on what they let me play. That's how I learned to play.

TERRY: Yeah, it was like a family, we all knew each other. It was a good time.

DICK: Yeah, the Union was great. Need a gig – and it would be you play here and etc.

TERRY: Yeah, in the East Bay all the hotels were all Union. And unless you had your card you couldn't even play. And they had guys who went around and checked on you. And they would have fired you if you weren't Union.

DICK: Eddie Burns was our agent. His real name was Tupo and he had two gorillas that whenever you went into his office, there would be these two guys standing there, these big tough looking guys. But he liked me; I took Pop Kennedy's place in the Streets of Paris. Pop Kennedy was the President of the Union. And he was a tough son of a bitch!

TERRY: Yeah, this guy tried to join the Black Union! They wouldn't let him in!

A Diary of the Underdogs

DON: Who was running that?

DICK: It was upstairs.

DON: I didn't realize there was a separation.

TERRY: Oh yeah. And you could only play certain parts of the City too.

DON: So that's why the Fillmore became famous?

TERRY: Sure.

DICK: Well partly, yeah. When are we talking about, the 60's?

TERRY: Early 60's. In April of 1960 they merged the Unions.

DICK: Well, in April of 1957 the white local voted down…

TERRY: Yeah, that's right. They got forced by the Nationals.

DON: They did have some power and they made sure things were taken care of. And they had those trust fund gigs. They still do that, I just talked to someone over on Green Street. So, tell me a little about your future and what you are going to do.

DICK: I am going to Ecuador in three weeks; probably for good. I am sort of famous down there in a strange kind of way. I have the advantage of being the gringo and I have the advantage of being married to an Ecuadorian, and a Jazz musician. I don't lift a vibraphone; people do things for you down there.

DON: Got the language down?

DICK: No, I am terrible. I will probably stay down there. It's still like it was twenty-five years ago down there.

DON: Yeah, Mom & Pop stores and the like.

DICK: Exactly.

DON: What about you Terry?

TERRY: Well, I am a life member of the Union, musicians union. I'm still doing that. There is a nice article in their quarterly newspaper. They did a nice article on me. And I still play at Bix. We are doing a lot of great music. Jules Rowel is such a great arranger. I still play with a group out of Napa, with Yancy Taylor. A lot of wine country stuff.

DON: You mentioned that you son was going to try and put a book together?

TERRY: Yeah, he wrote a book called the Soul of Rock'n Roll. It was about the influence of black musicians in Rock'n Roll. And the book has done well. It's on Amazon.

End: Terry Hilliard-Dick Saltzman

Interview: Abe Battat-pianist, singer, bandleader- with Don Alberts-July 29, 2009-San Francisco-about: Black Hawk, Helen Noga Guido, playing piano at the Saint Francis Hotel Compass Room, Roland's, Chet Baker, Mario Serrachi, Eddie Duran, John Rae, Cal Tjader, Vince Guaraldi, Bolo Sete, Johnny Mathis, President Bill Clinton, phantom tenor player with Chet Baker.

A Diary of the Underdogs

ABE BATTAT

ABE: I started with Cal Tjader.
DON: Yeah? Played the piano or vibes?
ABE: Vibes.
DON: Yeah he was a good guy, a sincere musician.
ABE: For a piano player he could be pretty boring, you know. Of course in those days, I mean Cal Tjader, if you look at the current vibe, Cal Tjader's vibe is pretty rustic.
DON: It was smooth, I liked it.
ABE: Yes I always enjoyed his playing. He was a really good drummer and actually, he went with George Shearing, not as a vibist but as a drummer. Yeah- in

Abe Battat

the late 50's. It was a big deal with Cal and Shearing. That was a huge break.
DON: Well how'd he come to prominence? Was it through Brubeck or something, as long as we're talking about Tjader? Or Jimmy Lyons promoted him? All of a sudden, this guy was there, right? Where was he from?
ABE: No, it wasn't all of a sudden. There was a group of people that were involved with Fantasy Records, the Fantasy record label. Brubeck was the mainstay of Fantasy. As Brubeck really started to sell, they had money to invest in new artists. (Max Weiss and Saul Zaentz)
DON: …And that was over on Tweet Street in the Mission, wasn't it?
ABE: Treat Street, yeah.
DON: I've been to that studio.
ABE: Yeah. So they had enough money to invest in newer people. So they started recording Cal. Then after Cal came it was Vince Guaraldi and Bola Sete. And then I did an album for Fantasy also.
DON: Oh, great! How'd that work out?
ABE: Well it worked out great. One of the tracks was a pretty good hit.
DON: I didn't know that you did something with Fantasy, that's news to me. Who did you have in your band at that time? Was it a trio recording?
ABE: Yeah.
DON: Anybody I might know; a drummer?
ABE: There were a couple of drummers. One was Gus Gustavson…I'm not sure if Vince Lateano is on it or not. Oh, that's a good question…
DON: Well we won't press it!
ABE: Let me see if I can find it! (Abe leaves table in search) You know Jim Stewart, the guitarist?
DON: No, I don't. Abe's going to find his first record he did with Fantasy…With drummer Joe Dodge…"*Once Around the Block*" with Abe Battat on piano. Oh that's great! San Francisco, Fantasy Records, High Fidelity. This would be what year?
ABE: The 60's.

A Diary of the Underdogs

DON: Oh they've got all of Fantasy's records listed on the back here. So we got personnel: Abe Battat, piano, guitar; Jimmy Stewart, bass; Jack Weeks and Wyatt Ruther!

ABE: Yeah.

DON: …Joe Dodge and Gus Gustavson. I had a chance to play a little bit with him. (*Reads titles*) Luck Be a Lady, Who's it Gonna Be, Listen Baby, Once Around the Block.. Side two is Shenandoah, Once You Were Mine, And I Love Her, There must be a Pony Somewhere, one of Batatt's compositions! *"Autumn Afternoon,"* written by the bass player. *"Once is Enough,"* written by Battat. *"Once Around the Block,"* at the piano, Fantasy stereo number 8368! Probably out of print by now?

ABE: Probably, yes.

DON: Well congratulations on that Fantasy Records, High Fidelity. And the year we're guessing is- late 50's?

ABE: '62 probably.

DON: (Reading) "National exposure was received in 1963 when Abe's first recording, *Once is Enough* was introduced on radio station KSFO and subsequently became one of the bigger hits of that year. Based on that- Abe was nominated to the Playboy Jazz Poll in that year, 1965."

So I had a couple of things I wanted to talk to you about. Of course, I'm real interested in the Chet Baker stint at Roland's when you were the house piano player. Of course this is early 70's, late 60's I would say. 1968- '67 maybe?

ABE: Ah well it was later than that. It was- '72 maybe, '71-72. I could find out because I have some press on it.

DON: Yeah, but *your* version of what it was like there? You had the house gig?

ABE: Yeah, a trio gig.

DON: On Sundays, or more than one night a week?

ABE: 6 nights a week… I wanted to go hear Charlie Bird play with Joe Pass at the Great American Music Hall. It was my night off; it must have been a Monday night. I was standing at the bar in the back and they introduced Chet Baker. And he came up and played.

DON: Really? Was it a big surprise?

ABE: Yeah. They just asked him to sit in.

DON: At the Great American Music Hall?

ABE: Yeah, it was really terrible, awful.

DON: What do you mean awful, he sounded bad?

ABE: He sounded really bad! 'Cause he had been in jail in Italy. They had beaten him severely and knocked all his teeth out. It was really difficult. And he was trying to get off of heroine. So he was on methadone. So when he finished playing, he came to the bar to get a drink, and I said, you know "It's nice to see you and hear you again". He said "Oh, it's really terrible. I just can't get back to where I was"! I said, "You know, you just got to keep at it. Practice everyday and play as much as you can." I said, "I have a gig out in the Marina if you ever want to come by to play with us, you're welcome to. It's not a big deal." So, sure enough he showed up! So we got along great. The next night he showed up again and again. Then Herb Kean found out about it and printed it in the paper. The next night there was a line outside the door.

DON: Oh my god!

ABE: People wanted to come in and hear Chet Baker. Chet saw that, and he figured he just better get paid! So he wasn't in the union. Oh, the union heard about it. They were going to fine me for allowing a non union player to sit in.

DON: That's right.

ABE: Imagine that, Chet Baker!

DON: Yeah!

A Diary of the Underdogs

ABE: So anyway, the owner of the club and I went 50/50 and paid his way into the union. So then he started getting paid, playing every night with us.

DON: So he was showing up on time and doing the gig?

ABE: Sometimes, yeah, he showed up on time. Sometimes he didn't show up. It was not a definite commitment. it was just that if he wanted to come out and play, he would get paid so much a night.

DON: Yeah. What do you think that was at that time? Was he asking for a whole lot of money?

ABE: No, he wasn't asking for a whole lot, but it ended up he owed a whole lot of money because then he started wanting advances, and then advances on the advances. Then he started meeting people in the parking lot and getting back to his old ways again.

DON: Yeah.

Abe: Then one night he said to me, "I'm going to be gone for a week". I said "Where you going?" he said, "I'm going to Las Vegas to play a Jazz tournament"…Or, Jazz-

DON: Festival, right?

ABE: So I said "How did you get that?" he says "The guy who was here the other night in the club". I said "Well, who is the guy?" and he said "Well what do you care?" I said "Well I care about you, you know. You don't just get on a plane or car and go to Las Vegas for some guy you've never seen before". He said "Why not?" I said, "It's not safe. You need at least half the money in advance *and* a paid-for round trip ticket and confirmation in a hotel room for a number of nights, and *then* you go. You don't even get in your car without having all that.

DON: You're right, Abe, you're right about that!

ABE: So he said, "Don't talk to me."

DON: Oh, he got defensive.

ABE: I said, "I'm just trying to"- he says, "Don't talk to me."

DON: I'll be damned…

ABE: So I said, "Okay." So he was gone for a week and came back.

DON: But he did come back?

ABE: I said, "What happened?" He said, "Don't talk to me." I said, "Did you get burned, is that what happened?" He said, "Yeah I did get burned, but don't talk to me." So, anyway, we start playing and he got into it with Johnny Rae, he was playing drums with us. They started arguing about the time and Chet said "We have to replace the drummer." I said, "I'm not replacing John Rae! He's an icon in the world of Jazz!" Plus John was playing other gigs with me, on vibes. So Chet Baker left owing us all money, a *lot* of money. And I never saw him again.

DON: That was it, huh?

ABE: Never heard from him again. I was happy to have played with him. Then he died…And I found some recordings, some tapes that we made together and I thought "Gee, he owed me all that money. Maybe I could put out some recordings, *Abe Battat and Chet Baker,"* (*Laughs*) But then I was afraid I'd get sued. I'll tell you when he died. So anyway, that's the Chet Baker story.

DON: Yeah well that's a pretty good story, Abe, I appreciate that! What about inside the music, anything going on there? Like, what did he like to play? I know he liked to play ballads like, "I Love You" and you used to play all those standards.

ABE: That's why we got along!

DON: Because of your sympathetic agreement on all those tunes, right?

ABE: I loved those tunes and all that music… I mean I really love melodic music, you know? That's why, when I first started trying to play Jazz, being a piano player you ended up in jam sessions, 3 horns, each horn taking 8 choruses and all you're doing is just comping! Then you play a couple choruses for a solo, bass player takes a solo, drummer takes a solo, then the horns play more…And I thought "This isn't

A Diary of the Underdogs

music!"

DON: Right...

ABE: I mean, it just wasn't music to me, sorry!

DON: Yeah, you're not getting what you want.

ABE: So anyway, Chet Baker was born December 23rd, 1929 in Yale Oklahoma. He died in Amsterdam, May 13th 1988.

DON: Oh, that's quite a while, 10 years later in '88. Did you ever meet Diane?

ABE: No. (*Reads)* "Specializing in relaxed, even melancholy music, Baker rose to prominence leading Cool Jazz in the 50's"...And his good looks, he had movie star looks.

DON: Yeah.

ABE: He was hammered by drug addiction. Then he was imprisoned.

DON: Where was he imprisoned?

ABE: He was in prison in Italy, I remember that.

DON: Oh the Italians, yeah.

ABE: And then he died after falling from a hotel window.

DON: That's the story I got too.

ABE: Yeah. It's too bad.

DON: Well Diane is another side story but Diane, his wife, was a friend of mine.

ABE: Did her mother work in San Jose in a super market?

DON: I don't know what her mother did but they had a house on Alum Rock Avenue, up there, high up above on the east side.

ABE: Where?

DON: On Alum Rock Avenue, a brick house.

ABE: Which town?

DON: San Jose.

ABE: See, because he didn't have a car and he was borrowing either his mother's car or his mother-in-law's car.

DON: Well when I saw him, we used to jam in places around. He'd call me up, "Hey Don! You wanna meet me at this bar?" And we'd go and play, so I'd meet him. I even came to Roland's a couple times with him and I saw you. But he was supposedly living with his mother in Fremont and he was on the Methadone program for a while.

ABE: Oh yeah, that's right.

DON: So I don't know where he got the car.

ABE: Yeah, it was her car.

DON: And he would come to San Jose into Ricardo's Pizza 'cause we all jammed there so we did that. Then he would call me for different things and say "Hey, let's go to the city"! But he wasn't coming to the city to score. He was coming to play at Roland's with you so I ended up coming a few times and I think I sat in on that gig.

ABE: Oh, and Mario Suraci was the bass player at Roland's.

DON: Oh, Mario, yeah!

ABE: Mario Suraci, Eddie Duran and John Rae. And one night Chet came and brought a friend, a tenor player.

DON: Who was that, do you remember?

ABE: No. (*chuckles)* But the guy got his horn out, put the strap on, stood there, we played the tune. Chet played his solo and then turned to the horn player to play and he just stood there like this...

DON: Nothing, eh?

A Diary of the Underdogs

ABE: Just like this…

DON: Couldn't do anything!

ABE: And I just kept playing with Mario. Now everybody in the band is looking at this guy and Chet taps him on the shoulder, "Hey, man, come on!" The guy looks around and just stood back to his position!

DON: (*Laughs*) The catatonic tenor player!

ABE: Mario will tell you. If you get a chance, talk to Mario. He'd be someone good for you to talk to.

DON: Yeah.

ABE: So, it was a really funny night. Mario can describe this guy.

DON: What was the guy's name? Didn't anybody get his name?

ABE: I have no idea.

DON: Where the hell was he from? He's just some mystery?

ABE: No idea, the guy never opened his mouth. Chet picked him up.

DON: The mystery Sax player who never opened his mouth.

ABE: Yeah.

DON: That's funny.

ABE: Chet just said, "You're embarrassing me! Get the fuck out of here!" you know?

DON: Oh really? Was Chet kind of taking over the front of the band when he was around, calling the shots and stuff?

ABE: No. He was at that stage where he was so insecure about his playing that he wasn't aggressive at all.

DON: Oh yeah.

ABE: You know, he was just kind of using us to get his lip back in shape.

DON: Trying to work through it, yeah. I always thought that you were very accommodating for him and I had a lot of respect for that 'cause you knew who he was and you knew what kind of problems he had, and what kind of things might be coming down the pike. I had a lot of respect for that. I mean, there were other people that played that gig but during that period, I remember that it was you.

ABE: Yeah, well the one thing about me that was different from everybody else; I never got into any kind of drugs whatsoever, never even tried it. I mean, I tried to take a puff of a joint one night and my throat got so raw just from that!

DON: (*Laughs*)

ABE: And I'm a singer! I said "Well, I guess I can't smoke grass!" you know? And I was the only one! Everybody else was into drugs!

DON: We were stoners, man.

ABE: You know, guys were dying! I worked with Lane Welch.

DON: Lane Welch the bass player, yeah!

ABE: Yeah, and he died, and then, Dennis the drummer.

DON: Who's that?

ABE: Dennis Allison.

DON: I didn't know him.

ABE: A great drummer. We took him on the road with us to a ski resort for a gig and he went through withdraw while we were there.

DON: Oh, terrible.

ABE: Mario, again, nursed him through withdraw and we fed him, kept him warm, and as soon as he started feeling better, he got into his car and he was gone, right back to the city to score more drugs.

DON: Right back to it?

ABE: So anyway that's I was empathetic towards Chet because I thought he was just too great a talent to down the tubes like those guys did, you know.

A Diary of the Underdogs

DON: He was! Yeah! It's a strange thing. I don't think he thought anything particular of me except that he knew I was a sympathetic drug user at the time and a piano player. We got along fine, he'd call me up and everything was automatic in a way. There was no inquiry or interview and we just got along. But I didn't want to go along with his trip if he was going to go downtown and try to find the guys because I was trying to get away from all that.

ABE: Yeah.

DON: But there was a brief period where I got to know Chet pretty good. We had some nice conversations and played some music together and I think that was important. But I had no idea where he was headed or where he was going or anything like that. He mentioned that he was living with his mother and he was on methadone. It seemed to be holding him. He was pretty much in control of whatever that was. If he was taking his doses on the regular schedule, he seemed to be ok!

ABE: And I think that was only at the times that he was with me!

DON: And that was it, huh? That was the time, eh?

ABE: It was just that one brief window.

DON: Yeah, however long it was; 6 months or whatever.

ABE: Yeah.

DON: So there's probably a lot of history written about Chet Baker but you don't get these stories. These come from personal, one-to-one, you know? But I like what you said about Mario. Mario's kind of a father figure, kind of takes care of people, eh?

ABE: Yeah. I'll tell you this 'cause I've already told Mario this; you can't always believe what he says. He's a very mendacious person.

DON: (*Laughs*) Oh, that's a good word! Not always truthful?

ABE: He would lie when the truth would do, about stupid things. He would never lie to you in a mean way, and he would never lie to you for any kind of personal gain. He just can't help it. He just can't help it. Even though I've told him many times; "I don't believe a word you tell me," he *still* lies to me.

DON: (*Laughs*) When you *know*, you got him!

ABE: He tells stories about the Tonight Show sending a limo for him and taking him to the airport to a private jet to LA to do a session because there was no one in LA who could read the chart or something like that. I mean something so outrageous! But he's a sweet guy and a good friend. He would do anything for you. You could call Mario at 4 in the morning and tell him you're stuck in Antioch or some place and he'd come and help you. So, you know; the other stuff you'd just overlook. So all I'm saying is if he's telling you stories, he embellishes a lot. He embellishes on who he's playing with lately. If you call him up and say "What are you doing next weekend?" It'll be some big deal!

DON: Some big deal and he doesn't have a gig.

ABE: Yup.

DON: Tell me about John Rae. People talk about John Rae as a very heroic kind of guy who kind of kept it all together. At one time he was the guy who answered the phone if you called the Union.

ABE: Yeah! And he had a little room. He lives there downstairs at the Union Hall, sort of next door in a little store front. (*Chuckles*) Women were his downfall.

DON: That's what someone else has said!

ABE: The women…

DON: So he had this charm, eh?

ABE: He had to marry them. If he fell in love with a woman, he had to marry her.

DON: That's puritanical.

ABE: And he kept marrying them and having kids, supporting them.

DON: And it just went on and on.

A Diary of the Underdogs

ABE: How could John Rae end up living in a store front under the musician's Union? This is a guy who played with everybody, first call! Show player, Jazz player, vibes player, drums, teacher...Busy all the time, never a spare minute, busy working, busy making money-

DON: No particular problems, like, he wasn't an alcoholic or anything?

ABE: Getting his cymbals from Zildjian.

DON: Oh, he had endorsements?

ABE: He had this cigarette lighter from Zildjian that said "In Honor of John Rae" and he always showed that to everybody. A wonderful musician, but I mean a *real* musician. Most drummers are drummers. John Rae, God, he would take those tunes apart and put them back together again, take them apart *again*...

DON: He played piano too?

ABE: He played piano with two fingers, one finger on each hand.

DON: Oh because he's a vibes player.

ABE: He had so many licks on vibes, he was really a monster!

DON: Well was there any communication with Cal or are we talking about a period after Cal had died?

ABE: You know; I never knew Cal.

DON: I mean did John Rae happen to?

ABE: Oh, John Rae, yeah!

DON: They must have been friends-

ABE: Yeah, they were.

DON: Through instruments?

ABE: Yeah. I don't remember if John Rae ever played while Cal was the drummer but I think maybe he did. I think he was the vibist and John was the drummer.

DON: Yeah, everything I've heard of John Rae has been very positive on the musician side. It's unfortunate, when I got back here from Oregon in 1991, very shortly thereafter people were going to a funeral at Peter and Paul's Church on Washington square and I didn't know who it was for.

ABE: Yeah, I was there.

DON: But I ran into Al Obidinski and I said, "What's going on?" and he says "This is John Rae's funeral." I thought, "Oh I've already heard of this guy. I'm not going to get to meet him."

ABE: I just saw Al Obidinski on Saturday. I went to the race track and he was there. Yeah, John Rae, he was...the women kept him running. It's too bad, really.

DON: Well what do you think was his demise? He wasn't old was he?

ABE: No, he wasn't old but he was a very heavy smoker and a very heavy drinker. He played Monday nights with us at the Saint Francis on vibes, every Monday night. His fans would come. One of his fans was some guy from Silicon Valley, with more money than God. He'd sit in that little alcove and sit and listen right behind from where John would be playing. When we'd take a break, John would go sit with him and the guy was ordering $100 shots of brandy! John would drink 3 or 4 of those and play the next set. John was very self destructive. I don't know what he died of, but it wasn't...

DON: How old of a man was he?

ABE: 50 maybe.

DON: A lot of my friends died young.

ABE: John Pompeo.

DON: Pompeo? So was he Puerto Rican or Italian?

ABE: Italian. John Pompeo, then he changed it to Rae.

DON: Oh, so he changed it; interesting.

ABE: It was r-a-e and the singer was r-a-y, John Rae.

DON: Ah, to separate himself from that. Well I noticed some information that I got on the internet that you played for a few presidents? What was it like playing for Clinton? What kind of music did he want? What did you play for him? He was then president, right?

ABE: Well it was Saint Francis, so…

DON: As president?

ABE: Yeah, yeah.

DON: With an entourage and security and all that?

ABE: Yeah. I'll show you a picture…

(*Both observe familiar faces with Clinton*)

DON: Wynton Marsalis!

ABE: Wynton and I are friends truly by accident. And this is Elvis!

DON: Elvis with Abe Battat, 1958! (*Both continue looking at various photos*)

ABE: Well, I didn't know exactly what to say to Clinton. People were gathered around, wanting to talk to him.

DON: Yeah well, tell me more about the Clinton thing and what you played for him.

ABE: You know what I said to him…Someone would say "Oh, Mr. President, I'm so-and-so from Fresno" and he'd say "Oh, it's nice to meet you" and go around to the next person. So when he took my hand, I said "When do you get time to practice your horn?" and with his other hand, he grabs my hand. Now he's hold my hand with both hands. He says "Let me tell you what happened to me the other night. I played with the Lionel Hampton band and I sat in with them. We played this and that". So we got to talking and I said "So you're in good enough shape that you can just pick up the horn and play?" he said "Well yeah, if I have just a couple of minutes to warm up, I'm ok". And we had this long conversation while the Governor's waiting.

DON: Yeah, and the world is waiting!

ABE: Yeah, and the world is wondering who the hell am I?

DON: (*Laughs*) that you're getting this kind of attention from him!

ABE: So anyway he was great, I liked him.

DON: Yeah, well I'm sure he's a gregarious, easy-to-get-along-with guy. But he didn't want any red neck music, he just, he liked music, right?

ABE: You know, I make it a habit, if I'm going to meet someone like that, to ask them something…Like Joe Montana, I said "Do you play any musical instrument?"

DON: Got to twist their head a little bit.

ABE: "No, my dad played a little piano" and I say "Oh well you have such a good sense of rhythm on the football field".

DON: Oh, that's a good observation. It's definitely true.

ANE: A lot of musicians are good sportsmen. A lot of musicians are good golfers, tennis players…

DON: And good dancers.

ABE: Dancers? Well I don't know. Not so much dancing.

DON: I tell students, I say "Dancing is part of music. You need the time. Don't be afraid to dance". But coordination, you're right. It comes back to coordination.

ABE: Yeah…So anyway, as far as the Jazz scene goes, I was kind of an outsider because I never got to really meet anybody. I only played with the guys I worked with and I hired a few guys. I was kind of always on my own. I never worked in anybody's band, I never got to meet any of the guys or hang out with any of the guys. Saturday nights we used to always go to Chinatown to the Far East Café and all the musicians would be there. You'd sit around and talk, and it was fun. I never got to play with very many musicians. Which, I didn't mind at the time but there are people that have critiqued my playing, who never actually heard me play-which really used to bug me.

DON: It's like making a review without *going* to it.

A Diary of the Underdogs

ABE: Yeah. They'd call me a "hotel musician"…

DON: who's successful!

ABE: Well yeah, but I was also playing with the best Jazz players in town.

DON: 'Cause they all needed gigs!

ABE: Yeah! I didn't care why they were playing with me, we were having fun.

DON: Sure! And you're playing on good pianos. I'd play a little Jazz club, play an out-of-tune piano and some of those don't work.

ABE: Yeah, and the owner wants to know why it wasn't tuned at the factory!

DON: Oh yeah, that's a good response.

ABE: Nah, I couldn't handle that. The first time I started playing Jazz, I'd say "What do you mean 'the check bounced'?" (*laughs*)

DON: Those insights, I think, are part of us. They're part of all of us. I think about that stuff. I mean you start talking to other people, you realize they were the same stuff, you know?

ABE: Well, there is a life. I mean there's a sports life, a political life, and there's a Jazz life.

DON: Yeah, so we're finding out.

ABE: And the Jazz life is not for everyone. It's really not. Not if you want to settle down, get married, have a family, have a nice place to live, you know? You're not going to get that, being a Jazz player, very often. There's only room for very few successful people in the Jazz world. And when I was coming along, if you were white it was 2 strikes against you right there. In fact, a funny story, when Vince Guaraldi made that Black Orpheus album that was such a hit, and recording with Bola Sete, there was a tour plan and Max Weiss will tell you about this. Some of the venues that Vince was going to play, they found out he wasn't Black and they were cancelling him. Cancelling concerts because they thought he was Black. It was predominantly Black Jazz enthusiast places.

DON: Racism was really strong there. With Bola Sete there, of course it was ok.

ABE: Vince and Bola could have been another Brubeck and Desmond. I always thought that. When they started fighting and not getting along I used to tell them "I'm just going to tell you, from a business standpoint, you guys have something really special going".

DON: What was that about them fighting? That's a story I haven't heard. Not getting along over music or more personal issues?

ABE: A lot of it had to do with just the billing.

DON: Bola said he wanted top billing?

ABE: Yes, he wanted top billing and he wanted to have his own career. He wanted to have an independent career which is really stupid. I used to tell him "Maybe Abbott and Costello didn't like each other, and Lucy and Ethel, they hated each other but they were so good together. You just go do the gig, go out 2 different doors, and rehearse once in a while. That's all you have to do". Vince and Bola could have been the biggest! Everybody loved Vince, and Bola had that smile when he played.

DON: The music was good!

ABE: But you know how guitar players seriously, and Bola was always smiling and he was like a show.

DON: Well what was Vince's take on all that? He wanted his billing too, I guess?

ABE: Vince didn't care that much, I guess. He didn't care enough to patch it up.

DON: Had Vince had his successful trios by that time?

ABE: Yeah. Vince had been on the road with Woody Herman which gave him a lot of credibility considering he never studied classical piano. He didn't read very well. But he had such raw talent. Everybody loved listening to him play. I used to listen to him play. I just loved listening to Vince. I'd watch him play and he would get his hands in the funniest positions. If you didn't watch him, and just listen, it was beautiful. But if you watched him you'd say "How is he doing that?"

A Diary of the Underdogs

DON: It's painful!

ABE: He kind of had his own fingering.

DON: Well that explains the percussive sound; crisp, like chopping… So that's a great take on him. People don't take the time to say anything about…I never knew him but I was taken when I first heard that music. Especially that Brazilian music, it's just beautiful, and he made it live.

ABE: I think he was ahead of his time, I really do.

DON: Well Leroy liked him a lot. Leroy played with him a little bit.

ABE: Leroy Vinnegar, yeah?

DON: Leroy Vinnegar, pulled him right along. There was an era there where Perkins, Carl Perkins, and Vince were around, Sonny Clark, and a lot of similar styles are going on at that time. They were feeding off of each other.

ABE: Oh yeah.

DON: And Vince really held his own there.

ABE: Then there's Hampton Hawes and that great bass player. Who's the bass player? He was from here. He was a Black guy, really tall, big guy, a sweetheart… He's still around, he's in LA.

DON: John Heard?

ABE: John Heard! Yeah!

DON: Yeah, he's played at Charlie O's.

ABE: There was a restaurant club in an alley in North Beach in the financial district called Just Fred's, and Fred was a big Jazz fan.

DON: I heard about that gig.

ABE: He hired Hampton Hawes to come and play from 9 to midnight and I played solo piano, the cocktail hour, from 5 to 8 just by myself. John Heard came in early one night, got out his bass, and played a couple tunes with me. John said "If you talk to Fred, I really need to make more money."

DON: He wanted to work with you.

ABE: "I'm afraid to ask him, but if you talk to him, maybe I could come in and play your last set with you". So that's what we did.

DON: Oh ok, so you had him for a while.

ABE: I saw him in LA years ago. I saw him and he remembered me. What a good bass player.

DON: I saw him recently. He's in Los Angeles and playing at a place called Charlie O's.

ABE: Yeah? Where is it?

DON: With Jack Sheldon…

ABE: No kidding!

DON: And, I can't remember, maybe Gregory Hutcherson as the drummer.

ABE: They had a big fund raiser at SF State and they asked the alumni to participate. It was a comedy night too. That's why Ronnie Schell was there. So Ronnie Schell got Merv Griffin to come, and Merv Griffin got Jack Sheldon to come.

DON: So Merv played?

ABE: Yeah, and I had Seward McCain and Jim Zimmerman

DON: I don't know that guy.

ABE: A drummer, Jim Zimmerman.

DON: Oh, yeah, Zimmerman. I like him.

ABE: And Seward and I were the basis. Jack Sheldon played trumpet with us and Merv Griffin sang with us. It was a whole night at SF State of different people doing different things. And that's where that photograph came from.

DON: You and Larry Vuckovich cross paths much?

265

A Diary of the Underdogs

ABE: We went to the same high school. I don't know him. He subbed for me often at St. Francis. You know, in this business, you have to draw a line. Or at least you have to be able to define who your friends are as opposed to who you know.

DON: Yeah, right. Who you play with and who you hang with, yeah.

ABE: So the question is, can I call Larry Vuckovich on his private phone on Sunday and ask him if he wants to go to a ball game? Or go to a movie? If he wants to come over and hang out, no, I can't.

DON: It's not like that. But you can call Mario.

ABE: I would call Mario, yeah.

DON: Well that's the way it's done.

ABE: So that's how I delineate between the acquaintances and friends. There are people I'm friendly with, but they're not my friends. Seward is definitely a close friend. He's a very special guy.

DON: Seward, I love Seward! A sweet guy!

After interview: -Helen Noga story: Helen Noga (1/3 partner in the Black Hawk Club) discovered and signed Johnny Mathis to recording and managing contract- Contract was 10% of first $1,000, 20% of $2,000, on up to 70% of $5,000 and above. Johnny had $6,000,000 coming from royalties which he tried to collect without Noga finding out but she still got 70% of it. Mathis finally got out of the contract years later.

End: Abe Battat

Interview: Bobbe Norris-jazz singer-Larry Dunlap-jazz musician, pianist-with Don Alberts-October 14, 2009-Pacifica, Ca.-About- Sausalito, Zack's, Frank Werber, Singers, Purple Onion, Enrico's Hungry I, Moulin Rouge, Ann's 440, Danny Patiris, Irwin Corey (Professor Longhair), Cannonball Adderley, Coffee Gallery, Nancy King, Beverly Kelly, Max Hartstein, Art Pepper, New York, Rainbow Room, Singers, Mary Stallins, Flip Nunez, Portland, Oregon, Tom Albering, Carl Smith, Benson Hotel, Braily Brown, Noel Jewkes, Wes Montgomery, Happy House, Buckwheat, Bill Lufborough, Virgil Gonsalves, No Name Bar, Trident, Vince Guaraldi, Soupy Sails, Paul Desmond, Scott LaFaro, Bill Evans, the Kingston Trio, Mike's Pool Hall, the Tropics, Bill Ham, Jerry Granelli, Mark Murphy, Jim Purcell, Bobby Burger, Harry Partch, Varda, Walter Kean, David Wheat (Buckwheat) Bob Dorough, Ornette Coleman, Don Cherry, Charlie Haden, George Andros, Fack's, Ernie Hood, Bill Hood, Steve Atkins, Bird's Saxophone, Lord Buckley, Sonny King, Bop City, Jimbo, Jane Getz, Howard Hesseman, John Coppola, Eldon Mills, Half Note (NY), Dick Saltzman, Jazz Workshop, Lee Crosby, Soulville, Red Garland, Inside at the Outside, Michael DuPont, Mike Montana, Benny Goodman, John Hammond, Vanderbilt, Herbie Hancock, Village Vanguard, Persian Room, Eddie Kahn, George Moffat, Al Plank, Mal Waldron, Cal Tjader, Buddy Hackett, Marian-Richard Williams, Paul Chambers, Pharaoh Sanders (Little Rock), Fred Marshall, Monty Waters, Art Lewis, Dewey Redman, Chris Ibanez, Paul Motian, Barney Kessel, Rea Brunell, Jo Ryder, Lee Coffee, Dick Stewart, Norm McKay, Brian Atchinson, Jim Pepper, Mike Nock, the Reunion, Pat O'Hearn, Ratzo Harris, Brent Rancone, George Muribus, Tony Lewis, Eddie Marshall, Pete Douglas, Dave Dunaway, Signe Anderson...

A Diary of the Underdogs

BOBBE NORRIS and LARRY DUNLAP

Larry Dunlap and Bobbe Norris

DON: OK, so you were talking about Croatia and Larry Vuckovich.

BOBBE: Yeah, I won't talk about Larry; he is always trying to give me a lecture about how the Croatians sympathized with the Nazi's.

DON: Yeah, I remember that.

BOBBE: But, the Croatians…they hate us because we have all the beach property, we have the whole coast, the beautiful Adriatic Coast. My family was from Dubrovnik and the Serbs have all the money, but they don't have the coast. They have the military and all that crap.

DON: Is that Montenegro?

BOBBE: Montenegro is near the coast, yes. I think that is where Larry is from, or least that is what he always said. He's Serbian, so I don't know. I should tell you that I first started singing in Marin, in Sausalito.

DON: What year?

BOBBE: Probably around 58. I graduated high school in 56 and then I went on the road for a while with this funny group called the Make-believe's, for about half a year. They were really funny, but they weren't from here. One of my first gigs was at the No Name in Sausalito and I worked with Jim Purcell.

DON: I have heard people talk about him, he is a piano player?

BOBBE: Yeah, and he is in bad shape. He had a stroke and he had cancer.

LARRY: He says he had the first hot-tub in Marin.

BOBBE: Yeah, he bought Frank Werber's house.

DON: Oh, I was hoping someone would talk about Frank Werber.

BOBBE: Well, I was the secretary, I was the Kingston Trio's secretary, before I started singing, well, I was still singing, but I got that job and it was great. And actually Jim Purcell got me the job because he bought Frank's house in Muir Beach. And I used to work at Zack's. And I used to, I was under age, I was maybe…well, I graduated high school at sixteen, so….and also it was the only other time I was a waitress. And I had to sing too, but I wasn't getting paid to and I was serving all my high school friends. And then Zack came up to me or whatever his name was…

DON: The manager of Zack's?

BOBBE: The owner guy. And he said that I should stop serving people because the beverage people or something were coming in. I was serving all my high school friends, and we were all under age. But then I worked at a great place called the Old Time Coffee Gallery and that was on Bridgeway but it was up; kind of going up the hill, its now a realtor office. But that was a very cool place and I worked there with a guy named Chubby Crank. I noticed you don't have him in there.

DON: No, I don't and nobody talks about Buck Wheat either.

BOBBE: I knew Buck Wheat too.

A Diary of the Underdogs

DON: And nobody talks about Bill Lufborough.

Insert from Wikipedia:

The boobam is a percussion instrument of the membranophone family consisting of an array of tubes with membranes stretched on one end, the other end open. The tuning depends partly on the tension on the membrane but mostly on the length of the tube. The boobams are probably an ancestor of the modern octoban. The tubes were originally made from lengths of giant bamboo although pipes of wood, plastic, metal, and cardboard also have been used. The membranes were originally goat or calfskin but most are now plastic. The name boobam was coined in Mill Valley, California in 1954 and was described as "bamboo spelled sideways." In 1948 Harry Partch, an American composer, developed a system of music that depended on the building of various exotic instruments that could play non-tempered scales. Some of them were based on Greek models and some on more primitive instruments like marimbas. Musician David Buck Wheat and his roommate in Sausalito, California, Bill Lufborough, a musician and electronic engineer, built such instruments for Partch as a marimba which was hit with a large soft mallet over the chamber. This device delivered low-cycled tones that were barely audible. Lufborough had scientific instruments borrowed from the Navy Yard, and using an oscilloscope and audio oscillator he and Wheat were able to work on a new technical level that had not been possible before.

Together they moved onto a Sausalito barge with Jack Simpson who in 1954 founded a business named the "BooBam Bamboo Drum Company." Buckwheat was working on the President Lines as a bass player, sailing to the Orient. In the Philippines he would buy large diameter giant bamboo and bring back sticks on the ship which they used to build the Pacific Island bamboo drums. Jazz groups were fascinated and added the boobams to their percussion sections. In 1956 Chet Baker's Ensemble used them on the Today Show. Their unique sound inspired Nick Reynolds of the Kingston Trio who eagerly included them on their tour with his percussion solo being featured on "O Ken Karanga" on the album College Concert recorded at UCLA in 1962.

BOBBE: I knew Bill. I had a key to Bill's studio over there and I used to go over there with this woman Bobbie Burger who played piano.

LARRY: She still around?

BOBBE: No, she died; I saw it in the paper. She was so horrible; I mean that woman drove me insane. But she showed me all the great tunes

DON: Oh, she knew?

BOBBE: Yeah, she was from back East. She came out here and lived in Sausalito and we had a key and we would go up there and Harry Partch. He built all these instruments. He built the Boobam drums that Bill had, but Harry made them. And people used to have parties at his house because he was never there. And also, Varda, a painter, I used to go on his boat, to his parties. I was just a kid and everybody was like out of it and I was like the little observer. And I was watching everybody and learning stuff. Walter Kean, I met Walter.

DON: The painter, and his wife?

BOBBE: Yes. I remember I had dinner with him one night, I was with my girlfriend and he picked her up and carried her down Bridgeway. He was really out of it. And Buck Wheat, Buck Wheat would come in to get his check when I was a secretary for Werber.

DON: Bass player right?

BOBBE: Yes. And then another time over at Bill Lufborough's studio, he was there, Bill and him and I recorded, I think it was – it was one of Buck Wheat's tunes, was it *Better Than Anything*? Did Buck Wheat write that tune?

LARRY: Yeah.

BOBBE: Yeah, ok, I was recording that song…

A Diary of the Underdogs

DON: What was his last name?

BOBBE: Well, his official name was David Wheat. Buck Wheat accompanied me… and I also did *Well You Need It*. And I think that was Bill's lyric. I wish I had a tape of that, I really do. And another time I walked up to the studio with my key and there was a band in there playing and I said oh, I guess we can't rehearse Today, it was Bob Dorough on piano and Don Cherry and Ornette Coleman and I thought – Oh my God what is this music, this was like 58, 59.

DON: Maybe James Black on drums?

BOBBE: I can't remember who the drummer was, but it was so cool. And another time, the guy who ran…the studio…with Bob, he was married to…it was Alan Watt's wife. Alan Watt's wife was a Japanese woman that played Koto. I didn't really talk to anybody, I was kind of shy back then – I was just an observer. They were going to put me in some magazine, like Life Magazine or one of those, because they really liked me and then Allen Watt's wife got the gig instead of me and she got the picture and the article and stuff.

DON: Was Allen living on one of those old ferryboats out the channel at that time?

BOBBE: He probably was, you know there was a whole community out there.

DON: Yeah, Chris Roberts had a boat down there, did you know Chris?

BOBBE: Sounds familiar, but I am not sure.

DON: I wanted to talk a little bit more about Frank Werber, because didn't he open the Trident?

BOBBE: Yes. That was after I worked for him. I worked for him around the time I worked at the Purple Onion. It was Columbus Tower, North Beach. And Frank and the trio were always on the road, and I had this great job – if I hadn't wanted to sing – the woman took my job there was there forever, she just stayed. It was such a great job. It was so easy, they were gone, I had an answering service, I would put the answering service on and go out and have a drink with people that were stopping by, and that's kind of how I met Mark Murphy. Also, Mark was singed with Frank at the time and Stan Kenton's wife, Ann Richards.

DON: Frank had a label?

BOBBE: No, he just managed them. This was before all of that. The trio was doing great, right and we had moonshine in the office, I remember that I got very drunk off of that one time, from Tom Dooley. That's another story. It was such a great job and so fun and they would go out of town and I would have all their sports cars to drive around, because I would have to take them in and service them and mount their gold records, so I had all this money, what a great job! But I wanted to sing and Frank said, don't sing, it's a terrible business, you will get fucked over and all of it – but you know how it is, you want to do it. He was a good guy, he was gone a lot, I remember one day I came in and he was sleeping on the couch, it was the time when he had those Hong Kong suits made and he had all those fabulous clothes. And after that, when I saw him later, when I lived in New York and came out here, and with the Trident, he was like a Guru guy, had the white robes on and the long hair and I think he got busted, he had that island out in the Bay with all this weed. He used to make these giant pot cakes for the holidays and give them to people. He turned into a total hippie and it was so weird because he had been so straight. And then I kind of gravitated to the City and worked at the Purple Onion. I have a great Hungry I story – I was going to do an audition at the Hungry I and it was with this woman, Bobbie Burger and I forget who the drummer was and we didn't have a bass player and we were on our way to the audition in Sausalito, because I lived in Mill Valley at the time and we were driving through Sausalito and this car was going by and it was Charlie Haden because Charlie lived in Marin at the time – this was the late 50's – and we said, Charlie, you want to go to an audition with us? So, he auditioned with us at the Hungry I and I was singing all these weird songs, I was like maybe eighteen by then, it was like all these songs, like *Love Lost* and *End of A Love Affair*, all these really serious heavy songs, *Lush Life* and I hadn't experienced anything much, you know, and Charlie, you know, it was still like he was a junkie and after the audition he just freaked out and he wanted money really bad, and we were trying to give him money, and none of us had any money. And he just totally freaked out and we didn't get the job anyway.

DON: Who did you audition for, Banducci?

BOBBE: No, I don't remember, it was one of his right-hand guys. He didn't like me.

DON: And Enrico's history is what?

BOBBE: Yeah, I worked with the Smothers Brothers and Phyllis Diller at the Purple Onion. That was fun.

DON: So, they had a showroom and they kind of had a little lobby and they had a piano in there, right?

BOBBE: Oh, you mean at the Hungry I. Yeah. Yeah, that was a great venue. I never did get to work there. But then I met George Andros, he owned the Fack's Clubs.

DON: Yeah, that's the guy who had one on Market Street.

BOBBE: He had one on Market and then he had one I think I was on Bush, maybe. And then I opened the new Facts in North Beach and I worked with this piano player that I can not think of his name. Actually, at the Purple Onion I worked with Steven Atkins and there was another guy too, but I can't remember his name. But he was real grouchy, the other guy, but Steve was real sweet.

LARRY: I want to interject something here – Don, in the emails that you sent out, somebody mentioned Ernie Hood, he was up in Portland. That cup that you are drinking out of is a cup that Ernie made!

DON: Oh, is that right! And there was Bill too...

BOBBE: Yeah, we knew Bill.

LARRY: I was watching TV about six months ago, there is this show that I like – its about detectives solving mysteries – and it was about 1am and I was flipping around and I saw something, Bill Hood was on the TV!

DON: Was he on there as an actor?

LARRY: No. You know he always claimed that he had this sax that belonged to Bird. And so these detectives were trying to find out if it really was Bird's sax and it turned out it was! Bird had played in Portland in like 1953 and put his horn in a pawn shop and Bill did something for him, probably got some drugs for him and he gave Bill the pawn ticket and said that he could go and redeem the ticket and so Bill got the horn! And he had this horn all his life and he didn't have any proof that it was Bird's horn, he just told everybody. And so his daughter, who is like in her sixties, was on the show, and she showed them the horn and the detectives went back to the pawn shop and there was a guy who was still alive who had been working there and the guy confirmed that Charlie Parker had brought his horn in and this guy Bill Hood came and picked it up!

DON: That is a great story; I don't think Ernie Hood is around anymore, right?

BOBBE: Oh, no, no. But I don't remember him being here.

LARRY: He was like a surrogate father to me. We were really close.

DON: How did you end up in Oregon?

LARRY: Well, that is where I am from. I grew up outside of Portland, Forest Grove.

BOBBE: He didn't get here until the 70's.

DON: I didn't know you then, but I saw your name around.

LARRY: I used to work with Brady Brown and those guys. I was part of that circle. But anyway, back to Bobbe.

BOBBE: OK, back to my interview! I remember one time at the Old Time Coffee House where I worked with Chubby Crane, Lord Buckley was there and Buckley stood up, right after we took a break and did the "Naz." He just stood up and did the "Naz." And he was all dressed very dapper and everything. That was very cool. So, lets see, I worked at the Coffee Gallery with Flip, the one in North Beach. Beverly Kelly worked there. She wasn't very nice to me.

DON: What about Nancy King?

A Diary of the Underdogs

BOBBE: Nancy stole my gig! I was working with Flip, Nancy and Sonny came in and worked cheaper. And it was cheap as it was! And I told Nancy that and she said, *Sonny did that, I didn't do it!* I used to go over to Jimbo's all the time, and when Nancy was in town, she wasn't here for very long, she was only here for several months, but they came down and stole my gig and then I guess they stayed…

DON: At the Coffee Gallery?

BOBBE: Yes, that's the only place I remember Nancy working.

LARRY: Let me tell this…she (Nancy?) went to Bop City in the afternoon and met with Jimbo to see about getting a gig singing there, and it was the middle of the afternoon and he said, come upstairs to my office. And she went up to the office and he asked her, *"Will you have sex with me?"* And she said, *"No, I won't!"* And he said, *"OK, I will hire you then*!"

BOBBE: That sounds like such a lie – he had such a big ego, I don't think he would say that.

LARRY: He was a pretty nice guy, I only met him once. There was a thing a Pearl's about seven, eight years ago. And Bobbe and I walked in and she said, you know, that she would introduce me and we went over and she introduced me and he said, *I knew her before you did!*

BOBBE: Yeah, he was always like that, I never saw his office.

DON: Did he hire you?

BOBBE: No, I would just sit in over there because Flip was there and Janie Getz, piano player. And we worked a lot together. I would sit in with Jane. But the Coffee Gallery was kind of cool because Howard Hesseman was the bartender. And we sat down one day and got really drunk on beer with Howard.

DON: And I think later on Robin Williams worked there too.

BOBBE: Oh, maybe I was in New York. I went to New York around 61 and I was there until 70. There was a lot happening here and I guess if I had stayed here I could have been Grace Slick! (Just teasing)

DON: I read in your bio that you had a contract and that it was confining and you had to get out.

BOBBE: Oh, yeah, it was bad. I had to declare Bankruptcy at twenty-seven. I declared Bankruptcy on Columbia Records, my manager, my agent, all of them. Bye….I stayed in New York and studied acting and became a hippie for awhile. And I had some fun; I wasn't having any fun with those guys. But out here I had fun too. I worked at the Moulin Rouge and it was Danny Patiris and Johnny Coppola. It was a great band. I would come out first and I would sing like twenty minutes and then the strippers would come out and it was really funny because at that time I was a little kid and I would wear these little high neck dresses with little funny sleeves and a couple of times they said take it off, but I was kind of embarrassing. I also worked at a place called Ann's 440. I won a singing contest there. And the prize was that you got a week or two to work there. They had a piano player and a drummer, no bass player. And I so I won, and I went in to do my gig and I didn't know where to put my stuff. The women's room was full of transvestites or whatever, because that wasn't typically a strip club; it was more of a gay club. And they were like, get out, get out. And then I tried to get in the men's room and they were like, get out, get out. And I thought it was all so weird. And then I was backstage and this beautiful, kind of Eurasian looking woman, but wasn't, came up to me and in this low voice, said, *Hi Bobbe, what are you doing here?* And it was my hairdresser – Eddie Akuna. I used to go to him for years, this little Philippine guy. He looked like Kim Novak when he dressed up! And then I sang and I did the night and there was a Black singer on the bill that was Ann's lover, this woman, and I heard her sing and then I heard her screaming, *if she stays, I go!* And that was Ann's lover and so I lost the job in one night! So, that was Ann's. There was guy called Elden Mills, he was an older gay man that had a really big house in Berkley and he used to let all the Black musicians stay there if they wanted to. And that's where I met Wes Montgomery and Wes had a crush on me. And I found out later from Mary Stallings that Wes really had a crush on me and every time he saw me, he would chase me. It was so funny. I know he was notorious for that and he had a lot of kids. But he was so cute and I loved Wes. And when I went to New York, he let me sit in at the Half Note. He and Joe Williams were really sweet. And that place was a trip; you had to climb up on to this big stage over the bar. It was way up there! That was the original Half Note, it was kind of downtown. There was a place called the Tropics that I used to sit in with Dick Saltzman. That was out sort of by Geary. That was a good place.

DON: Yeah, Brew Moore played there too.

BOBBE: When I was twelve, I started working around here on the backs of trucks with the Dixie Land guys. And we would open up all the shopping centers in the Bay Area.

DON: Who would that be, Turk Murphy and all those guys?

BOBBE: All those guys. I have a picture somewhere....oh, here it is. Lee Crosby I used to work with him. I worked with Lee. He had a big band and he had me doing all these shopping centers on the back of the trucks.

DON: Who are all these people?

BOBBE: Well, Lee Crosby on bass. I don't know who the others were, I was twelve!

DON: Oh, here is a photo, you look like Barbara Streisand. What was this 1960?

BOBBE: I think 1961. I have a nice picture of me and Cannonball, because I worked opposite him in New York- Here it is, and this is when I had a big space in my teeth, and there is Cannonball. This was in New York and I was in this magazine. Yeah, I knew Cannonball and I was at the Jazz Workshop all the time to hear him. And also a lot of those musicians like, what was his name, the piano player who used to stay with Marian and Dick Williams?

DON: Tell me a little about coming back from New York and meeting Larry and starting back here again.

BOBBE: I didn't meet Larry

Bobbe Norris with Cannonball Adderley-1961

until...oh, Soulville I used to go to a lot. There was a piano player there I just loved, Red Garland, he was so fabulous. There was another place I worked on the Peninsula called, Inside at the Outside. That was with Vince Guaraldi. That was around that time too.

DON: Was that Michael DuPont's Club?

BOBBE: Oh yes.

DON: And Jackie and Roy were there? Did you know them?

BOBBE: Sure. Yes, Mike Montana, he used to write up my charts. We didn't really use charts in those days, but he would write some. Benny Goodman – I turned the gig down, that was pretty good. John Hammond signed me to Columbia Records and John was Benny's brother in-law and he had married John's sister, the Vanderbilt's. And so, John said you can work with Benny, but he hates singers and he is a real pain in the ass, and you can work at the Rainbow Room and I turned it down – I didn't want to work with

A Diary of the Underdogs

someone like that – I wanted to have fun when I am singing! And I turned down Herbie Hancock too. I had a gig with Herbie at the Vanguard and Max Gordon signed me and my very favorite person in the whole world was Bill Evans, and so, I didn't know Bill, but I loved him. And I lived right around the corner from the Vanguard at the time in the Village, and so we sign this contract and I was going to work two weeks with Herbie and Tony, and Max called me up two days later and said, you can't work with Bill, its not going to work out, you can still work with Herbie and I said, no, I didn't want to do it then. I was getting ready to do this big scene at the Persian Room and I was going to try and be rich and famous, right…and so I was getting out of the Jazz thing for a minute. But I always regret that and I did get to do a rehearsal with Herbie and that was cool.

DON: And how about Bill, did you connect with him?

BOBBE: I never met Bill, but I used to sit down there at night and get sleepy and run up the street to my place, I would go in the back door there and I used to hear all of them. Miles and Monk, everybody came to the Vanguard. It was fabulous! Eddie Kahn was somebody you mentioned?

DON: Yeah, he was a bass player at Bop City…

BOBBE: I knew Eddie; he wanted me to run away with him at one point.

DON: Was he also a sax player?

BOBBE: No. And by the way, his name is spelled Kahn. He was very tall and real sweet. Max Hartstein. He is the one who changed my name to Bobbe with an E. He was doing some kind of weird…not Tarot, but something and he said that I should have my name Norris, numerology. He lived in this big house in the Haight that my friend George Moffett owned or rented. And George was a want to be singer; he ended up becoming an actor. He is still around, he is over in Berkley. But Max rented one of the rooms from him. Max is a very good bass player and he actually is still in touch with Rita. He just wrote her. He is trying to get $200 from everybody; he is losing his farm or something.

DON: Was that in Boulder Creek or something?

BOBBE: No, it's back in Indiana. He moved to Indiana where he was from. He was part of that Indiana group, the Montgomery Brothers and Al Plank, they were all from Indiana. Indianapolis. And Mel Waldron I knew, I worked with him a little in New York. In fact, some guy is writing a book on him and I just gave him some notes. Cal Tjader, Cal and Brubeck used to come to Drake High, where I went to high school and played for our rallies. I was madly in love with, not Dave, but Paul Desmond. I loved Paul Desmond. I never liked Dave. I never knew them, I was a high school student, I was like fifteen. I just loved his music, but I didn't like Dave. But I loved the band and of course Tjader would come too. And they lived in Marin. I lived in Mill Valley, on the road to Tiburon and I had a Triumph, you know, everybody had those sports cars in the late 50's and my car broke down and I had a job in the city. I was just kind of standing there and Cal Tjader drove by in his car, I think he had an MG, picked me up and drove me into the city and didn't say one word the whole time we were driving! All the way to North Beach and never said a word. Art Pepper, I lived in Santa Cruz during the 70's, and there was this guy who really liked my singing and he was an architect and he lived in Santa Cruz and he said that he wanted to drive me to Monterey, that night, to sit in with Jack Sheldon and his band. And so, I said I would go and so he drove…well, I went to his house, I drove to his house, he had this beautiful home and he asked me to stay in the living room because he needed to go upstairs. And he was a junkie too, I think, but I was sitting there and there was this music on, I think it was Art Pepper's music and it was real dark and I was sitting there and all of a sudden, over in the corner, was Art Pepper! He was like a Vampire or something, it was so spooky. He was over in the corner, it was real dark and he was dressed all in black and he had been there the whole time. And I thought it was so weird! And then the guy came down and we left.

DON: Did you ever talk to Art?

BOBBE: Nothing! He was in the corner, probably stoned. Soupy Sales, you mentioned him. When I worked the Persian Room in New York, I worked there a couple of times; he came up to my room with some people one night, holding this giant Soupy Sales doll! And I thought he was going to give it to me, but he didn't. Darn it!

LARRY: He was a big Jazz fan.

BOBBE: Buddy Hackett, you had that down, he was so mean to me! I hated that guy! Mary and Richard Williams, they had house over kind of in the Haight, they were the ones…like Joe Zawinul. I would be over there, Joe was staying there. I knew Joe from there and a lot of musicians. Noel Jewkes lived there. They would let all the musicians stay there that came into town.

DON: Was that the Happy House?

LARRY: It was on Oak.

BOBBE: They called it the Happy House?

DON: Well, people are talking about it – Vince talked about it.

BOBBE: My girlfriend Suzanne that was her parents. She was married to Flip. (Nunez)

DON: So, Dick and Mary from Sacramento, that owned the Iron Sandal.

BOBBE: Yes, that's whom I am talking about. And they also had an after-hours club in the city. I think I worked there one time too. But yeah, they were like really good friends and Suzanne and I we hung out because I used to work with Flip. She now lives in Mexico. Yeah, I used to visit the Mom and Richard up in Calistoga when they lived there. That house was so much fun, I would drop in and they would be having dinner and there would be all these famous people. Paul Chambers the bass player was there. He died really young. You would meet all these people and have dinner with them.

DON: Yeah, I knew that Wes was there and Noel Jewkes was there, Dewey Redman was there, Art Lewis was there.

BOBBE: Yeah, I knew all those guys, I had a band with Flip and Pharaoh Sanders, when his name was Little Rock and Dewey was in the band, Monte Waters was in the band, Monte Waters, Art Lewis was in the band. I was the only white person. We did a lot of army bases. We would go around and do gigs at the army bases. And Mary and Richard were fun. Elden Mills was another guy in Berkley that would let all the young black guys, like Monty, and Dewey and all those guys stay at his place. Fred Marshall I used to go over to his house a lot because and Jerry Granelli were my friends. I used to work with Jerry and Jerry I don't know where he is now, but he took a lot of acid.

LARRY: He lives in Europe.

BOBBE: He also lives in Nova Scotia and Berlin.

LARRY: Yeah, he came to San Francisco with his band from Berlin.

BOBBE: He was a very cool guy. We worked together up at Tahoe. We worked one time a whole summer up there with this guy, Johnny Hamlin, he was kind of a jazzer, but we had to be somewhat commercial. He played accordion.

DON: Where did you work in Tahoe?

BOBBE: We worked at Harvey's. And I also worked up at the North Shore with Chris Ibanez. That's where I met The Make-Believes, those crazy guys. And they took me on the road for half a year. It was pretty interesting.

DON: What were they?

BOBBE: They were piano, bass, drums. They weren't from here; I don't know where they were from. They traveled all the time. I would only do three songs a set. And I would do the same songs over and over. *Personality* was one- *You Came along Way from St. Louis* was another. And then I had one other song. And I just did those same songs for six months. They were funny and they also did all the Stanley Freeburg stuff. They did record pantomime.

LARRY: Stan Freeburg. I used to do his stuff as a kid. He would have these different characters on a record doing a funny story and people would pantomime all the characters.

BOBBE: Yeah, it was pretty funny. Scott LaFaro, I have one more story. I was at the workshop one night and he was with Bill, working with Bill Evans. I used to go down the street to the pool hall, it was Joe's Pool Hall or Mike's Pool Hall and I would have a hamburger. They had great hamburgers. And all of a sudden Scotty came in and sat down next to me and we hung out until he had to go back and we were just talking and talking about Big Sur and how he loved it and how he loved it here and he was dead, like two days later! It was that close – spooky. And he was talking about how he was so happy and God, it was so sad. He was just so wonderful and a wonderful player.

DON: And that was the trio at that time, Bill Evans, Scott LaFaro and who was the drummer?

BOBBE: Can't remember. There was another person I worked with, Irwin Corey, I worked with in New York and that was Professor Longhair. And someone said to me when I worked with him, I worked with him at a place called The Living Room. And they said to me, *Oh no! You are working with Irwin, he pinches your ass!* But he didn't. We had this little tiny dressing room, and that never happened. He was very sweet and his daughter was there, maybe that's why he was being good. And he was very funny and he was out here a lot. He was at the Hungry I a lot. And the story about Mark Murphy was when I worked for Werber, this lady came in, Dena Valli, and she and I were friends, and she was Mark's fan and Mark used to come out from New York and stay with her in Hillsborough. And I didn't want anything to do with this and Dena said, well let's go to lunch then, and we went to lunch and became friends. And Mark would fly out here and stay with Dena and I would go down there and practice, Mark would play the piano and I was probably eighteen or nineteen then, and we would do songs.

DON: Was Mark recording and traveling at that time?

BOBBE: Yeah, he was out here working at Fack's Two. And I heard him, which was a good place, they had Dick Haymes there one time with his new wife, she was a singer from out here. And Mark was so great then, he was young and cute. I had all his records and I was his secretary for a minute there. And I quit, I said, I have to sing!

DON: So, are you guys still in touch?

BOBBE: Yeah. He's coming out next week; we are doing a tribute to him.

DON: So, what would you say that circle would be you and Nancy King and Mark and maybe Madeline?

BOBBE: They came later, they were younger. I am seventy. Madeline and Kitty and all of them, they are in their fifties.

LARRY: So what singers were around then?

BOBBE: Mary Stallings. Mary and I hung out, we are the same age.

LARRY: You met in high school.

BOBBE: No. She was from the city. We used hang out a lot and we would go to all the clubs. And people always wanted to let Mary sing because she was black and beautiful. And I thought, well, if I hang out with Mary I will get to sit in too! And it was true, because I know we went to the Blackhawk one time and Barney Kessel let us both sit in. And then we went out to breakfast with Barney. And Mary told me another story and I always forget who the sax player was, a wonderful black man, he has been gone for a number of years, can't think of his name.

DON: Yusef Lateef?

BOBBE: No, but I did work opposite of him, sweet, sweet man. Anyway, the sax player was really, really famous, not Lester Young, not Coleman Hawkins.....well, anyway, Mary said, remember when we went up to blah, blahs room and he taught us to breathe? He was kind of like a Sonny Rollins guy, but it wasn't him. He was really nice.

DON: Ok, so who were some of the other female singers?

BOBBE: Rhea Brunell would cook me Italian dinners, she was married to a Rudy Salvini at the time and there was another woman, Jo Ryder. She was around and she worked at the Purple Onion too and she did a lot of obscure songs, she lived here, she went to New York and kind of disappeared.

DON: How about the woman who sang with Brubeck for a minute – John Coppola's wife?

BOBBE: I didn't know her. There was only about four of us. There weren't very many. Like Joe Ryder, the reason I worked at the Moulin Rouge was because she worked there and when she took a break she would hire me as a back-up.

DON: What about Barbara Dane?

BOBBE: I never knew her. She played with the Dixie guys. This guy Lee Crosby who was in that picture, I used to sing on KTIM, when I was twelve I would go over there on Holidays and stuff. I would sing along with Liberace with the records, *Easter Parade* and stuff. He had me singing and then I sang on the back of those trucks for the shopping centers and then we would have casuals. He had a big band that we used to play out in Marin at the beach out there, it was probably 1959, the beach near San Rafael, can't think of it (Muir Beach). And I also used to work with this guy and his big band – Dick Stewart. He had a show, kind of like Dick Clark. You know; a dance show on TV. And we worked at the Marin County Country Club. On my 21st. Birthday! The whole band got up and sang Happy Birthday! It was so cool!

LARRY: What about Jeannie Hoffman, was she around then?

BOBBE: She was but I didn't know her though. She was weird, she was like an alcoholic and you couldn't talk to her.

DON: Yeah, she had a trio, right, with Dean Reilly and Bill Young?

BOBBE: Yeah, and Al Pimentel, I used to work with him. He lives in England now. And there was another bass player I used to work with, Norman McKay, and then he went into a mental hospital or something. We skipped through Sausalito one night, I mean skipping! We went all the way down Bridge way, skipping. He was so cute and I did see him having an attack one time. He had epilepsy. Sometimes I would have to go find him, he worked at the Coffee Gallery. He and Flip both worked there. They would not be there, I would have to get into the car and go get them out of bed and bring them over. I was like their mother or something.

DON: Did you know Trevor Kohler?

BOBBE: No. And then there was my boyfriend, Stan Foster. Trumpet player. He died really young. He worked with that band that worked at the Hungry I, can't think of it, damn, he had a really nice band, he played baritone sax, the bandleader.

DON: Larry, do you want to add something?

LARRY: Well, I knew about Portland in those days, I didn't get down here until the early 70's, 72 or something like that. Growing up around Portland in the 60's, my idea of San Francisco would be that there would be all these Jazz clubs and a really vibrant scene happening. So I came here like in 72 and it was pretty much gone. Keystone Korner was happening and Jazz Workshop just barely hanging on. El Matador, just a tiny bit. But the whole scene that I expected to see happening was gone.

BOBBE: Well, I met Larry, I was down sitting in with Flip at a place down near Palo Alto and I was just sitting in because we were opening a club for these guys in South City or something, they were all there. And Larry came and he was listening and he left his date at the door and came back in and gave me his phone number and his name and I looked at it and I thought, "Who is this, some nut?" And so I never called him or nothing, but I was at the Matador one night, because I lived in Campbell then, and I said to Brian Atkinson, he was working with Jackie and Roy, the vibes player, and I said, do you know some guy named Larry Duncap? Because I couldn't read the name, it was all scribbles. And he said, oh, yeah Larry Dunlap he is one of the best! And then I thought, well maybe I better call him. And so I called him and that is how we met.

LARRY: My first day in San Francisco is a pretty interesting story, but it was like 72 and I came to San

A Diary of the Underdogs

Francisco and I only knew two people – Jim Pepper who I had played with before and Mike Nock who would come through Portland and park his van at my house for two weeks and lived at my house. So, I knew those two guys and I came to San Francisco on a Saturday with everything I owned in my car and both those guys were busy that night. And so I couldn't see them, I had a number of a guy's house where I might be able to crash over by Twin Peaks, and I didn't know this guy and I called him and he said well, there is about ten people crashing in the place already but you can stay there for a night or two. And so I did that and he was working as a doorman at a strip club in North Beach and so I went down there with him and I said, *"Where can I hear some Jazz?"* And he told me about this place called the Reunion, over on Union Street, the original reunion. And so I went over there and not knowing anybody and suddenly I hear somebody say, *"Larry Dunlap, what are you doing here?"* And it was a cocktail waitress who was working there and she had been a buyer for a department store and she used to come to Portland and stay at the Vincent Hotel where I was working all the time with Tom Albering and David Friesen and so she knew me from there. Oh, the owner Tony Lewis is playing piano; do you want to sit in? And I said, yeah! And so I sat in and Ratzo Harris was playing bass, Brent Ramponi, and so I sat in and Tony Lewis says, *Do you want to work here tomorrow night*? Yeah! I had only been in town like three hours. And then I said to these other musicians where else can I go tonight? And they told me to go over to the Japan Center. They told me that Flip Nunez was playing over there. And I knew Flip's name, Nancy King had talked about him. So, I went over there, Flip was playing there with George Muribus, Dave Dunaway, Eddie Marshall, Michael Howell, all those guys. I sat in there and met all those guys! And then the next day it just happened, it was Sunday, Pete Douglas was having a concert and it's Jim Pepper and Mike Nock playing together! And these are the two guys I know and so I go down there and Dave Dunaway and Eddie Marshall, whom I had met the night before, they are playing with them! And they said, *"You wanna sit in?"* And I said, Yeah! So, I sat in and also another guy sat in and it was Noel Jewkes and so I met him and then I came back to the city and worked a gig at the Reunion! That was my first day in San Francisco!

BOBBE: I remember that Jerry Granelli, Fred Marshall, and Noel Jewkes… I have a picture of them somewhere, but they used to work for this guy that put on the shows with all the famous light shows….

DON: Bill Hamm?

BOBBE: Yes! Bill Hamm, they worked for him. And they played this weird music and I think Flip was playing there sometimes.

DON: Noel was in on that too….

BOBBE: Yes, Noel was in on that. They would play music for the psychedelic stuff. But I missed a lot of that. I would come out here from New York. And I would hang out and I would go see Flip and I would go over to the Haight and buy some beads ands stuff, they didn't have that much….New York wasn't…it was later, they didn't really have beads and all the necklaces and stuff that I liked.

DON: Right, and then it was over and then when it was over it was pretty much over. They put the pipes in the streets and you couldn't drive down there.

BOBBE: Well, my Mom was real straight and she and my Grandmother and my sister used to go over there to park and here like Jefferson Airplane and my Mother would always say, *They were smoking weed all over the place!* And I would tell her that I smoked weed too and she would always say, *No, you don't.*

LARRY: Did you know the singer Signe Anderson? I used to work with her. She was the original singer in the Airplane!

BOBBE: I actually went to her house with you that time, because we lived up in Portland.

LARRY: Yeah, so when I got out of college, I went to Lewis & Clarke College, I had a senior recital where I did some classical stuff, because I was majoring in composition, I was studying piano, I played some classical music, I played some original compositions and I did some Jazz things for my graduation recital. And I got some musicians, I forget how I got them, but they brought some other musicians with them, some of the Jazz musicians, just to be in the audience. And this guy came up to me after the concert and said there was this guy putting a band together and he was looking for a piano player! And he asked me if I wanted to do it. I was just about to graduate and I didn't have anything to do and so I agreed and it was Braily Brown. And so, I played with Braily for a couple of years and all the guys in Bailey's band also played in Carl Smith's band.

DON: Carl Smith and Natural Gas!

LARRY: Yeah! And so I got involved in that and I started writing a lot of music for both of those bands. And I am still in touch with Carl.

BOBBE: Yeah, Carl was our best man when we got married.

LARRY: Yeah, and I wrote a lot of stuff for his band and he still plays. And he is like seventy-four or something.

DON: Yeah probably. He had a great energy. He used to rehearse right there on a hill that I lived right down the street.

LARRY: Yeah, by Goose Hollow.

DON: Yeah, on the hill above Goose Hollow.

LARRY: Yeah! I used to be there all the time. I used to stay in that house all the time.

BOBBE: What house?

LARRY: Carl's house.

DON: I think the street was named Montgomery Ridge. And the whole ridge caught on fire one time and burned about five houses down.

BOBBE: When I met Larry in the late 70's and we moved up to Portland and we worked a lot.

DON: Me too! I worked a lot when I was there. People don't know but there is plenty to do up there.

BOBBE: There probably is more happening up there then here. They didn't pay much I remember. And New York was good when I first went there, right around the late 60's the Beatles came and of course I was trying to be a superstar, but they wanted me to be a movie star and I didn't want to do that.

End: Bobbe Norris-Larry Dunlap

Interview: Frank Passantino-jazz musician, bassist- and Buddy Barnhill-jazz musician, drummer- with Don Alberts-October 21, 2009- in Los Altos-about: Playboy Club, Roland's, Cameo Club, Kingston Trio, Hawaii, Jimmy Borges, Frank Werber, Trident, Jeanne Hoffman, Oh Calcutta, Jim Zimmerman, Dick Fudge, Tom Reynolds, Al Plank, Puzzie Firth, Jerry Gilmore, Blackie Perry, George DiQuattro, Bobby Enriquez, Smith Dobson, Garden City.

FRANK PASSANTINO and BUDDY BARNHILL

FRANK: It says Sammy, a baritone player.

DON: Sammy, I never knew his last name.

FRANK: It was Sammy Simpson, right?

DON: Remember that little Black guy that used to hang out with Monty Waters and Jimmy Lovelace? I think he got hit by a car on the street one day, or something. He played baritone, a nice little Cat.

FRANK: Yeah, yeah.

DON: Do you know his last name?

FRANK: I'm thinking. Shit, there are a lot of guys I played with.

DON: It doesn't have to be formal, we're just hangin' out talking about our shit. But what it is, is you get to tell your stories. I interviewed Bobbe Norris. She had a little piece of paper, written on both sides, like an

A Diary of the Underdogs

envelope, all kinds of shit. She went through there and said "I found some names in there you didn't have!" She's talking about this Cat talking about this Cat talking about etc. etc.

FRANK: Well basically, I had the gig at Montefusco's and it was Tom, me and Smith to start off with.

DON: Smith Dobson.

FRANK: Yeah. So he says here, in this thing "The set I heard on Sunday night was somewhat compromised by the events of a nearby table who were auditioning for a local little theater production of King Kong. But Reynolds, Dobson and Passantino Trio was cooking and Joan Blackman was the singer. Joan Blackman's voice, rich and burnished, was a revelation."

Buddy Barnhill

DON: Wow!

FRANK: But he was saying here about whatever happens to old Playboy types when their club closes down forever? Nevertheless it turns out that Montefusco's Italian coffee and D'Acquisto's Lounge-" Johnny D'Acquisto's my cousin.

DON: Oh, ok!

FRANK: So they were partners and they both played for the Giants; Montefusco and D'Acquisto.

DON: Cool!

FRANK: And Buddie Deborough was working there after Tom was hooking up with her.

DON: Tom Reynolds?

FRANK: They were living together. The Cobra already moved out.

DON: The Cobra. That was Patti, right?

BUDDY: No, that was Genie! She was the original.

DON: Genie, she was the blonde who lived on top of Los Gatos Heights, up there with him?

BUDDY: Yeah, that was his wife.

DON: And his son's mother, right? What's his name- Zack?

BUDDY: Zach is one of them and Craig is the other.

FRANK: And then he had a daughter. Anyway, "all of whom were present at the Playboy Club in the final week of existence that summer." The Playboy Club closed in 1976. He goes on to say that "Montefusco and D'Acquisto Lounge, located at the corner of Powell and Bay featured music nightly led by Reynolds and various worthies including bassist Frank Passantino, pianist/singer Smith Dobson and fill-ins; Larry Dunlap, Flip Nunez, George Muribus", all pianists; drummer Steve Mitchell and Jim Nichols, guitar. Nichols, whose first instrument is guitar, on which he played a little bass, too, which he is exceptional; he's the only guy I know who could eat while he was playing!

DON: I know a guy who reads the newspaper while he's playing, that's Mike Lipskin!

A Diary of the Underdogs

BUDDY: Who was the bassist who always listened to the baseball game and played the gig? Vernon Alley! Yeah, he always had the game going while playing.

FRANK: Anyway, that's what was going on at the Montefusco thing.

DON: You've probably got some stories about Gatsby's in Sausalito, Frank, 'cause you lived there.

FRANK: Gatsby's? Oh yeah, we played some gigs there with George and Puzzie, shit I don't know who. Sometimes the bass player with the Headhunters...

BUDDY: Jackson.

FRANK: Yeah, Paul Jackson would be playing bass and we did it between Puzzie, me, and Paul.

DON: Yeah, you should hear what George said about Paul Jackson. He said the first time he met him, he was in the john, taking a shit and eating a sandwich! He was a bass player in Azteca, so that's how he knew him. And Al Pimentel was the drummer?

FRANK: Yeah, we called him the Captain's Paradise.

DON: Why?

FRANK: 'Cause he had a wife in Marin County and he had a wife in San Francisco at the same time! You remember the movie Captain's Paradise with actor Alec Guinness?

DON: (reading) "but her distinctive vocals were lost because of a Sausalito law that forbids amplification in public."

FRANK: Yeah we went through that for a while.

DON: (reading) "Her accompanists are the stirring bassist Chuck Metcalf and a deftly restrained drummer Al Pimentel."

BUDDY: Yeah, he was one of the best.

FRANK: I think that was after her and the bass player from Sausalito, a Black guy, lives in Felton.

BUDDY: A Black dude who lives in Felton, plays bass?

FRANK: Plays bass. He played at Glide, and all those places.

DON: I don't know who that is.

FRANK: Yeah you do!

DON: But her bass player was Dean Riley and her drummer was... God, it just slips my mind all the time, but she married the guy and he was wacko, they had this negative supportive thing going on.

BUDDY: Oh yeah, I ran into that when I was over in Hawaii, they came over.

DON: Oh, so you saw that.

BUDDY: Oh, I saw that. Matter of fact I had to take his place one night because he was arguing with her so bad he got sick!

DON: Yeah, it was that kind of thing.

BUDDY: Yeah, he got sick to his stomach so I got a call to go in and play.

DON: Yeah, and he wouldn't show up, or he'd leave or something...So I can't remember this guy's name but anyway a drummer that Jeanie Hoffman had when she was at the Black Hawk, I remember that. She was doing pretty well 'cause she was starting to sing and get some recognition.

BUDDY: She also had a gig on Van Ness Ave. with Pimentel on drums. A little Jazz pub, right before you make the turn to go down Lombard.

FRANK: Yeah, I remember that one.

DON: Well what was the name of the place?

BUDDY: I can't- I don't know. I would stop in several times because I liked the way she sang, It was fun!

DON: I did too; I thought she was pretty good.

FRANK: Usually by the third set her head was on the piano.

DON: Yeah I know! It's funny, I didn't know her over here but I knew her in Portland. She worked across the street, the East Bank Saloon, and I worked across the street at Digger Odell's. But I started at 5 and she

A Diary of the Underdogs

didn't start until 7.
BUDDY: What year was this?
DON: Mm, I don't know, '80 or '82. So she would come in, listen to me, have a couple of pops of vodka before she'd go across the street. Then I'd finish my gig and go to listen to her but by the time I'd get over there, *Hits table* she'd be down on the piano! I mean down!
FRANK: It's a wonder she didn't bring booze in her pocket like Puzzie!

Don Alberts, Buddy Barnhill, Frank Passantino

DON: Puzzie used to bring booze in his pocket?
BUDDY: Oh, you know about the famous leather coat?
DON: No, tell me about that!
BUDDY: Ah, you missed out on that?
DON: I wasn't here!
BUDDY: Oh you were up in Oregon.
DON: Yeah.
BUDDY: I was working' up at the hotel, Starlight Room with Richie Farrar, but I'd meet Puzzie, 'cause-
FRANK: Ok, the bass player was Nat Johnson.
DON: With whom?
FRANK: With Jeanne.
DON: Oh I see. And nobody else ever played with her?
FRANK: You know something? I was coming home from a gig, down Franklin Street, and I see him walking down the street. He was one block over from Van Ness Avenue from where they were working. I pulled over. I said, "Nat, what's going' on?" He says "hey, can you give me a ride to Sausalito?" I said, "Yeah!" He was fuckin' hot. Jeanne pissed him off and he walked off the gig.
BUDDY: Well she pissed a lot of people off, yeah.
DON: She did, because she had an alcoholic "jones" early on.
FRANK: She called him a "fuckin' n....... man, you know? And Nat of all people!
BUDDY: You don't do that to Nat.
FRANK: Nat is not a n .... He's a good guy.
DON: So he wasn't really a San Francisco guy, was he? How come he showed up here? When did that all

A Diary of the Underdogs

happen?

BUDDY: Well, he did a lot of work with Flip. I'd say he was a San Francisco guy; he just didn't live in the city. He was part of the players.

FRANK: He lived in Sausalito, played in the city. You know, he was the bass player at Glide for a long time.

BUDDY: But back to the leather jacket!

DON: Tell me about that.

BUDDY: Puzzie had a full length leather coat, this really great jacket going all the way down. But he had these pockets that were all lined inside the coat. At the end of his gig, we'd all meet up at... What was the name of that restaurant, Frank, right by the Playboy?

FRANK: We'd go to the Storyboard on Columbus and Montgomery.

BUDDY: That wasn't it... Scrooge's!

DON: Scrooge's!

FRANK: But Scrooge's wasn't a restaurant, it was a bar.

BUDDY: Yeah, that was the hang. That was it, and I'd get off the hotel gig dying to do something.

FRANK: We'd be drinking there 'til 4 o'clock in the morning.

DON: Don't you love those joints!

BUDDY: And we'd go there and Puzzie had this jacket with all these pockets, and we'd go from one club to another and he had a drink-

DON: A leather over-coat, and inside pockets and what did he have inside, half pints?

BUDDY: No! Glasses, drinks!

FRANK: Glasses with booze in 'em!

BUDDY: Yeah! So we'd go out and he'd be drinking' all the way to the bar, between the two bars! He'd hand you a vodka-soda here, and different drinks. Yeah, that was the hook up.

DON: So he'd do that on a gig too?

BUDDY: Oh sure he did.

FRANK: Are you kidding? Puzzie, Tom and I used to ride together to work at the Playboy club. First stop was the liquor store on Lombard to get a half of gallon of vodka, and whatever else we needed. It was one stop shopping and we'd pay it off on pay day.

DON: Then you'd go to the gig. Did you ever work the Playboy, Buddy?

BUDDY: Yeah, I worked the Playboy for two weeks. They had just opened up this one room and it was supposed to be a disco room. I started with Smith Dobson and the bass player was one of the brothers, John Nichols. I played that gig with them, and we had plaid pants and other weird shit going on, and it lasted two weeks, and then we were gone.

DON: Was that a formal gig? Did you guys have to dress up?

BUDDY: No, it was just a very modern thing.

FRANK: When you played upstairs in the living room, the play room and the pent house, that was coat-and-tie.

BUDDY: The other one was very casual.

DON: That was the lobby. George was talking about playing there when Oscar Peterson came in and started messing around with him.

BUDDY: That was the gig!

DON: So that was the lobby down stairs. Then there was a show room upstairs.

BUDDY: A big show room up at the top-

FRANK: Friday and Saturday night-

BUDDY: George Muribus.

282

A Diary of the Underdogs

DON: Jackson and Montgomery we're talking about, right?

FRANK: Yeah, it was kiddy corner from the Cypress Club. I went to work there; I went to work on the off-night band which was the best deal!

BUDDY: This is a good story.

FRANK: We'd work four nights a week. We'd take Monday nights; we'd do the living room. Wednesday nights we'd do the play room, and Friday and Saturday we'd do the pent house. So we had to do three rehearsals a week. Paid rehearsals, too! Just the same as if it was a gig! It was like getting paid for seven nights and working four. It was cool. So then what happened was, I went into the living room. I was hanging out at Gatsby's and I get a phone call. Steve Atkins, he'd just fired Don Prell after the first set!

BUDDY: Where have I heard that before?

FRANK: "Can you get down?" He said. I said, "I'll be right there!" I run home, put on my coat and tie, grab my bass and zip, I was there for the second set! So it's Steve Atkins, Vince and me, and we played that until the first of the year.

DON: Which was when?

FRANK: Oh I don't know, '68.

BUDDY: Jesus!

FRANK: So then, next thing that happened; Steve leaves. So now I'm in the living room.

DON: You the leader?

FRANK: I'm never the leader. Check this out; so now I'm in the living room with Jack Coker, drummer from Indianapolis. Willis Kirk, and like I said, I'm not the leader, I'm in the band. Ok after that, I get my knee operated on and they put this metal knee cap in. So I come to work. Now it's Gus Gustavson-

DON: Piano player.

FRANK: Yeah. I don't remember the kid on drums. Gus has his own bass player! I come in with my bass and they tell him, "No, you use Frank." Again, I'm not the leader but I'm always on the gig. Now figure that one out!

DON: That's cool, because they loved you, man! So Plank was the boss, huh?

FRANK: Plank was the musical contractor, the musical director. Bill Douglas was the bass player that had to go.

DON: Really? I thought he had good reputation.

FRANK: Well he did, but Plank wanted me on the gig. It had nothing to do with who played better.

DON: Yeah, that's right. Probably, who could hang with him!

FRANK: The drummer that played with us, nice kid, good drummer, and he became a vibe player too. Tall, thin kid, Jewish name....Jim Zimmerman!

BUDDY: Oh, yeah! Good drummer!

DON: He was around then, I remember him!

FRANK: Yeah, well he was the drummer on the gig. So then I played that until I got a call from the Kingston Trio. Then I went on the road with them.

DON: What was the guy's name who managed them? Frank Werber?

FRANK: He managed Kingston Trio Inc. Not so much the trio. Bobby Shane was pretty much the manager. He was the guitar player; scotch and soda.

BUDDY: He drank more than the other ones did.

FRANK: And he's still alive!

DON: Well Bobbe Norris told me she worked for Frank Werber, and his office was handling the Kingston Trio. She had a place over the Hungry Eye.

FRANK. Yes. Frank was in charge of Kingston Trio Inc. which was the building on the corner where Coppola is now.

A Diary of the Underdogs

DON: The Flatiron building.

FRANK: The Trident, the place upstairs, a couple of other houses in Sausalito, but as far as the trio itself that was like a separate entity. Frank ran the corporation. He had a house- you know Richardson bridge? You see a house on the point there by the water. That was his house. A beautiful wooden place, I mean really well designed, arty, and that was where Frank lived. Whoa boy, talk about a party pad!

DON: Did you have a lot of parties there?

FRANK: He got busted. That's where he got busted, at his house.

DON: Bobby Norris said that he changed from a business man to a party guru and started wearing all white clothes and a bunch of stuff.

FRANK: Yeah, he got out. It got to the point where, I think the guys were happy to get rid of him.

DON: Yeah? He was a problem?

FRANK: Oh yeah. I remember going into the Trident one time with the guys, the trio. And we're at the bar and they start throwing shit, and the little waiter guy is having a fit, so he goes over to the manager and the manager tells him "Keep your mouth shut. Those are the guys that pay your fucking check."

DON: So who booked Vince Guaraldi and eventually Bill Evans? All those various acts, was that all Frank Werber?

FRANK: Somebody else did the booking at the Trident, I don't know who.

BUDDY: How long did Trident last?

DON: Was it a long time, because a lot of good stuff happened there?

FRANK: Let me tell you something about the Trident; it was going when I left Sausalito in '75, it was still going.

DON: But it started in the '60s right?

FRANK: Yeah! They owned that whole pier; that belonged to Kingston Trio Inc. They own 4 or 5 house in Sausalito. They had a car one time, a Rolls Royce. You know what a shooting break is?

DON: No.

FRANK: It's a station wagon with wood sides. It was a white Rolls Royce with the wooden sides.

DON: Never seen one.

FRANK: That was their car!

DON: The most expensive car they could buy, right?

FRANK: Oh, are you kidding me! Later on I saw it in the window of the Rolls place on Van Ness Ave.

DON: As a used car?

FRANK: It was a collector's item, a classic. It was gorgeous but it drove like a truck, Jesus Christ!

DON: It probably weighed 5,000 pounds.

FRANK: The steering and everything was like a truck. You didn't have this nice power steering and all that shit.

DON: So they had it custom-made in London and shipped over to 'em, huh?

FRANK: Well they found it over there, it was already made. But it was a rare car, you didn't see many of those around.

DON: Tell me about the different personalities of the guys in the Kingston Trio.

FRANK: Bobby Shane was cool.

DON: He was one of the guitar players, and there were two guitarists and a bass?

FRANK: Two guitars and a banjo. Dave Guard was the first guy to play guitar and banjo. Nick Reynolds played the smaller guitar, the little short guy, and Bobby Shane played a regular Martin.

DON: So who was the dominant personality?

FRANK: Bobby. He was the guy who did scotch and soda and all that stuff..

DON: He was the lead singer and everything?

A Diary of the Underdogs

FRANK: Yeah.

BUDDY: He was the director, he was lead everything!

FRANK: Bobby was from Hawaii.

BUDDY: A funny dude, man! He'd just tear the place up.

DON: Did he look Hawaiian?

FRANK: No his family was from Hawaii. His mother's family was Castle Steamship. His dad was the sporting goods distributor for the islands. They all met here at Menlo College in Menlo Park.

DON: That's funny, that's where the Ungrateful Dead started, and Kenny G. that's funny.

FRANK: Yeah, that little rich boy school.

DON: So there's Bobby Shane and the other guys were kind of support musicians with supportive personalities?

FRANK: Well there are three originals; Dave Guard, Nick Reynolds and Bobby Shane. Then after a while, Dave went back to Australia which is where he is from. Then they got John Stewart. Total jerk, as banjo players usually are. So they had John for a while. Nick decided he was tired, moved up to Oregon to 200 acres up there. You know the name Reynolds, right?

DON: Yeah? Reynolds Aluminum? Are you serious?

FRANK: Yeah. I told you, this was a rich kid school.

DON: Reynolds Aluminum is a huge corporation in Oregon!

FRANK: So he went back there and went underground. No phone, nothing!

DON: I bet, no more press or anything.

FRANK: No nothing! He got tired.

DON: I don't blame him.

FRANK: So Bobby got a couple of guys; one from Kentucky and one from Alabama. The kid from Kentucky was pretty good. I liked him. The banjo player was from Gadson, Alabama which is where Lee Charleston's from.

DON: Lee the drummer.

BUDDY: Right, he should be in here *points to book*

FRANK: But this guy was a total asshole. When we were in The Philippines, we were in the car driving back from Subic Bay. I told him "If you don't shut up, I'm gonna take your banjo and shove it down your throat, big end first!"

BUDDY: He's so bad!

DON: Yeah, Frank's bad!

FRANK: I and the drummer bunked, split expenses on rooms and such.

DON: So to make it clear, the rhythm section is added?

FRANK: Yes, we were the back up rhythm section. Ok, so I call him a fucking asshole.

DON: Oh, right on.

FRANK: So he comes to my room, bangs on the door; "I think you owe me an apology!" I said "Yes, I apologize for calling you a fucking asshole, because you're a big fucking asshole!"

DON: So he went off smiling, right?

BUDDY: "It's Mister Asshole to you!"

FRANK: Then he wants to tell me "You know, we could send you back to the United States at your own expense!" I look at him and say, "You know, accidents happen. People fall down stairs and shit like that."

BUDDY: Whoa, that was a threat.

DON: So he got off your case?

FRANK: Yeah, he got off my back. We were actually in Japan. We went to the Philippines for a couple of days. We went to Okinawa, back and forth all over Japan. Then we went to Hong Kong and Bangkok. Then

A Diary of the Underdogs

when we got back here we went to Vancouver. That's where I ran into Oscar and talked to him. Then we did a couple of other gigs. We went to Boston. When we finally got to LA, we were at the Coconut Grove. I figured; "It's time to bail. I'm close enough." I got a plane ticket home to Sausalito, got my fucking car and I says "We're done!"

DON: And they called you and said "Frank-where you at?"

FRANK: Oh no, I went back. I finished the gig. I went home and got my car and drove it back to LA so I could split. I told them before I took the plane.

DON: They went on touring and you got out of it.

FRANK: I got out of it. That was enough.

BUDDY: The timing was just right.

FRANK: I figured that's as close to home as I was gonna get.

DON: Tell me about Roland's. You had that gig, didn't you Buddy?

BUDDY: I was gone, man.

DON: You were in Hawaii all this time?

BUDDY: All this time.

FRANK: I was in and out of Roland's in the '60s. Out of 20 years, I did about 15 there.

DON: Quite a while there, huh, with George DiQuattro?

FRANK: Yeah, George, and I did some with Abe Battat. I had my own band. I had Freddie Gambrell and Ron Marabuto. Freddie wanted me to fire Ronnie, I told him to go fuck himself. It's my band, you don't tell me what to do.

DON: With Ron you probably had a good time!

FRANK: I love him, man he's a good kid, a good player.

DON: He was a kid then.

FRANK: For the most part, I played there with George, and Jerry Gilmore, and Vince was on drums predominantly. For a while we had Curt Moore. I gave him a bad time, man. He didn't deserve it. And you know I was a prick at that time. I realized that he could play better than he did, so I kept on him. George was even worse on him than I was. But he's a good fucking player though! Curt's a good player. Then we got Steve Mitchell. He comes in with his Rock n' Roll drums, his fucking cymbals way up here. And I say "No man, put the cymbals down here. You're playing Jazz now. Turn the sticks around and use the tips!"

BUDDY: Like they were made to!

FRANK: We had a Latin thing going on. We had this kid from San Jose, Tim Gutierrez. He played steal pan and congas. Then we got Al Guzman. He played timbales and vibes. We smoked! And you couldn't get on the dance floor at any time.

DON: So the Roland's format was basically a drinking bar, right? They had a little dance floor...

BUDDY: That was down stairs though, the recreation room.

FRANK: I don't want to go into too much depth, but we always brought musicians down stairs and we'd smoke a little shit.

BUDDY: A little?

FRANK: So one time we're all around the table and Bobby comes downstairs. Chili is his nick name. So he comes downstairs and he's passing the coke around and he says "You take care of this half of the table, I'll take care of that half." I said, "Ok, no problem!" We gave everybody a little toot. Bobby's standing there and says "What about me?" I says, "Why don't you bring something down besides your fucking habit?!"

DON: He never brought anything to the table?

FRANK: That's right.

BUDDY: Same thing over in Hawaii too. He almost got killed over there.

DON: So you knew him in Hawaii?

A Diary of the Underdogs

BUDDY: Yeah he came to Hawaii.

FRANK: I played with Bobby Enriquez. We were good friends.

DON: He's a storming' piano player.

FRANK: I used to tell him "Who do you study piano with, Bruce Lee?"

BUDDY: He played with the elbows.

FRANK: He'd laugh though! He was a good guy and I liked him. You know what happened one time in Garden City; Hal Stein was playing, it was Smith's gig but he wasn't there. So Bobby Enriquez was sitting in. He had asked to sit in and when he went up, no one went up to play with him 'cause they're full of shit. You know, these chicken shit musicians were gonna make him go up and play by himself. I went up and played with him. He's my friend. You know what he played? I'll never forget it. That Chuck Mangione tune. He could play, man! I was having a ball. And these other guys were out there in the crowd with these long faces. He came down to Roland's one night, a couple of times.

DON: He played?

FRANK: Yeah, George let him sit in, of course! Then we'd be downstairs and he and I would be playing cribbage. I'd whoop his ass. He says "You're a good player!" Then he says to me "You know, Frank, you're the only musician in this band!" I don't know, man, it was a nice compliment but... This is at Roland's. There were a lot of good players there.

DON: I would say so, with Jerry Gilmore and all the guys that you're talking about.

FRANK: The people that would come there, there was always limos out front, a lot of the local bookies used to hang out in front there.

DON: It was a happening spot.

BUDDY: When I was in Hawaii, I heard about Roland's musicians coming through Japan.

FRANK: They heard about Roland's in Australia. All these people would come in. I'd get off the band stand and I'd look, there's Phil Harris and Alice Faye and Aldo Ray, Robert Walden, Jim Belushi, and all those kinds of people would come through. It was that kind of place where you go down to rub elbows.

BUDDY: There was a place just like that in Hawaii.

FRANK: And the place was always packed.

DON: And who was this bright guy who started this whole thing?

FRANK: Well the guy who owned the place, his name was Dick Tomey. It isn't that he was a genius but he hooked onto the right thing. He liked to dance. He was a swing dancer, so he knew it would get the people going.

DON: He was smart enough to put in a dance floor and a band that would play dance music.

BUDDY: Dance music; that was it!

DON: I was gonna ask Buddy about the early days in the Cameo.

BUDDY: Oh the Cameo club? Shit! I don't have too much. Finish off with Frank.

DON: So, Dick Tomey? He was the owner there, and he knew what sold. He sold the place a couple of times and he got it back both times. One of the buyers was a defrocked priest and a nun who got married and they bought the fuckin' place and they didn't know shit about running a bar. So dickey got it back. They didn't make the payments. Art Saltis was his last partner, a good guy. He had places around town; he was also a head bookie. He ran the whole drill. He even had Shelly Robins answer the phones. Shelly Robins the piano player, for $500 a week! Anyway Art was a really good Cat. Sometimes I'd say "Hey Art, I need $300." "Ok Frankie!" You know, he'd give it to me. I'd come by to give him back $100 and he'd say "No, give it to me the way you got it." He liked me, man! He'd call me Iron Man.

DON: You've been called a lot of things but I haven't heard that!

BUDDY: I haven't heard that either.

FRANK: Well, I went there every fuckin' night, and I always showed up on time.

A Diary of the Underdogs

DON: You get a badge for that!

FRANK: I left there around '84, and then I went to work in Napa for 5 months.

DON: Wasn't the Keystone Korner going on during the same time, in the '70s.

BUDDY: Yeah, I heard about that too.

DON: They had a Monday night trio; I don't know who that was. I think Vince was probably in on that and not too many people know too much about that but every body can tell you something about some body. It's all there.

FRANK: The guy that was running it put the place up his nose.

DON: Yeah, Todd Barkan. He's the manager of Dizzy's Coca Cola in New York at Lincoln Center.

FRANK: Funny how these guys survive?

DON: Now you wanna tell me more about the Cameo club?

BUDDY: With George DiQuattro and Jerry Gilmore.

DON: I never heard about this stuff.

BUDDY: It's a funny story. The gig was George and Jerry. No bass player. It was a total strip gig because we had a stripper. We had a comedian and a magician. Who was a weird asshole, really! The place was packed every night. That's why they came; there was a big card room in the back. George was really hung up on that. Whenever we couldn't find George, we found him in the card room.

DON: George actually had a gambling jones.

BUDDY: He was gambling all the time.

FRANK: He was always looking for the easy buck!

BUDDY: One night out in the parking lot with George and tenor player, Bob Ferrara. So, we're out talking about the high school days, and I was telling them that I was a jumper; hop-skip-and-jump in high school and I won trophies and shit. George asks "Well how does that go? You run, you hop, skip and jump?" "Yeah, I'll show ya!" Idiot! I'm out there in the parking lot and I'm running and I do the whole thing and I came down on my side.

FRANK: When you jump you land on the sand.

BUDDY: Yeah, I was landing on concrete! Concrete head! He had to carry me to the hospital. On the way in there were these two girls going into the ER, cute girls. And George is saying "We got a junkie, he OD'd!" He's doing this whole thing about me being a junkie. So I couldn't play the gig for a while. Dick Fudge, the drummer took my place. Then I was better so I came back to the gig and he and Bob unfortunately went on the road, got into the accident and Dick Fudge died. Bob was in the back so he was injured. Dick Fudge was a great drummer.

DON: I remember meeting him.

BUDDY: That gig went on and on.

DON: I had that gig and I gave it to George. There was a Jewish guy drummer playing with me and Gordon and we had a house trio.

BUDDY: So you were in on this before.

DON: The owner liked us, would buy me dinner. He'd say "I really happy with you guys." He'd bring in Strippers on Monday nights.

BUDDY: Oh, I remember Monday nights; a magician, comic and singer. That's how the show was set up.

DON: So I left there and George got the gig.

BUDDY: My dad died, so I had to leave the gig.

DON: I wanted to talk about the Broadway gig you did.

BUDDY: "Oh Calcutta" on Broadway, right across the street from Moulin Rouge, a big old two story theater.

DON: What was it like back stage?

A Diary of the Underdogs

BUDDY: Insane. Hanging out with the cast was the best part! I was playing with 3 pianists; Harpsichord, piano which was Gus Gustafson. Don Haas played the bass line and did singing. 3 pianos and drums, it was very strange. I watched the whole show through a mirror. The stage was behind me. I had to play and watch, try to catch their movements. It went on for a whole year, doing seven shows a week, with a Sunday matinee, so actually, 8! We were getting paid a fortune. For a whole year, we got busted, 3 or 4 or 6 times.

DON: What was going on?

BUDDY: On stage nudity.

DON: What was the show like? I never saw "Oh Calcutta".

BUDDY: They had the guy who wrote the music come in. It was strange stuff. It was all done in the nude. We had to play for the auditions and some funny shit went on there too. Some guys would get a hard on and you can't have that on stage. That just wasn't right. Back stage was fun. Went upstairs and hung out with the cast, bought all the dope and everything.

DON: You left for Hawaii after that?

BUDDY: I guess I did leave after that in '74.

DON: What about Jimmy Borges- was he a guy from here?

BUDDY: No, he's from Hawaii. He did a lot of work in Japan Town.

DON: So when you went back the second time you were in a group and you had something set up?

BUDDY: Yes with Jimmy Borges at Keoni's, that was the bar. It went on forever.

DON: You didn't come back for 18 years!

BUDDY: The first time Frank came over to play the gig with me.

FRANK: I left after 3 months.

DON: And Jimmy wasn't good to you, Frank.

FRANK: Well one night I'm sitting on my speaker playing electric bass, and he said something, I said something back, and he said "Bass player got no lines" and I said "All the lines are in your face!" Then he stiffed me $150! So I got a hold of Blackie Perry. He went over there and said "there's no chance of getting the bread there, it's all family. That mother fucker ever comes out here he's in trouble." Sure enough we were at the Miyako hotel in San Francisco. I get a phone call. "Frank! I can't start my show until I pay you." I say, "Ok, I'll be down. Bring it in cash." All I wanted was my $150; I could have got him for more. Blackie Perry took care of it, man!

DON: I love Blackie; he was a San Jose guy!

BUDDY: I was in the band, and Eddie Duran was the guitarist.

DON: Let's have a smoke.

End: Frank and Buddy

Interview: Richard Hadlock –musician, clarinetist, author, journalist, broadcaster-and Don Alberts-September 29, 2009-at Brannan's Restaurant, Berkeley, Ca. About Traditional bands and San Francisco Clubs, Kewpie Doll, Amelio's, Easy Street, Pier 23, Earthquake McGoon's, Club Hangover, Tim Angel, Say When, Burp Hollow,-Musicians, Thelonious Monk, Vince Cattolica, Sidney Bechet, Barney Baggard, Bob Mielke, Red Nichols, Earl Hines, Kid Ory, Turk Murphy, Mezz Mezzro, Lu Waters, Bob Wilber, Barbara Dane, Scott Anthony, Jim Rothermel, Burt Bales, Ray Skjelbred, Joe Sullivan, Dick Oxtot.

A Diary of the Underdogs

RICHARD HADLOCK

RICHARD: It's funny; so many people, who used to be outcasts, then became icons, like Thelonious Monk. Why did they even listen to this guy, he can't play piano, he's no Art Tatum. And he was just kind of awkward and angular, doesn't swing. So why bother with him?

DON: Do you know some of those guys?

RICHARD: At one time Miles was sort of an outcast because he didn't try to sound like Dizzy.

DON: Yeah, he was really intimidated playing with Bird which was the best gig he ever had. But one thing about Miles he pulled himself together and realized he had to play his own sound. As far as Thelonious Monk some article came out in Down Beat, which is what they were trying to get to all along, Monk can't play. One of the critics said that.

RICHARD: Leonard Feather said so.

DON: Was it Leonard Feather?

RICHARD: Leonard said that Sydney Bechet was corny and had a nanny goat vibrato, why would you waste time listening to that. Now, Wynton Marsalis has declared that Sydney Bechet is a national treasure and that makes it real.

DON: I just read recently that Sydney Bechet could get that Louis Armstrong sound.

RICHARD: But he was; he was swinging before Louie! 1919 Louie was still in New Orleans playing riverboats or whatever, Bechet was in England knocking out the critics and they said, "My God, who is this guy?"

DON: Well, it comes around, you know, very interesting. But I am interested in some of the things you have to say. I will read just a little of this. Trad Bands, "Traditional Jazz Bands." I want this story, I want to know those bands and I want to know those traditional players. They are just as passionate and driven and soulful as any of the modern Bebop players, and seem even more exotic at times. And the blues was a big part of that repertoire. Plus, their lifestyles as musicians were similar, but also different and unique. I think theirs is a story that could easily be a centerpiece of this foray into the life of Jazz in San Francisco and that's what I am looking for. These men seem unique and seasoned, road worn, eclectic, and epical. After talking with Mal Sharpe I really became interested and realized this can't be ignored in a book about Jazz.

RICHARD: I am glad you saw that because, well, I'll just give a random example – Vince Cattolica was one of the greatest clarinet players to ever come out of California.

DON: Was he blind?

RICHARD: He was blind. He started off on Goodman's show, can't think of that name, the guy who played for years with Tommy Dorsey. Suddenly I have gone blank, but anyway, those were his heroes. But then he carved something so special out of that. People like Larry Vuckovich would recognize Vince.

DON: Yeah, I talked with Larry; he had a lot to say about that.

RICHARD: But the hidden side of people in New York, you know like the standard crowd, would say,

A Diary of the Underdogs

Vince who? We don't need him. And that was always something that baffled me. Why do they think – modern guys – that Dixieland isn't Jazz and why do so many of the Trad players think that Bebop isn't Jazz, they are all crazy. It's impossible. They wrote these books about the "real" Jazz and so did that French guy, Tenacie. He even declared Mezz Mezzro the greatest white clarinet player, and Mezzro was a joke, he was a real pariah. The people that played with Eddie Condon, Jimmy Ryan, or any of those guys…you know if you talk to Hot Lips Page or even Bechet, who recorded with him, you know, he was willing to record with him and work with him, but they also said it was a joke. Mezzro said, "Yes, I am a genius. I worked with Sydney Bechet, you know, I am a genius!" It's kind of pitiful.

DON: Well, he was a salesman?

RICHARD: And then he gets lumped in with Vince Cattolica, you know, as if… "Well, they are all just Dixieland guys, who cares?" I have seen that over and over.

DON: Unfair, right, unfair and inappropriate? I remember early on, running across some music from Mezz Mezzro in my early days of playing piano when I was eighteen or nineteen years old.

RICHARD: He had one thing really going for him; he was the best pot connection in Harlem. All these musicians bought from him; maybe they owed him money.

DON: Was it called *Gage* or *George* or *Muggles* or something in those days, the pot?

RICHARD: They had all kinds of names; *Reppa, Mary Jane*. But he would get it from somebody like J.C. Higginbotham.

DON: What is his generation? What year was were they, early 40's?

RICHARD: 1930's. He started recording in the 30's. But they never took him seriously. I think what people in Europe did, besides the writers; Tenacie, Humphrey Littleton, you know, Mezzro did play pretty nice slow Blues. They named a couple of tunes after Mezz Mezzro, you know we have to be a little kindly sometimes.

DON: He is a clarinet player, right, a reed player?

RICHARD: Clarinet.

DON: As was Vince Cattolica also-and yourself too, right?

RICHARD: Yeah, I try. Comparisons are bad things. Somebody might say to you, Tony Scott wasn't really a clarinet player; but Tony Scott was really a great clarinet player.

DON: Of course, of course, so what is it, personal preferences, or somebody that they heard on a record?

RICHARD: Jazz is full of personal preferences. That's what Jazz is.

DON: Yeah, I think we hit on something there. Yeah, I am very much that way myself.

RICHARD: I try to disguise some of my prejudices when I do radio shows.

DON: Yeah, your radio shows are great.

RICHARD: Like last night, I was actually sifting through Keith Jarrett records. But I was looking for something special and I got it and realized that he made this, and made that, and I am sort of educating myself. That is what that show is all about.

DON: That is a great show Richard. It's on KCSM on Sunday nights. But I went through your bio and you have accomplished quite a bit. You have written at least two books on Jazz and they are very authentic.

RICHARD: One was a real book and one was sort of a booklet that goes with an album about Joe Sullivan.

DON: Yeah, piano player?

RICHARD: That took as long to write as the book. That one I got a Grammy nomination for, I didn't win. Not bad considering I never joined NARAS and usually winners are members of the inside group.

DON: NARAS – what is that?

RICHARD: National Association of Recording Arts and Sciences – The Grammy's. They are the ones who judge the content, but if the writer or the musician just happens to be a member, that gives them a leg up. It used to be, twenty-five years ago, a little more conservative in a sense that they didn't vote so heavily for rock. But then rock wiped out everything else. The one time I went there, when I was nominated, Michael

A Diary of the Underdogs

Jackson came out with all those record players statues; he had eight of them that he won that day. And Wynton Marsalis won best Pop and Classical awards that day, and he came out on stage and played a classical piece and then he played a Jazz piece that impressed me. You know it's very hard to change your brain right in the middle like that.

DON: Yes, he has done well, but he was very precocious at a young age.

RICHARD: That whole family should write a book. I think Branford is the outstanding Jazz player.

DON: Thank you very much, I agree with you. I think he is the most natural and advanced Jazz player. Some of the younger boys are coming along, but they are not as outstanding as Branford.

RICHARD: They are all talented. The father is talented. I wonder what it is like to be the mother of that family.

DON: Well, God Bless them, they advanced Jazz quite a lot, and it came at a time when Jazz was really struggling in the late 70's.

RICHARD: It's sort of poetic that they are all from New Orleans, you know, being the birthplace of so much of the music and all that. I think that is kind of nice.

DON: Can you fill me in on some of the clubs and some of the guys playing in San Francisco during the 60's? There was a place called the Kewpie Doll that Mal Sharpe talked about and I think that Vince Cattolica and Cuz Cousineau were playing there; and you mentioned Bob Nabors when we were talking on the phone.

RICHARD: Bob Nabors. The Kewpie Doll was Marty Marsala's stomping ground. Marty was Joe Marsala's younger brother.

DON: Where were they from?

RICHARD: Originally from Chicago. I met them on a milk run train going from New York up to Bridgeport, Connecticut. They were living in Hartford but they were on the same train. The milk run was about 3:30 or 4 in the morning. The pubs closed down around 3am, but you would see musicians on these little trains that would take two hours to go sixty miles because they stopped so frequently to unload the mail and take on milk or whatever. Anyway, Marty wound up in San Francisco and he got some work at the Hangover Club in San Francisco and he liked the city. This is such a typical story of Jazz musicians that come to San Francisco, they get a few gigs and they say, God it's nice here – this is a paradise. Doesn't freeze in the winter, everybody is hip, beautiful scenery – I'm staying. And they stay a year or they stay two years and then they realize there are no gigs. They realize they are on the road all the time going to New York, Paris or London. And then they leave. It is a typical story. The ones who stay, don't ever quote me on this, but the ones who tend to stay, including me, tend to be kind of the losers in a sense. They are less aggressive and they find this to be a charming place, and why should you want to be a big success if you can be totally happy here? What is success for anyway, except to be happy? So you already got the happiness without all that hustling and bustling. But not everyone feels that way, and people with agents, the agents typically don't feel that way. So, if you are Stan Getz you could say, hey I like it here in the Bay Area, but his agent is saying, like hell, we got things lined up in Denmark, Sweden, France, Germany; you are on the road Buster, right now! I used to joke that this was the place that people came to die. Not that bad, but, they were old alcoholics that wound up here, a good place to drink.

DON: Yeah! Good drinking bars here.

RICHARD: And if you were a piano player, you could usually find a bar, you know, they would say, ok, I'll take you on Friday and Saturday's, to try it out. So we had people like Joe Sullivan who was a confirmed alcoholic; and Arthur Schutt who was a major player in the twenties, on piano. He came out of Pennsylvania with all those guys like the Dorsey Brothers and others that came out of there. In the thirties when the swing era hit, after working with Benny Goodman, he was Benny's choice for piano and arranging, he wound up in Hollywood doing arranging, but the booze got him finally. He drifted into San Francisco to a flea-bag hotel at the foot of Broadway and his lady friend that was with him for a long time went across to the Embarcadero and was listening to a very talented local guy named Bill Erickson at Pier 23. Bill was a very well versed Jazz man, he knew his Jazz history. Good piano player and good arranger. One of his heroes was Arthur Schutt, but as far as he knew Arthur Schutt wasn't alive anymore. Arthur's lady goes over and she is sitting in the corner nursing a beer, listening to Bill Erickson and she got kind of juiced and yelled out, *"Hey kid, you are all right but you're no Arthur Schutt!"* And Erickson falls off the piano stool and is like, what! What did she say? Then he found out that Arthur Schutt was living two blocks away! So he went to see Arthur a couple of times and took some of Bix Beiderbecke's piano music and asked him if he could still read it, and he said yes. And he sight read it! What a musician. When Arthur died, I am not telling you what he died of, but I am assuming that it was cirrhosis of the liver; he had no money, he was taken to SF General Hospital, which is where you take the poor people. A guy, who was doing his residency at that point, becoming a medical doctor, was Denny Zeitlin, and I knew Denny. I knew Arthur and I knew that Arthur at any moment was likely to go. Denny called up and said, we got a patient here who says he is an important Jazz musician and he asked me if I had ever heard of Arthur Schutt. And yes, of course I had! Denny told me that Arthur was in the hospital and that it wasn't looking very good but that he is taking care of him and he is good hands. I thanked him.

DON: What a great story! And as far as you know, did Denny develop an appreciation for Arthur?

RICHARD: He might have. I don't know if he ever went back to listening to him because Denny was more into more modern avant-garde stuff. Arthur died shortly after that and the musicians union honored him by having a string quartet play at his funeral. Hardly anybody was there, his lady friend. My wife and I went, but almost no one else. They were like, "Arthur who?" So, that is just one story, you could almost make up another one about Brew Moore.

DON: Yeah, that was a little sketchy.

RICHARD: He wound up going to Europe and getting some of the attention he deserved. But also the booze got him. And it meant that when he was living in the Bay Area everybody had great regard for him, but can you quite trust Brew on a gig? If he has been drinking can you trust him? They weren't sure, and they would call another guy instead. And yet when Brew was "on" he was a delight. He had a great respect for the older guys. He played some of the Dixieland Jazz on clarinet. Most people don't know that. But he could do that, and he enjoyed it. One time I put together a big benefit for Burt Bales and my band included Brew Moore, nobody was paid, it was a benefit. So, I could call up anybody I wanted. And so my band was at the Jazz Cellar.

DON: Oh, up there on Green Street?

RICHARD: Yeah. That's where my band was. We had four different clubs lined up that night with eight bands. And we raised two thousand dollars, and in 1960 that was a fair amount. He was in the hospital with no medical insurance or nothing.

DON: Well that's interesting that you mention the cellar, because I thought it was strictly Bebop and more modern Jazz.

RICHARD: It pretty much was. Although one of the partners in that was a guy that you ought to have in your book named Jack Minger. Jack was, and is, still a trumpet player. Jack is a unique guy, he was brought up listening to everything and he liked Bebop and he sort of tended to play in that idiom but with kind of a swing feel. You know, it wasn't way out there or anything, just a great improviser, is what he was, and he became a partner. Bill Wejohn and those guys at the cellar played a lot with him. They used to tease him and they would say, *oh, you are you the trumpet player that played when Dickie Mills wasn't there!* And he didn't like that!

DON: There is a missing link here – Bill Wejohn's partner at the Jazz Cellar?

RICHARD: Sonny.

DON: Sonny Wayne or something like that? Was he a drummer?

RICHARD: Yes, he was a drummer. You are close when you say Wayne. It might even be that.

A Diary of the Underdogs

DON: And then there was Wilber Carlson – he was around too.

RICHARD: Wilber is one of my best friends, even though he is a real right-winger. He's always saying, *"Jesus Christ, what is that guy doing, he is a Communist! – he is a fucking Communist!"*

DON: That's right! That's Wilber! I have played a lot with him at Pier 23. Wilber would bring his lunch and go out in his pick-up truck to eat on breaks. Great, great guy! He could play! He loved to play.

RICHARD: Sometimes he would come to a gig and bring just a simple little snare with the brushes, one cymbal and it would sound good! He could swing the band. He had good time. But, I wanted to tell you more about Jack. Minger kind of drifted out of that partnership and he wound up driving a cab in the city. He never had a couple of nickels to put together, he was always broke, and either had bad luck or he just wasn't a business guy, no hustle. But a wonderful player, good reader, really reliable, had a big sound and he was wonderful, he would click right in with the trumpet section on any tune. You could call the most traditional tune, *Trouble in Mind*, he would play something great. And then you could call *Cherokee* or something, and boom, boom, boom, he had it all. And he wound up playing just to make a living with Dick Oxtot's traditional band. Oxtot was a banjo player.

DON: Yeah, I found him in some of my notes.

RICHARD: Out at the Point, in Richmond, Point Richmond, they played there for years and years. And Jack never stopped being kind of a modern player, but knew how to fit in a traditional band. It was always amazing how hip he could be. Because he knew how to lead the front-line of the band, which is what you have to do as a trumpet player in a Dixieland band. At the same time he is not trying to recreate who played in the twenties or even the thirties. He is a contemporary guy. He was so widely respected. He played in a band, I think it was at the Hangover, there was another club too, the guy who was a professor out at SF State and doubled trombone and vibes. He had a Dixieland band and he had sort of a swing band, Paul Desmond was in that band. And Vince Cattolica was in the band at different times. Anyway, this guy was a mediocre musician but hired these wonderful people.

DON: Before John Handy?

RICHARD: Yeah, before John Handy was well known. This was before Desmond was well known.

DON: Oh, yeah, that is much earlier.

RICHARD: We are talking about 1949 or 1950 maybe. He made some records – 78's – and one of them was *The Man I Love* where the leader is playing vibes and Desmond puts down the clarinet and picks up the alto and plays this absolutely beautiful song. It's pure, all Desmond – early, early. His name will come to me, that later. But Minger was with him for quite awhile. And when Paul Desmond died, lets see, that was in the 70's, 80's, can't remember now-

DON: I think 80's.

RICHARD: He was young, like in his fifties.

DON: Yeah, he was young, drank a lot of scotch.

RICHARD: Yeah, and a lot of cigarettes too. I had a call sometime after Paul's death, it was Jimmy Lyons, and I said, "Hello," and he said, "Hi and how are you, and blah, blah," and he said that Paul had named him Executor of his Estate. And he said that he had to take his ashes out over Monterey Bay and spread his ashes out over the ocean. That was his request. He wanted to be near the Monterey Jazz Festival and Jimmy said he had hired the pilot and set it all up. But he said in his "Will" he had a thousand dollars to some guy named Jack Minger, "who is that," he wanted to know? And I told him that Jack was a great trumpet player who used to play with Paul. And he asked me if I knew him and I told him that I was playing with him this coming Friday night! And then Jimmy said to tell him that there was a thousand bucks waiting for him. And for Jack Minger a thousand dollars was like millions for you. That was a lot for Jack. He was lucky if he had the rent. And so I called him up and I said, "Jack, you are not going to believe this story, but Paul Desmond wants you to have a thousand dollars, he admired your playing so much, and Paul even said in his Will that this was a guy who deserved so much more attention then he ever

A Diary of the Underdogs

got. And so maybe this will help." Anyway, Jack thought I was putting him on, but I assured him it was real and that he needed to call Jimmy Lyons, and he did. And I tell that story because Desmond really liked Minger's playing. And I talked to Paul one time about that band and he said that Dixieland playing, if you wanted to call it that, collective improvisation is a wonderful idea, but he said that none of them do anything with it. And I knew just what he meant – I got awful tired of the bands at Nick's, like Phil Napoleon, Pee Wee Erwin; they all sound alike. Turk Murphy sounds like the same as he did last year or a decade ago. But Jerry Mulligan came along and was playing collective improvisation with Chet Baker and then for one session which Dick Bock organized, they had Lee Konitz and the three understood, you can update Dixieland and this is what it is going to be like. And it was pretty and hip and everybody listened to everybody else and playing parts which is all that the Trad guys were trying to do all the time. But these guys happened to be geniuses on top of that. What a great session that was! It kills me still to listen to that.

DON: Yeah, those were great recordings. And that was in the early 50's?

RICHARD: 53, yeah. When Lee was out there with the Kenton band, Pacific Jazz, they tapped into the new sound.

DON: And it's really nice that you bring it up because it's a nice extension of that music into the modern era. And they brought it along.

RICHARD: Yeah. And I always wanted to find more of that, you know, more people thinking about doing that. Both Steve Lacy and Roswell Rudd had backgrounds in Dixieland and thought they understood it. But then they got it, and eventually they became quite disciplined. But for quite awhile there, they thought non-disciplined was the way to go and just play your head off in any direction you wanted to go.

DON: I think that crosses every musicians mind at one time or another, especially Jazz musicians.

RICHARD: But Steve eventually became almost conservative in a way. He wanted compositions, he wanted charts.

DON: He basically became a contemporary with Monk.

RICHARD: Well, Steve Lacy and Roswell Rudd had a band that played only Monk! They knew more Monk tunes then Monk knew! It's a fascinating thing – the other guys who could do this sort of thing were Lee Konitz and Warne Marsh. When they start intertwining ideas, it just floored me. And I would think, gee, if I could only do that!

DON: One of the most impressive things I've ever heard were the early Lenny Tristano recordings with Konitz and Warne Marsh. But you know that actually Paul Desmond and Dave Brubeck did that too.

RICHARD: Yeah, they worked with the full counterpoint roll.

DON: It was one of their formats.

RICHARD: And Paul, he made a couple of records with Mulligan; I wish he had done more. That would have been a very rewarding thing to hear.

DON: Mulligan was very at ease with that kind of playing.

RICHARD: Oh, absolutely. Well, he wound up playing with Brubeck after Paul, which surprised me because I would have thought that Jerry was a little too acidic.

DON: He has always been acidic, that's a good word!

RICHARD: I mean he might just turn around and say to Dave, *"For Christ sake, you're not swinging,"* or something like that.

DON: Well, he made a record with Thelonious too.

RICHARD: Yeah, and so did Pee Wee Russell.

DON: That's right Pee Wee Russell – that's right - you got a good memory.

RICHARD: Now, Pee Wee was one of the heroes of my kind of Trad guys, because in 1929 he made a record with Coleman Hawkins, *If I Could Be With You One Hour Tonight* and then they just shortened the title to *One Hour* so you wouldn't know that was the tune they were playing. They never played the melody. And that's very Tristano like. Like, Lenny doing *Yesterday's* or something. Those guys are so hip,

A Diary of the Underdogs

man, 1929 and all, but the general public wasn't very appreciative, I don't think those records ever went anywhere.

DON: Well, that's the example of art, art takes awhile.

RICHARD: Yeah. Whenever they re-issue Coleman Hawkins on the RCA label, that's the first track they put on there.

DON: Yeah, it's an artistic thing. Somebody gave me a copy of a handwritten letter that Sonny Rollins had written to Coleman Hawkins, talking about his great appreciation of Coleman Hawkins.

RICHARD: Yeah, he talked about that.

DON: And a very eloquent letter. It's amazing. But he went on and on in a very gentlemanly way and in language of the thirties, the language of Jack London, which really is amazing.

RICHARD: Hawk (Coleman Hawkins) was such an enormous force in tenor sax and very outgoing and Rollins was also outgoing – have you ever seen that video of Rollins stomping around on the stage with a remote mike on the bell of his horn so he wasn't attached to a mike cord – and he fell off the stage and landed five feet down on the ground and he was lying on his back and still continued to play? He never missed a beat! He belongs in some other world.

DON: He has really contributed a lot. Tell me a little bit about Lou Waters, Clancy Hayes, Pat Yankee, Kid Ory, those guys. Where they doing anything in early 60's?

RICHARD: You know Kid Ory was a link to the real beginnings of Jazz. He could sit down and talk to you about his discussions with Buddy Bolden, a direct link to the beginnings of Jazz. I played two nights with him at "On the Levy," that club that is right across the railroad tracks from Pier 23, down on the Embarcadero. He had a very distinct idea of what he wanted and some of the Trad people thought, he has got it, which is what a band is supposed to do. He played the trombone parts, Mutt Carey played the straight lead but with hot phrasing and the clarinet player filled in between that, and that's what part playing is all about. When Ory was playing in San Francisco, he was getting to be an old man, he is way up in his sixties or into his seventies, and he wanted everything so organized it made me uncomfortable and I couldn't deliver what it was that he wanted. He wanted to play his big hit tune, *Muskrat Ramble* in every set! And it always had to be the same. And he would play the same parts and expected me to play the same parts. And I just can't operate like that and that is also why I couldn't stay with Turk Murphy's band.

DON: You were with Turk also?

RICHARD: Yeah, six months. But he basically wanted a sound, he had a sound in his head for that band and no matter who played clarinet or trumpet in the front-line with him, he wanted the same sound. That's impossible; you can't replace Bob Helm or me, for example, and get the same band sound. And somehow Turk thought he could.

DON: Yeah, and it's basically with your instrument because it's a roaming polyphonic; everyone is going to do that differently.

RICHARD: I always felt that Jazz centered on soloists and I love the packaging of it, and I love ensemble playing, but first and foremost to me is what you play as an individual. That is not the way a lot of Trad people saw it. Some of the real fundamentalist bands didn't even want to hear soloists. All ensembles, thank you. And how you play your part in the ensemble is what is important. Ok, that is their outlook – it's not mine. And Turk would come up and sometimes say something like, "On such and such a tune you played the whole solo behind the beat." And I would say, "Yeah, that's what Lester Young would do." And he would respond by saying, "Don't let that happen again." He was very adamant. And he didn't want to hear about Pee Wee Russell or any of those people. He wanted everybody to be a rhythm section. That means for trumpet players – "da dat dat data dat da dat data," or your clarinet players; all night long. God, that's boring!

DON: It doesn't have any freedom.

RICHARD: Now if you have a great rhythm section you can get away with that and sound like a good band.

A Diary of the Underdogs

But it wasn't for me, that's all. I shouldn't knock Turk, he did some wonderful things. One wonderful thing was that he kept more guys employed full time then any other leader I can think of for more years. You know, for like forty years, he paid scale, five nights a week to a full band! How many leaders can do that?

DON: Where was his hangout in San Francisco?

RICHARD: He had various ones. One was – oh, I have forgotten his earlier one.

DON: I have the Earthquake McGoon's, Club Hangover, Tin Angel, Say When, Burp Hollow, and The Maltese Grill.

RICHARD: Yeah, those are short-term things, just to fill in….

DON: Easy Street?

RICHARD: The "Tin Angel" became the club that I was telling you Kid Ory had named, that was "On the Levy." That is the same building and the same place. That is one thing that is confusing, they keep changing the names. When I joined Turk Murphy he was getting funding from a very wealthy family in South Carolina that wanted to underwrite his new club. They took a place out in North Beach, I think it had been a Mambo club; it was a Latin band place, and they re-named it Easy Street. We opened Easy Street on New Years Eve, 1958. And it was a little wrong headed from the start, because the guy that was putting the money in wanted to hire a decorator. Turk wanted a nice old-fashioned saloon looking place; dark wood and captain's chairs, red velvet – that comfy old-fashioned look.

DON: So go ahead –

RICHARD: So, the first name that has come to my mind is Bill Napier. He is one of the great clarinet players, he and Vince Cattolica. He played with Bob Scoby for years; he played with everybody around here. He played in Chicago for some time, but essentially he was a Bay Area guy and he could have gone to Europe and made $1,500 plus travel expense or something. He was just one of those natural guys, I don't think he read very well but his ear was so wonderful and he played this beautiful limpid style, I guess you would say like Albert Nicholas from New Orleans, you know, just beautiful tone and smooth flowing ideas, sort of like Barney Baggard too, he had that quality.

DON: So these are your clarinet heroes.

RICHARD: Yes. Bill was a hero to the Bay Area too. And he was totally modest, he would always get embarrassed if you flattered him or complimented him. He lived with his wife in a house in Pacifica and would play little local gigs for a hundred dollars or a hundred and twenty-five or something, not bad, but he could make a nice little living that way and he had no interest in travel or being a big name or being recognized, he just didn't care about that stuff. Bill Napier is one who is now getting better known, but for years he was not. Noel Jukes though – oh he was wonderful.

DON: Yeah, we played a few weeks ago. Yeah, he is wonderful, but he has been here playing good like that for years.

RICHARD: Yes, I know. The first time I ever heard him, I was like, who is this – he is a major league guy. Joe Sullivan was a good friend of mine and plagued with bad luck all his life. He was one of the major players and he was kind of ignored in the Bay Area. He played intermission at the Hangover Club for years.

DON: But a very strong player?

RICHARD: Yes, a power player.

DON: Power player in the genre, right?

RICHARD: He came out of Chicago in the 20's.

DON: So, there are a couple of categories of piano players – stride, and also Scott Joplin.

RICHARD: The head liner that he was playing intermission for was Earl Hines. And I used to wonder, how can that little spinet piano take two powerful players? They banged the heck out of that piano every night.

DON: What was the name of the club? Was that the "Say When?"

RICHARD: The "Hangover Club." It was up on Bush. Bob Short was a tuba player who played with Turk and played with all those traditional guys; doubled on trumpet. But he was one the best tuba players you

A Diary of the Underdogs

will ever hear anywhere. Bob Short recorded with Bill Evans. Bob Mielke, you should talk to Bob, he is eighty-three now, but very available and he is still playing. And he has a unique style, there is nobody like him. And he knows the Tradition scene better then I do; a powerful guy. For years we had two guys who came down from the Northwest, Jim Goodwin, he died last spring.

DON: Yeah, Barbara Hauser spoke of him, they were good friends.

RICHARD: She was very close to Jim and helped organize the memorial that I just went to. Jim is a vastly underrated player. Ray Skjelbred was sort of his partner and lived in Ray's house, a pianist deserving of wider recognition. A piano player you may know is Al Plank.

DON: Yes, I knew Al.

RICHARD: I think Al was one of the best pianists ever.

DON: Yes. Where did Al come from? Los Angeles, Las Vegas?

RICHARD: Originally he is out of Indianapolis, I think, pretty sure.

DON: He had a great sense of humor.

RICHARD: He was with Benny Barth. I hired him and Benny one time for a concert and it was like old home week. They were reminiscing. Dean Reilly is another you might know.

DON: Yes, I have met with him.

RICHARD: Si Perkoff, do you know Si?

DON: I know Si. Si was my first interview.

RICHARD: I love Si. He's very imaginative. And he is like Minger in a sense, you can't throw him off – you can follow with a Jelly Roll Morton tune and follow it with a Thelonious Monk tune, he can get it. He is at home. The next one might be a Boogie Woogie tune, he is at home. Drummer Dave Black deserves more attention then he got. He used to be with Duke Ellington in the 50's. And he came and settled here and played local gigs mostly. And he is just one of those all around fine drummers. Died maybe a year ago or something like that. Good player.

DON: There are a couple of bands I am interested in – Salty Dogs, The Golden Gate Rhythm Machine, The Yerba Buena Jazz Band, I think that was Lou Waters.

RICHARD: I think the Salty Dogs are pretty nearly a Chicago band, the ones I am thinking of. The Yerba Buena is partly Leon Oakley's work. He's a wonderful trumpet player and wants to preserve that sound of the old Lou Waters band with the two trumpets and tubas, in its present reincarnation – if you can have a reincarnation of a reincarnation.

DON: For a time Red Nichols was here wasn't he?

RICHARD: He played here off and on. I interviewed him once when he was at the Palace Hotel. And I was talking to you before about Pee Wee Russell, who at one time was kind of a pariah. Well he worked with Red Nichols in the 20's and this was in the 50's and Redd was like, do you agree that Pee Wee Russell is a great Jazz clarinet player and I said, he is not even a clarinet player, with that sound? No way! That was just ugly, that wasn't clarinet playing. Benny Goodman – now that is a clarinet player. And I asked him if he would admit that he was a better Jazz man then Sal Franzello who is all over the place. And he said, no way! And he said that he was a far better clarinet player then Sal. Then I knew we were in separate rooms and we were never coming together. That Red Nichols was a friend of Lou Waters surprises a lot of people. Back in the 20's; Lou actually recorded in the 20's. So he was older then people thought.

DON: How about a guy named Lee Collins

RICHARD: I never got to meet him. He played at the Hangover a few times.

DON: Yeah, he was included in somebody's band here.

RICHARD: I think he might have played with Ralph Sutton. Ralph was around here for a long time – good piano player.

DON: You talked about Bob Wilber, I got a guy named George Lewis and Barbara Dane who I thought was a stripper turns out she is a singer.

A Diary of the Underdogs

RICHARD: She is a good singer. I worked with Barbara and so has Bob Mielke a lot. My teacher in New York, his name was Garvin Buschell; he recorded with Bessie Smith in the 20's. He recorded with Jelly Roll Morton and his history was incredible. But he wasn't locked into that era, he was playing bassoon with Gil Evans. But somehow the name came up about Barbara Dane and he said that he was playing some gigs with her and he said that she was the closest that he had ever heard to Bessie Smith. She really had it. She had that sound and that big voice and she had the phrasing and the feeling for it. So, I told that to Barbara.

DON: Well I saw some newspaper clippings from era, I think it was the early 60's and I think it was the El Cid, and El Cid had strippers of course, and the headliner was Barbara Dane, so all these years I assumed that Barbara Dane was one of the strippers.

RICHARD: I thought it might have been on Broadway, or maybe that was the original name, she took over a room there and I am not sure what it was called before, and called it Sugar Hill. And then she booked her own acts, she brought in Wellman Braud, a great bass player from Ellington's band to play with her, and Kenny Woodson, wonderful piano player. And then she booked people from the outside. Carmen McCrae.

DON: Carmen McCrae, I remember that. I have some other names for you, Bob Schultz, Scott Anthony and Jim Rothermel.

RICHARD: Yeah, Rothermel is a good clarinet player. Well, he plays all the reeds but he is very impressive as a clarinet player.

DON: What do you think of the success of Earthquake McGoon's?

RICHARD: Well, I didn't come to that part of Turk's story, after Easy Street folded, he tried booking name acts in there, he brought in Red Norvo and then he brought in the whole Ellington Orchestra. And that was a great moment for me because I was able to get in for free and sit down near the band and not pay anything. Anyway, he found this place; I think it was the William Tell Hotel on Clay Street. A funny, old-fashioned bar, stage and balcony overlooking a dance floor and they did Folk music on the weekend, I don't know if it was square dancing or Balkan music or something, but they did Folk music dancing. And they were just about to go out of business, they were right down in the heart the financial district, and Turk got a hold of it somehow and changed the name to Earthquake McGoon's, he got permission from Al Capp to use that name because Al invented the character. It worked out beautifully, it was a wonderful, warm, very woody, you know all dark woods, a basement room that they converted into a magic cellar and they had magic acts down there.

DON: They had seating and all that?

RICHARD: Yeah. They actually ran shows down there with name magicians. Who would sit at your table, as close as you and I are, and do this slight of hand, and you kept thinking you would catch it this time but you never did. The disappearing penny or whatever it was.

DON: Yeah, those guys are good. There is a guy named Mark Stock here in town, he is a great artist, an oil painter and a drummer. And I ended up working opposite him at a club called The Cypress Club.

RICHARD: I will tell you a club story mixed with a Mingus story. I was working with Mal Sharpe at a place called Tipsy's; sort of across the street from Burp Hollow on Broadway. And again, run by a couple of thugs, guys with no necks in suits. So Mal took it all humorously and he thought it was kind of funny and we launched the Jazz band. Mal couldn't play trombone at all but he was funny and it worked out. So one night I am sitting in there between sets and this guy comes in, kind of a threatening looking guy, and he says, *Are you Hadlock?* And I said, *Yeah.* And he said, *Mingus sent me, and he didn't like the review you wrote in the Down Beat and he told me to come and shoot you in the leg!* This guy had apparently been in San Quentin and somebody that Mingus knew in the Bay Area and so he really did have a rough background. And I got scared; I thought maybe he was going to do that! And then he said, *Don't worry, Mingus is like a big baby, he wouldn't do that.* But he had to deliver the message.

DON: He had to shake you up, huh? This is when you were writing the Jazz column for the Chronicle?

RICHARD: We were reviewing records at Down Beat and I gave him only four stars instead of five, and he

A Diary of the Underdogs

got enraged.

DON: And the evolution of that column was – you did work for the Chronicle also?

RICHARD: No, the Examiner. Yeah, Ralph Gleason was at the Chronicle and I was at the Examiner. And then I turned my column over to Phil Elwood because he was the guy I recommended to the paper. I went into teaching at that point. Phil was already in teaching and he became the full time…

DON: Where you teaching Journalism or Music?

RICHARD: No, I taught in a one room school on an Indian Reservation, grades one through eight. That was far more interesting then renewing Jazz groups. Let me mention club names that you can look into. One was the Black Sheep. Earl Hines went there after he left the Hangover. Basin Street West, Gold Nugget, Sail Inn; it was in that funny hotel where Arthur Schutt lived for awhile, and the Honey Bucket, a real low-life Dixieland club.

DON: Is that in the Tenderloin?

RICHARD: No, I think it's out in the Marina. I am not sure. Berkeley Square, I worked in Berkeley. And Nod's in Berkeley. The New Orleans Room at the Fairmont was another one, and Fack's and Fack's II.

DON: Wasn't there something that was pretty good for a while in Sausalito?

RICHARD: I am sure you know about Bop City. I played for three years and in Point Richmond. And that was with Jim Goodwin and that was a wonderful gig. Also there was the El Matador. And you know the Weiss Brothers at Fantasy, they owned the company.

DON: Max Weiss and Saul Zaentz. Is that correct?

RICHARD: Well, Max and Saul Zaentz, and George Weiss. There were three brothers. And they hired Saul Zaentz to sort of run the business end because they weren't terribly good at business. They were big personalities, and George had and maybe Max did too, had a big interest in the Blackhawk.

DON: Do you happen to remember the other partner with Helen Noga?

RICHARD: I am not sure what interest they had. Guido and Eleanor, sort of ran the club.

DON: That's the name I was looking for. Yeah, John Handy mentioned that he had an apartment next door, upstairs and he could look down at the Blackhawk and see the money coming out through a porthole.

RICHARD: Who knew at the Hang Over Club, all those years Earl Hines was there, his clarinet player, Darnell Howard was also a Hi- Fi nut and he stayed in the hotel next door and had all these AMPEX and ten inch reel to reels for recording and he ran a wire across the alley into the back window and under the bandstand and recorded the Hines Family without permission. And then sold it to Europe where they issued the albums. "Earl Hines with Muggsy Spanier and Darnell Howard" And the whole band was just down on Darnell because they never saw a penny.

DON: How about Earl Hines, did he find out about it?

RICHARD: Yeah he found out. He wasn't above such things himself. All those guys were kind of swift with the buck.

DON: So, this has been great, thank you.

RICHARD: Well, thank you. Please use discretion, especially with Turk. I don't want to embarrass him or myself. Turk had a lot of good qualities and I don't want to knock him. It just wasn't a good match for me. I would like to say a nice word about Burt Bales. He was not only an important piano player on the Traditional scene but was like a teacher to many, many young people including me, who came down to Pier 23 to sit in, and he would play a couple of numbers and say, you have to know the difference between a stomp and, whatever it was, I have forgotten now. He had the subtleties of Jelly Roll Morton.

DON: Could he imitate him pretty well?

RICHARD: He would say, *you were dying to play that too fast, you should slow that down. You are missing the meat of that melody.* And that was worth coming to California for. This was where I was really learning.

End: Richard Hadlock

A Diary of the Underdogs

Interview: Vince Wallace; jazz musician-tenor saxophonist-San Francisco jazz legend- with Don Alberts-July 28, 2009-Oakland Ca. About: Bop City, Black Hawk, Ed Eliot, Pony Poindexter, Helen Poindexter, Dexter Gordon, Sonny Simons, Frank Haynes, Ron Crotty, Colin Gleason, Jack Dorsey, Larry Vuckovich, Terry Rodriguez, Andy Woodhouse, Bishop Norman Williams, George Jones, Kermit Scott.

VINCE WALLACE

DON: I found a very extensive interview you did with Jerry Karp. That was pretty cool! They used to call you Hawk? Was that at the Black Hawk days?

VINCE: That's what they used to call me in high school- partially because of my beak and partially for playing the sax.

DON: Because you sounded like Coleman Hawkins?

VINCE: I guess.

DON: There was a guy you mentioned that I have never heard of before – Ed Elliot. What did he play and where was he from?

VINCE: He was an alto player He was local – he lived a couple of blocks from here, over on Dearing Street.

DON: Is he still playing?

VINCE: I haven't seen him for years. I think he moved to some other state.

DON: So you started going to the Blackhawk and every Sunday you had sessions?

VINCE: Yeah, Dean Reilly was playing bass over there and Frank Jackson on piano.

DON: Who was the drummer?

VINCE: Gus Gustafson was there, sometimes Forest Ellige.

DON: I did not know Forest.

VINCE: He plays out in East Oakland – East 14th Street.

DON: Yeah, I played there with Smiley – he was in and out of there. Then they sold it and it was called Top Drawer for a while.

VINCE: Same with Bop City – they moved over to Fillmore and it didn't last very long after that.

DON: Oh, was it still going when they moved over there? They moved those two houses right?

VINCE: Yeah. And that was great. They were still having sessions and I was playing with Walter Benton, the tenor player. And we all got raided by the tax squad and they herded us into a corner and searched us

(continued)

A Diary of the Underdogs

and made all the music stop right in the middle of it. We were playing *Night In Tunisia* when it happened.

DON: They stopped the song?

VINCE: They stopped the song right in the middle of *Night In Tunisia*. Same thing happened in Long Beach. I had a gig down there and I was playing *Night In Tunisia*, same thing happened. They stopped the gig.

DON: Same song?!

VINCE: Same song – it was weird.

DON: So, did anything happen with all that? Did they jack you up because they wanted taxes or something?

VINCE: Well, they didn't have an entertainment license and all that stuff.

DON: Well, Jimbo was still around when they moved that right?

Vince Wallace

VINCE: Yeah. He was around for many years after that. We all had our picture taken together over at City Hall. That picture in Harlem – they had all the......

DON: Yeah, I remember the picture.

VINCE: Well, they did the same thing in San Francisco.

DON: Yeah, I was in that picture.

VINCE: I don't have that; I gotta get a copy of that.

DON: Yeah, I just saw Mars Breslow. A lot of other people took pictures that day. And this friend of mine, Barbara sent me some pictures that she took little sections of the crowd.

VINCE: Eddie Duran?

DON: Yeah. Mel Martin. What part of that crowd were you in? I was up on the right.

VINCE: I was down on the left somewhere in the third row.

DON: Behind Jerome Richardson?

VINCE: Yeah, I was sitting next to them.

DON: So, tell me a little more about the Blackhawk.

VINCE: A lot happened there. Like most places, you would meet cats from there that would go to other places, you know. And then you could connect with other Jazz scenes.

DON: Well, Vuckovich was around in the 60's I guess, but this is like 50's?

VINCE: Yeah, like late 50's, early 60's up till about 1965 I think it was.

DON: Yeah, I saw all those guys there and it was a pretty romantic place.

VINCE: Yeah.

DON: You got to see everyone – Miles was there with the quintet one time with Philly Joe Jones and one time he had Sonny Stitt. I don't know if you saw that gig or not.

VINCE: Yeah I did. And they had J.J. Johnson for a while. Miles would take off and let the band take over and he would be gone for about an hour or so.

DON: Yeah. He was real pissed off at Sonny Stitt for a while for some reason. He wouldn't give him any room!

VINCE: Yeah. Miles didn't care for Freddie Hubbard either. Miles was always bad rapping him. He got too famous or something during that time.

DON: It bothered him huh?

VINCE: Yeah. Vince Guaraldi was there quite a bit at the Blackhawk.

DON: Yeah, those guys had a lot of steady gigs there. Yeah, I saw Vince there solo one time; I don't think he had been hooked up with anybody yet.

VINCE: Yeah, he was a regular on the Sunday thing usually.

DON: There was a drummer named Kenny Sherlin, no one seems to remember him.

VINCE: I remember a Kenny Sherlin; he was a Calypso guy from somewhere down in the Islands.

DON: Yeah, he was kind of wacky, but he could play.

VINCE: Yes he could.

DON: Do you remember Max Hartstein?

VINCE: Yes. I played a gig with Max Hartstein in Santa Cruz one time.

DON: Well, last time I saw you was at Simple Pleasures.

VINCE: Where was that?

DON: On Balboa Street.

VINCE: Wow, can't remember.

DON: Chuck Bernstein was playing drums. Obidinski; Al was playing bass, I was playing piano. We did an 80th Birthday party for Chuck Travis.

VINCE: He used to have a red sax.

DON: Yeah! He came in with a red sax! He helped me out and told me to get playing in the city.

VINCE: Did you ever know Richard Williams? "Notes" Williams. Not V. Williams, he played drums, he was from Utah or someplace.

DON: No. Do you remember some of those guys, the rhythm section, at Bop City? I remember Eddie Kahn- bass player.

VINCE: Oh, yes Eddie. He played tenor also. And then later on he was playing with the Jazz Crusaders up in Sacramento. A guy named Spook, a guy named Trevor Kohler.

DON: Trevor Kohler, baritone player?

VINCE: Yeah.

DON: You are the only guy who mentioned him!

VINCE: We used to have a workshop after Bop City was over we would go down to the street to the Plantation Club. They would give us grits and stuff to eat and we would play until about noon; Harold Wiley and Gary McFarland, the vibe player.

DON: Yeah, he ended up going to the same school as I did. And then he left and did time. He was great.

VINCE: Did you know Smitty? Alfred Smith? He was from Texas. I knew him from Santa Barbara also.

DON: Tenor player?

VINCE: No, a drummer, Alfred Smith and everyone called him Smitty.

DON: No, didn't know him. I remember Kermit Scott. He was 380lbs-a big guy!

VINCE: Yeah, and a big sound too!

DON: I don't remember him being that big when I saw him. He used to come in and play with us a lot. I was in that period when John Handy was coming in all the time.

VINCE: Yeah, he would be on his way to school to San Francisco State and he would come in the morning and play a few tunes. I remember Pony Poindexter too. He was the bandleader for a while.

DON: Yeah, Pony was there. He also played up at the Coffee Gallery. Did you know Nancy King?

VINCE: From Portland? Yeah.

DON: Did you know Sonny?

VINCE: Sonny King? Yeah. Do you know Johnny Baker?

A Diary of the Underdogs

DON: Yeah I know him. I used to hang with him as long as I could. Not too many people could do that.

VINCE: Yeah, he was great; he could really tear it up. He was kind of like Bud Powell.

DON: Yeah. And he was from Sacramento. A lot of guys were.

VINCE: Yeah. He was a Fresno Indian and part Armenian. I have some tape recordings of him that are around here somewhere.

DON: He made an LP with Vince.

VINCE: I didn't know that.

DON: I don't know who the bass player was, maybe Norm McKay. You know who has it – Tom Madden has it. Kent Glenn produced it.

VINCE: I am going to do a lot of Kent tunes next time I record, a Kent Glenn Memorial Album.

DON: Did you play a lot with Kent?

VINCE: Quite a bit, yeah. Twenty years. In fact I met Kent he was graduating from high school, he came into the Cascades Club down in Long Beach and he had a white tuxedo on and a red carnation and this girl that he took to the Senior Prom. He was amazing for how advanced he was for his years. He knew all the tunes and everything.

DON: Did you work at the Jukebox?

VINCE: Yes, with Danny. He smoked cigars and opened up an ice cream store later on. Danny, he was the owner of the Jukebox. Bishop was there for a while, and also across the street, the Haight Levels. It was called the Overcast Club too. They changed names a few times.

DON: Yeah, that's when I knew Kent; he was doing those gigs too.

VINCE: Right; and Bob Maize and Bill Douglas.

DON: Yeah, both bass players.

VINCE: Yeah.

DON: So Bill was around?

VINCE: Yeah, Bill plays with Marianne McPartland quite a bit.

DON: I didn't know he went that far back. Is he a San Francisco guy?

VINCE: No he lives up in Northern California, Grass Valley.

DON: OK. Where did he come from?

VINCE: I think he came from Grass Valley.

DON: OK. Yeah, I ran into him at Moose's. I think he was playing with Don Asher.

VINCE: Did you know Skippy Warren?

DON: I know the name – never met him.

VINCE: He played Bop City quite a bit on bass and he sang *My Foolish Heart* and things like that. He played with Bird.

DON: Yeah, Skippy Warren, he has done pretty well. What about Fredrico Cervantes?

VINCE: Yeah, Freddie Gambrell. He switched over to trumpet.

DON: Yeah I know he got in touch with me; he wanted to do some tunes. We ended up doing a record and he played trumpet. He was a strong player.

VINCE: Yes he was. He could really play.

DON: Yeah, he could play like Oscar Peterson too; a very talented guy. Do you remember Ben Tucker?

VINCE: Yeah, I used to work with Ben Tucker in L.A. Carla Bley Group. I went to high school with her. She was a weird girl. She used to wear green finger nail polish and blue lipstick and stuff like that. She would eat her lunch in the library.

DON: Back then in the 50's?

VINCE: Yeah.

DON: Well, she is not that much different now! Carla Bley – was that her married name?

A Diary of the Underdogs

VINCE: Yes, that was her married name with Paul. I met up with them too in L.A. We had Scotty Le Faro on bass for a while and Ben Tucker and Bobby Hutchison were still in high school then.

DON: Yeah, I hope to be able to talk with Bobby. So, you were in L.A.? You probably knew Sonny Park?

VINCE: Yeah, at one time or another.

DON: Yeah, he is one of my favorite guys, Sonny Clarke and Carl Perkins.

VINCE: Yeah, I love Carl Perkins.

DON: Did you know Carl Perkins?

VINCE: Yeah. Joe Albany is another one.

DON: Yeah, Joe and Kenny Drew.

VINCE: Did you ever hear of Speed Parsons? Dexter Parsons – he was a lot like Al Plank, he lived down in L.A.

DON: No, I didn't know about him, a piano player, right?

VINCE: Yes.

DON: Never heard of Dexter Parsons. There was a lot going on.

VINCE: Yeah, and it's always been a struggle. But we have a few bright moments.

DON: Yeah, well that is the thing; I had to examine my life. This thing got a hold of me and moved me all through my life man. That was it, music was what I wanted. The most powerful force I had ever encountered.

VINCE: Yeah. Especially when Bop City was open every night of the week, the door would open and somebody great would come through like Billie Holiday or Sonny Stitt.

DON: Did you ever go down to Fack's and those places?

VINCE: Fack's II. Scat man Crothers played there and Al Boletto Sextet.

DON: And Miles played there too. At Facks I- I think when it was new. He had just done a 10" LP and he had Art Blakey and Percy Heath and Horace Silver. Those guys didn't come out with him but Miles came.

VINCE: Miles used to live in Oakland for a while. And Billie Holiday used to play up at the 50's Street Club on Shattuck Avenue.

DON: Oakland has a lot of history too.

VINCE: Yes it does. It was an underground town – those things were happening in people's pads and private sessions and stuff like that.

DON: Yeah, there was the Gold Club or Golden Nugget or….

VINCE: Oh yeah, Don Rupo's Gold Nugget on Telegraph.

DON: Fred Murgy was over there.

VINCE: Yeah, mostly white guys from Stan Kenton's band. You never saw a black guy in there. Rudy Salvini, Jerry Coker.

DON: Coker was around quite a bit for awhile.

VINCE: Yeah, I used to work over at the music store selling reeds and equipment and stuff like that on the side.

DON: Yeah; and then there are a couple of places in Palo Alto. We played a place in Redwood City called Crackpot.

VINCE: I have been to the Satin Doll down there. They used to have an after hours sessions on weekends.

DON: Yeah and there was the Outside at the Inside. That was like a singer's club. It was off University Avenue in Palo Alto. So, I know we talked about Pony Poindexter, oh, Theresa Poindexter – was she a player?

VINCE: She was a waitress and they would make her wait till the end and then she would get to sit in around 6 O'clock. She worked there for a while and then they go married. Frank Haynes – my hero.

DON: Sax player from Texas and played flute.

A Diary of the Underdogs

VINCE: Actually he was from Ohio, Cleveland or something like that.

DON: OK, but didn't he come up through L.A.?

VINCE: I don't know about that. Do you remember a place called – it was on Telegraph – The Palladium Club? It was an indoor laundry mat later on.

DON: I remember the name. Was it an underground place to play Jazz?

VINCE: Yeah, just a place to go and play where the cats would go and hang out. I used to come up all the time over to Bop City with Harold Land, we would play – *There Will Never Be Another You.*

DON: Harold would play for half an hour? And then you would play for half an hour….you are famous for that!

VINCE: Well, I don't know about that.

DON: Well, that is your reputation. Did you ever run into Lee Konitz? He was around for a little while.

VINCE: Yeah, I ran into him later on – he was playing with Flora Purim, re-emerging on day at the Keystone Korner. That night he left for Italy or something and he never showed up for the gig. I heard him recently, he sounds pretty good.

DON: Yes, I think he does too. He did a good thing by hanging out here for a while and meeting people and sitting in and playing, trying to get the feel of the West Coast scene. I had a gig at the Hyatt Hotel in San Jose and he came in every night and played.

VINCE: Did you know Sammy Cohen? The drummer, he was from Chicago. He wound up teaching or something in San Jose. He was good friends with Johnny Baker also.

DON: No. I never ran into him. He played a lot with Johnny Baker?

VINCE: Yeah.

DON: So, who were some of the talented bass players around other then Max Hartstein and Eddie Kahn and Norm McKay?

VINCE: Dean Reilly.

DON: I talked with Dean. He said he was on the road a lot. I guess he was. I know he played with Jeannie Hoffman's Trio with Bill Young. And Jeannie was singing then.

VINCE: She played over in Sausalito quite a bit.

DON: So, bass players, so many of them, they come and go. Max Hartstein was the most impressive to me at that time. He was the strongest bass player but he wasn't always around. Bob Maize, he was around. And I mentioned Eddie Kahn but he didn't last too long, he left with Randy Weston; he took him on the road. And Dewey? Ever run across Dewey?

VINCE: Dewey Redman?

DON: Yeah.

VINCE: Yeah, we hooked up.

DON: Do you remember the Happy House? Did you ever go there? It was where all the guys hung out – it was on Fillmore and Oak.

VINCE: Mmmm, was it the same place that Jesse Hawkins used to live?

DON: No, Jesse Hawkins was on Haight Street.

VINCE: We had rehearsals over there with Philly Joe Jones on drums – for hours. And Joe used to play piano too and he knew all the chords and stuff and it was great.

DON: Yeah, it was in the back? There was a window there and an upright piano.

VINCE: Yeah.

DON: Hang out in Jesse's kitchen. Everybody would hang out.

VINCE: What about Lane Welch. He was from the Peninsula or Burlingame or something like that. I have been on the road with him. Santa Barbara.

DON: What about Paul Smith, the bass player.

A Diary of the Underdogs

VINCE: Yeah, I knew Paul down in L.A.

DON: He lives here now.

VINCE: Yeah, I play with him over at Café Trieste.

DON: Did you know the Both/And? Did you know those guys?

VINCE: Yeah, in fact, what's his name used to be my mailman? The owner of the Both/And…Delano. Yeah, he used to be a mailman over in Glen Park.

DON: Delano Dean. What was his partner's name?

VINCE: Lenny.

DON: And Richard Brown used to bartend there. He told me stories about Miles coming in late while his band was on the bandstand playing. OK, how about Big Bands, did you get into the Big Bands at all?

VINCE: Quite a bit, yes.

DON: Rudy's band?

VINCE: Yes, Rudy's band.

DON: Sal Carson?

VINCE: Yeah. They used to play a lot of those ballrooms, like Sweets.

DON: Yeah, I played in that band, one night Sal Carson crawled under the piano to listen to me, because he couldn't hear the piano with the rest of the band. Were you a Union guy?

VINCE: Well, I joined San Leandro because it only cost $50. They never helped me too much.

DON: Yeah, it used to be the Union was strong, collecting money for you and taking care of business. But when it comes retirement time, they suddenly forget all the gigs you played.

VINCE: Yeah, supposedly if you are in twenty-five years you get a gold card and you don't have to pay any more dues.

DON: Yeah…..Oh, I talked to Dick Saltzman.

VINCE: Oh, how is he doing?

DON: He is doing pretty good, 82 years old, very lucid, knew everything. He is moving to Ecuador.

VINCE: Yeah he stayed down there for a couple of years not too long ago, got married to some girl down there.

DON: Yeah; so, what fun. I don't know about you, but I was chasing after Miles and Coltrane in those days; that was the music I liked.

VINCE: Yes, me too. I fact, the other day I just heard some undiscovered Coltrane. Remember in the time of *Kind of Blue*, the same band went touring in other places and they recorded every night, all over the country. There was this guy who stopped by my house and played some Miles I never heard before. He never played it on any of his albums.

DON: Different stuff?

VINCE: Completely different. He is going to give me a copy of that.

DON: That would be nice, just like that hidden thing with him and Monk.

VINCE: Yeah it was like that. Wonderful!

DON: Yeah, those guys really had me man, that's all I wanted to do. Try and understand that music and try to play it. And before that it was Bud Powell and pretty much that's it; and later in the 70's a lot of McCoy Tyner. I remember Getz had a pretty strong impact about then.

VINCE: I saw Getz with Scotty LaFaro over at the Blackhawk. They were playing *Pennies from Heaven* in the Key of D and they were playing the original *Milestones, (the old one)*. Yeah, Getz was great.

DON: Yeah, that's one of my favorite tunes. So, let's see….I guess you were still talking about the Blackhawk – guys that used to come in – George Coleman?

VINCE: Yeah, George Coleman – I saw him mostly at Bop City. He recommended this book: *The Universal Saxophone* and I practiced everyday with exercises.

A Diary of the Underdogs

DON: And what about Dexter – did he come in?

VINCE: Yes, and Teddy Edwards.

DON: Yeah, you never knew who you were going to see.

VINCE: Never, it was always a surprise.

DON: One night Jimmy Garrison came in and played with us.

VINCE: Al McKibbon used to come in and play. He played with George Shearing.

DON: Right. And did he play with Tjader for a while?

VINCE: Yeah.

DON: Did you ever spend anytime with Leroy Vinnegar?

VINCE: Quite a bit, yeah. I played with him with Shelly's group at the Blackhawk when they were there. Charlie Mariano, Russ Freeman.

DON: And the trumpet player?

VINCE: Stu Williamson was one.

DON: Who played trombone?

VINCE: John Raider.

DON: Stu didn't play trombone?

VINCE: Not when I knew him.

DON: Gary Barone – did you know those guys?

VINCE: Yeah. He had a brother.

DON: Yeah and his brother was a trombone player.

VINCE: We used to play over in Oakland somewhere.

DON: Yeah, Gary is a great friend of mine, great player. Yeah, he was in Shelly's band? John Gross was in Shelly's band at the same time. And they both moved to Portland. So, John Gross is up in Portland now. And Gary was there for a long time and then moved to Freiburg, Germany. And he is still there. He went to the University – to do Classical and Jazz. The Jazz program, it's in the Black Forest.

DON: Oh. And then his brother, the trombone player came to Portland.

VINCE: Mike.

DON: Yeah, Mike. He started writing charts up there. And you know who showed up one day was Ernie Hood, and Bill Hood. Ernie could really write. He wasn't in good shape when he got there and his brother pretty much took care of him; great people.

DON: Let see, well everybody has a story about John Rae....

VINCE: John Rae – African vibes, a good drummer too.

DON: How about Richie Goldberg?

VINCE: Yeah, I knew Richie Goldberg. One of the greatest drummers I have ever played with. I played with Vi Redd quite a bit too.

DON: Vi Redd – the Birdcage-Richie Goldberg's ex?

VINCE: Yeah, and Fred Marshall. We used to have a gig at the Jazz Workshop on Monday nights. And *Back Screw* was our theme song. And Richie and Harley White.

DON: Who was the drummer?

VINCE: Richie Goldberg.

DON: Dick Saltzman used to run that thing for a while? A lot of people played there.

VINCE: Yeah, I was one of the first guys who ever played there. A guy named George Kimball on vibes, Stan Popper on drums.

DON: And I guess Terry Hilliard was around then too?

VINCE: Yeah. I think he was with the Board of Education.

DON: And did you know Claude Allen?

A Diary of the Underdogs

VINCE: Yeah, probably.

DON: Black guy at the door at the Workshop. It was a good thing Ralph Gleason was around then, every night he would write your gig up.

VINCE: Right. He used to play trumpet too. He sat in at the Blackhawk a few times.

DON: He was great. He really made sure you covered the scene. And he would come in to the Workshop and have a half pint stuck in his overcoat. Let see, I was going to ask you – well you probably didn't do much at Enrico's because that was a show place.

VINCE: I did later on.

DON: Yeah, I need to get some pictures of that joint.

VINCE: I remember Hewey Newton. He was always very nice to me, contrary to what they said in the paper about him. He had very good manners. He used to buy my cigarettes all the time and compliment my music.

DON: Did you get involved in any of the rock bands? Sitting in with them or doing any of their music?

VINCE: Yeah.

DON: I got involved with Big Brother.

VINCE: Yeah, I did some gigs with their new vocalist; they got a girl that sort of sounds like Janice. And my friend is in it, a guy named Jimmy, the guitar player. There is a famous poster where he is dressed up as an Indian and had a headband and stuff.

DON: Oh, that was him?

VINCE: Yeah.

DON: So, Terry, is he still around?

VINCE: Yeah, I still am playing with him every once in a while.

DON: Yeah? And Ron Crotty, you guys get together?

VINCE: Oh yeah. He works with me down at Van Cleef's every once in awhile.

DON: I don't know who Sean Kenner is, I never met that guy.

VINCE: He is another generation, he is a young guy and he is back in New York now.

DON: And Jason Sloda?

VINCE: Yeah, he plays drums with me.

DON: And Ben Adams?

VINCE: Ben moved to Colorado or something like that.

DON: What did he play?

VINCE: Vibes.

DON: And Colin Gleason – that's not related to the writer is it?

VINCE: No, no relation. His father is a teacher.

DON: And Jacky Dorsey. I know Jack.

VINCE: Yeah, I saw him yesterday.

DON: Andy Woodhouse – I like Andy's playing. But I don't think Andy likes Woodhouse playing. Andy is real self-critical. But he is a great player. OK, so let's see you have a long list of influences: Louis Armstrong, Coleman Hawkins, Earl Hines, John Coltrane, Ben Webster, Frank Foster, Duke Ellington, Count Basie, Frank Haynes, and Sonny Simmons.

VINCE: I just talked to Sonny on the phone the other day. We are the last of us.

DON: He is still touring?

VINCE: Yeah, he made a record in Norway with the Symphony not too long ago.

DON: Yeah, I have been talking with Art Lewis and he and Sonny Simmons go on the road with Michael Marcus. Do you know Michael?

VINCE: Yes. I just found a picture of Michael in the *Jazz Podium Magazine* from Germany.

A Diary of the Underdogs

DON: Really! How long ago?

VINCE: It is from 83.

DON: OK, continuing on: George Maddox, Johnny Cash, George Jones, Ray Charles. You would never think George Jones….

VINCE: Well, you never know. They had a place called the Garden of Allah out in Niles, out by Hayward…

DON: Niles Canyon?

VINCE: Yeah, and Friday nights they had Rock and Roll and Saturday nights they had Western and Country.

DON: Continuing on: Pony Poindexter, Shelly Robbins, Art Pepper, and Dexter Gordon. But what they say about you – one of the best tenor saxophonists alive today. I will go for that. OK, so you talk about where the music comes from: "Comes from out of the air, it comes from God, it comes from the source from which all life comes. It comes from the Cosmos, it's out there, and it doesn't belong to anybody. It is a reservoir that everybody who is a medium for music can tap into and share. It's something that belongs to everybody and should be shared with all the people on the earth. It is a powerful force and something that we can't live without. A world without music would be a terrible thing. It would be like being born without your senses. Music is very important. If you take it away life would get awfully sad very fast. Music can express so many different things, happiness, sadness, joy, pride, victory, and defeat, whatever. It is an all-encompassing thing. The more you are into it the more you feel its ability to express all these different feelings and emotions." (Vince Wallace)

DON: So, I was supposed to interview Abe Battat. We were going to meet tomorrow.

VINCE: Yeah, that's the guy – Abe Battat, he used to play with a guy we were talking about – Forest Ellige used to play drums with him a lot.

DON: OK, that's the guy. Abe is saying that I don't need to talk to him about all this. He says that he is just a lounge player and not really in the Jazz scene. But for one thing, he played that gig at Roland's and I know there was a lot happening there because Chet Baker used to come and I used to come in with Chet and we would play. And I left town and Chet kept coming in there and pretty soon Chet was asking for money. So, Chet would want the money before he played – he would want $300 and then Chet would take off and then he wouldn't come back.

VINCE: I played with Chet quite a bit.

DON: Yeah and Chet was around San Jose.

VINCE: Yeah, I remember when he was with Diane. We used to play at some pizza place out there.

DON: Yeah, Ricardo's Pizza or something like that.

VINCE: What about Diane?

DON: Her name was Diane Vavra. She actually married Chet. She lives in Boulder Creek.

VINCE: I used to play at the Brewtail a lot and used to live in Boulder Creek. I used to write for the San Lorenzo Valley Sun, I had an article in the paper. Did you ever know Barry Tillson? He played valve-trombone, from Alameda.

DON: No, didn't know him. Is he still around?

VINCE: No he passed away a few years back. He used to play with "One-Handed Mitts," the drummer, Mitch McGwen. He had just little stubs and he had these things that he could put on to hold the sticks with.

He was born like that. Max Roach told him what he had – even one-handed – he played better then Max.

End: Vince Wallace

Interview: Dick Whittington-Jazz Pianist, Educator, Presenter-with Don Alberts at Dog patch Saloon-

A Diary of the Underdogs

Sunday April 11th, 2010-about playing with LA cats-starting a band at the Lighthouse in Hermosa Beach with Charles Lloyd, Don Cherry, Billie Higgins, Scott LaFaro, Charlie Haden. About- Sonny Chris mentoring, piano players-Sonny Clark, Carl Perkins, Hampton Hawes and Victor Feldman. Working with Dexter Gordon, Leroy Vinnegar, and Lawrence Marable-coming to town to play the Jazz Workshop. Stories about Anita O'Day and Al Plank. Vernon Alley, Shelly Robbins, 12 Adler Place, Flip Nunez, Noel Jewkes, Moulin Rouge, Strip Clubs, The Plantation, the Black Hawk-asking Miles Davis for the piano gig-Miles response-Smiley Winters, Tsubo's (club) Teaching in Berkley schools-early jazz improvisation to young students with Phil Hardyman-early students-Rodney Franklin, Peter Apfelbaum, Steven Bernstein, Joshua Redman, and a Benny Green-story when in the fourth grade. Maybeck Hall- Carl Jefferson, Concord recordings and concerts-Joanne Brackeen story-how it became a series-the pianos, Walter Norris, Buddy Montgomery, John Campbell, Don Friedman, John Colianni, Ted Rosenthal...

DICK WHITTINGTON

DON: OK, So tell me what we are looking at? (Pictures)
DICK: That's at Tsubo-you know Tsubo's in Berkley? It probably went from 1959 to 1962, maybe three years.
DON: And who are the guys in here?
DICK: That's Johnny Apperson, drummer from Oakland, Billie Kiyou, bass player from Oakland, George Kimball from Contra Costa College, a vibes player, and me.
DON: This is you, Hal Stein, Dean Reilly, and Smiley Winters. What year is that?
DICK: Early 70's, maybe '73-74, something like that.
DON: And this is a picture of you and Dexter Gordon with Leroy Vinnegar at the Jazz Workshop.
DICK: And you can't see him, but also Lawrence Marable on drums.
DON: And what year was this?
DICK: 1962. And this is later – Fillmore Street, probably the 80's. And this is a bass player, Perry Lind who was around San Francisco until like, 64. He played with Chris Ibanez.
DON: Yeah, so that was an interesting time, I didn't realize, I mean I knew you back in the 60's, I didn't realize that you came out to San Francisco with Dexter and....well, we were in different places, you know? What about Basin Street? There is no information about Basin Street West. It's very hard to get.
DICK: Basin Street West? What were you doing in like '64 or '65?
DON: I was playing Bop City and doing gigs around with Virgil Gonsalves.
DICK: Yeah, Basin Street West. I remember like in 65 hanging out with Al

Johnny Apperson, Billie Kiyou, George Kimball,
Dick Whittington at Tsubo's

A Diary of the Underdogs

Plank and I remember the year because my first daughter was born and I just finished playing at the Moulin Rouge and I guess it was about that same time, they had Basie's band, I remember that was like 65, spring of 65. Plank was playing with Anita O'Day with Tom Reynolds and I can't remember who the bass player was....

DON: John Mosher?

DICK: Yeah.

DON: Yeah, that was Basin Street West?

DICK: Yeah.

DON: Did you play there?

DICK: I don't think I ever played there. I think I sat in there once. I played with Anita in L.A.

DON: Well she... There are some funny stories about her. She used to trash people and especially, piano players, in front of the audience.

Dick Whittington

DICK: Yeah.

DON: And I was there one night and I kind of thought that happened to you, and I have seen it happen in Portland and I've seen it on various gigs. She would always do that.

DICK: She never wanted to rehearse because if you had a chance to really get things tight, she might screw up, and then she wouldn't have any excuses.

DON: Oh, so that was her thing.

DICK: I mean, last time I played with her was in '73 at the El Matador, with Obidinski, and he'd be there for a rehearsal and sound check, so we show up and we're there and she comes in, we're there about three in the afternoon, that same night of the gig, and she comes in, not even with her old man – drummer – John Poole. She walks in and she gets up there and I think, you know that we got to rehearse some things, she says give me a B flat or an A flat on the piano and play a chord, and she goes LA LA LA LA on the microphone and that was the rehearsal. Next part of the rehearsal was we both had to go to the Greyhound bus station to pick up John Poole and take him back to the hotel. She was really something, I worked with her in L.A. on Sunset Strip, La Cienega or something, this was like 60 or 61, and she goes on the break, I had a car, she doesn't have a car and she wants a ride over to her hotel because she has to feed her cat. So we drive her over to her hotel with John Poole and they go inside and we wait for like, 30 minutes while Anita and John Poole take car of the cats.

DON: Yeah, we know what was happening...

DICK: She and John finally come back to the car and we drive back to the gig. On another occasion, one night at Basin Street West, I went to see Al Plank who was the piano player on the gig with Anita that night, and she gives him the "treatment." (Embarrass the piano player) she wanted to sing *Tea for Two* in A flat. Al was so cool. She says, "Give me an A flat arpeggio." Al plays an A flat arpeggio and she goes, "that's not right, give me another arpeggio." And Al goes with another arpeggio and she says, "No, that's not right. Give me another arpeggio." And Al gives her another arpeggio in a different key, and she says, "No, not that key. Give me another arpeggio." And Al says finally, "I've given you four keys now. Why don't you just pick one?" The audience laughed. She lightened up after that and went on to do the song. (In A flat)

A Diary of the Underdogs

I knew Miles was in town at the Blackhawk. I didn't know at the time he had hired Herbie Hancock so I didn't feel so bad. Herbie would be joining the band in about two weeks. He was still with... (Restricted info)... And so I went to the Blackhawk to audition for Miles Davis.

DON: Yeah, you got an audition with Miles?

DICK: It was 1963, and so I went to the Blackhawk to see Miles and when I got there, Miles was taking a break and he was sitting at the bar, and I came up to him and like, I had never met him, like god, Miles Davis; and I went up to him and I said... I introduced myself and, I kind of lied, I said I was referred by Victor Feldman, which was not true; and I said, "I'd like to play for you and see what you think. I just made some records and worked with Dexter Gordon, Gene Ammons..."

DON: What did Miles say?

DICK: *He was like, "cool man," and bought me a drink. And I said, "You know, would it be cool if I just play a tune, or I can come down tomorrow afternoon so you can see how I sound?" And Miles he says; "I can't let you sit in," And I said, "Why?" And he said, "Because I got to use this guy for another two weeks, and if you sound better than him, then you are going to make him twice as nervous as he already is...and if you sound worse than him... the band is going to sound twice as bad as it already does!*

DON: Yeah, Miles. That sounds like him.

DICK: Yeah, so I didn't know at the time that he had already hired Herbie Hancock, so I didn't feel so bad and Herbie was still finishing with the Jazz-tet and Benny Golson for two more weeks.

DON: So you didn't...?

DICK: No, he was very nice. Maybe he thought I was cute?

DON: You never know. That was a nice story about Miles, touching, because most of them are pretty bad.

DICK: He was very cordial, very much the gentlemen and he actually took me very seriously.

DON: Yeah, well, I compliment you for even approaching him. That is a big intimidating situation.

The Black Hawk-Turk and Hyde-San Francisco

DICK: Yeah.

DON: What year was that again?

DICK: That was 62 or 63. And you know at that time, just going back say five years since going out to intergraded clubs in parts of L.A., you would have never seen a racial problem and I had no idea that there might be some kind of scene with Miles about being white, I had never been in New York and I really didn't know what was cool. All the guys I played with, there were never any problems. If you could play man, you were accepted anywhere. You were really accredited.

DON: Yeah, as long as you were qualified.

DON: You had a pretty good time. You did everything I wanted to do.

DICK: Yeah and looking back on it, you're always going on to the next thing and think what will be next and sometimes you don't stop and savor the moment like you could have at the time, you know?

DON: Yeah, right.

DICK: I mean I was just worried about how to... I remember playing with Lawrence Marable and, I was

A Diary of the Underdogs

Dick Whittington, Hal Stein, Dean Reilly and Smiley Winters

just worried about how to keep up.

DON: Well, it is pretty obvious you are a good player, because certain things have to happen.

DON: You stayed here after the gig at the Jazz Workshop with Dexter, Leroy and Lawrence Marable.

DICK: Yes, I liked the Bay Area, there were some gigs around and I got a job at the Plantation in the Fillmore and the Moulin Rouge and met Noel Jewkes and Flip Nunez and Vernon Alley, and Shelly Robbins at the 12 Adler Place (Now Specs Bar). I soon moved into a place in the East Bay but kept working in San Francisco clubs. I went back to teaching in the Berkley public schools. I taught music classes in the lower grades because there was no funding for Jazz as it was not considered a legitimate music form yet for education in schools. But some kids came to me for that kind of information and I did what I could. One was young hyper-active Benny Green. He was in the fourth grade and he wanted me to teach him to play the piano. I said go get some lessons and come back to me and I'd work with him. I didn't know who his early teachers were but later, when I got together with Phil Hardyman and we established a jazz education format in Berkley High School Benny was there and he had made a lot of progress. We actually were successful in establishing a Jazz curriculum for Berkley High students. Some of those students are people you now find in the Jazz mainstream, some have done very well, some were outstanding talents in the music, Benny Green, Rodney Franklin, Peter Apfelbaum, Steven Bernstein, Joshua Redman and others.

DON: Tell me about early years in L.A. Were you involved in the jazz scene there in the mid 50's?

DICK: Well, yes I was. I met Sonny Chris and he kind of took me under his wing and mentored me. He

Al Plank

took me to Central Avenue to hear those piano greats; Sonny Clark, Carl Perkins, and Hampton Hawes, Victor Feldman. Man, those guys were really playing. I had a lot of catching up to do, but I did, and there was a good scene there. Victor Feldman was working with the movie studios so he was really busy playing vibes, drums and piano, so I got calls to do some of his gigs.

I sat in a lot at the Lighthouse in Hermosa Beach and met Howard Rumsey. He asked me to put a band together for the Sunday afternoon gig so I hired Charles Lloyd, Don Cherry, Billie Higgins, Scott LaFaro, or Charlie Haden. Those guys were around because they were in the music program at UCLA. It was a great time to be in L.A. I learned a lot.

DON: Well, we have a few more minutes, I know you got to play this gig Today at Dog patch with Vince Lateano and the guys; looks like Michael Zisman and Andrew Speight. Good band, you'll have fun. Just tell me a little bit about the Maybeck Recital Hall and the concert series, and what it

A Diary of the Underdogs

was like to have those kind of great musicians around and be in situations like that, performing and recording. It can't be ordinary.

DICK: No. It was really a once in a lifetime kind of thing. It went on for about ten years, but the recordings went on for about five or six years. We secured the property, it had three mortgages when we bought it, but I didn't know you had to get a permit from the city to have music performances because it was in a residential neighborhood. If we wouldn't have been able to get that permit we would have been screwed. We had to find a way to generate income. We only had fifty seats in the auditorium and we only had license to do it on Sundays. So I started booking people that I knew and then for about a year we had already had some pretty good players, people heard about what a great place it was to play, but it was sort of difficult to get people to play with a group because the money wasn't there, and to pay for a band was a lot more. And we would go a night when traveling people would come through and get them for one night. And Carl Jefferson from Concord Records was considering a series and we talked about who we could get. So I made some calls. We started with Joanne Brackeen in L.A. and she called me. So I asked her about it, if she wanted to do it and she said yes. She came and I picked her up at the airport. I hadn't seen her for twenty years, she was Joanne Grogan when I knew her in L.A.-and she said, *"I got to do a solo recording for Concord; I got one more, you know, to fulfill my contract."* And I said, *"We could probably get Carl Jefferson to record it and put it out."* She said, *"No he would never come."* And I said, *"Well, what are you going to do?"* Well, I'll come sometime in the next couple of months. I said, *"The piano is there in a beautiful hall, the acoustics are wonderful."* And she said suddenly; *"I want to do my record here."* And I said, *"Well good, next time you come back I will try and set it up."* And she said, *"No; I want to do it tonight!"*

DON: Was she the first?

DICK: Yeah-1989. She called Carl; he used to work with her and he tried to find her a recording engineer. Carl said he couldn't do it on such short notice. And so I called around and I got Bud Spangler. At about 5pm we had already sold some seats; we had about twenty people coming. So Bud Spangler showed up with a couple of other guys and all this stuff; he broadcasts on Sunday nights you know? Well, he and Ron Davis, and we set up, you know, and we didn't even have time to tune the piano, but it wasn't bad.

DON: Was that the C7?

DICK: No the Yamaha S400, which is a better piano but it is a little bit smaller, 6'4".

DON: Yeah, I remember I liked the smaller one.

DICK: And so she recorded it and Carl heard it was knocked out and he said, well, I want to record somebody else, and he said, how about Dick Hyman. And I said we already have him booked. We already had some really pretty big names, we have Dave McKenna, and Carl goes, *"Yeah, ok-why don't we start a series?"* And so I got Walter Norris and I gave Carl his record to listen to and said, *"What do you think of this guy?"* Carl said, *"Kind of far-out isn't he?"* *"No, I said; he's a great New York piano man, one of the best piano players in the world."* So, Walter came and, we I made a deal with him, and it was all set, the program was standards. He and Carl made the deal the day before.

DON: That he would play standards?

DICK: Yeah, and Carl sat down and Walter played the first four bars and Carl looked over at me and smiled and Walter played *The Song is You.* So we just went on from there and so, he got a lot of the guys, I got a lot of the people that I knew and then there were a lot people that I wanted that we didn't get because they were too expensive, and a lot of people that he wanted that were cheaper and I didn't want them because I didn't think they were good enough. And then we all did some forty some records, you know man, they just kept coming.

DON: Just an amazing thing.

DICK: And people would hang out with these guys, lot of people stayed over for a week, and people would

A Diary of the Underdogs

come in a few days before, play the piano, get used to it. It was very business like, we had a set list. If you Google Maybeckpiano.com, there is a website and it tells the story about the Maybeck Recital Hall and there are interviews there with the musicians.

DON: I was there Today and I looked at it. Who is Ted Rosenthal?

DICK: Ted Rosenthal won the Thelonious Monk Piano Award probably around the year he recorded. He was with Jerry Mulligan- a very good piano player. And Carl Jefferson, he would go to New York and he would get these guys that were killer; John Colianni, Mel Torme's piano player; Kenny Drew Jr.-a marvelous piano player, Kenny Werner, I got him. I got Don Friedman; he was an old friend from L.A. He was burning when he was 19.

Maybeck Recital Hall-Berkley

DON: Yeah, he's around here once in awhile, Mel Martin uses him.

DICK: We had Fred Hirsch, John Campbell, from Chicago, and Andy Laverne; all great players. And we had Denny Zeitlin with David Friesen. They came to play a lot. I fact maybe twice a year Denny would stop in.

Oh, one last story. In 1962 I was working with Lee Konitz on Sundays at the Black Hawk. Perry Lind, our bassist, had been asked by Jimmy Lay, a less than mediocre tenor player, to hire a rhythm section and an alto player to join him on his New Year's Rotary Club dance gig in Vallejo. Perry Lind asked Lee Konitz to play the gig and Lee agreed. He told Jimmy Lay he had hired Lee Konitz to do the gig but Jimmy thought Perry was putting him on. For weeks he kept asking, *"Did you really hire Lee Konitz to play the gig?"* *"Yeah,"* he said, *"Lee Konitz."* You can imagine the look on Jimmy's face when he came back stage at the Casa Vallejo Hotel ballroom and saw Lee Konitz warming up. Lee played the gig beautifully, and Jimmy, completely intimidated by Lee, (as we all were the first time we played with him) could hardly get anything to come out of his horn. Privately to Perry he said, *"Why didn't you tell me you were bringing Lee Konitz?"*

DON: You said you played the bar on Columbus, behind Pearl's- Specs?

DICK: So, you know the bass player Vernon Alley? He always listened to the Giants baseball game on his little battery powered radio with an ear-piece stuck in his ear on every gig. Yeah, well anyway we're playing the gig at Spec's (12 Adler Place) one night for Johnny Copper, Vernon's regular piano player, and we are getting ready to do another song and I said to Vernon, *"How about- All The Things You Are?"*-He took his ear-piece out and said- *"Giants-7 to 4!"*

End: Dick Whittington

A Diary of the Underdogs

Chapter 16-Quotes

Conversations in Bars:

At Puccini over a cappuccino, I wondered about Italians in North Beach. Are they homesick or glad to be out of here? What about when Carlo from Capri comes to town to see San Francisco and meet some Italians, like needing somebody to talk Italian? Hard to see the old districts fade, replaced by imitations of the once magical North Beach neighborhood. They closed the Savoy! One more spot for a Chinese laundry, and another step toward a faceless neighborhood. Now the tourists walk along looking for signs of the old culture and see broad marquees touting; *"Italian Dinners, Espresso, Garlic!"* "Ah, that's the place, run by Chinese with an Italian bartender."

Herb Caen: It was all over when he left, really over. Now it stumbles for an identity, clutching at remnants, looking for old Italians on the street that would sooner be left alone. Tourists photograph them and go on gleefully to Fisherman's Wharf, now run by Filipinos and Hispanics.

Ah, the old days; that lofty whiff of old San Francisco when it was real; Flour D'Italia, the Golden Spike, Ernie's, the Castle, the Coffee Gallery, the U.S. Restaurant, Sugar Hill, Original Joe's, Vanessi's, the Matador, the Condor, Carol Doda, El Cid, the Committee, the Moulin Rouge, the Chi Chi, Ann's 440, Finocchio's. It was a real *place* then and you talked about it. Everyone talked about Howard Kean and the "big eyes" girl paintings and Vince Guaraldi, the Hungry I, the Purple Onion, On Broadway, Enrico's, Tosca, Vesuvio's, Specs, (12 Adler Place), and the original Clown Alley, Steve Silver and Beach Blanket Babylon, (Fugazi Hall), Mike's Pool Hall, the Jazz Workshop. That was Broadway! Sabella's, Fisherman's Grotto No.9, the Giants at Candlestick with Mays and McCovey, the Castro… Oh, well, some things only belong in memory. But it is nice to meet someone who knows what you're talking about, in fact it's vital.

But the faces don't seem as happy, as relaxed and beaming, taking on the day as it comes, un-angry, maybe a little drunk in the afternoon, rosy cheeked and friendly with a mile of stories about the concerts at Winterland or the Fillmore. We miss the sidewalks with Gregory Corso, and Bob Kaufman and Lawrence Ferlinghetti and the City Lights bookstore, and Melvin Belli and Bill Graham and Ralph Gleason, the Hell's Angels, Sonny Barger, the Berkley Barb, and the Haight; the Panhandle and Chet Helms, the Polo Fields, Playland and Ocean Beach, the Cliff House and Sutro Baths, and Lenny Bruce, Professor Longhair, Phyllis Diller and Mort Sahl, and the Kingston Trio; Harry the Hipster, Jazz, and Bop City, and Jimbo Edwards. "A honeymoon in Cairo, in our brand new auto-gyro, I'll buy that Dream" and I played "Easy Livin' at Moose's and Herb Caen came over and said, "Easy Livin,' huh? I love that song... the bridge goes to D flat!" And I said, "thank God!"

And Herb's gone, and we all begin to realize what's missing, and it *is really* missing! Come on, where's the spy bird in the park, the ear upon the street, the gentle confidant? "Oh, how we miss you Herb, you and Glen Dorenbuch." And I could walk into Pearl's like twelve people beaming, an entourage of one, and own all twelve of me, like twelve people beaming- an entourage of one. Yeah, I'm here! And now Vince Lateano says, "Want to sit in, man-all of you?" "All of me?" No-*"All of You!"* Vince was very perceptive, he could see these things.

A Diary of the Underdogs

"God must be an "F" Blues- Everyone knows it, everybody understands it, but they all play it their own way." Don Alberts

"Do you know Thelonious Monk?" "No... Who is the loneliest Monk?"
(Anonymous)

"It's better to be in life's battle than to stand aside." Don Alberts

I like the girls to match the upholstery of the car.
Charlie Barnet-

I wish you wouldn't make the strings such an important part of your arrangements because frankly they're only a tax dodge! -Tommy Dorsey
(to arranger Nelson Riddle)-

Tastes are created by the business interests. How else can you explain the popularity of Al Hirt?
Charles Mingus-

The outer space beings are my brothers. They sent me here. They already know my music.
Sun Ra-

I discovered early in life that if you take gym first period, you can
go into the wrestling room and sit in the corner and sleep.
Paul Desmond-

I was very happy and secure until I went into the army. Then I started to feel there was something I should know that I didn't know.
Bill Evans-

I've never heard anything Wynton (Marsalis) played sound like it meant anything at all. Wynton has no voice and no presence. His music sounds like a talented high-school trumpet player. To me he's jazzy the same way someone who drives a BMW is sporty. Keith Jarrett-

Jazz is the folk music of the machine age.
Paul Whiteman-
As long as I've been playing, they never say I done anything. They always say that some white guy did it.
Miles Davis-

I don't expect people who listen to Emerson, Lake, and Palmer to come hear me. I accept that reality.
Cecil Taylor-

Are big bands coming back? Sure, every football season.
Woody Herman-

Blues is to jazz what yeast is to bread-without it, it's flat.

A Diary of the Underdogs

Carman McRae-
Giving jazz the Congressional seal of approval is a little like making Huck Finn an honorary Boy Scout.
Melvin Maddocks-
Playing "bop" is like playing Scrabble with all the vowels missing.
Duke Ellington-

My feeling is, music is a more eloquent international language than Coca-Cola or McDonalds.
Paul Horn-

I don't want no drummer. I set the tempo.
Bessie Smith-

I am the world's laziest writer.
Oscar Peterson-

If someone has been escaping reality, I don't expect him to dig my music.
Charles Mingus -

Miles was a soul man, a sound, a black Bogey. He was also an
insufferable prick.
Albert Goldman-

How could you not be influenced by reading the same idiocies in ten different jazz journals?
Boris Vian-

It's taken me all my life to learn what not to play.
Dizzy Gillespie-

I don't mind being the butt of a joke-if it's a funny joke.
Kenny G.-

Some stances are just conducive to swinging. If I stand up straight for too long it's harder to swing. Plus my feet hurt.
Wynton Marsalis-

Those people were mavericks. The only person who wanted them was me. I mean, was Gene Krupa hard to get? Was Bunny Berigan hard to get?
Benny Goodman-

I spent a lot of time playing in miserable places that were not a lot of fun. Somebody once said it is character building and I was like, "My character is just fine."
Diana Krall-

Too soon; Grasshopper. -David Haskell

I used to roll joints for the Doobie Brothers.-Don Alberts

There are only two things worth dying for – love and purpose. –Don Alberts

A Diary of the Underdogs

THREE WISHES

Jazz Greats-answers from: "Three Wishes" by Pannonica Koenigswarter and Nica Koenigswarter, Published, 2006 Harry N. Abrams Inc.

"If you were given three wishes, to be instantly granted, what would they be?"

Thelonious Monk: "To be successful musically," "To have a happy family," "To have a crazy friend like you."

Philly Joe Jones: "Money, Money, Money!"

Dizzy Gillespie: "Not to play for money," "Permanent peace in the world," "A world where you don't need a passport."

Coleman Hawkins: "Perfect health," "Great success in my music," "To be extremely rich!"

Elvin Jones: "Peace on earth," "Complete acceptance and recognition of this music as a pure art form," "To see an end of suffering for humanity."

Johnny Griffin: "I wish I knew myself better," "I wish there was more love in the world," "I wish to live to see the day when jazz is recognized."

Art Blakey: "That you love me," "That Art Junior gets through this shit that he's in," "That I get divorced and we get married."

John Coltrane: "To have an inexhaustible freshness in my music. I'm stale right now," "Immunity from sickness or ill health," "Three times the sexual power I have right now and something else too; more natural love for people. You can add that on to the other."

Ornette Coleman: "Eternal life," "Love," "Happiness."

Sonny Clark: "Money,""All the bitches in the world," "All the Steinways."

Barry Harris: "Peace in the world," "a room with a Steinway and a good record player, where I can be alone with all the Charlie Parker and Bud Powell records," "The end of all soul, funk, and rock 'n' roll jazz!"

Wilber Ware: "That I could get my life straightened out, so that I could be accepted otherwise, as well as musically," "To be able to play music, and out of my musical ability, to be able to have security for my family as well as myself," "For the world to live in peace and harmony."

Al Haig: "Coitus." "Hurry over to the Algonquin and I'll tell you what two and three are."

Clark Terry: "To be assured of health, so as to have happiness and a long life," "To be wealthy enough never to have to worry about money," "I would like to have something happen to everyone to abolish that old racism shit."

A Diary of the Underdogs

Horace Silver: "Immortality," "To be rich," "A baby."

Bobby Timmons: "To have some money," "To have a nice house of my own," "Oh, you can't put that in your book? All right, then. I wish I may give something to the world."

Arthur Taylor: "That Charlie Parker was alive," "That Bud Powell was in town, playing like he used to. No, just playing any way," "Money."

Mal Waldron: "That clubs should have better acoustics, and that they should all have good pianos," "Tremendous exploitation of my records," "That selections should be made purely on an aural, or should I say auditory basis."

Billie Higgins: "To have the genius of Thelonious Monk," "To send my wife and two babies something," "A set of drums."

John Ore: "To be able to play, play well," "To be all over the world, in good health," "To have a time machine."

Freddie Hubbard: "Happiness," "Musical success," "I can't get that third one. I'm trying to find that third one. I know! I want a baby."

Julius Watkins: "To have three nice young ladies," "Three more," "To put the six of them to work."

Joe Zawinul: "To be able to play better my instrument," "Love, Period." "To make a decent living and not play no bullshit!"

Kermit "Scotty" Scott: "I wish I could get on a good recording date."

Billie Strayhorn: "I wish that music would become even more beautiful than it is, and that I would be able to listen to it forever, and write it forever."

Oscar Peterson: "I wish I could play the piano the way I want to," "I wish that everyone was born with innate understanding of all art forms." "Love throughout the world, individual to individual."

Kenny Dorham: "Money." "Happines'd take care of all that shit." "To have the ecstasy granted to me of music."

Ruminations of a Music Presenter by Prentice "Pete" Douglas, founder of the Bach Dancing and Dynamite Society

The best Jazz is art and entertainment going on at the same time.

Artistry is a subjective thing to describe, but you are usually certain when you witness it. (Quote from drummer Jeff Tain Watts)

A Diary of the Underdogs

Real artists can take the most familiar music to another level of experience.

Most Americans do not grow in their interest in music beyond the music of their formative years. Quality by definition is in limited supply, especially in the performing arts.

The wheelers and dealers in the music business know the price of everything and the value of nothing.

A good intimate venue pulls one right into the music, whether they intend to be or not.

The only proof one might need for the existence of God is music.

The only thing that saves live music from extinction is that people need to get out of the house occasionally.

The music business is a cruel and shallow money trench, a long plastic hallway where thieves and pimps run free, and good men (musicians) die like dogs. There's also the negative side. –Quote: Hunter S. Thompson.

A Diary of the Underdogs

Chapter 17-What is a Jazz Musician

Closing comments:

What is a Jazz Musician?

It has to do with the substance of our lives, the dedication to the music and the art form and to what it gives us in joy and identity and the life it provides, the ongoing work and learning, the friends, the community, the songs, the study and excitement of jazz music, and the life force that it contains. We never imagined that it would take over our lives, but it has. Jazz has become part of our names, the explanation of who we are. "I play jazz," is what you say after you say your name. That is a big statement, "I play jazz, and that's my life." I'm both proud and delighted to say, "I play jazz."

It lets other people know who I am; it defines me, in a broad sense, to others that are not musicians. But musicians know exactly what that means, all of it, the good and the bad, and it has been plenty of both. But the music seems to offset all of that and somehow remain pure and worthy of our life dedications. It is something we are, something we all share.

When you say, "I'm a jazz musician," it means you're a humble soul, it means you like to perform, it means you have night club skin, and you've drunk about everything there is to drink behind that bar, and you've seen every hustle there is, and even pulled off a few of your own, and seen all the beautiful women, and the bimbos, the housewives, and divorcees, and you played for them, sometimes to roaring room noises, and at other times to quiet sensitive listeners. But, still you played, you played your best, your most loved songs for them, with a hope that they got it, and they had a good evening, and you get paid.

But there is nothing like musician friends, they know how you feel, they feel the same things you feel, sometimes tired, sometimes a little drunk, but they love the music, they way you do, and it's always there, like a reverence, and they sing some bebop song to you because they love it and they want to talk about it and about playing it together or about someone who did play it. That's life, man, what else? That's the gig.

So, one night he fell in love with her because she said she liked his music and she was beautiful. And they went to his pad and he played his Miles Davis records for her and they made love. That's what it is, man, that's what it is to be a jazz musician...

A Diary of the Underdogs

The Age of Jazz

So it appears the age of Jazz is about 19 or so. That's when the music seems to stick with you. Songs become important, and Jazz becomes a part of your revolving thoughts. There are exceptions of course, some younger, some older; like in hip hop music, which can begin early. The quickest way to teach anything is in rhyme and rhythm-"the beat." But in jazz there is a melodic and rhythmic passion, a memory of a felling or an emotion. We like to isolate that feeling as our own world, the world of jazz music and of those who played it and introduced you to your life-long passion and delight, and something that would never leave you. Good that it is worthy of a world filled with musicians and advocates of a lasting and fulfilling art form and a unique society to which you have found you now belong.

The following is a good example; "Describing the Music of Horace Silver"

Describing the Music of Horace Silver

Horace Silver's music comes with that gritty modern blues and hard bop cacophony that romps through hard edged chords and funky soul beats filling you like a vodka tinged lemonade and leaves you wanting more, more of the heat, more of the resonant blend of saxophone and trumpet that gets you right in the gut the first time it storms into you.

That sound defined Art Blakey's Jazz Messengers with the voluminous roar of Horace Silver's piano and its urgency, like a revolution waiting, seeming as though if it didn't happen right now it may never happen at all. You heard it, and it filled you, sending your previous indifference about jazz music to become an opinion of excellence, "music with commitment" is all you'll have now.

Like when you play Horace's "Lonely Woman" for your girlfriend and it becomes an exotic perfume that fills the room and makes her eyes shine and you soon forget about the world outside. Horace is thumping gently through the chords, playing, waiting, singing, sighing low. It is so right, so hard perfect, and so unassailable, like a truth you had forgotten, a sound that always seems to be going somewhere. And that sound becomes part of you, it goes with you, like a soft breeze that moves the curtains and slides in to cool your naked body in the heat, like round full notes that can clear a murky pool to crystal. His hand is a fervent hammer, a claw chipping out melodies and Cape Verdean rhythms fused into an urgent pronouncement of the blues.

A Diary of the Underdogs

City Hall, San Francisco, May18, 1999-Mars Breslow's famous "Giants of Jazz" photo shoot. Photo courtesy of Barbara Hauser-here is a partial list: Front row, left to right-Jerome Richardson, unknown, Willie Brown, unknown, Sonny Buxton, Jimbo Edwards-next row to left-unknown, Vince Wallace, unknown, Eddie Duran, unknown, Dick Berk, Frank Jackson-next row up to right-Wyatt Ruther, Earl Watkins, Bobby Domingus, Wanda Stafford, Wesla Whitfield, David Hardiman, Ed Wetland, John Handy, Dottie Dodgion, Margie Baker, unknown-up to left-Ed Kelly, Chuck Travis, Al Obidinski, Larry Vuckovich, unknown, Orrin Keepnews, Bishop Norman Williams, Mike Greensill, unknown, John Goodman, unknown-

A Diary of the Underdogs

City Hall, San Francisco, May18, 1999-Mars Breslow famous "Giants of Jazz" photo shoot.
Top left-Don Prell, to right-Colin Bailey, Bruce Forman, Al Bent, unknown, unknown, Al Molina, below-Noel Jewkes, to left-Chuck Bennett, John Hettel, unknown-down-Paul Distel, to right-Buddy Barnhill, Don Bennet, Jeanne Hoffman, Don Alberts, down-Scotty MacLaine, to left-George DiQuattro, Rudy Salvini, Chris Pitts-below-Al Obidinski. Photo: courtesy of Barbara Hauser.

A Diary of the Underdogs

City Hall, San Francisco, May18, 1999-Mars Breslow famous "Giants of Jazz" photo shoot. Photocourtesy of Barbara Hauser. Top left to right: Graham Bruce, George Cotsirilos, Charles McNeal, Jeff Pittson, Don Haas, Joe Ellis, Danny Spencer (behind Joe) Bill Langlois, below-Mimi Fox, to left, Frank Passantino, Max Perkoff, Bishop Norman Williams, Si Perkoff, unknown, Don Alberts, Jeannie Hoffman, Noel Jewkes, Al Molina, Mark Levine, below to right, Buddy Barnhill, Rudy Salvini, George DiQuattro, Scotty MacLaine, Dave Gonzales, Dick Conte, Ed Kelly, down and back left, Brown, Al Obidinski, Chris Pitts, down, Chuck Travis

Chapter 18-Index and Credits

The Underdogs

The following is a list of musician who kept the music playing and appeared on most gigs providing the city with the music of the time. These are the true underdogs, the supporting musicians, the unsung heroes of San Francisco and what has become the true heritage of jazz music in the 1960s. It is with honor and appreciation their names are added here. Thanks for the music.

Index of names

A Diary of the Underdogs

A Diary of the Underdogs

A Diary of the Underdogs

A Diary of the Underdogs

D

A Diary of the Underdogs

A Diary of the Underdogs

A Diary of the Underdogs

A Diary of the Underdogs

H

A Diary of the Underdogs

A Diary of the Underdogs

A Diary of the Underdogs

A Diary of the Underdogs

A Diary of the Underdogs

A Diary of the Underdogs

A Diary of the Underdogs

A Diary of the Underdogs

A Diary of the Underdogs

R

A Diary of the Underdogs

A Diary of the Underdogs

A Diary of the Underdogs

A Diary of the Underdogs

A Diary of the Underdogs

Y

Z

A Diary of the Underdogs

Index of Bands

A Diary of the Underdogs

Index of Photos

A Diary of the Underdogs

A Diary of the Underdogs

Page-326- City Hall, San Francisco, May18, 1999-Mars Breslow famous "Giants of Jazz" photo shoot. Top left-Don Prell, to right-Colin Bailey, Bruce Forman, Al Bent, unknown, unknown, Al Molina, below-Noel Jewkes, to left-Chuck Bennett, John Hettel, unknown-down-Paul Distel, to right-Buddy Barnhill, Don Bennet, Jeanne Hoffman, Don Alberts, down-Scotty MacLaine, to left-George DiQuattro, Rudy Salvini, Chris Pitts-below-Al Obidinski. Photo-Barbara Hauser

Page-327-City Hall, San Francisco, May18, 1999-Mars Breslow famous "Giants of Jazz" photo shoot. Top left to right: Graham Bruce, George Cotsirilos, Charles McNeal, Jeff Pittson, Don Haas, Joe Ellis, Danny Spencer (behind Joe) Bill Langlois, below-Mimi Fox, to left, Frank Passantino, Max Perkoff, Bishop Norman Williams, Si Perkoff, unknown, Don Alberts, Jeannie Hoffman, Noel Jewkes, Al Molina, Mark Levine, below to right, Buddy Barnhill, Rudy Salvini, George DiQuattro, Scotty MacLaine, Dave Gonzales, Dick Conte, Ed Kelly, down and back left, Brown, Al Obidinski, Chris Pitts, down, Chuck Travis-photo Barbara Hauser

A Diary of the Underdogs

Index of Interviews

A Diary of the Underdogs

Credits:

Editors: Beth A. Hoffman, Barbara Hauser, John Wiitala

Transcribers: Cocco Savelli, Maia Wiitala

Photos: Barbara Hauser, Pearl Wong, Don Alberts, Tosh Leventhal, Bobbe Norris, Nora Maki, Dick Whittington, Larry Vuckovich

Book Design: Don Alberts-lulu.com

Eric Whittington-Bird and Beckett Books-Directing and Publishing support

Bibliography and Index: Don Alberts

Chapter 3- January 1966 interview with Francis Davis for Atlantic Monthly re: "Bud's Bubble" (pg 15)

Chapter 6- Joel Selvin, San Francisco Chronicle-December 24th 2004 (pg 23)

Chapter 6- "On the Town"-column by Ralph Gleason-San Francisco Chronicle 1965 (pg 24)

Chapter 6- "On and Off the Record" –from "This World" April 18th 1962-San Francisco Chronicle-column by Ralph Gleason (pgs 25-27)

Chapter 7- "Who's Playing Where (the Districts)-Courtesy of Larry Vuckovich (pgs29-30)

Chapter 8-"Carol Doda and the Condor Club" from Wikipedia 2009 (pgs 33-34)

Chapter 10- "The Black Hawk"-The Black Hawk, a San Francisco Jazz Club-History: from Wikipedia (pgs 38-40)
Chapter 14-"Kerouac and Cassady"- notes from SF Weekly, July 29th to August 4th 1998 by Jack Boulware-website reference-PEN Oakland International Writer's Organization (pgs 49-50) "My Beat Journal" by Eric Anderson-"Book of the Beats" published by Rolling Stone, 1999-Hyperion New York.

Chapter 15- Insert from Wikipedia- Bill Lufborough re: boobam drums (pg 288)

Chapter 16-Quotes- "Three Wishes-An Intimate Look at Jazz Greats" published by Harry N. Abrams Inc.

Chapter 16-Quotes- "Ruminations of a Music Presenter"-Pete Douglas, Founder Bach Dancing and Dynamite Society-by permission.

A Diary of the Underdogs

DON ALBERTS BIOGRAPHY

A jazz musician through most of his life, Don took up writing soon after leaving San Jose State College where he studied with concert pianist Thomas Ryan and majored in Music Composition and English. His early works of writing were inspired by writers Ken Kesey and Neal Cassady with whom he toured for a short time on the Joy Bus, and the work of Jack Kerouac, Allen Ginsberg, Charles Bukowski, Henry Miller, Gabriel Garcia Marquez, Ernest Hemingway, Pablo Neruda, Billie Collins, and others.

Ultimately, writing and music became his bitter-sweet joy. He continued to develop his skills spending more and more time writing, and playing music at night. In 1990, under the pen name, *Whitney Louis,* he completed his first full length novel, *"Beyond the Grand Matoeba,"* a wild outdoor adventure involving a young Sheriff with a personal vendetta. With the experience of writing *"Beyond the Grand Matoeba,"* which consumed thirteen months of his life, he came to realize the dedication and responsibility required of an author and also the passion.

"Play Melancholy Baby," originally titled, *"Frankie and Pauline,"* a work of fiction, first appeared in a group of short stories submitted to a San Francisco editor in 1994 but never published. It has become one of the author's favorites. It possesses the power to be a great motion picture in the hands of someone like Francis Coppola or Clint Eastwood. *"Play Melancholy Baby"* has raw power, a story that moves forcefully through scene after scene, pushed on by the seductive power of the characters and their dubious intent.

This collection of short stories and poetry is now available at the internet site *www.lulu.com/donalberts.* *"Small Unrested Desires,"* also includes *"Play Melancholy Baby,"* and five other significant short stories; *"Bain," "Walking on Heaven," "The Romance of Desolation," "Mooney,"* and *"Sassa,"* plus a list of *Affirms. "Ancient Warrior, Selected Poems from 1995 to 2005"* is also available.

In the period of the 1960's, Don found himself embroiled in the after hours jazz night life, employed by Jimbo Edwards at the famous "Bop City" in San Francisco playing piano until dawn. Don has documented much of these times in his novel *"The Rushing,"* describing the life of a jazz musician. Much of this experience prompted a work of non-fiction, "A Diary of the Underdogs, Jazz in San Francisco in the 60's," a work of social and historical documentation accompanied with musician's interviews.

Don has written ten volumes of original jazz compositions. Volumes 5, 6, 7, 8 and 9 have won the ASCAP jazz composers award for 2005-2006-2007-2008-2009. Don has taught jazz composition at the Jazz School in Berkley, California and has published a course book. He has recorded 7 CDs with his own groups. All CDs are available at www.cdbaby.com. Don now lives in San Bruno and is frequently plays piano at clubs in San Francisco.

A Diary of the Underdogs

Author's Correspondence:
Don Alberts
San Bruno, Ca. 94066
email: jznotes@yahoo.com
Published by Chill House 2009

Other books by Don Alberts:

Small Unrested Desires: Short Stories and Poetry-2003
Absolute Time: Poetry-2007
Ancient Warrior: Poetry-2005
Play Melancholy Baby: Crime Fiction-2003
The Rushing: Crime Fiction-2009-xlibris.com
Bad Boys Fan Club Photo Book: Photo Book-2008
Don Alberts Original Jazz Compositions Volume 8-2008
Don Alberts Original Jazz Compositions Volume 9-2008
Don Alberts Original Jazz Compositions Volume 10-2009
All publications available at: www.lulu.com/donalberts

A Diary of the Underdogs